Imagining the Arabs

Imagining the Arabs

Arab Identity and the Rise of Islam

Peter Webb

EDINBURGH
University Press

Edinburgh University Press is one of the leading university presses in the UK. We publish academic books and journals in our selected subject areas across the humanities and social sciences, combining cutting-edge scholarship with high editorial and production values to produce academic works of lasting importance. For more information visit our website: www.edinburghuniversitypress.com

Edinburgh University Press Ltd
The Tun – Holyrood Road
12 (2f) Jackson's Entry
Edinburgh EH8 8PJ

Typeset in 11/15 Adobe Garamond by
Servis Filmsetting Ltd, Stockport, Cheshire

A CIP record for this book is available from the British Library

ISBN 978 1 4744 0826 4 (hardback)
ISBN 978 1 4744 0827 1 (webready PDF)
ISBN 978 1 4744 0828 8 (epub)

Contents

Acknowledgements

The inspiration for this book stems from a gracious invitation. When Bryan Ward-Perkins invited me, then a rather uninitiated PhD student, to speak at the 2012 After Rome Seminar Series at the Oxford Centre for Late Antiquity, my searches to decide what to say stumbled upon the almost entirely critically unexamined monolith of historic Arab identity. At the time, I was only able to grasp that something was wrong with the way ancient Arabs have been studied, but as the magnitude of interrogating Arab origins steadily dawned upon me thereafter, the direction of my PhD was transformed, and now, another metamorphosis later, this book has materialised.

If it is correct that 'from the mouths of the innocents flows truth' and that 'Paradise lies at the feet of mothers', then my first nod of acknowledgement is properly due to my mother who, as an absolute non-specialist, patiently read the drafts, often several times, and in so doing removed untruths and unclogged some of the prose. Doubtless, I have not followed enough of her advice, and this book goes to press a little less prepared than its mother would like, but such is the way of the world.

In researching and writing, I accrued equally substantial debts to scholars. As this book's origin lies in my PhD, great thanks is due to my supervisor, Hugh Kennedy, whose enthusiasm and encouragement are one of the principal causes of this book's very existence. Equally fundamental was the funding of my PhD at SOAS by the Arts and Humanities Research Council, which provided all the material needs this intellectual endeavour required. I am grateful too for my thesis' examiners, Geert Jan van Gelder and Andrew Marsham: their suggestions and meticulous attention offered a bridge over difficult theoretical and evidential matters which showed the way, which I hope I have followed, to transform the thesis into this new form. And that form which unfolds across these pages was further moulded in seminar discussions: thank you Benjamin Fortna, Stefan Heidemann, Derek Mancini-Lander and Walter Pohl for inviting my presentations through which the embryonic *Imagining the Arabs* grew.

I was able to complete the writing of this book thanks to the generosity of an Art Histories and Aesthetic Practices postdoctoral fellowship 2014/15 at the Forum Transregionale Studien, Berlin. Hosted at the Museum für Islamische Kunst under the auspices of its director, Stefan Weber, I found a happy environment, amidst beginning a new project, where I was afforded time to accomplish the task of editing and reshaping the draft into its final form. The progression of this book in the past year is also indebted to its anonymous reviewers, whose excellent ideas prompted further rounds of refinement. If the result yet has impurities, it is the fault of the alchemist, not his instructors – and I thank you all for taking the time to apply your expertise to make those instructions. And throughout the process of revision when the draft found itself ever expanding and buffeting against its deadlines, Nicola Ramsey and the staff at Edinburgh University Press well deserve my final word of thanks for their patience!

Note on the Text

Readers' attention is drawn to three conventions followed in this book. For dates, all references to events before the Islamic Hijra year reckoning's commencement (622 CE) are written with Before Common Era (BCE) and Common Era (CE) notation. Almost all dates following 622 CE are written in a dual Hijra/Common Era format, for example, '250/864'; centuries are indicated likewise, for example, 'second/eighth'. Because the Hijra lunar year is not contiguous with the longer solar year, dates that are not known precisely are written as a range: that is, '250/864–5' since the beginning of Hijra year 250 corresponds to mid-February 864, while the end of Hijra year 250 was in January 865.

For transliteration of Arabic words, I follow the American Library Association/Library of Congress system, except were words have entered common English usage, for example, Qur'an, Muhammad, hadith, Mecca, Baghdad.

Arabic texts cited herein are rendered in translation; other than transliterated key words and phrases, I have not written the Arabic in full for reasons of space, and readers are invited to refer to the noted sources. Unless otherwise stated, translations from the Qur'an are from Abdel Haleem (2004); all other Arabic translations are mine, unless indicated otherwise.

Introduction

A book about the history of the Arab people strikes its path into seemingly well-worn ground. There is nearly a millennium-worth of Arabic literature and a several century-strong tradition of European writing that portrays the Arabs as Arabia's original population, an array of ancient Bedouin tribes roaming vast expanses of solemn sand-sea until the dawn of the seventh century when Islam's rise stirred them from their long Arabian subsistence into a wave of rapid conquest and settlement across the Middle East that laid the ground for today's Arab World. This familiar story has persuaded many, and the sum of much historical writing about the Arabs has erected a venerable icon of the 'original' Arab as a camelback desert nomad. Accordingly, a writer of Arab history may seem to have little left to achieve, save adding some names and dates to the great tableau of the Arabian–Arab Desert, but when research recently began probing some of the time-honoured stereotypes of Arab origins, the entire model began to wobble, and it now appears that we need to rethink the Arab story with entirely new orientations.

The root of the problem of Arab history is a crisis of plausibility. The traditional Arab origin story is too facile and the conventional image of the original Arab as a bescarved nomad astride his camel is more a romantic fancy than historical reality. Recent studies have encountered difficulties finding even any expressions of Arab identity in Antiquity,[1] and it now seems wrong to assume that all inhabitants of the Arabian Peninsula can legitimately be counted as Arabs,[2] or that Arabs originated as Bedouin.[3] The date when Arabs emerged as a distinct group of people is also currently disputed: some even venture that no Arab communities existed before Islam.[4] The beginnings of

Arab history have become uncertain, and there are yet deeper misunderstandings still awaiting due evaluation.

The traditional stereotype that Arabs originated as Bedouin tribes provided a tidy concept of 'the Arab' which enabled us to think of Arabs as one demographic category neatly segregated from other populations of the Late Antique Middle East, but in so doing it lumped generations of people into a static snapshot of Bedouin primitivism. This had the disadvantage of prompting us to imagine early Arab history as a cyclical pattern of pastoralism and raiding that lacked a narrative of change and development. Pre-Islamic Arabians were thereby robbed of their history, as if their existence revolved without perceptible interruption in the desert until they were activated by the divine intervention of Islam which ushered them into linear, progressive and 'real' history.[5] We should like to better understand the actual history of Arab origins to uncover the paths by which Arab communities formed.

Recovering early Arab history is further hampered, however, by the tendency to label both pre-Islamic Arabians and early Muslim Middle Eastern communities by the single term 'Arab'. This approach treated 'Arabs' as an enduring and homogenous bloc of humanity, and took Arab identity as a 'given', one of the constants that did not change despite the tumultuous transformations of imperial fortunes and religious movements accompanying the rise of Islam. The stance now appears untenable since recent research demonstrates that societal changes over the first centuries of Islam profoundly affected other Middle Eastern communities such as the Persians, Syriac Christians and Jews, and in many respects, actually propelled them to become recognisable ethnicities with new concepts of kin and identity.[6] It seems remote that the 'Arabs' – the social group at the very centre of the transformations during early Islam – could maintain one cohesive (and culturally conservative) community, and modern theoretical approaches are necessary to disengage from generalisation and interrogate the historical development of Arab communal identities. Unless we pay attention to the contours of communities and the significations of identities, we lose the opportunity to perceive how people responded to Islam's message, and ultimately we risk misunderstanding the early development of Islam itself.

The need for critical appraisal of early Arab history is all the more pressing since studies of the contemporary Arab World now avoid generalising about Arab culture,[7] and conceptualise today's Arabs as a patchwork of sometimes only faintly connected peoples. Hence, on what basis can we continue to maintain that early Arabs were, conversely, so cohesive and culturally uniform? And herein we reach the crux of the matter: groups of people do not neatly reduce into archetypes, nor do real communities actually exist like the faceless stereotypes which historic Arabs have been oft-compelled to adopt. We must move beyond treating Arabs as one social and cultural monolith in order to investigate Arab history as the story of an ethnic identity: a plastic intellectual construct which people can join, discard and change.[8]

This book broaches the change by directing analysis to the history of Arabness – the bed of ideas upon which Arab communal identity was constructed. We shall tell the Arab story by tracing the history of what it meant to belong to an Arab community, investigating the range of meanings associated with the word *al-ᶜarab*, the ways in which primary texts about 'Arabs' relate to real or imagined Arabian communities, how Arab communities imagined their own identities, and how others imagined the Arabs. Instead of assuming that Arab communities simply can be 'found' in the historical record of ancient Arabia, our search is for the more ephemeral, evolving and mobile consciousness of Arabness, which compels us to study Arab history as a process – an ethnogenesis – as various groups imagined and reimagined the meaning of being Arab.

A New Trajectory for Arab History

Studying the meaning of historic Arab identity converts the reconstruction of Arab history from an operation of imposing to a task of listening. We jettison assumptions in order to avoid forcing predetermined, anachronistic ideas about the Arabs onto the past and thereby invent historical narratives to validate our own models. Clearing away potentially misleading preconceptions, we can then listen to the sources to determine what they intended when they used the word 'Arab'. Most importantly, we especially want to listen for people calling themselves 'Arabs' to plot when and where those communities emerged and how they articulated their own sense of self. The result will produce a string of data about 'Arabs' as described both by others and by themselves, with rich material dating from Late Antiquity to early Islam (*c.*300–1000 CE). To construct a new, coherent narrative of Arab history, the material will need to be synthesised, and here we employ methodology from anthropological theories of ethnogenesis.

Studies of Arab history have yet to integrate what has now become a substantial body of theoretical scholarship on ethnogenesis into a model that can help explain the development of Arab community and identity.[9] Anthropological theories are indispensible for reconstructing Arab history since they articulate ways to study people and analyse the complex web of ideas that constitute ethnic identities. The theories offer explanations for how sociopolitical contexts help form ethnic identities, and so allow us to transcend bare statements about when Arabs came into existence by enabling us to better understand why Arab communities emerged. Such theories have been valuably applied to study the emergence of other identities in pre-modern Europe and the Middle East, and Arabness now needs similar theoretical rigour.[10]

The model of ethnogenesis directs us to view the Arab story as a fluid process of intellectual and social development by which disparate peoples interacted under specific socio-economic and political conditions that induced them to begin calling themselves 'Arabs' and to reshape their diverse old identities into a new sense of over-arching Arab community. We shall appreciate Arab identity as a constantly evolving idea too: once the first groups called themselves 'Arabs', new groups joined the community, others left, and the ways of imagining Arabness shifted in step. The Arab story thus detaches from DNA and mapping population migrations, and turns into a *longue durée* history of the 'formation' and then the 'maintenance and renewal'[11] of a potent idea which peoples adopted, negotiated and adapted over time as they imagined themselves to be 'Arabs'.

When research takes the question of Arabness as its target of analysis, a number of Arab history's perplexing conundrums can be resolved. Part One of this book traces the formation of Arab communal consciousness: Chapter 1 surveys references to 'Arabs' in ancient records and evaluates them with models of ethnogenesis, Chapter 2 probes deeper into Arabian voices around the dawn of Islam to explore expressions of pre-Islamic communal identities and the emergence of self-expressed 'Arabs', and Chapter 3 studies the origins of the word 'Arab'/*ᶜarabī* and its transformation into an ethnonym (the label of an ethnic community). Contrary to the longstanding belief that Arabs are an ancient ethnos from the Arabian Desert, Part One argues that groups only gradually began to identify themselves as 'Arabs' as a consequence of social, linguistic, political and doctrinal changes inaugurated by the rise of Islam. Prior to the seventh century, Arabian populations were too fragmented to constitute a cohesive group which we can realistically treat as a single people, and these peoples did not call themselves 'Arabs'. They instead used an array of different names such as Maᶜadd, Ghassān, Ḥimyar and Ṭayyiᵓ that distinguished group and regional identities, and hence the notion that there was one pre-Islamic 'Arab' identity seems quite anachronistic.

The creation of an Arab community and the imagination of a pre-Islamic Arab past are accordingly major intellectual achievements of early Islam. But while the circumstances following Islam's rise prompted early Muslims to begin identifying their community as 'Arab', not all imagined Arabness in one uniform fashion, and the cohesion of the Arab community was not stable. Part Two explores Muslim-era literature and society to trace how the idea of the 'Arab' changed during the maintenance and renewal of Arab identity through Islam's first four centuries. Chapter 4 investigates the core components of Arab identity: the definition of the name *ᶜarabī* and the construction of the Arab 'family tree', and uncovers how Muslim writers debated and developed the senses of Arabness and Arab kinship over time. Chapter 5 evaluates how the shifting status of Arabs in Abbasid society between the second/eighth and fourth/tenth centuries influenced senses of community and constructions of pre-Islamic history, and Chapter 6 investigates the remarkable change in the way 'Arab' was conceptualised when third/ninth century philologists started to codify the Arabic language and redefined Arab identity to suit new discourses. Many of the Bedouin stereotypes familiar today emanate from this later literature which fashioned a classical, 'canonical' notion of Arabness that has influenced so much writing about Arab origins ever since. With that development our book closes, leaving questions of Arab identity from the fifth/eleventh century to modern times for further study.

Arabic Literature, Islam and the Arabs

The comprehensive construction of Arabness in the early Muslim period means that this book required survey and interpretation of a wide array of

Arabic literature written between the late second/eighth and fourth/tenth centuries. The constituent parts of the Arab story appear across many genres of writing, and compelled me to pull together unwieldy threads. In so doing, I have stuck out my neck into highly specialised fields from Qur'anic exegesis to philology, poetry to genealogy, hadith to history – each genre alone prompts myriad questions worthy of dedicated research, but the importance of our quest to understand Arabness as an identity in the round demanded a broader approach. Too often modern writers use the label 'Arab' to generalise about both pre-Islamic Arabians and early Islamic-era Muslims, and so leave scant space to study the complexities of Arabness as an idea, as an identity of human beings in different historical circumstances. In order to start the enquiry, the need for integration and cross-reference is essential: the wide swathe of cultural producers who developed notions of Arabness were in dialogue with each other, and it is vital to harness their various disciplines and bring their dialogues back to life. I therefore explore texts that will be familiar to scholars, but I read them together from the perspective of Arabness, which aims to open new opportunities to probe the meanings of Arabic literature's ubiquitous hero, 'the Arab' and the contexts of his creation, to investigate the strategies, power structures and survival of the Muslim Conquest society, and to consider the construction of Muslim identities by tracing how ideas of Arabness were used to effect the Middle East's gradual transition into the 'Islamic World'.

While this book closely evaluates non-Arabic pre-Islamic evidence, Arabic-language sources are specially privileged to reconstruct Arab identity since ethnogenesis is fundamentally about individuals' consciousness of belonging to a community, and hence it seems inappropriate to write Arab history without listening to Arabic voices. Muslim-era Arabic writings reinterpreted pre-Islamic history to reshape the past into an 'Arab origin' story, but this ought not dampen interest in Arabic literature's historical worth given that most modern historiographers doubt that we can reconstruct history 'as it really happened' as a matter of theory,[12] and a history of the Arabs should in any event be most interested in the period when Arabs began to construct history into their own communal story. The moment when self-styled 'Arabs' began to imagine an ancient history for themselves is precisely when meaningful Arab ethnogenesis was underway: the consolidation of disparate older memories into one 'Arab story', the invention of new stories, and the forgetting of other memories are the nuts and bolts from which ethnic identities are constructed.

As we shall see in Part One, the paucity of pre-Islamic Arabic literary records does not entail that we are missing vital chunks of the earliest *Arab* story. As Chapter 2 traces, pre-Islamic Arabian poetry mirrors indications of community and identity from non-Arabic pre-Islamic sources in pointing to the beginnings of Arab ethnogenesis as contemporaneous with the proliferation of Arabic-language records in the early Muslim-era. And in Chapter 4 we uncover the heterogeneous and contested definitions of *ᶜarabī* ('Arab') and the only gradual steps taken to harmonise an Arab origin story and family tree, which underline that the key elements of creating a sense of Arab ethnos were incomplete even in Islam's second and third centuries.[13] There is a wealth of early Muslim-era Arabic literature waiting to tell us the many ways in which Arabness was conceptualised, and this book seeks their stories. Much can be learned from reappraising how Arabic literature represents Arabs, and by interpreting the literature without a priori assumptions that the Arabs 'must have' entered Islam as an already formed identity, we enable ourselves to witness the creation of Arabness across the pages of our sources.

Readers will find that much of this book, and particularly Part Two, focuses on the idea of Arabness in Iraq during Islam's first four centuries. The nature of our sources necessitates this: the majority of the extant literature was written in Iraq and Western Iran (or, to use fourth/tenth century Arabic geographical terminology, the 'two Iraqs'), and in order to interpret the literature, it was paramount to link it to the specific Iraqi contexts and discourses into which it was disseminated. Theories of ethnogenesis (detailed in the next section) instruct that the idea of Arabness, like other identities, evolved across periods and locales, and hence the only means to adduce legitimate conclusions is to ensure that analysis is informed by gathering evidence from texts produced in the same place and time. I accordingly refrain from referring to our sources as 'classical Arabic literature' – as the term breeds presumptions of homogeneity from Spain to Central Asia which are as misleading as the monolithic notions of static Arab identity which this book critiques. Each text has its geographical and temporal context, and, to the greatest extent possible, they are studied here in their contexts, compared with sources written at the same time, and contrasted against those written in subsequent generations.[14] By paying attention to dates, a diachronic picture of evolving Arabness comes into view, but since our texts are Iraqi, our conclusions are expressed in relation to Iraq. Iraq was the political and cultural centre of the Muslim world for most of this period, so it is perhaps the most important region for the early history of Arabness in any event, but this does not at all imply that Arab identity was everywhere articulated uniformly. Spain produced vibrant Arabness discourses, but they are geographically outside the purview of this book. Likewise, the extensive encyclopedias of Arabian lore written in Ayyubid and Mamluk Egypt and Syria chronologically post-date this book's focus. Our goal is to probe the subtle evolution of Arab identity in early Islam: our sources for that period are Iraqi, and hence Iraqi society and its discourses are our focus.

By proposing that Islam was a catalyst for Arab ethnogenesis, this book will cross lines of current debates over both (1) the role of religion in generating senses of ethnic identity, and (2) the causes for the rise of Islam. Traditionally, early Islam has been interpreted as an Arab 'national movement', its success explained by assuming the existence of pre-Islamic Arab communal cohesion, under the speculation that religious belief of itself would not have facilitated the unprecedentedly rapid 'Arab conquests' in the decades after Muhammad.[15] Against this trend, Donner's 2010 *Muhammad and the Believers* rejects notions of pre-Islamic Arab unity, and explains the conquests as pietistic and apocalyptic movement of 'Believers' in which faith constituted a driving force.[16] Donner accordingly rejects the term 'Arab conquests',[17] and traces the gradual evolution of the 'Believer movement' into a specific Muslim identity, and since his theories often tally with various archaeological and textual sources contemporary with the conquests, Donner presents compelling challenges to the traditional monoliths of both Arab and Islam.[18] This book welcomes the invitation to reconsider Arab ethnogenesis, and by investigating the idea of Arabness within the developing sociopolitical and religious contexts of the post-conquest Middle East, we offer insight to evaluate Donner's thesis and new explanations for the roles of faith and society in driving varied conqueror groups (whom I will call 'Conquerors' or 'early Muslims'[19]) to adopt 'Arab' identity.

Because identities are composite ideas conjured in the minds of peoples who sometimes disagree with each other, there are uncertainties inherent within Arabness that cannot always be cut and dried. But since the label 'Arab' has so frequently been marshalled to describe very important groups, there is a need to better appreciate its origins and the ranges of its significations. The available evidence, when read in a theoretically grounded fashion, will indicate that early Muslims were the first to imagine themselves as Arabs and initiated a process of ethnogenesis which led them to retrospectively Arabise Arabian history, turning *al-^{c}arab* into the central protagonist of a complex mythology which subsequent Muslim writers narrated to explain their history and their place in the world. From an array of Arabian peoples, to the political elite of a massive, yet divided empire, to a device of later *littérateurs*, the idea of Arabness enjoyed an exciting career in the minds of diverse and very influential people. We now explore how each has imagined the Arabs.

Ethnogenesis and Arab History

We begin the Arab story with an explication of this book's theoretical framework, as it will be referenced throughout to evaluate textual indicators and to identify the drivers of Arab ethnogenesis. Theory is particularly important in the Arab case given the uneven survival of textual evidence from the early centuries of Islam. Anthropological theories have been refined from the observation of actual populations, and hence offer the precision of a coherent structure upon which we can pin the evidence we possess about the early Arabs, finessing gaps in our sources with theoretically grounded assumptions.

Theories of ethnogenesis critique the homogenising generalities of 'race' that would treat each and every 'Arab' as representative of one archetype. The theories originate in Max Weber's celebrated essay, published posthumously in 1922, which argues that kinship is symbolic, not biological, that race is imagined, not objective, and that awareness of common ancestry between members of a group is a consequence of collective action, not its cause.[20] The passage of time and experience of events make people aware of unity which they express as an ethnic bond, but as time moves on, their awareness will change to suit new circumstances.

Anthropologists found Weber's theory has wide application to communal identities around the world,[21] and for our study, Weber's model of subjective, evolving identity erases the possibility of simply alighting upon *al-ᶜarab* as a single blood-interrelated community in pre-Islamic Arabia and the early Islamic Middle East. Immediately, therefore, we can deconstruct much pre-modern Arabic literature which presents 'Arabs' in one uniform way and uses the monolithic term *al-ᶜarab* to describe many groups. Whilst such literature has prompted contemporary scholarly assumptions that pre-Islamic Arabians and Arabic-speakers in the early Caliphate were all equally 'Arab',[22] Weber inspires caution that this is a false homogenisation, and when studying the rise of other peoples around the world, historians found that we indeed cannot always accept the names of ethnic groups in source texts at face value. The sources were written in particular historical moments when ethnic communities had already formed, and writers often anachronistically backtrack their own ethnicity into an ancient past to construct an imagined sense of historical cohesion that obscures the process by which the group actually formed.[23] Theories of ethnogenesis possess the advantage of moving beyond conceptualising identity as a static marker of a genetically related kin-community, and instead study groups of people as 'ethnos':[24] an evolving idea and a product of history.

A community can be studied as an ethnos if its members articulate a matrix of features which theorists identify as indicative of the existence of consciousness of shared ethnic belonging. Each ethnos has its own particularities, but for studies of ethnogenesis in Late Antiquity, scholarship refers to Hutchison and Smith's list which delineates an ethnos as a group possessing (1) a proper name expressing its identity, (2) a myth of common ancestry, (3) shared historical memories, (4) a link with territory, (5) elements of common culture, and (6) a sense of solidarity.[25] Building from these criteria, historical context is the next consideration, for we need to grasp the circumstances and the webs of significance in which an ethnic identity is expressed. This is key since people always have various options when choosing how to identify themselves, and as a consequence, we need to know how different notions of community intersected with each other in specific historical moments, and why a certain identification (in this case, 'Arab') became sufficiently popular to fuel ethnogenesis.[26] To then propose a cogent narrative, we need to sustain a rigorous diachronic approach because the contexts in which people live and the ideas that are important to them change over time, and so ethnic identities change too, sometimes taking radical new paths. A history of an ethnos must inevitably be one of evolving significations.[27]

To reconstruct the drivers that unite formerly disparate people into an ethnic group, Weber's theory directs us to examine economic and political factors.[28] Subsequent theorists observed more factors at play, and their detailed schemes now articulate varied instrumentalist/transactionist or constructivist models. No single theory dominates the field today, and we can follow modern anthropologists who employ a blend of both instrumentalism and constructivism to explain ethnic development.[29] The variations are, in any event, complimentary, as Fredrik Barth, the founder of the instrumentalist/transactionist 'school', maintained,[30] and the model of ethnogenesis applied in this book begins with the widely accepted premise that ethnicity is about consciousness. Ethnicities must be believed in order to become real – for a slogan, we could say 'there is no *kin* or *race*, but thinking makes it so'. What then are the factors that explain how groups in the Middle East first thought their way into Arab ethnicity?

I deliberately speak of groups in the plural since 'it takes two, ethnicity can only happen at the boundary of us'.[31] Consciousness of collective unity needs an outsider, the other who is 'not us', whose alterity drives us to construct our own ethnic unity. People will become aware of such an 'other' when interacting with groups in a network which ethnographers call transactions across boundaries.[32] The nature of the transactions and the location of the boundaries can take many forms: they may reflect commercial interactions, political and ideological divisions, and divergences in lifestyle and environment, but in each case of ethnogenesis, a network of interactions, physical or conceptual, must be established that enforces division and recognition of difference. Ethnic identity takes shape on the boundaries, and new ethnicities can form when boundaries change. In the case of Arab origins, we need to consider the groups in opposition to whom Arabs could have defined themselves, and relate the earliest expressions of Arab communal consciousness to changes in social boundaries that prompted the friction from which sparks of Arab ethnogenesis flew. It will be apparent that we cannot expect Arabs to 'materialise' from a void in the middle of Arabia; rather, awareness of Arab community should be sought in a dynamic environment where population movements, new political, economic and confessional divisions, and changing relationships altered webs of interaction and compelled the redrawing of group identities.

When a new network of transactions becomes stable, groups have time to perceive the boundaries and develop consciousness of 'inside' and 'outside' – 'us' and 'them'. On the 'inside', people find themselves undertaking a common and regular array of activities that reveals to them their shared interests and common sense of difference from those on the other side of the boundary, and so solidifies consciousness of community. That consciousness is then crucially aided by 'cultural stuff',[33] traits such as language, religion, mythology, symbols, dress and cuisine, for these visible traits and physically performed actions can be seen and felt on a daily basis as 'real evidence' of shared belonging and distinct community.[34] Once aware of their unity of interests and cultural commonalities, people can then begin the process of imagining blood-ties to construct a common genealogy and history. And in this way, groups formed from shared political/economic/social transactions can begin to 'feel ethnic' and maintain their cohesion and sociopolitical status.[35]

In this study, the role of religious belief as a 'cultural stuff' component of ethnogenesis is central, given the intriguing evidence of the emergence of expressions of Arab kin-belonging following the rise of Islam. If we are to ascribe the stirring of Arab communal consciousness to a consequence of Islam's spread, we need to consider whether a sense of shared religion can prompt disparate groups who formerly did not recognise common community to unite as one ethnos. Is there historical precedent where communities practising a common religion began to rethink their confessional bonds into one ethnic community, that is, one with its exclusive name, genealogy, and unique sense of shared history and symbols that demarcate them from others?[36] We shall consider specific examples in Chapter 3, where we find that while religion is usually not a driver of ethnogenesis on its own, nor necessarily even a 'first resort' that prompts a group to articulate an ethnic identity, there are precedents during Late Antiquity where co-religionists in particular circumstances did construct a sense of ethnic kin-interrelation to maintain their communal cohesion. The Arab case offers pertinent data to elaborate the theory.

Taking the varied factors together, the combinations of transactions and the array of 'cultural stuff' commonalities that drive ethnogenesis are intrinsically fluid. As populations move, embrace new practices, and change their social standing and relations with others, the very basis of the identity evolves. An ethnic identity therefore does not form 'once and for all', but exists with a constant potential for transformation, and analysis of a group consequently needs to pursue its changing forms over time. In the Arab case, camel nomadism, tent dwelling, a penchant for poetry, or any other cultural/ lifestyle trait cannot be upheld as an unchanging touchstone of Arabness. Instead, we should expect membership of an Arab community to fluctuate as groups opt in and out of expressing themselves as Arabs, and we can expect the meaning of 'being an Arab' to evolve in turn. The evolution can be traced in historical records and linked to sociopolitical changes in society, and theories of ethnogenesis proffer key factors for consideration.

First, changing boundary transactions and the attendant interactions with new transactional partners and new senses of the 'other' will alter the manner in which an ethnic group articulates its identity, history and unity. Second, as lifestyles and power relationships change, groups will join the community if it is advantageous to do so, and groups will leave if the identity loses its value as an asset in the wider social context. Third, and equally important, ethnic groups are subject to assimilation. Whilst boundary transactions initially prompt consciousness of difference, when transactions flourish and persist, the common social context develops into an increasingly cooperative, mutual relationship which can dissolve the boundaries, and with them, old consciousness of difference.[37] It is often the case, however, that difference flares a second time, brightly, but fleetingly like a dying star in a phenomenon known as 'ethnic revival' that occurs when the inexorable process of assimilation has nearly run its course.[38] Ethnic revival is a reaction to decreasing cultural difference: people, often those who have most assimilated with the 'other', make the loudest claims of ethnic particularism for a period before homogenisation finally overrides all old notions of difference, and the former boundaries fade into oblivion.[39] In the Arab case, the long view of history spans the momentous sociopolitical and doctrinal changes inaugurated by the dawn of Islam, the redrawing of the political map of the Middle East and its urban networks, and the assimilation of Arabian Conquerors and the diverse panoply of conquered populations into the new system. We shall find that the idea of the 'Arab' was an important rallying point for communities across these transformations, but the circumstances of Arabness' use and the scope of its usefulness changed as new situations prompted new ways to imagine the Arabs.

The act of imagining the meaning of an identity is thus ultimately reliant upon the individuals who jointly conceptualise and embrace their ethnic unity, and analysis must ask: who is imagining the community? A group can be described by its own members, and by members of other groups, and different factions within each of the inside/outside camps may also make different claims. Competing discourses each assert the 'correct' interpretation of a group's 'true character', but given the subjective nature of identity, there are no empirical grounds to resolve 'accuracy' – objective criteria only establish a range of credible definitions. The dominant conception of identity can be ascertained by measuring its ability to generate consent and to silence dissent, and here power enters the structure: the relative power of different actors promulgating an ethnic identity determines the ambit of who is inside the community and who is outside, as well as the 'canonical' articulation of the community's identity from time to time. Following Gramscian notions of negotiation between hegemons and subalterns, the 'canon' will shift as the most powerful group establishes its view, plus or minus some concessions to subaltern views.[40]

When accounting for the voices of our narrators to determine where they can be placed on the continuum of imagining the Arabs, we need also be aware that texts are not created in a vacuum. Texts describing ethnic identity exist in dialogue with past legacies as well as contemporary writings, and theorists demonstrate that writers do not have complete freedom to describe a people and their history in any way they choose. Ethnicity is 'real': real people imagine their community, and membership tangibly affects how they live, speak, pray and interact with others.[41] Ethnic identity thus acquires a tradition which constricts the ways it can be imagined,[42] as Attwood neatly epitomised Australian Aboriginal ethnogenesis, 'the aboriginal is both determined and determining'.[43] He explains how English/Australian administrators categorised Indigenous populations and so 'determined' the tribal composition of Australia, but at the same time, their determinations were not made in a vacuum: pre-existing local groups shaped colonial categorisations to an extent,[44] then, later, when Indigenous Australians gained power to express their own identities, they inherited the old categorisations and reinterpreted them in turn, taking the old template but 'determining' new trajectories. Regardless of how strongly new agendas strove towards articulating new ethnic ideas, Attwood demonstrated the influential legacy of the past.[45] Hence the long view is again essential: writings about an ethnos are all partially determined by past writings and reflect legacies of different interest groups and changing power relations. Arab identity competed with old forms of communal organisation when it came into existence, and its subsequent development built on its earlier foundations.

Telling Arab history accordingly demands an integrated approach of the widest possible array of sources, rigorously separating their discussions of Arabness chronologically to identify how people articulated Hutchison and Smith's 'building blocks' to develop 'Arab' ethnic identity over time, and to interpret the texts against their historical and discursive contexts. Drawing inspiration from Anderson and Rodinson, Part One searches for self-awareness of an expressly 'Arab' imagined community[46] within theoretically grounded circumstances that can explain why people alighted on the idea of Arabness to imagine a new unity, and used the name 'Arab' to describe themselves.[47] Having uncovered the first stirrings of Arab identity, Part Two pursues the ways in which the idea of Arab identity was maintained and renewed over subsequent generations, exploring what the idea of Arabness has meant, how it attracted new members, how history changed its fate, and how changing power relations and communal organisation altered the range of its meanings. We can then finally begin to state, with some confidence, when and why Arab groups originated and how they survived through history, thereby gaining unprecedented access into the minds and lives of the peoples who experienced and drove the rise of Islam, and laid the deep historical foundations for today's Arab World.

Notes

1. The equation of authentic Arabness with Arabia was well established: von Grunebaum writes 'the Arab, by etymology and cultural convention was the Bedouin' (1963) p. 12; Crone (2008) p. 8 investigates the Bedouin Arabs' 'barefoot and naked' deportment at the dawn of Islam; see Gibbon's classic work (1776–89) vol. 5, pp. 231-45; also Nöldeke (1899), Caskel (1954) p. 38,

Carmichael (1967) pp. 6–7, Rodinson (1981) p. 15, Robin (2010) p. 85, Dousse (2012) pp. 42–3, Robin (2012) p. 48. Corm and Foissy equate 'the genuine Arab 'ethnic' group' with Arabia (2012) p. 26; the Oxford English Dictionary repeats the paradigm, defining 'Arab' simply and succinctly as '[o]ne of the Semitic race inhabiting Saudi Arabia and neighbouring countries' (vol. 1, p. 597). But difficulties in finding express references to actual pre-Islamic populations calling themselves 'Arabs' are noted: von Grunebaum (1963), Robin (2006) p. 124 and (2012) p. 48; Retsö (2003) p. 236 and Hoyland (2015) p. 65. Reconciling the long-held notions of Arab origins with the absence of reference to 'Arab' identity is a significant stumbling block.

2. The assumption that all inhabitants of Arabia constitute members of one Arab community fuses spaces with race. Macdonald rejects the generalisation (2009(a) p. 2); Potts reveals the wealth of pre-Islamic non-Arab Eastern Arabian civilisations, dating the arrival of 'Arabs' only in the first century CE ((1990) vol. 2, p. 227); Hoyland (2001) pp. 5, 8, 48 and Robin (1991) argue against the 'Arabness' of pre-Islamic Yemenis. See Ghabban (2010) for surveys of different Arabian regions and cultures. Al-Azmeh's recent avowal of pan-Arabian Arabness (2014a) p. 100 is becoming a minority opinion (see Hoyland (2015) pp. 21–7).
3. See Macdonald (2009a) pp. 2, 20, (2009b) pp. 312–13; Retsö (2003) pp. 1–8; Lecker (2010) pp. 153–4; Berkey (2003) pp. 40–9, though he does not appear to distinguish between 'Arab' and 'Arabian'.
4. See Chapter 1 for the varied current theories about Arab origins. Donner (2010) pp. 217–20 and Millar (2013) pp. 154–8 suggest that the idea of pre-Islamic Arab identity is 'anachronistic', and that the notion of 'Arabia and the Arabs' in a pre-Islamic context is untenable.
5. The paradigm presenting Arabs as primitives or even 'barbarians' (Goldziher (1889–90) vol. 1, p. 202; Cook (1986) p. 478; Khalidi (1994) pp. 1–3) engenders sweeping notions that pre-Islamic Arabians had no sense of 'real history' before Islam (Robinson (2003) p. 14; Duri (1962) p. 46).
6. See Boyarin (1999) and Millar (2013) for various views on the development of Jewish identity in Late Antiquity; Savant (2013) for the idea of 'Persian', and Haar Romeny et al. (2010) for Syrians. Against this background, the study of Arabness now lags behind in the academy.
7. Said (1991) pp. 284–321 famously deconstructed prior racialist thinking about the Arabs; see also Ibrahim (2011) p. 14. For examples of such 'traditional' discourses, see Carmichael (1967) and Polk (1991).

8. For classic studies highlighting the subjectivity of identity and a community's sense of its past, see the 'Vienna School' of Wenskus (1961) and the work of like-minded scholars Pohl (1998), Pohl and Reimitz (1998), and Geary (1983). For other theoretical work, see Hobsbawn (1990) and Anderson (1991). There are now many invaluable case studies: see Nora (1996–8) for French identity; Pohl, Gantner and Payne (2012) for the Late Antique Middle East. Theories of ethnogenesis are detailed at the end of this Introduction.
9. Al-Azmeh (2014a) pp. 100, 138, 147 cites the word 'ethnogenesis' in his discussion of pre-Islamic Arabs, but his work, like that of previous scholars, does not consult the key anthropological theories which inform the notion of ethnogenesis, and hence cannot engage with the vital question of how Arab communities developed.
10. See the studies listed above, Notes 6 and 8.
11. For the cogent division of ethnogenesis into 'formation' and then 'maintenance and renewal' stages, see Haar Romeny et al. (2010) p. 9.
12. White (1980) and (1987), Ricoeur (1988) and Lowenthal (1985) deconstruct the empirical veneer of positivist historiography; Donner (1998) urges the employment of such narratological historiographical approaches to study early Islam.
13. The awareness of an identity as a distinct community with its exclusive name and own mythic origins, genealogy and shared history constitute the vital features Hutchison and Smith identify as constituting an ethnic identity (1996) pp. 6–7.
14. The method of chronologically dividing and contextualising sources stems from Vienna School: for a summary, see Haar Romeny (2012) pp. 185–94.
15. In Western scholarship, reading Islam as an 'Arab movement' is an Enlightenment discourse crucially underpinned by Gibbon's classic study (1776–89). Gibbon accorded substantial role to the 'Arab' Conquerors' religious motivation; the secularisation of interpretations to view Islam's rise as a racial/national movement correspond to the rise of secular nationalism in Europe: see Renan (1857) and Becker (1913), and later iterations in Crone and Cook (1977) and Hoyland (2015).
16. Donner (2010) pp. 56–92.
17. Donner (2010) pp. 88–90, 217–20.
18. Another major contributor, Robert Hoyland similarly hypothesised about the Islamic-era shaping of Arab identity (2001) pp. 243–7 and (2015) pp. 59–61, 213–19, but Hoyland is critical of Donner's notion of religiously-motivated conquests (Hoyland (2012) p. 574), and so ultimately returns to the familiar

model of pre-Islamic Arab cohesion and 'Arab conquests' terminology, and suggests the existence of specifically Arab communities in pre-Islamic Arabia (2001) p. 230; (2015) pp. 22–7. Evaluating Islam's rise and Middle Eastern society from the alternative angle of Byzantine Late Antiquity, Fergus Millar (2013) pp. 53, 154–8 likewise questions the legitimacy of speaking of a pre-Islamic Arab identity or sense of Arab community before Islam. By directing analysis to both pre-Islamic Arabia and Islamic-era Iraq, this book proposes a bridge to tie together Millar and Donner's impressions.

19. While this book welcomes Donner's critiques of traditional paradigms about the 'Arab conquests', it seems premature to replace reference to 'Muslim' with 'Believer'. 'Muslim' did have important meanings in early Islam and more textual analysis is needed to develop Donner's 'Believers' thesis; moreover, it would probably be preferable to render 'Believer' untranslated as *Muʾmin*, since we do not call Muslims 'Submitters'. By 'early Muslim', I intended the still nascent parameters of Muslim confessional identity that developed over the 100–150 years after Muhammad.
20. Weber (1996) p. 35. Weber's theory is the root of all modern work, though his approach did not become widespread until after the Second World War. See Raum (1995), Vermeulen and Govers (1997), Banton (2007) and Jenkins (2008).
21. Vermeulen and Govers (1997) p. 5.
22. The influence of Muslim-era archetypes about Arab identity appear in modern conflations of Arab origins with the idea of a nomadic, poetically-gifted pre-Islamic Arabian community (Hourani (1991) p. 12, Conrad (2000), Hoyland (2001) pp. 241–4, Dousse (2012) p. 45). The theoretical lens of ethnogenesis would prefer Rodinson's observation that Arabness changes between 'periods and locales' ((1981) p. 9), priming a radical rethink of Arabness as an intellectual construct.
23. Haar Romeny (2012) pp. 189–93.
24. Some call the race/ethnicity distinction merely semantic – Wallerman called it a 'quibble' (see Jenkins (2008) pp. 23–4), but Boas' 1940 *Race Language and Culture* explained the difference as 'race and biology' vs 'ethnicity and culture'.
25. Hutchison and Smith (1996) pp. 6–7. Cited, for example, in the essays in Haar Romeny (2010).
26. Hofstee (2010) pp. 60–3.
27. The diachronic approach incorporates methods of the Vienna School, and the pioneering studies of Geary (1983) and Pohl (1998).

28. Banton (2007), although Raum (1995) pp. 81–5 argues that Weber did not intend to be so narrow.
29. Vermeulen and Govers (1997) pp. 19–22. Pure 'instrumentalism' can be too rigid, as it subordinates ethnicity to sociopolitical processes, taking insufficient account of the persistence of cultural legacies and their ability to survive changes, even in attenuated forms (see Haar Romeny et al. (2010) pp. 8–9. Whereas pure 'constructivism' relegates ethnicity to a mere intellectual discourse, thus overlooking how actual sociopolitical contexts drive the imagination of identity.
30. Barth (1994) pp. 17–18.
31. Wallman (1979) p. 3.
32. Barth (1969) p. 15.
33. Barth (1969) p. 15, (1994) pp. 17–18; Jenkins (2008) pp. 25–7.
34. Anderson (1991) p. 15, Hutchison and Smith (1996) pp. 6–7; Jenkins (2008) pp. 25–7.
35. Though Weber demonstrated that notions of kinship are not related to real blood-ties, Roosens (1994) argued that a believable, imagined kinship is key to constructing an ethnicity, and Lancaster's 1981 study of the Rwala Bedouin reveals the importance of this 'generated genealogy' for identity articulation in modern Jordan.
36. Enloe (1980) p. 361 and Jenkins (2008) pp. 111–27 ascribe religion a determinative role in ethnic formation, especially before Europe's secular nation states (which have received disproportionate attention in studies on identity such as Anderson (1991), Gellner (1983) and Hobsbawn (1990)).
37. Epstein (1978) p. xii. See also Vayda (1994) p. 320 for further discussion of ethnic boundaries.
38. Steinberg calls ethnic revival a 'dying gasp' in a process of homogenisation ((1989) p. 76). Roosens (1989) elaborates a similar argument; see Eriksen's fieldwork in Mauritius (1997) and Sansone's in Bahia (1997) for field studies.
39. Sansone (1997) found that black identity in Bahia is more pronounced among the young educated population which has most contact with whites. The less educated population, living in supposedly more 'traditional' black Bahian culture, are less vocal in cultural defence.
40. Jenkins (2008) pp. 22–3.
41. Ethnic identity is thus not completely subjective as it retains cultural baggage, and hence a non-dogmatic employment of Barth's instrumentalist theories remains useful to ground the identity in its specific contexts.
42. Ethnicity resembles history in its mediation between reality and fiction. White's

narratological argument that equates history writing with fiction strayed too far as Ricoeur (1988) vol. 3, p. 154 rightly notes. History can be reinterpreted, but the underlying real events limit the realms of creativity in ways fiction writers do not experience. Ethnicity is similar: it is an intellectual construct, but can only be reconceptualised within boundaries imposed by social realities.

43. Attwood (1989) p. 150.
44. Attwood (1989) pp. 136–7.
45. Vail (1989) and Ranger (1983) argued that colonial powers created the ethnic composition of Africa, Ranger (1993) reversed his views and confirmed the two-way process of ethnogenesis in colonial and post-colonial southern Africa as Attwood noted in Australia.
46. Anderson (1991); Hutchison and Smith (1996). Rodinson anticipated these later theories to a remarkable degree (1981) p. 12; though he did not pursue pre-Islamic and early Islamic evidence, and so this present study adduces different conclusions.
47. The search for instances of the word 'Arab' is in part an onomastic exercise, the pitfalls of which have been noted (Beeston (1977) p. 51, developed by Macdonald (2009g) pp. 187–9). But Arab identity can only have been meaningful at the point when people began to call themselves Arabs and recognised their mutual connections (Rodinson (1981) p. 12), so we need to find instances of the name 'Arab', and we can overstep the shortcomings of rigid onomastic analysis by undertaking close consideration of our sources' historical and discursive contexts.

PART ONE

THE RISE OF ARAB COMMUNITIES

1

Imagining Ancient Arabs: Sources and Controversies

The evidence about pre-Islamic Arabian populations emanates from two perspectives: (1) the writings of peoples from outside Arabia who, across the 1,500 years from the Assyrians in the ninth century BCE to Islam's rise in the seventh century CE, recorded many stories about Arabians, and (2) voices from within the Arabian Peninsula itself, preserved in inscriptions from as early as the eighth century BCE. Both bodies of sources contain numerous and intriguing references to an array of ancient peoples whose names resemble 'Arab', and it may seem logical enough that Arab history can be written by synthesising the material, but, curiously, it has not transpired this way. Several generations' worth of modern analysis produced a number of different narratives, and the field remains divided between surprisingly divergent opinions. Different approaches to the evidence enabled some to argue that Arabs existed across Arabia since time immemorial as its original (or at least very early) inhabitants,[1] while another imagines Arabs as a distinct militarised religious community that formed around the ninth century BCE.[2] Another posits that Arabs only emerged as a group circa the first century BCE in south-central Arabia and only consolidated a sense of political unity in the fourth century CE;[3] whereas a further body of scholars imagines the first Arabs as a conglomeration of north-west Arabian Bedouin who formed a loose sense of a community around a shared oral/poetic culture between the fourth and sixth centuries CE.[4] Yet another theory argues that Arab ethnogenesis occurred not in Arabia, but on the Byzantine–Syrian frontier in the fifth and sixth centuries CE,[5] whereas other recent observations radically hint that 'Arab' communities did not emerge until after the dawn of Islam.[6] The theories are rather mutually exclusive, but the origins of an Arab community must lie somewhere, and hence the array of options are in need of better resolution. The task inspires this chapter.

As Christian Robin and Michael Macdonald each note, we cannot recreate Arab history by simply searching for instances of the word 'Arab' in ancient records, as this produces an unmanageable array of references, many of which do not point to what can be understood as a community of Arabs.[7] And we need add further circumspection regarding the nature of the sources themselves. It is material to note that most modern writers of Arab history have relied primarily on outsiders' testimony as those sources are more copious and detailed than the pre-Islamic Arabian inscriptions,[8] but as this chapter explains, outsider texts actually distort the understanding of Arab origins and exacerbate scholarly disagreement. The outsiders' sources are unwieldy: they cross divides of time and space, delivering an array of voices that include Assyrian scribes, Persian administrators, Greek geographers and Roman soldiers, and their differing points of view and varying levels of knowledge about the Peninsula make it hard to consolidate their many stories into one single Arab story. And it is even more material to note that textual references to ancient groups with 'Arab'-like names have not yet been evaluated through theories of ethnogenesis to probe Arab communal consciousness. As a result, we currently have not been able to theorise how references to 'Arabs' in an ancient literary source written outside of Arabia relate, if at all, to senses of Arab identity within. Herein, critical enquiry could at last relate the textual evidence to theories of identity and offer a grounded appraisal of ancient Arabian communities and Arab origins. Through such analysis, this chapter investigates whether we can in fact legitimately speak of 'Arab' ethnic communities in the Ancient and Classical periods, and proposes an alternative approach to draw sense from the varied testimony of outsiders and ancient Arabians themselves.

I Arabs and Pre-Islamic Textual Traditions

Assyrian Testimony: 853–612 BCE

The Arabness puzzle begins in 853 BCE when the Assyrian king Shalmaneser III recorded a battle against the *Arba-ā*, a people from the deserts southwest of Damascus led by king 'Gindibu'.[9] If *Arba-ā* can be read as the first Arabs, and if the name Gindibu is in fact an old form of the modern Arabic *jundab*,[10] then the Arabs enter history some 1,500 years before Islam under the leadership of 'King Locust', and stereotypes of Arab origins as a militant horde of menacing Bedouin have ancient pedigree! But while some do identify Shalmaneser III's pesky nomadic neighbours as the ancestors of Muhammad's Arabs,[11] most are hesitant: Djaït calls Gindibu's group only 'proto-Arabs',[12] and others are more sceptical, arguing that the lexical similarity between Assyrian *Arba-ā* and today's 'Arab' does not signify an ethnic bond across the centuries.[13] The scepticism is reasoned, since building the *Arba-ā* into a narrative of Arab communal identity is hampered by the absence of any records indicating that Gindibu's people called themselves 'Arabs' and/or imagined communal affinities with their neighbouring groups such that we could classify the people whom Shalmaneser III called *Arba-ā* as members of one wider Arab ethnos. Moreover, the first histories of the Arabs written in Arabic 1,500 years after Shalmaneser III never recall wars with Assyrians, or other events so long before Islam,[14] nor did any self-designated Arab groups in early Islam claim descent from an ancestral 'Gindibu'. The *Arba-ā* occupied land which many centuries later was populated by self-designated Arabs, and there may be some diluted blood relations, but the idea of ethnicity discounts racial bloodlines and focuses instead on communal memory, and Gindibu's *Arba-ā* left no legacy for Arab memories. From the perspective of ethnos and Arabness, therefore, the *Arba-ā* seem a false start for the Arab story.[15]

The name *Arba-ā* does resemble 'Arab' so closely as to beg a connection, but fusing a name with a sense of ethnic identity is not straightforward as a matter of theory, particularly in the *Arba-ā*'s case. It was the Assyrians who recorded the name *Arba-ā*, and consideration of its Akkadian etymology reveals that as opposed to being one specific group's own ethnonym, the term was perhaps an Assyrian creation coined to represent a type of people in general. *Arba-ā* is similar to the common Semitic word *ᶜarabah* meaning 'steppe',[16] as well as Assyrian words for 'the west' (*erebu*),[17] 'fields'/'uncultivated land' (*arbu*),[18] and 'outsider'/'person without family' (*arbu* and *arbutu*).[19] Robin and Dousse suggest that *Arba-ā* thus connoted generic 'westerners', 'outsiders' and/or 'steppe nomads',[20] and since the *Arba-ā* mentioned by Shalmaneser III lived in western deserts outside of Assyrian control, the explanation is logical. Another possibility which has hitherto escaped emphasis is the affinity between *Arba-ā* and Assyrian words for 'locusts' (*erbū*, *aribu* and *arabū*).[21] Given that Gindibu's name may also connote a kind of locust, it may be that Assyrian administrators viewed outsider nomadic groups as threats to the stability of their Syrian borders, and coined the term *Arba-ā* to articulate their impressions of that existential threat. Assyrian locust-words were elsewhere used metaphorically for plagues and affliction, and *arbutu* also means 'devastation' or 'ruin' (compare with *arbu*, 'uncultivated/unworked land'),[22] revealing semantic associations between 'Arab'-sounding words in Assyrian and the sort of menace posed to agrarian communities by nomadic marauders.

Arba-ā thus appears to be readable as an Assyrian invention, a designation applied by a settled empire for the idea of dangerous (western) nomads, and the word would accordingly be neither an ethnonym nor a reflection of how peoples inside Arabia expressed their own senses of community. This suggests that long before any community used the name 'Arab' to describe itself, the word 'Arab' was a term of imperial administrative jargon, and administrators conceptualised 'Arabness' as a category of outsider. Consequently, it is vital to reappraise ancient evidence with a view to considering how imperial administrative references to 'Arabs' relate to senses of belonging to a community; otherwise if we cobble all references to 'Arabs' from disparate sources into one cohesive 'Arab story', we risk unifying separate peoples who never sensed kinship amongst themselves and only shared the coincidental common trait of being seen as 'outsiders' in the Assyrians' eyes. Numerous 'Arab'-sounding names reappear in later Assyrian records, and our task now turns to explore whether they do connote one cohesive Arab ethnos (as often maintained, most recently in Retsö's detailed study),[23] or if Assyrians instead used the word 'Arab' idiosyncratically.

Assyrian records after Shalmaneser III fall silent on Gindibu's *Arba-ā*, but 125–200 years later (between the eighth and seventh centuries BCE) they report *Aribi*, *Arabaa*, and other 'Arab'-cognates as nomadic groups on Assyria's desert fringes in what is now Syria, Jordan and Iraq.[24] These peoples are depicted in wall reliefs as tent-dwelling, simply-clothed, lightly-armed warriors on camelback,[25] which dovetail with traditional archetypes about original Arab Bedouin identity,[26] and Assyrians cite *Aribi*/*Arabaa* as collective labels under which tribal names are sometimes subsumed,[27] also similar to the manner 'Arab' was employed to group an array of tribes in the early Islamic period. With our knowledge in hindsight that Arabs currently inhabit the desert steppes south of the Fertile Crescent, it is again tempting to read the Assyrian records as evidence of the first 'Arabs', but there are cogent reasons for circumspection, and even to doubt that Assyrian administrative texts evidence the origins of the Arab community connected with Islam's rise, some 1,300 years later.

The names by which the Assyrians referred to their nomadic neighbours all sound like 'Arab' to us, but they are not identical, and it is unclear whether the Assyrians intended them as references to one single ethnos. Consider, for example, the term *Urbi* which appears in Sennacherib's reign (705–681 BCE) to describe groups in both the Levant and southern Babylonia. If *Urbi* was yet another alternative Assyrian rendering of the name 'Arab', then it would evidence a wide geographic spread of the Arab ethnos, but *Urbi* could instead have meant 'mercenaries' without ethnic associations, and this may be the more accurate translation.[28] Even interpreting the more commonly encountered 'Arab'-cognates as connoting one Arab people is hampered since the Assyrians used the names unsystematically,[29] and sometimes conflictingly. For example, records of the Assyrian Sargon II (721–705 BCE) expressly distinguish *Arbāya* from *Arabaa*.[30] In other texts, Sargon II's scribes refer to *Aribi* living between Palestine and Egypt, but one generation earlier, during Tiglath-Pileser III's reign (744–727 BCE), scribes named some inhabitants of that same region *Aruba* and others *Idibiʾil*. Retsö, who interprets Assyrian testimony to prove that 'Arabs' constituted one ethnic group in ancient times, reads the *Aruba* of Tiglath-Pileser III as one and the same as the *Aribi* of Sargon II, and subsumes the *Idibiʾil* into the same Arab ethnos too, but he admits difficulties in maintaining the interpretation.[31] The array of names and their idiosyncratic usage make it difficult to grasp how the Assyrians differentiated their nomadic neighbours, and prompts questions of whether they understood or indeed cared about Arabian ethnic composition at all.

Theories of ethnogenesis erect additional challenges to read Assyrian records as evidence for the development of an Arab ethnic community. The transactionist model outlined in the Introduction (p. 11) stresses that consciousness of community arises from regular transactions between groups across boundaries: did the Assyrian/Arabian frontier constitute such a boundary that could have sustained the growth of an Arab imagined community? In search of answers, we recall that ethnic boundaries are not simply lines on a map, and in order for a group on one side to develop consciousness of kinship, they require a unity of interests amongst themselves and continuity of interaction across stable boundaries to sustain ethnogenesis. In the Assyrian/Arabian case, groups of people on the non-Assyrian side of the border shared a commonality inasmuch as they were non-Assyrian, but this neither axiomatically requires that they all must have banded together, nor that they even imagined broad communal ties expressible as 'the Arabs', particularly because the typical drivers of ethnogenesis are absent. At different times, some groups were at war with the Assyrians, others (like *Urbi*) seem allied, some were subject to Assyrian authority,[32] others settled peacefully around the borders, and yet others remained at large and warlike in the Arabian interior. Assumptions that all the peoples whom the Assyrians labelled with words resembling 'Arab' constituted one socially and even politically cohesive ethnos,[33] overlook the varied transactional environment and the differing interests of the various Arabian groups. The commonalities needed in order to realistically gel a sense of unity within Arabia appear absent.

When reappraising the Assyrian evidence about Arabian populations, it becomes apparent that interpretations hitherto privileged the perspective of empire, which engenders substantial risks of misjudging peoples outside imperial boundaries. The imperial view treats ancient Arabia analogously to nineteenth-century European conceptions of Africa that viewed its peoples as an interchangeable array of tribes all categorisable as 'Negroid'. The outsider is unaware of local differences, the imperial outsiders' perceived superiority prompts a disregard of distant peoples as unworthy of closer scrutiny in any event, and the imperialists' power enables them to write history in their own voice. From the Assyrian perspective, Arabian peoples were desert dwellers and non-Assyrian, and this entitled Assyrian imperial administrators to generalise about them. But if we draw straightforward interpretations about Arabian communities from Assyrian records, we become Assyrians ourselves and adopt their prejudgements. Modern theories of ethnic formation instruct that the mere fact that Arabians were not Assyrian would not of itself compel them to marshal that difference to unify themselves, nor that they were aware that they could call themselves *Aribi* or *Arabaa*. The notion that 'Arab' signified a definite, ethnically distinct and cohesive community,[34] accordingly pays too little attention to the ways in which changing lifestyles and transactions over a vast area from the Sinai to southern Mesopotamia may have altered the consciousness of ethnic identity, especially in the face of significant sociopolitical transformations in Syria and Mesopotamia during the quarter-millennium between Shalmaneser III and Ashurbanipal.

Claims that the Arabs constituted one ethnically cohesive community in the Assyrian period also place undue reliance on 'cultural stuff' (see p. 12), particularly camels, to delineate that community. For example, from the observation that Arabs were camel experts, Retsö concludes that whenever pack-camels are referenced in historical records, they were 'probably handled by Arabs', and extrapolates the existence of Arab groups from the presence of camels between Palestine and Western Iran.[35] Here Retsö adopts an enduringly popular, though misleading, topos that assumes Arabs are inextricably linked with camels,[36] and hence he (and numerous previous scholars) finds 'Arabs' even where evidence is 'admittedly scanty'.[37] Ethnographers would shun the notion that a particular form of animal herding can drive cohesion on its own, and the varied transactional environment coupled with the different relations between the various communities of camel herders and the succession of Assyrian regimes between the ninth and seventh centuries BCE leave little scope to understand how camel handling expertise enabled so many different groups to perceive unity amongst themselves.

Other factors, particularly commonalities of language and employment in frontier defence, are also adduced to explain ancient Arab ethnogenesis, but these too lack explanatory power. Language is another 'cultural stuff' trait: the uneven changes to a language over time and space can drive people apart as easily as similar dialects can glue them together, and mutual intelligibility between speech groups does not, of its own, prompt ethnogenesis. Furthermore, proponents of ancient Arab ethnogenesis, such as Retsö, are unable to find substantial evidence of the Arabic language creating one speech community of Arabs beyond scattered onomastic evidence which they do not problematise,[38] and instead find Arabs where the records merely proffer individual names which 'we would classify as a form of Arabic'[39] – a difficult a priori assumption – since we should instead like to find indication that the people who went by those names classified themselves as 'Arabs' and recognised ethnic interrelations. The second proposition that Arab identity coalesced from a common task of frontier guardianship is also static and breeds generalisations that all desert frontier guards across centuries must have been Arabs, even when the records do not use a cognate of 'Arab' to label them, as if border patrolling was the Arabs' hereditary monopoly.[40] The argument is, moreover, insensitive to the transactional ramifications of frontier guardianship: guards are allied to empire and wield coercive force against those further into the desert; as such, even if the frontier guards and nomads shared cultural traits, language and/or common heritage, the guards' status, power and disruptive activities bring their interests more into line with empire than with outsiders, and so divide what may have been former unities.[41] The assumption that an 'Arab' community always maintained its single, stable core throughout Assyrian times does not discharge the burden of explaining how 250 years of changing alliances and conflicts with Assyria could have kept 'Arabs' together between the Sinai and Iraq: we are left with an array of names, but little else to understand how a single Arab community formed in these circumstances.

One crucial and sometimes overlooked congruency across the sum of Assyrian evidence is the variety in the ways Assyrians discussed peoples in Arabia. The Assyrians engaged in a variety of different interactions with Arabians, and they gave them various names: *Aribi*, *Idibiʾil*, *Urbi*, *Arabaa*, *Arubu*, *Qi-idri*, *Qadari* amongst others.[42] Assyrian records accordingly afford glimpses into a plurality of groups across a wide area, often acting independently of each other. Many of the names sound like 'Arab' to us, but the records give no sense of a swelling cohesive ethnic community that permits conceptualising one Arab unity which endured 1,500 years from Shalmaneser III to the Islamic era – especially considering that Arabic-language records have no memory, not even mythological tales, of such early generations.[43] Since the Assyrians never employed one name to describe Arabians, and since they never described all Arabians in identical terms, the varied 'Arab'-cognates in Assyrian records do not, at face value, need to be consolidated. It seems that names resembling 'Arab' conjured generic images of nomadism in the minds of Assyrian administrators, and modern interpretations have anachronistically marshalled Assyrian texts into sources for the pre-history of the Islamic-era Arab community. Upon reflection, observers could be commended for siding with Ephʾal's cautious analysis that avoids drawing direct connections between Assyria's desert neighbours and the Arabs of Muhammad's day.[44]

From Babylon to Rome: 612 BCE – 106 CE

Notwithstanding the grounds to doubt the origins of a cohesive Arab community in Assyrian times, the Arabness puzzle is yet more convoluted since cognates of the word 'Arab' persist in records after the Assyrian collapse. Neo-Babylonian (612–539 BCE) scribes chronicle their kings' campaigns against the *Arabi*, particularly around Palestine and the Sinai,[45] and the succeeding Mesopotamian power, the Achaemenids (539–330 BCE) refer to *Arabāya* variously located between Gaza and Dedan (north-west Saudi Arabia).[46] Classical Greek writers chime in from the fifth century BCE with Herodotus' description of Arabs whom he identifies as all those people living between the east bank of the Nile and Mesopotamia.[47] He was unaware that the Red Sea divides the region, but once it was discovered during Alexander's naval explorations, Hellenistic writers revised the map, demarcating the Peninsula which they called *Αραβια*, and labelled its population *Αραβιή*.[48] Greek nomenclature initiated the enduring meld of Arabian space and Arab race which still influences conceptions that 'Arabia' is synonymous with 'Arab',[49] and the Romans, the next Middle Eastern superpower, seamlessly continued the Greek tradition of describing Arabia and its 'Arabs' into the first century CE.[50]

The Hellenistic invention of the idea of Arabia as uniform 'Arab land' ought to be emphasised. Greco-Roman discourses were transferred across the centuries to form the 'classical tradition' and the foundational blocks of European scholarship, and with regards to the Middle East, Robert Irwin's absorbing study of the intellectual background of early modern European scholars reveals the effects of their study of the Classics on their outlooks.[51] Eighteenth and nineteenth century European writings in turn formed the foundations of Orientalism and our contemporary Academy, and hence the Hellenistic meld of Arabian space and 'Arab' race is deeply engrained across generations of European scholarship. The manifold contemporary theories that the Arabs were Arabia's earliest populations can almost certainly trace their genealogy to Hellenistic discourses.

Interpretations of Arab origins are thus pulled in conflicting directions. On one hand, we have seen that the varied transactional boundaries between Assyria, Babylon, Achaemenid Iran and their nomadic neighbours are of the sort which confound ethnogenesis, and the 'locust' connotations of 'Arab'-cognates in Akkadian hint that the 'Arab'-sounding names in the sources were externally applied labels to what were actually disparate peoples with different senses of their own identities. The idiosyncratic manner in which the Assyrians and others used 'Arab'-cognates seems to confirm that there was no single shared sense of Arab imagined community amongst Arabian groups across these eight centuries, and assumptions of ancient Arab-Arabian origins stem instead from Hellenistic generalisations. But on the other hand, the repetition of 'Arab'-sounding names to label people in the deserts south of the Fertile Crescent across nine centuries and five imperial regimes seems curiously consistent. There may be a solution, however, if we explore the hypothesis that the 'Arab'-cognates was never intended to refer to one Arab ethnos: the terms are not identical, and pictorial depictions occasionally differ too (for example, Achaemenid palace reliefs show *Arabāya* in various dress rather unlike the *Aribi* depicted by Assyrian sculptors).[52] Most importantly, the textual evidence may be misleading us: all sources considered so far were written by peoples living outside Arabia who neither recorded how Arabian populations conceptualised their own communities, nor whether Arabians were conscious that one Arab community united them. We should like to link the outsiders' evidence with analysis of the Arab ethnonym inside Arabia, and herein Arabia's own pre-Islamic epigraphic record offers unexpected testimony.

II Arabs in Arabia: Ethnonyms, Interpretations and Problems

In order to identify Arab origins in the historical record, we seek a meaningful sense of group identity – evidence of consciousness of communal cohesion between transacting groups who used the name 'Arab' as the symbol for their conceptual unity.[53] With this in mind, one of the most salient impediments to locating Arabness is the surprising absence of reference to 'Arab' people or 'Arabian' land in any ancient records from the Peninsula. Archaeologists have unearthed thousands of pre-Islamic inscriptions from Yemen to Syria, dated between the eighth century BCE and sixth century CE,[54] but in no case do texts refer to homeland as 'Arabia'.[55] The absence of reference to common homeland/place of shared origin implies an absence of broad communal consciousness, and that Arabian groups instead conceptualised their identities in more fragmentary, localised terms. This accords with the array of different names by which outsiders refer to Arabian populations, and supports the inference that in Ancient and Hellenistic times, there was no Arabian–Arab ethnos which imagined central Arabia (or any substantial part of the Peninsula) as its proprietary space.

An ethnic community indeed can exist without leaving many written traces of its sense of homeland, but the question of ancient Arabian communal organisation becomes even more surprising when we consider that from the thousands of Arabian inscriptions, there are perhaps only eleven references to 'Arabs' as a people.[56] Instead of sustained signs of a self-expressed Arab community, we have instead a sparse and staccato record: two references to ^{c}*rb* ('Arabs') in circa seventh–sixth century BCE Yemen,[57] 500 years of silence, five Yemeni inscriptions mentioning ^{c}*rb* between the first century BCE and the third century CE, one fourth-century Syrian epitaph of an enigmatically entitled 'King of the Arabs', and three references to Arabs in Yemeni inscriptions between the fourth and sixth centuries.[58] The small sample size is significant because pre-Islamic Arabians, even nomadic groups, did leave many written records referring to their communities, and inscription writing proliferated across Arabia from the fifth century BCE onwards. Hence the complete absence of reference to 'Arabia' as homeland, coupled with the only trace reference to the word 'Arab' hinders attempts to adduce a swelling sense of Arab communal identity.

The minute quantity of references to 'Arab' over 1,500 years of Arabian inscriptions is further complicated by the inscriptions' context and meaning. Christian Robin has worked most closely with the material, and while he suggests there are 'about sixty' references to 'Arab'-sounding words in South Arabian texts,[59] some 'Arab'-cognates in South Arabian languages are no longer deemed reference to groups of people,[60] and connecting any of the words with a sense of ethnic identity confronts difficulties. Robin identifies three lexical items from South Arabian inscriptions dated between the first century BCE and fifth century CE: ^{c}*rb* (^{c}*arab*), ^{c}*rby* (^{c}*arabī* – an adjective 'Arabic') and ʾ^{c}*rb* (*a*^{c}*rub* – a plural (?) of ^{c}*rb*).[61] Like the Assyrian texts centuries before, the terms in the South Arabian inscriptions resemble the word for Arabs (*ᶜarab*) familiar today, but, also akin to the Assyrian case, it is challenging to declare the sum of South Arabian writing as evidence of one Arab ethnos. First, the inscriptions are not in Arabic and predate the earliest examples of Arabic language inscriptions by several centuries.[62] Second, and moreover, the 'Arab'-sounding words are used to describe groups of 'tribesmen', 'hill-dwellers',[63] or 'Bedouin'/'Bedouin mercenaries':[64] these 'Arabs' are outsiders in the eyes of the inscriptions' writers who never called *themselves* Arabs: instead they referred to their own South Arabian identities and territories as Sabaᵓ, Ḥimyar, Ḥaḍramawt, amongst others.[65] In the fifth century CE, the South Arabian Ḥimyar kingdom made significant advances into central Arabia and counted *ᵓᶜrb* as conquered peoples, yet inferring from these records that *ᵓᶜrb* connoted a political unity of 'the Arabs' extrapolates quite far from the bare statement in the Himyaritic political titulature, and it would be equally possible (and supported by the earlier usage of the word *ᵓᶜrb* as generic nomads) to interpret the title to mean rule over 'the tribal groups' without ethnic tones. Other research into central Arabian political culture in the fifth century CE does not support the impression that a broad Arab 'political entity' existed, and hence favours non-ethnic interpretations of the Himyarites' references to *ᵓᶜrb*.[66]

Third, the term *ᵓᶜrb* occurs much more frequently that *ᶜrb*, and while Robin reads them both as reference to one and the same people, the approach is insensitive to the nature of Arab communal consciousness. We will see in Chapters 3 and 4 that populations who first enter historical records referring to themselves as 'Arabs' (*al-ᶜarab*) specifically distinguished themselves from *ᵓᶜrb/aᶜrāb*. And given the long tradition in Semitic languages (originating with the Assyrians' *Arba-ā*) to use the word *ᵓᶜrb* to connote the idea of nomadism and otherness,[67] it would seem incorrect to retrospectively reinterpret South Arabian citations of outsider *ᵓᶜrb* and *ᶜrb* as both references to one Arab ethnos unless we can find evidence that people did use the word *ᵓᶜrb* to describe themselves, and herein the evidence indicates otherwise.

The South Arabian texts, like all other ancient Arabian inscriptions almost never contain 'Arab'-cognates as a reference to 'self'. Robin notes that 'is very exceptional that [people] declare themselves as Arabs',[68] and there are only two South Arabian texts dated to the third century CE in which individuals are called *^{c}rby*.[69] This is surely significant: if words resembling 'Arab' mean 'nomadic outsider' and are also invariably the property of someone else who imposed the label on an outsider population, how legitimate is it for us to vacuum up these references and assume they refer to one consciousness of 'Arab' ethnos? The two South Arabian examples are a case in point: if the 'Arabs' did connote a sizeable community, the survival of only two inscriptions where people are self-identified as Arabs is very puzzling. The names of the individuals listed on those inscriptions are also not, to my knowledge, Arabic-language names: ^{c}tybt, Gdwt and Snd. Could it be, therefore, that these three people were members of varied nomadic communities who settled in the towns of South Arabia and were called *^{c}rbī* on account of their nomadic origins, thus meaning *^{c}rbī* designated their nomad identity in the eyes of settled South Arabians, not their ethnic group? Individuals can operate with multiple designations, and there is no evidence that those people called themselves *^{c}rbī* when communicating with their own kin, which bears the interpretation that they used *^{c}rbī* as a label specifically when dealing with sedentary others.[70]

The evidence is ultimately better stacked to indicate that nomadic Arabian groups did not call themselves 'Arabs', since the epigraphic corpus contains a wealth of more localised tribal names, and not one over-arching term indicating broader collective consciousness of community which is crucial for ethnogenesis. The plethora of tribal names, the absence of self-designations of 'Arabs', and the fact that 'Arab'-sounding words carried nomadic/outsider connotations, all combine to make it rather remote to adduce the evidence as the basis of Arab origins. South Arabian inscriptions paint a picture of central Arabia filled with scattered, independent nomadic groups lacking both a sense of over-arching community and evidence of a political system to unite them.

And here we return to the crux of the matter. None of the inscriptions have been tested through the lens of ethnogenesis. Pre-Islamic history is approached with the intention of finding 'Arabs': the stark absence of any populations calling themselves 'Arabs' is noted as 'disappointing',[71] but narratives of Arab origins are nonetheless constructed from references to nomads written by outsiders. The mentions of 'Arab'-sounding cognates in the South Arabian inscriptions therefore much resemble the Assyrian-era material:

both point into an external distant desert where some groups of people are generalised as being *ʾʿrb* or *Aribi* or *Arba-ā*. And since conclusions about Arab origins from this material are based on primarily onomastic observation, there is some arbitrariness as to which 'Arab'-cognates scholars choose to count as referring to 'ethnic' Arabs, and which ones are merely generic terms for 'nomads'.[72] Without more recourse to the theoretical considerations of ethnogenesis, we still do not know if anyone used the word 'Arab' as a designator for 'self', and equally, we cannot evaluate whether transactional boundaries, sociopolitical forces and cultural affinities could have sparked Arab ethnogenesis.

The inscriptions reveal that various peoples on the edges of the Arabian Desert used words resembling 'Arab' to describe other groups in the interior as nomads/outsiders, but no groups emerge proclaiming their own Arabness. (Syria's al-Namāra inscription and its phrase 'King of the Arabs' may seem to affirm the existence of an Arab identity – but its meaning will become clearer via our next chapter's closer contextualisation of central Arabia in the three centuries before Islam). Cognates of the word 'Arab' meant 'nomads', and never 'the Arab people': in pre-Islam, 'Arab' seems to be a label without a people, an idea lacking a precise group to which it referred. In contrast, Arabs are visible as a self-aware community in Islamic times, and so we are now obliged to wonder how far back into pre-Islam Arab communal origins should be plotted. When and why did Arabians become conscious of an Arab unity, and how can we tell? Referring to Weber and the models of ethnogenesis, we cannot tell from DNA – we seek indications of formerly disparate peoples gathering around a consciousness of Arabness, and we shall want to know what it meant to be an Arab.

A Radical Theory Revisited

We can now appreciate the current divergence of opinion regarding Arab origins. We only possess indications about an array of varied groups labelled as 'nomadic outliers' from the ninth century BCE to the dawn of Islam, who neither expressed their own unity nor can be tied together in the ways theorists identify as conducive to ethnogenesis. The puzzle of Arab origins now crosses two millennia of history, and since names and labels in pre-Islamic epigraphy proffer no conclusive answers, new interpretations are needed.

One alternative is D. H. Müller's now much-overlooked 1896 proposal that Arab identity only came into existence with Islam when the Prophet Muhammad coined the term 'Arab' as a novel means to gather tribes into a 'nation' as a 'religious-state collective' (*Glaubens- und Staatsgenossenschaft*).[73] Müller's theory was perhaps too radical for its day: Weber's thesis about ethnicity's subjective and plastic nature was yet unpublished, and late nineteenth and early twentieth-century Europeans adhered to nationalist and primordialist doctrines which imagined that nations rose from ancient racial bloodlines. The Arabs were counted as such a race/nation, and it would have been inconceivable for most of Müller's contemporaries to imagine that ethnicities could be made and un-made by sociopolitical circumstances, or that Arabs only came into existence in the seventh century CE. Accordingly, scholars rejected Müller: Nöldeke's 1899 essay on Arabs marshalled comparative philology to 'prove' that ancient Semitic words related to ᶜ-r-b connote 'desert' and 'nomad', and so 'confirmed' that the Arabs indeed existed as nomads for centuries before Muhammad.[74] Nöldeke buttressed the racial stereotype, banished Müller's theory, and most over the last century have imagined the first Arabs as pre-Islamic Bedouin.[75] But the replacement of 'racialist' thinking with the more nuanced theories of ethnogenesis, the inconclusive pre-Islamic evidence reviewed here, and Donner's recent hypothesis that Arab unity could be conceptualised as a Muslim-era phenomenon, do suggest that it may be time to give Müller a second chance. To do so, we can first evaluate justifications for challenging Nöldeke's Bedouin thesis, given that it remains the dominant archetype for conceptualising pre-Islamic Arab identity.

Arabs in a Vacuum

Nöldeke left opinions about Arab history in a bind. Avowals that Arabs 'must have' existed in pre-Islamic Arabia contradict the absence of Arab self-awareness across pre-Islamic epigraphy, and so when we read Muslim-era accounts of people expressly calling themselves *al-ᶜarab* (Arabs), the Arab ethnos seems to emerge from nowhere to take centre-stage in Arabic literature. In order to explain the abrupt conjuring of Arabs into history during early Islam, much recent scholarship resorts to finessing the lack of evidence by proposing that Arab ethnogenesis took place during the two–three centuries before Islam in al-Ḥijāz, a mountainous and desert region in north-west Arabia where the argument states that nomadic groups began coalescing into a super-tribal cultural community that called itself 'Arab'.[76] The Ḥijāzī theory appeals because we know little about north-west Arabia in Late Antiquity: until very recently, few inscriptions and scant archaeological material datable to the third–sixth centuries CE had been found in al-Ḥijāz, and few Latin or Byzantine observers recorded anything about its history. Hence Late Antique al-Ḥijāz is a nearly empty void offering a silence from which Arab origins cannot easily be *dis*proven. But here the theory begins to lose explanatory power: it cannot positively identify nascent Arab communities (no inscriptions mentioning 'Arabs' have been found in al-Ḥijāz), and instead it relies on what James Montgomery's cogent critique refers to as the 'seductiveness of the Bedouin' and the convenience of the 'Empty Ḥijāz' as a 'hermetically sealed' receptacle to project Arab origins.[77] The theory leaves us having to accept, effectively on faith, that a sense of Arab community matured in a 'pagan reservation'[78] of the Ḥijāzī deserts during the centuries before Islam.

From our perspective of ethnogenesis, we can further deconstruct the Ḥijāzī theory's insinuation that 'Arabs' spontaneously emerged from a way of life shared between Bedouin communities because the theory relies on 'cultural stuff' as the primary component of Arab ethnogenesis. It argues that Arab unity was formed around language and poetry, as if similar language idioms and participation in a poetry-based system of cultural values prompted nomads to become aware of their distinct ethnic identity.[79] Such approaches render Arab identity beholden to culture, and are thus theoretically suspect because cultural traits are usually too arbitrary and too susceptible to change to drive otherwise disparate people into a cohesive community. Shared culture can accelerate the pace of ethnogenesis where groups are already coming together via more dynamic sociopolitical drivers, but where such drivers are absent, cultural traits do not build bridges to unity on their own. When scholars seek the more tangible drivers to explain Arab ethnogenesis – such as a common political system, economic interests, creed or otherwise – the Ḥijāzī theory's desert vacuum is empty-handed: it offers only intangibles to imagine Arab origins.

In the Arab case, the 'cultural stuff' approach risks distorting the past. It defines historical Arab identity via a set of 'Arab traits' which we determine today, and so withholds the right for pre-Islamic Arabians to identify themselves. The Ḥijāzi theory does not take the notion of communal identity seriously: it determines 'Arab' now and imposes it on then; this is primordialist and overlooks how pre-Islamic Arabians ordered their own communities.[80] Moreover, the 'Arab traits' of poetry and cultural practices are not evidenced in the archaeological record: they are instead derived from Muslim-era sources about pre-Islamic Arabs. Before we can use those traits to reconstruct a totality of pre-Islamic Arab life and community, we need to consider that Muslim-era writers lived centuries after pre-Islamic times and they were not empirical positivists. They reconstructed pre-Islamic history under various guises, and it is methodologically unsound to plumb an assortment of their books for 'raw facts' without critical analysis. Part Two of this book examines the array of Muslim discourses and Abbasid-era guises which invented an apparent homogeneity for pre-Islamic Arabica, and thus obscured the real divisions and diversity of the Arabian past. If critical analysis is not undertaken when employing these Arabic literary records, writers will perpetuate millennium-old Muslim agendas in their reconstructions of the pre-Muslim past today.[81]

The pernicious result of the Ḥijāz–Bedouin model of Arab origins is an air of platitudinous generalisation that reconstructs Arabs as faceless archetypes with preset and homogenised beliefs, activities and identity. Maps of Arabia are drawn marking the diffusion of tribal names, but each is equally and interchangeably 'Arab' and there is little sense that they constitute different cultural areas.[82] Powerful groups such as Kinda, Ghassān and Lakhm[83] are depicted patrolling the desert, but their wars and interactions are portrayed as internal 'Arab family' affairs – they are presumed to have acted and looked alike. Pre-Islamic Arabia certainly housed nomads and witnessed conflicts, but to what extent are our impressions of these peoples' Arabness the result of Muslim historians homogenising pre-Islamic history for us? We assume Muslim writers knew what 'Arab culture' was – but their static depictions of pre-Islamic 'Arabs' across all of Arabia are curious and offer convoluted parallels when compared with Late Antique records.[84] We lack answers as to when, where and, most importantly, why groups first chose the name Arab as their ethnonym, and by retreating into cultural archetypes to conceptualise Arabness, pre-Islamic Arab identity settles into a static nativism which ultimately bears remarkable parallels with an ill-conceived discourse formerly employed to generalise about the ethnic unity of native North Americans. Highlighting these intriguing parallels can inspire a reorientation in our study of *Arabica.*

The Problems of Nativism

Until the later twentieth century, American history writers conceptualised 'Indian' identity as a certain essence shared between pre-Columbian groups within the geographical unit of 'America' in ways similar to the manner Arab is used to circumscribe the identity of pre-Islamic Arabia. The idea of 'Indian-ness' constructed an internal pre-Columbian American homogeneity in which Indians interacted with each other in contrast to the portrayal of Europeans arriving as definitive outsiders. Writers articulated a tribally organised 'Indian culture' that subsumed Aleutian fishermen, Navajo farmers and Algonquian hunter-gatherers, akin to the manner in which 'Arab culture' constructs a tribal system subsuming Bedouin, the 'Bedouinising' principalities of Ghassān and Lakhm,[85] as well as traders and agriculturalists across Arabia into one 'Arab' mould. Huron and Iroquois played a role analogous to that of Ghassān and Lakhm, acting at the behest of external imperial powers to control their fellow 'natives'. Likewise, descriptions of 'Indian tribes' such as the Sioux and Cheyenne resemble Arabian Bakr and Taghlib (or other neighbouring pairings): their mutual enmity was imagined to have maintained a string of desultory tribal squabbles, whilst their perceived Indian-ness and Arabness, respectively, purportedly explained how they banded together for 'national' struggles such as Little Big Horn and Dhū Qār.[86]

Pre-Islamic Arabia is, in short, ghettoised by Arabness in the same way pre-Columbian North America was by the paradigm of Indian-ness. And in both cases, the 'Arab' and 'Indian' ethnonyms were imposed from the outside. Pre-Columbian peoples could never have called themselves 'Indians' (they did not live in India, after all!), nor, does it seem pre-Islamic Arabians called themselves 'Arabs'. Accordingly, the 'Arab' idea appears as an outsiders' invention to whitewash and/or simplify contours in Arabian history and identity. Recent American histories debunk Indian-ness essentialising, and scholars no longer work under misconceptions that Native Americans can be analysed via broad cultural unities with neat tribal subdivisions.[87] Modern

Arab identity has also been freed from former misconceptions about the 'Arab mind' and 'Arab world', and the new model ought to be applicable to ancient Arabness.

In the case of ancient Arabs, scholars have been aware of the evidential problems, but the will to prove the existence pre-Islamic Arabs in (at least some) parts of Late Antique Arabia is overriding, and engenders curious assertions. Consider von Grunebaum's argument that pre-Islamic Arabs were a *Kulturnation*,[88] a community whose members recognised their unity from their shared cultural practices, yet never felt the need to leave express records of their community's name.[89] It is difficult to fathom that whole generations of Arabians would never state their name, and it seems more likely that twentieth-century paradigms about the ancient fixedness of racial archetypes compelled von Grunebaum to articulate his theory. Some recent studies vigorously assert the existence of pre-Islamic 'Arab identity' without substantiation beyond reference to the familiar 'Arab' cultural traits,[90] but building on Montgomery's critique of the 'seductiveness of the Bedouin', we need also be wary of the seductiveness of poetry and culture as the trigger for Arab ethnogenesis. The pervasive Muslim-era assurances in Arabic literature that one Arab ethno-cultural community encompassed pre-Islamic Arabia do not tally with the pre-Islamic evidence, and trying to navigate the material to reconstruct pre-Islamic Arab history had consistently yielded unwieldy results. Hoyland's recent study of Islam's rise reveals the extent of the paradox: in parts he affirms pre-Islamic Arab identity, but elsewhere he considers evidence suggesting Arabs did not exist at the dawn of Islam.[91] At this juncture, a rethink is needed.

Returning to first principles, the observation that 'Arab', akin to 'Indian', originates as an externally applied label to categorise an 'Arabian other' 'over-there' is significant since stories of ancient Arabness are almost always told for a purpose serving the interests of outsiders. Some employ the antiquity of Arabness to establish Arab rights to land in the Middle East,[92] others use it to reverse old European stereotypes that the Arabs were backward Bedouin,[93] while others need a broad community of Arabs to have existed in order to articulate secular explanations for the seventh century conquests as an ethnic (Arab), not religious (Muslim), undertaking.[94] In each case, pre-Islamic Arabness is a commodity – an object imagined by an outsider and marshalled to bolster competing visions of history. Like the top-down cultural definitions of Arabness itself, the idea of Arab identity loses autonomy and becomes subservient to modern reconstruction. Since pre-Islamic Arabs themselves refuse to speak up and proclaim their community's existence, we may be backtracking Arab history too far into Antiquity. The remainder of this and the next chapter consider the evidence afresh, reappraise how pre-Islamic Arabians organised themselves, and re-evaluate the genesis of Arab communal consciousness.

III An Arabness Pretence: Pre-Islamic 'Arab'-Cognates Reconsidered

Reinterpreting Arabness returns to the *Arba-ā/Aribi/Arabāya/Αραβιή* names of Assyrian, Babylonian, Persian and Greek records. Their resemblance to today's 'Arab' suggests that the names in ancient records must represent varied attempts by different foreign observers to reproduce the native ethnicon *ᶜarab* by which Arabian people must have referred to themselves, but most historians reject this and propose that only some of the Arab-cognates refer to the Arab people.[95] We discussed above the attendant arbitrariness in deciding which textual 'Arabs' were actual ethnic 'Arabs', and we need a resolution grounded in sustained interrogation of the precise relationship between outsiders' labels and Arabian senses of community.

We noted at the outset of this chapter that the Assyrian Shalmaneser III's scribes may have coined the name *Arba-ā* themselves from Akkadian words for 'western/desert/outsiders', and/or 'locust/destructive menace'. The name is apt for Assyrian ears given the threats they perceived from certain nomadic groups, and lends to the interpretation that Assyrians invented the term *Arba-ā* independently from the actual names of Arabian communities. It then follows that the term became part of Assyrian administrative jargon to convey the idea of pesky western nomadic outliers, and this would explain why subsequent generations of Assyrian administrators reused *Arba-ā*-like cognates over the next 250 years as new groups buffeted the imperial frontier. The various and idiosyncratic forms of *Arba-ā*-cognates are products of an Assyrian nomenclatural model, representing varied attempts across generations of Assyrian scribes to try (or not try very hard) to distinguish different nomadic groups for the purpose of imperial records. The similarity between the terms can be explained as reflecting the undifferentiated impressions

Assyrians had of distant nomadic groups, and need not bear relation to the names the groups applied to themselves, nor would it imply that the nomadic groups imagined themselves as members of one cohesive community from the ninth-century BCE *Arba-ā* to the seventh-century BCE *Aribi*.

When the Neo-Babylonians defeated the Assyrians in 612 BCE, they inherited the Assyrians' Akkadian-language administrative system, and with it, its Arab-cognate jargon, which Babylonian officials employed when they needed to identify outlying nomadic groups to their south-west. In 539 BCE, the Neo-Babylonians fell to the Achaemenids, but since Achaemenid administrators had to maintain similar control on their frontiers, they perpetuated the Arab-cognates in turn, changing the pronunciation to a Persianate *Arabāya*. By this time, if not earlier, the original Assyrian meaning of *Arba-ā* may have been forgotten, but the legacy of the term's long-repeated use ensured that the word survived as the label for nomad/outsider-ness. Crucially, during the flow of 400 years between Shalmaneser III's *Arba-ā* and the Achaemenid *Arabāya*, neither the succession of scribes, nor the military networks reporting to them had substantial physical presence inside Arabia – the generations of administrators had little opportunity to gain familiarity with the Arabians' own terms of self-identification, and the history of the 'Arab'-cognates can be read as a legacy passed from one Iraqi-based administrative regime to the next, independent from how Arabian groups described themselves. The generic meanings of 'Arab'-cognates manifest in the Achaemenid case where *Arabāya* did not constitute one specific demographic in the empire's detailed schema categorising tax-paying subject nations, but was 'merely a general noun' for peripheral nomads in the 'Land Beyond the River',[96] i.e. west of the Euphrates and away from the Achaemenids' Mesopotamian heartlands. What looked from the outside as a world of 'Arabs' for the sake of administrative convenience need not resemble the lines of ethnic division on the inside, and this offers an explanation as to why the Arab-cognates could persist so prominently in Mesopotamian writing notwithstanding the absence of 'Arabs' in Arabian epigraphy.

Arab-cognates entered Greek parlance via similar external borrowing. Herodotus, the first Greek writer to describe 'Arabs', derived his information about Arabia from Persian and Achaemenid–Egyptian informants, and not from direct interaction with the region, since he erroneously assumed that Arabia extended from Egypt to Mesopotamia (had he made an expedition, he would have found the Red Sea), and his fantastic descriptions of Arabia transcend what actual travellers to the region would have witnessed. There is 'fact' reported second-hand to Herodotus, for example, the Arabian oaths which Herodotus describes share similarities with later reports,[97] but his description of Arabia is primarily wondrous fancy: consider his accounts of flying serpents 'abundant in Arabia, and nowhere else', the Arabian sheep with tails so enormous that shepherds needed to fasten carts to their posteriors to enable them to walk, and Arabia's apparently pervasive frankincense which 'breaths from Arabia, as it were, a divine odour'. Herodotus expressly counts Arabia as one of the 'extreme parts of the world' and 'the furthest of inhabited countries towards the south', and his ensuing narrative serves the purpose of exciting Greek readers about such remoter corners of the 'barbarian' world.[98]

Herodotus' successors copied him and continued referring to 'Arabs', though they too enjoyed little direct contact since Greek, Hellenistic and early Roman power did not extend far into the Peninsula. The Mediterranean sources about 'Arabs' were written from afar, just as their Mesopotamian administrator precursors had done in the centuries before, and the fanciful representations of a wondrous, remote Arabia constituted a common trope in Latin writing, betraying literary creativity rather than observational empiricism.[99] The disastrous failure of Aelius Gallus' campaign to Yemen in 26–24 BCE would abet impressions in Rome of faraway Arabia's inaccessibility and fantastic perils, and the contemporary observer, Strabo, expressly noted that Gallus' failed expedition 'did not profit us to a great extent in our knowledge of those regions'.[100]

The Greek and Latin stories we read today were consequently produced without substantiation from actual experience. Consider, for example, Agatharchides' report of the

> fragrance which greets the nostrils and stirs the senses of everyone – indeed, even though those who sail along the coast may be far from the land, that does not deprive them of a portion of the enjoyment . . . the sweet odours exhaled by the myrrh-bearing and other aromatic trees penetrate to the near-by parts of the sea.[101]

Agatharchides' passage further underlines the difference between reality and fancy, expressly contrasting the starkly different aromatic effects of his imagined 'full bloom' incense in Arabia with his actual experience of 'old and stale' resin imported to the Mediterranean.[102]

Greek literature has a rich tradition of creating ethnic stereotypes for peoples of different geographical regions, especially regions they deemed exotic, and these archetypes multiplied in their literature. The elaborate descriptions and detail feign acquaintance with such regions, but the familiarity was not empirical, it was instead produced by fecund imaginative expansion, and little is corroborated by modern archaeology.[103] There are accordingly strong grounds for circumspection when appraising the Greek tradition of depicting Arabs, and the direct line of administrative succession between Shalmaneser III and Trajan offers a means to understand that the word 'Arab' was passed from one outsider regime to the next without input from voices inside Arabia. What appears today as a cohesive textual tradition of pre-Islamic 'Arab' history is instead the independent outgrowth of an Assyrian administrative label in the ninth century BCE.

The prospect that outsiders perpetuated 'Arab' cognates by copying each other, and not from investigating Arabia's ethnic composition leads us to questions of what the generations of administrators thought 'Arab' signified? In modern parlance, 'Arab' is an ethnonym, but such words can be used in multifarious non-ethnic senses, and perhaps because 'Arab' signified the idea of 'locust' and 'desert nomad' to Mesopotamian administrators, the term enjoyed its longevity in their records as a convenient generalisation to label each of the successive, separate communities of nomads who contacted imperial frontiers over the centuries.

The hypothesis that the 'Arab' in Mesopotamian/Hellenistic administrative jargon did not refer to an actual underlying Arab ethnos in Arabia finds uncanny precedent in the similar misapplication of the ethnicon 'Saracen' that generated a millennium of inaccuracy in European writing about the Middle East. The word 'Saracen' originates as a Roman administrative term coined in the second century CE (its genesis is considered presently) either replicating the name of an autonomous group of people in the Syrian Desert, or an indigenous term meaning 'Easterners', a reference to nomads who annually migrated east–west between Roman Provincia Arabia to the deeper deserts.[104] This group subsequently disappeared (no reference to 'Saracens' has been found as a term of self-identity in Late Antique Arabia), but the term persisted as the dominant ethnicon for Arabians in Latin and Byzantine Greek writing, and European writers in turn extended the tradition for a millennium, using 'Saracen' to describe all Middle Eastern peoples up to the Enlightenment.[105] Pre-modern European writers had very limited access to the Middle East, but they did possess the old Latin literature about Saracens, and so when they wrote about the Middle East, they reasoned that its contemporary populations must still have been as 'Saracen' as they were in Late Antiquity. In European consciousness 'Saracen' also became synonymous with Muslim, and the Qur'an was described as written in 'Saracen',[106] a remarkable development since Romans identified Saracens as an ethnicon centuries before Islam, and Muslims never called themselves 'Saracens'. But because Muslims occupied the lands which Latin texts described as belonging to the Saraceni, Western Europeans continued what had become a long outdated, fallacious tradition to label Middle Eastern people.

During the millennium-long reign of 'Saracendom' in European ethnic jargon, 'Arab' is nearly absent. The Crusades brought some awareness that Middle Eastern people could be called 'Arabs', but it was insufficient to replace the Saracen paradigm,[107] and only during the eighteenth-century Enlightenment, when European scholars first began concerted academic translations of Arabic literature and engaged with Middle Eastern historiography did they realise the error and finally replace 'Saracen' with 'Arab'.[108] The European labelling of Middle Eastern peoples shows how familiarity begets accuracy, and how unfamiliarity perpetuates inaccuracy. The ancient Mesopotamian/Hellenistic tradition of 'Arab' resembles the 'Saracen' tradition also because the administrators across the succession of the Fertile Crescent empires from 853 BCE – *c.*100 CE, like the European writers *c.*600–1700 CE, had limited direct contact with Arabia, and derived their ethnicons from the literary traditions of their predecessors. If today we interpret the two words as connoting 'Arab' and 'Saracen' peoples, respectively, we mistakenly read our sources with misplaced trust in their sensitivity to the actual ethnic boundaries of the people they describe. Arab-cognates in historical records trace their terminology (not genealogy!) to Shalmaneser III's *Arba-ā*, and since his *Arba-ā* did not connote a cohesive ethnos of pan-Arabian communities, none of the later writings need to be interpreted as such.

The hypothesis that the ancient outsiders did not intend their 'Arab' cognates to denote one specific ethnic group is supported by Michael

Macdonald's survey of the idiosyncratic use of the toponym 'Arabia' and the ethnicon 'Arab' to label a wide and unconnected array of peoples across the Middle East in Greek and Latin writings. Some writers situated 'Arabs' in the mountains of Lebanon, others in what is now south-east Turkey, some in the Sinai and others in the deserts of the Peninsula.[109] The various peoples they labelled as 'Arabs' share general characteristics of non-urban communities outside of the direct control and quotidian familiarity of Greek writers, but there is no indication that pan-regional ethnic unities were intended. The literature presents the 'Arab' as a genre of people rather than a cohesive community, and such ambiguities of Arabness dovetail with the absence of reference to 'Arabs' in the Arabian record: 'Arab' was the property of Hellenistic writers who used it independently and according to their own logic.

If unfamiliarity with the Peninsula perpetuated fictional Arabs in literature, familiarity could be expected to correct the error. This transpired. In 106 CE, Trajan's Roman Imperial armies conquered the Nabataean kingdom in modern Jordan and north-west Saudi Arabia, opening unprecedented access to Arabia. Unlike any previous imperial regime, Roman administrators interacted with Arabian communities through permanent settlements in their land, and fascinatingly, from this moment, Latin texts stop calling Peninsular people 'Arabs'. They named the land of the former Nabataean kingdom *Provincia Arabia* (following Greek geographic tradition), while inhabitants of the semi-desert steppe between Syria and Iraq and the Arabian Desert became labelled *Saraceni*/*Σαρακηνοί*. The more the Romans interacted with Arabians, the less they called them Arabs, and by the third century CE, 'Saracen' supplanted 'Arab' to describe actual Arabian groups. The word 'Arab' survived in Roman literary consciousness, but it was transformed into an archaic term redolent of an ancient desert ideal, an epitome of either nomadism or past peoples, and not a term for groups of contemporary Arabian populations.[110] The replacement with 'Saracen' was absolute, and, crucially, for over 300 years before Islam, 'Arab' never appears in Latin or Greek literature to identify Arabian communities of familiar interaction.

The disappearance of 'Arab' was not only a Hellenistic phenomenon: when the Sasanian Persians began to establish deeper interaction within Arabia as part of their wider policies against Rome, 'Arab' cognates also disappear from their records. It seems that the last Mesopotamian reference to 'Arab' occurs in the title of a late first-century CE Parthian ally identified as *Malkā dhī ᶜArabh*,[111] and whilst modern historians speak of Sasanian-*Arab* relations,[112] the Sasanians actually called Arabians *Ṭayyāyē*. This is a borrowing from Syriac and a rendering of the Arabian group Ṭayyiᵓ: an instructive development since it indicates that the Sasanians adopted the term from the name of a real group with whom they interacted, and between the third and seventh centuries CE, when their interest in Arabia intensified, they ceased using *Arabāya*/'Arab'. The modern tendency to translate all Late Antique references to *Saraceni* and *Ṭayyāyē* as generic 'Arabs', and hence uphold a purported ethnic unity of Arabian populations is expressly critiqued as potentially obscuring the meanings of source texts.[113] The choice of ancient authors to abandon the word 'Arab' needs due attention indeed when translating their works, as the comprehensive and abrupt disappearance of 'Arabs' in both Hellenistic and Mesopotamian records reveals that when outsider observers were able to interact with the Peninsula, they seemed to realise that 'Arab' was an inappropriate ethnonym, and their terminology shifted into line with actual names found inside Arabia.

The notion of 'Arabia' as a geographical term persisted in the Roman provincial nomenclature *Provincia Arabia*, and the Sasanians also named the semi-desert between the Tigris and Euphrates *Beth ᶜArbāyē* (another borrowing from Syriac).[114] Both terms are, however, continuations of previous geographic traditions and the ambit of these 'Arabias' did not extend to cover the broader region between the Sinai and the Euphrates, and neither did they bare ethnic connotations: the Romans described *Saraceni* living around Arabia, and Syriac writing described *Ṭayyāyē* living in *Beth ᶜArbāyē*. Furthermore, the sixth-century CE historian Procopius is explicit that the land south of Gaza 'used to be called in olden times Arabia',[115] indicating the earlier Hellenistic association of the entire Peninsula with 'Arabia' had become a past relic, lacking contemporary signification in the century before Islam. As 'Arabia' receded from Greco-Roman geographical imaginations, their notion that 'Arabs' constituted one ethnic community inhabiting the steppe and deserts between Syria and Iraq fell away too, and there is accordingly cogent reason to consider that 'Arab' was never a term pre-Islamic Arabians used to identify a meaningful consciousness of community.

The indications that 'Arab'-sounding words were the property of outsiders who used them to categorise undifferentiated nomadic populations find additional support in Semitic philology. Above, we saw that the South Arabian word *ʾʿrb* connoted outsiders, and on the opposite side of the Peninsula, the Hebrew Bible references 'Arab'-cognates to describe either a way of life practised outside Israel,[116] or a group living outside the boundaries of Israelite lands.[117] Hebrew and South Arabian employment of 'Arab'-cognates thus mirror the (earlier Semitic language) Assyrian connotations of *Arba-ā/Aribi*, and unfurls a long history of the word 'Arab' connoting the idea of outsiderness, redolent of foreign nomadism and neither indicative of nor translatable as one 'Arab people'. Outsiders used the word 'Arab' for convenience's sake and not because pre-Islamic Arabian populations were culturally cohesive and conscious of their overarching 'Arab' identity.

By interpreting the literary tradition of 'Arab' cognates in Mesopotamian and Hellenistic writing as the legacy of an externally imposed label, we can understand why foreigners spoke so frequently about 'Arabs' from 853 BCE to 106 CE, why Arabian records offer no corroboration, and why references to 'Arabs' disappear in historical records during the centuries before Islam. The key result is the observation that words resembling 'Arab' are older than consciousness of an Arab community: there was no tradition in ancient times of groups using the word 'Arab' to describe themselves. But deconstructing ancient 'Arab' terminology is not an end in itself: while it allows us to confidently decouple 'Arab' cognates in Mesopotamian and Hellenistic testimony from the narrative of Arab ethnogenesis, it imposes a new challenge to reappraise the historical record and determine when the tables turned and transformed 'Arab' into the marker of a community's own identity. The next chapter proposes a date for the emergence of self-styled Arabs.

Notes

1. Claims connecting Arabs with first Arabian camelback nomads in the second millennium BCE coincide with the height of politicised Arab nationalism (Nāfiʿ (1952), ʿĀqil (1969) pp. 52–60, Sālim (1970) pp. 411–45, Carmichael (1967) pp. 6–7); more recent works somewhat less ambitiously count all Arabians, Bedouin and settled, since Assyrian times as Arabs (Hitti (1946)

pp. 23–9, Hourani (1991) p. 10, Bosworth (1983) pp. 593–8, Shahid (1984), (1989), (1995–2009) and Potts (2010) pp. 74–6). Al-Azmeh (2014a) deems all Arabians, at least since the Common Era as Arabs. Such methodology is critiqued (see Fisher's (2011b) pp. 248–9 rejection of Shahid), even the Palmyrene and Nabataean trading kingdoms in Syria and Jordan, respectively, long classified as 'Arab', are now moving out of scholarly opinions about the Arab ethnos (Macdonald (2009b) pp. 306–7, Retsö (2012) pp. 77–9).

2. Retsö (2003).
3. Robin (2006).
4. von Grunebaum (1963); Conrad (2000) p. 680; Pietruschka (2001) p. 214; Dousse (2012) p. 44.
5. Hoyland (2009); Fisher (2011a).
6. Donner (2010); Millar (2013). See Introduction, n.18.
7. MacDonald (2009a); Robin (2006).
8. For detailed studies of this material, see Ephᵓal (1982); Retsö (2003); Macdonald (2009a); Fisher (2011a).
9. Shalmaneser *Monolith* II: pp. 90–97: see Grayson (1996) p. 23.
10. Or perhaps *jindab* (Ibn Manẓūr (1990) vol. 1, p. 257). Retsö, citing Lane, notes that the name is only known in Arabic in more recent times (2003) p. 126, and thereby argues for Gindibu's certain Arabness.
11. ᶜAlī (1968–73) vol. 1, pp. 574–6; Retsö (2003) pp. 623–5, 577–8. Crone (2006), without venturing into ethnicity, equates the culture and lifestyle of Arabs from Assyrian to early Islamic times as largely homogeneous.
12. Djaït (1986) pp. 181–3.
13. Ephᵓal (1982) pp. 7–9; Rodinson (1981) pp. 13–14. Hoyland (2001) p. 230 infers some continuity; Robin (2010) p. 85 and Dousse (2012) p. 44 argue the *Arba-ā* were a nomadic group lost in history without relation to today's Arabs.
14. Hoyland (2009) pp. 389–90 and Retsö (1993) p. 32 note that Muslim-era Arabic writers were mostly unaware of events occurring more than 150–200 years before Islam.
15. It could be argued that the *Arba-ā* only entered 'Arab history' via the coincidence of the mid-nineteenth-century British discovery and decipherment of the Assyrian records with the rise of new forms of Arab nationalism in need of ancient evidence in order to construct an autochthonous communal history.
16. Rodinson (1981) p. 14. Nöldeke (1899) pp. 272–3 invokes Semitic philology to interpret 'Arab' as originally meaning 'Bedouin' via the word's 'steppe' connotations.

17. *The Assyrian Dictionary* vol. 4, pp. 258–9; cf. modern Arabic *gharb*.
18. Ibid. vol. 1.2, p. 239.
19. Ibid. vol. 1.2, pp. 239–41; cf. modern Arabic *aʿrāb*.
20. Robin (2010) p. 85; Dousse (2012) p. 44.
21. *The Assyrian Dictionary* vol. 4, pp. 256–7.
22. Ibid. vol. 1.2, p. 240.
23. Retsö (2003) and ʿAlī (1968–73). Here I engage primarily with Retsö, as ʿAlī is vague as to his basis for identifying people as 'Arabs'. ʿAlī inflates the sense of Arab community by melding space and race, treating Arabians as Arabs, and accords little account to narrative and context of the textual records to amalgamate pre-Islamic and Islamic-era evidence into his narrative.
24. Ephʾal (1982) p. 113: Assyrians tend to use *Aribi* for Syrian and *Arabaa* for Iraqi groups, but not consistently. See Retsö (2003) pp. 129–66 for examples. There is a reference to an *Arba-ā* individual in Esarhaddon's (r. 681–669 BCE) court (Retsö (2003) p. 161), but linking him specifically with Gindibu's group last mentioned 160 years earlier is tenuous.
25. See British Museum reliefs from the eighth (118901) and seventh (124926 and 124927) centuries BCE.
26. Crone comments on the continuity of Bedouin Arab dress, remarking on the similarities between Assyrian visual depictions and Late Antique writings (2008) pp. 6–8.
27. Ephʾal (1982) p. 83.
28. Ephʾal rejected interpreting Urbi as an ethnonym (1982) pp. 74, 76; Retsö argues for the Urbi's Arabness, associating them with camel breeding in Judah (2003) p. 156. *The Assyrian Dictionary* (in 2010) renders Urbi 'band of mercenaries' (vol. 20, p. 213), thus supporting Ephʾal.
29. Ephʾal (1982) p. 83.
30. Retsö (2003) p. 150.
31. Ibid. pp. 136, 148.
32. Records indicate *Arbāya* as allied to Assyria during the later eighth century BCE, Ibid. p. 152.
33. Retsö's notion of Arab cohesion from Mesopotamia to the Syrian Desert prompts his argument that the Arabs were not only in contact with each other, but were also capable of collective action, for instance, in deciding on a 'definite change in policy' vis-à-vis the Assyrians during Sennacherib's reign', Ibid. p. 154.
34. This underpins Retsö's thesis, Ibid. pp. 191–2.

35. Ibid. p. 192. See also pp. 127, 131, 151, 191.
36. Macdonald (2009a) p. 25. Rodinson (1981) pp. 10–11 similarly critiques the prevailing definition of Arabness via desert culture.
37. Retsö (2003) p. 151.
38. See, for example, Retsö's identification of ethnic Arabs in instances where Assyrian records report what he calls a 'good Arabic name/word', Ibid pp. 126, 131, 153. Venturing conclusions about ethnic identity on the basis of onomastic indicators is problematised in Macdonald (2009g) pp. 187–9. Consider also how the presence of 'Arabic' names in Nabataean inscriptions, long held as evidence that the Nabataeans were 'Arabs', is no longer seen as proof of their Arabness (Healy (1989) and Macdonald (2009c) p. 109).
39. Retsö (2003) p. 153. Interestingly, he hedges his bets too, arguing later that one does not need a common language to be 'ethnic' (p. 592), therein revealing some methodological inconsistency.
40. Ibid. p. 136. Hoyland's (2015) and Fisher's (2011a) theories that frontier guardianship in Late Antiquity prompted Arab ethnogenesis use similar logic, though for a different period.
41. Barth explores how different strategies by different interest groups in a given transactional environment affect senses of ethnic cohesion (1969) pp. 4–7; the impediments that frontier guardianship pose to pan-regional ethnic cohesion are material.
42. Retsö's exhaustive summary of Assyrian records reveals the full panoply of names (2003) pp. 124–66.
43. Retsö (2003) p. 157 adduces references in Muslim literature to Nebuchadnezzar's forced deportation of Arabs as a memory of ancient communal history, though this rather badly misreads Muslim-era narratives: their references to Nebuchadnezzar seem much more likely a borrowing and rebranding of the Biblical tale of Nebuchadnezzar's war against Israel; see further analysis below, Chapter 5(II) pp. 253–4.
44. Ephʾal (1982) pp. 7–9. He does not elaborate his reasons; it is hoped this section's ethnogenesis lens provided some grounds.
45. Ephʾal (1982) pp. 170–9; Retsö (2003) pp. 176–91.
46. Retsö (2003) pp. 235–40.
47. Herodotus (1992) Book III, §§107–14.
48. All analysis of Greek writing on Arabia is indebted to Macdonald's excellent and insightful survey (2009a).

49. Macdonald (2009a) p. 21 critiques the pervasive and problematic meld of 'Arab' and 'Arabia'.
50. e.g. Strabo (1930) 16.1.26 describes the 'Scenitae Arabs, a tribe of brigands and shepherds' in Mesopotamia, and the '[Arabs] far away and near Arabia Felix' (Ibid. 16.1.28); see also Ibid. 16.3.1–2.
51. Irwin (2006) pp. 82–5, 88; see also Tidrick (2010).
52. Compare the varied Achaemenid depictions of Arabians – the Terrace throne-bearer E12 (Schmidt (1953) p. 136), the Apadana East Stairway delegation 20 (Ibid. p. 89) and the Council Hall throne-bearer 24 (Ibid. p. 120) with the Arabians on the British Museum Assyrian reliefs (see above, Note 25).
53. Rodinson (1981) p. 12 counts awareness of Arab identity as '[likely] the most important criterion' to locate Arab populations. Theories of ethnogenesis outlined in the Introduction stress even more emphatically the importance of communal consciousness.
54. The earliest inscriptions date to *c.*750 BCE (Robin (2010) p. 81). The epigraphic corpus is in process of digitisation: see <http://dasi.humnet.unipi.it (South Arabia)> (last accessed 15 November 2015); <http://krc2.orient.ox.ac.uk/ociana (North Arabia)> (last accessed 15 November 2015).
55. Robin (2010) p. 85. Macdonald (2009b) pp. 311–13 demonstrates that 'Arabia' as a geographical term was invented by outsiders. Robin (2006) pp. 125–6 cites the South Arabian inscription Ja 560 which contains the phrase *ʾrḍ ʿrb* ('Land of the Arabs'), but this resembles the Greek concept of 'Arabia' – a term South Arabians used to identify an outside place, not their own homeland.
56. Robin (2010) p. 85 also includes Nabataean inscriptions citing 'Arab', but these are rejected by Macdonald as labels referring to the Roman Province of 'Arabia', not ethnic groups (Macdonald (2009b) pp. 306–7). Retsö offers a nuanced, open-ended discussion of Nabataean Arabness (2012) pp. 77–9. Robin (2006) also includes references to *ʾʿrb* in South Arabian inscriptions as instances of 'Arabs' – this has significant difficulties when considering the shape Arab communal conscious would take, as considered below.
57. Inscriptions RES 3945 and Mafray ash-Shaqab 3 from Jawf north of Sana'a (Robin (1991) p. 72). Note that Robin (2006) p. 133 now rejects that either refer to the Arab people.
58. South Arabian inscriptions CIH 79, Ja 560 and Ja 629 date first–second centuries CE; Ja 950 and Ja 961 the third century CE; the Syrian al-Namāra inscription is considered in Chapter 2(II) pp. 75–6; South Arabian inscriptions

Ir 32, Ja 1028 and CIH 541 date fourth–sixth centuries (see Retsö (2003) pp. 552–66 for interpretations).

59. Robin (2006) p. 121.
60. Robin (1991) and Retsö (2003) count a number of Minaean and Sabaic references from the seventh to fifth centuries BCE as evidence of 'Arabs'; Robin (2006) p. 135 argues they are not ethnonyms.
61. Robin (2006) pp. 122–3. See inscriptions Ja 561 bis, CIH 353, Ry 502, RES 4658, Nami 72, Ja 635 and Ja 665; and Retsö (2003) pp. 536–66.
62. See Chapter 2(I) for discussion of pre-Islamic Arabian languages and the development of Arabic.
63. Biella (2004) p. 383.
64. Beeston et al. (1982) p. 19.
65. Rodinson (1981) pp. 4–15 noted that pre-Islamic Yemenis considered themselves separate from *ᶜrb* and *ᵓᶜrb*, though he did not consider the ramifications for this on the Arab ethnos, and concluded that the Yemenis still acknowledged 'a distant kinship with these savage Arabs'. Current scholarship more firmly distinguishes pre-Islamic Yemenis from 'Arabs' (Hoyland (2001) p. 9).
66. Robin (2006) pp. 128–30 argues for Arab 'political entity'. Montgomery (2006) p. 50 and Conrad (2000) p. 680 reject the imposition of a political unity onto pre-Islamic Arabs, and Nehmé's recent findings in western central Arabia also point to a fragmentary system of small kingdoms, none of which refer to themselves as Arabs. Robin's inference of Arab political unity is derived from outsider political titulature and needs substantiation from more than onomastic interpretation.
67. *Aᶜrāb* connote groups of undifferentiated Bedouin who can be the object of attacks or employment as mercenaries, and the term is used this way in both the Hebrew Bible and South Arabian records (see Notes 116 and 117, below). From the Qur'an and early Arabic poetry and into Muslim-era Arabic texts, the tradition of othering *aᶜrāb* continues (see Chapter 4(I) and 6(II), below). In a fifth-century South Arabian inscription of Abīkarib Asᶜad (see Robin (2006) p. 129), the writing of *ᵓᶜrb-hmw* in a possessive construction 'their nomads' similarly suggests not a reference to a community of Arabs, but rather to a generic type of person.
68. Robin (2006) p. 124.
69. Inscriptions Ja 950 and Ja 961.
70. The Marṭadum and Dharḥān inscription J629 (Jamme (1962) p. 128) counterpoises 'all the people' (*wkl ᵓns*) with 'nomads'/*aᶜrāb*' (*ᵓᶜrb*) in lns. 7–8. Lns.

5–6 list the various settled/agricultural communities familiar in Sabaic inscriptions. This presumably led Biella (2004) p. 383 to interpret ʾʿ*rb* as the opposite of 'town-dwellers', and suggests a generic sedentary/nomadic distinction was intended. The distinction of 'nomads' from 'the people' also underscores the usage of ʾʿ*rb* to connote otherness – 'not us'.

71. Retsö (2003) p. 236.
72. While Robin (2006) critiques Retsö's use of Assyrian terminology to construct Arab history, the South Arabian references upon which Robin relies treat central Arabians with rather the same generic aspect as earlier Assyrian records.
73. Müller (1896) p. 344.
74. Nöldeke (1899) pp. 272–3.
75. For reiterations of Nöldeke's paradigm, see Caskel (1954) p. 38; von Grunebaum (1963) p. 12 'the Arab, by etymology and cultural convention, was the Bedouin'; Rodinson (1981) p. 15; Robin (2010) p. 85; Dousse (2012) p. 43. Rare critique of Nöldeke appears in Bashear (1984) and (1997): Bashear does not cite Müller, and is more radical, rejecting even that Muhammad imagined himself as an Arab. Bashear proposes that Islam was originally a Jewish/Byzantine sect which Arabs usurped in the Umayyad period ((1984) pp. 331–69). Bashear did not refer to ethnogenesis; Chapter 3(III) p. 151 reinterprets his findings via our theoretical framework and wider source material.
76. For detailed summary of the Ḥijāzī theory, see Montgomery (2006).
77. Montgomery (2006) pp. 46, 50.
78. Al-Azmeh (2014a) pp. 101, 154, 249–63 coins the term to describe Late Antique al-Ḥijāz, mirroring the tenor of the 'Empty al-Ḥijāz'.
79. Montgomery (2006) pp. 58, 97 and Conrad (2000) 680 accord poetry the central role of gelling sense of Arab community. Al-Azmeh (2014a) pp. 100–54 gathers an even wider array of 'cultural stuff'. Hoyland identifies 'shared values and experiences' reinforced in poetry as paving the way for Arab Empire (2015) p. 25.
80. For a case in point consider the ʿEn ʿAvdat inscription, dated to the first century CE. Its final three lines are in a rhyming language resembling Arabic familiar to us. Because Arabs are axiomatically associated with the culture of poetry, modern readers of the ʿEn ʿAvdat inscription expended great efforts to interpret it as poetry (Bellamy (1990), Snir (1993)), as if this, perhaps the earliest Arabic inscription, must represent the first stirrings of Arabic poetry too. But the inscription should not be read as a precursor to the poetry that emerges 500 years later (Testen (1996) p. 292; al-Azmeh (2014a) p. 149 also expresses

reservations), and reveals pitfalls of the a priori approach to finding Arabs based on anachronistic assumptions about their 'national traits'.

81. Pre-Islamic 'Arab history' is often written by amalgamating Muslim-era Arabic records into a consolidated archetype of Arabness (see ᶜAlī (1968–73); Conrad (2000); al-Azmeh (2014a)). As a result, there is a tendency to assume Arab cultural uniformity for at least several centuries before Islam, for example, Hoyland's remark about the 'homogeneity' of Arabic poetry and therefore of Arab identity (2015) p. 25. Poetry specialists, on the other hand, stress the pitfalls of this approach since old poetry filtered through an 'Abbasid guise' of third/ninth-century agendas that influenced its recording (Jones (1996) p. 58; see also S. Stetkevych (1993) p. 122; Montgomery (1997) pp. 8–9). This book examines the extent to which the wide-scale construction of pre-Islamic Arabian history by Muslim authors actually created the discourse which enabled subsequent writers and Western scholars to think of pre-Islamic Arabia as an 'Arab' land.
82. See, for example, the consideration of ethnicity in the pre-Islamic Syrian desert near Palmyra in Genequand (2012) pp. 33–6, where the appearance of a name in historical records which, in the Muslim-era was counted as an 'Arab tribe', is used to date the entrance of 'Arabs' to the region. The one-to-one equation of tribal name with pan-Arab communal identity takes Arabness for granted, obviating vital questions of when, how and why certain groups decided to become 'Arab'.
83. Fisher (2011a) suggests replacing the tribal 'Ghassanid' and 'Lakhmid' with Jafna and Naṣr, respectively, repeated in the latest study, Genequand and Robin (2015). But since Arabic sources always use *Banū Ghassān* and *Lakhm*, and contemporary Late Antique sources generalise them all as Saracens, I prefer the familiar Ghassān/Lakhm nomenclature. 'King of Ghassān' is also expressly mentioned in epigraphy: see ThNJUT 65 (Nehmé (2015) p. 17).
84. For example, Procopius (1914) 2:16:18/2:19:38 describes a two-month holy season during the Vernal Equinox during which 'Saracens' refrained from fighting. Muslim texts also mention prohibition of fighting in holy months, but they enumerate a three-month period (Dhū al-Qiᶜda to Muḥarram) and add a fourth (Rajab) without reference to the Equinox: general parallels ought not obscure considerable variation in detail.
85. Montgomery's 'Bedouinising' term is most appropriate (1997), p. 8, n. 11, and Ghassān and Lakhm's culture, aspirations and identity should be distinguished from inner Arabian Bedouin communities.

86. Holm (2002) p. 154 noted a Western historiographical tendency to project warfare in 'civilised' societies as total and decisive, whereas societies deemed 'primitive' are accorded only desultory conflict of revenge killings lacking strategic goals. Holm discussed how this engendered misleading conceptions of pre-Columbian history; the parallels with historians' model of the 'pre-civilised' pre-Islamic 'Arab' battles (*ayyām al-ᶜarab*) vs the Islamic-era 'civilised' Arab conquests are striking.
87. Ethnohistory and 'new subjectivity' effected an about-face in modern scholarship about American Indian peoples (see Washburn and Trigger (1996) pp. 82–97); critical historiography has elegantly shown the many faces of Indianness in European and American writing (see Berkhofer Jr. (1978)).
88. von Grunebaum (1963) pp. 5–7.
89. Ibid. p. 20.
90. Hoyland (2015) p. 25, 61; al-Azmeh (2014a) pp. 100–46.
91. Hoyland (2015) asserts the existence of pre-Islamic Arab identity (pp. 24–7), becomes equivocal (pp. 60–1), and then rejects it (p. 102). As this book was going to press, a similar critique of other aspects of a prevailing homogenising treatment of Arabs and Arabness in *In God's Path* was published: see Donner (2015) pp. 138–9.
92. Bāshmīl (1973), written at a climax of Syrian–Israeli tensions, reconstructs an ancient Arabness in Syria, expressly predating the Israelites.
93. Hitti (1946) pp. 87–9.
94. Hoyland (2015) p. 5 argues for the existence of pre-Islamic Arabs so as to label the conquests 'Arab' in distinction to Donner's (2010) p. 17 theory of the conquests' religious motivations.
95. Proponents of what is now a relatively widely held belief in Arab ethnogenesis between the third and sixth centuries CE are listed in Note 4, above. They accordingly discount pre-Roman references to 'Arabs' as connoting generic Bedouin and not 'real', self-aware Arabs. Robin (2006) discounts Assyrian references to 'Arabs', but admits Sabaic 'Arab' references as ethnic Arabs.
96. Cuyler Young Jr (1988) p. 88, Ephᵓal (1988) p. 148. The ambiguity of *Arabāya* may also explain the difficulties which Schmidt faced in positively identifying 'Arabians' in Achaemenid palace reliefs (1953) pp. 120, 136.
97. Marsham (2009) pp. 24–5 discuses Herodotus (1992) Book III, §107.
98. Herodotus (1992) Book III §§106–13.
99. The disjoint between Hellenistic literary production and actual contact with Arabia is detailed in Macdonald (2009a) pp. 21–30.

100. Strabo (1930) 16.4.24–5.
101. Cited in Diodorus (1935) 3.46.4–5. Distant South Arabia, the real source of incense was linked with the fantastic in the Roman imagination, and earned the name *Arabia Felix* (Lucky Arabia), though Retsö (2000) pp. 191–2 shows the idiosyncratic use of this name to label various 'wondrous' places around the Peninsula.
102. Cited in Diodorus (1935) 3.46.4.
103. Geographical archetyping in Greek perceptions of outsiders is well documented (see the essays in Gruen (2011a)). As an example, consider the Greek reduction of the image of Thracian peoples into one male archetype of lightly armed peltasts, and one female archetype of tattooed slaves, neither of which accord with modern archaeological finds (Martinez and Mathieux (2015) p. 30).
104. The traditional reading of Saracens as a specific group follows the tenor of the citations in Ptolemy and Stephanus Byzantinus (see Retsö (2003) pp. 491–3). Macdonald (2009a) pp. 20–1 and (2009d) pp. 1–5 argues for the 'Easterners' interpretation and rejects association of Saracen with one tribe. For further summary of different opinions, see Ward (2008) p. 128, for the transition from Arab to Saracen, see Hoyland (2009) pp. 392–3.
105. For an excellent survey of the Saracendom idea in European writing, see Tolan (2002).
106. Mandeville (1953) vol. 1, pp. 97, 101.
107. French and English dictionaries evidence the name 'Arab' in writings from the twelfth century onwards: Roland combats with 'Franceis et Arrabit' (Roland, éd. Bédier, 3481), Garin le Loherain (1e chans., IX, P. Paris ds GDF) refers to 'chevaus arrabis et corans', though a sense of Arabic meaning 'Le langage des Arabes' does not appear until 1680. Nicot's *Thresor de la langue française* defines 'Arabe' as 'ou qui est d'Arabie' (1606) p. 41: i.e. Arabian and not a pan-Middle Eastern people. The earliest dictionary to describe 'Arabes' as 'Il se dit des persones et du langage; un arabe, une arabe' is Jean-François Féraud, *Dictionaire critique de la langue française* (Marseille, Mossy 1787–88, A142B). In English, the word 'Arab' is very rare before the eighteenth century (see *Oxford English Dictionary* vol. 1, p. 597). Early French and English writers knew of 'Arabie/Arrabe/Arabia' which housed, in Chaucer's words 'arabiens', but this Arabia was a distant, fabulous part of the world – a land of perfumes, herbal potions, phoenixes and unicorns borrowed from Herodotus – on display in Shakespeare's nine references to 'Arabia' and 'Arabian' (For Phoenixes (the 'Arabian Bird') see *Anthony and Cleopatra* III.2, *Cymbeline* I.6. For herbals,

see *Macbeth* V.1; *Othello* V.2; *Tempest* III.3). As for real people of the East, Shakespeare never used 'Arabs', instead he identified Saracens (e.g. *Richard II* IV.1). European writing mirrors Late Antique Greek and Latin usage whereby 'Saracen' connoted real Eastern populations, whereas 'Arab' was redolent of a more distant, fabulous ideal.

108. Between Howell's 1685 *History of the World* with its '*Mahomet* was Captain of the *Saracens*', vol. 3.3, p. 280, and Gibbon's 1776–89 *Decline and Fall* and its 'Mohammed . . . sprung from . . . the most illustrious of the Arabs', vol. 5, pp. 254–5, the European literary tradition of *Arab* history was born.
109. Macdonald (2009a) pp. 17–20.
110. A case in point is the fourth-century CE Ammianus Marcellinus' citation of 'Arabs' in his *Res Gestae* (1989) Books 24–5. Ammianus uses the term *Saraceni* when describing real people in Arabia, whereas he only cites 'Arabs' when quoting earlier authors. The sixth-century CE Procopius evidences further distancing of 'Arab' from connotations of contemporary people: he refers to 'Arabia' and 'Arabs' as ancient names used in 'early times' by the king in Petra (i.e. the Nabataeans) (Procopius (1914) 1:29:20–1). Retsö notes such usage of 'Arab' served to give a 'more antique flavour' in later Latin writings (Retsö (2003) p. 520). See fuller discussion in Retsö (2003) pp. 505–21 and Macdonald (2009d).
111. Bosworth (1983) p. 596. First- and second-century CE inscriptions from Hatra and Edessa (states neighbouring Parthia) record similar titles where 'Arab' connotes a land in northern Mesopotamia.
112. See, for example, Daryaee (2009) pp. 16, 22, 29; Bosworth (1983) pp. 597–609.
113. Millar (2013) pp. 162–3.
114. Aramaic *bēth* *ᶜarbāyē* was formerly used to connote various different parts of Mesopotamia (Macdonald (2009b) p. 312).
115. Procopius (1914) 1:29:20.
116. Isa 13:20; Jer 3:2.
117. Jer 25:24; Ezek 27:21; 2 Chron 9:14. See Pietruschka (2001) p. 214 and Dousse (2012) p. 44.

2

Pre-Islamic 'Arabless-ness': Arabian Identities

The analysis thus far presents the spectre of an 'Arabless' pre-Islamic Arabia which may appear an extreme reaction to the familiar notion of Arabs in Antiquity, but we pose these radical challenges as there is a need to provoke critical questioning of the idea of Arabness and the timeworn practice of labelling peoples 'Arab' without considering how they related to senses of Arab community. An array of groups inhabited pre-Islamic Arabia and some of their descendants would come to identify themselves as Arabs, but outsiders' evidence and anachronistic paradigms about 'original Arab characteristics' have not been able to give a sense of the process which caused formerly disparate groups to recognise and rally around a shared sense of community as 'Arabs'. To grasp the process of Arab ethnogenesis and the meaning of early Arabness, we need to probe deeper and evaluate the articulations of communal identity inside pre-Islamic Arabia. The findings shall explain what we mean by the 'Arabless' centuries before Islam, and uncover the first communities who expressed their consciousness of Arab communal ties.

I The Arabic Language: a Signpost to Arabness?

The ever-growing body of pre-Islamic inscriptions found in archaeological surveys in Saudi Arabia is prompting a new approach to rethink Arab ethnogenesis by tracing the emergence of the Arabic language. The research proposes that language is a key component of Arab identity,[1] and that the first truly Arab communities can be located by determining when and where the Arabic language developed.[2]

Linguistic searches reveal a wide array of languages spoken in pre-Islamic Arabia, and amongst the thousands of pre-Islamic inscriptions uncovered to date across Arabia, the Syrian Desert and surrounding steppe, a small number have been classified as 'Old Arabic', inasmuch as they share characteristics that potentially differentiate them from other attested languages and herald the beginnings of the Arabic language familiar from the Islamic period. But it is difficult to precisely enumerate the 'Old Arabic' inscriptions. Michael Macdonald notes that the small number of samples, the variety of scripts used and the brevity of the texts make it difficult to ascertain definitively whether a given inscription is Arabic, or in a related language, or an attempt by a proto-Arabic speaker to write in a different (but related) language.[3] Additionally, there are several texts containing a mixture of what appears to be 'Old Arabic' and other pre-Islamic Arabian languages:[4] these could evidence an Arabic speaker trying to write in a 'foreign' language of which he had only limited knowledge, or it could imply an attenuated bilingualism where closely related languages without standardised literary traditions mixed and produced haphazard results. The precursors to the Arabic language are thus mostly hiding: they were presumably transmitted orally, which is itself interesting given that a number of other Arabian languages were widespread in graffiti, more elaborate inscriptions, and on papyri. The absence of 'Old Arabic' inscriptions and the almost complete absence of development of the Arabic script itself implies that Arabic lacked a body of writers promoting its use in pre-Islamic times, and that it perhaps lacked prestige too. Pre-Islamic 'Old Arabic' speakers, whoever they may have been or whatever group 'Old Arabic' represented, were possibly a tiny minority or, at least, pre-Islamic Arabic lacked appeal as a means for fixing messages in physical form.

In the wake of the enigmatic corpus of inscriptions, there is much debate over their meaning and the number which can legitimately be called 'Old Arabic'. Macdonald counted thirteen in his 2008 survey,[5] but several have been recently discounted,[6] a few new texts have been proposed for inclusion,[7] and in sum, it seems that one certain conclusion can be drawn, with chronological and geographical inferences attached. What is certain is the paucity of pre-Islamic 'Old Arabic'. The paucity is salient given the myriad inscriptions recorded in Sabaic, Dadanitic, Nabataean, Safaitic, Hismaic, Greek, Aramaic and other languages across Arabia, indicative of a widespread pre-Islamic interest in writing and an amply attested ability, even amongst nomadic populations, to write.[8] There were surprisingly few 'Old Arabic' writers, but from the small corpus of inscriptions, patterns relatable to time and space seem discernable to launch inferences about pre-Islamic Arabness. In terms of chronology, two (now debated) 'Old Arabic' inscriptions date circa first century CE,[9] while the others are dated between the third and sixth centuries CE. The third-century pseudo-'Old Arabic' inscriptions tend to group in northern Saudi Arabia,[10] while the majority of clearer examples of Arabic emergent by sixth century are situated further north (four inscriptions).[11] The concentration immediately preceding the Islamic era implies that an Arabic speech community did not exist in very ancient times, bolstering our last chapter's conclusion that the *Arba-ā*, *Aribi*, *Arabāya*, and related names were indeed terms coined by foreigners and not reflective of ancient Arabic communities. In terms of geography, the first signs of the Arabic alphabet's development appear in circa fourth-century CE inscriptions from al-Ḥijāz, but they are archaic: the earliest inscriptions bearing the grammar and script familiar as classical Arabic date from the fifth century and are clustered in modern Syria, Jordan and the Sinai.[12] Since all of the agreed 'Old Arabic' inscriptions are Syrian/Palestinian or from the adjacent north-west Arabia (al-Ḥijāz),[13] it seems that Arabic was not used across all pre-Islamic Arabia even shortly before Islam. The findings prompt a new theory that Arab ethnogenesis began when groups migrated towards Syria from central-western Arabia and were established as frontier guards for the Byzantine Empire during the fifth and sixth centuries.[14]

While the epigraphic evidence demonstrates that the Arabic language did not exist in very ancient times, one shortcoming of the current body of evidence is its small sample size and the brevity of the surviving inscriptions.[15] Arabia's pre-Islamic epigraphic corpus contains manifold different languages, and while epigraphists are sanguine that the formative history of the Arabic language can be reconstructed,[16] the question of why there is so little evidence for pre-Islamic Arabic is muted. If Arabian kingdoms in Late Antiquity conceptualised themselves as constituent members of an Arab ethnos, we could expect that they would have called themselves 'Arabs' and that their collective local power and influence would generate more than a dozen texts across a

500-year period.[17] The absence of peoples expressing their own identity as 'Arabs', coupled with the scarcity of Arabic-language inscriptions constitute evidence against wide-scale pre-Islamic Arab ethnogenesis, and moreover, substantiating the presumption that each of the pre-Islamic inscriptions is in *the* Arabic language is also challenging. The inscriptions resemble Arabic as codified by Muslim grammarians 300–400 years later, but prior to their encyclopedic efforts, the definite term *al-ᶜarabiyya* (the Arabic language) is not attested and we do not know whether pre-Islamic speakers of related languages across north-west Arabia realised they all spoke one language, a single unifying 'ethnolect'. The inscriptions are varied, not all are in the Arabic script and most are difficult to interpret within the confines of Arabic grammar.[18] An observer could thus ask whether it is legitimate to assume that each pre-Islamic 'Old Arabic' inscription represents successive steps in one ladder to Arabness. Building from Macdonald's reservations noted above,[19] have we vacuumed up texts which have tolerable relation to classical Arabic in order to construct one unified, linear progression towards *the* Arabic language? And more pressingly, how does language development relate to emergence of communal identity? Such theoretical issues need consideration before concluding that the small body of texts are *al-ᶜarabiyya* and expressions of an emerging community which knew of itself as *al-ᶜarab*.

Herein theories of ethnogenesis suggest caution since language is a 'cultural stuff' trait that does not create consciousness of ethnic identity on its own. A community needs to exist within a common framework before it can alight on shared language as a means to express its unity, and the privileging of inscriptions to plot the emergence of an ethnos puts the proverbial cart before the horses. Languages are fluid constructs: for example, the modern dialects of Arabic are related, but some are barely mutually intelligible, yet they are all usually called Arabic. On the other hand, Italian and Spanish or Swedish and Norwegian are very similar idioms, yet they are classified as different languages, while Germans and Austrians speak the same language but constitute separate nations. The vital role of language in cementing a sense of mutual communal belonging is not in dispute, but theorists who pursue the links between language, culture and identity elsewhere in the world stress that communities form as the result of negotiation, and that language cannot be treated as a direct reflection of identity.[20] A language, once established, does not become the fixed marker for an ethnic community – it is more accurate to move beyond a one-to-one relationship between language and ethnicity to study the two in a constantly developing relationship. Language production is a cultural act, one of an array of methods by which people articulate similarity and difference, authority and legitimacy, and therefore, when considering the emergence of communities, social and political considerations are ultimately more determinative than mere linguistic mutual-intelligibility.

Directing the theory to pre-Islamic Arabia, there has been recent debate as to whether the thousands of Safaitic inscriptions found in the Ḥarra region on the Syrian/Arabian frontier indicate the presence of a Safaitic people or *ethnos*. Despite the significant linguistic uniformity of Safaitic graffito, al-Jallad's recent survey of the inscriptions and the lineage groups they mention argues that the writers did not constitute one single social group.[21] The fact that several writers of Safaitic inscriptions expressly self-identified as Nabataeans (who had their own distinct language and script) further underlines the difficulties of extrapolating ephemeral notions of identity from the empirical boundaries of language and philology.[22] Given that the copious and grammatically consistent corpus of Safaitic inscriptions offers insufficient grounds to assume that one 'Safaitic' community inhabited the pre-Islamic Ḥarra, much greater circumspection should be applied to theories of Arab ethnogenesis from the minuscule and erratic body of 'Old Arabic' texts. Reading pre-Islamic 'Old Arabic' inscriptions as monuments of Arabness will reduce Arab identity to a function of language without offering explanations for the important question of why certain speakers of mutually intelligible dialects chose to imagine communal cohesion at the exclusion of others in Late Antique Arabia.

The privileging of *the* Arabic language as the Arabs' 'ethnolect' also replicates a narrative of some Muslim-era grammarians who argued that proper *fuṣḥā* (grammatically correct Arabic) defines Arab identity, and that, by extension, all Arabic speakers must have been, *ipso facto*, members of the Arab ethnos. Such an argument is one of several discourses developed by Muslim writers in the third/ninth and fourth/tenth centuries to construct a sense of cultural traits by which Arabs could be exclusively identified, but many of their arguments can today be appreciated as entirely false – consider, for example, their adamant claims that Arabs were the only people on earth capable of producing poetry.[23] From a modern anthropological perspective, we can interpret such claims as typical devices groups invoke to ground their sense of communal identity in tangible traits, and such definitions of an ethnic group necessarily post-date the formation of the ethnos itself. Part Two of this book will reveal how these 'Arab traits' and notion of 'the Arabic language' were gradually developed in the early Muslim period; focusing on pre-Islamic evidence and the origins of Arab ethnogenesis here, it is imperative to look through the later Muslim 'cultural stuff' definitions of Arabness, and to appreciate, as a matter of theory, that imagining an Arab community as a function of language alone is fraught, and we need probe beyond linguistic evidence to reconstruct Arab history.[24]

A more cautious approach proposes that Arabian linguistic uniformities created a potential for unity (without actually triggering it).[25] This is reasoned, but it still does not delineate the beginning of Arab communal consciousness since it neither explains why, nor investigates the extent to which language was actually standardised in pre-Islamic Arabia.[26] The model supposes that an Arabic speech community must have existed in pre-Islam in order to explain the rapid uptake of the Qur'an's message, but such does not necessarily follow. Early Muslims did not need to understand the Qur'an in order to believe it: the Christianisation of non-Latin, non-Greek speaking peoples in early Medieval Europe is a case in point. While Muslim traditions elaborate upon the purity of the first three generations of believers to present a rather romantic picture that all Muslims partook in memorising and reciting the Qur'an as an exercise in their national language, the notion that the Qur'an's Arabness caused wholesale 'Arab' conversion accepts the Muslim-era narrative that all pre-Islamic Arabians were Arabic speaking 'Arabs' at face value. From the perspective of ethnogenesis, the budding consciousness of Arab community should conversely pre-date Arabic language standardisation: when a community forms, its previously disparate members harmonise their idioms, and with this in mind, it is noteworthy that the number of Arabic inscriptions and graffito from the first Islamic century alone is at least six times greater than the sum of all 'Old Arabic' writing from the five centuries before Islam, with particularly marked increase in the last quarter of the first/seventh century.[27] The existence of a pre-Islamic 'Arab' community is not a theoretically necessary condition precedent for the widespread conversion to Islam, and the epigraphic record indicates that Arabia's decisive Arabisation was indeed primarily an Islamic-era phenomenon.

In sum, pre-Islamic Arabian inscriptions and pre-Islamic Arabian records are complimentary. There is an intriguing silence in both corpuses about 'Arabs' and Arabic language during pre-Islam, and the silence is emphatically broken with ample references to Arabs and Arabic in the Islamic period. Linguistic development is discernable in the centuries before Islam, but its pace and direction towards Arabic are markedly limited, and pre-Islamic Arabia does not speak to us as a font of Arabness. What we now want to know is what prompted linguistic homogenisation? Why did increasing numbers of people adopt a language, call it Arabic and assert exclusive possession over it, using it as a means to distinguish themselves from others and imagine the Arab community? In short, we want to know when Arabic became *the* Arabic language, but the answer cannot be teased from the small, tendentious corpus of pre-Islamic inscriptions alone. The first consciousness of an imagined community around the idea of Arabness will become clearer by re-examining a vast and underutilised source of pre-Islamic lore: Arabian poetry.

II The Search for Arabs in Pre-Islamic Poetry

Collections of pre-Islamic poetry contain tens of thousands of verses ascribed to poets who lived (predominantly) in northern Arabia and the Syrian Desert during the two centuries before Islam. Quantitatively, poetry constitutes the richest source of material to examine how groups expressed their senses of self, but it has been underutilised in the study of Arab origins. In a large part, the inattention stems from the fact that the poetic corpus was surveyed once by Nöldeke (in 1899) to prove that ancient Arabians called themselves 'Arabs'.[28] Nöldeke unearthed six individual verses citing the word *ᶜarab* in pre-Islamic poetry, thus declaring the case closed, reassuring his readers that Arabs existed as Arabian Bedouin centuries before Islam. Subsequent scholars accepted Nöldeke's word,[29] and the pre-Islamic poets are now assumed to be quintessentially 'Arab', but there is need to refresh the scene. The old racialist paradigms of Nöldeke's day are no longer tenable, and we now possess more advanced understanding of early poetry and the ways to use it in historical analysis. We shall find that the poetry is much less self-consciously 'Arab' than assumed, and that alternative notions of communal consciousness are decidedly more prevalent.

The 'Arab' in Pre-Islamic Poetry

The evident starting point for reassessing identity in pre-Islamic poetry is the strikingly small number of times the word *ᶜarab* appears. Nöldeke did not question why the assemblage of just six references is so minuscule; he took it as sufficient that the word *ᶜarab* is cited in a handful of scattered verses, but from modern theoretical and source critical perspectives, more circumspection is in order: and it begins by reducing Nöldeke's body of evidence. His six citations of *ᶜarab* appear in two verses ascribed to Imruᵓ al-Qays, two lines by obscure poets mentioned in the fourth/tenth-century *Kitāb al-Aghānī*, one verse attributed to Ḥassān ibn Thābit (a contemporary of Muhammad), and a line in the pre-Islamic history section of the fourth/tenth-century al-Ṭabarī's *Tārīkh al-rusul wa-l-mulūk*.[30] From the set, the verse of Ḥassān ibn Thābit should be discounted since he was a Muslim-era poet, and the two verses ascribed to Imruᵓ al-Qays can be discounted too because they seem to be spurious, and are not recorded in the modern scholarly edition of Imruᵓ al-Qays' *Dīwān* edited by Muḥammad Abū al-Faḍl Ibrāhīm in 1958.[31] We are thus left with only three verses mentioning the word *ᶜarab* (and I suggest it is more likely only two),[32] attributed to obscure poets recorded in later Islamic-era compendiums. This is very scant evidence indeed, and it uncannily resembles the virtual absence of reference to 'Arab' in pre-Islamic epigraphy.[33]

We now possess fuller editions of pre-Islamic poetry than those available to Nöldeke a century ago, but in this much larger corpus, I found only one further line referencing *ᶜarab*. It appears in a poem ascribed to the pre-Islamic Zuhayr ibn Abī Sulmā:

> Ah Fate! You have bereaved me of men,
> They were kings of the Arabs and non-Arabs (*mulūk al-ᶜarab wa-l-ᶜajam*)[34]

The verse's dichotomy of Arabs/non-Arabs depicts a group identity in contrast to an outsider 'other' which is a typical device to form ethnic consciousness, and the phrase is invoked here to demarcate status of lordship over both 'us' and 'them', that is, 'everyone', but this particular verse may not actually have been composed by the pre-Islamic Zuhayr. There are three early scholarly collections of Zuhayr's poetry: two by the early Iraqi grammarians Thaᶜlab (d. 291/904) and Muḥammad ibn Hubayra al-Asadī Ṣuᶜūdāᵓ (d. 295/907–8), and a later commentary by the Andalusian belles-lettrist al-Shantamarī (d. 476/1084), and none contain the above line mentioning 'Arab', nor do they narrate any other poems citing the word *ᶜarab*.[35] The 'Arab' verse only appears in a fragmentary version of the poem which al-Buḥturī (d. 284/897) narrated in his *al-Ḥamāsa*.[36] Al-Buḥturī's narration is also defective: it only relates seven of the poem's twenty lines, it omits the poem's *nasīb* (opening section) entirely and begins the poem with the 'Arab verse'. The verse may therefore be an alternative opening for the poem which contemporary collectors of Zuhayr's poetry ignored. The peculiar context of the verse's narration could mean it was inserted into Zuhayr's original poem by later hands, and there is a logic behind this. The poem is politically potent: it praises Harim ibn Sinān's clan, a group active in the Islamic era, and it and similar poetry was circulated by the clan's partisans.[37] The clan would welcome relishing their past merits and embellishing them with some new insertions, especially claims of mastery over an Islamic-era epithet for all humanity (that is, Arabs/non-Arabs). But poetry specialists appear to have counted the line as a spurious addition and withheld it from the *dīwān* manuscript tradition, akin to the scholarly omission of the two lines citing *ᶜarab* ascribed to Imruᵓ al-Qays. Taking stock, therefore, reference to *ᶜarab* in pre-Islamic poetry is absent from the poems of all important poets, and the references ascribed to minor poets in Muslim-era collections are accordingly suspect: they could all, in reality, be Muslim-era fabrications, and we now need to address the central methodological issue of how poetry can be used for historical research.

Pre-Islamic poetry originates from an oral performative milieu, and was transmitted orally across three or four hundred years before Muslim scholars in the urban centres of Iraq began recording it into the collections we possess today. The collectors and their peers wrote voluminously about pre-Islamic Arabia, and there is a risk that they could have inserted references to 'Arab' into genuine pre-Islamic poems, or fabricated poems outright in order to give an archaic sense for Arabness. The tiny number of references to 'Arab' indicates that they did not do this concertedly, but the verses of Zuhayr and Imruᵓ al-Qays seem to be examples of tampering, evocative of the scepticism advocated in Margoliouth's and Ḥusayn's 1920s assertions that Muslim anthologists wholly fabricated the poetry to serve Islamic-era discourses.[38] Such claims render pre-Islamic poetry useless for historians of pre-Islam, but subsequent scholars rallied to the poetry's defence,[39] and the spectre of forgery has now receded, though it has not entirely disappeared. We lack tidy authoritative collections; there are variant narrations for many pre-Islamic poems, and classical-era Iraqi anthologists themselves admitted to forgeries and false ascriptions.[40] But in favour of authenticity, poems' meter and rhyme make them easy to remember and help maintain their form over time, and the mere fact that poems were transmitted orally for three centuries does not mean they must have been transformed beyond recognition.[41] Specialists today mostly affirm that Muslims did not fabricate the whole corpus, but much may have been lost or altered as it passed through the hands of Iraqi narrators.[42] So, as a practical matter, there are enough lingering prospects of forgeries of individual lines to worry historians who wish to derive empirical data about pre-Islamic Arabia from specific verses. To better ascertain communal identity expressed in poetry, we cannot suffice with extracting references as Nöldeke did a century ago;[43] we need more cautious methodology.

New methods can borrow from the more developed field of hadith studies. Both pre-Islamic poetry and Prophetic hadith were recorded during the same period in Iraq, and while the mechanics of narrating poetry and prose differ, in the case of both disciplines, the narrators' expressed interest in authenticity competed with urges to fabricate and alter texts for varied ulterior motives. The resultant corpuses present similarly varied windows into the past, which they purport to preserve, and from amongst the debate over hadith's authenticity, Wael Hallaq offers a useful analytical rubric with recourse to basic statistics. Hallaq reminds us that hadith narrators were themselves sceptical about all but a score of definitively authentic hadith (the *mutawātir*), and as for the rest, they 'engender probability, and probability . . . allows for mendacity and error'.[44] Applying Hallaq's logic to poetry, we could propose that many individual lines of poetry bear probability of being fakes, but trends that appear across a wide cross-section of the entire poetic corpus have better probability of authenticity since it is improbable that all verses bearing a similar message were fabricated, whereas messages endorsed by only single or a small number of verses could indeed be fabrications inserted by Muslims into the pre-Islamic corpus.

To use poetry for analysis of Arab ethnic identity, therefore, we need to search for unambiguous expressions of community across a wide spectrum of poetry. It would also be helpful if we can corroborate testimony from poetry with pre-Islamic epigraphy and Greek and Latin literature too, since names and events mentioned in both poetry and independent pre-Islamic sources have enhanced probability of reflecting social realities in which the poetry was first sung. Amidst the tens of thousands of recorded pre-Islamic verses, the three (or just two) lines containing the word *al-ᶜarab* are insufficient to prove that all poets unequivocally conceptualised their community as 'Arab', and the poetic silence is particularly material since pre-Islamic poetry is dated to the two centuries before Islam – the precise period in which we noted the word 'Arab' disappeared from contemporary descriptions of Arabia. Nöldeke's essay accordingly instructs us to believe that pre-Islamic poets knew that they constituted an 'Arab community' even though (1) they do not mention 'Arab' in their poetry, (2) the term 'Arab' is not attested in epigraphic finds from the same period, and (3) no other contemporary outsider observers used the word 'Arab' to describe Arabian populations either. Adherents to Nöldeke's theory are left conceding that the third-century CE disappearance of 'Arab' as an ethnicon is 'odd', yet nonetheless argue that Arabians must have 'began to call themselves Arabs' at this time.[45] Instead of reiterating paradoxes, we can re-examine the poetry to see if it expresses alternative forms of identity which researchers may have missed on account of their predisposition to find 'Arabs'.

Pre-Islamic Poetry and Maᶜadd

In contrast to the absence of the word *ᶜarab*, 'Maᶜadd' emerges as a salient label of collective identity across pre-Islamic poetry. We shall revisit Maᶜadd in Chapter 4's exploration of the construction of Arab genealogies in the Islamic era, but in brief, Muslim genealogists identified Maᶜadd as one of the key Arab ancestors, and after some wrangling (considered in Chapter 4(IV)), they divided the Arab family tree between 'Northern/ᶜAdnān' and 'Southern/Qaḥṭān' Arabs, and identified Maᶜadd as the son of ᶜAdnān, thus memorialising him as the common ancestor of most Arabian groups from the deserts south of Syria and Iraq. This is where pre-Islamic poetry was primarily composed, and it is pertinent that the poetry accords significant emphasis on Maᶜadd.

Maᶜadd's importance has been noted as connoting a collective wider than merely 'Northern Arabs',[46] but previous research has been driven to find pre-Islamic 'Arabs', so there has been no attention to the question of whether Maᶜadd was in fact the communal identity by which some pre-Islamic poets identified themselves instead of 'Arab'. Consider the line of the poet Labīd:

> Their virtue is known across Maᶜadd:
> Those with true knowledge know the truth.[47]

Labīd's poem aims to exaggerate the renown of the group he praises, hence logic and rhetoric dictate that the poet should select the largest conceptual community. Labīd's reference to Maᶜadd alone indicates that Maᶜadd served this function, and was not merely a subdivision of a larger 'Arab' community. In another line, Labīd boasts that:

> I chased off Maᶜadd, the ᶜIbād and Ṭayyiᵓ
> Kalb too, like thirsting camels drive others from the well.[48]

Goldziher adduced a similar line where Labīd mentions Maᶜadd, Kinda and Ṭayyiᵓ which Goldziher concluded must intend the three peoples constituting the pre-Islamic 'Arabs',[49] but neither in these lines, nor any other poem does Labīd mention 'Arab', and Maᶜadd's primacy in pre-Islamic imaginations should be taken more seriously since neither Ṭayyiᵓ, Kinda or Kalb are cited as frequently, as revealed when considering more poetry.

The poet Imruᵓ al-Qays, when praising his father, a 'Southern' king from Kinda near Yemen, referred to him as:

> He, the best of Maᶜadd, most virtuous and generous[50]

In another poem, Imruᵓ al-Qays praises a different king, the 'Northern' Saᶜd ibn Ḍabāb al-Iyādī with the same formula: 'the best of Maᶜadd' (*khayr Maᶜadd*).[51] Given the Islamic-era interpretation that Maᶜadd refers only to 'Northern Arabs', this dual citation confused later commentators who made an odd grammatical assumption to change the meaning of the first verse such that Maᶜadd would not be an adjective of Imruᵓ al-Qays' father.[52] Since

Muslim genealogists have taught us that no 'Southerner' would claim descent from Maᶜadd, such interpretation seems necessary, but the most straightforward reading of the verse renders Imruᵓ al-Qays' father himself the 'best of Maᶜadd',[53] so on the clearest interpretation of the verse, either the poet got his own father's ancestry wrong, a later scribe made a mistake, or Maᶜadd actually had wider connotations than we attribute it today. Further consideration of the *khayr Maᶜadd* epithet suggests the third possibility is likely: it was cited across Arabic literature about pre-Islamic Arabia, not as specific identification of ancestry, but instead as a broad expression of praise.[54] Although Muslim genealogists separated Arabians into 'Northern' and 'Southern' camps, pre-Islamic poets and their patrons 300 years earlier seemed to have expressed wider consciousness of shared affiliation with Maᶜadd.

The hypothesis finds support by reading more poetry. Zuhayr ibn Janāb al-Kalbī, perhaps the earliest poet whose work has survived, invokes Maᶜadd in a line about the Banū Nahd:

> I have not seen any tribe of Maᶜadd scatter other than the Nahd
> Quite like the scattering of al-Fizr's goats.[55]

Here the Nahd is depicted as part of Maᶜadd, and Maᶜadd is invoked as the greatest collective Zuhayr could imagine in order to achieve the rhetorical effect of specifically singling out the Nahd. If a consciousness of a community greater than Maᶜadd existed, it would have behoved Zuhayr to cite it. Similarly, the pre-Islamic poet, al-Aᶜshā says:

> We came upon men, who, when the chargers of Maᶜadd are gathered
> Are most respected and awed[56]

Al-Aᶜshā seeks to praise one tribe by indicating that its warriors stand a cut above all others. Al-Aᶜshā also cites Maᶜadd to praise his own people:

> If all of Maᶜadd had mustered with us at Dhū Qār,
> Glory would not have eluded them.[57]

Again, Maᶜadd should be read here as the byword for the largest group amongst which the story of the tribe's exploits could be expected to extend. Shouldn't we expect al-Aᶜshā to select a name which signifies the largest conceivable community?

When praising the tribal leader al-Nuᶜmān ibn Wāʾil al-Kalbī, the poet al-Nābigha al-Dhubyānī invokes Maᶜadd in his summa of al-Nuᶜmān's distinction:

> You outstrip the nobles in nobility
> Like a stallion outstrips hunting dogs in the chase,
> You surpass all of Maᶜadd as a patron sought and enemy feared,
> From the abundance of praise, you are its first recipient.[58]

Again, if a collective greater than Maᶜadd existed, would not the panegyrist's voice mention it instead?

Further indications of Maᶜadd's status appear in Abū Tammām's *al-Ḥamāsa* collection of shorter poetry fragments. The poet Ḥujr ibn Khālid invokes Maᶜadd in a tribal self-praise, again as an allegory to what seems, in his conception, the largest conceivable collective above individual tribes:

> Our subalterns, they could be leaders of any other tribe;
> And our leaders: they could head an army of Maᶜadd, no doubt.[59]

Abān ibn ᶜAbda ibn al-ᶜAyyār boasts of his own tribe's self sufficiency, claiming:

> Leave us; we could fight all of Maᶜadd alone![60]

Al-Ḥamāsa contains three further citations of Maᶜadd as 'all the people',[61] and analogous citations occur across other classical collections: for instance, five verses collected in the tribal anthology of the Banū al-Asad, including a line of Jumayḥ who, in the vein of T. S. Eliot's Tiresias, exclaims

> I have met all that Maᶜadd – in its entirety – has seen;
> And [now] I have lost the joys of youth and vigour.[62]

And Maᶜadd is also found in poems of dispraise; Muhammad's poet Ḥassān ibn Thābit, for example, disparages a rival contending that

> [Your tribe] is a symbol of disgrace, all of Maᶜadd knows it.[63]

Ḥassān invokes Maᶜadd in six other poems,[64] notably in the last line of a long praise of his tribe where he expresses the summa of their character:

We've dealt equity to all of Maᶜadd:
Recompensing ill for their ill; goodness to their grace.[65]

Yet again, Maᶜadd operates as the chosen signifier for the notion of 'all people' to achieve the effect of expressing the certainty of Ḥassān's claim.

In contrast to the two/three references to 'Arab', we find dozens of Maᶜadd, consistently and frequently repeated across the spectrum of pre-Islamic poetry to invoke the idea of 'all the people'. The citations engender the impression that poets conceptualised Maᶜadd as the byword for a super-collective communal identity, neither the property of one tribe, nor a tribal designation itself – Maᶜadd is cited on its own, I have not found it in the familiar tribal composite *Banū Maᶜadd*. Its usage accordingly reflects pan-family attributes to articulate the idea of 'all of us', typical of an ethnonym, and it mirrors the manner in which the ethnonym 'Arab' is used to circumscribe an imagined community today. The poetry indicates that Maᶜadd should not be read through the prism of later Islamic genealogy that restricts it to a subdivision of a larger Arab entity; for a large segment of poets, Maᶜadd represented the ultimate conception of community. Mentions of Kinda, Ṭayyiᵓ and al-ᶜIbād indicate that poets were aware of, and interacted with other groups, but there is no term uniting all of them into a greater collective. 'Arab' does not stand for such a pre-Islamic collective: poets primarily invoke Maᶜadd alone. A reader, unaware that the corpus of poetry would later come to be called 'pre-Islamic *Arabic* poetry' could perhaps be excused for considering that many poets belonged to the people of Maᶜadd.

Maᶜadd in Other Pre-Islamic Sources

Poetic expressions of Ma'addite identity find parallels in non-Arabic pre-Islamic texts too. For example, the sixth-century Byzantine historian Procopius identifies Arabians living beyond imperial control during the reign of Justinian as *Maddenoi* or 'Maddene Saracens', a people whom Procopius counts as a distinct group in western Arabia and 'subjects of the *Homeritae* [Ḥimyar]'.[66] Procopius, unlike the earlier Hellenistic writers about Arabia noted in the last chapter, is familiar with the region and gives an empirically reasoned account of a land inhabited by various peoples. Procopius never uses the word 'Arab' to group them: Procopius' references to Maᶜadd indicate an independence mirrored in the manner Ma^{c}add is cited to delineate a particular group in pre-Islamic poetry. In addition, Zwettler's survey of Greek and Syriac writings reveals multiple citations of Arabian Ma'addites which leads him to conclude that Ma^{c}add was the byword for militarised, camel-herding Bedouin of northern Arabia during Late Antiquity.[67] There is accordingly a significant congruence of sources: both outsider literature and pre-Islamic poetry make no reference to Arabness in the three centuries before Islam, whereas both invoke Ma^{c}add when conceptualising central Arabian populations.

A reference to Ma^{c}add in the funerary monument erected in 328 CE at al-Namāra in southern Syria for a king named Imru$^{\circ}$ al-Qays also informs our analysis. The inscription is difficult to translate since it was written in archaic Arabic and in Nabataean script,[68] but it does identify Imru$^{\circ}$ al-Qays as 'King of the Arabs' (*malik al-^{c}arab*) and 'King of Ma^{c}add' (*malik ma^{c}add*).[69] The inscription appears to be the first Arabic-language reference to an individual calling himself an Arab, but drawing conclusions about fourth-century Arab ethnogenesis from the al-Namāra epitaph is difficult since the interpretation of the king's titles is contested. Most scholars shy away from reading the inscription's 'Arabs' as referring to a pan-Arabian community.[70] Retsö notes the epithet 'King of the Arabs' was an old Imperial Roman honorific granted to leaders on the Syrian/Arabian frontier (and by the second century CE perhaps specifically for rulers on the borders of Rome's *Provincia Arabia*), and the same honorific was used by Persians for their *Beth ^{c}Arbāyē*, suggesting the term's origins in Hellenistic geographical notions of Arabia as a place, not a specific community or ethnos.[71] The title thus asserts Imru$^{\circ}$ al-Qays' sovereignty over a place known to the Romans as Arabia, not sovereignty over the people whom we know as Arabs. The broader context of the al-Namāra inscription's 'Arabs' is also telling: after the fourth century, there is no further reference to 'King of the Arabs' in Greek or Syriac prose, nor in pre-Islamic inscriptions, and Latin and Greek records ceased referring to 'Arabs' altogether (noted in Chapter 1(III), pp. 47–8).

Al-Namāra's inscription ought to be evaluated in the context of pre-Islamic poetry too, for much of the poetry was performed for Arabian leaders who called themselves 'kings' (*malik*/*mulūk*), yet across the entire poetic corpus the honorific 'King of the Arabs' is absent. This seems substantial, for if 'Arab' was an important ethnonym or title of status in Late Antique Arabia, poets from the fifth and sixth centuries should have liberally used the term to curry favour with their patrons. That they did not cite the term despite their custom of excessively praising their patrons, again mitigates against imagining a continuity of Arab ethnos and kingship from the fourth century al-Namāra's inscription up to the seventh century dawn of Islam. To this point, consider also Labīd's reference to *mulk maᶜadd* (sovereignty over Maᶜadd) in praise of a ruler, and not *ᶜarab*.[72] I am also unaware that any inscriptions relating to fifth- and sixth-century kingdoms in al-Ḥijāz invoke the 'King of the Arabs' boast either. The al-Namāra epitaph's Arabness seems the end of a road: the last reference to an archaic imperial honorific, not the first reference to a new ethnic community of Arabs.

Al-Namāra inscription's mention of Maᶜadd helps qualify its 'Arab' puzzle. The manner in which it lists the 'King of Maᶜadd' phrase indicates it was a separate sovereignty from 'King of the Arabs'. This may be the earliest reference to Maᶜadd from any source, and as we have seen, reference to Maᶜadd became increasingly common in both non-Arabian texts and pre-Islamic Arabian poetry following the fourth-century. Given the significance of Maᶜadd in communal consciousness in poetry dated to the two centuries following al-Namāra's epitaph and the contemporaneous disappearance of 'Arab', al-Namāra's epitaph is an intriguing monument offering the last surviving employment of an archaic sense of 'Arab' as Hellenistic geographic nomenclature, while also pointing forwards to a new significance of Maᶜadd as a sense of community for people living to the south of the Roman *Provincia Arabia* in the centuries preceding Islam.

In sum, attempts to find a pre-Islamic Arabian community of 'Arabs' are confounded by the appearance of Maᶜadd in both poetry and prose to describe many of the peoples whom tradition assumes should have been Arabs. Maᶜadd acts like an ethnonym to express a collective identity which no one group possesses or dominates, but to which a wide array of subgroups conceptualise a shared belonging. The reference to Maᶜadd alongside other collectives in al-Namāra's inscription implies that it was between the fourth and sixth centuries CE that Maᶜadd grew into a sense of community for widespread, vigorous, militarised peoples in central Arabia. As will be explored in Chapter 4, Muslim genealogists originally posited Maᶜadd as the oldest grandfather of the Arabs, and hence the evidence points to the origins of the Arab ethnos as an expansion from a previous community of Maᶜadd. The texts urge us to move beyond von Grunebaum's *Kulturnation* theory noted in Chapter 1(II) that 'Arabs' existed but did not express their identity, since the prevalence of Maᶜadd indicates that pre-Islamic Arabians did indeed express specific identities – but none were 'Arab'. Müller's instincts were right after all: 'Arab' did not connote an ethnos in pre-Islamic Arabia.[73] More time and change was needed for groups to articulate a sense of Arabness.

The status of Maᶜadd sheds new light on pre-Islamic Arabic epigraphy too. We have seen that the small number of inscriptions reveal that Arabic was neither concertedly codified, widely written, nor a marker of status amongst pre-Islamic Arabian populations, and this aligns with the absence of reference to *ᶜarabī* or *al-ᶜarab* in the lexicons of pre-Islamic Arabian poets. Their conceptions of community were not informed by Arabic language homogeneity, and they did not establish a sense of self via collective awareness of a non-Arabic other. Arabian communities were divided in other fashions, pitting kin-conceptualised groups of Maᶜadd against other Arabians.[74] Idioms which would become 'Arabic' were developing, and a number of groups which would become 'Arab tribes' were in existence, but the sense of wider community that could promote Arabness and homogenise the Arabic language was absent. We have no indications that pre-Islamic groups were making perceptible progress towards creating consciousness of an Arab community as something bigger than or a substitute for the idea of Maᶜadd.

Our texts are 'Arabless' and full of Maᶜadd and we now seek to know what this means and why the pre-Islamic textual record contains no evidence of pan-Arabian Arab community. For answers, exploration of pre-Islamic Arabia's sociopolitical conditions, transactional boundaries and lines of cultural affinities offer explanations why we found no Arabs across Arabia, but instead Maᶜadd in central Arabia before Islam.

III Contextualising the 'Arabless' Poetry: Ethnic Boundaries in Pre-Islamic Arabia

The absence of reference to *al-ᶜarab* in pre-Islam's textual record makes it difficult to substantiate the term 'pre-Islamic Arabs', for we have neither textual indications of what the label could have meant nor evidence that groups ever adopted it to define their sense of community, and hence extrapolating backwards from Muslim-era records to call pre-Islamic Arabians 'Arabs' seems anachronistic. When pursuing the evaluation of pre-Islamic Arabia's complex web of politics, power, faith and culture, we shall further perceive how factors pointed not towards pan-Arabian cohesion, but rather to zones of fragmentation which traditional assumptions about Arab origins have overlooked. And through this exercise we can move beyond 'must have been' statements that accompany the idea of pre-Islamic Arab origins and adduce evidence confirming the hypothesis proposed by both Müller and Donner that it is indeed anachronistic to imagine that 'Arab' constituted a mobilisable form of communal belonging before Islam.

From the perspective of politics and power, Arabia's most significant players in the century before Islam were on its fringes: the Byzantine and Sasanian Empires vied for influence inconclusively in Arabia, dividing it between their spheres of influence. The Byzantines allied with Ghassān in the north-west, the Sasanians employed Lakhm to the north-east, and their wars are well known.[75] In Iraq, Islamic-era sources written 300 years after the fall of the Byzantines and Sasanians count Lakhm based in Iraqi al-Ḥīra, Ghassān based around Syrian al-Jābiya, and nomads deeper in Arabia as all subgroups of one pan-Arab community, but such ethnic homogenisation sits uneasily with pre-Islamic transactional boundaries. Lakhm and Ghassān, being frontier guards employed by distant empires to extend influence into Arabia, interacted with other Arabians on unequal terms. Lakhm and Ghassān were ex-nomads, and so shared 'cultural stuff' with Arabians such as similar language, customs and perhaps a taste for particular kinds of poetry, but the imbalanced power differential between the agents of empire and independent peoples constitute the type of political barrier which anthropologists typify as conducive to creating ethnic difference. The helpful dichotomy James Montgomery articulated between Arabian 'Bedouin poets' and the 'Bedouinising taste' of poetry audiences in Lakhmid Iraq feeds into the consideration of the transactional divide between Lakhm and the central Arabian interior.[76] Lakhmid nostalgia for an 'othered' Bedouin world points to the different cultural approaches to poetry attendant upon the differing transactional environments of the poets and their patrons. It would be remarkable if a sense of Arab communal cohesion could have incubated across northern Arabia in the face of such divisions, contradicting interests, and lifestyles.[77]

Further cultural barriers inhibiting opportunity for groups to rally around consciousness of a single pan-Arabian identity can be identified as stemming from the divisive political boundaries. Ghassān was drawn into the Hellenistic world via its contacts with Byzantium; Lakhm fostered links with Sasanian court practices. Their regimes endured for over a century, and hence we need to account for the long period when Ghassān's and Lakhm's different facing allegiances entailed adoption of different models of kingship, patronage rituals and historical traditions. The different cultural trappings would have enabled them to feel distinct from one another, and furthermore, as they acculturated towards their northern benefactors, their awareness of differences from independent groups within Arabia would increase, etching substantial fault lines confounding putative pan-Arab *Kulturnation* unity.

The political and cultural difference between inner Arabian groups versus Ghassān and Lakhm suggest that recognition of kinship difference should follow, and this is substantiated in the textual indications about Maᶜadd. I am unaware of poetry in which Ghassān and Lakhm are described as members of Maᶜadd, and neither group were included in genealogies of Maᶜadd (genealogists grouped Ghassān and Lakhm into a different family) – a telling legacy that the uneven transactional boundaries obstructed consciousness of shared interests and fragmented kinship alignments. The power differentials are reflected in awareness of Maᶜadd identity on the 'inside' amongst central Arabians to specifically exclude imperial 'bullies' on the 'outside'.

Doctrinal difference also abetted communal fragmentation. Ghassān were Christian Monophysites, Lakhm were polytheistic, and many of the peoples within Lakhm's sphere of influence were East Syriac Christians, especially around al-Ḥīra.[78] Late Antique inter-Christian feuding over Christological issues flared in violence, and whilst Monophysites and East Syrians could coexist peacefully in some circumstances,[79] doctrinal disagreement, separate places of worship, and the different political allegiances associated with different sects play a material role in shaping divided communal identities. Consider also the significance of the annual festival which Ghassān organised for St Sergius on 7 October at their north-easterly centre al-Ruṣāfa, and Ghassān's establishment of a shrine for St Sergius in their south-western stronghold in

Buṣrā.[80] Veneration of St Sergius was a central aspect of Christian identity across the Euphrates and Syrian Desert frontier region between the Byzantine and Sasanian Empires,[81] and Ghassān's adoption of St Sergius would seem to serve political interests by filling Ghassān's polity with the symbolically potent St Sergius, and thereby presenting Ghassān as an attractive and legitimate authority in the eyes of Christians across the region, including those on the Sasanian/Lakhmid side of the frontier. Christians on the Tigris river accordingly negotiated political boundaries that pointed them eastwards to Lakhm, but since the Lakhmid rulers were predominantly pagan, confessional boundaries presented paths of redrawing allegiance towards Ghassān and their cults of St Sergius. The shrines to St Sergius at both termini of Ghassān's settled zone circumscribe Ghassān's sphere, and participation in the festivals establishes a spiritual framework to create a sense of 'inside' Ghassān, bolstering transactional barriers against outsiders, and thereby enabling participating groups to apprehend their belonging to Ghassān's system. The role of regular festivals more generally in cementing identities and political legitimacy in Late Antique Syria have elsewhere been noted on localised bases.[82] In the charged environment of Late Antiquity, the competing religious identities, different boundaries and cultic practices across a patchwork of peoples seeking to distinguish themselves should be evaluated instead of extrapolating from presumptions that a single Arab faith system linked the communities of pre-Islamic Arabians.

Arabia's religious map was also divided by Jewish communities which entered the Peninsula after the revolts against Rome in 67 and 132 CE, and which, by the dawn of Islam, had developed population centres throughout western Arabia and in Yemen where Jewish converts asserted substantial political power.[83] Further still, there were polytheistic elements in western Arabia, visible in some inscriptions, referenced in the Qur'an, and noted by contemporary Byzantine observers who recount conversions of pagan 'Saracens' to forms of monotheism.[84] Modern studies on religious practice in pre-Islamic Arabia, particularly al-Ḥijāz, debate the extent of Christian and Judaic penetration, but akin to the tendency to generalise about 'the Arabs', modern texts also subsume 'Arab Christians', 'Arab Jews' and 'Arab pagans' into one homogenous Arabness monolith without considering how doctrinal difference could have fragmented communal consciousness across Arabia.[85]

While members of different confessions did on occasion share religious spaces and syncretism occurred, pre-Islamic Arabia's variegated pantheon needs investigation instead of whitewashing a cohesive Arab identity onto pre-Islamic society.[86]

Religious divisions were exploitable for political aims to disrupt balances of power in pre-Islamic Arabia, witnessed famously in the mid-sixth-century CE Christian Byzantine interference with the Judaic-leaning South Arabian kingdom of Ḥimyar which sparked violent conflict, the martyrdom of Christians in Najrān, Christian Ethiopic invasion of Yemen, and Sasanian counter-attack.[87] The Ethiopians also invaded central Arabia,[88] and memories of their campaign appear in Qur'an 105 and later Muslim writings,[89] where it is adapted it into a story of a single-minded attack on Mecca's sanctum, indicating a degree of trauma induced in al-Ḥijāz.[90] Since the Qur'an ascribes victory against the Ethiopians to a miraculous intervention of Heaven, and since no groups claimed participation in Mecca's defence, it seems that no pan-Arabian force was mustered to ward off the Ethiopic threat, again indicative of an absence of the putative 'Arab' communal solidary as a politically mobilisable body in the century before Islam.[91]

As noted above, the presumption that pre-Islamic Arabia was full of Arabs follows the legacy of Muslim-era literature which cites an array of cultural activities to delineate a putative pan-Arabian Arab identity.[92] Such assertions are not only unsupported, given the 'Arabless' pre-Islamic epigraphy and poetry, but they are equally theoretically suspect given the shortcomings of purely 'cultural stuff' approaches to ethnogenesis. Consider, for example, the linkage of pre-Islamic Arab unity to the system of fairs, *aswāq al-ᶜarab* ('the Arab markets' as Muslim-era literature calls them), supposedly held at fixed times in and around Arabia during which communities met, mixed and recognised their common culture.[93] Mixing populations in a trading environment could theoretically foster ethnic cohesion, but it is difficult to substantiate in pre-Islamic Arabia's circumstances. Market centres possess demographic heterogeneity, not homogeneity, and a degree of political centralisation or permanent settlement is needed to enable transacting groups to regularise interactions and then begin the process of assimilation. While the Muslim literary references have been used to underwrite assumptions that a political system unifying the Arabs existed,[94] there is no indication from

Late Antiquity itself suggesting such a pan-Arabian structure: stories about the markets' 'Arabness' derive exclusively from Muslim-era literature. Pre-Islamic poets mention some individual markets, but never the collective term *aswāq al-ᶜarab* common in the Muslim-era narratives, prompting a suspicion that Muslim writers gathered tales about the markets and subsumed them under a novel 'Arab' umbrella as part of creating a narrative of Arabia's past in homogenous 'Arab' communal terms. It seems more accurate to propose that the actual pre-Islamic Arabian groups, lacking political unity, gathered in markets and then dispersed into their separate spheres of influence and theatres of war. The noted swift disappearance of the markets in the Islamic period[95] further indicates that there was no engrained system of the sort which the Muslim-era sources insinuate, but instead more local arrangements which could be easily abandoned when social situations changed. It may be more fruitful to conceptualise the Arabian markets in the guise of the Silk Road: Central Asian trade flourished through interlocking webs of localised trading networks even though political unities existed only rarely and populations remained ethnically diverse. Only from the vantage of hindsight does the Silk Road appear today as a cohesive system. The Silk Road was brisk in trade, but not in fermenting ethnic cohesion.

Assumptions of pre-Islamic 'Arab' communal cohesion also draw on Muslim-era stories about the Hajj, since later Arabic literature presented the pilgrimage to Mecca as the central ritual of all pre-Islamic Arabians. Reliance upon these stories as a source for the putative cohesion of pre-Islamic Arabs, however, is anachronistic. I found that reference to the Hajj or Mecca in pre-Islamic poetry is intriguingly absent. Poets give no indication that the Hajj had ritual significance for them, and the Hajj and Mecca are only referenced in poems praising the Quraysh tribe.[96] Since Quraysh constituted the caliphal family and ruling elite of early Islam, poetry about Quraysh is precisely the sort which bears enhanced probability of Islamic-era fabrication to cloak Quraysh's manifest sovereignty in the Caliphate with anachronistic assertions of pre-Islamic precedent. Although almost all signs point to the fact that Mecca's sanctum pre-dated Muhammad, there is no need to overestimate its importance as a pan-Arabian centre of worship common to all 'Arabs'. Mecca's 'ethnic' sobriquet *bayt al-ᶜarab* (the Arab Sacred House) only appears in Muslim-era histories written from the third/ninth century, whereas the earlier references to Mecca and its sanctum in the Qur'an and Prophetic hadith have no such Arabising terminology, and instead restrict Mecca's significance to worship of Abrahamic monotheists, never expressly 'Arabs'.[97] When Muslim-era writers constructed a pan-Arabian 'Arab' past, they alighted upon Mecca's Islamic-era status as *the* focus of Muslim prayer and pilgrimage and made it the equivalent focus for their imagined Arab community's roots.[98] Reading Mecca's signature 'pan-Arab' pre-Islamic significance as the fruit of Muslim historical reconstruction, and not the glue for pre-Islamic ethnogenesis, perhaps also explains why modern scholars are unable to find pre-Islamic evidence to substantiate Mecca's supposedly central status in Arabian society.[99] By unburdening ourselves from the notion of a pan-Arabian cultural community, we can conceptualise Mecca's devotees as a localised group: they may have been rich and even influential, but the lack of communal cohesion within Arabia kept their pre-Islamic significance muted in records of those residing at a remove from Mecca.

The signs pointing towards communal fragmentation in pre-Islamic Arabia also explain why a significant cross-section of pre-Islamic poets opted to identify themselves as Maᶜadd. As opposed to being a byword for an idea of 'high nomads' as recently proposed,[100] Maᶜadd emerges as a more tangible community and its significance is theoretically sustainable given the specific circumstances in central Arabia. The poets who cite Maᶜadd lived in the contested region to the south of Byzantine and Sasanian influence, and the exclusion of the imperial allies (Ghassān and Lakhm) from Ma'addite genealogies indicates that differing interests and power differentials generated a transactional boundary, on the southern side of which the weaker independent groups became cognisant of their shared commonality. Maᶜadd also did not extend far into southern Arabia: the kingdoms of Ḥimyar and the settled agricultural populations of Yemen had their own long history, political independence, religious institutions and trading links with each other, and likewise Yemenis were excluded from Ma'addite genealogy.[101] Geographically, the idea of Ma'addite community occupied a central Arabian transactional sphere, and chronologically, the community developed from its earliest attested beginnings as one of several groups mentioned in the early fourth-century CE al-Namāra inscription to become the dominant form of expressed communal consciousness in sixth-century CE poetry. To account for such expanded cognisance of 'Maᶜadd-ness', we need neither postulate a violent takeover of central Arabia, massive migration nor above-average birth rate: instead, we can link Maᶜadd's rise as generated by the specific pressures that prompted groups to embrace union against the backdrop of the particularly intensified Byzantine, Sasanian, and Himyarite and other Southern Arabian interest in, competition over and interference throughout Arabia from the late fifth century to its climax towards the end of the sixth.[102] Central Arabian groups exposed to such sudden forces from their north and south can be expected to recognise their precarious position, and hence begin to apprehend some common interests, which leads to a mutual drive towards defensive solidarity, and thence to the articulation of a new form of community to identify themselves. The rise in expressions of Ma'addite belonging in poetry and inscriptions in the sixth century are an anticipated result of politicking and division which left an array of groups in central Arabia with the attractive choice of articulating a sense of exclusivity around the idea of Maᶜadd against the array of intruders.

We can thus grasp how similar languages and aspects of Bedouin culture offered a basis upon which Late Antique Arabian populations could interact, but the absence of a common pool of interests divided Arabians internally, and they lacked one common 'other' against whom an exclusively Arabian identity could be conceptualised. Pre-Islamic Arabians had ample opportunity to dislike and compete with other Arabians before imagining that they constituted anything like a common band facing ethnically different others. The inroads of outsider powers into Late Antique Arabia influenced senses of community, but they evidently did not promote new awareness of 'Arab' community given the silence of both the inscriptional and textual record. Instead, the closing pincers of power from the north and south left a middle ground which texts reveal engendered consciousness of the smaller-scale Maᶜadd. Were it not for the vociferous avowals of Arab unity in Muslim-era literature, we would never expect to find 'Arabs' spanning pre-Islamic Arabia, and the absence of 'Arab' in pre-Islamic poetry is accordingly natural.

The traditional belief in a pre-Islamic Arab ethno-cultural community can thus be discarded as the anachronistic end product of selective citation of later Muslim-era texts without source critical method. The notion of an

'Arabless Arabia' of more fragmented groups proposed here demands less conjecture and marries with models of ethnogenesis.[103] It is now pertinent to return to texts to determine when the term 'Arab' actually appears as a form of self-reference in order to begin understanding how the culturally, doctrinally and politically divided Arabians were reorganised into one Arab imagined community.

IV The Rise of 'Arab' Poetry

In contrast to the silence of pre-Islam, self-expressions of Arabness burst into history in the Islamic-era, particularly in poetry dated to the later Umayyad Caliphate. The coincidence of the emergence of people who called themselves 'Arabs' and the sociopolitical changes accompanying the rise of Islam is suggestive, and invites consideration of the poems to determine the meaning and significance of these first references to Arabness as a term for self.

At the dawn of Islam, Ḥassān ibn Thābit, one of the oft-called 'official-poets' of the Medinan Muslim community refers to the 'tribe of the Arabs' (*ḥayy min al-ᶜarab*) to identify a group from a larger collective.[104] In the following generation, two verses ascribed to Abū Dahbal al-Jumaḥī marshal a binary pair 'both *al-ᶜarab* and *al-ᶜajam*' to refer to 'all people':

> Abū al-Fīl's virtues are innumerable
> They have spread, well known amongst the *ᶜarab* and *ᶜajam*.[105]

Al-Jumaḥī's expression of *ᶜarab*/*ᶜajam* signals the conception of a group of language speakers (*al-ᶜarab*) united against those who do not speak their idiom (*al-ᶜajam*).[106] This typically binary conceptualisation of identity of us/them signals the importance of the 'other' in articulating the identity of Arabness, which accords the modern theory that ethnicity 'takes two', and that ethnogenesis occurs upon the occasion of new awareness of differences across boundaries.[107] The *ᶜarab*/*ᶜajam* distinction is established in the later Umayyad-era, witness the *Dīwān* of al-Farazdaq:

> Your claim to not know him is baseless:
> Both Arabs and non-Arabs (*al-ᶜarab wa-l-ᶜajam*) know what you deny.[108]

And al-Farazdaq's peer, Jarīr, twice invokes a collective notion of 'Arabs' to lampoon al-Farazdaq:

Al-Farazdaq has no glory to protect him
Except, perhaps, his cousins, who carry wooden staffs,
Be gone cousins! You should settle in al-Ahwāz
And the river Tīrā; no Arabs know you![109]

Al-Farazdaq and Jarīr's contemporary al-Rāᶜī al-Numayrī cites the Arab collective in praise of his own tribe:

Numayr is the burning ember of the Arabs
Burning all the brighter when war flares.[110]

And the Umayyad Caliph and poet al-Walīd ibn Yazīd (r. 125–6/743–4) cites 'Arab' to describe the lineage of one of his love interests:

I wish for Sulaymā, my cousin
From the noble Arabs.[111]

The Arabian domiciled Umayyad-era poet Dhū al-Rumma cites Arabs four times, referring to the 'dialects of the Arabs', the 'absent Arab girls', and 'the Arab noblewomen'.[112]

Since early Islamic and Umayyad poetry was preserved only from the late second/eighth century, empirical study faces questions of authenticity, but it is intriguing that the word 'Arab', absent from poetry ascribed to pre-Islamic Arabia, should make its appearance in poetic memories from the dawn of Islam as a widely cited expression of the collective in the fashion which Maᶜadd had been used in pre-Islam. Müller's thesis of the Muslim-era 'invention' of Arabs is herein substantiated, but the evidence does not permit Müller's clear-cut dichotomy, and suggests a more gradual development of the Arabness idea as postulated in Donner's *Muhammad and the Believers*.[113] The expressions of belonging to an Arab community eventually eclipsed attachment to the pre-Islamic Maᶜadd, but the persistence of Maᶜadd in Umayyad-era records indicates an only gradual reorganisation of Arabian communities around the idea of Arabness. Most Umayyad poets mention 'Maᶜadd' as a term of the ultimate collective identity, citing it more frequently than 'Arab';[114] for instance, Jarīr chides al-Farazdaq:

Al-Farazdaq is disgraced throughout Maᶜadd.[115]

The Umayyad caliphs also reportedly employed Ma'addite nomenclature to describe themselves: Hishām (r. 105–25/724–43) was addressed as 'the Lord of Maᶜadd and non-Maᶜadd' (*rabb Maᶜadd wa-siwā Maᶜadd*),[116] and al-Walīd ibn Yazīd's *Dīwān* contains reference to his entourage as 'elite of Maᶜadd' (*ᶜulyā Maᶜadd*).[117] Maᶜadd's substantial footprint in Muslim genealogies as 'father of the Arabs' (detailed in Chapter 4) underlines the continued relevance of Ma'addite kinship in early Islam, alongside intriguing references to Islam as the religion of Maᶜadd,[118] and a remarkable anecdote preserved only in Ibn Abī Shayba's early collection of hadith, *al-Muṣannaf*, which expressly contrasts Maᶜadd with Arabic, reporting: 'Recite the Qur'an Arabic-ly (*aᶜribū al-Qurʾān*), for it is Arabic (*ᶜarabī*). You must act like Maᶜadd because you are Ma'addites (*wa-tamaᶜdadū fa-innakum maᶜaddiyyūn*).'[119] The anecdote's meaning will become clearer in Chapter 3 where we consider the connotations of 'Arab' in the Qur'an: it is a fascinating indication of the contested nature of identity where early Muslims were faced with reconciling familiar terms (such as Maᶜadd) with novel parameters of the previously unattested *ᶜarab* which articulated community with other groups formally outside of Maᶜadd's boundaries. Later Muslim writers forgot these memories by not repeating such hadith, and hence forged a more straightforward history of Arabness than actually existed at the dawn of Islam.

Maᶜadd's persistence alongside increasing citation of 'Arab' paints Islam's first 125 years as a period of transition when the Ma'addite ethnicon eventually gave way to Arabness. Interestingly, amongst Umayyad poets, the Arabian Dhū al-Rumma is the only poet I have encountered who refers to 'Arab' more pervasively than Maᶜadd – the three references to Maᶜadd in his *Dīwān* are all in one unusual poem,[120] perhaps evidencing that the militarised communities of Maᶜadd left Arabia for Syria, Iraq and beyond during the conquests, and Maᶜadd lost its significance for an Arabian-domiciled poet one century later. Does Dhū al-Rumma indicate that we could better conceptualise the conquests as Ma'addite rather than Arab?

Reading the poetry from the pre-Islamic and early Islamic periods together, and tracing the shift from Maᶜadd's connotation as the expression of the largest meaningful collective to the gradually increasing citation of 'Arab' for the same meaning, plots a process with its nodal point after the dawn of Islam. Readers familiar with later third/ninth- and fourth/

tenth-century writings (which we consider in their chronological place in the following chapters), will know that Abbasid-era writers constantly described all pre-Islamic Arabians as 'Arabs' and left no room for Maᶜadd as a meaningful social group, relegating Maᶜadd's memory to genealogical curiosity and bygone tribal rivalries (*ᶜaṣabiyya*). But the poetry prompts reconsideration of the earlier Islamic-era rivalries: as opposed to viewing them as 'Arab family feuds', the alliances and conflicts of Islam's first century may have actually created the sense of Arab community as formerly disparate groups negotiated their status and undermined the value of membership to Maᶜadd identity.

The transition from pre-Islamic Maᶜadd to the third/ninth-century literary memorialisation of pre-Islamic Arabia as homogeneously 'Arab' was, therefore, a major rewriting of pre-Islam to forget old identities and homogenise the ethnic and cultural map of the Late Antique Middle East and nascent Islam. Opposite to the familiar narrative in which Islam's first century marks the transition of Arab *Kulturnation* to *Staatsnation*, it seems more accurate to read Arab identity as retrospectively constructed, and the Arabisation of the past as a momentous legacy of early Islam, second only to (and perhaps a central part of) early Muslims' codification of Islam's message. Parameters of the transition can be seen at work in the memorialisation of a seminal historical event just before the dawn of Islam: the Battle of Dhū Qār.

V Transition from 'Maᶜadd' to 'Arab': Case Study of Dhū Qār

Dhū Qār is now remembered as an epic pre-Islamic battle pitting Arab against Persian, Bedouin against Empire, and memories of the Persians' defeat at Dhū Qār resonate as the portentous herald of the Muslim conquest of Iraq and annihilation of the Persian Empire about twenty years after the battle.[121] If our argument that a cohesive 'Arab' ethnos did not exist before Islam is right, however, then there is a serious disjoint between the pre-Islamic battle and its 'Arabised' memory in later Muslim narratives. The Arab versus Persian ethnic struggle projected into pre-Islam must be anachronistic, and the depiction of Dhū Qār as the first 'Arab victory' would thus be a retrojection imparting ethnic significance to the battle which its actual participants never knew. Later tampering with Dhū Qār's memory is apparent in its dating: al-Iṣfahānī (d. 356/967) places it within a grand pan-historical narrative of Arab versus Persian by dating Dhū Qār as contemporary with Muhammad's victory over the pagan Meccans at Badr, elevating Dhū Qār to a pendant-piece of Islam's most famous military victory.[122] But this chronology seems to be a Muslim innovation 300 years after the event – earlier texts are both less specific and impute less significance to the battle.[123]

Modern re-examinations of Dhū Qār also support the suspicion that the battle lacked the strategic and ethnic significance later imputed. Bosworth suggests Dhū Qār may have been merely a 'skirmish',[124] and Donner critiques the traditional depiction of the battle as pitting the 'Arab' Bakr ibn Wāʾil tribe against the Sasanian Empire, because not all of the sub-tribes which Muslim genealogists classified as 'Bakr' participated in the battle (the combatants were from the group of Shaybān and some units from Qays), and moreover, because it appears that Bakr did not actually constitute a unified political collective in the early seventh century CE in any event. Notions of Bakr's pre-Islamic tribal unity and *ᶜaṣabiyya* solidarity are hence a fiction of Muslim historiography.[125] It is thus unlikely that Shaybānī and Qaysī warriors at Dhū Qār could have believed they represented the collective interests of the tribe Bakr, let alone the supposed nation of 'Maᶜadd' and certainly not the then non-existent 'Arabs'. And on the other side, the Sasanians were aided by Lakhmī (and likely also Taghlibī) units[126] – groups later classified as 'Arabs' in Muslim genealogies. To construct an Arab versus Persian image of Dhū Qār, therefore, third/ninth-century Muslim historians downplayed Arab presence in the Sasanian camp[127] and rebranded Shaybān and Qays as both 'Arabs' in order to retrospectively make them appear as representatives of an 'Arab' cause. A diachronic survey of poetry about Dhū Qār reveals these transformations in progress as succeeding generations of poets summoned evolving memories of the battle, rewriting Dhū Qār in tandem with negotiating Ma'addite and Arab identities.

Dhū Qār in Pre-Islamic Poetry: al-Aᶜshā

The Qaysī combatants at Dhū Qār counted the famous pre-Islamic poet al-Aᶜshā as one of their kinsmen, and his poetry sings the battle into historical memories. Whilst the historical al-Aᶜshā was a contemporary witness, the literary recollection of al-Aᶜshā survives only in Muslim-era texts, and, like any early poetry, his verses passed through the hands of Muslim cultural producers who recalled Dhū Qār as the signature Arab victory of pre-Islam. But they do not appear to have tampered significantly with al-Aᶜshā's Dhū Qār poems: if we read them without prose commentary added later, we find three poems which are widely and consistently cited in Arabic literature without debate over their ascription or authenticity, and which describe Dhū Qār in terms which do not accord with the manner in which later Muslim narrators represent the battle.[128] The trio seem to permit a glimpse into a first level of Dhū Qār's memorialisation.

Given Dhū Qār's significance in Muslim narratives as an Arab victory over the Persians, it is intriguing that Al-Aᶜshā's pre-Islamic poetic descriptions of the battle have no emphasis on 'Persian' ethnicity: the words *ᶜajam* and *furs* are absent, and the poems tend away from projecting the battle in ethnic terms.[129] In one line al-Aᶜshā refers to 'Kisrā' (the Sasanian monarch) as the opponent of his kinsmen:

Who will inform Kisrā when my
Dismaying messages come in:
'I say we will not surrender our boys
As hostages to corrupt as he has done before'.[130]

But the Sasanian monarch is a distant figure: al-Aᶜshā elsewhere mentions the Persian commander Hāmarz as the chief opponent,[131] and nowhere does he give an impression that the Sasanian Empire was threatened by the battle, that Kisrā was the intended target of the 'Arabs', that the Persian 'race' was an inferior foe, or that the Persians were destined to lose by virtue of their ethnicity.

Crucially, and in line with the findings from the rest of pre-Islamic poetry, al-Aᶜshā makes no mention of 'Arab', nor does he imply the battle has any significance beyond an example of the bravery of the combatants involved. One line suggests al-Aᶜshā conceptualised his kinsmen as 'a furious wave of Wāʾil',[132] and his poems reserve praise solely for those who fought at the battle, in particular the Banū Dhuhl ibn Shaybān, a group to whom al-Aᶜshā was tangentially related:

May my camel and I be ransom for Banū Dhuhl ibn Shaybān
(Though we be meagre!) on the day of battle.
At al-Ḥinw, Ḥinw Qurāqir,[133] they crashed blows

Down upon al-Hāmarz's ranks until the rout.
Blessed are the eyes of those who saw this band,
As they beat down foes thrusting from the plain
With gleaming white helmets under high flags.[134]

The style in which al-Aᶜshā derides one of his kinsmen, Qays ibn Masᶜūd for siding with the enemy is also noteworthy. Al-Aᶜshā mentions Qays' journey to the opponents (perhaps to curry favour with the Sasanian administration?),[135] but he does not depict Qays as a traitor who crossed ethnic boundaries, nor even a traitor at all, rather he upbraids Qays as simply a fool for not trusting the might of Shaybān's warriors:

If you had been satisfied with Shaybān,
You would have spacious tents, a thronging tribe, and massed cavalry,
. . .
But you foolishly left them, though you were their leader.
I hope I hear no more from you![136]

Al-Aᶜshā's poetic remembrances of Dhū Qār are reminiscent of the many pre-Islamic battles (*ayyām al-ᶜarab*) in pre-Islamic poetry. Rewards of victory are the property of the winning combatants, and the aftermath is devoid of ethnic or grand strategic consequence. Al-Aᶜshā makes no reference to prolonged struggle with the 'nemesis' Kisrā, and those Arabians not present at the battle have no share in the glory. Neither does al-Aᶜshā elevate the battle to a symbol for the collective glory of Maᶜadd: in another poem he invokes Maᶜadd to frame his boast of Shaybān's unprecedented glory:

If all of Maᶜadd had mustered with us at Dhū Qār,
Glory would not have eluded them.[137]

Al-Aᶜshā is thus aware of Maᶜadd as the greater collective, but leaves them as the audience who will awe at Dhū Qār as Shaybān's exclusive achievement.

Dhū Qār in Umayyad Period Poetry

One century after Dhū Qār, its memory was summoned by Umayyad poets with strikingly different emphasis. Both Abū ᶜUbayda and the poet/

anthologiser Abū Tammām (d. 231/845)[138] record a poetic duel between the famous Umayyad poet-rivals Jarīr and al-Akhṭal where al-Akhṭal chides Jarīr's kin:

> Did you assist Maᶜadd on the ferocious day,
> Like we supported Maᶜadd at Dhū Qār?

Al-Akhṭal's Dhū Qār is elevated to the status of Maᶜadd's signature collective victory. Akin to Shakespeare's transformation of Henry V's St Crispin's Day escapade into a retrospective national triumph which any able-bodied Englishman should wish to have attended, al-Akhṭal's version of the battle presents it as waged by a (mostly) united Maᶜadd, so that he can accordingly deride Jarīr's Ma'addite tribe for not participating. It is a significant departure from al-Aᶜshā's pre-Islamic Dhū Qār where Shaybān monopolised the battle's glory and expressly needed no help from other Ma'addites. And Jarīr reiterates Dhū Qār's changed significance in an extraordinary twist by inserting his own tribe Tamīm's memory into the battle's lore:

> I am a Muḍarī at root.
> You cannot hope to vie with me and my prestige!
> We sent the horsemen to battle at Dhū Bahdā and Dhū Najab
> And we stood out on the morn of Dhū Qār.[139]

Jarīr's Dhū Qār reference puzzled the later commentator Abū Tammām who wondered how Jarīr, a Tamīmī tribesman, could lay a claim to the battle. Abū Tammām reasoned that there must have been a separate battle of the same name between Tamīm and Bakr,[140] but Abū ᶜUbayda attempts a more detailed justification. He relates one narrative reporting that a number of Tamīm tribesmen were captured by Shaybān before Dhū Qār, and, on the eve of battle, the Tamīmīs offered to fight for Shaybān in return for their freedom, and, according to Tamīmī partisans like Jarīr, they acquitted themselves manfully. The anecdote, and Jarīr's poem evidence an Umayyad-era allure of Dhū Qār and a major reworking of its memory, raising its reputation such that groups sought to insert themselves into its narrative in any way possible, even by claiming that they arrived at the battle as prisoners. Extending the St Crispin's Day analogy, Jarīr's poem is reminiscent of Pistol's duplicitous intention to rebrand ignoble wounds as scars from Agincourt!

Explaining the shift from al-Aᶜshā's Shaybān-focused battle to Jarīr and al-Akhṭal's memory of Dhū Qār as a seminal event of Ma'addite heritage is straightforward. Al-Akhṭal and Jarīr wrote at two generations' remove from the Muslim conquest of the Sasanian Empire, and both poets were employed by the descendants of its conquerors. As Umayyads looked back into the past, they could alight on Dhū Qār as the 'beginning of the end' of Sasanian power and elevate the battle's significance with hindsight beyond what its actual combatants could have imagined. In terms of Arabness, al-Akhṭal's invocation of Maᶜadd without mention of 'Arab' also supports the hypothesis that Ma'addite identity only gradually shifted towards 'Arab' in early Islam. While history was evidently being reinterpreted during the Umayyad period, memories of pre-Islamic Arabians were not yet axiomatically homogenised as 'Arab', and at least some felt that Maᶜadd still symbolised their collective 'nation'.

Other Umayyad-era poems exhibit similar shifts towards emphasising Dhū Qār as a grand Persian defeat without assertion of Arabness. Abū ᶜUbayda records two poems attributed to very minor Muslim era poets from the ᶜIjl tribe that refer to Kisrā, the Sasanian monarch, as the *jabbār* (the despot), betraying influence of the Qur'ānic portrayal of Moses' Pharaoh to whom Kisrā was linked in Muslim literature.[141] Another paints the victory as a crushing blow to Persian imperial might:

> We took their booty, our cavalry was grim,
> On the day we stripped all Kisrā's knights (*iswār*) of their armour.[142]

Al-Aᶜshā neither referenced the evil of Kisrā, nor whole might of Sasanian Iran and its *iswār, asāwira* (Farsi: *savārān*) cataphracts, but in Islamic-era literature these cavalrymen become a byword for Sasanian nobility, and as the 'Persian' aspect of the battle ascended, and its significance as harbinger for the end of Persian Empire took root, it can be expected that such vocabulary would be employed to embed the stereotypical topos of Persian versus Muslim/vainglorious Persian king versus plucky Arabian (Ma'addite, not yet 'Arab') warriors into the memory of the pre-Islamic battle.

Dhū Qār in the Abbasid Period

Abbasid-era literature evidences shifts in the depiction of Dhū Qār, which at last transform it into the seminal Arab victory, as it is famous today. Abū ᶜUbayda achieves this with no less than a hadith from the Prophet referencing the battle in ethnic Arab–Persian terms: Muhammad reportedly remarks that Dhū Qār 'is the first battle in which the Arabs have become the Persians' equal'.[143] Abū ᶜUbayda's hadith lacks *isnād* (chain of authorities), but it would spread in the third/ninth century and acquired both *isnād* and some key narrative additions. Ibn Saᶜd (d. 230/845) reports that Muhammad said, 'On this day the Arabs diminished Persian kingship',[144] and Khalīfa ibn Khayyāṭ (d. *c*.250/854–5) records a version in which Muhammad elaborates, 'Dhū Qār is the first battle in which the Arabs became the Persians' equal; they were granted victory through me.'[145] This latter Prophet-assisted representation of Dhū Qār was included in the hadith collectors Ibn Ḥanbal's *Faḍāʾil al-Ṣaḥāba*[146] and al-Bukhārī's *al-Tārīkh al-kabīr* (though, perhaps tellingly, not in their respective *Musnad* and *Ṣaḥīḥ*, which were compiled according to stricter standards of hadith authenticity),[147] and historians repeat the hadith thereafter.[148] The hadith reveals how express Arabisation of the battle's memory appeared in tandem with prophetic history, and by the fourth/tenth century, this underpinning became even more express, for instance in a new and colourful anecdote (without *isnād*) which al-Iṣfahānī (d. 356/967) narrates:

> The battle was made manifest before Muhammad's eyes while he was in Medina, and he raised his hands and prayed for victory for the Shaybān (or the Rabīᶜa). He continued making the prayer until he was shown the Persians' [*furs*] defeat.[149]

To support the new Arabisation of Dhū Qār, Abū ᶜUbayda and most narrators who followed him also insert a poem attributed to the otherwise unknown pre-Islamic poet Bukayr al-Aṣamm[150] which includes the verse:

> They attacked the *Banū Aḥrār*[151] on that day
> With sword thrusts to their heads;
> Three hundred Arabs against a squadron[152]
> Two thousand-strong: Persians (*aᶜājim*) from *Banū Faddām*.[153]
> Ibn Qays found a battle
> The fame of which was heard from Iraq to Syria.[154]

The verse is one of the six Nöldeke counted as a reference to 'Arab' in pre-Islamic poetry, and while it is impossible to prove the verse's Abbasid-era fabrication, there are several red flags. Bukayr is an entirely unknown figure, and an easy target for false ascriptions of poetry. Moreover, on a lexical level, the references to the Islamic-era nomenclature *Banū Aḥrār/Faddām* for Persians and to Iraq and Syria (a typically Islamic-era division of space)[155] suggest Islamic-era fabrication, and hence the poem's reference to 'Arab', in distinction to the narrow tribal poetry of al-A^{c}shā and al-Akhṭal's Ma'addite reference seems yet another indication of its Abbasid-era invention to facilitate the Arabisation of Dhū Qār's memory.

From tribal conflict against the Persian lieutenant Hāmarz to a divinely guided Arab national victory, the transformation of Dhū Qār takes us to the heart of early Islamic-era myth-making which reconfigured memories of the past not just to explain the rise of Islam, but also to create an antiquity for Arab identity. Islamic myth-making seems to be part of 'making Arabs', homogenising the peoples of the Arabian Peninsula into one Arab ethnos. Abbasid eyes saw the pre-Islamic history of Arabia as a single Arab story, but pre-Islamic Arabians neither imagined the same sense of ethnic unity nor used the term 'Arab' to identify themselves.

VI Pre-Islamic Arabian Identity: Conclusions

The evidence from pre-Islamic Arabia frustrates the search for pre-Islamic Arab communal consciousness. We found that the inhabitants of the geographical area now known as Arabia did not call themselves Arabs, they struggled with divisive political alignments, they neither possessed a common religious creed nor shared similar lifestyles, and they did not speak one standardised language. Old texts and modern theories of ethnogenesis are in harmony: we found neither expressions of cohesive pan-Arabian 'Arab' communities, nor conditions in which we should expect consciousness of them to arise. Modern generalisations about the 'Arab character' of pre-Islam are outsiders' retrojections to give pre-Islamic Arabia an Arab identity.

The evidence presents the broad sense of Arab community as a Muslim-era phenomenon, rendering the expression 'pre-Islamic Arabs' meaningless and misleading. The label homogenises distinct peoples and bequeaths a false sense of history, misrepresenting pre-Islamic Arabia via one, totalising more recent construct, confusing pre-Islamic society with subsequent agendas.

Since we lack both textual indications and theoretical grounds to posit that one 'imagined community'[156] existed around a sense of pan-Arabian belonging or even cultural homogeneity in pre-Islamic times, it is best to avoid any one label to speak of pre-Islamic populations south of the Fertile Crescent. If it is necessary to discuss the region's population as a whole, the geographic 'Arabian' is preferable to 'Arab' – though 'Arabian' should not be used to buttress generalisations about Islam's formative milieu in the way 'Arab' was traditionally employed.

We have now opened exciting opportunities. The Arab community can be studied like other 'imagined communities' to trace the process by which groups began to construct a notional Arab family, negotiated solutions to define what Arabness meant, and rewrote history to articulate a past for their new identity. The Islamic-era Arabisation of Dhū Qār and the pervasive appearance of 'Arab' as a term of self-reference in early Islam links Arabisation to Islamicisation. The next chapter explores the history and discourses of early Islam to propose why 'Arab' was chosen as a name expressing early Muslim communal consciousness and how the community's first members began to imagine Arab identity.

Notes

1. For recent discourses associating Arabness with language, see Muṣṭafā et al. (2006) and Suleiman (2003).
2. Al-Azmeh (2014a) pp. 147–50; Hoyland (2009); Nehmé connects the emergence of Arabic language to the rise of Arabian principalities in the late fourth- and fifth-century al-Ḥijāz (2015) p. 17; Al-Jallad (forthcoming pp. 3–5) traces the emergence of 'Old Arabic' in Greek-script writings from the southern Levant in the fifth and, particularly, sixth centuries.
3. Macdonald (2008) vol. 3, pp. 465–6.
4. Macdonald lists the 'Old Arabic mixed texts' (2008) vol. 3, pp. 470–1. The haphazard nature of the inscriptions as a function of the lack of formal teaching and a standard system of writing is discussed for the case of Safaitic in Macdonald (2009h) pp. 87–90.
5. Macdonald (2008) vol. 3, pp. 467–70.
6. Hoyland (2010) identifies the Jabal Ramm and the Nebo inscriptions, formerly counted as Arabic, as being in Nabataean Aramaic and Christian Palestinian

Aramaic, respectively. Al-Jallad (2014) discounts the Qaryat al-Faw text, once thought to be the oldest Arabic inscription.

7. Al-Jallad (forthcoming) argues that a number of Greek-script texts should be classified as 'Old Arabic'.
8. Macdonald (2009h) pp. 78–98 considers literacy in pre-Islamic Arabia and the intriguing phenomenon that some Arabian nomadic communities left significantly more written records than populations in settled agricultural villages. Safaitic writers left the great bulk of records and some of the most informative graffito on the Syrian–Arabian frontier: the corpus of inscriptions is extensively surveyed in al-Jallad (2015), see especially pp. 201–20 for the contents and detailed formulae in Safaitic inscriptions to express quotidian events and experiences.
9. The two earliest inscriptions are problematic: the Palestinian ᶜEn ᶜAvdat text is dated only conjecturally, and while the southern Saudi Arabian Qaryat al-Faw text is of a more certain early date (see al-Anṣārī (1982) p. 63), recent analysis argues that it is not in fact an Arabic-language text (al-Jallad (2014)).
10. At Madāᵓin Ṣāliḥ, the Raqūsh inscription dates to 267, but seems better classified as Nabataean, not 'Old Arabic'; three graffito from Jabal Umm Jadāᵓid near al-Ulā (mostly in Nabataean with some words possibly in 'Old Arabic', Macdonald (2008) vol. 3, p. 469); and three enigmatic graffito from Sakkaka near al-Jawf.
11. The generally agreed sixth-century inscriptions are Zebed, Jabal Usays, Ḥarrān, Umm al-Jimāl. For lists and varied discussions of individual inscriptions, see Gruendler (1993) with a counter-argument regarding the Jabal Ramm inscription in Hoyland (2010) pp. 39–40; al-Ghul (2004); Hoyland (2008) pp. 53–60; Macdonald (2008). The Nebo inscription was often counted as a sixth-century 'Old Arabic' text, though Hoyland (2010) deconstructs the arugment.
12. Nehmé et al. (2010) details the fourth–fifth-century transitional Nabataean to Arabic scripts; Nehmé (2015) discusses Arabic's early emergence.
13. The non-Syrian/Palestinian/Ḥijāzī inscriptions include the al-Fāw inscription which al-Jallad (2014) pp. 17–18 rejects as Arabic; Macdonald (2008) vol. 3, pp. 471–2 notes other South Arabian, two eastern Arabian and one Egyptian inscription which have been claimed as 'Arabic', but seem certainly to be in another language.
14. Hoyland (2009) and Fisher (2013). Al-Azmeh notes the role of Arabian interaction with Imperium as a component of Arab ethnogenesis, but constructs

a different argument from the epigraphic evidence to reconstruct a wider-ranging system of 'Arab principalities' (2014a) pp. 150–3.

15. Of the inscriptions from the Syrian/Arabian frontier between the third and sixth centuries, only one (Raqūsh from Madāᵓin Ṣāliḥ) is more than five lines long; two (Petra and Nebo) contain just one noun/noun phrase, though Hoyland rejects counting the Nebo inscription as 'Old Arabic' in any event (2010) pp. 30–1, 37, and Macdonald suggests discounting the Petra '*nāyif* papyrus' as a pre-Islamic text (2008) vol. 3, p. 467.
16. Robin (2010); al-Ghul (2004); Hoyland (2009); al-Jallad (forthcoming). Macdonald (2009e) pp. 50–60 traces possible routes between 'Old Arabic' into 'Classical Arabic', but notes the conjectures and complications inherent in modern reconstructions.
17. Macdonald (2009g) pp. 180–1 considers the role of prestige in determining an inscriber's choice of script, and problematises the connections of script and ethnicity (Ibid. pp. 183–5). Nehmé (2015) considers the growing principalities in the fifth-century al-Ḥijāz as possessing sufficient power to merit changing scripts to Arabic, but interestingly, they make only tentative changes from Nabataean. Al-Jallad's study of Greek-script Arabic (forthcoming) implies that a form of Arabic was used in the southern Levant – but without proliferation of Arabic script, which is intriguing considering the power of Ghassān. Arabic seems to have lacked prestige and/or a group to promote it in pre-Islamic times.
18. I noted the difficulties in interpreting the ᶜEn ᶜAvdat inscription as an 'Arabic poem' (see Chapter 1 n. 80); assumptions that the Nabataeans spoke 'Arabic' caused similarly strained interpretations of onomastic evidence from their inscriptions (see Macdonald (2009e) pp. 46–8). Longer inscriptions such as those at ᶜEn ᶜAvdat and Namāra have spawned numerous competing interpretations (ᶜEn ᶜAvdat: Negev et al. (1986), Bellamy (1990), Testen (1996); Namāra: see Bellamy (1985) and Retsö (2003) pp. 467–73.
19. See note 3.
20. On the importance of language see Kramsch (1998) pp. 70–2; in addition to general works on ethnogenesis cited in the Introduction, my understanding of language and identity to interpret Arabian inscriptions is particularly indebted to the case studies of language usage and social contexts in Duranti and Goodwin (eds) (1992) and the theoretical overview of Bucholtz and Hall (2004), especially pp. 382–3 and see the detailed bibliography pp. 388–94 for further leads.

21. Al-Jallad (2015) pp. 18–21.
22. Two examples of people identifying as *nbṭy/nbṭwy* (Nabataeans) and a further reference to a Nabataean person are translated in al-Jallad (2015) p. 19.
23. Al-Jāḥiẓ (1998) vol. 1, pp. 51–7; Ibn Qutayba (1998) pp. 149–50.
24. Rodinson problematised the centrality of language in unifying Islamic-era Arabs (1981) pp. 5–6, 22. Why should the pre-Islamic situation be different?
25. Al-Azmeh distinguishes 'sociolect' and 'ethnolect' on this basis, but concludes that linguistic homogenisation did occur in the centuries before Muhammad (2014a) pp. 150, 154.
26. Al-Azmeh argues that political cohesion caused linguistic standardisation, but his interpretation of the evidence within a pan-western Arabian context lacks evidence of political institutions (2014a) pp. 148–54, and he begins his linguistic excursus with a somewhat contradictory statement (which he does not resolve) that the Arabs may have 'had no sense of emergent common political identity' before Islam (2014a) p. 147. Hoyland (2009) and Fisher (2011) restrict the ambit of political cohesion to the Syrian–Byzantine border for their theories of Arab origins.
27. At least fifty-five Arabic inscriptions and graffito (not including the monumental inscriptions on the Dome of the Rock or the vast numbers of coins) are expressly dated to the first century of Islam; a further fifteen undated inscriptions are ascribed to the first century AH. Well over half of the total date from 73/693 to 100/718 (a helpful, though now slightly dated, list is online: <www.islamicawareness.org/History/Islam/Inscriptions> (last accessed 15 November 2015). Numerous new discoveries and up-to-date discussion of the epigraphy are not integrated into its list). Islamic-era inscriptions are often longer than the pre-Islamic as well.
28. Nöldeke (1899) pp. 272–5.
29. Von Grunebaum (1963) pp. 20–1; Rodinson (1981) p. 15.
30. The same verse is cited in Abū ᶜUbayda's (d. 210/825) earlier *al-Naqāʾiḍ* (1905–12) vol. 2, p. 645. Bevan published his edition of *al-Naqāʾiḍ* six years after Nöldeke's essay.
31. von Grunebaum also deemed the attribution of the lines to Imruʾ al-Qays as 'spurious' ((1963) p. 20, n. 7).
32. One of the three verses concerns the Battle of Dhū Qār, and, as discussed herein pp. 94–5, the verse mentioning 'Arabs' is likely an Abbasid-era fabrication.
33. See Chapter 1(III) pp. 33–6, 47–9.
34. Zuhayr (1988) p. 123.

35. Tha^c^lab (2004) pp. 274–6 and Zuhayr (1988) p. 123, n. 8.
36. Al-Buḥturī (1910) p. 105.
37. Ibn Qutayba counts Zuhayr's poetry in praise of Ibn Sinān as paradigmatic examples of pre-Islamic poetry's use to praise Islamic-era groups (1998) pp. 157–8; al-Ṭabarī (n.d.) vol. 4, pp. 222–3 cites one of Zuhayr's praises of Ibn Sinān's clan in a politicised context.
38. Margoliouth (1925); Ḥusayn (1926).
39. See Arafat (1966), (1970). Agha (2011) p. 8 describes the retreat from earlier 'vigorous' doubts about authenticity.
40. See al-Jumaḥī (n.d.) vol. 1, pp. 5–6, 7–8. For analysis of the 'vagaries' of recorded poetry, see Montgomery (1997).
41. Monroe (1972) pp. 7–13 adopted the Parry and Lord hypothesis of oral performance of poetry, though it did not convincingly explain the transmission effects in Arabia. See also Zwettler (1978).
42. Jones (1996) p. 58 and S. Stetkevych (1993) p. 122 allude to the impact of the 'Abbasid guise' in shaping the preserved form of pre-Islamic poetry, but it is generally left unproblematised: there is tacit assumption of the poetry's basic authenticity, exemplified in S. Stetkevych (1993), Montgomery (1997) and (2006), and Farrin (2011).
43. Elsewhere, Nöldeke (2009) pp. 63–80 advises caution, but primarily where verses have obvious connection to Islamic-era political debates; Nöldeke tends to accept 'non-politicised' poetry as accurate.
44. Hallaq (1999) p. 90.
45. Robin (2012) p. 48; see also Hoyland (2015) pp. 24–5. Elsewhere, Robin (2010) p. 85 argues that 'shared language and culture' forged pan-Arab unity, though does not explain the disappearance of the ethnicon 'Arab' at the time when Greeks and Romans finally became acquainted with Arabia. Hoyland also notes that 'Arab' is 'extremely rare' in pre-Islamic poetry (2015) p. 60, but the question of poetry's alternative terms of identity remains open.
46. Goldziher (1889–90) vol. 1, pp. 88–9, von Grunebaum (1963) p. 20.
47. Labīd (1962) p. 24.
48. Ibid. p. 216.
49. Goldziher (1889–90) vol. 1, p. 89. See also a similar formula with Ma^c^add, Kinda and Ṭayyi^ʾ^ in Imru^ʾ^ al-Qays (1990) p. 198 and the Banū Asad collection (Diqqa (1999) vol. 2, p. 501).
50. Imru^ʾ^ al-Qays (1990) p. 134.
51. Ibid. p. 207.

52. Ibid. p. 134, n. 4.
53. A reading von Grunebaum also preferred (1963) p. 20.
54. See, for examples a poem ascribed to 'One of the Aznam' in al-Zamakhsharī (1992) p. 315; an anonymous poem in al-Zabīdī (1994) vol. 8, p. 36; Ibn ᶜAbd Rabbihi (n.d.) vol. 2, p. 140. Muslim-era figures use the term less frequently: though it appears in poetry connected with Muhammad's Tabūk Campaign (Ibn Kathīr (n.d.) vol. 5, p. 43); and the Umayyad-era poet Ibn Mayyāda invoked to praise Bedouin from Banū ᶜUyayna (Abū al-Faraj al-Iṣfahānī (1992) vol. 2, pp. 328–9).
55. Zuhayr ibn Janāb (1999) p. 69. Only one verse of the poem survives and its meaning is unclear, hinging on the interpretation of the word *fizr*: the reference to Fizr's goats is used a metaphor for anything that can never be gathered (see al-Madāᵓinī (2011) vol. 3, p. 130)
56. Al-Aᶜshā (1974) p. 135.
57. Ibid. p. 361.
58. Al-Nābigha (1990) p. 140.
59. Al-Marzūqī (1968) vol. 2, p. 513.
60. Ibid. vol. 2, p. 634.
61. Ibid. vol. 1, pp. 293, 353; vol. 2, p. 974.
62. Diqqa (1999) vol. 2, p. 23. See also vol. 2, pp. 25, 245, 437, 501.
63. Ḥassān ibn Thābit (1974) vol. 1, p. 167.
64. Ibid. vol. 1 pp. 18, 35, 36, 109, 199, 366.
65. Ibid. vol. 1 p. 36.
66. Procopius (1914) 1:19:14; 1:20:9.
67. Zwettler (2000) pp. 280–6.
68. Bellamy's 1985 interpretation is measured; subsequent scholarly debate is summarised in Retsö (2003) pp. 467–73.
69. Bellamy (1985) pp. 35, 46. Bellamy prefers reading the inscription 'he subdued Maᶜadd' (*malaka Maᶜadd*). See Retsö (2003) pp. 468–9 for the array of interpretations.
70. Shahid interprets the inscription to announce the king's sovereignty over the Arab ethnos. Shahid equates Imruᵓ al-Qays with the 'Lakhmid king of al-Ḥīra' (1984) p. 32, but such interpretations must be read cautiously since Shahid espouses a largely unproblematised interpretation of Arabness which paints a cohesive Arab unity across most of pre-Islamic Arabia and relies on a problematic labelling of Hatra and Palmyra as 'Arab towns', an elevation of al-Ḥīra to the centre of the Arab political world in the third century CE, and a convoluted

explanation for why a Lakhmid king would be buried in Syria (Ibid. (1984) pp. 35–6). Fisher (2011b) pp. 248–9 offers further critique of Shahid. Hoyland (2009) and Retsö (2003) urge distinction between the fourth-century inscription's reference to 'Arabs' and modern notions of pan-Arabian Arabness.

71. Retsö (2003) pp. 471, 485. An example of the same honorific is the first-century CE Parthian title *Malkā dhī ᶜArabh*, see Chapter 1 n. 111. Hoyland (2015) p. 26 offers a similar interpretation.
72. Labīd (1962) p. 257.
73. See Chapter 1, p. 37.
74. For example, Maᶜadd was distinguished from the Syrian-based groups of Ghassān and the kingdoms of Yemen: see the next section's discussion.
75. See Shahid (1995–2009); Hoyland (2001); Fisher (2011a) pp. 72–127; Genequand and Robin (2015).
76. Montgomery (1997) p. 8, n. 11.
77. The disruptive nature of frontier guardianship also casts doubt on a theory articulated in Hoyland (2009) and Fisher (2011a) that consciousness of Arab ethnicity arose by virtue of Byzantine employment of Ghassān and other groups as frontier *foederati*. The argument operates by analogy with Rome's Rhine and Danube frontiers where client tribes employed by the Romans developed into ethnic groups. Application of the model to Arabia is difficult, however, since the Europeans splintered into different nations, whereas 'Arab' would embrace a more cohesive unity across a wider area. The European model would expect Ghassān and Lakhm to form different ethnicities, given their different regional bases and political alignments, yet they both became 'Arabs', suggesting Arabness emerged from different drivers. See Chapter 3(I) for more consideration of Arab ethnogenesis contrasted to the European cases.
78. East Syriac Christians are now better known as Nestorians, though the communities only began calling themselves Nestorians in the eighth century (Reinink (2010) pp. 219–20). Al-Ḥīra's religious milieu is detailed in Toral-Niehoff (2014).
79. In Singara both Monophysite and East Syriac monasteries were founded in the sixth century (Alexander (1985) p. 28) and Tannous (2013) pp. 84–90 argues for substantial communal coexistence, at least up to the late sixth century CE.
80. Sauvaget dated the St Sergius Festival to 15 November (followed in al-Azmeh (2014a) p. 122), though Fowden (1999) p. 156 corrects Sauvaget and proposes 7 October instead (Ibid. pp. 22–3). For more detail on St Sergius and Ghassān, see Fowden (1999) pp. 143–4.

81. Fowden (1999) pp. 101–29. For the importance of the shrine at Ruṣāfa 'manifesting' imperial presence in the region, see Ibid. pp. 67–9. Fowden (Ibid. p. 139) proposes that common veneration of St Sergius also fostered a pan-Arab unity in the Syrian Desert, though this seems a difficult extrapolation. Followers of St Sergius are called 'Saracens', and never 'Arabs' in the sources. Also, references to Saracen veneration of St Sergius derives from Greek and Syriac ecclesiastical texts, whereas Arabic literature and pre-Islamic poetry is almost entirely silent on 'Sarjis', and the spread of the name Sergius in sixth century CE Greek populations did not replicate in Arabia. Greek sources are not as insistent on the ingrained importance of St Sergius amongst the Saracens as Fowden imputes, either (compare Procopius (1914) 2:20:10–16 with Fowden (1999) p. 135), and moreover, when the Umayyads occupied the Euphrates, they changed the name Sergiopolis to al-Ruṣāfa, forgetting almost all vestiges of Sergius veneration in the process.
82. Binggeli (2007) pp. 579–81.
83. See Lecker (1995b); Newby (1988); Stillman (1979) and Wasserstrom (1995).
84. Sozomen describes pagan 'Saracens' converting to Christianity (1890) 6:38). Images of Abraham and/or Mary reportedly drawn in Mecca's Kaᶜba could be interpreted as poly-monotheistic syncretism (al-Bukhārī (1999) *al-Ḥajj*:54, Ibn Ḥanbal (1993) vol. 1, p. 362). As for paganism, see Q29:17, 53:19, and Procopius' allusions to Saracen pagan fighting practices (1914) 2:16:18/2:19:38). Hawting (1999) alternatively argues that much of pre-Islamic Arabia's apparent 'paganism' is a Muslim construct, but some polytheistic groups must have existed (al-Azmeh (2014a) pp. 252–65 is sanguine about al-Ḥijāz as a 'pagan reservation' and engages variously with Hawting); see also Chapter 5(III).
85. Berkey (2003) pp. 45–9 and Shahid (1995–2009) note the doctrinal violence without questioning their effects on putative Arab unity. See Munt (2015) pp. 252–3 for an up-to-date summary of views on monotheism in al-Ḥijāz.
86. Late Antique syncretism and sharing of ritual sites is noted (see Sozomen (1890) 2:4 for the sharing of the sanctuary at Mamre), Fowden (1999) p. 97 notes similar multi-faith participation at Sergiopolis, though Boyarin's work (1999) and (2004) on the development of Jewish communal identity notes significant changes from the fifth and sixth centuries which fostered more proprietary senses of Jewish and Christian religious communities, and which became even sharper with the advent of the Caliphate. For alternative approaches to Jewish identity, ethnicity and faith in the Middle East, see Millar (2013) pp. 54–105.

87. The reign of the Jewish Dhū Nuwās (Yūsuf Ashᶜar/Masruq) in Yemen, his persecution of Christians in Najrān and the wider geopolitical issues are much discussed (see S. Smith (1954) pp. 456–63; Shahid (1970); Hoyland (2001) p. 52; Berkey (2003) pp. 47–8; and see the *Book of the Himyarites*).
88. Abraha, Ethiopic Christian ruler of Yemen (r. 525/530/543–after 559), inscribed a record of his victorious campaigns in central Arabia *c.*540–50 (CI. Sem 4.541).
89. The invasion of Mecca is a key narrative in the *Sīra* (e.g. Ibn Hishām (n.d.) vol. 1, pp. 45–57), and the extensive *tafsīr* on Q:105.
90. The momentous nature of the events is reflected in the likely contrived Muslim tradition of dating the invasion to the year of Muhammad's birth (Conrad (1987)).
91. The lack of response to Abraha's invasion and the absence of memory of senses of communal struggle to defend Mecca would seem central evidence to support Donner's hypothesis that Arabness had no political traction to mobilise military units in pre-Islamic times (2010) pp. 218–19. The story of Abraha's invasion features in all early Prophetic biographies, and the absence of any assistance in Mecca's defence from other 'Arabs' is an important aspect of the narrative, since the stories include a role for the Prophet's (and the Abbasids') ancestor ᶜAbd al-Muṭṭalib, who is said to have met Abraha and demonstrated his piety in declaring Mecca's defence is a matter for God alone (see al-Balādhurī (1979–) vol. 1.1, pp. 170–1, Ibn Saᶜd (1997) vol. 1, pp. 73–4). Only Ibn Hishām's comprehensively pro-Yemeni version of the Prophet's biography claims that a group of Yemenis led by Dhū Nafar attempted (unsuccessfully) to block Abraha's advance on Mecca ((n.d.) vol. 1, p. 46). This outlying tale, absent in all but the one manifestly self-serving Yemeni narrative underlines the lack of an 'Arab' response when their supposed 'shared' sanctum was attacked. It seems that Muslim historians either invented the entire story to purport Mecca's importance in pre-Islam, or Abraha did invade towards Mecca, though the site lacked the pan-Arabian significance later imputed.
92. Prominent studies include von Grunebaum (1963); al-Azmeh (2014a).
93. See al-Yaᶜqūbī (n.d.) vol. 1, pp. 270–1 for a list of the fairs.
94. Al-Azmeh (2014a) pp. 137–40.
95. Binggeli (2007) pp. 560–1.
96. Webb (2013b) p. 7, n. 3.

97. The phrase *bayt al-ᶜarab* appears in Ibn Ḥabīb (1985) p. 74 and a boast of the Quraysh poet al-Faḍl ibn al-ᶜAbbās (al-Zubayrī (1999) p. 90; Ibn Qutayba (1994) p. 126). In Islam's earliest generations, Mecca's sanctum was called *bayt Ibrāhīm*, referencing its Abrahamic foundations: its interweaving with Arab history dates to third/ninth-century elaborations (Webb (2013b) pp. 7–8).
98. Muslim-era Arabic sources mention an array of other pre-Islamic sanctums as satellites emanating from the central site of Mecca (Ibn al-Kalbī (1924) p. 6). If, however, we remove a priori assumptions that Arabia was unified, Mecca no longer occupies the centre, and the various sites can be seen as competing or localised places of litholotry, the memories of which were homogenised by later Muslims to construct an Arab story. Serjeant (1962) pp. 42, 52–3 gives insightful indications of a diffuse system of ritual practices around shrines in south-east Arabia, perhaps reflective of the genesis of Mecca's sanctum as one of many places of pre-Islamic pagan worship.
99. Crone (1987) critiqued accounts of Mecca's pre-Islamic importance. Heck (2003) offers alternative interpretations, though also grounds to maintain that Mecca was not a shrine of pan-Arabian significance.
100. Al-Azmeh (2014a) p. 105.
101. Consider the classic early genealogical text, Ibn al-Kalbī's *Nasab Maᶜadd wa-l-Yaman*, revealing the old nomenclature and divisions at work.
102. Fisher (2011a); Bowersock (2013); Shahid (1995–2009); Genequand and Robin (2015).
103. Herein this book questions the references to 'ethnogenesis' in al-Azmeh (2014a) pp. 100, 138, 147 since he affirms Arab communal formation via selections from Muslim-era texts without citation of anthropological theorists. Al-Azmeh's methodological approaches outlined in (2014b) likewise do not reference theories of ethnicity, imagined community and construction of communal memories.
104. Ḥassān Ibn Thābit (1974) vol. 1, pp. 135, 370, 443.
105. Abū Dahbal (1972) pp. 78, 94.
106. *ᶜAjam* implies 'non-Arab', it would be hasty to transpose *ᶜajam*'s much later axiomatic association of 'Persian' here. The lexical connotations are considered in Chapter 4(I) pp. 179–83.
107. Epstein (1978) p. xii. This approach is the central consideration of Barth's (1969) and (1994) transactionist/instrumentalist theory.
108. al-Farazdaq (1983) vol. 2, p. 353. See also Dhū al-Rumma (1972–4) vol. 1, p. 23.

109. Jarīr (1969) vol. 1, p. 441. See also vol. 1, p. 437.
110. Al-Rā^cī (1980) p. 18.
111. Al-Walīd (1998) p. 14.
112. Dhū al-Rumma (1972–4) vol. 1, p. 418, vol. 2, p. 979, vol. 3, p. 1553. See also vol. 2, p. 1164. Dhū al-Rumma's poetry is also notable since he was not politically involved and his poems are accordingly less likely targets for later tampering.
113. Donner's suggestion (2010) p. 220 that '"Arab" political identity remained weak (until the nineteenth century) and never seriously challenged the tribal identity of most Arabians' could be modified somewhat by the Umayyad-era poems considered here. The poetry and further evidence discussed in Chapter 4(I–III) indicate that Arabness did become quite potent in the early Abbasid Caliphate.
114. For example, Jarīr cites Ma^cadd twelve times (1969) vol. 1, pp. 180, 202, 224, 246, 366, 461, 470, 472, 474; vol. 2, pp. 606, 818, 888 and al-Rā^cī three (1980) pp. 117, 274, 287. For Ma^cadd's role as an early Muslim identity see Webb (forthcoming (A)).
115. Jarīr (1969) vol. 2, p. 818
116. Goldziher (1889–90) vol. 1, p. 88.
117. Al-Walīd (1998) p. 81.
118. Al-Ṭabarānī (198-) vol. 8, pp. 165–6 contains an unusual hadith relating the words of Moses who discusses 'Ma^cadd', noting 'God will permit them to enter Heaven if they say, "There is no god but He", because their prophet is Muhammad . . .'. The place of this hadith in early Umayyad discourses is elaborated in Webb (forthcoming (A)).
119. Ibn Abī Shayba (2010) vol. 15, p. 433.
120. Dhū al-Rumma (1972–4) vol. 2, pp. 644, 653, 655. The poem's emphasis on Ma^cadd and other tribal identities are unusual for Dhū al-Rumma's *oeuvre* and suggest a later forgery.
121. Landau-Tasseron (1996) vol. 7, p. 575; Morony (1984) pp. 152–3, 220; Heath (2011) pp. 48, 50–2; al-Azmeh (2014a) p. 119 refers to Dhū Qār as an 'Arab' victory, but notes difficulties in the sources too (Ibid. p. 127).
122. Abū al-Faraj al-Iṣfahānī dates Dhū Qār 'a few months' after Badr (1992) vol. 24, p. 72.
123. Abū ^cUbayda's (d. 210/825) *al-Naqā^ciḍ*, the earliest extant source for Dhū Qār's date, dates the battle loosely to the period of Muhammad's prophecy (with no mention of Badr or Muhammad's *hijra*) (1905–12) vol. 2, p. 640.

Neither al-Yaʿqūbī (d. *c.*284–92/897–905) nor al-Ṭabarī (d. 310/922) date the battle, but al-Yaʿqūbī notes it was 'the first victory of the Arabs over the Persians' (n.d.) vol. 1, pp. 215, 225; al-Ṭabarī precedes the battle narrative with a telling section detailing signs of the Arabs' impending destruction of the Persian Empire (n.d.) vol. 2, pp. 188–93). The fourth/tenth-century al-Masʿūdī (d. 346/956) connects the battle to symbolic dates of the Prophet's career: either forty years after his birth, shortly after the *hijra* or four months after Badr (1966–79) §648.

124. Bosworth (1983) p. 608.
125. Donner (1980).
126. Lecker's 'Taghlib b. Wāʾil' *EI*[2] discusses the tribe's alignments from pre-Islam to the conquests. Note also that al-Ṣanāʾiʿ, one of the five fabled squadrons of Lakhmid cavalry (*katāʾib*), were (according to Muslim-lore) from Bakr ibn Wāʾil (al-Mubarrad (2008) vol. 2, p. 606), suggesting that part of 'Bakr' could even have fought against other members of 'Bakr' at Dhū Qār.
127. Al-Yaʿqūbī admits the Persian army included some Arabs, noting Iyās ibn Qabīṣa al-Ṭāʾī and 'other brothers of Maʿadd and Qaḥṭān' (n.d.) vol. 1, p. 225. Al-Ṭabarī also mentions Arab fighters with Kisrā, but does not name them, and al-Ṭabarī expressly changes Iyās' role, giving him Arab sympathies (n.d.) vol. 2, pp. 208–9.
128. Al-Aʿshā (1974) pp. 233–5, 277–83, 309–11. See partial narrations in Abū ʿUbayda (1905–12) vol. 2, pp. 644–5; al-Ṭabarī (n.d.) vol. 2, pp. 211–12. There is a fourth poem (al-Aʿshā (1974) pp. 349–53), but its authenticity is doubtful. It contains unusual vocabulary only common in Yemen (for example, the poem refers to the Sasanian commander as *qayl* (lns. 12, 19)), and the poem is ascribed to Yemenis in other sources: Ibn Isḥāq's Prophetic biography narrates five lines as part of the story of the Sasanian conquest of Yemen, ascribing the poem to the Yemeni leader Sayf ibn Dhī Yazan. Ibn Hishām's edit of Ibn Isḥāq's text notes that one narrator ascribed one line of the poem to al-Aʿshā, but Ibn Hishām affirms the whole poem's ascription to Sayf (Ibn Hishām (n.d.) vol. 1, p. 65). Elsewhere, Abū ʿUbayda (d. 210/825) claimed the poem was written by either Sayf or another Yemeni poet (ʿAbd al-Kallāl); only one early narrator, Abū ʿAmr Isḥāq al-Shaybānī (d. 206/821), ascribed the poem to al-Aʿshā (see al-Aʿshā (1974) p. 348). Abū ʿAmr's Shaybanid connection is noteworthy! I discount the poem given its troubled ascription, but it does evidence that Muslims associated al-Aʿshā with poems about battles against the Sasanians. Since al-Aʿshā was one of the first poets for whom Muslim anthologists collected

a *dīwān* (Ibn al-Nadīm (1988) p. 178 counts al-Aᶜshā behind only Imru᾿ al-Qays and Zuhayr ibn Abī Sulmā in terms of early scholarly attention), poems of uncontested attribution have reasoned probability of authenticity, hence my confidence in the three other poems considered in this section.

129. Note that in separate poem, where al-Aᶜshā boasts of his own tribe's might, he cites the battle of Dhū Qār to awe other Arabians, and there he notes that his people had defeated 'a mighty army of the vainglorious king of the *Aᶜājim* (non-Arabic speakers?) with pearls in their ears' (1974) p. 361. Even if this is authentic, the poem stops short of depicting the victory over the Persians as a shared glory of all 'Arabs' – al-Aᶜshā actually cites the victory as an example of his own tribe's superiority over other Arabians whom he calls Ma'addites.
130. Al-Aᶜshā (1974) p. 279.
131. Ibid. pp. 309–11.
132. Ibid. p. 283.
133. One of the names of the Battle of Dhū Qār. Abū ᶜUbayda's *Naqā᾿iḍ* (1905–12) vol. 2, p. 638 lists eight different names by which the battle was known.
134. Al-Aᶜshā (1974) p. 309.
135. Ibid. p. 233.
136. Ibid. pp. 233–4.
137. Ibid. p. 361.
138. Abū ᶜUbayda (1905–12) vol. 2, p. 646; Abū Tammām (attrib.) (1922) p. 135. Sezgin (1967–84) vol. 2, pp. 320–1 doubts the attribution of *al-Naqā᾿iḍ* to Abū Tammām, ascribing it instead to the contemporary al-Aṣmaᶜī.
139. Abū Tammām (attrib.) (1922) p. 143.
140. Ibid. pp. 143–4.
141. Abū ᶜUbayda (1905–12) vol. 2, p. 646.
142. Ibid. vol. 2, p. 646.
143. Ibid. vol. 2, p. 640.
144. Ibn Saᶜd (1997) vol. 7, p. 54.
145. Ibn Khayyāṭ (n.d.) p. 43.
146. Ibn Ḥanbal (1983) vol. 2, pp. 1045–6.
147. Al-Bukhārī (1941–64) vol. 2, p. 63. Pointedly, he also reports the hadith without Muhammad's promise of future victory (Ibid. vol. 8, p. 313).
148. Al-Yaᶜqūbī (n.d.) vol. 1, pp. 215, 225; al-Ṭabarī (n.d.) vol. 2, p. 193 (in a second version of the narrative copied from Abū ᶜUbayda, al-Ṭabarī relates the hadith without Prophetic promise of victory (n.d.) vol. 2, p. 207); see also al-Masᶜūdī (1966–79) §648.

149. Abū al-Faraj al-Iṣfahānī (1992) vol. 24, p. 72.
150. I found no mention of Bukayr al-Aṣamm in the major poetry anthologies or biographical dictionaries of poets. Reference to him in *al-Aghānī* is restricted to the single poem about Dhū Qār.
151. The 'free born', a sobriquet for Persians, referencing their stereotyped nobility.
152. I read this verse to imply Arabs against Persians. This is clear in the poem's narration in *al-Aghānī* (Abū al-Faraj al-Iṣfahānī (1992) vol. 24, p. 73) as the word *ᶜarab* is *marfūᶜ*, though in al-Ṭabarī's narration (n.d.) vol. 2, p. 211, it is *manṣūb* and could thus be an object of the verb 'attack' in the previous line, implying that Arabs and Persians were on the same side. I find this a strained reading, however: the numbers, 300 Arabs against 2,000 Persians implies a heroic interpretation of a victory for the numerically inferior Arabs, much suited to the poem's thrust.
153. *Faddām* allegedly refers to the veils (singular *fidām*) Persian Zoroastrian wine-servers would wear when pouring wine (al-Khalīl (1980) vol. 8, p. 54), and it became a (rare) sobriquet for 'Persian'.
154. Abū ᶜUbayda (1905–12) vol. 2, p. 645. Repeated with slight variation in al-Ṭabarī (n.d.) vol. 2, p. 211 and Abū al-Faraj al-Iṣfahānī (1992) vol. 24, p. 73.
155. The division of space along the Euphrates between *al-Shām* and *al-ᶜIrāq* is a quintessential spatial reference system in third/ninth-century Arabic literature (see Webb (2015) pp. 22–6). Whilst pre-Islamic Syriac writers also conceptualised the Euphrates as a frontier (Fowden (1999)), it is neither a spatial narrative of pre-Islamic Arabian poets nor of early hadith: the Arabian texts express the geographical binary not as East–West, but as North–South with the terms *al-Shām* and *al-Yaman* (see Webb (2015) pp. 10–12 and the spatial metaphors invoking the *Shāmī* town of Buṣrā). The East–West significance for Arabic writers arises in Islamic times, a logical corollary of the shifting worldviews resulting from early Muslim settlement and power relations in the generations after the conquests.
156. Anderson (1991).

3

Arabness from the Qur'an to an Ethnos

The novel appearance of *al-ᶜarab* in Umayyad-era poetry as a term of self-reference points decisively to the period when ideas of Arab communal consciousness gained wide acceptance to articulate a shared identity, but the verses alone do not explain why early Muslims during the later first/seventh century chose the name 'Arab' to identify themselves. The word *al-ᶜarab* appeared as an understood byword for the large collective – but where did early Muslims find the word and why did it become their ethnonym? These questions are important because peoples' choice to identify as 'Arabs' would not have been idle: Arabness replaced earlier identities and subsumed formerly disparate groups under a new umbrella – people changed who they thought they were and how they related to each other. Such transitions are contested processes that produce fissures and inconsistencies in the historical record, and the following chapters trace the flow of Arabness ideas over Islam's first centuries. As a prelude, this chapter tackles the genesis of Arabness as a symbol of community, a task that leads us to investigate the source of the word 'Arab' as an ethnonym and the ways which sociopolitical structures during Islam's first century prompted the formation of Arab identity.

I 'Arab': an Ethnonym Resurrected?

The reason why early Muslims identified themselves as Arabs remains obscure. Chapter 1 traced the extensive use of 'Arab'-cognates to connote 'outsider nomads' since Antiquity, but we lack an explanation as to why a group of people would transform 'Arab' into a reference for their own community. In order to elucidate the emergence of the Arabs' name, there is an ostensibly analogous case in Late Antiquity where a label for 'other' did transform into an ethnonym for 'self': this was the name 'Berber'. The genesis of the Berber ethnonym appears analogous to 'Arab' inasmuch as 'Berber' was initially a Greek and Latin term connoting 'outsiders', and in Late Antiquity an array of communities on the fringes of Roman/Byzantine control in North Africa embraced the name as a term of their own self-reference.[1] But notwithstanding the apparent congruence between 'Berber' and 'Arab', their circumstances and usage have material differences. In the Berber case, Roman and later Vandal hegemony over the Mediterranean littoral conferred power to them to apply the name 'Berber' on populations in the hinterland, and since those peoples never formed one cohesive kingdom of their own, but instead only established autonomies on localised bases, they adopted the ethnonym 'Berber' as a consequence of accepting what more powerful others had called them. Umayyad-era Muslims, on the other hand, wielded wide power and authority, and while they kept local elites in charge of conquered locales, there is little indication that Umayyads held the conquered in any great esteem; on the contrary, expressions of Arabness under the Umayyads emerged during the period when the new Caliphate was imposing the Arabic language and new government in a sustained fashion such that the 'Arab World' emerged from the lands first conquered by the first caliphs.[2] Unlike the fragmented Berber kingdoms, the preponderantly powerful political elite of the new Muslim empire would not have had to accept a name imposed on them by subalterns. 'Berber' and 'Arab' also crucially differ because 'Berber' had been employed continuously over centuries to describe North Africans before they adopted the name for themselves, whereas Chapter 1(III) demonstrated that Greeks, Romans and Persians stopped calling Arabians 'Arabs' three centuries before Islam. If early Muslims were minded to adopt the name by which outsiders identified them, they would have called themselves 'Saracens' in Syria and 'Ṭayyāyē' in Iraq. The old tradition of calling Arabian peoples Arabs had ended in the third century CE, and the name 'Arab' was not figuratively waiting in the Fertile Crescent for the Muslims to adopt as their own ethnonym. The genesis of the self-styled Arab community in early Islam thus defies explanation as a straightforward borrowing of earlier nomenclature.

An alternative theory proposes that 'Arabs' derived their name from the land from whence they emerged. In 106 CE 'Arabia' became the name of a Roman province in what is now Jordan and northern Saudi Arabia, its residents called themselves 'Arabs', and popular attachment to the province is argued as the root of the Arab ethnonym and Arab ethnic unity.[3] But connecting Roman 'Arabia' provincial nomenclature and Muslim 'Arab' identity is also difficult to substantiate. *Provincia Arabia* was never so big as to encompass the homelands of all those who called themselves Arabs in early Islam: the conquering armies included large contingents from Yemen, eastern Arabia and Iraq, and since those lands were so far outside *Provincia Arabia*'s borders, it seems too much an extrapolation to suggest that the limited geographical ambit of Roman 'Arabia' could appeal as the name capable of uniting people who lived so far from it. Arabia's provincial borders did not extend as far south as Islam's original heartland in Mecca and Medina either: one inscription records Roman activities to the north of Medina 450 years before Islam,[4] but their foothold was distant, fleeting, and we lack Arabic records expressing cognisance of proximity and respect for Roman Imperial power. Accordingly, it seems unlikely that seventh-century Meccans would seek to identify with old and distant Roman imperial nomenclature.[5] The marked absence of textual reverence for Roman 'Arabia' in our sources does logically flow from the collapse of Roman control in inner Arabia in the third century CE: over the 300 years before Islam, central Arabian kingdoms were no longer in awe of Roman might from 'Arabia', but rather faced Byzantine incursions which lacked the hegemonic power of the earlier Roman territorial control.[6] The symbolic value of Roman Arabia appears debased by the dawn of Islam, lacking the power which a new and vigorous state would wish to harness in its name. Furthermore, the Byzantines reorganised *Provincia Arabia* at the end of the fourth century, renaming it *Palestinia Tertia Salutaris*, and hence for two centuries before Islam, even memory of the name 'Arabia' was becoming archaic.[7] A legacy survived in popular recollection witnessed by reference to the name 'Arab' in several tombstone inscriptions up to the sixth century CE, where 'Arab' connotes provincial belonging,[8] but pre-Islamic poetry never remembers the toponym nor people identified as Arabians, and so connecting a sense of belonging to provincial/geographic 'Arabia' with the communities of Muslim conquerors is obtuse. Why would Muslims embrace a name they previously never cited by resurrecting old provincial nomenclature after dismantling the province in their conquests?[9]

The theory that the 'Arab' ethnonym emerged from the geographical context of Roman 'Arabia' perhaps also overemphasises a European historiographical outlook to trace Arab ethnogenesis. In Europe, new peoples emerged in Late Antiquity (and constituted the origins of modern European nations) as a consequence of the rising power of newcomers in different regions of the collapsing Roman Empire, and while it is tempting to read Arab origins as a similar end product of Roman decline, the analogy is flawed. The European groups are known as 'successor peoples' since they inherited the Roman Imperial system on localised bases and were attracted to the symbolic trappings of Rome as part of the process of legitimising their own power.[10] Conversely, Arab imagined communities did not look to Imperial Rome for legitimacy: they did not feign Roman identity, and I have found neither pre-Islamic nor Islamic-era Arabic references to Roman provincial belonging as a valued asset that could be a source for their community's sense of self and right to rule. Furthermore, the first signs of Arab identity were expressed far beyond the Roman–Arabian frontier: much early Muslim activity focused in Iraq and hence negotiated Sasanian, not Byzantine/Roman legacies.[11] And moreover, the context of Arab ethnogenesis differs from the processes in Europe from the perspectives of the sweep of historical events and cultural developments. Unlike Germanic groups' gradual incorporation into Roman frontier systems, the early Muslims entered the Middle East via a flash of rapid conquests, and unlike Germanic peoples, the Conquerors concentrated themselves in new urban settlements (*amṣār*) which they constructed exclusively for their own settlement, and which appear to be an 'intentional reconstitution of the social organisation of the conquered lands'.[12] The early Muslims also established governance over a vast area, within which they broadcast new symbolic capital – their Qur'an, a new script, its Arabic language – cultural legacies of a very different magnitude to those of the Germanic 'successor peoples' in Europe.[13] In contrast to the Middle East, European historical records do not adduce Lombard pretensions to 'caliphate' as a means to unify the array of Germanic groups under a religio-political order like the Umayyad *amīr al-muʾminīn* (Commander of the Faithful/Caliph), nor does Gothic or other Germanic-language scripture appear as the symbolic capital of the new peoples and catalyst for the emergence of a new script and official language as was the case of Arabic.[14]

By accepting that the conquests had momentous long-term effects which catalysed Arab ethnogenesis, we do not simply embrace the later Muslim-era traditions about the conquests wholesale. The Arabic sources have manifold contradictions in detail regarding battles, dates and the sequence of events,[15] and it is naïve to imagine that one cohesive Muslim politico-religious system was in place at the time of the conquests, or that each of the Conqueror communities was identical.[16] But probing the details ought not obscure the broad tenor of the novelty of Islam's symbolic capital, the speed of conquest, and the cohesion of the early Caliphate.[17] The Conquerors did not unload pre-Islamic Arabian 'Arab' culture onto the Middle East as much as they constructed something unprecedented which did become remarkably uniformly articulated across the conquered lands. The exceptional consistency of the Qur'an's dissemination,[18] the intentional founding of Conqueror settlements in sequestered communities from North Africa to Central Asia,[19] and the centralised attention to government revealed in papyrological evidence from Egypt,[20] suggest considerable confidence by which the Conquerors marshalled their symbolic capital and left it in the archaeological and epigraphic record. The extant material reveals the character of the conquests as not so dissimilar to the manner in which Muslim literary narratives later described them; and as a consequence, modern accounts of the conquests based on the framework of the Muslim-era sources, such as Kennedy's, remain cogent,[21] and analysis of non-Arabic writings contemporary with the conquests corroborates the outlines of the later Arabic tradition.[22] Modern historians can legitimately interrogate Arabic sources for new precision, and this book participates in such an enterprise by investigating Arabness, but it seems insensitive to blinker ourselves from the very reason we study early Islam with such interest: the conquests initiated a series of processes that unfolded with profound world significance and their considerable potential to inspire new formations of communal organisation could be anticipated, and Arabness as a form of expressing a community emerges as a central legacy of the seminal historical processes.

In sum, early Muslims appear to have been conscious of their particularism, and most importantly from the perspective of contrasting their experience with the 'successor peoples' in Europe, we lack indications that they tried to be Roman. Reading Arab origins as beholden to the Roman Syrian frontier therefore constitutes a rather narrow prism to tackle the very broad sweep of Arab ethnogenesis, and instead, we need to account for the generations of changes that gave rise to Arab communal consciousness against the background of the momentous forces in the decades following the conquests. Since pre-Islamic Roman *Provincia Arabia* legacies seem insufficient to explain why the broad-based community of early Muslims began to call themselves 'Arabs', we should perhaps pursue the reason behind their choice by looking within their own world for nomenclature possessing symbolic power in their systems of knowledge and identity.

II The Qur'an and Arabness

The Qur'an presents an intriguing candidate for the spark prompting the Arabness idea in early Islam. In complete contrast to the dearth of reference to the word 'Arab' in pre-Islamic Arabian epigraphy and poetry, the Qur'an emerges as the first Arabian record that makes multiple, unambiguous and self-reflexive references to the word *ᶜarabī*, citing it eleven times. It calls itself 'an Arabic Qur'an' (*qurʾān ᶜarabī*) on six occasions,[23] and refers to variants of 'an Arabic language' (*lisān ᶜarabī*) and 'a clear Arabic' (*ᶜarabī mubīn*) in the others.[24] Given that poetry begins to describe people as *ᶜarab* only following the dissemination of an *ᶜarabī* Qur'an, closer investigation seems warranted.[25] We shall find that the Qur'an accords special privilege to places in the Arabian Peninsula, but its relationships to senses of Arab people and community are complex, and the Qur'an constitutes only the beginning of a long process of ethnogenesis, not a fait accompli construction of Arab identity.

Space and Audience in the Qur'an: Arabia and Arabians

Whilst the Qur'an never mentions the toponym 'Arabia' (or any equivalent of the later-coined *Jazīrat al-ᶜarab* (the Arabs' [Pen]insula)), it does accord unique spatial emphasis to the Peninsula. The Qur'an is perhaps the earliest extant text (sacred or profane) to give Arabia a central role in a narrative of world history: unlike all earlier Judeo-Christian scripture, the Qur'an promotes the region's footprint in the story of monotheism by venerating Mecca as the centre of worship (in contrast to Judeo-Christian Jerusalem),[26] and by memorialising Peninsular peoples ᶜĀd and Thamūd and their prophets Hūd and Ṣāliḥ, whom Judeo-Christian traditions never mention. The Qur'an thereby reorients narratives of monotheism around Arabian loci, and while this is pointed and significant, it does not follow that the Qur'an was therefore targeted towards an Arab ethnos. Arabian space does not axiomatically equate to Arab race, and closer review confirms that the Qur'an offers no grounds to suppose otherwise.

The Qur'an neither refers to Mecca's sanctum as an 'Arab' establishment, nor does it call the Arabian peoples ᶜĀd and Thamūd 'Arabs' – it refers to them as destroyed peoples of an ancient past.[27] Two centuries after the Qur'an's revelation, some Muslim writers called Mecca's holy space *bayt al-ᶜarab* ('the [Sacred] House of the Arabs'),[28] but the Qur'an itself fixes its horizon of Meccan history on Abraham and his son Ishmael,[29] and never calls them *ᶜarab* either. Avoiding ethnic labels, the Qur'an adjectives Abraham as *ḥanīf* (of 'upright religion'[30]/'true religion'[31]). *Ḥanīf*'s etymology is debated,[32] but in half of its twelve Qur'anic citations, it describes the 'religious community (*milla*) of Abraham',[33] Abraham's 'people/nation' (*umma*),[34] and *ḥanīf* accompanies *muslim* in verse 3:67: 'Abraham was neither a Jew nor a Christian, but a Muslim *ḥanīf*'.[35] The Qur'an's association of *ḥanīf*, Abraham and Mecca is noted as central to Muhammad's legitimacy, for it presents the Prophet as Abraham's successor,[36] and Mecca is accordingly depicted as the sanctum of the *dīn ḥanīf*: Abraham's 'pure religion', Islam.[37] Akin to the Qur'an's depiction of ᶜĀd and Thamūd as chapters in the global history of monotheism and not a particularised Arab history, the Qur'an renders Mecca the global sanctum of true monotheists, not exclusively of Arabs. The Qur'an unambiguously orients its narrative around Arabian space, but we shall see that it conversely leaves the identity of its audience rather open-ended.

If the traditional dating of the Qur'an's verses reflects the order of revelation, it is instructive that the references to Mecca's Abrahamic connections are contained in Medinan verses – that is, verses revealed when Muhammad's Muslim community was at war with pagan Meccans. Emphasising Mecca's merger with Abraham would have obvious practical utility to justify Muhammad's political conflict by projecting it as the struggle to restore Abraham's rituals in Mecca, and there is accordingly little logic for the Qur'an to portray Muhammad as an 'Arab Prophet' leading the whole 'Arab people', since during most of the Medinan period, Muhammad led only a small northern Ḥijāzī community at war with its immediate neighbours. The Qur'an's discourse is shaped to confer priority right to Mecca on Muhammad's *ḥanīf* community and to challenge the legitimacy of Quraysh's control over Mecca. It thus lacks motive to depict the town as a shared 'Arab' sanctum, and, as noted, the Qur'an never uses the word *ᶜarabī* to describe Mecca, its sanctum or any other place.

The absence of the word *ᶜarabī* in Qur'anic stories about Abraham, Mecca and Muhammad is in harmony with verse 3:68 which states 'those of mankind who have the best claim to Abraham are those who followed him, this Prophet and those who believe'.[38] Akin to impressions of early Muslim community articulated by Donner and Bashear, the Qur'an constructs believers as a confessional group and not an ethnicity,[39] and so offers no tangible impressions of an Arab homeland, unlike the Judaic Israel ordained for the Hebrews. Interpreting the Qur'an like Judaic scripture in this sense is accordingly misleading: the Qur'an neither bolsters a racial identity nor confers right to land. Read on its own, the Qur'an tallies with our present theory of Arab ethnogenesis since the absence of self-styled 'Arabs' in pre-Islam leaves little scope to imagine that a broad consciousness of ethnic Arabness existed in the Qur'an's day. The Qur'an's early audiences would have been Ma'addites, Kindites, Christians, Jews and others who did not listen to revelation with pre-existing notions of kin-interrelation, and perhaps this explains why the Qur'an so avoids overt ethnic overtones. It did not have an already cohesive, unified population to receive its message, and so it articulated itself around the more theoretical (and perhaps ecumenical)[40] categories of *ḥanīf*, *muslim* and *muʾmin* (believer).

The claim that the Qur'an was addressed to one Arab people thus needs correction. The Qur'an articulates its believers as an *umma*, which Muslim exegetes since the fourth/tenth century explained as meaning 'the people', and, by extension, 'the Arab people', but if we follow this tradition,[41] we impose later Muslim interpretations onto the Qur'an. There are neither textual nor historic grounds to link the Qur'an's *umma* with its *ᶜarabī*: the words are never cited in the context of each other, and we lack indication that Muhammad, whose military campaigns were concentrated in al-Ḥijāz alone, ever spoke to a cohesive Arab pan-Arabian people or appealed to a sense of shared ethnos to make peace with his opponents or to convert them.

Furthermore, we shall see in the next sections that the Qur'anic narratives distinguish *ᶜarabī* from *aᶜrāb* (Arabian nomads), casting asunder attempts to adduce a pan-Arab/Arabian message in the Qur'an. Whilst several commentators accept that the Qur'an never mentions 'Arabs' by name, they nonetheless extrapolate from Qur'anic references to itself as an Arabic Qur'an (*qurʾān ᶜarabī*) that it was addressed to an 'Arab ethnos',[42] but such statements are unsubstantiated from the Qur'anic text, and obstruct our understanding of what the Qur'an means by *ᶜarabī* and how it conceptualises Arabia's populations.

Interpreting the Qur'an's ᶜArabī

The Qur'an's use of *ᶜarabī* is very consistent, and can be grasped by reading the scripture on its own. Each of the eleven Qur'anic occurrences of *ᶜarabī* is adjectival and specifically descriptive of the Qur'an: it is an *ᶜarabī* Qur'an (*qurʾān ᶜarabī*), and it is illegitimate to impute ethnic connotation here. *ᶜArabī* did later become an ethnonym, but the Qur'an's *ᶜarabī* is an adjective of revelation, not people: 'We have sent it down as an Arabic Qur'an perchance that you may understand',[43] and elsewhere, the Qur'an reveals that its 'Arabic-ness' is linguistic: 'Truly, this Qur'an has been sent down by the Lord of the Worlds: the Trustworthy Spirit brought it down to your heart, so that you could bring warning in a clear Arabic tongue (*lisān ᶜarabī*)'.[44]

ᶜArabī is an adjective for the Qur'an's sacred idiom, a language which 'contains no crookedness' (*ᶜiwaj*),[45] and in another verse it describes the purity of God's judgment contained in the Qur'an (*ḥukm ᶜarabī*).[46] The Qur'an's association of *ᶜarabī* with *lisān* (language) and *mubīn* (clear) disclose a conception of 'Arabic' as signifying an idiom possessing miraculous purity and clarity, conveying the sacred message and prompting its listeners to comprehend and respond by embracing Islam.

The linguistic connotation of the Qur'an's *ᶜarabī* may seem to imply that it is the language of Muhammad's 'Arab' people, and Q14:4 states that God's message is revealed in the language of its intended audience, but Q14:4 makes no mention of *ᶜarabī* and its passage (Q14:5–8) describes Moses, not Muhammad's audience. An express reference to *ᶜarabī* in Q16:103 offers more clarity on the place of *ᶜarabī* in Qur'anic discourses. The verse states: 'We know very well that they say, "It is a man who teaches him," but the language of the person they allude to is *aᶜjamī* [non-Arabic], while this revelation is clear Arabic [*ᶜarabī mubīn*].'

The verse depicts Muhammad as understanding both the *ᶜarabī* of the Qur'an and the *aᶜjamī* of the man alluded to, and it therefore does not seem that *aᶜjamī*/*ᶜarabī* is a distinction between different languages, but rather distinguishes different modes, messages and messengers. The Qur'an's *aᶜjamī* connotes something nonsensical or a sullied message of a non-divinely inspired messenger, whereas the verse affirms that *ᶜarabī* connotes a transcendently clear koine from God, not a terrestrial vernacular. Hence the Qur'an presents *ᶜarabī* as a particularly revered means of communicating a pure message. *ᶜArabī* is intelligible to Muhammad, but there is no indication that it connotes a common idiom, or that people used 'Qur'an-speak' in their everyday lives to delineate the boundaries of an ethnic community (as the much more codified language standardisation achieved in delineating nations in early modern Europe).

Qur'anic *ᶜarabī* is transcendent: it is proof of the Qur'an's miracle, and in this respect, the meanings of verbs derived from the root ᶜ-r-b such as *aᶜraba* and *ᶜarraba*, are instructive. They connote 'to clarify', 'to express' and to 'speak clearly' which correspond to the Qur'an's usage of the adjective *ᶜarabī* as a means to exalt itself by allusion to its pre-eminent clarity.[47]

Qur'anic *ᶜarabī* is further removed from the sphere of a specific community's language by virtue of its invariably indefinite and masculine form. The Qur'an refers to itself as '*an* Arabic Qur'an', not '*the* Arabic Qur'an'; it never speaks of '*the* Arabic language', only '*an* Arabic language' (*lisān ᶜarabī*).[48] The Qur'an's vision of Arabic is indefinite, unlike the rigidly defined (and feminine form) language that *al-ᶜarabiyya* would later connote in classical grammatical texts as *kalām al-ᶜarab*, '*the* language of *the* Arabs'. The transition from the Qur'an's indefinite *ᶜarabī* to Muslim grammarians' definite *al-ᶜarabiyya* points to the role of intellectual processes during the early centuries of Islam in developing new meanings for *ᶜarabī* and codifying Arabic as *al-ᶜarabiyya*, and underscores the difficulties in treating exegesis written four centuries after the Qur'an's revelation as reflective of the single, 'correct' interpretation of Qur'anic *ᶜarabī*. A definitive sense of codified language lends itself to ethnogenesis, but the indefinite Qur'anic *ᶜarabī* calls for a more fluid interpretation in a revelation/performative/oral-ritual sense. Such readings also better match the dearth of 'Arabic' inscriptional evidence before Islam: in reserving *ᶜarabī* as something exclusive to its revelation, the Qur'an implies that *ᶜarabī* is special and pure – not an idiom we could expect to find on graffito in the desert. The manner in which the Qur'an monopolises its conception of Arabness precludes extrapolation that its *ᶜarabī* connoted an ethnic community at the dawn of the seventh century. The expressions *qurʾān ᶜarabī* and *lisān ᶜarabī* therefore seem best captured by translating them as 'clarion Qur'an' and 'pure speech', dissociating them from the now ethnic sense embedded in our understanding of the word *ᶜarabī*.

ᶜArabī, Aᶜrāb *and* Taᶜarrub: *Misleading Homophones*

Having determined the consistently restricted and specific intention of the Qur'an's *ᶜarabī*, we should next like to investigate how the Qur'an's audience might have interpreted the word. This invites consideration of *ᶜarabī*'s root and the meaning of related words formed on the ᶜ-r-b triliteral, and here we shall find that *ᶜarabī* is intriguingly obscure: the Qur'an seems intent on carving out a unique meaning for its *ᶜarabī* that excludes associations with other words formed from the same root.

Students of the Arabic language are familiar with the classical-era philological paradigm that each triradical root in Arabic has one 'mother-meaning' shared by derived words. Several words from the ᶜ-r-b root relate to nomadism, and so suggest the Qur'an's *ᶜarabī* may connote nomads' language, but drawing such conclusions and proposing in turn that Arab ethnic identity originates in nomadism, unnecessarily falls back into the outdated, and much critiqued Orientalist paradigm that weds Arabness to the desert.[49] Exceptions to the philological 'rules' are legion, and the tidy semantic system bequeathed by classical Muslim grammarians obscures an earlier, less cohesive history of Arabic as it developed, buffeted by neighbouring languages and cosmopolitan contact over centuries during which many words were imported.[50] Thus, words containing the letters ᶜ-r-b neither necessarily relate semantically to *ᶜarabī*, nor need be derived from the same source. As an example of the diversity of ᶜ-r-b cognates in Arabic, consider the word *ᶜarūba* (an archaic name for 'Friday'). Though phonetically similar to *ᶜarab*, *ᶜarūba* carries no semantic connection to Arabness or nomadism whatsoever: it was a direct borrowing of the Aramaic/Syriac name for Friday.[51] We must be cautious therefore when considering the origins of the word *ᶜarabī*.

An ostensible relation to the Qur'an's *ᶜarabī* is the word *aᶜrāb* (nomads). But while the Qur'an makes ten references to *aᶜrāb*, it never describes them as *ᶜarabī*, and moreover, it paints a consistently negative picture of *aᶜrāb*, distancing them from the Muslim community.[52] We have seen that pre-Islamic Semitic languages used the word *aᶜrāb (ʾᶜrb)* to connote 'nomadic outliers',[53] and the Qur'an perpetuates that tradition, using *aᶜrāb* to describe Bedouin (*bādūn*)[54] situated outside the municipal Medinan Muslim community,[55] and derides them as 'the most stubborn of all peoples in their disbelief and hypocrisy . . . the least likely to recognise the limits that God has sent down to His Messenger'.[56] The Qur'an also doubts the sincerity of the *aᶜrāb*'s faith by noting their unwillingness to participate in communal actions,[57] and relegates them to an inferior status compared to the Believers (*muʾminūn*), telling the *aᶜrāb* that 'faith has not yet entered your hearts.'[58] The Qur'an's *aᶜrāb* appear much like the unnamed and undifferentiated *ʾᶜrb* in pre-Islamic South Arabian inscriptions, as well as the *Aribi* and *Αραβιή* of Assyrian and Greek writing: they are distant outsiders, and in the Muslim context, this means *aᶜrāb* are apart from the Qur'an's inside space where the Qur'an's *ᶜarabī* message is delivered and believed.

Bearing in mind that the Qur'an reserved the word *ᶜarabī* for itself alone, the outsider, non-perfected believer status accorded to *aᶜrāb* renders them quintessentially opposite to the Qur'an's *ᶜarabī*. Whilst one might argue on purely philological grounds that *aᶜrāb*/nomad is the plural of *ᶜarab*/Arab, pursuing this reasoning overlooks the context of the Qur'an's discourse.[59] An 'Arabic Qur'an' sees nomads as outsiders. The Qur'an is also the first extant text in history to repeatedly use the word *ᶜarabī* to describe itself, and shortly thereafter, we find Muslims adopting the same word and same self-reflexive practice to call themselves Arabs, and those early Muslims specifically distinguished themselves from *aᶜrāb* too in a manner similar to the Qur'an's separation of its *ᶜarabī* revelation from outsider *aᶜrāb*.[60] The marshalling of Arabness to connote a sense of community seems therefore to borrow from the novel connotations and mechanics of the Qur'an's self-reflexive *ᶜarabī*, and does not reflect a transformation of the old tradition using *aᶜrāb* to connote outsider–nomadism into a term expressing insider self-identity.

The distancing of the Qur'an's *ᶜarabī* from notions of nomadism is also underlined in early Islamic-era discussions of a related verb, *taᶜarraba*, which classical dictionaries defined as 'to go and live with/as nomads'.[61] The verb's form could be interpreted as meaning 'to become Arab', again purportedly suggesting the Arabs' roots in nomadism,[62] but the morphological similarity once again overlooks the semantic differences between Qur'anic *ᶜarabī* and the verb *taᶜarraba*. The difference materialises in early Muslims' application of *taᶜarraba* to describe individuals who shunned Muslim community, abandoned their *hijra* (emigration, the vital act of perfecting belief[63]), and entered the desert. The *hijra* was the defining criteria of early Muslim communal belonging: the action of *taᶜarraba* thus implied becoming non-Muslim, as both Bosworth and Marsham reveal through analysis of the verb's citation where it is used synonymously with words signifying apostasy (*irtadda*, *irfaḍḍa* and *fitna*), the religious discord axiomatically opposed to Islam.[64] Against this background where believers were evidently dissuaded from ever leaving their *hijra* communities, early Muslim jurists appear to have been asked to opine as to whether a return to the desert was legally permissible at all, and the records of their opinions in Ibn Abī Shayba's (d. 235/849) *al-Muṣannaf* suggest temporary desert visits of up to two months were allowed, but any more constituted *taᶜarrub*, and, as the texts adds: 'He who pursues Bedouin life becomes boorish' (*man badā jafā*).[65] It seems perverse to consider that Arab identity sprung from the 'boorish life' or that *taᶜarraba* shared associations with the Qur'an's *ᶜarabī*.

In other records from early Islam, the word *ᶜarabī* also appears as an adjective in the term *bayᶜa ᶜarabiyya*, an oath of allegiance given by nomads to the Muslim state during the early Caliphate and perhaps as early as the Prophet's lifetime.[66] *Bayᶜa ᶜarabiyya* is the opposite of *bayᶜat al-hijra*:[67] the latter involved physical settlement in a Muslim community, whereas the former applied to those who pledged allegiance to the Muslim state but did not emigrate to Muslim towns. Ostensibly, this *ᶜarabī* in pledging terminology appears to describe a 'nomad oath', and thus suggests the idea of *ᶜarabī* was synonymous with nomadism, but yet again there are difficulties in establishing a semantic link between the oath *ᶜarabī* and the Qur'an's *ᶜarabī*. If *bayᶜa ᶜarabiyya* was indeed referencing nomadic *aᶜrāb* and meant 'nomad oath', it is curious that it was called *ᶜarabiyya* instead of the usual adjective for Bedouin, *a*ᶜ*rābiyya*. Moreover, the Qur'an's self-reflexive use of ᶜ*arabī* for 'revelation' sits uncomfortably as equivalent to an adjective for an 'outsider's oath', and indicates the likely separate genesis for Qur'anic ᶜ*arabī*. Instead of sharing one meaning, the Qur'anic and the oath ᶜ*arabī* may be only homophones, and Old South Arabian philology can help elucidate their distinct origins and meanings.

The Old South Arabian noun ᶜ*rb* means 'guarantee of good conduct',[68] or 'pledges in token of submission'.[69] At law, pledges, guarantees and other securities are granted to secure obligations that are otherwise practically difficult to enforce, and this would suit an oath of allegiance given by an outsider since his obligations cannot be enforced directly because he does not settle within the remit of the state's power (that is, because he did not make a *hijra*). The outsider must provide more notional security to evidence his allegiance, and *bay*ᶜ*a* ᶜ*arabiyya* appears as such a legal solution for converts who did not move within the boundaries of the state (the *hijra* communities) and hence remained outside the direct observation of Muslim authorities. Early Arabian Muslims borrowed this securities nomenclature when they needed to articulate the new kinds of agreements they found themselves making with groups outside their direct control, and the adjective ᶜ*arabiyya* can be explained as deriving from pledging terminology and not from nomadism. That is, *bay*ᶜ*a* ᶜ*arabiyya* should be translated as 'oath by guarantee', the counterpart to the 'oath by emigration' (*bay*ᶜ*at al-hijra*).[70] The hypothesis has support from precedent of other borrowings of technical terminology in the early Muslim polity: the term for the Conqueror new towns (*miṣr*/*amṣār*) appears to derive from the South Arabian word for 'military expeditionary force',[71] and given that pre-Islamic South Arabia had more developed systems of administration than evidenced in al-Ḥijāz, the need for early Muslims to borrow from their southern neighbours aligns with their similar co-opting of Byzantine and Sasanian practices following the conquests too.

In the context of nascent Islam, those living outside of the *hijra* communities would, as a practical matter, almost always be Bedouin in the Ḥijāzī and Najdī deserts, hence the borrowed technical pledge term ᶜ*arabī* would meld with the word *a*ᶜ*rāb*, and this would become confusing by the Umayyad era when ᶜ*arabī* subsequently developed into an ethnonym connoting the Muslim 'Arab' elite (see the poetry considered in Chapter 2(IV)). A Muslim

^{c}*arabī* would not want to be associated with an outsider's oath, so to avoid confusion, the *bay*^{c}*a* ^{c}*arabiyya* would need to be dropped from pledge terminology, and it does indeed quickly disappear in Muslim-era literature contemporaneously with the rise of self-expressed 'Arabs'.

The Qur'an's Arabness: a 'Clarion Qur'an' in a 'Pure Tongue'

Distinguished from nomadic connotation and other cognates of the root ^{c}-r-b, the Qur'an's ^{c}*arabī* occupies a unique space, monopolised by the Qur'an, separated from profane matters, and accorded unprecedented connotations of divinely clear communication, and equally unprecedented use in a self-reflexive manner. The Qur'an neither appeals to a pan-Arabian ethnos nor addresses itself to Bedouin, and it certainly does not equate its ^{c}*arabī* with the idiom of the *a*^{c}*rāb*. In sum, Qur'anic Arabness asserts itself as a pure idiom of expressive communication, perhaps a language of ritual performance,[72] or sacred koine. ^{c}*Arabī*'s invariably indefinite state hearkens a language practice which pre-Islamic Arabians understood, but not a closed-ended concept with definite parameters such as the 'cultural stuff' traits which social groups marshal to conceptualise exclusive identities. The Qur'an's ^{c}*arabī* is neither the stuff of ethnic consciousness nor connected to a particular geographic place, and this harmonises with the sum of evidence adduced hitherto indicating the absence of a consciously Arab community in pre-Islamic Arabia. There is accordingly no requirement to presume that the Qur'an directed its message to a preformed community of Arabs: the first Muslims possessed an ^{c}*arabī* Qur'an which they understood in terms redolent of 'clarion revelation' not in terms of a national movement.[73]

As the next section will trace, the 'Arab' community of the Umayyad and Abbasid periods can be seen as deriving its name from the Qur'an via a century-long process of converting the purity of Qur'anic ^{c}*arabī* into a new sense of ethnic *al-*^{c}*arab* for the post-conquest religious community, but it is worth pausing first to reflect upon the phonetic correspondence between the Greek and Roman word 'Arab' which had been used to describe inhabitants of ancient Arabia and the *al-*^{c}*arab* Arabic people in Muslim times. The resemblance suggests some connection, yet as a practical matter, we have seen that the two traditions never coincided: there is the 300-year gap between the last reference to Arabs by the Romans and Persians and the emergence of self-styled Arab communities[74] and the Greco-Roman 'Arab' words connoted outsiders. The sudden outpouring of self-expressed Arab identity amongst Umayyad-era Muslim populations corresponds to the new and unprecented ways in which the Qur'an marshals *ᶜarabī*, thus pointing to the Qur'an, not Greek geography, as the inspiration for the emergence of the Arab enthnonym into history. But there may nonetheless be a bridge to explain the phonetic similarity between Muslim *ᶜarab* and pre-Islamic *aᶜrāb*.

We could propose that the Qur'an's *ᶜarabī* may be a development from the long Semitic-language tradition of referring to Bedouin as *aᶜrāb* on the hypothesis that Qur'anic *ᶜarabī*'s novel meaning of 'clarity' derived from notions of ritual practice, divination and the respected clarion *koine* of pre-Islamic *kuhhān* desert soothsayers (singular: *kāhin*). Shamans and soothsayers are de rigueur outsider characters: as far as we can tell, the pre-Islamic *kuhhān* lived in secluded areas and were thus *aᶜrāb* from a terminological standpoint, and the pre-Islamic *kuhhān* are reported to have revealed the hidden and the future in their coded statements, hence their performances produced 'clairvoyant revelation'. If their coded messages gained some cultural capital and ritual acceptance (which apparently was the case given the Islamic-era lore about them), a sense of reverence for *ᶜarabī* sayings as a byword for the communication of pure/special knowledge could emerge in pre-Islamic Arabia, bridging *aᶜrāb*'s notions of desert domicile and the verbs *aᶜraba*/*ᶜarraba*'s connotations of clarion speech (especially given the absence of other explanations for the origin of the clarity connotations). The Qur'an's coded idiom, its obscure or outright unknown vocabulary,[75] internal rhyme structure, and its emphasis on oral performative recitation do resemble the style of the *kuhhān*, and the Qur'an's repeated indefinite references to *ᶜarabī* imply that it is consciously a part of a wider practice. The Qur'an held itself as more than a mere *kāhin*'s performance, but it employed the *kuhhān*'s register, and it is noteworthy that the Qur'an twice stresses that Muhammad is not merely a *kāhin*.[76] Hence the Qur'an's sense of *ᶜarabī* may have indirectly descended from the Bedouin/*aᶜrāb* semantic universe, developed from centuries of pre-Islamic desert ritual practice which the Qur'an then Islamised and exalted for itself alone. Muslim 'Arabs' would thus be construable as people of a pure Qur'an episteme, and not 'outsider' Bedouin.

More consideration of pre-Islamic ritual is needed to affirm conclusions, but returning to the text itself, the Qur'an's Arabness is a linguistic register specific to divine revelation. While Müller's 1899 theory was therefore right in dating the dissemination of 'Arabic' as a symbolic expression to the beginning of Islam,[77] ethnicities are not simply invented by a single act: they evolve, and in the case of Arabness, the Qur'an appears to initiate the process by glorifying itself and its message with a new emphasis on the word *ᶜarabī*, but it reserves the adjective to itself. The Qur'an's *ᶜarabī* does not connote a group of terrestrial people, and the transformation of performance *ᶜarabī* to ethnic *ᶜarab* must have been wrought by later hands. The processes can be seen in action through investigation of events following the Qur'an's revelation.

III Early Islam and the Genesis of Arab Identity

Our analysis of pre-Islamic Arabia through the lens of ethnogenesis in Chapter 2(III) revealed the region's fractious and divided sociopolitical boundaries that militated against generating consciousness of one pan-Arabian 'Arab' communal cohesion, and so explains why Qur'anic *ᶜarabī* lacks ethnic connotations. In contrast to the 'Arabless' pre-Islamic Arabia, however, evidence of groups expressly conscious of an Arab identity abounds in the earliest surviving Arabic prose literature written in the late second/eighth and early third/ninth centuries. There is accordingly a window of less than 200 years in which a self-aware Arab ethnos formed, and we need to seek its drivers. In Chapter 2(IV), we found that poetry gave indications that the first bulk of expressions of belonging to an 'Arab' community emerged in the later first/seventh century, and this coincides with the period of a major proliferation of Arabic language inscriptions across Arabia and the Levant. The window of Arab ethnogenesis is thus offered some precision to a period of marked evolution two or three generations after Muhammad, which accords with the expectations from anthropological theory that the creation of a new sense of ethnic community requires a protracted and gradual development. No lengthy Arabic narrative texts survive from Islam's first century to provide clearer indications of the process, but we do possess a reasonable grasp of historical events, and our theoretical framework of ethnogenesis can allow us to interpret that history and pin the textual indicators we have onto a framework, and thus finally offer a grounded explanation for the origins of Arab communal consciousness.

Arab Ethnogenesis: the First/Seventh-Century Historical Background

Events occurring in the aftermath of Muhammad's death reorganised Middle Eastern communities. The Prophet's religious message invited expansion, communities of early Muslims pushed outwards, and within two years of Muhammad's death in 11/632 (if not even earlier[78]), conflict was advanced in both Syria and Iraq. Within less than a decade, early Muslims had scored a series of major victories over Byzantine and Sasanian imperial armies, and by the early 30s/650s, military operations conquered the whole region between Tunisia and Eastern Iran. The Conquerors adopted a unique settlement pattern: they rarely inhabited conquered towns, but instead constructed new settlements for themselves (*miṣr/amṣār*) nearby or adjacent to conquered towns on what are known in today's construction terminology as greenfield sites.[79] Contemporary with the establishment of the *amṣār*, the Conquerors established a new political system, the Caliphate, into the form of legitimate authority to rule their vast new territories.

To interpret the historical events and evaluate their effects on social groups and identities, it is material to observe that the Caliphate arose in circumstances quite unlike other empires across history. The rate of conquest was almost unprecedented: within the span of one generation, early Muslims advanced beyond what had likely been the length and breadth of their known world. Their maintenance of control was also unprecedented for its time: unlike the nearly contemporary operations of 'barbarian' outsiders on other edges of the Late Antique Byzantine and Sasanian Empires, early Muslim expansion was not followed by communal fragmentation, but rather inaugurated a new form of governance and, eventually, widespread expressions of Arab communal belonging.[80] Alexander's conquests are perhaps the nearest comparator in terms of land acquisition as a function of time, but herein the early Muslims were again unique, for unlike Alexander's Hellenic heritage, the Muslims lacked a long-established set of institutions and government to impose on their conquered territories. It does seem that the conquests were quite centrally directed from the outset under the one 'Commander of the Faithful' (*amīr al-muʾminīn*),[81] but the institutions that would eventually become the trappings of the 'Islamic State' initially lagged behind the pace of territorial expansion, and a cohesive ruling structure is dated to the

40s–50s/660–70s at the earliest, with better evidence of a state emergent from the reign of ᶜAbd al-Malik 65–86/685–705,[82] while the conceptual underpinnings of the Caliphate as embodying legitimate authority underwent even more protracted developed.[83]

The combination of speed and lack of state institutions may thus prompt comparison with Mongol successes in the seventh/thirteenth century, but the Muslims are yet again unique. The Mongols were a culmination of several centuries of well-documented nomadic expansion, and their conquests represented a climax of the state-building and territorial consolidation of the Uighurs, Qarakhanids and, especially, the Qara Khitai. No such expansive state development over vast and diverse regions are evidenced in pre-Islamic Arabia, and most pertinently, the early Muslims were also distinguished in terms of the symbolic capital of their belief system. Whilst there is debate over the motivation of the conquests,[84] it would be one-dimensional to view the conquests in purely military terms, overlooking the role of faith as an important factor given the Conquerors' careful preservation of their distinctive form of scripture despite the lack of a clergy,[85] and the proliferation of Arabic script, the faith's main symbolic capital, in the generation after the conquests. The nature of the Conquerors' settlement further underlines the keen efforts early Muslims expended to maintain a sense of special community encapsulated in the term *hijra* (emigration and establishment of the new *amṣār* as communities of co-confessionalists).[86] They were uninterested in converting conquered populations,[87] they neither destroyed the countryside nor razed towns,[88] and instead of leaving a legacy of destruction and then assimilation, the Muslim Conquerors essentially forged the opposite: they eschewed substantial cultural assimilation and developed a new faith and system of governance that turned the Greco-Persian Middle East into the heartland of the Islamic World, and constructed the major foundations for what is now familiar as the Arab World too.

In sum, two decades of conquest and a century of consolidation created a web of new *amṣār* towns inhabited by people sharing common religious aspirations as well as status as Conquerors, and a new system of governance under a Caliphate seeking to establish a sense of cohesion and centralisation. The result was a new state and a new society that sat on top of the conquered territory. The segregated populations held a monopoly over power and their faith.[89] If we now extend our theoretical lens to peer into the new social and political orders following the conquests, we shall perceive that the changes prompted new transactional boundaries, 'cultural stuff' affinities and power relations which rather precisely match conditions anthropologists identify as potent catalysts for ethnogenesis. By pursuing the theoretical indicators with the available evidence, we can grasp why the Conquerors were compelled to develop an exclusive identity, why that identity would need to be new, and why it would come to be expressed as 'Arab'. The following sections focus on post-conquest Iraq, since Iraqis in the third/ninth century wrote the majority of Arabic sources describing pre-Islamic Arabica, and their ideas of Arabness developed from the legacies of earlier Iraqi Arab ethnogenesis.

Arab Ethnogenesis: Transactionist Perspectives

The results of conquest were significant from the perspective of transactional boundaries. The early Muslims eliminated Sasanian and Byzantine imperial control in the Middle East and so changed the nature of interactions across the formerly divisive Mesopotamian/Arabian border and ended the divide-and-conquer politics that had marked the progress of imperium into Arabia during the century before Islam. Inner Arabia and the entire Fertile Crescent were now brought into one broad political sphere, permitting more peaceable and regularised interaction. The Conquerors' pattern of establishing themselves almost exclusively in the segregated *amṣār* towns further obviated competition over living space, while still enabling regular transactions with the nearby conquered towns and countryside. And in addition, the Conquerors controlled Arabian nomadic populations,[90] and so eased settled versus nomad friction too. As there is almost no evidence of armed resistance against the early Muslims after the Sasanian armies were defeated in Iraq, the conquests yielded a non-militarised and regularised interaction between Conqueror *amṣār*-dweller and indigenous Iraqi agriculturalist.

The stable post-conquest system nurtured a new and enduring shared social context which a transactionist analysis of ethnogenesis expects to facilitate new perceptions of communal difference and new awareness of ethnic cohesion. Spatially, *amṣār* settlement abetted the potentials for Conquerors' new communal formation as the demographic segregation of Conqueror from conquered erected clear physical boundaries between groups. Because power was concentrated in the *amṣār*, the physical boundaries were conceptually strengthened by the stark power differential between *amṣār* and surrounding countryside, and hence hardened the boundary, making it more enduring and readily perceptible. The Conquerors' physical choice of settlement seems primed to foster the formation and nurture the development of a new sense of community.

Within the *amṣār*, populations were gathered from groups originating from far-flung regions of the Peninsula: Ḥijāzīs (who initially constituted the political leadership in Quraysh and Thaqīf groups), other central and western Ma'addite Arabians (for example, Qays ibn ᶜAylān, Hudhayl), large populations of Yemenis, and more local Ma'addite groups from the fringes of Iraq (for example, Bakr ibn Wāᵓil groups).[91] With the view of hindsight, those groups are all identified today as 'Arab tribes', but the creation of consolidated genealogy necessary to bring all these groups under one shared 'Arab' kinship umbrella was protracted, as will be detailed in Chapter 4(II–IV), and given the absence of reference to 'Arabs' in pre-Islamic Arabia, we ought to question the grounds for a priori presumptions that such groups possessed awareness of shared Arabness at the outset. The groups' articulation of a hitherto unexpressed Arab identity after a century of living in the new conditions suggests that those new conditions themselves were the catalyst, and significant transactional forces offer support to explain what the new sense of 'Arab identity' could have meant.

While the *amṣār* may have been internally divided by tribal unit,[92] on the wider scale, the *amṣār* constituted cohesive and concentrated population centres distinguished from the indigenous Iraqis.[93] Borrowing Barth's theory, the shared space inside the *amṣār* and the political/spatial differentiation between Conquerors and Iraqis facilitated *amṣār* populations to conceptualise themselves as an immigrant 'us' against the indigenous 'them'. Such recognition of a common sense of 'other' was a novel phenomenon. Prior to the conquests, pre-Islamic Arabian groups had been organised in patterns that atomised communities within Arabia between, for example, Yemeni kingdoms, Ghassān's allies, Ma'addite tribes and mountain pastoralists. Territorial diversity and conflicting interests precluded perception of a single 'other' – the sense of a recognisable 'non-Arabian' 'them' against whom populations could imagine one cohesive Arabian community. Once the varied

Arabian groups left Arabia, on the other hand, they faced, for the first time, a common, conquered 'outsider', both physically and politically placed outside the *amṣār*. As the Conquerors apprehended the novel and shared sense of difference, conditions were primed to begin imagining a newfound collective sense of belonging inside the confines of the *amṣār*. Barth's theories urge due recognition of the dramatic shift in transactions and domicile attendant upon the conquests and their effects on novel communal awareness.

The close-quarter habitation within the *amṣār* could naturally abet the development of shared community between the various ex-Arabian groups on the inside as a practical matter, and moreover, the sense of a shared 'inside' identity was assisted by status and economic factors too. Firstly, the notion of the puritanical *hijra* community with its emphasis on shared monotheism and nominal equality between believers prompts a situation where former differences can be forgotten in the interests of achieving the Qur'anic exhortation to a sense of brotherliness:

> Remember God's favour to you: you were enemies and then He brought your hearts together and you became brothers by His grace; you were about to fall into a pit of Fire and He saved you from it.[94]

Qur'anic equality may be ultimately idealistic, but in the context of early Islam, the *amṣār*-dwellers also possessed unique power and status as Conquerors, which prompted senses of community across the same demographic lines as their religious feelings. Religious aspiration and worldly power accordingly coincided to enable awareness of a common sense of difference from non-Muslim, non-*amṣār*-dwellers which the Arabians never had the opportunity to experience in pre-Islam. And secondly, groups within the *amṣār* possessed shared interests in enjoying the economic fruits of conquest, and, as the beneficiaries of tax from conquered lands and shared spoils from further conquest, the identity of the 'winners' in the new system would be clear, abetting their sense of cohesion as a means to ring fence economic gains.

The conquests therefore laid new boundaries of interaction for ex-Arabian groups in which their domicile, interests and power manifestly aligned towards union against the external, lower-status conquered populations. The novel situation made fertile conditions for the incubation of a new sense of community, shaped around the idea of Conqueror elite. The unprecedented nature of the conquests and their sociopolitical ramifications meant that the transactional boundaries inaugurated a wholly new demographic system and urban networks, and accordingly, we should expect the form of communal consciousness emerging from these circumstances to be novel as well. Transactionist theory thus precisely anticipates the rise of Arabness as a new form of communal organisation. The former circumstances and interrelations of pre-Islamic Arabian groups no longer represented the realities of life imposed by post-conquest settlement, and the various Arabian communities who participated in the conquests would need to react accordingly, conjuring a new paradigm of community reflective of their transformed social status and contexts. Herein we can begin to understand why the senses of 'Arabness' expressed in early Islam lack precedent from the records of pre-Islam: Arab identity was not a legacy from pre-Islamic times, but a new solution for post-conquest questions of self and community.

In the Introduction, however, we noted that transactionist theory on its own does not offer a complete picture of ethnogenesis because transactional boundaries do not always turn into ethnic boundaries. Groups with common economic and political interests do not necessarily obliterate old identities and replace them with new labels for the sake of practical expedience alone. More factors are needed to generate new senses of community, and herein constructivist perspectives suggest that 'cultural stuff' commonalities enable transacting groups to 'feel ethnic' and agree to new identifications. In the case of early Islam, such salient factors can be adduced to explain the sustained construction of a novel 'Arab' kin-community amongst *amṣār* settlers.

Cultural Affinities and Becoming 'Arab'

Developing the spatial analysis of the *amṣār*, the importance of geography extends beyond transactional boundaries and prompts questions of the conceptual aspects of space in forming communal identity. In particular, did cognition of a novel kind of 'home space' within the *amṣār* open possibilities to foster a novel cognition of shared kinship amongst *amṣār* inhabitants?[95] The segregated nature of the *amṣār* populations, the common feeling that the populations had all 'immigrated' into a new home (*hijra*), and the towns' locations outside old population centres seem productive aspects to enhance feelings of both separation from the conquered and communal unity amongst the Conquerors. The *amṣār*-dwellers' adoption of the name 'Emigrants' (*muhājirūn* – discussed presently) implies that a sense of 'moving home' did inform their consciousness of community, and when constructing an identity, therefore, the conceptual and emotional aspects of forgetting pre-conquest homes in favour of the new community is material.

Further pursuing the idea of *hijra* and identity, we need also reiterate that whilst the Conquerors hailed from the region which modern geography terms 'Arabia', it is now established that such an idea of 'Arabia' as a cohesive territorial unit was not an indigenous conception of space, but rather an invention of Greek geographers.[96] We saw in Chapter 1(II) that no pre-Islamic inscriptions outside of Roman *Provincia Arabia* express senses of belonging to 'Arabia' either, and hence we should avoid imposing one value-laden consciousness of 'Arabian-ness' on all Conqueror groups, and instead consider it unlikely that they emerged from their disparate places of origin with a consolidated sense of shared Arabian homeland around which they could imagine their community. This is pertinent since awareness of ancient homeland is usually a potent means to articulate an identity, yet the Conquerors lacked such commonality, and instead their common sense of 'home' was embodied in the their new *hijra* towns. In the absence of a common origin land, the shared sense of *hijra* would doubly embed the symbolic importance of the new space as definitive of their *muhājirūn* identities. Thus, unlike the conquered communities in the Middle East who possessed awareness of long continuity of land occupation which enabled them to articulate independent regional identities,[97] the Conquerors were newcomers, and it could be almost anticipated *ipso facto* that they might seek a novel form of communal expression to maintain cohesion following their expansion into widely spread new lands. The emergence of the hitherto unexpressed form of Arabness in the century after the conquests would seem to coincide with their similarly unprecedented occupation of new space.

The Conquerors also experienced significant linguistic affinities. Not all Arabians spoke one standard language at the dawn of Islam,[98] but the early philologists' discussions of tribal dialects and the research of Arabists today reveals that the Arabians spoke broadly similar dialects (perhaps only the Yemeni were less intelligible to other Arabians).[99] While in pre-Islamic Arabia, the shibboleths and linguistic differences between Arabian groups would have abetted disunity against the background of pre-Islamic political and confessional divides, the mutually cooperative environment of the *amṣār* would highlight linguistic similarity, and the similarity between Arabian languages would rise into unprecedentedly recognisable relief when compared with the emphatically non-Arabian Syriac, Pahlavi and other Iraqi vernaculars outside the *amṣār*'s physical boundaries. The Conquerors' communication with Iraqis would immediately demarcate collective 'non-Iraqi-ness' inside the *amṣār* and enhance cognisance of similarities between Conqueror languages. The change from a competitive pre-Islamic intra-Arabian transactional environment to a cooperative Islamic-era intra-*amṣār* system also permits a different approach to appraising language and identity, leading towards greater awareness of communal affinity between the Arabian dialects. And moreover, close-quarter living in the *amṣār* necessarily catalysed homogenisation of dialect to enable formerly separate groups to speak together on a day-to-day basis, shifting the perception of difference even more starkly outside the *amṣār*'s precincts and fostering a common sense of 'us' around converging vernaculars on the inside.

The Conquerors' shared belief similarly constituted a common difference between *amṣār* settler and indigenous Iraqi. Religions entail a wide array of communal customs – prayer, diet, fasts, ethics and marriage and burial practices – and in the case of first/seventh-century Iraq (where conversion was initially limited outside of the *amṣār*),[100] the dual process of (1) awareness of community engendered by their shared Islam, and (2) the contrasting customs, behaviours and beliefs outside the *amṣār* could accelerate ethnic cohesion within. In the early Muslims' case, even if the first communities were ecumenical and open to other monotheists,[101] the impulse of monotheistic reform embedded in Islam's messages, the emphasis on communal prayer and the communal aspects of most other essential Muslim quotidian practices would rapidly combine to enforce distinctiveness of Muslim communal identity from the different practices and systems of religion in the conquered countryside.

Early Muslims specifically appear to have nurtured the sense of Islam as their community's exclusive property, evidenced in fascinating reports from the hadith of strategies employed to regulate the relationship between Conquerors and conquered. Reading anti-Zoroastrian, anti-Jewish and anti-Christian hadith from the perspective of anthropology illustrates how the process of constructing a religious identity for 'Muslim' influenced senses of ethnos and communal belonging.[102] For example, a hadith in Ibn Abī Shayba's *al-Muṣannaf* reports that the *amṣār* settler Abū Burza ordered the rejection of food (except fruit) gifted by Zoroastrians (*majūs*) on festivals.[103] Rebuffing the gift of food is a powerful symbolic denial of communal ties, and is the type of act ethnographers would expect in a town seeking to segregate itself from other communities to nurture its own exclusive identity.

To relate the hadith to a chronology of settlement and identity construction, there are a number of possible interpretations dependent upon one's vision of early Islam's articulation, but they seem to lead towards similar ends. If Islam was relatively coherent at the outset, the establishment of puritanical *hijra* communities and the rigorous maintenance of boundaries against others are to be expected as part of the very essence of being Muslim. Hence, when Muslim groups faced new circumstances in the post-conquest world where non-Muslim 'outsiders' constituted massive demographic majorities, the need to develop new approaches to maintain segregation would logically arise. The expressions of Arab identity as an exclusive community can thus be related to the process of Muslims settling in a foreign land. If, on the other hand, Donner's notion of ecumenical Islam, which entails that the Conquerors initially welcomed participation from others[104] is correct, the webs of transactional boundaries inaugurated by *amṣār* settlement in which wealth, status and power were monopolised would inexorably harden what may have been earlier openness. As a means to maintain status and to control material privilege, the Conquerors and their descendants would have found it most convenient to redefine the belief structure into a more exclusive confessional community, and the *amṣār*'s demographic segregation makes it easy to draw confessional lines that excluded the masses of Christians, Jews and Zoroastrians in the conquered countryside. A resultant closed-ended sense of 'Arab belonging' again emerges from ring-fencing material gains gathered by early Muslims. Another alternative could relate the expressions of Arabness in the later first/seventh century to the success of the Caliphate as a political institution. By the reign of ʿAbd al-Malik (65–86/685–705), the Caliphate entered a new maturation, permitting its elites to express newfound confidence in the sense of community, consequently breeding increasingly partisan senses of difference and natural drivers to increasingly articulate particularism as apparent in the hadith. The emergence of broad expressions of Arabness as a group identity do also coincide with the era of ᶜAbd al-Malik and the reigns of his successors.

Hence Arab ethnogenesis seems tied to the articulation of Muslim belonging and elite religious identity as the post-conquest Middle East settled into a new political order. The establishment of emotive bonds between Muslim groups to the exclusion of others alongside their shared political and cultural commonalities logically spawned new senses of kinship – which we see in the sources as expressions of Arab community – to cement the basis of Muslim Conqueror community.

Faith, Arab Ethnogenesis and the Caliphate

The cultural commonalities and tangible markers of identity which *amṣār* dwellers could marshal to imagine their community were essentially new, or newly recognised as a consequence of the social changes following the conquests. The 'cultural stuff' commonalities of the Conquerors' faith, language and sense of *amṣār* home also bear relation to the religious system of the Conquerors, and offer explanations as to why they chose the name 'Arab' to express their identity. Given the absence of pre-Islamic evidence of Arab cohesion or self-expression, the Qur'an's references to itself as *Qurʾān ᶜarabī* in a *lisān ᶜarabī*, and the Conquerors' common worship of that *ᶜarabī* Qur'an, coupled with their unique ability (compared to the indigenous Iraqis) to understand its *ᶜarabī* language, promote the name *ᶜarabī* as a focal point of collective difference between Conqueror and Iraqi.[105] Since many Conquerors and many of their leaders were settled peoples in pre-Islam, it is also unlikely that they chose the name 'Arab' from the Bedouin *aᶜrāb* nomenclature, and herein we need reconsider the relationship between nascent Arabness and Arabia's deserts.

It is insightful that the earliest layers of articulating the geographical idea of 'Arabs' land' in Arabic are imprecise. There are at least three terms used to express Arab origin space, *jazīrat al-ᶜarab*, *arḍ al-ᶜarab* and *bilād al-ᶜarab* (literally the Arabs' 'Island', 'Land', or 'Country'), and upon investigation of their citation, these terms seem impossible to subsume as synonymous with one static concept of 'Arabia' as the Peninsula familiar today. The term

'Arabs' Island' (*jazīra*) most closely resembles our current notion of peninsular Arabia, but early layers of texts referencing 'Arabs' land' intriguingly use *arḍ al-ᶜarab*,[106] and jurists' discussions refrain from identifying 'Arabs' land' as the whole Peninsula too, instead restricting it to space redolent with Islam's origins, counting Muhammad's *hijra* city of Medina as the actual place of 'Arabia', or expanding 'Arabia's' ambit to include Mecca and the wider al-Ḥijāz as well.[107] In the light of this book's proposal that senses of Arab identity emerged amongst the early Muslim political elite, the association of 'Arabs' land' with 'Muslim space' around the elites' homeland in al-Ḥijāz is significant, as the second/eighth-century terminology suggests a fusing of Arab with Muslim origins. But by the third/ninth century, the now common [pen]insular term *jazīrat al-ᶜarab* became dominant, and hence again points to a development, whereby the idea of 'Arabia' was expanded outwards to encompass the entire Peninsula, meaning that more groups could share in a common sense of origin space.

The ramifications of conceptualising 'Arab space' intersect with our reconstruction of Arab ethnogenesis: the flux and uncertainty evidenced in defining even the most core component of Arab identity – their putative place origins – suggest that notions of who the Arabs were and from whence Arabs originated were open and reflective of a process of formulation and refinement as membership of Arab communities became clearer. The early jurists who offered diverse conceptions of *arḍ al-ᶜarab* would not have been able to so play with Arabia's boundaries if the term was associated with a definitive sense of place. Since certainty evolved during the progress of Islam's early history, the dawn of Islam was thus not equipped with tidy terminology to allow people to conceptualise Arabness. We cannot take terminology for granted, nor can we impose our own conceptions of value-laden words such as 'Arabia' onto early Arabic terms, nor even assume that early Muslims divided space and ethnicity in the ways we presume today. Terms need historicisation and consideration in relation to Arab ethnogenesis, and in this case, the equation of the 'Arabs' land' with al-Ḥijāz and the territory of Muhammad's early polity underlines that the early sense of Arab origin land was not equated with the wider Peninsula and Bedouin, and instead revolved around a sense of Arab origins in holy territory which memory associated with the land where the *ᶜarabī* Qur'an was first revealed and believed.

The indications prompt consideration that the lexical universe of 'Arab' when first applied to describe a community connects to the religious identity of the Conquerors and their Qur'an's *ᶜarabī* revelation, and not an old attachment to land, Bedouin culture or pre-Islamic community. Hence Arab ethnogenesis is the process by which early Muslim elites in the post-conquest Middle East constructed a sense of kinship from the foundations of the new puritanical community of co-religionists after Muhammad, endorsing Müller's thesis and Gibb's conception that '[a]ll those are Arabs for whom the central fact of history is the mission of Muhammad and the memory of the Arab Empire . . .'[108] Given the connotations of purity in the Qur'anic *ᶜarabī* name, there is a logic in its attractiveness as the label for a religious movement promoting its new faith and empire, but the proposal brings us to the substantial theoretical question of whether religion can explain ethnogenesis. Is faith a glue that can make a confessional community develop ethnic ties? We seek historical precedent where a group of co-religionists from different backgrounds constructed a new name for their community that reflected an ethnic, not purely confessional identity by generating a new genealogy, history and traditions to create an imagined communal cohesion purporting to predate the religious conversion that actually created the community.

The Introduction noted that shared religion does not often of itself prompt ethnogenesis, but analysis of ethnic communities elsewhere in the Late Antique Middle East, particularly the cases of Armenians, West Syrians and perhaps also Jews, offers what seem to be important parallels to understand why Muslims began calling themselves 'Arabs' in historical records at the end of the first/seventh century. Morony's thesis that Late Antique Middle Eastern communal boundaries were primarily sectarian has encountered some obstacles given the evidence of confessional heterogeneity in Syrian and Iraqi towns before Islam where members of theoretically different sects did not seem to know that they should constitute separate communities.[109] But the hardening of confessional boundaries does become visible in some cases by the late sixth century CE, and certainly in the seventh – contemporary with the expression of ethnic Arabness as a distinct community, suggestive that Morony's proposed sectarianism was not innate, but instead was abetted by common circumstances felt between social groups attendant upon the Caliphate's rise. The West Syrian, Armenian and Jewish communities emergent in Late Antiquity shared salient commonalties of being communities with a distinct religious creed, yet lacking political independence and state institutions.[110] Their status was precarious, old imperial favours upon which they had relied were cleft from them, and clerical groups stepped into the vacuum to provide institutions and discourses which enabled the communities to redefine themselves as ethnic groups. As Haar Romeny's major project on the West Syrians reveals, the expression of confessional identities in increasingly cohesive ethnic terms was a potent force that enabled the communities to not only survive, but to establish a sense of community in the face of their unstable and fluid sociopolitical contexts.[111]

The situation of early Muslims was commensurately precarious. They possessed power, but their wide conquests spread their numbers extremely thinly, and they lacked established institutions to impose a uniform order at the outset. From a practical perspective, early Muslims can be expected to wish to maintain their wealth and status by keeping the venture of Islam on track, but their varied geographical backgrounds and origins offered scant common traditions of symbolic capital around which the disparate communities could rally. They were rich, however, in symbolic capital emanating from their new faith, and under the specific transactional circumstances conducive to generating new senses of belonging in the post-conquest Middle East, their shared faith and experience as Conqueror elite coincided to mobilise Islam as an attractive asset to make the newly formed post-conquest elite community feel tangible and give them a more solid sense of cohesion. Early Islam lacked a clergy, but it could compensate with a religiously legitimated form of leadership: the Caliphate and its self-titled 'Commander of the Faithful' (*amīr al-muʾminīn*). The Caliphate can be seen as fostering Arab identity creation as part of cementing its Muslim identity. Islam was thus not created by Arabs, but rather a sense of Arabness emerged from the particular shape of Umayyad Islam – or more specifically the Marwanid Islam articulated in the later first/seventh century (since the first perceptible swelling of expressions of Arab belonging in poetry correspond with the Marwanid-Umayyad caliphs).

The early Muslims would thus define Arabness in their own image – a religious and linguistic marker of the political elite. But when we pursue the model of ethnogenesis, we are reminded that the process of forging an 'Arab' identity from the circumstances of the post-conquest Middle East would necessarily be uneven: different Muslim groups possessed varied pre-Islamic identities, and the will to unite under a homogenous Muslim/Arab community faced obstacles given that power seems initially to have been monopolised by groups operating under the name Maᶜadd. The persistence of Maᶜadd in early Islamic-era poetry (see Chapter 2(IV)) indicates that Ma'addite particularism remained important, and its expression in poems specifically addressed to caliphs and the ruling elite seems to imply that becoming 'Arab' rubbed uneasily with the initial order and may have impinged upon Maᶜadd's political monopoly.[112] Accordingly, Arabness will have had a fitful start as it was mobilised to reorganise groups in the Caliphate, and its interaction with political forces becomes inevitable.

Very wide questions now emerge in need of closer study. How did individual groups 'become Arab', what happened to identities such as Maᶜadd, did other new identities rival the uptake of Arab consciousness, and what was the role of the Caliphate in persuading its elites to call themselves Arabs? This book's primary purpose of studying the idea of the Arab and the development of Arab imagined communities will need to leave particular group identities to the side for reasons of space, and it must move beyond Islam's first century too, in order to demonstrate how the 'Arab' idea changed its faces during subsequent centuries as the identity was 'renewed and maintained', but in order to better grasp the Umayyad 'formation'[113] stage of Arabness, we shall want to demonstrate the accordance of theory with textual and other historical evidence.

Analysis so far has significant crossovers with Donner's articulation of Islam's early identity, as Donner dates the decisive shift towards redefining the 'Believers movement' into a 'Muslim' exclusive confessional identity to the reign of ᶜAbd al-Malik (65–86/685–705),[114] which corresponds with the rise of self-expressed Arabs in the poetry composed during the period of ᶜAbd al-Malik's successors. ᶜAbd al-Malik's legacies also included the imposition of the Arabic language on the Caliphate's administration, and given *ᶜarabī*'s connotations of purity, it would seem an apt nomenclature if he was indeed attempting to reorient the Caliphate around the notion of a particularly narrow puritanical community. The drive to centralise the state and promote a specifically 'Muslim' identity of Caliphal institutions coincide remarkably well with the first expressions of Arab communal belonging, pointing to the confessional aspect of the early sense of Arab community. Donner is ambivalent as to whether the rise of 'Muslim' identity was a top-down design from the Caliphate, or whether the wider society compelled the caliph to rearticulate Islam in its new guise (he tends to privilege the role of the state):[115] and into the debate, our suggestions here would propose that the underlying society ought not be overlooked. Transactional boundaries and the circumstances of managing post-conquest society on a localised basis seemed to have been poised to prompt Arabness to emerge in early Islam as a symbol of power and as a reaction to the radical otherness of conquered populations. From ᶜAbd al-Malik's caliphate onwards, state and society were aligned to redefine their identities and create a new sense of exclusive community in which the powerful ideas of 'Arab' and 'Muslim' were articulated together.[116]

From Emigrant to Arab: Community and Changing Names in Nascent Islam

Turning from theory to texts, we are not blessed with a wealth of material securely datable to the first generations of Islam, but a mixture of papyri, Greek and Syriac records, and Arabic hadith in pre-canonical collections permit pertinent glimpses into a variegated period of naming the Conquerors. Communal identity in Islam's first century emerges as a complex, changing array of ideas as Conquerors negotiated the major sociopolitical changes, and this section explores strategies employed to articulate senses of self, paying particular attention to Ibn Abī Shayba's (d. 235/849) *al-Muṣannaf*, the largest pre-canonical hadith collection which, because it was only recently published in a reliable format, has yet to receive due analysis as a trove of conflicting snapshots (some of which were supressed, ignored or rewritten in later collections) into early Islam.[117]

Documentary sources and non-Arabic texts often refer to the Conquerors as Saracens or *Ṭayyāyē*, a continuation of the nomenclature Greek and Syriac writers employed to describe Arabians before Islam. My searches of non-Arabic sources written during the first decades of Islam have not uncovered reference to 'Arab' at this early period, tallying with the only gradual emergence of 'Arab' in Umayyad-era poetry. Hence all available evidence indicates that 'Arab' was not used during the initial period of conquests. Instead, as alluded above, the Conquerors called themselves *muhājirūn* (Emigrants), in reference to their religiously motivated migration (*hijra*) during the conquests and settlement in the *amṣār*. Patricia Crone and Ilkka Lindstedt demonstrate the wide application of the words *hijra* and *muhājirūn* in early Arabic hadith to refer to the identity of the Conquerors,[118] and their findings are supported in non-Arabic writings from Islam's first century too, since we frequently encounter references to the terms *Mhaggrāyē* in Syriac and *Magaritai* in Greek. These terms were not used previously to describe Arabians, and are therefore Greek and Syriac approximations of the word *muhājirūn* which Greek and Syriac speakers presumably heard the Conquerors calling themselves.[119]

The name *Mhaggrāyē*/*muhājirūn*/Emigrants can be appreciated as more apt than 'Arab' as a means for the first Conquerors to identify themselves. At the dawn of Islam, Arabians did not possess a tradition of recognising broad kinship via the idea of Arabness: developing such a sense of kinship takes several generations of close-quarter living and shared experiences, and before such processes matured, it is logical that Muslims could interpret their identity through the idea of emigration. Their migrations, conquests and settlement of new towns were *hijras*, the Qur'an relates multiple exhortations to 'emigrate in the way of God' (*hijra fī sabīl Allāh*), and emigration from former communities to Muslim settlement was the marker of perfected belief.[120] For examples of early references to *muhājirūn*, readers are directed to Crone and Lindstedt; in order to illustrate the role of the term as a sense of communal identity and Arab ethnogenesis, we can relate an example from Ibn Abī Shayba's *al-Muṣannaf* in the context of rules of combatting non-Muslims:

> [f]irst invite the people to Islam, and if they comply, do not fight them and accept them. Then invite them to move from their abode (*dārihim*) to the Abode of the Emigrants (*dār al-muhājirīn*) and inform them that if they move, they will have the rights and obligations of the *muhājirūn*, but if they refuse and chose to stay in their land, tell them that they will be like the Bedouin of the Muslims (*aʿrāb al-muslimīn*, and God's judgment for the Believers (*muʾminīn*) will apply to them.[121]

The hadith imparts that *muhājirūn* applies to the broad notion of Conqueror communities, and the hadith's terminology delineates community and space along confessional lines, revealing the response of a group of conquering Qur'an believers to manage territorial expansion. This emerges from the hadith's distinguishing of believers into two classes: (1) Emigrant/*muhājirūn* (the preferred) and, (2) *aʿrāb* and others (lower, but expressly Muslim), which replicates the Qur'an's own binary distinction of full Believers (*muʾminūn*) and lower-status *aʿrāb al-muslimīn*,[122] but with the slight modification of using the term of *muhājirūn* to connote full-status believer, a predictable development considering the extensive emigration across the Fertile Crescent after the Qur'an's revelation. The hadith's spatial connotations invoke the sense of 'inside' via the 'abode' (*dār*) of the Emigrants.[123] Later Arabic writings define 'believers' and their 'inside' space via the idea 'Islam' (*Muslim*, *dār al-Islām*), so Ibn Abī Shayba's hadith both evidences that the confessional outlook of identity and space was established early in the Conquerors' communal development, but terminology was not static. The way of describing a believer (and hence perhaps the composition of believer society too) was the subject of reinterpretation that initially began with *hijra*-based ways of thinking about Conqueror identity, but developed into new terminology in subsequent generations.[124]

The change is signalled by the disappearance of reference to *Magaritai*/*Mhaggrāyē* in Greek and Syriac writings during the eighth century and the contemporary narrowing ambit of the meaning of *muhājirūn* in Arabic literature to connote Muslims during Muhammad's early prophecy only, and we can relate the shift away from the use of *hijra* terminology in defining Conqueror identity to the development of the Conqueror communities themselves. The *amṣār* rapidly prospered as the new administrative centres of the Caliphate, and by the second half of the first/seventh century, the original *muhājirūn* and their children had good reason to settle and enjoy the fruits of the conquests. Furthermore, the rate of conquest slowed after the initial outburst between 632 and 650 CE, so Muslims had less opportunity to establish new *hijra* communities elsewhere in any event. The descendants of the first conquering *muhājirūn* were therefore becoming rooted, but at the same time, local/conquered peoples were beginning to convert to Islam and to move into the *amṣār*. These Iraqi converts could accordingly call themselves *muhājirūn* when they took residence in the *amṣār*, and so perfect their new faith, and this provoked a difficult status issue. If *hijra*/physical emigration was the mark of perfected belief, an Iraqi convert–emigrant technically possessed a higher-rank faith than original Conquerors' sons who never left their *miṣr*/hometown and thus never actually performed a *hijra* themselves. There was manifest disadvantage for the Conquerors' scion in having to surrender privilege to new converts on the basis of a technical notion of *hijra*, and so downplaying *hijra* becomes a key tool for Conqueror elites to maintain power.[125] Decoupling *hijra* from religious standing consequently entails that the collective name *muhājirūn* would need to disappear too: cue its disappearance from historical records in the second/eighth century.

When the word *muhājirūn* no longer operated terminologically to uphold the status of Conqueror elites, they would need a new name. One may think that *muslim* or *muʾmin* (believer) would do, but such names also entailed power concessions since conversion was technically open to new peoples. *Muʾmin* perhaps already had overly broad connotations of monotheist–believer which would fail to differentiate the high-status Conquerors from the massive majority of monotheists they encountered in the conquered countryside of Iraq, Syria and elsewhere,[126] and since conversion was theoretically open to new peoples, *muslim* did not offer a means to distinguish the Conquerors either. The major changes which communities experienced during Islam's first generations rendered such Qur'anic terms connoting 'belief' somewhat archaic as a practical means to conceptualise society. Since the Prophet's early first/seventh-century fledgling community in al-Ḥijāz lacked a prosperous homeland and needed new recruits/believers to establish itself, it was initially expedient for the Qur'an to impose no ethnic restrictions on membership, but by the later first/seventh century, Conquerors possessed a powerful and lucrative domain which they can be expected to not wish to share with 'neophyte' converts. Hence the Conqueror elites needed a different paradigm from the notions of identity expressed during Muhammad's lifetime, and herein we can grasp how confessional and material interests conjoined to prompt calls for a more closed-ended notion of community in order to ring-fence Conqueror status. I suggest the impetus to choose 'Arab' gained momentum at this point of imperial consolidation.

The hypothesis that *ʿarabī* only gained traction as a term of identity once the Caliphate had substantially matured is borne by the meaning of Qur'anic *ʿarabī* and its linguistic idea of pure revelation which could not have been a natural choice for an ethnonym at the dawn of Islam, especially since *muhājirūn* terminology so precisely encapsulated Conqueror activity and identity in the first generation. The crisis in power relations, wrought by the dwindling pace of conquest and the mixing of convert populations within the *amṣār* during the late first/seventh century, on the other hand, offer the sort of catalyst necessary to transform Qur'anic Arabness from koine to kin, from language to an ethnos. The Arabness idea had manifest practical potential for ethnogenesis because it tied language and religion together. Arabness qua Muslim Arabic speaker constructs barriers to entry greater than conversion alone can surmount. New Iraqi convert immigrants into the *amṣār* could become Muslim by professing faith in God and the Prophet, but they could not easily adopt the 'Arab' linguistic traits, and hence the post-conquest status quo could be maintained. A hadith from Ibn Abī Shayba's collection (never repeated elsewhere, according to my searches) offers intriguing corroboration. It instructs:

> If buried treasure (*kanz*) is found in the Abode of the Enemy (*dār al-ᶜaduw*) then it will be taxed as war spoils. If it is found in the Abode of the Arabs (*dār al-ᶜarab*), it will be liable to *zakāt* [tax].[127]

Leaving aside the niche taxation questions and focusing on the hadith's terminology, we perceive that the binary division of space does not permit interpretation of *dār al-ᶜarab* as 'Arabia', rather, it is in the insider space of a militarised community. *Dār al-ᶜarab*'s resonance with the terms *dār al-hijra* and *dār al-Islām* to signify what we now conceptualise as 'Muslim land' engenders the interpretation that the *dār al-ᶜarab* 'Arab Space' was confessionally delineated, that is, 'Arab' was synonymous with 'believer'.

We lack conclusively dated texts to determine whether the term *dār al-muhājirīn* predates the *dār al-ᶜarab* spatial nomenclature to express the inside of Conqueror community, but given that the early non-Arabic sources call the Conquerors *Mhaggrāyē* and never 'Arab', and that the Conquerors did not express their identity as 'Arab' either, it seems that the *dār al-ᶜarab* terminology was a later graft of the 'Arab' ethnonym onto the concept of Muslim elite community, marking one of the early steps in transforming the memories of early Islam into 'Arab history'. Both *ᶜarab* and *muhājir* are derived from the Qur'an's lexicon,[128] hence we can see scripture and a conviction of Muslim identity was the source for names, and the sociopolitical circumstances of Islam's first centuries offer reasons to understand the beginning of 'Arab' ethnogenesis, but the first generation of Conquerors were not yet Arab and their conquests were not 'Arab conquests'. The term '*Muhājirūn* conquest' seems apt:[129] *muhājir* terminology informed the initial choice for a name to forge a sense of Conqueror identity amongst the disparate pre-Islamic populations who participated in the conquests.

The process by which the Conquerors navigated the possibilities of Arab community as a replacement for their old allegiances appears protracted and complicated by the absence of a well-articulated sense of Arabness from pre-Islam.[130] Imagining the Arab had no one 'right' answer in early Islam, and this proposed novelty and consequent ambiguity of Arabness helps us grasp the substance of the hadith we saw above from Ibn Abī Shayba's *al-Muṣannaf*: 'Recite the Qur'an Arabic-ly (*aᶜribū al-Qurʾān*), for it is Arabic (*ᶜarabī*). You must act like Maᶜadd because you are Ma'addites (*wa-tamaᶜdadū fa-innakum maᶜaddiyyūn*).'[131] The hadith interprets Qur'anic Arabness as we have here – something Arabic to itself and separate from a people's sense of community. For so long as Maᶜadd retained its pre-Islamic status as a term uniting certain Arabian populations, 'Arab' would not have traction. The fact that the hadith feels the need to expressly distinguish the two, however, tellingly discloses that some Ma'addites were shifting towards Arabness and away from the sense of their old identity, merging with non-Ma'addites in the process, and prompting a rift within Ma'addite community. We shall see that other references to *ᶜarab* in Ibn Abī Shayba's *al-Muṣannaf* add further gloss to early Islam's Arabness negotiation.

In further indication that *ᶜarabī* first circulated as a term for the Qur'an's idiom and not a community, hadith generally do not employ *ᶜarabī* in an ethnic sense. For example, to explore the narrative context of the above Maᶜadd hadith further, it is reported in *al-Muṣannaf*'s section 'Virtues of the Qur'an' (*Faḍāʾil al-Qurʾān*) where it is preceded by two shorter hadith (one from the Prophet's authority and frequently cited elsewhere) exhorting Muslims to 'Recite the Qur'an Arabic-ly (*aᶜribū al-Qurʾān*)', and it is followed by a hadith ascribed to the Qur'an reader Ubayy ibn Kaᶜb that reads: 'Learn Arabic (*taᶜallamū al-ᶜarabiyya*) as you must learn to memorise the Qur'an.'[132] Herein, Muslims are depicted as non-natural *ᶜarabī* speakers, supportive of the notion that 'Arabic' was not originally conceived as an 'ethnolect', but was a more restricted koine. This message repeats in the section's following thirteen hadith. They strongly censure solecism (*laḥn*), urging people to learn solecism (presumably to avoid it, such that they can recite the Qur'an with the due purity signified by the Qur'an's *ᶜarabī* nature), and report that the Caliphs ᶜUmar and ᶜUthmān exhorted proper Arabic reading of the Qur'an, and mentioning that the language of Heaven is *al-ᶜarabiyya.*[133] Only in the section's last hadith (30548) is there a reference to an Arabic person (*rajul ᶜarabī*) who can act as an authority on the reading of the Qur'an, but elsewhere there are express remarks that even members of Quraysh do not always perform the Qur'an with due Arabic-ness (30540, 30541, 30543, 30544).

Ibn Abī Shayba's selection mirrors the Qur'an's own discourse: the Qur'an is 'Arabic' and people are classified as something else. Notions trumpeted in fourth/tenth-century grammatical texts that the early Muslims did not make mistakes in their Arabic or that Bedouin speak proper Arabic[134] are absent in the early third/ninth-century *al-Muṣannaf*'s section on *Faḍāᵓil al-Qurᵓān* where Arabic emerges as pure and focused on the Qur'an, not a characteristic of people or property of ethnic identity (perhaps herein is the origin of the idea that people in Heaven speak Arabic because 'Arabic' (*al-ᶜarabiyya*) was believed to signify a pure idiom not sullied by this world). Only the final hadith in *al-Muṣannaf*'s section indicates that Arabness can be inherent in a person, which could be interpreted as the 'last word' on the matter, but it is interesting that Ibn Abī Shayba could not muster other hadith exhorting people to consult 'Arabs' on the Qur'an (or more hadith praising historical figures for their Arabness), which is in keeping with the sparse reference to *ᶜarabī* and *al-ᶜarab* in *al-Muṣannaf* generally. When Ibn Abī Shayba relates hadith containing words ascribed to the Prophet himself (*ḥadīth marfūᶜ*), Muhammad almost invariably calls his community 'my/this *umma*' (religious community/people). Reference to the first Believers as an *umma* and not *al-ᶜarab* replicates the Qur'an's depiction of righteous community as a prophet-led *umma* without expressed ethnic (and never *ᶜarabī*) boundaries.[135] Hadith containing messages and terminology that harmonise with the Qur'an appear good candidates to reflect genuine worldviews held in nascent Islam, as an earlier study I conducted on the history of the Hajj argues,[136] and the dearth of any reference to kin-based Arab community in each of the Qur'an, the majority of hadith, pre-Islamic and very early Islamic-era poetry, and documentary sources seem to underline the absence of specifically Arab communal expression in Islam's first generations.

As additional indication that the early interpretation of the Qur'an's *ᶜarabī* was directed towards notions of purity and monotheism, and not kin–ethnic identity, we can consider the word *ḥanīfiyya* where it is used as an apparent synonym for *ᶜarabī* in some early sources. We saw at the outset of this chapter that the Qur'an invokes *ḥanīfiyya* to express the idea of 'pure monotheism', and in a few scattered anecdotes in very early Arabic literature, there are remarkable references to the Arabic language itself as *al-ḥanīfiyya*. For example, Ibn al-Kalbī's (d. 204/819 or 206/821) *Ansāb al-khayl* refers to Ishmael as the first speaker of 'the pure/true Arabic (*al-ᶜarabiyya al-ḥanīfiyya*) in which God revealed His Qur'an to His Prophet'. The interrelation of *al-ᶜarabiyya* and *al-ḥanīfiyya* points to the genesis of Arabness from a religious ideal of purity and monotheism, and specifically the 'language of pure monotheism'. Ibn Abī Shayba also narrates a terminologically charged hadith: 'Muḥammad ibn Saᶜd ibn Abī Waqqāṣ heard people speaking Persian [*al-fārisiyya*], and he exclaimed: "Why is it that [they speak] Majian [*al-majūsiyya*] instead of the Pure Language [*al-ḥanīfiyya*]!?"'[137]

Here we have an express link between language, religion and sense of community, similarly invoking *al-ḥanīfiyya* in place of *al-ᶜarabiyya*. In this period before language standardisation, the Conqueror's special koine leans towards conceptualisation as 'the clear tongue' of revelation, and not 'Arabic' as the ethnolect of 'the Arabs'.

Al-ḥanīfiyya is not, to my knowledge, reported as a linguistic adjective in Arabic literature after the second/eighth century, which again accords with our proposed model of Arab ethnogenesis inasmuch as the Qur'an's Arabness would have been interpretable as meaning monotheistic purity only in a time before Arabness was commonly equated with a particular ethnos. Once peoples began to call themselves Arabs and argued to conceptualise Islam as their proprietary religion, open-ended terms such as *al-ḥanīfiyya* lost useful purpose. In the wake of a transformation of Muslim community from faith to kin, *al-ḥanīfiyya* would be discarded, and its disappearance in later Arabic writings indicates this was the case.

The hadith corpus further supports our interpretation that the few hadith which are ascribed to Muhammad and which do expressly mention 'Arabs' as a people have issues of authenticity, suggestive that during Muhammad's lifetime the ethnic associations of Arabness were not established, and that later hands tampered with the hadith to forge an anachronistic sense of ethnic Arabness around the Prophet. Scholars have noted the apparent forgery of such hadith: for example, Aḥmad Shākir roundly rejects the authenticity of several pro-Arab hadith statements, noting their variance with the 'tenor of Prophetic hadith', and relating negative opinions which hadith scholars expressed about the credibility of the narrators of such traditions.[138] Hadith containing references to *al-ᶜarab* in Ibn Abī Shayba's *al-Muṣannaf* are similarly suspect: many are weak, either *mursal* (ascribed to Muhammad, but not narrated by people contemporary with him) or simply *ḍaᶜīf* (weak).[139] In other cases, narrators seem to have taken hadith where Muhammad referred to his community as *al-nās* (the people) or *umma*, and replaced those ethnically neutral words with *al-ᶜarab*.[140] 'Arab' does not emerge as a word familiarly associated with Muhammad.

The process of inserting Arabness into the hadith may have gained particular momentum during the caliphate of ᶜUmar ibn ᶜAbd al-ᶜAzīz (r. 99–101/717–20). A wide array of hadith in *al-Muṣannaf* expressly mentioning *al-ᶜarab* is actually ascribed to ᶜUmar ibn ᶜAbd al-ᶜAzīz himself, not Muhammad,[141] and ᶜUmar's caliphate was contemporary with the generation when poets such as al-Farazdaq, Jarīr and al-Rāᶜī began to cite *al-ᶜarab* as a collective in the way Maᶜadd pervades earlier poetry. ᶜUmar's biography is also noted as an important watershed in the management of intra-communal relations regarding the original Conquerors and subsequent converts, as the Caliph appears to have defended tax rights of non-Arabians (*mawālī*), while also enacting discriminatory policies to maintain the superiority of the original Conqueror groups.[142] ᶜUmar's reign was one generation removed from the end of the most extensive conquests (and hence the end of new *hijra* possibilities for the Conquerors), and ᶜUmar's reign also followed less than two decades after ᶜAbd al-Malik's imposition of Arabic as the official language of the Caliphate. ᶜUmar coincides with the period when transactional boundaries in the *amṣār* were blurring, when *hijra* lost its efficacy to delineate the Conqueror elite, and it would be a propitious moment for the Conquerors to seek a new form of exclusive identity, building on the efforts of ᶜAbd al-Malik in the previous two decades to construct the imperial identity of Islam's polity, and it seems not coincidental that we find increasing references to *al-ᶜarab* in poetry and hadith connected with this period.

Documentary sources also proffer signs to date articulations of Arabness. The earliest documentary references to 'Arab' after the advent of Islam appear in references to the calendar. Whereas an Arabic papyrus in 42/662 refers to the reckoning of years as *qaḍāʾ al-muʾminīn* (the jurisdiction of the Believers, not 'Arabs' – and there is similar reference in a papyrus from 57/677),[143] also in 42/662 a Greek building inscription at Hammat Gader (Gadara) refers to *kata arabas* (years of the Arabs).[144] References to 'years of the Arabs' also appear in Nessana entagion (papyrus receipts usually for tax) from the mid-670s (for example, *P. Ness.* 60–7);[145] however, seventh century Syriac writers refer to time reckoning in terms of 'years of the *Mhaggrāyē*'s power', in keeping with the usual *hijra*-based term Syriac sources use to describe the Conquerors.[146] The conquests' effect to change the reckoning of time shows the speed in which the Conquerors imposed their authority (and the change in the basis for reckoning time reveals the evidently effective and assertive form of that authority), but the sharing of nomenclature between *Arabas*, *Mhaggrāyē*, and *muʾmin* (in Arabic) is an interesting array perhaps indicative of regional differences in the ways the Conquerors were perceived (or projected themselves). That mid-first/seventh-century Conquerors refer to time via *īmān* and not *hijra* is very significant, for if *hijra* was ongoing during the first/seventh century (as argued herein), the significance and finality of Muhammad's *hijra* would not have been as apparent as it would in a post-*hijra* world one generation later, and hence Muhammad's *hijra* would not logically present itself as the decisive calendric reference point. Terminological flux is evident, and seventh-century documentary sources reveal no thorough Arabness expression, akin to early Arabic texts.

It is also material that the shift to labelling Conquerors as 'Arabs' in non-Arabic records rises in the eighth century CE, for example the Greek language Papyrus 1375 dated to 711 CE refers to 'Arabs and Christians', using *Araboi* as synonymous with Muslim,[147] and the earliest non-Arabic literary texts of which I am aware that refer to Muslims as 'Arabs' (and not as *Ṭayyāyē*, Saracens or *Mhaggrāyē*) are the *Chronicle* of Jacob of Edessa,[148] the Spanish *Chronicle of 754* and the Syriac *Chronicle of Zuqnin* written *c.*774–5 CE. The appearance of 'Arab' in these texts after the centuries' long tradition in Greek, Latin and Syriac of referring to Arabian populations as *Sarakenoi*, *Saraceni* and *Ṭayyāyē* implies the impetus for terminological change came from outside the Syriac and Greek communities, and stems instead from the 'Arabs' themselves, indicative of an increasingly self-aware community of Conquerors expressing their identity in 'Arab' terms only from the end of the first/seventh century.[149]

Our present theory of Arab ethnogenesis invites a revival of another earlier study of Arabness in early Islam. When examining the hadith corpus, Suleiman Bashear revealed that hadith containing references to 'Arabs' were forged in the second/eighth century, and he concluded that the very first generation of Muslims did not think of themselves as 'Arabs' or their faith as an 'Arab religion'.[150] Bashear was inspired by late twentieth-century radical critiques of Islam's origins, and he interpreted the initial absence of Arabness as as indication that 'Arabs' captured Islam from its original Judaic believers and grafted themselves onto its early history by fabricating hadith to make themselves appear to be Islam's 'chosen race'.[151] The theory that Islam emerged as a fringe Judaic group is now less tenable, and Bashear did not consider theoretical questions of community formation in early Islam, implicitly assuming, like others, that 'the Arabs' long existed as a cohesive ethnos in pre-Islam. But our study both deconstructs the primordialist paradigm by introducing the lens of ethnogenesis to read the material, and also searches for references to Arabness in a wider array of sources (Bashear limited himself to hadith and exegesis). In so doing, we can now recognise that what Bashear's extensive analysis revealed to be the novel appearance of *al-ᶜarab* in hadith is also mirrored in poetry and other sources, and we can relate all of these textual Arabisations to the gradual development of Conqueror society into an Arab guise.

We have, therefore, uncovered a crucial process whereby early second/eighth-century Muslims were imagining themselves as Arabs and projected their novel Arabness onto their own past. We can thus reorient Bashear's findings: 'Arabs' did not wrest Islam from someone else; rather, the sudden appearance of Arabs in hadith and the fabrications to portray Muhammad as an 'Arab' Prophet stem from the Muslim elite's growing consciousness of their own 'Arab' identity in the later first/seventh century. The novel expressions of Arabness are not the result of second/eighth-century 'Arabs' converting to Islam, but are instead the product of a century of ethnogenesis during which Muslims reconceptualised their own identity into Arabness.

Once Muslim elites began to call themselves Arabs, they were compelled to manipulate hadith in order to forge a new vision of the history of earlier, nascent Islam that conformed to their present, more matured Muslim imagined community. Our analysis of poetry and ethnogenesis, coupled with Bashear's work with hadith and exegesis point to the turn of the first/seventh and second/eighth centuries as the period when we can first meaningfully speak about actual communities of Arabs in the Middle East.

Arabness in Early Second/Eighth-Century Iraq: Between Unity and Fragmentation

Arabness as a self-reference for the Muslim elite thus gained ground in the later first/seventh century, and, like identities in other parts of the world, there was no grand entrance of Arabs onto the world stage, but only a gradual swelling of consent amongst the Conquerors to express their elite status around Arabness. The process developed distinctly 'ethnic' trappings of identity to wrap around groups of early Muslims, and resembles similar processes of entrenching confessional identities in ethnic guises amongst other groups in the post-conquest Middle East.[152] Analysis thus confronts the impression that the conquests inaugurated reciprocal forces by which groups maintained communal boundaries by a mixture of faith and ethnos in a pronounced fashion, implying that the Conquerors' transformation of their confessional identity into ethnic 'Arabness' marked a seminal, if not paradigmatic change across Middle Eastern communities.

Hence, post-conquest Iraq was a place where 'interest in pre-Islamic Arabian history crystallized . . . as an historiographical theme' and tribal genealogies were developed into new family trees that tied formerly disparate groups into 'Arab families' which were projected backwards into pre-Islamic times, not as an exercise of historical curiosity, but as an act of communal legitimisation.[153] The emergence of self-designated 'Arabs' in the second/eighth and third/ninth centuries indicate that Arab ethnogenesis was a real and successful process stemming from the particular conditions of post-conquest social boundaries, but the process of articulating one new 'Arab community' to unite Conqueror groups also faced opposing forces threatening fragmentation. This chapter has emphasised the crucial ethnogenic factors that nudged 'Arab' towards ethnic connotation, but we do not find documentary or poetic sources with expressions of monolithic Arab identities even by the end of the Umayyads, and this chapter accordingly closes with observations of the factors that prevented Arab identity from becoming more completely articulated within the early Caliphate.

Arabness' connection with the power and status of the Conqueror community rendered it sensitive to fissures within the empire's elites. The conquests nurtured awareness of unity, but the Conquerors had not been unified before Islam, and Muslims thus contended both with legacies of pre-Islamic fissures and new ruptures amongst competing elite groups. Each marshalled different constructions of history and faith to jockey for position,[154] and regarding the path of Arab ethnogenesis, the pluralities disrupted Arabness' smooth process towards one cohesive idea as multiple groups rewrote the past in different guises.

The power structure into which Arabness was articulated was not only divided by differing group allegiances and competition over the spoils of conquest, but it was also violently contested, as witnessed in the four or five major conflicts (*fitna*) between 35/655 and 132/750 alongside the difficult experimentation to develop a form of authoritative political leadership. Whilst hindsight sees the Caliphate as the 'natural' embodiment of Muslim sovereignty, the first 150 years of Muslim history involved the process of inventing the Caliphate as a form of governance which initially lacked an established tradition to legitimate itself.[155] The Umayyad inability to centralise power, even by the end of their era,[156] makes it difficult to generalise about pan-Muslim unities in the early period, including a cohesive notion of Arabness.

In the absence of consistent central, unifying leadership, the *fitnas* exacerbated awareness of difference between Conquerors that manifested in regionalism and tribalism: two alternative forms of identity evident in the historical record. Regionalism was relevant to the Iraqi milieu, as Iraqis often competed with the Umayyad caliphal centre in Syria (al-Shām), and the respective elites embraced territorial nomenclature of *ahl al-Shām* (People of Syria) and *ahl al-ᶜIraq* (People of Iraq) which feature in the record of their interactions since the first *fitna* of 36–40/656–61,[157] epitomised in a statement recorded in Abū ᶜUbayda's *al-Naqāʾiḍ* in which the Iraqi Qutayba ibn Muslim exhorts his followers against the (Syrian) Caliph Sulaymān:

> Oh people of Iraq, consider my lineage . . . by God you will find me to be an Iraqi, son of an Iraqi; al-Shām is a father obeyed, Iraq is a father disobeyed, for how long will you let the People of al-Shām luxuriate in your houses?[158]

Qutayba refers lineage to Iraqi space, not Arab genealogy, and such sentiments are logical if we consider that notions of Arab unity would be otiose for Iraqi belligerents as any sense of community that implied unity under Umayyad caliphs manifestly benefitted their rivals in al-Shām. The expression of political organisation in terms of regional factions in the early Islamic period is not merely a device of later Arabic historians – Haldon and Kennedy have demonstrated the power of regionalism as a device to maintain ruling structures, economic privilege and elite identity in both the pre-Islamic and early Islamic periods.[159]

Akin to regionalist identities, *ᶜaṣabiyya* (rivalries articulated on kin-group/tribal lines) couched in terms of the collectives Yamān, Maᶜadd, Muḍar/Nizār/Qays and Rabīᶜa added layers of politicised identity across the Caliphate in competition with pan-Islamic Arabness. These tribal groups may not have been fully cohesive political parties,[160] but the emphasis on tribal lore, contested genealogies and the masses of Umayyad-era poetry in which struggles even between subtribes appear as serious sociopolitical matters, indicate that tribal rivalries were disruptive forces against the articulation of one unified Arabness. To speak of the first generations of Islam in totalising terms of 'Arab history' imposes a unity which the fledgling Caliphate never enjoyed.

While division is the most obvious ramification of conflict, conflict also facilitates new forms of solidarity as groups find strength in unity and marshal identities as a means to alleviate conflict and gel truces into more lasting peace. The repeated conflicts of early Islam therefore ultimately (and perhaps haltingly) fostered the unifying power of Arabness to resolve *fitna* and centralise power. Arabic literary sources contain indications that towards the end of the Umayyad period narratives of 'Arab history' were being employed as a means to unify opposition to the Umayyads: the narratives isolated the Syrian Arabs, but unified the Arab Muslim elites in other parts of the Caliphate.[161] Also tied with politics, the creation of the state stipends to every 'Arab' (*dīwān al-ᶜaṭā*) suggests the central authority's attempt to forge unity and consent by appealing to a sense of Muslim Arabness amongst the Conquerors and their kin.[162] We should, however, consider the possibilities of retrospective 'Arabisation' of the stipend system too, as some records indicate it was initially paid on the basis of *hijra*, not Arabness,[163] which would be in keeping with our findings in the last section that *muhājir* pre-dated *ᶜarabī* as a means to organise the Muslim elite. Early hadith-style opinions about *ᶜaṭā* stipend do not often expressly refer to Arabs, and it is perhaps a legacy of the traditional assumptions about pre-Islamic Arab communal cohesion that stoke the belief that the caliphs initiated the system as part of the Arab *Staatsnation*. By the reign of ᶜUmar ibn ᶜAbd al-ᶜAzīz, the *ᶜaṭā* may have been converted to a specifically Arab right, but it is not clear that the earlier caliphs defined it in such an ethnic manner.

We thus enter the second/eighth century with a convoluted communal map of the Middle East. Previously divided Arabian groups had banded together under a religious creed with a militarised outlook that exhorted expansion and settlement. The creed was centred on a sacred Arabic/'pure' book, and its adherents were multi-ethnic, but as they concentrated in new towns where shared power, wealth, language and creed created fecund transactional boundaries to nurture ethnogenesis, they began to rethink their identities towards a more uniform Arabness. They were imagining a community, an Arab community, but their imaginations pulled in different directions since the processes were marked by competing pressures to band together to maintain status as Conquerors, and to fragment as they competed over the riches of their new empire.

The Qur'an can accordingly be ascribed its due place in forming Arab community. Whilst it did not itself designate ethnic Arabs, the Qur'an did bestow an enduringly potent and unprecedented value to the word *ᶜarabī* as a signifier of religious purity. The success of the Conquerors over the succeeding generations enabled the Qur'an's *ᶜarabī* to become established within a dynamic polity, and – for the first time it seems – *ᶜarabī* entered common parlance meaning something other than 'nomadism'. *ᶜArabī* was established with the potential to be an attractive identity for a puritanical religious community, but the early Conquerors already had a name: *muhājirūn*. However, as circumstances conspired to degrade the symbolic value of *hijra*, new names and a new basis to unify Conqueror groups were sought. Here Arabness entered the breach, but only tentatively at first, for Arabness' connection to the Qur'an melded Muslim and Arab identities, and so bestowed conceptual problems aplenty. Christian groups which had assisted the first Conquerors but did not subsequently convert to Islam faced intractable troubles for they could not easily become 'Arabs' without nudging their monotheistic belief towards Islam too, and they accordingly faced inevitable loss of status when 'Arab' became the symbol of the new elite in the second/eighth century.[164] And the Muslim community itself faced the difficult task of rethinking its past and religious identity into an Arab guise. 'Orthodox' Islam would need a radical reorientation to appear an exclusively 'Arab faith' to suit the needs of the newly 'Arab' second/eighth-century Muslim elites. And simultaneously, Arabness competed with other forms of communal organisation, regional and tribal, resulting in the creative and heterogeneous conceptual universe in which early Muslims began to imagine the Arabs.

When Abbasid-era writers picked up the pieces of old memories a century later to write history, they were confronted by the contradictory legacy of the different ideas of Arabness, history and community. When they recorded Umayyad history, they applied their own idealised notions of centralised Caliphate and Arab unity on the early period, but those concepts were initially underdeveloped, and we should accordingly speak of Umayyad history as 'Arab' only in caveated terms. In order to demonstrate the process by which the fractured early Muslims were turned into a tidy, unified group of Arabs in our source texts, the next chapter turns to the literature to explore how its writers defined Arabness, and how they crafted a sense of ethnic cohesion for the Arab people.

Notes

1. For recent work on the Greek–Barbarian dichotomy see Gruen (2011b) pp. 76–7 and the essays in Gruen (2011a) pp. 185–272. For origins of 'Berber', see Brett and Fentress (1997) pp. 5–6, Merrills (2004) pp. 5–6.
2. The concerted establishment of a Muslim state on conquered territories is demonstrated with reference to Egypt in Sijpesteijn (2013).
3. Hoyland (2015) p. 23.

4. An inscription (IGN 132) written by members of the Roman Legion III Cyrenaica is dated 175–7 CE (Nehmé et al. (2010) p. 304).
5. Memories of Roman Arabian past and the Nabataeans are almost non-existent in Arabic literature: the old centre of Madāʾin Ṣāliḥ was completely forgotten, witness its descriptions in connection with Muhammad's campaigns in the region (al-Wāqidī (1966) vol. 3, pp. 1006–8). Had memories of earlier regimes lingered even in the Prophet Muhammad's day, some vestiges could be expected to linger in Arabic literature's early acquisitive collections.
6. The rise of Arabian principalities in al-Ḥijāz in the centuries before Islam occurred after rather complete Roman withdrawal from the region which seems datable to the early fourth century at the latest (witness the end of constructions and even occupation at the major site of Madāʾin Ṣāliḥ (Nehmé (forthcoming) p. 37). It is noteworthy that fifth-century Ḥijāzī kings did not continue using the Bostran calendar from the old regime of *Provincia Arabia,* indicating further break with the Roman past.
7. Millar (2013) 26 outlines the changes in Byzantine provincial administration and the end of 'Arabia' terminology.
8. Macdonald (2009b) pp. 306–7; Hoyland (2015) p. 23.
9. Two 2008 PhD theses add pertinent observations. Ward's 'Palaestina Tertia' discusses the Christianisation of the renamed province of Arabia in the centuries before Islam and the antipathy its inhabitants expressed about 'Saracens' whom they portrayed as an external threat. 'Saracens' were outside the administrative world of pre-Islamic 'Arabia'. Stroumsa's 'People and Identities in Nessana' rejects the notions that there were Greek–Arab relations in the Late Antique southern Levant, noting that even 'Saracens' cannot be termed an identifiable ethnic group. Accordingly, it seems that pre-Islamic *Provincia Arabia* neither evidences a swelling pre-Islamic Arab community nor a set of symbolic ideas which could be relevant for Muslim identities. Millar (2013) pp. 154–8 draws similar conclusions on the 'anachronism' of referring to any sense of Arab identity in the pre-Islamic Levant.
10. For the classic considerations of early Medieval European ethnogenesis, see Geary (1983) and Pohl and Reimitz (1998).
11. The Syrian-frontier theory is primarily articulated via analysis of Greek and Latin writings (Fisher 2011a) and the methodology of analysis from the European cases (Hoyland (2009)), whereas Persian material and Arabic writing are de-emphasised. As a consequence, the Syrian legacy looms disproportionately large – elsewhere I trace how distant a region Syria (al-Shām) was in very early Muslim imaginations,

indicating significant disjoints between central Arabian conceptions of 'home' and a more alien Ghassān and Syrian frontier (Webb (2015) pp. 150–2).

12. Whitcomb (1994) p. 28.
13. The contrast in doctrinal features of European and Arab ethnogenesis seem particularly material. Most European groups began to take shape following their adoption of monotheism, and almost all of their monastic and priestly circles, from the Anglo-Saxons to the Lombards, embraced Roman Christianity, mirroring their political elites' backward-looking political aspirations to portray themselves as the legitimate continuity of late Rome. See Pohl and Reimitz (1998); for theoretical considerations of the rise of ethnicities from religious sects, see A. Smith (2003). Consider the importance of clerical writers cooperating within the framework and memories of the Roman Church in the Late Antique/early Medieval European cases: Gregory of Tours (Franks), Bede (English) and Paul the Deacon (Lombards). As this chapter will argue, while the Arabs similarly formed following the adoption of monotheism, their creed (whether or not its origins derive in past precedents) was portrayed by the nascent Muslims as independent of previous churches, mirroring their political proclamations of independence.
14. As this book was going to press, the theory expressed in Hoyland (2015) equating Arab ethnogenesis with the emergence of Germanic 'peripheral peoples' in Europe was also critiqued on similar grounds in Donner (2015) pp. 136–9.
15. For excellent evaluations of the tropes, confusions, and narrative in the construction of Muslim Conquest narratives, see Noth (1994) and Donner (1998).
16. The process of developing well-articulated senses of Muslim identity and political organisation is much researched: see Berkey (2003), Crone and Hinds (1986), Crone (1980) and Donner (2010).
17. Dating the beginning of the 'Muslim state' is difficult, and entirely dependent on the definition of 'state' applied in analysis. Donner (1986) ascribes the emergence of a 'state' to Muᶜāwiya (41–60/661–80), a view somewhat corroborated in Humphreys (2006); whereas Johns (2003) and Hoyland (2006) date the 'state's' emergence to ᶜAbd al-Malik (65–86/685–705). Taking stock, significant steps were taken towards developing a sense of state structure under the central leadership figure of the Commander of the Faithful (*amīr al-muʾminīn*) in the immediate aftermath of the conquests, whilst greater bureaucratisation and organisation emerged at the end of the first/seventh century. The search for the 'Islamic State' may in any event be a red herring: even in the caliphate of Hishām (105–25/724–43), the state was not wholly centralised

as demonstrated in Blankinship (1994), and the Caliphate may never have achieved centralisation to the extent of its rulers' wishes. The will to centralise control under novel principles derived from interpretations of Islamic belief is perhaps the better indicator of the activity of the early Muslims, and this seems present from the outset, and important vestiges of a version of an early Muslim state in Egypt are elaborated in detail in Sijpesteijn (2013).

18. The Qur'an's novelty is apparent in the absence of early Arabic-language scripture: Shahid (1989) pp. 422–9 and (1995–2009) vol. 2.2, pp. 295–6 argues for sixth-century CE Arabic translations of the Bible, beginning with small Arabic liturgies in fourth century CE, but the claim is largely unsubstantiated, and stems from assertions of the putative Arab identity of pre-Islamic Middle Eastern monks, which this book argues is anachronistic. The proliferation of Arabic inscriptions following the Qur'an seems to underline that the Qur'an was the first widely written liturgical text in Arabic, and the absence of any physical evidence of the contrary seems to bolster that conclusion. Likewise, Luxenberg's argument (2007) that the Qur'an is a translation from Syrio-Aramaic is conjectural and lacks material substantiation. For the concordance of early Qur'anic manuscripts, see Déroche (2003) and the Corpus Coranicum project in Potsdam: <http://www.corpuscoranicum.de> (last accessed 15 November 2015).
19. The settlement of Conquerors in new towns or independent parts of older settlements as indicated in Arabic narrative sources is becoming increasingly well attested in archaeology across the conquered lands. In Khurāsān, remains of a very early Conquerors' settlement in Merv were uncovered at Shaim Kala, about one kilometre south-east of Sasanian Merv (Herrmann et al. (1995) pp. 57–9; in Syria, a number of *amṣār*, in particular Ayla (ᶜAqaba) have been studied, see Whitcomb (1994) and (1995); Egypt's *miṣr* at al-Fusṭāṭ is well known (Kubiak (1987); Fenwick (2013) p. 15 indicates a greater settlement in existing towns in North Africa, but brownfield constructions and a change in the significance of urban centres indicates similar changes of occupation as witnessed elsewhere. The *amṣār* in Iraq have not been well excavated, but al-Baṣra, al-Kūfa and al-Wāṣiṭ are well known, see Djaït (1986). In Northern Iraq, the swift eclipse of Sasanian Nineveh and the massive urbanisation of Mosul represents the rise of yet another brownfield *miṣr* (Robinson (2000) pp. 36, 64–5).
20. Sijpesteijn (2013).
21. Kennedy (2007).
22. Hoyland (1997) pp. 546–59.

23. Q12:2; 20:113; 39:28; 41:3; 42:7; 43:3.
24. Q16:103; 26:195; 41:44; 46:12. Q13:37 presents an analogous variant linking *ᶜarabī* with revelation.
25. I read the Qur'an as an Arabian document from the seventh century CE. Against radical critiques of the text's provenance, recent manuscript analysis seems to confirm codification by at least the later seventh century, which also corresponds to the first widespread stirrings of the 'Arab' references in Umayyad-era poetry. For discussions of scholarship on the history of the Qur'an, see Donner (2008), Gilliot (2006) p. 48, Déroche (2003), Böwering (2008).
26. Some question whether the Qur'an actually situates the *bayt*/sanctum in Arabia, and argue that later Muslim exegetes forged the Arabian spatial association (Crone (1987), Hawting (2003) vol. 3, p. 79). Saḥḥāb (1992) and Heck (2003) make a case against Crone's thesis; in response to Hawting, note that the clusters of verses describing *al-bayt* have a lexical unity with words associated with Hajj and Mecca such as *ḥajj*, *maqām Ibrāhīm*, Bakka, Makka, *al-masjid al-ḥarām* and *al-bayt al-ḥarām* (Q2:124–8; 3:95–7; 5:97; 8:34–5; 22:25–9), hence even without recourse to later exegesis, the verses seem internally consistent in intending pilgrimage to Mecca.
27. See Chapter 4(IV) for the process by which ᶜĀd and Thamūd were incorporated into Arab history and genealogy by Muslims in the third/ninth century.
28. See Chapter 2, pp. 82–3.
29. Q2:127. See Webb (2013b) pp. 7–8 for analysis of the Qur'an's Abrahamic portrayal of the pre-Muhammadic Hajj.
30. Rippen (1991) p. 159.
31. Abdel Haleem (2004) p. 41.
32. Rippen (1991) opines the Qur'an uses *ḥanīf* in differing contexts; Rubin (1990) relates it to pre-Islamic Arabian monotheism; Beeston (1984) proposes a possible Sabaic origin as the 'High God'. Rippen (1991) pp. 165–6 rejects Beeston, though the Qur'an's association of *ḥanīf* with some form of monotheism seems clear.
33. Q2:135; 3:95; 4:125; 6:161; 16:123.
34. Q16:120. *Umma* could also refer to religious community (al-Khalīl (1980) vol. 8, p. 427).
35. See also Q22:31; 22:78.
36. Waardenburg (1981).
37. Aligned with the Qur'anic discourse, hadith describe Mecca's foundation as *asās Ibrāhīm* (Abraham's Foundation) Webb (2013b) pp. 7–8.

38. Pickthall's translation <http://www.sacred-texts.com/isl/pick/003.htm> (last accessed 15 November 2015).
39. Bashear (1997) pp. 2–5 noted the absence of ethnic Arabness in nascent Islam: we evaluate his findings herein, pp. 151–2. Donner's notion of an ecumenical nascent Islam (2010) likewise stresses the absence of ethnic particularism in messages and discourses of the first Believers. Non-ethnic sentiment accords with a literal interpretation of the famous verse 49:13: 'People, We created you all from a single man and a single woman, and made you into races and tribes so that you should recognize one another. In God's eyes, the most honoured of you are the ones most mindful of Him: God is all knowing, all aware'.
40. The lack of ethnic tones in the Qur'an has been overlooked in much modern scholarship, where assumptions that the Qur'an pitched its message to an Arab ethnos predominate (see the following note). Donner's account of Islam as a movement of monotheists, not 'Arabs' (2010), is accordingly supported in this analysis of the Qur'an; whether his further thesis that Islam began as an ecumenical movement of monotheists remains open: the Qur'an contains some negative statements against Jews and Christians (noted in Hoyland (2015)), but in the complex confessional map of the Late Antique Middle East, the division of confessional communities may indicate that the Qur'anic invective was not directed against all Christians and Jews; further research is needed.
41. The equation of *umma* with Arab and/or Arabian race is widely endorsed: Wensinck (1932) p. 6; Duri (1987) pp. 29–30 (but note Duri's rather primordialist notions of Arabness (Ibid. pp. 17–23)); Calder (1990); Naṣṣār (1992); Günther (2002) p. 10, (2006) p. 40. The essential ethnic 'Arabness' assumed for the Qur'an's audience is a key underpinning of various modern discourses, including even Qur'anic ethics, see Izutsu (1966). The attendant generalisations about Arab character and Muslim ethics seem hollow and are in need of reconsideration.
42. Khalidi (2001) vol. 1 p. 145; see also Naṣṣār (1992); Duri (1987).
43. Q12:2 (my translation).
44. Q26:192–5.
45. Q39:28. See also Q16:103; 41:44; 46:12.
46. Q13:37. The verse echoes a sentiment opposite to the *ḥukm jāhilī* (Q5:50), i.e. a non-divine judgment, suggesting the significance of *ᶜarabī* is something beyond the human, let alone 'ethnic'.

47. The verbs ᶜ*araba* and ᶜ*arraba* do not readily appear in pre-Islamic poetry, which indicates they could have been coined, or at least proliferated, after the Qur'an's ᶜ*arabī*, but since they do not carry ethnic connotations either, it supports the impression that Qur'anic ᶜ*arabī* was originally conceptualised in terms of communication, not ethnos.
48. Brustad (forthcoming) also argues that before language standardisation in the third/ninth century ᶜ*arabiyya* was a performance koine lacking 'clear borders' and that Qur'anic ᶜ*arabī*'s indefinite sense should prevent axiomatic linkage to modern notions of *the* Arabic language.
49. As argued by Nöldeke (1899) pp. 272–3; Pietruschka (2001) p. 214. For critiques of melding Arab origins and Bedouinism, see Introduction, n. 3.
50. Versteegh (1997) pp. 76–7 summarises alternative approaches to the history of the triradical system.
51. ᶜ*Arūba* is defined as 'Friday' in the first Arabic dictionary, *al-*ᶜ*Ayn* (al-Khalīl (1980) vol. 2, p. 128), and was attested as the 'old word' for Friday 'amongst the Arabs of *al-Jāhiliyya*' (al-Masᶜūdī (1966–79) §1311; al-Wazīr al-Maghribī (1980) p. 102). The word is borrowed from Hebrew (Mahler 'ᶜArūba', *EI*[1] vol. 1, p. 463) or Syriac ᶜ*rubtā* which seems to have been derived from the Syriac verb ᶜ*rab* 'for the sun to set', connoting the eve of the Sabbath (Payne Smith (1903) p. 427) or because 'Friday is accustomed to making the living set at its evening' (Sokoloff (2009) p. 1134). Most Arabic writers were unaware of the origin and attempted to explain its semantic connection to the root ᶜ-r-b (see al-Wazīr al-Maghribī (1980) pp. 102–3); it confounded Ibn Fāris (1946-52) vol. 4, p. 301; al-Zabīdī was the most circumspect, noting 'it is as if the word is not Arabic' (1994) vol. 2, p. 218).
52. The Qur'anic citations of *a*ᶜ*rāb* are discussed in Binay (2006) pp. 78-89; Pietruschka (2001) pp. 214–5.
53. See Chapter 1, pp. 34–6, 49.
54. Qurʾān 33:20 states 'there are those who wish they were nomads (*bādūn*) amongst the *a*ᶜ*rāb*'.
55. Q9:101, 120; 33:20.
56. Q9:97–8.
57. Q48:11.
58. Q49:14–15.
59. Pietruschka (2001) p. 214 identifies *a*ᶜ*rāb* as the plural of ᶜ*arab*: see Chapter 6(II) for discussion.
60. For the early Muslim-era Arab–nomad distinction, see Chapter 4(I), and see

Chapter 6(II) for the process by which fourth/tenth-century writers reimagined the Arabs and established the now familiar nomadism stereotypes.

61. Al-Azharī (2004) vol. 2, pp. 167–8; see related discussion in Athamina (1987) p. 11.
62. Athamina (1987) pp. 5–6.
63. See Crone (1994b) pp. 355–63 and Lindstedt (2015) p. 73.
64. Bosworth (1989) p. 359 and Marsham (2009) pp. 97–8.
65. Ibn Abī Shayba (2010) vol. 17, p. 503–5.
66. Kister (1991) pp. 279–80, Marsham (2009) p. 98.
67. See Athamina (1987) p. 8.
68. Beeston et al. (1982) pp. 18–19.
69. Biella (2004) p. 382.
70. Beeston et al. (1982) p. 18, Biella (2004) p. 381: both modern dictionaries of Old South Arabian place the 'pledge' (^{c}*rb*/*t*^{c}*rb*) family of words in a separate category from the 'Bedouin' ($^{\supset c}$*rb*/^{c}*rbn*). The verb ^{c}*rab* also means 'to pledge/give security' in Syriac liturgical texts, also without relation to Arabness (Sokoloff (2009) p. 1133). It is possible, therefore, that Arabic borrowed this usage from Syriac. The Arabic *qurbān* (offering/sacrifice) is obviously derived from the root, but the legalistic usage and retention of initial ^{c}*ayn* in early Islam suggests the ^{c}*arabī* of *bay*^{c}*a* ^{c}*arabiyya* was a direct loan.
71. Biella (2004) p. 431. See also Donner (2010) p. 137.
72. See Note 48.
73. The Qur'anic conception of Arabness provides support for Donner's thesis of Islam's origins as a religious, not ethnic movement (2010).
74. Retsö (2003) pp. 625–6 explained the absence of reference to 'Arabs' in the centuries before Islam as reflecting the fact that the previously numerous Arabs were 'on the verge of disappearing' before gaining new momentum with Islam. For the reasons adduced in Chapter 2, we would counter that the notion of pre-Islamic Arabness as a form of community is anachronistic, and the appearance of 'Arabs' in early Islam needs another explanation, considered here.
75. The undeciphered opening letters of various Qur'anic chapters are an example of deliberately obscure expressions; the style of the chapters traditionally identified as the earliest revelation are closely aligned with Arabic literary records of *kuhhān* divinations.
76. Q52:29; 69:42.
77. See Chapter 1 p. 37.
78. Pourshariati (2008) pp. 170, 281–3.

79. See Note 19.
80. The spread of the appeal of Arabness over such a wide area which emerged across the scope of the conquered territory, but only after some generations strongly suggests that an Arab ethnic cohesion was not the cause of the conquests themselves, but was a product of the forces abetting and resulting from the establishment of a Muslim state across that region; and thus again distinguishes Arab ethnogenesis from the plurality of processes of Germanic ethnogenesis in early Medieval Europe.
81. The term 'Commander of the Faithful' (*amīr al-muʾminīn*) is attested in inscriptions from Muʿāwiya's caliphate: see Donner (2010) pp. 99, 120–1, 135–6.
82. See Note 17.
83. Crone and Hinds (1986); Marsham (2009).
84. Early accounts of the conquests stressed violence and the details of military movements and strategic command (e.g. Becker (1913), a tenor frequently revisited since). The lack of evidence of widespread destruction would question why such emphasis is placed on warfare, the construction of a community seems to be a vital task of the early Conquerors, and herein lies the appeal of Donner's thesis of pietistic Islam (2010) which proffers to gain access into the minds and aspirations of the Conquerors by considering their faith and its role. Such a communal/confessional lens enables closer consideration of ethnic identity and Arabness.
85. The unprecedented coherence of the Qur'anic text and its maintenance across the widespread conquest communities, along with the spread of Arabic script inscriptions in the second generation after the conquests indicates a remarkable degree of coherence and spread of the Conquerors' symbolic capital.
86. The Conquerors' identification of themselves as Emigrants (*muhājirūn*) to the *hijra* towns (*amṣār*) seems a key factor when evaluating their sense of self, their aims and worldview. For the evidence of the *muhājirūn* name, see Crone (1994b) and Lindstedt (2015).
87. The speed of conversion is difficult to measure. Bulliet's classic 1979 survey cautioned against assuming it was rapid, as does Crone (1980) pp. 49–50. Dennet (1950) argues for economic drivers; recent studies suggest conversion progressed in different regions at different rates as a response to varied factors: see Levtzion (1979); Levy-Rubin (2000); Wasserstein (2010).
88. Donner (2010) p. 107.
89. Donner (2010) argues a more open-ended ecumenical approach to Islam

marked the first generation of Conquerors, while a more closed-ended 'Islam' as the exclusive property of the Conquerors was articulated, particularly from the late first/seventh century. Donner notes (2010) p. 142 the importance of the Conquerors 'monotheistic reform' which, while, just by virtue that it was 'doctrinally not obnoxious' to Middle Eastern Christians (Ibid. p. 142), does not imply that it was wholly inclusive, even in the earlier period: the Conquerors perhaps derived more pride from their possession of Muhammad's message than Donner implies (2010) pp. 111–15, 205–11, and the very early period remains open for more research.

90. Donner (1981) pp. 218–20, 263–7, and (2010) pp. 121–6; Kennedy (2007) pp. 58–9.
91. For the diverse affiliations of settlers in al-Baṣra al-Kūfa, see Ibn Khayyāṭ's *al-Ṭabaqāt* (n.d.) and Ibn Saᶜd's nearly contemporary *Ṭabaqāt* (1997). For modern study of Yemeni settlement in Iraq, see Mad'aj (1988) pp. 85–7.
92. Djaït describes the tribal *khiṭaṭ* arrangement of the neighbourhoods of al-Kūfa (1986) pp. 117–32. Djaït does not problematise the notion of tribe, however, and assumes that they arrived with pre-Islamic cohesion, and Djaït does not pursue the notion that al-Kūfa helped create a sense of unity around the Arabness idea: he accepts the traditional model of ancient Arabness and treats all Arabian settlers of al-Kūfa as equally 'Arab' in an almost racially-stereotyped study of 'Arab settlement tendencies' (Ibid. pp. 190–203).
93. The importance of the *amṣār* model for the Conquerors' concept of organising community can be gauged by the repetition of the settlement pattern from North Africa to Central Asia (see Note 19).
94. Q3:103.
95. For the theoretical aspects of conceptualising space, see the classic text of Lefebvre (1991) and for notions of 'inside' and 'home space', analysis borrows from Bachelard (1994) pp. 105–35, 211–31.
96. See Macdonald (2009b) pp. 311–13 and discussion in Chapter 1(II–III).
97. Examples of Late Antique Middle Eastern expressions of ethnic communities via notions of long habitation in 'home' territory manifest in the case of Armenians (van Lint (2010)) and West Syrians (Haar Romeny et al. (2010)).
98. Brustad (forthcoming) notes the slow emergence of a standardised version of *al-ᶜarabiyya*, and the nebulous relationships between the variety of tribal dialects and the eventually standardised Arabic language (*al-lugha al-ᶜarabiyya*).
99. Reference to the difficulties of other 'Arabs' understanding Yemeni languages are noted in Ibn Fāris' (1993) pp. 54–9, and the chequered linguistic map

of Arabia on the eve of Islam is detailed in Versteegh (1997) and Macdonald (2009e).

100. Morony (1984) pp. 178, n. 55, pp. 199, 431 considers that conversion would have begun in substance towards the later first/seventh century, which, given the nature of Iraq's close population centres and the tremendous power and wealth of the *amṣār* seems reasonable. He notes 'pagans' could be found in remote areas in the eighth century (Ibid. p. 398).
101. The central thesis of Donner (2010).
102. Kister (1989) is an example of methods that can be used to probe inter-confessional ritual; closer attention to the construction of confessional identities (now more commonly considered) would assist analysis: Morony (1984) pp. 445–58 considers burial rituals and Muslim communal development; Halevi (2007) offers stimulating analysis within an anthropological approach.
103. Ibn Abī Shayba (2010) vol. 17, p. 415 (33342).
104. Donner (2010) pp. 68–74, 108–18.
105. Müller's instincts again appear correct when he posited that the Arab 'Nation' came together under 'einer 'arabischen' Sprache und einem 'arabischen' Koran' (1896) p. 344.
106. Mālik (1994) p. 684, al-Shāfiᶜī (1996) vol. 9, p. 70. Both Mālik and al-Shāfiᶜī were late second/eighth-century jurists, and they report the term *arḍ al-ᶜarab* in one hadith which they both narrate from earlier generations. Commentators on these texts and jurists in the later third/ninth and fourth/tenth centuries only use the now more familiar *jazīrat al-ᶜarab* terminology, suggestive of a significant semantic change to rearticulate the idea of 'Arabia' into an unequivocally peninsular concept: see al-Bājī (1999) vol. 9, p. 255; al-Bukhārī (1999) 4431, Muslim (1999) 4594, 4232, Abū Dāwūd (1999) 3030.
107. A rich source of early definitions for 'Arabs' land' (*jazīrat al-ᶜarab*, *arḍ al-ᶜarab* or *bilād al-ᶜarab*) is the juridical rulings on the famous hadith about expelling non-Muslims from *jazīrat*/*arḍ al-ᶜarab*. Munt (2015) pp. 256–66 surveys evidence in the early hadith collection of ᶜAbd al-Razzāq al-Ṣanᶜānī (d. 211/827) where Arabia's borders were expressed in an idiosyncratic matter, particularly focused on al-Ḥijāz, and Munt suggests that the jurists were constructing 'legal definitions on the back of legal traditions' (2015) p. 263. A detailed survey of all early texts defining 'Arabs' space' is beyond the scope of this note, but a number of preliminary observations indicate that there was perhaps more at stake than juridical matters. Firstly, the notion of 'Arabs' space' is conceptually loaded in terms of ethnic identity: a community needs a common origin

home, and given the absence of self-designated 'Arabs' in pre-Islam and the absence of any record of 'Arabia' as an indigenous term for home, the coincidence of both the emergence of self-styled 'Arabs' and references to 'Arabs' land' in early Islam suggests early Muslims were thinking about constructing a notion of their origins, hence moving the articulation of the space out of the exclusive hands of jurists. The jurists can then be seen as participating in a wider discourse. This lens can help make sense of their varied definitions of 'Arabs' space', given the non-peninsular references to *arḍ al-ᶜarab* and reference to al-Ḥijāz in Mālik (d. 179/795) and al-Shāfiᶜī (d. 204/820) (see previous note). The interchanged references to 'Arabs' land' with al-Ḥijāz reflect the original lands controlled by the early Muslim state (for the Ḥijāz-centred nature of Muslim elites, see Donner (1981) pp. 182–3; Kennedy (1986) p. 56): supportive of the notion that the first people to call themselves 'Arabs' were the elite of the early Muslim state who posited their origins as the 'Arabs' land' (see also, for example, Muslim (1999) *Jihād*:61–3 (4591–5) for the interchanging of al-Ḥijāz and *Jazīrat al-ᶜarab* in different versions of the same ruling). The curious reference to 'Arabs' space' as just Medina (reported on the authority of Mālik in Ibn Ḥajar (2011) vol. 7, p. 302, see also al-Bukhārī (1999) *al-Jihād*:176 where it is extended to Mecca and Yemen too) adds indication of the religious associations invested in early senses of Arab origins. By the early third/ninth century, manifold references to the [pen]insular *jazīrat al-ᶜarab* appear (e.g. Mālik (1979) p. 312, Ibn Abī Shayba (2010) vol. 17, pp. 514–17, and the dictionary *al-ᶜAyn* (al-Khalīl (1980) vol. 6, p. 62) defines *jazīrat al-ᶜarab* as 'the Arabs' source' (*maᶜdin-hā*)): these could be explained via a change in the constituency of the Arab ethnos to encompass *all* people of the Peninsula, and hence 'Arabs' space' would need extension beyond al-Ḥijāz of the early Muslim elite. Arabic geographical texts all post-date the third/ninth-century settling of 'Arabs' space' as the whole Peninsula, and hence have no hesitation in defining its borders quite clearly, but jurists had more obligation to rehearse old opinions, even if to refute them, and hence retained vestiges of earlier uncertainty. Further work, viewing the construction of Muslim senses of 'Arabia' as a process, like the process of Arab ethnogenesis itself, would seem rewarding, given the intriguingly variegated sources.

108. He continues, 'and who in addition cherish the Arabic tongue and its cultural heritage as their common possession' (Gibb (1940) p. 3).
109. Morony (1984) p. 227, Tannous (2013) pp. 84–90.
110. The formation of confessional/ethnic identities and their changes into

increasingly ethnic guises accompanying sociopolitical developments appears to have formed the West Syriac community (Haar Romeny (2010), modified notions of Armenian identity (van Lint (2010)), and perhaps also catalysed the adoption of the name 'Nestorian' and organisation of East Syriac communities in the eighth century CE (Reinink (2010)). Price (2010) indicates that the Byzantines, conversely, did not reorganise themselves around 'Chalcedonian' confessional identity. The Byzantine case seems significant: they retained political autonomy and strong, ancient institutions during the period, and hence, unlike the other groups listed above, they did not 'need' to rally around a religious idea to defend the boundaries of their community.

111. The articulation of these Middle Eastern identities in increasingly ethnic forms in the eighth century CE seems to contrast expressions of civic and aristocratic identities in Sasanian Iraq which were negotiated around Sasanian ethnic exclusive identity as *ērīh* (noted in Payne (2012) p. 220). It is tempting to suggest that when Muslims began organising their community into an increasingly 'Arab' guise in the late first/seventh and through the second/eighth centuries (as discussed presently), Iraqi Christian groups in turn redirected their discourses to negotiate the more confessional-inspired Muslim/Arab nexus, and fit their Nestorian, West Syriac and Armenian identities into the new discourse environment. The expression of Christian confessional communities as ethnicities in the second/eighth century would therefore be, in mirror, a reflection of the contemporary transformation of early Muslims into Arabs.
112. Webb (forthcoming (A)).
113. The useful terminology 'formation' and 'maintenance and renewal' are from Haar Romeny (2010) p. 9.
114. Donner (2010) pp. 206–16; Robinson (2005) pp. 66–80 also detailed the substantial 'innovations' of ᶜAbd al-Malik in his exercise of state formation.
115. Donner (2010) pp. 220–1.
116. The proposal here that 'Arab' was coined to express the identity of the Muslim elites of the later first/seventh and second/eighth centuries, and that it was a function of the development of post-conquest society suggests a reinterpretation of the use of 'Arab' to describe Christian groups in pre-Islamic Arabia, such as Ghassān, Tanūkh and Taghlib. Given the absence of any groups calling themselves 'Arabs' before Islam, the paradigm of 'Christian Arabs' seems a misnomer applied as a consequence of modern-era Middle Eastern politics. Writers of 'Christian Arab' history project the name 'Arab' back into the pre-Islamic past to vacuum up an array of Christian groups in order to

create a sense of ancient origins for the important groups of Christians who self-identified as Arabs in nineteenth-century Lebanon, Syria and Palestine and who became key political stakeholders in the modern Middle East (See Griffith (2008); Courbage and Fargues (1997) pp. 10–25; Wessels (1995); Cragg (1992) and Levtzion (1990)). The validity of retrospective Arabisation is questioned in Millar (2013) pp. 154–60, and on a theoretical level, the labelling of pre-Islamic Christian 'Arab' communities progresses on assumption of Arabness without interrogating identity and ethnogenesis (see Cheikho (1890) and Shahid (1984), (1995–2009) as seminal works of Arab–Christian identity construction). Analysis of 'Christian Arab' communities also overlooks the unusual treatment of them in early Muslim-era sources. Muslim jurists were unclear as to their legal status: in terms of taxation their faith suggests they were liable to *jizya* tax, but most 'Arabs' only paid *ṣadaqa*, and *jizya* seems to be interpreted as a non-Arab tax (indicating again the close association of Arab with Muslim) (al-Shāfiᶜī (1996) vol. 9, pp. 444–8). There was competing precedent as to the solution: following a ruling ascribed to Muhammad, such Christian Arabs could be liable for *jizya*, but a ruling ascribed to ᶜUmar ibn al-Khaṭṭāb stated that 'Christian Arabs' were neither Christian *dhimmīs* nor Muslims, and hence must either convert to Islam or be killed (Ibid. p. 445)! The array of opinions can perhaps be connected to the Caliph al-Mahdī's order to force the Christian Tanūkh to convert to Islam in 162/779. In a similar vein, a poem in which a pre-Islamic Christian group from al-Ḥīra was praised for their 'sterling lineage' (*ᶜurūq ṣāliḥāṭ*) apparently invoked the ire of Umayyad-era 'authorities' (*al-sulṭān*) who seemed to deem the expression of good lineage in an Arabic poem about Christians impermissible (see al-Mubarrad (1998) vol. 1, pp. 58–9). The Christian 'Arab' legal conundrum coincides with Donner's (2010) 'Believers' thesis of early ecumenical Islam: Donner proposes that some Arabian Christians supported the Conquerors, and hence were part of the original 'Believers' movement and shared the status of Conquerors. When the 'Believers' increasingly defined themselves as 'Muslims' and as 'Arabs' in the later first/seventh century, Christian groups which did not convert to Islam found themselves in a paradoxical position: in terms of political status and cultural traits, they were like the Muslims/Arabs, but as Christians, their Arabness lacked a crucial basis, and hence spawned questions as to how they should be identified and treated. Via a different analysis, the early Conquerors may have accepted opportunistic Christian groups and pragmatically overlooked religious difference in order to swell their armies. In light of the above, Griffith's terminology 'Arabic speaking Christian' ((2008) pp. 198–9) seems preferable to 'Arab'.

117. See Lucas (2008) for remarks on Ibn Abī Shayba's enigmatic text.
118. Crone (1994b) links *hijra* to settlement of the *amṣār*, Lindstedt (2015) affirms the application of *muhājirūn* as a name for early Muslim communities.
119. The term *Magarites* appears in the Egyptian papyrus Perf 558; the letter of Patriarch John of Sedreh *c.*640 is the earliest Syriac reference to *Mhaggrāyē*: see a list of Syriac examples in Brock (2005) p. 277. An alternative interpretation of *Mhaggrāyē* is 'children of Hagar', a reference to the Muslim Arabians' belief in their Biblical lineage from Abraham via Ishmael, son of Hagar (Crone and Cook (1977)). As will be discussed in Chapter 4(IV), Muslims only embraced Hagarene genealogy in the early second/eighth century, i.e. two or three generations after the first appearance of *Mhaggrāyē* references. Hoyland (1997) pp. 156, 180, 414 and Donner (2010) pp. 86, 118 interpret the word as *muhājirūn* (as does Crone (1994b)), which seems sounder philologically given the 'm' at the beginning of *Mhaggrāyē*, and historically, given that ethnonyms related to Hagar are not evidenced in Arabic texts: we neither find reference to names derived from Ishmael in pre-Islam (see al-Azmeh (2014a) p. 125, n.151 for discussion of Ishmael) nor the affiliation *hājarī* lingering in records about early Islam, whereas *muhājir* and the related term *hijra* are ubiquitous. Like we found vestiges of Maᶜadd in pre-Islamic poetry, if the first Muslims called themselves Hagarenes, we would expect some of these voices to survive.
120. Q2:218; 4:89; 8:74; 16:41; 22:58. See also Crone (1994b); Athamina (1987).
121. Ibn Abī Shayba (2010) vol. 17, pp. 401–2 (33300).
122. Q49:14–15 contrasts the *muᵓmin* 'Believer' status of Muhammad with the *muslim* 'Submitter' status of the Bedouin *aᶜrāb*, noting also the importance of joining the community in jihad as a point of differentiation: 'The Bedouin say, "We believe." Tell them, "You do not believe, you have but submitted since belief has yet to enter your hearts." . . . the Believers are those who believe without any doubt in God and His Prophet and expend their possessions and their lives in God's Path: they are the true ones.'
123. For similar versions of the hadith and its 'Emigrant' space terminology to connote the Conquerors' territory, see also al-Shāfiᶜī (1996) vol. 9, pp. 52–3; al-Tirmidhī (1999) *al-Siyar*:48; Abū Dawūd (1999) *Jihād*:82.
124. Donner (2010) p. 220 considers the 'reformed vocabulary' imposed to rearticulate aspects of early Islam into new language that corresponded with new interpretations of Islam's rise. The disappearance of *muhājirūn* as the term for

all Conquerors, and the restriction of the term's ambit to refer just to emigrants during Muhammad's lifetime appears an example of terminological 'reform'.

125. Could this practical change to the community's demographics be linked to the vigorous spread of the versions of *lā hijra baᶜd al-fatḥ* hadith ('There is no emigration following the conquest [of Mecca]') (e.g. al-Bukhārī (1999) *Jihād*:1,27)? See also the array of hadith in al-Nasāʾī (1999) *al-Bayᶜa* :15 exhibiting more experimentation with the trigger for the 'end of *hijra*'.
126. Donner (2010) pp. 68–74, 112–15 argues for the designation of a range of monotheists as *muʾminūn*/Believers.
127. Ibn Abī Shayba (2010) vol. 17, p. 421 (33365).
128. Q29:26 uses *muhājir* in a sense wider than its familiar narrow definition of Meccan emigrants to Medina, see also Q24:22; 59:8.
129. Hoyland (2015) p. 102 also discusses '*Muhājirūn* conquest', but he otherwise retains the traditional 'Arab conquest' and 'Arab state' terminology throughout.
130. The value of Maᶜadd as an asset in early Islam is the topic of Webb (forthcoming (A)).
131. Ibn Abī Shayba (2010) vol. 15, p. 433 (30534).
132. Ibid. vol. 15, pp. 431–3 (30532–30535).
133. Ibid. vol. 15, pp. 433–5 (30535–30548).
134. See Chapter 6(I-II) for analysis of the development of Arabness in grammatical discourses.
135. For Muslim *umma* see Q2:128; for *umma* as a group of specifically righteous peoples within a wider community, see Q3:104; 7:159. Q10:47; 16:36; 23:44 link *umam* with their prophets.
136. Webb (2013b) pp. 7–8, 10–11.
137. Ibn al-Kalbī (2009) p. 12; Ibn Abī Shayba (2010) vol. 13, p. 403 (26807).
138. See al-Mubarrad (2008) vol. 2, p. 646 n. 2.
139. Consider, for example, the hadith where Muhammad declares 'I am the head of the Arabs' (*sābiq al-ᶜarab*). Ibn Abī Shayba (2010) vol. 16, p. 465 (32388) relates debate over the hadith's authenticity, Ibn Ḥanbal narrates it in his *Faḍāʾil* (1983) vol. 2, p. 909, but tellingly does not narrate it in his more authoritative *Musnad*. *Mursal* and *ḍaᶜīf* hadith mentioning 'Arab' in Ibn Abī Shayba (2010) include vol. 17, p. 41 (32612), p. 331 (33136), p. 332 (33138).
140. See Ibid. vol. 17, p. 349 (33170 and 33171) where the Tamīm tribe are praised as the 'sturdiest' Arabs, though in al-Bukhārī (1999) hadith 2543, Tamīm are praised as the 'sturdiest of this *umma*'.
141. Some of the ᶜUmar ibn ᶜAbd al-ᶜAzīz hadith referring to 'Arabs' are repeated

in *al-Muṣannaf*, ascribed to the earlier Caliph ᶜUmar ibn al-Khaṭṭāb and Muhammad himself (e.g. Ibn Abī Shayba (2010) vol. 17, pp. 422–3 (33372, 33375–6), 400 (33298). This seems to be a case of backtracking a statement of ᶜUmar ibn ᶜAbd al-ᶜAzīz to earlier authority figures which was not uncommon in second/eighth-century hadith codification (see Borrut (2005) and (2011) pp. 306–20).

142. See Levy-Rubin (2011), Chapter 3.
143. Ragib (2007).
144. Blau (1982) p. 102. It is instructive that this inscription is from a state sponsored construction mentioning the Caliph Muᶜāwiya and his official title, showing correspondence between expressing statebuilding and Arabness terminology.
145. Millar (2013) pp. 161–2 discusses these papyri as indicative of the 'novel system of personal nomenclature' that arrived with the Muslim regime and emergence of 'Arab' identification in the first century of Islam.
146. Kerr (2014) pp. 26–7.
147. Bell (1910) p. 49.
148. Millar (2013) p. 163 notes Jacob's reference to Muhammad (*mḥmṭ*) as 'King of the Arabs' (*mlk ᶜrby*): Jacob died in 708 CE, Millar dates his Chronicle to the last decades of the seventh century.
149. *Chronicle of Zuqnin* pp. 151–2 refers to the Caliph Sulaymān as 'Caliph of the Arabs'; Ibid. p. 155 refers to 'testimony of a Syrian against an Arab', implying the association an interchangability of Muslim and Arab.
150. Bashear (1997) p. 112.
151. Bashear (1997) p. 121.
152. See above, pp. 138–9.
153. Donner (1998) pp. 197–8.
154. Donner (1998) p. 198, Goldziher (1889–90) vol. 1, pp. 61–97, though Goldziher's notions of tribalism and innate pre-Islamic 'Arab character' that led to the spirited rivalries in early Islam are dated.
155. See Marsham (2009) and Crone and Hinds (1986) for the evolving nature of the early Caliphate.
156. Blankinship (1994) details the struggles of the Caliph Hishām to centralise the caliph's control.
157. See, for example, the earliest surviving text about the first *fitna*, Ibn Muzāḥim (1981) where the *ahl al-Shām* vs *ahl al-ᶜIrāq* dichotomy is pervasive. Haldon and Kennedy consider the interaction of regional identities with tribal in the Umayyad period, and, arguing from an economic perspective, note the

'common interest' ((2012) p. 543) the militarised elite had with their tax-paying farmers, and hence the enhanced importance of regional transactional relationships and identities (2012) pp. 541–53.

158. Abū ᶜUbayda (1905–12) vol. 1, p. 355
159. Haldon and Kennedy (2012).
160. Crone (1994a) argues that Qaysī and Yamānī never constituted cohesive political parties as Shaban maintained ((1971) pp. 135–7), though Crone accepts the divisive nature of tribal factionalisation, arguing that on a provincial level amongst the Umayyad-era military, *ᶜaṣabiyya* rivalries articulated on tribal lines were a significant issue facing central administrative management (1994a) pp. 42–3, 50–2.
161. The developing tribal consciousness and shared 'Arab past' seem perceptible in reports from the Muhallab revolt during the reign of Yazīd ibn ᶜAbd al-Malik (101–5/720–4), and they become pronounced during fall of the Umayyads. For example al-Dīnawarī (2001) p. 514 relates a fascinating anecdote in which an alleged pre-Islamic alliance between 'Yemenis' and 'Qaysī' Arabs against Muḍar was cited by anti-Umayyad agitators in Khurāsān who called for the alliance to be 'renewed' to unite Yemeni and Qaysī 'Arab' groups against the 'Muḍarī' Umayyads.
162. See Bashear (1984) pp. 10–11. Hadith ascribed to ᶜUmar refer to the recipients of *ᶜaṭā* and *fayʾ* as *muslimīn* (Ibn Abī Shayba (2010) vol. 17, p. 491 (33583), p. 511 (33649).
163. Ibn Abī Shayba (2010) vol. 17, pp. 472–6 (33539). See discussion in al-Qadi (2010).
164. As discussed above, Note 116, it is material to ask how 'Arab' Arabian Christians expressed their identities in early Islam, and the less ethnic terms of 'Arabian Christian' (Griffith (2008) pp. 198–9) or Conqueror elite perhaps better convey the boundaries between groups in the environment when the majority of the elites were construing 'Muslim' and 'Arab' as synonymous.

PART TWO

THE CHANGING FACES OF ARABNESS IN EARLY ISLAM

4

Interpreting Arabs: Defining their Name and Constructing their Family

When third/ninth-century Iraqi writers began their efforts to gather the many pieces into which memories of Islam's rise had scattered, they imagined that Islam's first believers all constituted a unified community of Arabs, and they set about assembling narratives of Islam's rise into an Arab story. The sum of their writings had the seminal result of creating the impression that pre-Islamic Arabia was inhabited by 'Arabs'. Akin to the construction of communal identities across the world, the Muslim-era writings obscured the Arab community's origins in early Islam and cast Arabness back into a deep, ancient pre-history, cobbling memories of tribes, nomads and poets into a robust icon which has long been misread as *the* 'history' and 'culture' of the 'original Arabs', and which has long fuelled assumptions that Arab communities 'must have' existed in pre-Islamic Arabia.

The history of pre-Islamic 'Arabs' ought therefore be approached afresh as the history of the Muslim invention of pre-Islamic 'Arabs', and when we interrogate the sources from this perspective, we can begin to grasp the challenges that third/ninth- and fourth/tenth-century writers faced in order to create the cohesive 'Arab story', and the creativity they employed to overcome them. We saw that pre-Islamic Arabians had not called themselves 'Arabs', and hence Muslim-era writers faced the primary challenge of creating a sense of pre-Islamic 'Arab identity' to replace the heterogeneity of pre-Islamic Arabian memories with the homogeneity of one overarching Arabness. There were yet further complications too, because Arabness did not ossify in the third/ninth century into one static archetype. Arabness is an idea, it was the property of Muslim society and it consequently developed in correspondence to changing needs of Muslim discourses. The corpus of Arabic literature written between the late second/eighth and fifth/eleventh centuries is thus a truly unwieldy organism, and it would be naïve to assume that all narratives about Arabs and Arab history can be treated identically.

The interpretation of literary references to the word *ᶜarab* will benefit from circumspection that pays due accord to their history – their chronology on the continuum of Arab ethnogenesis that changed the faces of Arabness over time. Part Two of this book investigates the extent of Arabness' evolution, and this chapter begins with a diachronic interrogation of two fundamental underpinnings of Arab identity: (1) the definition of the name *ᶜarab* itself in pre-modern Arabic dictionaries and (2) the construction of the Arab family tree, particularly in third/ninth-century texts. The dictionary writers afford us a window into how a sense of community was imagined around the word 'Arab' from time to time, and the development of an Arab family tree connecting the early Muslim groups into one shared genealogy signals key evolutions in the sense of Arabness as an ethnic identity. By the third/ninth century, the conception of Arabs as a distinct 'nation' was certain, but the rich array of Arabic terminology to delineate social groups – *umma, shaᶜb, jīl* and others – was variously interpretable.[1] The fluctuations and disputes which we shall encounter reveal the vitality and thus the practical importance of the Arabness idea in early Islam, and the major issues underwriting the process of imagining the community of Arabs over time.

I 'Arabs' Defined

'Arabs' in Pre-modern Lexicons

The oldest surviving dictionary definition of the word *ᶜarab* appears in what is also the oldest Arabic dictionary, al-Khalīl ibn Aḥmad's (d. 175/791) *al-ᶜAyn*,[2] the extant form of which dates to the late second/eighth and early third/ninth century. *Al-ᶜAyn* defines *ᶜarab* through a range of statements, opening with a mention of *al-ᶜarab al-ᶜāriba* whom it calls 'the pure of them' (*al-ṣarīḥ minhum*).[3] *Al-ᶜAyn* thus conceptualises *al-ᶜarab* as a group, but does not elaborate upon the basis of *al-ᶜāriba*'s purity. Third/ninth-century texts would later identify *al-ᶜāriba* as the first Arabic speakers (the scion of Yaᶜrub ibn Qaḥṭān),[4] which is perhaps the thrust of *al-ᶜAyn*, particularly since it emphasises the importance of language in defining Arabness by adding that the related verb *aʿraba* means 'to speak correctly/clearly' (*afṣaḥa*),[5] and by defining non-Arabs (*ʿajam*) as 'the not-Arabs' (*ḍidd al-ʿarab*), the people 'who do not speak correctly/clearly' (*alladhī lā yufṣiḥ*).[6] It also describes prayer in which no Qur'an is recited (aloud) as *ʿajmāʾ*, and any speech which is 'not Arabic' as *ʿajam*.[7] *Al-ʿAyn*'s impression is that those who speak Arabic in a pure/clear form fit within the universe of *al-ʿarab*, and the description of Qur'an-less prayer as *ʿajmāʾ* indicates a connection to the performance and sacred idiom of an 'Arabic Qur'an'.

Al-ʿAyn's linguistic emphasis leaves the now familiar Arabness stereotypes of tribes, Arabia and Bedouin out of its definition of 'Arab'. The dictionary mentions the word *aʿrāb*/Bedouin, though it admits no connection between them and *ʿarab*/Arab; *al-ʿAyn* only records *aʿrāb*'s plural form (*aʿārīb*).[8] The attention to the 'correct' plural of *aʿrāb* can be contextualised when read with *al-ʿAyn*'s contemporary grammatical book, Sībawayh's *al-Kitāb*, which explicitly classifies *aʿrāb* as neither a plural of nor a collective noun related to the word *ʿarab* (Arabs), and thus seeks to lexically distinguish Bedouin from Arab.[9] By establishing grounds to cleave Bedouin-ness from Arabness, the philologists' approach consigns Arabness towards language, delineating *ʿarab* as those who comply with a set of speech rules. These definitions tally with other evidence already encountered: we saw in Chapter 3 that the Qur'an separates linguistic *ʿarabī* from nomadic *aʿrāb* and that Ibn Abī Shayba's *al-Muṣannaf* reports hadith using *ʿarabī* in a specifically linguistic sense and refers to Bedouin as *aʿrāb*, not *ʿarab*. The texts erect a barrier between Bedouin and Arabness, and related verbs reflect a similar dichotomy: the verb *taʿarraba* connoted residence outside the Muslim community (and hence reads as 'to become *aʿrāb*'),[10] whereas the verb *istaʿraba* is cited in cases of learning to speak Arabic, or becoming part of an Arabic religio-linguistic community, without connection to nomadic *aʿrāb* (and hence translates as 'to become Arab/Arabic').[11]

Chapter 6 considers Bedouin otherness in more detail; as far as the specific definition of *ʿarab* is concerned, early Muslim social status was evidently at stake via the *ʿarab*/*aʿrāb* distinction, as indicated in a verse of poetry circulating in the second/eighth century which levels invective against non-Arabs (likely Persians or ethnic Iraqis):[12]

They call us *a^c^rāb*, but our name is *^c^arab*!
We call them 'sack necks'!

The poem's binary friction between 'us' and 'them' touches the transactional divide between the conquering elite and the conquered populations within Iraq, and it is instructive that the budding elite also articulated their Arab identity to the exclusion of Bedouin groups. Texts from Islam's first 150 years thus speak to a distinction between *ᶜarabī* and *aᶜrāb*, assigning Bedouinism a vile, outsider status, while seeking to link Arab community to *ᶜarabī* with its connections to a unique, pure speech idiom derived from religious practice.[13] The linkage of Arabness with language, scripture and status forms the contours of the context in which the first peoples proclaiming their own Arabness emerged into the historical records, as visited in Chapter 3. The parameters of Arabness considered here point to an outgrowth from the seed of Qur'anic *ᶜarabī* and its potent connotations of divinity and purity, whereby the Qur'an-following urban elites of the Conqueror communities who understood *ᶜarabī* communication reformatted the Arabness idea in their own image as a means to articulate their sociopolitical status and independence as the conquests settled into a more exclusive and confident sense of Muslim-run Caliphate.

After another 150 years of societal and intellectual development, a new dictionary, al-Azharī's (d. 370/980) *Tahdhīb al-lugha*, presents Arabness with different emphasis and different terminology. It repeats the language-based definition of *al-ᶜAyn* (expressly citing the earlier dictionary), but specifically contradicts it with a counterstatement: 'others say an Arab (*ᶜarabī*) is someone whose lineage (*nasab*) can be securely established as Arab, even if he cannot speak correct Arabic (*faṣīḥ*)'.[14] Herein we have a significant debate in view: was Arabness defined by language, as *al-ᶜAyn*'s definition suggested, or by lineage? Al-Azharī prefers kinship, the now more familiarly ethnic model of Arab community, as he emphasises it by adding a new term into the dictionary: *muᶜrib*, which al-Azharī defines as a speaker of correct/clear Arabic 'even if he is of non-Arabic lineage (*ᶜajamī al-nasab*)'.[15] Al-Azharī thus lexically distinguishes language from lineage, and enables the assertion that a learner of Arabic can never become an Arab (*ᶜarabī*), but only *muᶜrib*.[16]

Al-Azharī erects a similar dichotomy for the 'non-Arab', adducing separate ethnic (*ᶜajamī*) and linguistic (*aᶜjamī*) terms. *ᶜAjamī* connotes 'one whose lineage traces to the non-Arabs, even if he speaks correct [Arabic] (*yufṣiḥ*)'; whereas *aᶜjamī* describes one who 'does not speak correctly (*faṣīḥ*) even if he has Arabic lineage (*ᶜarabī al-nasab*)'.[17] *Tahdhīb al-lugha* thus rejects and rewrites *al-ᶜAyn*'s definition of the 'not-Arab', transforming *ᶜajam* from non-Arabic speech to non-Arabic lineage, and establishes that mastery of the Arabic language is neither a necessary nor sufficient condition of Arab identity. By al-Azharī's logic, an ethnic *ᶜarabī* Arab could, if he cannot speak correct Arabic, be *aᶜjamī* (a non-Arabic speaker), but this is merely a linguistic adjective without prejudice to his belonging to the Arab people – an Arab by birth can never turn into an *ᶜajamī* (non-Arab).[18] The reverse is identical – a non-ethnic Arab could learn enough Arabic to be called *muᶜrib*, but he can never become *ᶜarabī*.

Al-Azharī further downplays the role of language in defining Arabness by adding spatial restrictions too. Unlike *al-ᶜAyn*'s space-neutral definition of 'Arab', al-Azharī defines *ᶜarabī* with mention of the 'land from which Arabs derive' and 'the country of the Arabs' (*bilād al-ᶜarab*).[19] In another departure from *al-ᶜAyn*, al-Azharī incorporates both Bedouin and settled populations as component parts of the Arab people. The full ramifications of his inclusion of Bedouin *aᶜrāb* into the ambit of Arabness (he calls them 'people from the desert lands of the Arabs' (*qawm min bawādī al-ᶜarab*))[20] will be revisited in Chapter 6, but as far as his definition of Arabness is concerned, both desert-dwellers (*aᶜrāb*) and residents of towns/villages (*ᶜarab*) are 'Arabs' by virtue of their origins from Arab lands, and are counted as Arabs 'even if they do not speak [the Arabic language] correctly/clearly' (*wa-in lam yakūnū fuṣaḥāʾ*)[21] – note again al-Azharī pointedly dismisses language's role in defining Arabness. Al-Azharī reiterates Arab space through a discussion of the five 'Arab prophets' (Ishmael, Hūd, Ṣāliḥ, Shuᶜayb and Muhammad), explaining their Arabness by virtue of their residence in various parts of the Arabian Peninsula.[22] Al-Azharī's additions thereby reverse *al-ᶜAyn*'s earlier thrust: if Arabness can be conceptualised primarily via language, there is no need to restrict it to a specific place; however al-Azharī (writing 150 years after *al-ᶜAyn*) presents Arabness around fixed notions of Arab lineage and space.

Lastly, when considering the origin of the word *ᶜarab*, al-Azharī considers two possibilities: does the name derive from (1) the descendants of the purported first speaker of Arabic, Yaᶜrub ibn Qaḥṭān, or (2) the descendants of Ishmael who reportedly lived in the town ᶜAraba, and from thence, spread across Arabia?[23] The options again divide between language and place. Are we to identify Arabs as an eponymous linguistic community or an ethnos with a common homeland after which they were named? Consistent with his pervasive downplaying of language's role in defining Arabness, al-Azharī prefers the second option, rooting Arabness in notions of land.[24] His final word on the matter admits some equivocation by concluding that Arabs are 'all those who lived in the land of the Arabs and their Peninsula and spoke the language of its people'.[25] While this retains some role for language, al-Azharī's substantial departures from the earlier *al-ᶜAyn*'s linguistic model are apparent: in al-Azharī's definition, shared language did not create Arab unity; Arabness is constructed around shared lineage and land.

Subsequent classical dictionaries perpetuate al-Azharī's slant, effecting an eclipse of *al-ᶜAyn*'s linguistic Arabness. Al-Jawharī's (d. *c.*393/1002–3) *al-Ṣiḥāḥ*, written one generation after al-Azharī, is the first lexicon to use explicitly ethnic terminology to define *ᶜarab*, defining them as an 'ethnic group' (*jīl min al-nās*),[26] distinguished as the people of 'clear Arabness' (*bayyin al-ᶜurūba*) and the inhabitants of the first cities of Islam (*al-amṣār*). Like al-Azharī, al-Jawharī does not strictly segregate Arabs from Bedouin, notwithstanding their distinct domiciles; he defines the *aᶜrāb* as 'those [Arabs] who specifically inhabit the deserts'.[27] Al-Jawharī is not explicit about the meaning of 'Arabness'/*ᶜurūba*, but he does cite it as a verbal noun connected with speaking Arabic,[28] suggesting, as al-Azharī also accepted, that language remains a factor of the identity, but unlike *al-ᶜAyn*, there is no stipulation that 'Arab' connotes a speaker of correct/pure Arabic, al-Jawharī's terminology embeds the kin-based touchstone of Arabness as designating an identifiable *jīl*/ethnos.

Al-Jawharī's contemporary Ibn Fāris' (d. 395/1004) *Maqāyīs al-lugha* similarly defines Arabs with terminology bearing ethnic connotations by calling them a people/nation (*umma*). Pursuant to *Maqāyīs al-lugha*'s purpose of relating words to their roots, Ibn Fāris relates the name 'Arab' to ᶜ-r-b, and considers it 'feasible' (*laysa bi-baᶜīd*) that the name arose because of what he reasons was the perfect clarity of Arabic speech. This, however, is a philological theory about the name's root and not a criterion to establish contemporary members of the Arab *umma*: Ibn Fāris' dictionary has a fixed notion of the Arab people that is not open to new Arabic learners.[29]

The sixth/twelfth-century Nashwān al-Ḥimyarī's (d. 573/1178) *Shams al-ᶜulūm* also mirrors al-Azharī, defining *ᶜarab* as 'the opposite of the non-Arab' (*ᶜajam*),[30] and distinguishing ethnically non-Arab *ᶜajam* from linguistically not-Arabic *aᶜjam* in the same manner as al-Azharī: *aᶜjamī* is 'one who does not speak Arabic correctly/clearly, even if he is from the Arabs'.[31] Lastly, Ibn Manẓūr's (d. 711/1311) *Lisān al-ᶜarab* repeats all of al-Azharī and al-Jawharī's definitions, but (pointedly) not *al-ᶜAyn*'s: he speaks of the Arabs as a *jīl* (ethnic group) who share blood relations, making several express mentions of *nasab* (kinship/lineage).[32] Ibn Manẓūr notes that a speaker of correct Arabic should be called *ᶜarabī al-lisān* (Arabic-tongued), a decisive remark intimating that an Arabic learner can never become truly *ᶜarabī* (Arab) himself, only his tongue can earn association with Arabness.[33] By eclipsing *al-ᶜAyn*'s linguistic Arabness and defining Arabs into a kin group, the progression of dictionaries suggests that the ways of conceptualising 'Arab' experienced paradigmatic changes during the third/ninth–fourth/tenth centuries, and this deserves scrutiny.

Arabness Caught Betwixt Language and Lineage

Why did dictionaries shift their definitions of 'Arab' from a speech idiom to a dogmatically kin-based model? The historical context of early Islam offers some indication since, as traced in Part One of this book, Arabness only gradually developed as a broad communal identity from the first/seventh century, and hence we could propose that Arab genealogy was in fact initially incapable of acting as the touchstone for Arabness. The original Conquerors were drawn from an array of regions and possessed disparate senses of kinship, and so cobbling them together under a novel umbrella of 'Arab family' would initially be unwieldy. The Conquerors' linguistic and confessional similarity, on the other hand, provided an easier means to articulate communal identity under the puritanical early Muslim movement and its *ᶜarabī* symbolic capital, and when they first began calling themselves 'Arabs', it appears they had yet to devise a definitive model of kin-interrelatedness. Herein, the results of our lexicographical survey accord with other examples of ethnogenesis in Late Antiquity, whereby the role of shared creed is identified as a catalyst for ethnogenesis during the early centuries of Islam.[34] Arabic dictionaries point to the contours of similar processes inasmuch as definitions of Arabness in genealogical terms emerged only in the generations after Muslims had refined Islamic doctrines and established accompanying state structures.

The Caliphate and Islam again emerge as key catalysts to prompt early communities of Conquerors towards embracing Arab identity. First, 'Arab' acted as a marker of elite status identified by the special *ᶜarabī* language of the Conquerors' faith, but gradually a family tree was articulated to redefine Arabness around genealogy. The kinship Arabness in the later dictionaries heralds a seismic reorientation of the basis of Arab identity into a fixed sense of one 'Arab family', and the only gradual recognition of kinship to define Arabness in the lexicons suggests that the construction of an agreed, cohesive Arab genealogical system was protracted and only came to full fruition by the fourth/tenth century. Indicators thus point to the third/ninth century as a formative period of debate between linguistic Arabness versus ascendant genealogical Arabness.

Such debates over the ways to conceptualise Arabness appear in early disagreement over the interpretation of Qur'an 41:44's challenging verse 'If We had revealed it as a non-Arabic (*aᶜjamī*) Qur'an, they would ask "Why are its verses not clear? What! Is it non-Arabic and Arabic?" (*[a]aᶜjamī wa-ᶜarabī*)'.[35] One interpretation reads *ᶜarabī* as a linguistic feature of the Qur'an, and accordingly reads the words *aᶜjamī wa-ᶜarabī* to mean that the Qur'an does not contain a 'mixture of non-Arabic and Arabic language'. To follow the translation of Qur'anic *ᶜarabī* proposed in Chapter 3(II), the verse erects a contrast between 'impure and pure language'. This interpretation is aligned with *al-ᶜAyn*'s linguistic definition of *ᶜarabī*, and al-Ṭabarī's (d. 310/923) exegesis, *Jāmiᶜ al-bayān*, lists several early scholars, contemporary with *al-ᶜAyn*, who read the verse with the linguistic interpretation.[36] But other readers imputed ethnic meanings into the verse. Both al-Ṭabarī and the grammarian al-Farrāᵓ (d. 207/822–3) in his *Maᶜānī al-Qurᵓān* note that the verse's words *aᶜjamī wa-ᶜarabī* could alternatively be interpreted as the Qur'an's response to claims that the ethnically 'Arab Prophet (Muhammad) had received revelation in a foreign tongue'.[37] The two possible readings mirror the debate al-Azharī noted in the definition of *ᶜarabī*: should Arabness be associated with a system of speech or with a kin-ethnos? It seems that both exegetes and lexicographers were debating the fundamentals of *ᶜarabī* along similar lines.

To explore the conundrum, it is noteworthy that the verse's context in the Qur'an does not impose ethnic interpretations. The verses affirm the purity, clarity and unchanging nature of the Qur'an's message: compare with the preceding lines (41:41–3): 'It is an unassailable Scripture which falsehood cannot touch from any angle . . . you [Prophet] are not told anything that the previous messengers were not told.' The citation of *ᶜarabī* in 41:44 continues the discourse about the Qur'an's clarity and pure truthfulness of its message, and an interpretation of the verse to assert Muhammad's ethnic Arabness is an exegetical imposition onto the text, wrought by later hands searching for Qur'anic justification for their opinions about Muhammad's Arab identity.[38] We saw in Chapter 3(III) that labelling Muhammad an ethnically 'Arab' prophet was indeed a later reinterpretation of Muhammad's identity as Muslim elites in the second/eighth century sought to reconceptualise Islam in terms of an 'Arab faith'.[39] Since the Qur'an elsewhere makes no reference to Muhammad as an Arab prophet, it does seem anachronistic to interpret 41:44 as imputing Arabness upon Muhammad, whereas the linguistic reading of 41:44, which focuses on the purity of Qur'anic revelation and leaves Muhammad's ethnicity open-ended, matches both the verse's specific context and the general meaning of *ᶜarabī* throughout the Qur'an. Hence we behold the tension faced by writers 200–300 years after the dawn of Islam: they were conscious of a sense of Arab ethnic community, but the historical memories they possessed pre-dated the maturation of Arab ethnogenesis, and did not corroborate their present notions of Arabness. Muslim writers accordingly bridged the gap by creative reinterpretation in order to make old texts like 41:44, which were initially devoid of ethnic implications, speak to new notions of Arab ethnicity. The reworking of 41:44 also mirrors the contemporaneous forging of texts like Dhū Qār stories and hadith to represent the past in 'Arab' terms.[40]

Another early text which discusses Qur'an 41:44, Muqātil ibn Sulaymān's (d. 150/767) *Tafsīr*, adds some further indications to the competing concepts of Arabness between a language system and a family tree. It interprets the verse as: 'They say the Qur'an is non-Arabic (*aᶜjamī*) and it is revealed to Muhammad and he is Arabic (*ᶜarabī*), so [ordering Muhammad] say: "God revealed it Arabic (*ᶜarabiyyan*) so that you may understand it"'.[41]

By describing Muhammad as *ᶜarabī*, Muqātil gives the Prophet an Arab identity, as Muqātil's contemporary hadith narrators were beginning to articulate, but further probing of Muqātil's descriptions of Muhammad, his community and the concept of Arabness, reveals intruiging equivocation. Muqātil never mentions Muhammad's *nasab* (lineage) in his exegesis. This is significant since later exegetes (explored below) make unfailing comment about Muhammad's genealogy, expressly defining his Arabness through tribal *nasab*. His *Tafsīr* engages with ethnic categories, inasmuch as he discusses Persians (*ahl Fāris*), Copts (*al-Qibṭ*) and Byzantines (*Rūm*), but reference to *al-ᶜarab* as a single category appears less frequently. Muqātil mentions 'Arabs' as one of the groups descended from Noah via his son Sām, interestingly counting the people of Lakhmid al-Ḥīra as a separate group of Sām's descendants,[42] and hence Muqātil's *Tafsīr* can conceptualise the Arabs as a 'race' in genealogical terms, but when Muqātil engages in his many discussions of groups which would later be classified as 'Arab tribes', I have found few declarations of their communal unity as Arabs.[43] Muqātil is cognisant that Arabness constitutes a community, but he is reticent to define it with particular emphasis, and when he glosses the Qur'an's references to 'Arabic revelation' (*tanzīl ᶜarabī*), Muqātil never equates it to the 'language of the Arabs' (*lughat al-ᶜarab*) as later exegetes do,[44] and instead interprets the Qur'an's *ᶜarabī* as something essential for its audience to understand/conceptualise (*fahima*/*ᶜaqala*) the revelation itself,[45] reflecting the proposal here that Qur'anic *ᶜarabī* resonated with purity before community. Likewise, Muqātil navigates Qur'an 9:128: 'We have sent you a messenger from amongst yourselves' without any reference to Arab nation or genealogy, in stark contrast to commentators from the fourth/tenth century onwards who invariably construe the verse as a sign of Muhammad's Arabness. As examples of the exegetical development over time, al-Ṭabarī inserts express ethnic tones by remarking: 'God said *to the Arabs*: "Oh people (*qawm*), the messenger of God has come from amongst you"';[46] al-Zamakhsharī (d. 537/1143) is more explicit: '"from amongst you' means from your race (*jins*) and from your genealogy (*nasab*), Arab, Qurashī';[47] and al-Qurṭubī (d. 671/1273) further still: 'the verse entails praise of Muhammad's genealogy – he is from pure Arab stock'.[48] Al-Zamakhsharī and al-Qurṭubī's references to *jīl* and *nasab* notably echo the precise terminology used to define *ᶜarab* in dictionaries written by their contemporaries. They impose such terminology to substantiate the Qur'an's undefined *qawm*, whereas Muqātil interprets the verse without mention of Arab *nasab* or even Quraysh tribe, and suffices with saying the verse was addressed to the 'people of Mecca',[49] the immediate audience of revelation.

Elsewhere Muqātil's exegesis also refrains from extrapolating Qur'anic references to Meccans and other Arabian groups into generalisations about pre-Islamic Arabs, whereas later exegetes assume such statements are references about the entire Arab community at the dawn of Islam.[50] And so, if we disengage from the hindsight of later exegesis, we find that Muqātil's text (like the Qur'an itself) does not proffer a pre-Islamic Arabian world filled with one genealogically cohesive Arab community, and neither does Muqātil employ the Qur'an as a platform to discuss Arabness.

The early textual indicators and their conceptions of *ᶜarabī* assist our interpretation of the gradual emergence of Arab ethnic consciousness. One single Arab kin-community did not exist in pre-Islamic times, so the Qur'an is naturally interpretable without imposing a sense of 'the Arab people' into its narratives, and Arabness remains predominantly linguistic. But ethnogenesis was in process, and while senses of interrelation between Arabian tribes emerged in early Islam in the form of consciousness of Arab community, they were also checked by fragmenting experiences of Umayyad-era enmities that prevented the full convergence of disparate peoples with clashing sociopolitical, doctrinal and regional interests. The resulting equivocation in the dictionary definitions of *ᶜarab* reflect that context, but by the fourth/tenth century, debate seems to have ended, and early Islamic history was reinterpreted as part of the Arab national story with a fixed sense of Arab genealogy/*nasab*. On a theoretical level, both Weber's 1922 ethnicity essay and Smith's elaboration of Weber's thesis anticipate the shift towards an increasingly fixed consciousness of kin-interrelation as a result of ethnogenesis and nation building,[51] and we now turn to genealogy to determine how the Arab family tree was constructed.

II Arabness and Contested Lineage

The hypothesis that pan-Arab genealogical unity was not systematised by Islam's second century is reflected in various sources. In Abū ᶜUmar Muḥammad al-Kindī's (d. after 355/966) *Kitāb Quḍāt Miṣr*, for example, we encounter a peculiar situation that arose in the town of al-Ḥaras in Egypt's Eastern Delta during the caliphates of al-Rashīd (170–93/786–809) and al-Amīn (193–8/809–13), that is, shortly after *al-ᶜAyn* was written. The inhabitants of al-Ḥaras reportedly claimed to be Arabs of the Quḍāᶜa group in order to be included on the official *Dīwān* for entitlement to government stipend,[52] but their claim was not accepted, and despite being offered a bribe of six thousand dinars to include them on the *Dīwān*, the Egyptian presiding judge deferred decision, referring the matter to the Caliph. The Ḥarasīs' subsequent delegation to Baghdad was also expensive,[53] but they eventually forged or bribed their way into an opinion from an Iraqi scholar of genealogy, al-Mufaḍḍal ibn Faḍāla, that proved their lineage to the Arab tribe of Quḍāᶜa. The Caliph al-Amīn accepted the 'evidence' and ordered their names entered on the Egyptian *Dīwān*, but in Egypt the governor still demanded further Arab witnesses to confirm that the Ḥarasīs were indeed Arabs, and while they were eventually successful, al-Kindī notes that the witnesses were all from the Syrian Desert and al-Ḥawf (the edge of the Sinai), implying that the other Arabs in Egypt did not accept the Ḥarasīs' Arabness, and the domicile of the witnesses – exterior to *Jazīrat al-ᶜarab* (Arabia) – may also be a mark against their true Arabness-credibility. Al-Kindī closes the story with a pointed remark that the Ḥarasīs 'hounded' the judge day and night in their petition,[54] further implying that the final acceptance of their Arabness was perhaps more a matter of acquiescence than conviction of the genuineness of their claim. Al-Kindī also relates an invective poem against the Ḥarasīs from an Egyptian Arab:

> How strange a matter it is that a gang,
> Copts from amongst us have become Arabs!
> They say 'Our father is the [Arab] Ḥawtak',
> But their father is a Coptic lout of uncertain past,
> They brought witnesses – brutes from al-Ḥawf

Who shouted out daft allegations of their relation;
May God curse those satisfied with their claim 'til the very last setting of
the sun![55]

The story indicates that proving Arabness was evidently of substantial practical value at the end of the second/eighth century, but the Ḥarasīs' travails also reveal how contested (and fluid) kinship was (in keeping with the premise that Arab genealogy was not yet wholly systematised). Al-Kindī's account was only recorded in the fourth/tenth century, but it mirrors other examples of genealogical confusion in the early Abbasid Caliphate. Consider the much-discussed genealogical conundrum of the Quḍāᶜa's lineage. During the later Umayyad era, Quḍāᶜa sided with the Yamāniyya faction of other 'Yemeni' tribes, whereas groups of the Quḍāᶜa had aligned with opposing collectives of Maᶜadd and Muḍar during Muᶜāwiya's Caliphate, and hence later genealogists were unclear as to whether the Quḍāᶜa was a Yemeni or Ma'addite tribe.[56] Finding the 'true' genealogy of Quḍāᶜa is a false hope, obstructed by both politics and the ephemeral notion of 'tribe' itself. Quḍāᶜa, as a collective name for groups residing in Syria before the Islamic conquests, found opportunities to offer services to the early Umayyads who, as noted in Chapter 2, were closely affiliated with a sense of belonging to a community of Maᶜadd. Quḍāᶜa's initial Ma'addite leanings thus seem more readily explainable as a matter of political expedience to show solidarity with their paymasters rather than being a 'memory' of actual, empirical genealogy. As Syrian politics fragmented after Muᶜāwiya's death, groups realigned, prompting new claims about Quḍāᶜa's lineage to fit them within a newly vigorous group (backed by stakeholders in the important towns of Ḥimṣ and Damascus) of *al-Yamāniyya*. And moreover, a priori assumptions that Quḍāᶜa even represented one certain cohesive group are difficult to substantiate since both the underpinnings of the Maᶜadd, Muḍar and Yamāniyya factions evolved during early Islam, and various smaller subgroups likely joined and seceded from Quḍāᶜa over the same period. The multivalent complexity of Quḍāᶜa's lineage was never resolved, and confounded attempts to settle one, static and tidy family tree from the conflicting memories generated over generations of flux and political turmoil.

To the array of fluid genealogy, we can also proffer an anecdote written in the early third/ninth century by al-Jāḥiẓ in *Kitāb al-Ḥayawān*,[57] where he reports a story from his informant Abū al-Jahjāh about

> an old man who claimed he was from the tribe of Kinda before looking at all into the lineage (*nasab*) of Kinda. I asked him one day when he was with me: 'Who are you from?' He responded: 'From Kinda', to which I asked: 'From which [sub-tribe] of them?' He responded: 'This is not the place for such speech, God bless you!'[58]

Al-Jāḥiẓ places this anecdote in one of his many sections of witty diversions, classifying it as a droll tale (*nawādir*), but it depicts an environment of uncertain Arab tribal lineages. For a scholar such as al-Jāḥiẓ, ignorance of the proper proof of lineage was amusing, but for the old man, he had either circulated in society falsely masquerading as a Kindite, or actually was a Kindite but was unable to establish his connection to one of the tribal subgroups which genealogists had determined to be 'correct'.[59]

The development of Arab communities after the conquests, *al-ᶜAyn*'s non-lineage definition of 'Arab', Quḍāᶜa's complications, al-Kindī's tale of contested lineage, and al-Jāḥiẓ's sarcastic recounting of a curiously unsubstantiated claim to Arab lineage each suggest an early third/ninth-century Arabness fluidity when genealogy was for sale and pan-Arab family trees were imprecisely articulated. From the perspective of ethnogenesis, uncertainty and competing claims about a community's membership are markers of periods when the symbolic value of belonging to that community was high. For so long as Arabness was an asset of real people who were actively asserting their own senses of being 'Arabs', Arabness would not settle into a stable, static concept that could be cut-and-dried by dispassionate scholars as an academic exercise.[60] The early third/ninth century can accordingly be appreciated as a time when being 'Arab' meant a great deal as a practical matter, and in this context, al-Jāḥiẓ is again instructive for his remarkable description of Arabness in *Risāla fī Manāqib al-Turk* (written between 218 and 227/833 and 842)[61] that articulates Arab unity in a manner that sidesteps genealogical uncertainty:

> If you ask: how can all of the children of [ᶜAdnān and Qaḥṭān – the progenitors of the 'Northern' and 'Southern' Arabs, respectively] be Arabs since they come from different fathers?

> We reply: when the Arabs became one, they became equal in their land, language, characteristics, motivation, pride, zealotry, ethics and character. Then they were [as if] cast into one mould and poured out as one, they were all in one form; their component parts were similar. When that similitude became pronounced in all generalities and particularities . . . they reached a decision about noble descent [*ḥasab*], this became the cause for a second birth, such that they married along these lines and became in-laws because of it. ᶜAdnān absolutely prohibited intermarriage with the tribe of Isaac, the brother of Ishmael, but over time they openly welcomed intermarriage with the tribe of Qaḥṭān, son of ᶜĀbir[62] . . . This proves that genealogy was agreed between them, and these concepts took the place of close relationships of common birth.[63]

Al-Jāḥiẓ's Arab example is part of a discourse on the theoretical relationships between *umma* (people/ethnos) and genealogy (*nasab*); al-Jāḥiẓ pointedly fudges precise lineage by proposing that the Arab *umma* did not arise from one eponymous ancestor, and that instead, different peoples who recognised their similarities on account of various commonalities (including shared domicile) agreed amongst themselves to form a kin-relationship and maintained it, achieving the 'second birth', that is, the basis of lineage-based Arabness. In this argument, al-Jāḥiẓ seeks to convince his readers that similarity engendered blood ties, not the other way around.

Al-Jāḥiẓ's text, perhaps the fullest direct Arabness discourse surviving from the early Abbasid period, has attracted modern attention. Jan Retsö compares al-Jāḥiẓ's statement with notions of Arabness expressed by the eighth/fourteenth-century Ibn Khaldūn and twentieth-century North African nomads, and concludes that al-Jāḥiẓ's text should be interpreted as prototypical, an empirical fact proving that 'at least from the beginning of the Abbasid age', Arabs defined themselves via an attenuated genealogy.[64] On the other hand, Lassner reads al-Jāḥiẓ's Arabness passage as convoluted and 'problematic', interpreting it as a relic of a very particular moment in the mid-third/ninth century when the Caliphate in Baghdad was in systematic decline and when the Caliph was retreating into increasingly private confines, surrounded by Turkic private armies.[65] Lassner considers al-Jāḥiẓ's position as an occasional figure at court and an intellectual who was nostalgic for

Baghdad's political heyday during the decades before, and held out hope that the Turks could be integrated to reinvigorate the system. Under Lassner's reading, al-Jāḥiẓ's thoughts on Arab identity are not really about the Arabs at all, but are instead a cleverly constructed mirror to express his aspirations about how the Turks could be integrated into Iraqi cosmopolitan society.[66] And so, al-Jāḥiẓ's apparent discussion of Arabness seems yet another example of his slippery ideas which Montgomery discusses at length, noting how difficult they can be to capture.[67] Like Lassner, I am nonetheless sanguine that the 'real al-Jāḥiẓ' does speak his mind sufficiently for us to make sense of him, though bearing Montgomery's warnings in mind, our readings require careful contextualisation in order to apply his rich discourse about Arabness to aid our reconstruction of Arab ethnogenesis.

To interpret al-Jāḥiẓ in this study, we return to the basic framework of ethnogenesis and its call to place evidence on a chronological continuum. Since theorists have shown how the 'Aboriginal is both determined and determining',[68] it is remote that a given statement about ethnic identity can be taken as a static definition that will last for centuries, and it is equally unlikely that an author can concoct a discourse about a ethnic group from nothing. When al-Jāḥiẓ wrote about the Arabs, the scope for his ideas, howsoever independent minded he was as an author, can be expected to have been determined in part by the many Arabness debates surrounding him. Such debates included the linguistic definition of Arabness as a speech community and the difficulties Arabs and others faced when trying to construct genealogical interrelations. Al-Jāḥiẓ's notion of subjective, consensual Arabness thus sits rather neatly between the open-ended linguistic definition of 'Arab' in *al-ᶜAyn* (originally written about fifty years earlier) and al-Azharī's closed lineage-based model (written a century later), and his essay is an appropriate compromise in an environment where precise genealogical models exhibited flux and where notions of Arabness as a language were being increasingly undercut by new definitions which as yet lacked a solid genealogical model to 'prove' the correctness of their senses of Arab kin-community.

The interpretation of al-Jāḥiẓ's Arabness puzzle can be augmented by shifting to a similar, though much less commented upon, passage in his *al-Bayān wa-l-Tabyīn*.[69] Al-Jāḥiẓ repeats the debate between linguistic and genealogical Arabness, and rejects both the arguments that Arab identity flows from speaking Arabic or that Arab identity is beholden to lineage, again in favour of positing Arabian land as the incubating ground for the true 'Arabs'. This passage is not concerned with Turks and the caliphal army, suggesting therefore an amendment to Lassner's thesis, inasmuch as we have alighted upon an Arabness idea which al-Jāḥiẓ held with wider application. The discourse in *al-Bayān* concerns language and the unique identity of the Arabs, and al-Jāḥiẓ (for reasons that will be detailed in Chapter 6(I)), is keen to deny that mastery of Arabic is something exclusive to people born of Arab parents. Accordingly, al-Jāḥiẓ critiques those he calls 'the Nizaris' (*ᶜawwām al-Nizāriyya* – that is, the descendants of the most important Ma'addite groups) whom he describes as pursuing an argument that Arabness is essentially a function of language in order to promote the pre-eminence of their Arabness over South Arabians. Al-Jāḥiẓ proposes instead that 'real knowledgeable people' (*al-khawāṣṣ al-khullaṣ* - that is, al-Jāḥiẓ's longhand for himself!) know that Arab identity is a function of the special qualities of the Arabs' land of origin: its soil, air and water.[70] Al-Jāḥiẓ's discursive construction indicates he was writing against a body of opinion (and hints a Ma'addite/Nizārī interest group was the faction who sought to uphold Arabness as a function of language),[71] and the passage, read together with the excerpt from his *Risāla* above, reveal a waning of the persuasiveness of defining Arabs by their tongue, and a scholarly search for new ways to imagine the Arabs.

If al-Jāḥiẓ's sentiments can be read as an indication of one of Arabness' meanings in the cosmopolitan Iraq of the early third/ninth century, they, and the other anecdotes considered herein, indicate that pan-Arabian Arab genealogy was a Muslim-era construct to forge a sense of Arab identity through novel lines of kinship. Developing from the earlier fractured everyday negotiation of kinship in the growing cities of Muslim Iraq, we could thus see Muslim scholars during the third/ninth century as creators of a new, more cohesive Arab kin-identity by which they projected the idea of 'Arab blood' into an ancient past, and thus gave 'Arabs' (who only began to imagine their community in Muslim times) new-found, primordial imagined kinship. Once the genealogical construction site was finished, we can see why al-Jāḥiẓ's subjective conception of Arabness would not be repeated – it was no longer necessary and it could give way to the tidier lineage-based definitions in later dictionaries. Close diachronic consideration of the construction of the Arab family is accordingly our next order of business.

III Arab Genealogy Reconsidered: Kinship, Gender and Identity

Investigating the constructedness of Arab genealogy confronts the well-worn stereotype that 'Arabs' always and naturally envisage history through a 'genealogical imagination'.[72] From the fourth/tenth century, Muslim authors maintained that Arabs possess a special expertise in the 'science of genealogy' (*ᶜilm al-nasab/ansāb*),[73] and modern scholars have tended to follow suit,[74] but invocations of innate 'Arab penchants' are sweeping generalisations of the sort this book seeks to challenge, and the impressions about 'Arab genealogy' are no exception. To this point, it is significant that in contrast to fourth/tenth-century texts, Ibn Qutayba's (d. 276/889) *al-Tanbīh*, the most generously detailed third/ninth-century discourse on the knowledge of the Arabs, has no mention of *nasab* as an Arab science.[75] Since Part One of this book maintained that pre-Islamic Arabians left no indications that they imagined a kin-community as Arabs, the relatively early writer Ibn Qutayba's silence is anticipated: the Muslim-era constructions of pan-Arab genealogy did not emanate from actual pre-Islamic populations, and it was up to Muslim-era writers to link the various groups, tribes and memories into neat genealogical models.[76] Only once the models were established could subsequent writers, for the first time, conceptualise ancient Arabs as a single community of interrelated tribes. The constructedness of third/ninth-century Arab genealogies has been noted,[77] but the actual mechanisms and the significance of their constructions are yet not fully tested, as there has been little diachronic survey of the layers of Muslim-era Arab genealogy. Such survey alongside fresh attention to the constructedness of genealogy as a matter of theory can now open new avenues to grasp the consequences of the emergence of a widely articulated Arab identity in the second/eighth century.

Genealogy and Identity

Genealogy is, in many respects, the predecessor of today's concept of DNA. Both are concerned with blood, and both employ tables of interrelations to show how blood connects people to each other. Both have been employed to answer one of the most enduring human concerns: who is family and who is kin? And both genealogy and DNA, therefore, have weighty resonance in the human psyche: genealogy has long been the arbiter of inheritance, war and peace, and DNA currently stands as nearly unimpeachable evidence in courts of law. The power of both DNA and genealogy is located in their claim to reveal the truth, but herein they mix most uneasily with history and identity. A number of scientists and historians attempted to plumb the DNA of national populations to determine the 'real history' of humanity, but their results are not always helpful. For very ancient population movements across thousands of years, DNA offered new ways to test the dispersal of *Homo sapiens* and theories of migrations 'out of Africa', but for more delicate questions of mapping specific historical migrations or determining the origins of modern nations,[78] DNA fell short, resulting in what Patrick Geary dubs 'bad history'.[79] Max Weber would doubtless agree with Geary's assessment: we have seen that Weber's 1922 essay on ethnicity stressed the role of human agency and choice to determine who we want to be, and this is never a matter predetermined by blood or genes, but one chosen by the brain. Theorists of ethnogenesis accordingly consign DNA's role in studying communal identity to the outdated nineteenth- and early twentieth-century notions of 'race': the material question for studying an identity is not whether people are actually related to one another, but rather, whether (and why) they imagine they are related.[80] As a result, our studies need to appreciate the paradox of genealogy, for it is both an important edifice for community's identity, but equally a chimera for scholarly research. Genealogy was the 'truth' marshalled to explain the deep historical blood connections between members of a community, but as its membership changed, so the 'truth' needed to evolve in step.

For the study of Arab ethnogenesis, therefore, modern theory instructs us to deconstruct genealogy's empirical veneer. Instead of the traditional belief that by following family trees we can construct narratives of Arab history, we would propose that by following history we can see how Arab family trees were constructed. The absence of a pan-Arabian community in pre-Islam (as set out in Part One of this book), together with the indications from dictionaries and other sources surveyed at the outset of this chapter that the construction of Arab genealogy was yet incomplete even in the third/ninth century, direct us to investigate the processes which prompted Conqueror groups to experience a shared sense of Arabness in the later first/seventh and second/eighth centuries, and gave rise to the contours of an Arab expressed by linking groups into new family trees. If the Conquerors did invent genealogy to gel their Arab imagined community, we can expect at least two findings: (1) the different ways in which different groups approached genealogy and kinship would need to be homogenised into a single overarching system, and (2) 'origin' Arab ancestor figures would need to be created in order to back-track each of the Conqueror groups to 'shared' roots. As society developed and new groups sought membership in the Arab community, each of these aspects of genealogy would need to change, and we seek these changes in the sources.

Our searches are further inspired by Lancaster's and Shryock's analyses of Jordanian tribal society in the twentieth century which, in line with the theoretical stance of this book's method, revealed that modern Jordanian genealogical trees are indeed generated and evolve to suit changing needs of present realities. Both Lancaster and Shryock call genealogy a strategy, a 'malleable'[81] 'asset' which tribesmen 'manipulate . . . to fit in with the working arrangements of groups on the ground'.[82] Their researches found that purported kin-relationships embody shared political/economic interests in the present, and instead of indicating ancient blood-ties, they construct a sense of belonging to present political/economic interest groups by generating a consensual fiction of past kin-relationships.[83] Supposed tribal ancestor figures are unlikely to have ever really existed,[84] there is a gap of many generations in remembered genealogy between an individual's immediate ancestors and his tribe's supposed 'founding fathers',[85] and kin groups could just as easily form on matrilineal as patrilineal lines – matrilineal relatives are made to fit into the conventional patrilineal system by recasting them as relations via *ibn ᶜamm* (sons of an uncle).[86]

Akin to Benedict Anderson's theories of European nationalism, whereby the nation is constructed to appear to 'loom out of an immemorial past',[87] notions of lineage construct a 'genealogical nationalism'[88] by which seemingly cohesive ethnicity emerges. Models of shared genealogy post-date the emergence of a community's consciousness of unity, and in the case of early Arab communities, the third/ninth-century appearance of kin-based arguments to define Arabness suggest a dynamic second/eighth-century Arab ethnogenesis which necessitated the transformation of disparate older family lines into one new consolidated Arab family tree. The timing again accords with the stirrings of the word *ᶜarab* in poetry and hadith, and similar kinds of construction strategies which Lancaster and Shryock observed also appear in third/ninth- and fourth/tenth-century models of Arab genealogy. For example, the ubiquitous use of the verb *daraja* ('he left no offspring') in the genealogists' discussions of ancient ancestors permits efficient streamlining of early steps in the family tree to connect near contemporaries with eponymous ancient ancestors without unwieldy bifurcated models. The '*daraja* device' allowed genealogists to effectively 'kill off' past generations to traverse memory gaps similar to those explored by Lancaster. Furthermore, Hugh Kennedy indicates the likelihood that the encyclopedic pan-Arab family trees constructed during the generation of Hishām ibn Muḥammad al-Kalbī (d. 204/819 or 206/821) were fluid constructs, generated on a 'must-have-been' basis, analogous to Lancaster's findings in modern Jordan.[89] Others note that the synthesis of genealogy dates from Ibn al-Kalbī,[90] but Kennedy's proposal that Ibn al-Kalbī and his contemporaries actually created the very sense of an Arab family tree is what we develop here.

Gender, Genealogy and Arabness: from Women to Men?

There are intriguing indications that the sociopolitical drivers of Arab ethnogenesis had fundamental transformative effects on the underlying ways by which early Muslim groups consolidated and imagined their kin-interrelations. It can be expected that major alterations in the very organisation of genealogy are a natural by-product of ethnogenesis: different groups have their own ways of reckoning kinship, and as they begin to unite into a new shared identity, their different traditions yield to one, new overarching model of genealogy in order to unite them all. The appearance of new forms of kinship organisation is therefore a useful barometer to trace a process of ethnogenesis, and in the case of Arabness, intriguing shifts towards homogenisation of various pre-Islamic ways of reckoning ancestry appear when the sources are evaluated from the perspective of gender.

Arab genealogical models familiar today are patrilineal since groups are identified by their shared fathers and uncles, but the system of organising tribes into patrilineal lines may in fact be a comparatively late innovation. Ḥayāt Qaṭṭāṭ uncovered a wealth of matrilineal links between the first generations of Muslims which later genealogical writings obscured, thereby revealing that matrilineal kinship ties had more importance in pre-Islam and early Islamic times than they were accorded in later Arab genealogical constructs written after the second/eighth century.[91] The political importance of female figures in early Islam is also noted,[92] and the 'traditional' patriarchal interpretations of the Qur'an are likewise being challenged via arguments that the 'textualising of misogyny' is the compound result of several generations of interpreting the Qur'an in early Islam, and that the Qur'an itself promotes the status of women, particularly (but not exclusively) mothers.[93] The third/ninth-century patrilineal overwriting of early Muslim groups' matrilineal genealogy parallels the promotion of patriarchal interpretations of the Qur'an in exegesis of the same period, and it thus appears that we are uncovering a point of key significance. From Qaṭṭāṭ's groundwork, it bears consideration that a number of pre-Islamic Arabian groups were organised matrilineally, and that they brought such systems of communal organisation into the nascent Muslim world, but their genealogical thinking was reorganised into patrilineal kinship over the course of Islam's first two centuries. Such reorganisation goes to the heart of ethnogenesis: the switch from matrilineal to patrilineal succession transforms the very ways individuals conceptualise themselves and their interrelations with others, and would indicate the emergence of a new kind of 'imagined community' – in this case, the 'Arab community'.

Evaluating the development of nascent Muslim society from the perspective of gender, and linking the changing role of gender in political movements, the organisation of power and, not least, the structure of families in Islam's first two centuries to Arab ethnogenesis emanates from Pohl, Reimitz and Geary's observations that the adoption of identities elsewhere in Late Antiquity occurred at both a communal and individual level.[94] Gender and identity should be connected in respect of both clan and nuclear family, and enables deconstruction of the Arab genealogical monolith that projects patrilineal 'Arab kinship' into time immemorial, allowing us to then uncover how factions and families would have been able to imagine their senses of self, and why, by the third/ninth century, the contours of the new Arab identity came to be defined on starkly patrilineal tribal lines.

From the perspective of power, the role of matrilineal links factored in key events of early Islam's political history underscores Qaṭṭāṭ's observation of the initial importance of female lines in early communal imagination. For example, consider the succession of the first caliphs. The Prophet had no male issue, but the first two caliphs were both Muhammad's fathers-in-law: Abū Bakr was the father of Muhammad's favoured wife ᶜĀᵓisha, and ᶜUmar was the father of Ḥafṣa, another important wife. With the third caliph, succession naturally shifted one matrilineal level down from the fathers of the Prophet's wives to men who married the Prophet's daughters: ᶜUthmān=Ruqayya (and then a second wife, another daughter of the Prophet, Umm Kulthūm) and ᶜAlī=Fāṭima. It seems material that each of the first caliphs, each in need of presenting their novel form of leadership in a legitimate fashion, possessed intimate matrilineal ties to the Prophet.

Whether or not gender legitimately featured in early caliphal succession, a gendered lens does reveal that alliances in the First *Fitna* struggles (36–40/656–61) during ᶜAlī's caliphate divided between distinct matrilineal clusters:

1. ᶜĀᵓisha (wife of the Prophet and daughter of Abū Bakr) and her brothers-in-law (a) Ṭalḥa (married to both ᶜĀᵓisha's sister Umm Kulthūm and the sister of another wife of the Prophet, Zaynab), and (b) al-Zubayr (married to ᶜĀᵓisha's sister, Asmāᵓ); versus
2. ᶜAlī and the *Ahl al-Bayt* (Family of the Prophet) traced through the female line of Muhammad's daughter, Fāṭima; versus
3. Muᶜāwiya, brother of one of Muhammad's less notable wives, Ramla bint Abī Sufyān.

In the case of each faction, power seems articulated through, and factions divided along different female connections to the Prophet, but the *Fitna*'s eventual winner, Muᶜāwiya's party, had the most flimsy matrilineal pedigree. Ramla, Muᶜāwiya's only female connection to Muhammad, is a very minor figure in the sources of the Prophet's biography with only a few stories associated with her memory.[95] They report that she was initially married to ᶜUbayd Allāh ibn Jaḥsh, both were early converts to Islam, and they emigrated from Mecca to Ethiopia where Ramla stayed until almost the end of Muhammad's life. In Ethiopia, her original husband is said to have abandoned Islam in favour of Christianity (and most accounts add that he swiftly drank himself to death thereafter), but Ramla remained Muslim, and once widowed (and by this time over the age of thirty), sources report that Muhammad married her *in absentia*, and several years later she returned to Arabia. Very little else is reported of her relations to Muhammad, except that the marriage was seen as a bridge between Muhammad and Mecca's most powerful family with whom he was warring, as expressed in Qur'an 60:7 (a verse reportedly revealed on the occasion of the marriage): 'God may still bring about affection between you and your present enemies – God is all powerful'.[96] Interpreting these stories today is difficult because the accounts of Ramla's Ethiopian sojourn and her betrothal to Muhammad are obscure: there is some disagreement regarding the connection of Qur'an 60:7 to Ramla's marriage, there are evident marks of storytelling and narrative embellishment, and there is stark contrast between the extensive detail on Ramla's marriage and the essential silence regarding the rest of her biography. The texts are at least unanimous in agreeing that Ramla was a wife of Muhammad, and whilst the details of the Ethiopian stories may be skewed to portray the circumstances in a more pious light, what does make sense is that Muhammad arranged the marriage for political reasons, given the utility of cementing an alliance with his most powerful rivals in Mecca, and this perhaps explains why the sources have scant further detail about Muhammad's actual relations with Ramla.

From our perspective of gender and the First *Fitna*, Ramla's story is pertinent for it reveals that Muᶜāwiya's camp lacked truly intimate connections with women of the Prophet's family, and that Muᶜāwiya's powerbase focused on the prestige of pagan Mecca's most powerful clan. Given the impeccable pedigree of Muᶜāwiya's chief opponent, ᶜAlī, the Prophet's son-in-law, there is logic in seeing that Muᶜāwiya had little to gain by promoting his claims to the Caliphate in matrilineal terms, as it would only benefit his rival. To this end, it is also relevant that Muᶜāwiya's faction was also the first to effect patrilineal succession to the Caliphate when Muᶜāwiya appointed his son Yazīd as heir. Muᶜāwiya's move is often seen as an impious importation of principles of worldly kingship into Islam,[97] but it could also be understood as a move to keep power away from his main rivals, the Alids, by introducing a novel form of caliphal legitimacy through the patrilineal line.

Muᶜāwiya's Umayyad successors of the following generation were faced with a similar crisis of legitimacy traceable to their lack of strong matrilineal pedigree compared to their rivals. During the Second *Fitna* (60–73/680–92), the patrilineal Umayyad clan was challenged by ᶜAbd Allāh ibn al-Zubayr. Ibn Zubayr was traditionally branded in histories as a traitor/usurper, though recent scholarship stresses the legitimacy of his pretensions to the Caliphate,[98] and to this point, we can add that if Ibn Zubayr's cause is evaluated in matrilineal terms, we could venture that he was the most legitimate contender in the ring, for he possessed impeccable pedigree via both his aunt Khadīja, Muhammad's first wife and mother of all Muhammad's surviving children, and Ibn Zubayr's own mother, Asmāᵓ, daughter of the first caliph, Abū Bakr, Muhammad's father in law. Though doubly related to the Prophet and first caliph, Ibn al-Zubayr nonetheless lost the war and was rebranded by later historians as a usurper, and further Umayyad victories over the Alid *Ahl al-Bayt* set up three further generations of clustering power in a patrilineal guise through the Marwanid dynasty. Like Muᶜāwiya's Sufyanid line before them, the Marwanids lacked their rivals' matrilineal pedigrees, and instead promoted a notion of Caliphate based on claims of legitimacy through oaths of allegiance to the chosen male successors whose position was cloaked in Divine authority.[99]

The Third *Fitna* and the rise of the Abbasid dynasty further exerted pressure against the prestige and practical value of matrilineal genealogy in the Caliphate's power structures. Like the Umayyads before them, a pillar of Abbasid legitimacy was paternalist (the line from al-ᶜAbbās was on the Prophet's uncle's side), whereas swelling Alid discontent continued emphasising the female line from the Prophet's daughter Fāṭima. The relevance of the distinction materialises in letters ascribed to correspondence between the second Abbasid caliph, al-Manṣūr (r. 136–58/754–75), and the Alid leader Muḥammad ibn ᶜAbd Allāh ibn Ḥasan which debate the relative merits of matrilineal versus patrilineal genealogy. Since the Alids had manifestly stronger maternal relations to the Prophet, the practical advantage of promoting patrilineal links in Abbasid rhetoric is palpable, as al-Manṣūr's letters reveal.[100]

Taking stock, the power structures in the century following the First *Fitna* in 35/656 worked against matrilineal prominence at each crucial juncture of the Caliphate's path. As the succession of caliphs during the course of 150 years between the first Umayyads and the first written genealogies all promoted patrilineal dynasties, the conception of power would inevitably shift away from earlier notions of matrilineal prominence, and groups of the Conqueror elite, that is, those who would become the Arabs, would be prompted to follow suit, reorganising their senses of kinship and interrelations into increasingly patrilineal models.[101] We can thus perceive that the patrilineal manner in which Abbasid-era scholars organised Arab genealogies echoed their contemporary structures of power, and in so doing, fundamentally reorganised the community's kin-structure, overlooking (and perhaps overwriting) the older matrilineal links which Qaṭṭāṭ's research uncovered.

We discern more of the process of shifting genealogy towards a patrilineal model through the narrative context of a version of the al-Manṣūr/Alid letters reported in al-Mubarrad's (d. 285/898) *al-Kāmil*. The letters are a culmination of a lengthy (and typically for al-Mubarrad, omnivorous) discourse that touches on Arab/ᶜ*ajam* identity, the status of Arabs and new converts (*mawālī*), and the effects of mothers' social standing on their children's status. Al-Mubarrad exhibits interest in negotiating issues of status, especially where sons are born of noble Arab fathers and slave-girl or low-status mothers, and while his style never forces conclusions (except in the case of coincidental grammatical issues arising in the source anecdotes!), his presentation of anecdotes casts status as emanating through fathers, irrespective of mothers' identity, and from the outset this betrays Abbasid/Alid competition.[102] His first anecdotes recount the status of the descendants of the freed (male) slave Abū Rāfiᶜ, whose manumission by Muhammad makes him a client (*mawlā*) of the Prophet and thus, in al-Mubarrad's view, of no lower ranking than the Alid *Ahl al-Bayt*. To prove it, al-Mubarrad presents the story of a confrontation between al-Ḥasan ibn ᶜAlī and Abū Rāfiᶜ's son, in which al-Ḥasan's claim of superiority is debunked via poetry from a partisan of the Abbasid family:

> You challenge the legitimacy of al-ᶜAbbās' father
> But you do not argue from a noble corner:
> When did sons of girls become inheritors –
> Who can claim the rights of a father?[103]

More poetry follows, denigrating matrilineal lineage, promoting paternal uncles and substantiating their good lineage via the Qur'an's inheritance rules, which are skewed in favour of male descendants. Al-Mubarrad's defence of sons of ignoble mothers is pointed, and the identities of several characters in the anecdotes betray connections to Abbasid–Alid rivalry. The discourse is also relevant to the nobility of the Abbasid caliphs of al-Mubarrad's own day, since they were all born from non-Arab mothers.[104] By marshalling the Qur'an along with poetry to support the status of the Abbasid caliphs, al-Mubarrad goes to some lengths to ground his discourse in legitimate authority.[105]

Shifting from the organisation of the highest echelons of power to the wider post-conquest society of early Muslims who would constitute the basis of the 'Arab community', we can perceive that changes to family organisation also conspired against matrilineal thinking and prompted impetus to articulate status through descent from fathers. The shift is apparent from the practical realities of status confronted by the children of the original Conquerors on account of the identities of their mothers. As a consequence of the widespread conquests and the permissiveness of polygamy, powerful men in the post-conquest Middle East had unprecedented access to captive girls, and as the *amṣār* swelled, all of the Emigrant men had opportunities to marry local women along with the daughters of fellow Emigrants. The long-term effects of such marriages created contradiction: Emigrants and their scion constituted the political elite and naturally wished to maintain their status as the community of original Conquerors, but increasing numbers of the Emigrants' descendants were born of non-Conqueror women. If status remained tied to mothers, individual families would be torn from within between high-status sons of Emigrant women and lower-status brothers born of local women and *umm walad* (slaves), and hence a rapidly growing portion of the elite faced an embarrassing drop in status and dilution in pedigree simply because of their mothers. The problem could, of course, be obviated if the Emigrants/Muslims reconceptualised the sense of status and community belonging by tracing identity through fathers which could unite all the sons into one cohesive family.

It is difficult to peer through the thicket to view the pre-Islamic genealogical imagination, but we behold an array of reasons why third/ninth-century Muslims would have been influenced to re-think genealogy in patrilineal terms. The third/ninth-century cultural producers lived in a world commanded by caliphs born of ignoble mothers, they navigated a political system that had evolved in favour of patrilineal groups, and the individual constituent members of the 'Arab community' had long needed to promote patrilineal lineage to maintain status. The situation seems to contrast the pre-Islamic past, given the weight of matrilineal importance in nascent Islam, records of women leaders in pre-Islamic Arabia,[106] indications of legacy matrilineal chains in genealogical texts,[107] and the cover-up of matrilineal linkages, which Qaṭṭāṭ identified. We can thus envision that some Arabian groups, in the process of their Islamisation and Arabisation, had to reverse their conception of genealogical succession to a patriarchal model in order to fit the changing realities of the post-conquest Middle East, and that the pan-Arabian patrilineal descent system offered to us in classical-era genealogies is a fiction, a retrospective rewriting of the past to fit the lineage models which had become the vogue with Islam and its Caliphate. The phenomenon of third/ninth-century writers 'record[ing] the past as a back projection of more current events' to serve discourses of the elite has been noted in respect to other genres of historiography,[108] and the entrenchment of patrilineal lines in the construction of historical tribal genealogies seems another facet of this process of Abbasid-era cultural production.

There is no need to proclaim that all pre-Islamic Arabians were organised in matrilineal clans: one of the principal aims of this book is to critique the habit of imagining one social/cultural/communal cohesion in pre-Islamic Arabia. Our argument is that pre-Islamic heterogeneity experienced homogenisation in line with the trajectories of the wider developing post-conquest society. The *longue durée* approach under the theoretical presumptions that neither Arab identity nor Arab genealogy were created in one stroke offers the possibility to observe how the act of becoming Arab was linked to the power relations favoured by the caliphs and the elite, and how the patrilineal predilection of Islamic identity influenced the way groups coordinated their interrelations. From the perspective of Arab ethnogenesis, the findings are a key indication of the scope of imagining new communities in the first centuries of Islam. Beyond merely tinkering with genealogical lineages to join formerly disparate groups, an entire system of conceptualising genealogy was constructed to suit the needs of the Muslim elite: this was a fundamental aspect in shaping how people becoming 'Arab' could imagine their interrelations with other 'Arabs', and reveals the extent to which the sociopolitical changes following the conquests reworked old memories, reconceptualised communities and gave rise to new forms of identity expressed as Arabness.

Shifting from the fundamentals of genealogy to the particulars, the next section investigates the ways in which Arab genealogies identified the 'first Arab'. This takes us on another journey across the generations of early Islam, as shifting senses of Arab community engendered new interpretations of Arab ancestry to write an imagined pre-Islamic 'Arab' past into history, and uncovers traces of the evolution that eventually yielded what is today known as 'traditional Arab genealogy'.

IV The Creation of 'Traditional' Arab Genealogy

The familiar model of Arab genealogy is bipartite, dividing Arabs into Northern and Southern branches, descendants of ᶜAdnān and Qaḥṭān, respectively. The tradition identifies Qaḥṭān as a very ancient figure, dated to the dispersal of the world's people from the Tower of Babel, thereby making Arabs appear to be a very ancient ethnos. Traditions also identify two prophets frequently mentioned in the Qur'an, Hūd and Ṣāliḥ, as descendants of Qaḥṭān and, therefore, the pair are identified as ancient 'Arab prophets' and precursors to Muhammad.[109] But herein considerable chronological problems arise. As Chapter 3 revealed, the broad sense of Arab identity only materialised from the later first/seventh century, and so the stories of ancient Qaḥṭānī 'Arabs' and the specific identification of Hūd and Ṣāliḥ as ethnically 'Arab prophets' would seem to be Muslim-era fabrications, back-projected into bygone pre-Islamic time in order to give Arabs an obstensibly ancient past and to forget that the Arab community only emerged after the dawn of Islam. Proving the fact of fabrication is not easy, however, since medieval Muslim writers confidently made manifold references to pre-Islamic 'Arabs', the ancient 'Arab prophets', and the fixed ᶜAdnān/Qaḥṭān genealogy. So, we would like to agree with Donner that the medieval literary assertions of pre-Islamic Arabness are indeed fabrications and that their use of the word 'Arab' is part of the 'reformed vocabulary' which Donner postulated second/eighth-century Muslims coined to rewrite history and redesignate past peoples as 'Arab ancestors',[110] but to prove the case we need to adduce textual evidence. This section directs close scrutiny to the traditions about the purported 'Arab' ancestors, drilling down from the 'canonical' medieval writings into the earliest textual layers.

To probe the foundations of the 'traditional' Arab genealogy, we can begin with the work of a prominent and prolific medieval scholar of Muslim traditions, the Ḥanbalite jurist Ibn al-Jawzī (d. 597/1200–1). Ibn al-Jawzī wrote a chronological universal history, *al-Muntaẓam*, which he expressly introduces as an orthodox history, free from 'legends' (*khurāfāt*) and 'far-fetched details' (*baᶜīdat al-ṣiḥḥa*), and with rigorous *isnād* and attention to chronology throughout.[111] *Al-Muntaẓam* contains a number of sections relating to pre-Islamic 'Arab' history and ancient 'Arab prophets', and its narrative includes a *marfūᶜ* hadith on the authority of the Companion Abū Dharr in which Muhammad is reported to have said that there have been 124,000 prophets since Creation, listing the well-known ones, that is, those commonly encountered in the Qur'an and later exegesis, and adding:

> Four are *Suryānī*: Adam, Shīth [Seth], Akhnūkh [Enoch] – he is Idrīs, the first to write with a pen – and Noah. Four are from the Arabs [*min al-ᶜarab*]: Hūd, Shuᶜayb, Ṣāliḥ and your Prophet, Muhammad . . . The first of the Israelite Prophets was Moses, and the last was Jesus.[112]

Abū Dharr's hadith is recorded in *al-Muntaẓam*'s chapter on the summa of prophetic history and invites an ethnic conceptualisation of prophecy, grouping prophets by their respective peoples. The approach enables readers to think about 'Arab prophets' as a distinct category, and the inclusion of Muhammad in the Arab group naturally privileges 'Arab prophecy'. Ibn al-Jawzī emphasises the cohesion and importance of 'Arab prophecy' by next relating further hadith with ethnic insinuations: one from Ibn al-ᶜAbbās tells that 'the Persians had no prophet',[113] and another from Ibn Ḥayda tells that Muhammad informed his companions that they are 'the fulfilment of seventy nations (*umma*) . . . the best and most honourable [people] before God'.[114] Ibn Ḥayda's hadith makes no express mention of the word 'Arab', but given its context in *al-Muntaẓam*, where it is narrated after Abū Dharr's hadith identifying Muhammad as an 'Arab prophet' and the pointed remark about the absence of Persian prophets, the insinuation of Muhammad's Arabness is apparent. In overview, *al-Muntaẓam*'s arrangement of anecdotes and ascription of most of them to the Prophet Muhammad himself[115] enables Ibn al-Jawzī to present the Arabness of the ancient prophets Hūd and Ṣāliḥ as a fact, a purportedly Prophet-endorsed view maintained since Muhammad's day. Such is the customary strategy of orthodoxy: by articulating its views in an unambiguous fashion and via unimpeachable authority, it lays claim to settle a truth. But when we analyse *al-Muntaẓam*'s material more closely, we can begin deconstructing its 'truth' claim about the ancient, pre-Islamic 'Arab prophets'.

The innovativeness of Ibn al-Jawzī's 'orthodoxy' is hidden within the Abū Dharr hadith. Ibn Qutayba (d. 276/889) narrated a nearly identical anecdote 300 years earlier in *al-Maᶜārif,*[116] but with the key difference that Ibn Qutayba did not ascribe it to Muhammad or even to the Companion Abū Dharr. Instead, Ibn Qutayba relates it on the authority of Wahb ibn Munabbih and Ibn ᶜAbbās, two narrators who commonly appear in Arabic literature as sources of material from biblical and other pre-Islamic traditions, and whose trustworthiness is often critiqued.[117] Ibn Qutayba studied hadith,[118] and it is curious that he would narrate the anecdote from a weaker authority if he had the option to ascribe it to Muhammad. But he may not have had that option: analysis of the Abū Dharr hadith's citation outside of Ibn al-Jawzī's *al-Muntaẓam* reveals that the anecdote may not have actually existed in the form of a Prophetic hadith in the third/ninth century – it only first appears in mid-fourth/tenth-century hadith compilations of Ibn Ḥibbān (d. 354/965) and al-Ājurrī (d. 360/970).[119] When Ibn Qutayba mustered evidence for the concept of 'Arab prophets' in the third/ninth century, therefore, the Prophetic hadith was probably not available, thus calling into question whether Muhammad and the first Muslims ever expressed opinions about the Arabness of earlier prophets, as *al-Muntaẓam* would have us believe. The early fourth/tenth-century shift in the anecdote's ascription from Wahb ibn Munabbih and the Judeo-Christian source milieu to a saying of Muhammad is suggestive of an attempt to generate enhanced credibility for the notion of Arab prophethood by invoking the higher authority of Prophetic hadith. It also implies that Hūd and Ṣāliḥ's Arabness was contested, and that scholars eventually shifted 'proof' to Muhammad in order to silence doubts. By Ibn al-Jawzī's sixth/twelfth century, the ascription of the hadith to Muhammad was long-established, and so Ibn al-Jawzī could cite it as evidence of proper 'orthodoxy', but the existence of earlier dispute underlines fundamental questions of Arab identity: if early generations of Muslims did not always believe that Hūd and Ṣāliḥ or their respective peoples, ᶜĀd and Thamūd, were

Arabs, then later hands must have invented a history and genealogy to extend Arabness back to an ancient past. The integration of these stories into Arab history and the intertwining of Arab origins and Arab prophecy has evident parallels with the discourses noted in Chapter 3(III) and our interpretation of Bashear's findings on the second/eighth-century push to rewrite history with an Arab/Muslim identity.

Suspicions that early Muslim writers neither assumed that ᶜĀd and Thamūd nor Hūd and Ṣāliḥ were Arabs are bolstered by the earliest extant text describing their history: Muqātil ibn Sulaymān's exegesis, *Tafsīr al-Qurʾān*. We noted above that Muqātil refrains from references to the Arabs in general, and his discussions of ᶜĀd and Thamūd are no exception. According to my readings of Muqātil's *Tafsīr*, he never mentions *ᶜarabī* in connection with ᶜĀd and Thamūd, he describes them as 'past people' (*al-umam al-khāliya*) destroyed by God,[120] and never as *al-ᶜarab al-bāʾida* (the 'disappeared Arabs') or *al-ᶜarab al-ᶜāriba* (the 'Arabic Arabs'), as later exegetes and historians identify them.[121] Muqātil also invokes the word *umma* (race/people) to classify Thamūd as a distinct and past group,[122] never implying that they were either part of Muhammad's or an Arab *umma*. Muqātil links Thamūd with the people of Lūṭ (Lot) by virtue that both shared neighbouring homelands on the borders of the Arabian Peninsula and the Levant, though Lūṭ's community would never, to my knowledge, be counted as 'Arabs' in later exegesis.[123] Muqātil's treatment of ᶜĀd and Thamūd and the doubtful authority of the 'Arab prophets' hadith in Ibn al-Jawzī's *al-Muntaẓam* together point to a second/eighth- or third/ninth-century shift that brought the *Arabian* ᶜĀd and Thamūd into a new *Arab* system of history and cast the Arab family tree into unprecedentedly ancient pasts.[124]

Literary Accounts of Arab Origins: Sources

A rich source for exploring the steps by which Muslims backtracked Arab origins into increasingly ancient history is the Prophetic hadith. Hadith contain an array of opinions about Arab ancestors, but they relate so many divergent statements about the first Arabs that it is impossible for Muhammad himself to have articulated all (or any!) of the views ascribed to him. The fact that Arab genealogy was expressed through the voice of the Prophet – the highest form of terrestrial authority – underlines the importance which early

Muslims attached to debates about Arabness, but the evident volume of forgeries prompts questions as to how these hadith can be evaluated.

The long tradition of academic hadith criticism unfortunately is of limited direct help to make sense of the Arab origin hadith.[125] Hadith studies focus on the development of legal texts, whereas the Arab origin hadith markedly differ from the legal material in terms of structure, content and context, inasmuch as the Arabness statements (1) have no manifest legislative value, (2) they record the direct words of the Prophet,[126] and (3) almost none are contained in well-known hadith compilations. The *aṣḥāb al-ḥadīth* (hadith experts) may have been aware of the Arab origin hadith, but they did not record them (with only one exception).[127] Those hadith were instead recorded in histories, genealogies and prophetic biographies which conformed to different standards of scrutiny. We have noted that the vast majority of hadith make no reference to 'Arabs',[128] and the genealogical statements about Arab origins, preserved not in dedicated hadith collections, but in genealogical compendiums, seem to be extreme outliers of Wael Hallaq's hadith authenticity spectrum:[129] that is, they can be treated as fabrications masquerading under the authority of the Prophetic voice to ground their content in an authoritative-sounding shell.[130] To interpret them, therefore, the context of their narration is key, and by reading them diachronically, we shall uncover vibrant discourses across the third/ninth century debating fundamental questions of Arab identity expressed through genealogy.

Arabs and Maᶜadd

In striking parallel to the prominence of the Maᶜadd collective in pre-Islamic and Umayyad-era poetry, the earliest extant genealogies posit Maᶜadd as the ultimate derivable Arab ancestor. A hadith reported in Ibn al-Kalbī's *Jamharat al-nasab*, Ibn Saᶜd's (d. 230/845) *al-Ṭabaqāt*, Khalīfa ibn Khayyāṭ's (d. *c.*250/854–5) *al-Ṭabaqāt* and in the *Nasab* section of Ibn Wahb's (d. *c.*197/812–3) *al-Jāmiᶜ* details Muhammad's ancestry, stating that 'when Muhammad recited genealogy and reached [the ancestor] Maᶜadd ibn ᶜAdnān he would stop and then say, 'the genealogists lie''.[131] Maᶜadd was dated about twenty generations removed from Muhammad,[132] but the lineage has no connection with ᶜĀd, Thamūd or other ancient Arabians. If Maᶜadd was the oldest-known Arab progenitor, the Arab ethnos was not imagined in early Islam to be as ancient as later historians would intimate.

Ibn al-Kalbī's *Jamhara* respects the hadith and retains Maᶜadd's seniority on the Arab family tree, but interestingly, by the later third/ninth century the hadith's citation dwindled and its text was altered to downplay Maᶜadd's position atop the Arab family tree. Al-Balādhurī's (d. *c.*279/892) *Ansāb al-ashrāf* repeats the hadith's formula 'the genealogists lie', but replaces the reference to Maᶜadd with 'Udad ibn ᶜAdnān ibn Maᶜadd', Maᶜadd's grandfather,[133] and al-Balādhurī adds further anecdotes (considered later in this section) that completely forget Maᶜadd's status as Arab progenitor, focusing on ᶜAdnān, Udad and Yemenis in ways bestowing much greater antiquity to Arab origins than the Maᶜadd model permits. Fourth/tenth-century writers almost unanimously ignored the hadith too – I have found it cited only in Ibn Durayd's (d. 321/933) *al-Ishtiqāq*,[134] and like al-Balādhurī, Ibn Durayd also gives no indication that he believes Maᶜadd represents the terminus of Arab lineage. Rather, he infers that the hadith intends that the names of prior generations are 'Syriac [*sūriyānī*] names' which cannot be studied as Arabic language derivatives.[135] Ibn Durayd was a philologist, and his *al-Ishtiqāq* is not a strict genealogical text, but rather an etymological enquiry into Arab tribal names, and while it is interesting that he noted the generations of 'Arabs' prior to Maᶜadd did not have 'Arabic' names, he gives no indication that he suspected them to have been ethnically non-Arab.[136] The fact that Ibn Durayd did not deem non-Arabic names as incompatible with Arab ethnicity also supports this chapter's findings from the dictionaries of Ibn Durayd's contemporaries that indicate fourth/tenth-century writers had shifted to consider bloodlines, not language, to be the primary hallmark of Arabness.

The Maᶜadd model thus appears a relic of the second/eighth century, extinguished by rewordings and new hadith to be considered presently. In a second/eighth-century context, the Maᶜadd model conceptually fits early poetry that conceptualised Muslims as the people of Maᶜadd, and the hypothesis that Maᶜadd was then indeed imagined to be the original father figure in early Muslim memory is reflected in the fact that the genealogy between Muhammad and Maᶜadd is consistently reported, yet there is no consensus on Maᶜadd's ancestors. It is as if the more ancient generations were filled not from traditional memories, but from creative constructions of later genealogists.

The dwindling citations of the Maᶜadd model after the early third/ninth century suggest that Maᶜadd was an imperfect father figure for the developing Muslim community, and Maᶜadd's deficiencies are rather apparent since his persona lacks prophetic significance and many early Muslims were not related to pre-Islamic Ma'addite groups. If a sense of Arabness was to be constructed on a more inclusive basis for all Conquerors, the Arab family tree would need to be extended, and this is what happened. Mirroring Lancaster and Shryock's observations of genealogy's malleability, Maᶜadd's identification as primogenitor did not survive. Ibn al-Kalbī's *Jamhara* is both the earliest and the only text to accept Maᶜadd's seniority as the oldest Arab: as our next section demonstrates, an alternative model of Arab genealogy, supported by its own hadith and *akhbār*, was to gain wide acceptance in the generation after Ibn al-Kalbī, and enabled genealogists to backtrack Arab lineage and history far earlier than Maᶜadd.

Arabs and Ishmael

The root of the Maᶜadd–Arab family tree is expressly undercut by a hadith where Muhammad declares: 'All the Arabs are descendants of Ishmael son of Abraham'.[137] Ishmael lived long before Maᶜadd: al-Zubayrī's (d. 236/851) *Nasab Quraysh* provides two enumerations of either ten or forty generations between Maᶜadd and Ishmael, and other third/ninth-century texts reflect a similar range.[138] The hadith thus makes the Arabs an older ethnos and creates a prophetic origin for their bloodline. The establishment of kinship between Muhammad and a previous prophetic family is attractive, and it explains why third/ninth-century texts concerned with sacred topics such as Muhammad's ancestry[139] and the caliphal Quraysh tribe (unlike Ibn al-Kalbī's *al-Jamhara*)[140] narrate this hadith and drop the Maᶜadd model.

Ibn Saᶜd's *Ṭabaqāt* also glosses the Ishmael hadith with anecdotes that illustrate how arguments over Muhammad's ancestry related to different reconstructions of Arab history in the first half of the third/ninth century. He narrates first that Ishmael was the 'first to speak Arabic', and that before Ishmael travelled to Mecca with Abraham, he spoke Hebrew (*ᶜibrāniyya*).[141] Ibn Saᶜd also reports an opinion that Ishmael was inspired by God to speak Arabic from birth.[142] While he curiously follows it with a contradictory statement that Ishmael did not speak Arabic and that only his children did, Ibn

Sa^c^d reveals his preference for the 'Arabic speaking' Ishmael by narrating more anecdotes in support of it and by giving authoritative finality to the debate by closing with the Prophetic hadith 'all of the Arabs are the children of Ishmael son of Abraham'.[143] Ibn Saᶜd next describes Ishmael's construction of Mecca's sanctum and then lists his descendants to Maᶜadd.[144] And so Ibn Saᶜd's narrative deftly intertwines Ma'addite community, Arab history and Arabic linguistic origins with sacred history to promote a perception of Arabness emanating from prophecy.

There is modern debate regarding the antiquity of the Ishmaelite model of Arab genealogy, but most posit that it was first articulated in the Muslim era, and, in Hawting's view, originates from ideas acquired outside of Arabia.[145] Such opinions harmonise with our proposal here that Iraqi Muslim-era writers asserted the Ishmaelite lineage system over the Maᶜadd kinship model which had been widespread in pre-Islamic Arabia. It is apparent that Muslim writers essentially grafted Ishmael onto Ma'addite genealogy, taking an existing genealogical unity of Maᶜadd with already well-articulated kinship bonds, and augmenting it by backtracking its lineage into prophecy.[146] The nature of the sources which relate the Ishmaelite hadith betray the motive behind its adoption: the hadith appear in biographies of the Prophet Muhammad and genealogies of the caliphal Quraysh group, evidencing writers' desire to recast the origins of the Arabs and the leadership of the Muslim community beyond north-west Arabian tribalism and into the Judeo-Christian prophetic tradition. The fact that none of these particular Ishmaelite hadith were recorded in the main hadith collections of the later third/ninth century are also cause to doubt their connection to Muhammad's own consciousness of kinship. My readings of pre-Islamic poetry likewise found no expressions of connection to Ishmael, and Chapter 2, pp. 70–4, 86–8 revealed the pervasiveness of Maᶜadd as the sense of community in the poetic corpus. Moreover, the Qur'an does not use the word *ᶜarabī* in any of its six references to Ishmael (as noted in Chapter 2(II)), and Ishmael's quite minor footprint in the Qur'an, together with the absence of Qur'anic stories of Ishmael's own prophethood (outside the two generic verses in Q19:54–5)[147] add further indication that Ishmael's importance in Arab–Muslim imaginations had a post-Qur'anic genesis. In sum, it was the process of Arab ethnogenesis during the first two centuries of Islam in the Fertile Crescent that prompted early Muslims to appreciate the need to both construct one pan-Arabian ancestor, and connect him to a prophetic milieu.

For the bulk of the early Conquerors from central Arabia, a combination of Maᶜadd and Ishmael answered the dual needs of constructing an Arabian–monotheistic genealogy, but this was not the end of the story. The Maᶜadd/Ishmael genealogical model lacks an apparatus to connect Hūd/Ṣāliḥ and ᶜĀd/Thamūd into the Arab family. The identification of either Maᶜadd or Ishmael as the first Arab leaves earlier Peninsular peoples outside the Arab family, and while it accords with Muqātil's early *Tafsīr* which classifies ᶜĀd and Thamūd as 'destroyed peoples' from the past without blood connection to Muhammad's *umma*,[148] other pressures in the developing Muslim society arose to expand Arabness further and widen its family tree.

Arabs, Yemenis and Ishmael

Exactly why Arab history would be amended to extend beyond the Maᶜadd/Ishmael model and why the legendary Thamūd and ᶜĀd would retrospectively muscle their way into Arab history is a complex question that can be explored, at least in part, via another set of Arab origin hadith connected to Yemeni interests. 'Yemenis' was the name adopted by large groups of South Arabian and other early converts to Islam who participated in the Islamic conquests,[149] and a 'third way' set of hadith seem intended to redress the absence of Yemenis in the 'Arab family' by arguing that Qaḥṭān, the legendary Yemeni ancestor, was himself related to Ishmael. The workings of this narrative are on display in Khalīfa ibn Khayyāṭ's mid-third/ninth-century genealogical text, *al-Ṭabaqāt* where Ibn Khayyāṭ appears at the outset to endorse the most restrictive concept of Arab origins by reporting the Maᶜadd hadith on the authority of both Muhammad and the Caliph ᶜUmar ibn al-Khaṭṭāb,[150] but adds, on the lesser authority of the narrator Ibn ᶜAbbās, that Yemenis constitute a separate group of Arabs who were not related to Maᶜadd, but nonetheless related to Ishmael.[151]

Ibn Khayyāṭ's narrative still maintains that all Arabs descend from Abraham/Ishmael's prophetic family, but now Maᶜadd's group are no longer portrayed as the only descendants of Ishmael, since Ibn Khayyāṭ's new model counts Yemenis as a second, equally Ishmaelite Arab group descended from a separate line from Ishmael through Qaḥṭān. The discourse again suggests that the Ma'addite genealogy was the incumbent and that new groups were compelled to negotiate around it, and in order to achieve this, Ibn Khayyāṭ explains that Yemenis had called themselves the sons of Ishmael until the time of al-Ḥajjāj ibn Yūsuf, the Umayyad governor of Iraq (75–95/694–714).[152] This is a defensive self-justification: it admits that the assertion of Yemeni descent from Ishmael sounded novel or unfamiliar to his readers, and it attempts to bolster credibility with reference to the past – that is, by stating that this was the manner Yemenis *originally* thought of themselves. The fact Ibn Khayyāṭ does not adduce any reason why Yemenis stopped claiming that ancestry prompts doubt as to the real historicity of his anecdote, and, as if anticipating incredulity, Ibn Khayyāṭ marshals two hadith, this time in the voice of Muhammad himself, to support the claim in his section on Yemeni genealogy. Both hadith are similar: one narrates that when the Prophet passed a group from the Aslam tribe (Yemenis related to Khuzāᶜa) who were contesting an unspecified matter, the Prophet said to them: 'Shoot, children of Ishmael! Your father was an archer!'[153] The second hadith relates the same statement, but sets it in the context of the Prophet speaking to the Anṣār (the people of Medina, another branch of 'Yemen' Arabs).[154] The connection of Ishmael and archery derives from Genesis 21:20; Isaiah 21:17 describes Ishmael's descendants, the Qedarites (who are attested as an Arabian people in Assyrian records) as archers too. The process by which Yemenis sought inclusion into the newly forming community of 'Arabs' via discourses and imagery from the Bible again point to the dual forces of faith and politics invoked in the process of creating Arabness as an identity capable of circumscribing groups who imagined their community around a combination of common faith, reverence for the *ᶜarabī* Qur'an and allegiance to the 'Commander of the Faithful' (*amīr al-muᵓminīn* – caliph). For Yemenis to establish parity with Ma'addite elites, they needed authentically phrased prophetic blood too.

As further indication of what appears a swell of very early opinion that argued Yemenis were Arabs via Ishmaelite lineage, Ibn Wahb's *al-Jāmiᶜ* contains two hadith in which the Prophet specifies that the tribes of Ashᶜar and Ḥaḍramawt (Yemenis by all accounts) were 'sons of Ishmael'.[155] These didactic expressions of genealogy are devoid of context and arouse suspicion: under what circumstances would Muhammad need to inform the Ashᶜarīs and Ḥaḍramīs that they were Ishmaelites? Did these tribesmen really need to learn their lineage from the Prophet? It seems more likely that the terse statements were fabrications to embed certain tribes within Ishmaelite models of Arab origins. It is also noteworthy that these hadith, according to my searches, were never repeated in later texts, indicating that they were connected to a discourse that became obsolete. Analysis of later writings indicates that this was the case.

The attempt to link Yemeni ancestry to Ishmael appears to have come from groups of Yemenis themselves, likely in the second/eighth century, as Ibn Hishām's early third/ninth-century biography of the Prophet notes that 'some of the people of Yemen say that Qaḥṭān is one of the sons of Ishmael and that Ishmael is the father of all Arabs'.[156] But Ibn Hishām does not endorse this view, and by the early fourth/tenth century, even the Yemeni scholar al-Hamdānī notes in the genealogical section of his *al-Iklīl* that hadith in which Muhammad appears to call Yemenis the 'sons of Ishmael' have been misinterpreted, and that the Prophet never intended that Ishmael was the progenitor of the Yemenis.[157] After the fourth/tenth century, I have not found any writers repeating the model, except the fifth/eleventh-century genealogist Ibn Ḥazm who only mentions it to categorically reject it.[158]

Diachronic reading of our sources thus reveals that early Yemeni attempts to link themselves to an ancestral Qaḥṭān and Ishmael, and thereby expand the Ishmaelite–Arab genealogy to non-Ma'addite groups were ultimately unsuccessful. But Yemenis ventured another model which eventually gained widespread consent and paved the way for the 'orthodox' history of Arab origins we find in later texts. In the wake of the new Yemeni model, the Maᶜadd and Ishmael genealogies virtually disappear from the fourth/tenth century.[159]

'Arab' Origins and 'Arab' Prophets in the Third/Ninth Century

Ibn Hishām's *Sīra* provides a construction of Arab genealogy which separates the Yemeni father figure, Qaḥṭān, from Ishmael and declares that both were progenitors of different strands of the Arab people: 'All Arabs are descendants of [either] Ishmael [or] Qaḥṭān.'[160] A genealogical text ascribed to Ibn al-Kalbī, *Nasab Maᶜadd wa-l-Yaman*, also divides genealogy into two branches: Maᶜadd and Yemen, but as it is a very early text, it unsurprisingly reports uneven details regarding the origins of the Arab groups. Ibn al-Kalbī emphasises Ma^c^add as forefather of the Northern Arabs without connecting them to Abraham/Ishmael,[161] suggestive that the Ishmaelite model was not yet universally articulated at the end of the second/eighth century; and while Ibn al-Kalbī's depiction of Yemenis evidences movement to promote their equal Arabness to the Ma'addites, it is noteworthy that he does not mention Hūd and Ṣāliḥ within the Yemeni branch, and he equivocates as to whether Qaḥṭān was a descendant of Ishmael or an earlier figure with a separate ancestry.[162] It would take almost one hundred more years for the non-Ishmaelite–ancient Qaḥṭān model to mature, and in the interim numerous variations and disputes were aired.

Ibn Wahb's *al-Jāmi^c^* offers one early version narrating the familiar 'All Arabs are the children of Ishmael' hadith, but adds an unusual exception for the tribes Thaqīf and Ḥimyar.[163] The hadith describes Thaqīf as descendants of Thamūd, and Ḥimyar Yemenis as descendants of Tubba^c^ (a mysterious figure mentioned in Qur'an 44:37, and about whom Yemeni historians later greatly elaborated tales of pre-Islamic Yemeni history).[164] The intrusion of Tubba^c^ and Thamūd (who appear in the Qur'an without any connection to Arabness or contemporary Arabians) into Arab history reveals how early Muslims grasped ambiguous historical figures from the Qur'an and co-opted them into genealogical stories of Arabness.[165] As Shryock observed, narratives of the past offer fertile ground for groups in the present to weave novel stories of their origins, and in a similar vein, Ibn Ḥabīb's (d. 245/859) *al-Muḥabbar*[166] reveals further efforts to include the ancient Peninsular peoples mentioned in the Qur'an into Arab history. Ibn Ḥabīb reports that the first speakers of Arabic were émigrés from the fall of the Tower of Babel who populated the Peninsula many generations before Abraham and Ishmael,[167] thus counting various groups, including ^c^Ād and Thamūd as 'Arab tribes' (*qabā'il ^c^āriba*).[168] This use of *^c^āriba* is interesting. The word is an active participle which implies an underlying verb *^c^araba* or *^c^aruba* ('to be an Arab', 'to speak Arabic'?), but, to my knowledge, neither verb appears in poetry or early sources. *^c^Āriba* must instead have been derived from the noun *^c^arab* itself and, as such, derives from its fluid meanings. Ibn Ḥabīb's historically ancient *^c^āriba* outright contradicts the Ishmaelite model of the first Arabic speaker, and hence the word's interpretation is intertwined with debates over Arab origins. Later lexicographers define *^c^āriba* as the 'Ancient Arabs',[169] which corresponds with the disappearance of the Ishmaelite 'first Arab' narrative in the later sources, and hence *al-Muḥabbar* seems to evidence the vanguard of a movement to tweak Arab history, extending its horizons far further than hitherto in order to link ancient Arabian peoples like ᶜĀd and Thamūd into the Arab family's heritage.

The history of the *al-ᶜarab al-ᶜāriba* term merits further consideration, as the later third/ninth-century al-Balādhurī makes interesting remarks when defining the idea, identifying *al-ᶜāriba* as 'the first to speak Arabic', aligned with incipient notions of Arabness defined around language.[170] Al-Balādhurī ascribes the opinion to an obscure figure, ᶜAbbās ibn Hishām al-Kalbī: the connection with the Kalbī family of genealogists and historians proffers authority, but ᶜAbbās is not a usual conduit for historical facts, and in the surviving work ascribed to ᶜAbbās' father, Hishām, *Nasab Maᶜadd wa-l-Yaman*, there is no mention of *al-ᶜāriba* in the section on the Yemenis, the supposed kin-group constituting *al-ᶜāriba*.[171] If al-Balādhurī's narration is faithful, ᶜAbbās appears to have built the *al-ᶜarab al-ᶜāriba* label onto his father's account of Yemeni genealogy, indicating perhaps an increasing acceptability of the term to discuss Arab ancestry in the early-mid third/ninth century, which in turn corresponds with the generation of Ibn Ḥabīb with his *al-Muḥabbar*, the earliest extant text employing the *ᶜāriba* label to articulate a particular narrative about the antiquity of the Arabs. From the laconic reference to *al-ᶜāriba* in the dictionary *al-ᶜAyn* to the rather confident certainty of Yemeni genealogy's origins as constituting *al-ᶜāriba* in al-Balādhurī's *Ansāb*, the sweep of the third/ninth century again bears witness to scholarly development towards codifying an Arab history.

Al-Muḥabbar further consolidates the narrative of ancient Arabness elsewhere. For example, the text pays special attention to anecdotes about the circumcision of prophets which, though at first glance appears a rather abstruse area of study, does, on closer inspection, develop a sense Arab antiquity and a privileging of the Arabs. *Al-Muḥabbar* relates an anecdote which states that of all the prophets, only Hūd, Ṣāliḥ, Shuᶜayb and Muhammad were born circumcised.[172] This appears to be the earliest reference to the quartet later familiar as the 'Arab prophets' as a distinct group, and the fact that they share the miraculous trait of circumcision at birth seems a thinly veiled lauding of Arab prophethood as the most divinely favoured group. Since it does not include Ishmael, we see further decoupling of Arabness from the Ishmaelite model in favour of associating Muhammad with the earlier 'Ancient Arab' (*ᶜāriba*) Qaḥṭān-branded prophets Hūd and Ṣāliḥ instead.

Reading *al-Muḥabbar* as a text seeking to produce a novel approach to Arab history from gathering scattered material accords with Julia Bray's observation that Ibn Ḥabīb's 'objective as a historian' was to organise material in order to yield 'a new order of data' and to create 'a new kind of cultural memory'.[173] Ibn Ḥabīb's selection of data on pre-Ishmaelite peoples and his presentation of them as Arabs (while neglecting to record data about Maᶜadd-Arab genealogies) does prompt readers to grasp a new kind of Arab history which deconstructs earlier bounds of Arab origins in favour of an ancient past where Arabness is equipped with more prophets and with the status of one of the world's oldest nations stemming from Babel. The old Ma'addite genealogy lacked such ambition to plot Arab history so deep into prehistory, which is perhaps explainable given that Maᶜadd was a relic of a very different, pre-Islamic central Arabian people. Once Maᶜadd and others conquered the wider Middle East, a grander historiographical perspective behoved the new Conqueror society, but it would need to be rather thoroughly contrived, bringing attendant problems of incredulity as the new genealogical models asked their audience to imagine the Arabs in starkly new ways.

The novelty of the efforts to convert the Qur'an's ancient Arabian past of ᶜĀd, Thamūd, Tubbaᶜ and others into 'Arab history' can be gauged from scholarly suspicion expressed in early third/ninth-century literature. For example, the aforementioned Ibn Wahb hadith about Thaqīf's Thamudic ancestry was roundly rejected in al-Jāḥiẓ's *al-Bayān wa-l-tabyīn*. Al-Jāḥiẓ did not cite the hadith directly, but addressed those who made its claim that some Arabs were Thamūd's descendants, and declared that Thamudic lineages plainly contradict the two clear statements in the Qur'an that God completely destroyed Thamūd.[174] Al-Jāḥiẓ concluded: 'I am amazed that anyone who considers the Qur'an to be the Truth would allege that some tribes of Arabs are survivors of Thamūd . . . I seek refuge in God from that!'[175]

In more comprehensive fashion, the poetry anthologist Ibn Sallām al-Jumaḥī (d. 231/845–6) critiqued the claims of Thamūd and ᶜĀd's Arabness reported in Ibn Isḥāq's Prophetic biography which, in the surviving sections preserved in Ibn Hishām's abridgement, contains a lengthy section on ancient

Yemenis and their relationship with prophecy.[176] Ibn Sallām commences like al-Jāḥiẓ, citing no less than five Qur'anic verses that emphasise the total destruction of ᶜĀd, Thamūd and other ancient peoples.[177] Ibn Sallām follows with two separate anecdotes describing Ishmael as the first Arab and first Arab speaker, and a third anecdote arguing Ishmael is the ancestor of all Arabs other than Ḥimyar and some of Jurhum.[178] Ibn Sallām, revealing his adherence to what was in his day the more traditional notion of Ma'addite Arab origins, continues the deconstruction in a fascinatingly revealing direction, arguing that even the Arabic allegedly spoken by Ishmael was 'not the Arabic of the age of the Prophet Muhammad, it was a different Arabic, and not our language'.[179] Ibn Sallām also avows that no pre-Islamic poet (other than one verse ascribed to Labīd) mentions any ancestor beyond Maᶜadd and remarks that poems used as evidence for more ancient genealogies are fabrications, expressing his utter disbelief that anyone could adduce Arabic poetry from as far back as ᶜĀd or Thamūd.[180] Not yet finished, Ibn Sallām reiterates that Maᶜadd is the oldest ascertainable Arab ancestor and adds 'the tongue of Ḥimyar and the furthest South (*aqāṣī al-Yaman*) today is not the same as our Arabic' (note how he pointedly refrains from associating his contemporary Yemenis' tongues with Iraqi 'Arabic'). He concludes that any discussion of ᶜĀd's Arabness or speaking Arabic is preposterous.[181]

To understand why some Yemeni partisans would so blatantly forge a version of genealogical history that was unbelievable to early scholars, one can return to Shryock's observations that genealogical models may appear incorrect to outsiders, but they are perfectly understandable to insiders involved in the relevant sociopolitical contexts.[182] In the case of hadith proclaiming Thaqīf and Ḥimyar's pre-Ishmaelite Arabness, the explosive power relations in Umayyad-era Iraq provided ample opportunity for repackaging memories of the past for present political aims and generated anecdotes which would confuse later scholars seeking to reconstruct Arabness. Thaqīf and Ḥimyar were key political factions in Umayyad Iraq: Ḥimyar constituted a significant part of the Emigrants settled in al-Baṣra and al-Kūfa,[183] while Thaqīf were the governors of Iraq, allied to the Umayyads and often very unpopular.[184] Read in the context of late first/seventh- and early second/eighth-century Iraqi politics, therefore, the hadith is a manifest political statement suiting the purpose of a disenchanted Iraqi. The 'bad' governors, Thaqīf, are cast as descendants of the evil Thamūd whom the Qur'an repeatedly describes as being punished by God, while the 'good' Iraqi population, descendants of Ḥimyar, are the descendants of Tubbaᶜ, a character more cryptically mentioned in the Qur'an as a possible ancient believer.[185] Because the pointed genealogies are given an authoritative form via ascription to the Prophet Muhammad, Iraqi politics is consequently conceptualised as a war of good versus evil.[186] A century later, when Thaqīf no longer ruled Iraq and Ḥimyar was no longer oppressed, scholars such as al-Jāḥiẓ and al-Jumaḥī would understandably react with dismay and confusion when encountering these references which had, by their time, lost all operative context.

The multiple strands of Arab origins posited via genealogy thus attest to the essential fluidity of the Arabness idea in early Islam. Far from a clear 'orthodox' concept of who the Arabs were, Arab origins were indefinite, and Muslims could pluck characters from the Qur'an and weave them into novel genealogies. Over the passage of time, the resultant anecdotes and hadith did not harmonise with new narratives of Arab history, and hence they could be so strongly censured as erroneous interpretations and blatant misuses of history. But the strong objections to the ancient Qaḥṭānī Arabness of the Yemenis cease after the mid-third/ninth century when the biting critiques were forgotten, and the Yemenis firmly planted themselves into Arab history, obliterating the Maᶜadd and Ishmaelite hadith formerly dominant in early third/ninth-century sources. The integration of Yemenis into the Arab fold is itself an enormous study, but survey of later third/ninth-century writings on Arab genealogy reveals gradual scholarly acquiescence to the Qaḥṭān model. For reasons of space, I trace here the process in the major surviving historical works.

Al-Balādhurī's (d. *c.*279/892) *Ansāb al-ashrāf* narrates a version of the Ibn Wahb hadith, but pointedly removes reference to Thamūd as the ancestors of Thaqīf, a response to earlier criticism, perhaps? Al-Balādhurī's version modifies the hadith, counting the tribes al-Salaf, Thaqīf, al-Awzāᶜ and Ḥaḍramawt as the only Arabs not descended from Ishmael,[187] but by al-Balādhurī's late third/ninth century, notions of Arab origins were shifting ever backwards beyond Ishmael, and he narrates the above hadith as a minority report, while furnishing other anecdotes to prove that even more Arab groups pre-dated Ishmael, tracing their roots through Qaḥṭān, Yemen and *al-ᶜarab al-ᶜāriba*.[188]

Taking the various hadith and early texts about Arab origins together, Arab history during the mid-third/ninth century possessed two contradictory narratives: Arabs were either (1) intimately tied to the Abrahamic prophetic family, or (2) their origins were more ancient and inclusive of a broader range of Peninsular peoples. Later third/ninth-century histories embrace both models simultaneously, narrating Prophetic hadith and other anecdotes to support both camps and giving only tentative, if any, indication of what they believed to be the correct version. Al-Yaᶜqūbī (d. 275/888 or 292/905) leaves the issue unresolved,[189] al-Balādhurī seems to prefer the Yemeni/pan-Arabian notion of Arabness, but leaves some room for doubt,[190] and Ibn Qutayba's (d. 276/889) *Maᶜārif* is also ambivalent, though it tends towards accepting the Yemeni Arabness model.[191] We can speculate that later third/ninth-century readership was aware of the conflicting opinions about Arab origins and that both the Ishmaelite and Yemeni/pan-Arabian models had sufficient scholarly support to keep both alive, but instability, by nature, tends to resolution, and what would become the 'traditional' Muslim narrative of Arab origins begins to assert itself with increasing confidence in the last half of the third/ninth century. At the dawn of the fourth/tenth century, al-Ṭabarī's *Tārīkh al-rusul wa-l-mulūk* introduces certainty at last, declaring forthright (and, pointedly, without *isnād*) that ᶜĀd and Thamūd 'were Arabs of *al-ᶜarab al-ᶜāriba* (the ancient Arabs)'.[192] Al-Ṭabarī does not often add his own editorial comments such as this to his historical narrative, since he typically opts to narrate history via anecdotes attributed to earlier sources. His short comment thus appears directed to curtailing doubt which is not surprising, given the unclear status of Arabness over the preceding century. Al-Ṭabarī declares the debate ended: ᶜĀd and Thamūd are Arabs via an ancient genealogy, and, in giving no indication of contrary opinions (as previous authors had done), al-Ṭabarī leaves little room to reopen the debate. We are to accept them as Arabs and proceed accordingly – much as Ibn al-Jawzī did in *al-Muntaẓam*.

It is noteworthy that al-Ṭabarī is also the first Qur'an commentator to expressly interpret Qur'an 9:128's statement about 'A Messenger has come to you from among yourselves' as a reference to Muhammad's mission to 'the *Arab* people', specifically rewriting the second/eighth-century Muqātil's restriction of 'yourselves' mean just to Muhammad's contemporary Meccans.[193] As later *akhbārī* history writers would follow al-Ṭabarī's model of

Arab origins, so exegetes followed al-Ṭabarī's interpretation of the Qur'anic verse,[194] indicating that the ethnic Arab context of the Qur'an was affirmed during the third/ninth century in tandem with the expansion of the ambit of historical Arabness and the systematisation of 'Arab lineage'. And al-Ṭabarī's certainty surfaces in wider *adab* literature too: witness al-Ṭabarī's younger contemporary Ibn Durayd, who, in his dictionary, *Jamharat al-lugha* enumerates the *ᶜarab al-ᶜāriba* as a defined set of seven tribes (*qabāʾil*) without any alternatives or dispute, and, in the same passage, resolves al-Jāḥiẓ and Ibn Sallām's earlier reservations about their Arabness, stating 'all of them became extinct except some remnants who survived in the tribes'.[195] Via the unnamed 'remnants', Ibn Durayd's statement enables readers to conceptualise ᶜĀd/Thamūd et al. as both bygone peoples *and* ancestors of later Arabs, presenting a genealogical continuum from ancient Arabia to Muhammad's community, sealing Arabia in a sense of undiluted and perpetual Arabness.

V Defining Arabs: Conclusions

The third/ninth century emerges as a pivotal period for imagining the Arabs. Writers articulated novel notions of Arab unity and identity, giving Arabness an ancient past, projecting it backwards to the age of Noah, resplendent with genealogical constructs and Prophetic hadith in support.[196] Whilst Arabic literary sources have been critiqued for presenting pre-Islam and Islam's rise as a homogenised 'Arab story', our survey of the building blocks of Arab ethnic identity now reveals that such critique oversimplifies the sources somewhat. The early texts are not monolithic, they do not possess one canonical idea of Arabness, and by listening to their voices for their own conceptions of Arab community, varied discourses unfurl to reveal that Qur'anic *ᶜarabī* invoked senses of purity and revelation in contrast to *aᶜrāb* nomadism, and that the first Arabs drew their ethnonym from *ᶜarabī*, and consequently articulated Arabness as focused on the purity of their language and system of nascent Muslim belief. When *ᶜarabī* came to represent a sense of Conqueror community, Maᶜadd seems to have been the dominant group, and its members championed Ma'addite genealogy as synonymous with Arab lineage, while they also backtracked Maᶜadd-ness to Ishmael to inject prophetic blood into their Arab idea which perfected *ᶜarabī*'s connotation of purity in an ethnic guise. But non-Ma'addites also participated in the Conquerors' elite society, and Arab kin would need expansion and also paradigmatic changes to embrace the patrilineal power structure that emerged over the four generations following the conquests.

As the Arabic language spread amongst urban Iraqis alongside their conversion to Islam, and as Arab genealogy became more coherently articulated, Arabness discourses took refuge within the increasingly tangible boundaries of kinship, and open-ended notions of linguistic Arabness gave way to the closed-ended models of defining Arabs by genealogy. Literary codification began at the end of the second/eighth century with Ibn al-Kalbī, but Arab genealogy remained fluid and contested as Iraqi writers tried to codify 200 years' worth of disparate oral memories, and third/ninth-century Iraqi writers were 'outsiders', to borrow Shryock's terminology: the original discourses about Arab lineage were contested in political wrangling during the two centuries before scholars began consolidating the Arab family tree. The process of consolidation took a century to mature into the cohesive pan-Arab genealogical system that enabled subsequent fourth/tenth-century philologists to confidently define the Arabs as a kin-community, as evidenced in al-Azharī's *Tahdhīb*, al-Jawharī's *al-Ṣiḥāḥ* and later lexicons.

The streamlined simplicity of the resultant model of Arab kinship indicates that more processes were operating than mere scholarly codification of Arab opinions. The frequent references to Arab genealogy in literature from the fourth/tenth century onwards, in tandem with the consistency of the genealogy's portrayal and the absence of substantive debate over the details presents Arabness in later Muslim-era literature as a theoretically important idea, but yet also an idea lacking vitality. The Arab kin codification into two sets of 'Northern/ᶜAdnān' and 'Southern/Qaḥṭān' branches betrays the onset of a period when Arabness was no longer influenced by the whims and allegiances of influential factions on the political stage, and when Arabness had been rarefied beyond a quotidian identity of actual living communities. The ability of scholars to so cut-and-dry Arabness by setting and ossifying a kinship edifice that would endure for centuries without discernable change implies that the value of Arabness as a living asset had dissipated, and with these inferences in mind, we should now like to investigate the changing faces of Arabness in the context of the society which consumed the source texts we have examined. In the absence of a bureaucratic state to impose Arabness as a 'national identity', what drivers can be adduced to explain the development of Arabness as a closed-ended genealogy, and why did the bipartite ᶜAdnān/Qaḥṭān model become so widely accepted (and acceptable) by the late third/ninth century, given the sharp scholarly reservations expressed two generations before? We shall query both Arab identity's value as an asset (as it was evidently changing given the textual shifts we have encountered so far), and how groups fit themselves into the developments. The next chapter's task is to relate how the changing senses of Arab community in the early Abbasid period (mid-second/eighth to third/ninth centuries) impacted the ways in which Arab history was narrated in this formative period of Arabic literature.

Notes

1. Arabness as an ethnic identity engages with the conceptual categories delineating boundaries between groups. Early dictionaries discuss at least fifteen terms connoting 'social group', and several, e.g. *umma, qawm, jīl, maᶜshar*, accord significant role to shared faith as determining membership of a 'people'. The term *shaᶜb*, on the other hand, had clear 'racial' connotation, defining a people via shared kinship; Arabs were particularly associated with tribal terminology too. See Webb (forthcoming (C)) for discussion of the terms.
2. For discussion of the date and authorship of the extant version of *al-ᶜAyn*, see Schoeler (2006) pp. 142–63.
3. Al-Khalīl (1980) vol. 2, p. 128. I translate *ṣarīḥ* as 'pure' based on *al-ᶜAyn*'s own definition of the word as *maḥḍ, khāliṣ* (Ibid. vol. 3, p. 115). It also states that *ṣarīḥ* can mean *ḥasab* in the case of men and horses which it defines as noble (*sharīf, karīm*) (Ibid. vol. 3, p. 148), but I am unaware of any classical uses of the term *al-ᶜarab al-ᶜāriba* as equivalent to noblemen.
4. A common theme in early pro-Yemeni writing (see Wahb ibn Munabbih (1996) pp. 34, 37–38) and endorsed widely afterwards. The third/ninth-century articulation of *al-ᶜarab al-ᶜāriba* around a specific genealogical notion of primordial Arab ancestry is considered below, pp. 216–17.
5. Al-Khalīl (1980) vol. 2, p. 128.
6. Ibid. vol. 1, p. 237.
7. Ibid. vol. 1, p. 237. Ibn Fāris interprets *ᶜajmāʾ* as the silent daytime prayers (1946–52) vol. 4, p. 240.
8. Al-Khalīl (1980) vol. 2, p. 128.
9. Sībawayh (1966–77) vol. 3, p. 379.

10. See Chapter 3, p. 122.
11. See for example al-Ḥarbī (attrib.) (1999) p. 75 referring to a black slave who 'adopted/learned Arabic and understood' (*zanjī ista^c^raba wa fahima*); and Ibn Abī Shayba (2010) vol. 15, p. 417 (30502), 'I seek refuge from God from the evil of an Iraqi countryman if he becomes Arab' (*sharr al-nabaṭī idhā ista^c^raba*). Ibn Abī Shayba's hadith continues, also chiding the 'Arab if he becomes an Iraqi countryman' (*al-^c^arabī idhā istanbaṭa*), which seems to be cultural, as the hadith explains 'becoming Iraqi' involves 'taking their ways and clothes' (*akhadha bi-akhdhihim wa ziyyihim*). The capacity for individuals to feign identities seems instructive in a period before genealogical models would be strictly delineated (see herein, pp. 188–94).
12. Attributed to al-Aṣma^c^ī in al-Zamakhsharī (1992) p. 244; al-Mubarrad (2008) vol. 2, p. 579. The later al-Wazīr al-Maghribī (1980) p. 115) ascribes the poem to al-Ashhab al-^c^Ukaylī (a rather unknown early Umayyad-era figure mentioned in al-Jumaḥī (n.d.) vol. 2, p. 791). The wear on provision-sack necks from tying makes the leather red – redness was a sobriquet for *^c^ajam* non-Arab, usually Persians.
13. The association of 'Arabs' Land' (*bilād al-^c^arab*) with the lands Muhammad conquered in al-Ḥijāz also suggest the connection in early discourses between Arabness and 'Islamic' origins. See Chapter 3(III), pp. 136–9.
14. Al-Azharī (2004) vol. 2, p. 166.
15. Ibid. vol. 2, p. 166.
16. It is perhaps pertinent that a dictionary written about two generations earlier, *Jamharat al-lugha* by Ibn Durayd (321/933), does not contain the term *mu^c^rib* to lexically separate an Arabic speaker from a person descended from Arab lineage. Likewise, Ibn Durayd defines Arabness by both lineage and language: he notes possible genealogies of the first Arabs, and mentions tribes that constitute Arabness, but he also identifies the first Arab as Ya^c^rub ibn Qaḥṭān on the basis that he was 'the first whose tongue was changed from Syriac to Arabic' (1987) vol. 1, p. 319 (Syriac was widely believed to be the universal world language from Adam to the fall of the Tower of Babel). Speaking Arabic is an apparent condition for the beginning of Arabness, and the connection of Arabness with communication is repeated – for example, Ibn Durayd notes that some (he specifies Yemenis from Ḥimyar) defined *^c^arabiyya* as a synonym for 'language' (*lugha*), and the verb *^c^arraba* to mean 'repeating a saying' (Ibid. vol. 1 p. 319). Ibn Durayd's definition of *^c^arab* is not as lengthy as al-Azharī's in *Tahdhīb al-lugha*, and we cannot tell how Ibn Durayd would wish us to classify an

individual who relates to an 'Arab tribe' but does not speak 'Arabic': it is left open. The conclusions reached by his successors, al-Azharī and subsequent philologists are considered herein.

17. Al-Azharī (2004) vol. 1, p. 352.
18. One generation after al-Azharī, Ibn Fāris writes that philologists discussed the logical corollary that an Arab could be *a^{c}jamī* (1946–52) vol. 4, p. 240. For further discussion of Ibn Fāris' context, see below, pp. 312–19.
19. Al-Azharī (2004) vol. 2, pp. 167, 171.
20. Ibid. vol. 2, p. 167.
21. Ibid. vol. 2, p. 167.
22. Ibid. vol. 2, pp. 170–1.
23. Ibid. vol. 2, p. 171.
24. Ibid. vol. 2, pp. 170–1.
25. Ibid. vol. 2, p. 171.
26. Al-Jawharī (1956) vol. 1, p. 178. He defines *jīl* as a 'type of people' (*ṣinf min al-nās*), giving examples of the Turks and Rūm as distinct *jīl* (Ibid. vol. 4, p. 1664).
27. Ibid. vol. 1, p. 178.
28. Ibid. vol. 1, p. 179.
29. Ibn Fāris (1946–52) vol. 4, p. 300. See Webb (forthcoming (C)) for the Arabic philological discourses on *umma* and other pre-modern Arabic terms used to delineate 'ethnic groups'.
30. Al-Ḥimyarī (1999) vol. 7, p. 4456.
31. Ibid. vol. 7, pp. 4381, 4383.
32. Ibn Manẓūr (1990) vol. 1, pp. 586–7.
33. Ibid. vol. 1, p. 588. Here Ibn Manẓūr also cites *al-^{c}Ayn* (referring to Layth ibn Muẓaffar, the student of al-Khalīl and the dictionary's transmitter), noting it contains the related term *^{c}arabānī al-lisān* as meaning a particularly correct speaker of Arabic (al-Khalīl (1980) vol. 2, p. 128). As discussed at the outset of this section, *al-^{c}Ayn* refrains from mention of Arab lineage (*nasab*), whereas Ibn Manẓūr subordinates the passage to his lengthy section on Arab ethnos, genealogy and Bedouinism, effecting a different emphasis in articulating Arabness (1990) vol. 1, pp. 586–7.
34. See Chapter 3(III), pp. 134, 138–9. The confessional connotations of *umma, ma^{c}shar* and even *ahl* accord with faith-based paradigms for conceptualising community alongside the *sha^{c}b* (racial/kinship) model (see Webb (forthcoming (C)).

35. Q41:44, my translation.
36. Al-Ṭabarī (1999) vol. 24, pp. 157–8.
37. Al-Farrā᾽ (n.d.) vol. 3, p. 19; al-Ṭabarī (1999) vol. 24, pp. 157–8.
38. Bashear briefly describes how later commenters used the verse to 'set forth the notion that Muḥammad was an Arab prophet' (1997) p. 49.
39. See p. 151 for my interpretation of Bashear's findings.
40. See Chapter 2(V) and 3(III), pp. 147–51 for discussion of the Arabisation of Dhū Qār and hadith, respectively.
41. Muqātil (1979–89) vol. 3, p. 746.
42. Other sons of Sām include the people of al-Ahwāz, the Persians (*ahl Fāris*), and Mesopotamians (*ahl al-Sawād*) (Ibid. vol. 4, p. 353–4).
43. I found an example, related to the text on Noah noted above, where Muqātil's *Tafsīr* references South Arabian idols as vestiges from the time of Noah, and which he notes were subsequently 'worshiped by the Arabs' (Ibid. vol. 4, p. 354). Herein Yemeni groups such as Ḥimyar and Hamdān are within the ambit of Arabness. Ibid. vol. 3, p. 330 also mentions 'Arab' to discuss the unclear ethnicity of the Queen of Sheba.
44. See, for example, Ibn Kathīr (1994) vol. 2, p. 432, vol. 4, p. 114.
45. Muqātil (1979–89) vol. 2, p. 318, vol. 3, p. 735.
46. Al-Ṭabarī (1999) vol. 11, p. 101.
47. Al-Zamakhsharī (1995) vol. 2, p. 314.
48. Al-Qurṭubī (2000) vol. 8, p. 191. Later commentators repeat the notions of Arab race (*jīl* or *jins*) and lineage (*nasab*): see Ibn Kathīr (d. 774/1373) (1999) 2:372 and al-Bayḍāwī (d. 791/1389) (1999) vol. 1, p. 426.
49. Muqātil (1979–89) vol. 2, p. 204.
50. See his exegesis of references to *jāhiliyya* in Webb (2014) p. 80.
51. Weber (1996); Smith (1986).
52. Al-Kindī (1912) pp. 397–9.
53. They are said to have spent a 'great sum of money' (*māl ᶜaẓīm*) (Ibid. p. 397), al-Kindī notes it may have cost a further two thousand dinars (Ibid. p. 398).
54. Ibid. p. 399.
55. Ibid. pp. 398–9.
56. For lengthy discussion of Quḍāᶜa and its contested genealogy, see Kister EI[2] 5:315–8 and Crone (1994a) pp. 44–9. For late third/ninth-century discussion of Quḍāᶜa's lineage, see al-Balādhurī (1979–) vol. 1, pp. 40–7.
57. Pellat (1984) p. 139 dates *al-Ḥayawān* 'anterieur à 232'.
58. Al-Jāḥiẓ (1998) vol. 3, p. 5.

59. In a modern anthropological context considered below, Lancaster observed that actual living memories do not recall the complete lineage of a given tribe (1981) p. 26. The wide, unfilled gap between supposed founding fathers and actually remembered ancestors left much conjecture; a problem al-Jāḥiẓ's Kindite aspirant evidently encountered!
60. The relationship between definitional uncertainty and practical utility of an ethnic identity seems to hold in pre-modern times; the advent of the nation state and its manifold apparatuses aimed at creating a sense of nationhood are better able to construct and enforce monolithic senses of community. Herein modern and pre-modern identities can be distinguished from a theoretical perspective, but the importance of belonging to a group greater than one's own 'tribe', and the need to imagine such an overarching community seem amply demonstrated in the pre-modern Arabs' case. Arabness presents itself as an important body of material to debate nationhood before the nation, and develop Anthony Smith's theories in his *The Ethnic Origins of Nations* (1989).
61. Dates proposed in Pellat (1984) p. 161.
62. i.e. the sons of ᶜAdnān descended from Ishmael did not marry into their own kin (Isaac's descendants), but accepted marriage into the descendants of a different lineage: Qaḥṭān.
63. Al-Jāḥiẓ (1963–79) vol. 1, p. 11.
64. Retsö (2003) pp. 18-22.
65. Lassner (1980) pp. 119–124.
66. Lassner (1980) pp. 129–136.
67. Montgomery (2013). For another view on making sense from al-Jāḥiẓ, in particular his notions of cultural identities, see Webb (2012a); we return to a second Jahizian discourse at length in Chapter 6.
68. See Introduction, pp. 14–15.
69. Al-Jāḥiẓ (2003) vol. 3, pp. 290–1.
70. Ibid. vol. 3, p. 291.
71. The proposal that Nizārī/Ma'addite groups sought a uniquely qualified membership to Arabness through a notion that they possessed the correct Arabic language (via the Qur'an and their Ma'addite pre-Islamic poetry) has support from the opinion expressed in Ibn Durayd's *Jamharat al-lugha* where the Yemeni Ḥimyarī group is said to have defined *ᶜarabiyya* as 'language' in general (1987) vol. 1, p. 319. Together, possible parameters of an argument emerge: the Nizārī faction argues for their exclusive Arabness because they speak *the* Arabic language, whereas their rivals, the Yemenis, argue to reduce *ᶜarabiyya*

to a range of languages, thereby denying the Nizārīs' monopoly, and promoting instead the Yemeni claims as being better Arabs via their more ancient genealogies. Yemeni genealogies are considered below; Iraqi Ma'addite claims to possess superior Arabic language are developed in Webb (forthcoming (A)).

72. I borrow the apt term from the title of Shryock (1997).
73. See, for example, al-Shahristānī's heresiographical *al-Milal* (n.d.) p. 662; Ibn Fāris' philological *al-Ṣāḥibī* (1993) p. 76; Ibn Ḥazm's genealogical *Jamhara* (1999b) pp. 4–5 notes the Arabs' expertise in genealogy, the Prophet's knowledge of it and the second caliph ᶜUmar's exhortation for Muslims to study it.
74. Qaṭṭāṭ (2006) p. 190 identifies genealogy as a unique hallmark of pre-Islamic Arabs. Khalidi (1994) p. 5 refers to pre-Islamic genealogy as 'the well-known Arabian tribal preoccupation', and Rosenthal proposes that genealogical writing was the basis for Arab historical consciousness (1968) pp. 21–2, 99. See also Rosenthal *EI*[2] 'Nasab' vol. 7, p. 967 and Duri (1987). See also al-Azmeh (2014a) pp. 125–6, where he notes a stage of 'operative' genealogies before the Muslim-era systematisation of Arab lineage.
75. Ibn Qutayba (1998). For his opinions of 'Arab sciences' see Chapter 6(III).
76. Ibn Qutayba's *al-Maᶜārif* contains a section on genealogy (1994) pp. 63–111, but as we explore in the next sections, it lacks the tidy pan-Arab cohesion upon which fourth/tenth century writers elaborate, and as such, it is perhaps understandable why Ibn Qutayba refrained from counting genealogical precision as a quintessentially Arab 'science' (*ᶜilm*) in his *al-Tanbīh*.
77. Though 'Arab genealogy' is supposed to record an oral tradition preserved since pre-Islamic times, modern scholars note the reign of al-Maᵓmūn and the generation of Ibn al-Kalbī as a seminal period in *nasab* writing (Kister and Plessner (1976) p. 50). Medieval Arabic writers call Ibn al-Kalbī the 'head of genealogy' (*raᵓs fī al-nasab*), they frequently cite him and Ibn Ḥazm's famous genealogy *Jamharat ansāb al-ᶜarab* owes its model to Ibn al-Kalbī. For references to Ibn al-Kalbī's influence: see W. Atallah *EI*[2] vol. 4, p. 495; Szombathy (2002) p. 5; Kennedy (1997) p. 531.
78. Several states, e.g. Turkey, encouraged genome research to match national mythologies, though Yardumlan and Schurr (2011) show the shortcomings of DNA to prove migration narratives. For DNA-based history writing regarding the English, see Oppenheimer's *The Origins of the British*. His re-evaluation of exaggerated narratives of 'Saxon genocide' in the fifth and sixth centuries CE and his problematising Gildas and Bede are welcome fruits, but the scientific data seems to run out of explanatory power when considering English identity

(Oppenheimer (2007) pp. 481–4), indicative that empirical methods fall short of the cognitive aspects of ethnicity.

79. See Geary's 2013 introduction to his project on DNA and mapping migration: <http://www.ias.edu/about/publications/ias-letter/articles/2013-spring/geary-history-genetics> (last accessed 2 August 2015).
80. The subjectivity of kinship is the basis of Weber's conception of ethnicity (1996), and subsequent theories of ethnogenesis, discussed in the Introduction.
81. Shryock (1997) p. 34.
82. Lancaster (1981) pp. 23, 34.
83. Ibid. p. 35; Shryock (1997) pp. 146, 212.
84. Lancaster (1981) pp. 24–5.
85. In relation to this fundamental gap between living memory and ancient ancestors, Lancaster observed that no one 'attempted, even as a joke, to invent ancestors to fill in between' Ibid. p. 26.
86. Ibid. pp. 20–2, 29–30.
87. Anderson (1991) p. 11.
88. Shryock (1997) p. 326.
89. Kennedy (1997) pp. 539–44; Kennedy cites Lancaster (1981) p. 32.
90. Robinson (2003) p. 41; Khalidi (1994) p. 50.
91. Qaṭṭāṭ (2006) pp. 192–209.
92. For discussions of female political figures in pre-Islamic Arabia, see Abbott (1941); ᶜAlī (1968–73) vol. 4, pp. 616–54. These studies are somewhat dated, for example Abbott begins with the 'Queen of Sheba' as the grand entrance of 'Arab Queens' into history, though the connection of Solomon's Sheba to the South Arabian Sabaic Kingdom is no longer supported in terms of chronology. The references to female leaders are nonetheless intriguing: neither pre-Islamic Arabia nor early Islam were necessarily matriarchal, but it does bear consideration that pre-Islamic male status may have been in part determined matrilineally. Onomastic references to 'sons of a mother' in pre-Islamic poetry and variations of words related to *khāl* (maternal uncle), such as *mukhwil* (possessing illustrious maternal uncles) suggest wide value in matrilineal status.
93. See Wadud (1999) and Barlas (2002) pp. 87–9, 167–202; 'textualising of misogamy' (Barlas (2002) p. 9). Barlas (2002) pp. 6, 65, 77–8 and Wadud (1999) pp. 80–8 assume that the original Muslim community was 'Arab' and therefore patriarchal, but their evidence is derived from third/ninth-century texts. This book problematises such assumptions about 'original Arab ways', and suggests that the stereotypes were gradually created by Muslims: hence

it would seem that the third/ninth-century patriarchal writings are the products of early Islam and not an actual reflection of pre-Islamic Arabia, but our approaches converge inasmuch as the third/ninth century does appear as a well-entrenched patriarchal system.

94. Pohl (1998); Geary (1983); Pohl and Reimitz (1998).
95. The fullest accounts are in Ibn Sa^c^d (1997) vol. 8, pp. 76–80 and al-Balādhurī (1979–) vol. 1.2, pp. 1086–90. Ibn Hishām's *Sīra* (n.d.) vol. 2, pp. 362–3, 645 and al-Zubayrī's *Nasab Quraysh* (1999) pp. 121–2 contain much less, and Ibn Ḥabīb's *al-Munammaq* (1985) – the other major third/ninth-century collection of Qurayshite lore – omits Ramla's memory entirely. The purpose of *al-Munammaq* involves extolling the Abbasid branch of the Quraysh, perhaps explaining its inattention to the Sufyanid Ramla.
96. For connections of the verse's revelation to Muhammad's marriage to Ramla, see Ibn Sa^c^d (1997) vol. 8, p. 79; al-Balādhurī (1979–) vol. 1.2, pp. 1088–9. Muqātil Ibn Sulaymān's early *Tafsīr* reports an abbreviated, but similar interpretation, though it intimates that the marriage was only concluded after the Meccans all converted to Islam (1979–89) vol. 4, pp. 301–2. Al-Ṭabarī's interpretation of the verse in his *Tafsīr* (1999) vol. 28, pp. 82–3 makes no mention of the marriage, and also implies the verse refers to events after Muhammad's conquest of Mecca; likewise al-Ṭabarī's *Tārīkh*, when recounting Ramla's marriage in Ethiopia, does not mention the Qur'anic verse (n.d.) vol. 2, pp. 653–4.
97. The lambasting of Mu^c^āwiya for his dynastic aspirations seems odd given that his chief opponent, ^c^Alī, whom most Muslim historiographers lauded for his piety, also had similar dynastic designs via his sons al-Ḥasan and al-Ḥusayn. Perhaps one of Mu^c^āwiya's problems was his selection of a successor who had no Prophetic matrilineal pedigree.
98. Robinson (2005) pp. 37–9 argues for the legitimacy of Ibn al-Zubayr's caliphate and dubs the Umayyad ^c^Abd al-Malik's attack on Ibn al-Zubayr as a 'rebellion'. Accordingly, he cogently critiques earlier scholarship branding Ibn al-Zubayr as the 'rebel' as superficial readings of later Arabic chronicles.
99. See Marsham (2009) for the development of the oath of allegiance (*bay^c^a*); Crone and Hinds (1986) for the evolving models of caliphal legitimacy.
100. Al-Mubarrad (2008) vol. 2, pp. 649–50; vol. 3, pp. 1490–4; al-Ṭabarī (n.d.) vol. 7, pp. 566–71.
101. Lancaster also noted that actual matrilineal links are easily converted into patrilineal-looking genealogies ((1981) pp. 20–2, 29–30).

102. In my reading, al-Mubarrad enters this discourse from Jarīr's verse *bīʿū al-mawāliya wa-staḥyū min al-ʿarabī* (2008) vol. 2, p. 576, and continues to vol. 2, p. 652 where the discourse switches (via deft digression through beards) to marriage. Matrilineal status issues are highlighted from vol. 2, pp. 618–50.
103. Ibid. vol. 2, p. 619.
104. Ibid. vol. 2, p. 643.
105. Ibid. vol. 2, pp. 618–20, 642–5.
106. Female political leaders appear with some frequency in records of interactions between Arabians and powers in the Fertile Crescent.Ephʾal (1982) records Assyrian campaigns against women leaders, the Palmyrene Zenobia is certainly a historical figure, and Shahid (1984) pp. 120–1 comments on 'Queen Mavia' of Tanūkh. See also Abbott (1941). Claims that the 'Arabs' began as an ancient matrilineal people who then became patrilineal (e.g. Shahid (1995–2009) vol. 2.2, p. 83) is an unnecessarily sweeping generalisation, as not all Arabians can be homogenised into one 'Arab mould', and the evidence is not so clear cut, as male rulers are also recorded. Again, the evidence points to Arabia's broad demographic diversity and different ruler-ship traditions.
107. Al-Mubarrad reports several matrilineal links (1936) pp. 6–7. The groups Bāhila and Khindif are two prominent examples of pre-Islamic tribes that took their name from their mothers on a matrilineal basis: later Muslims genealogists would identify their 'actual' lineage in patrilineal terms.
108. Lassner (1986) p. xiii. See also Khalidi (1994) p. 70 for discussion of early third/ninth-century relations between political power and cultural production.
109. The identification of Hūd and Ṣāliḥ as 'Arab Prophets' flows from the conceptual meld of Arab/Arabian. The stories of these prophets are located in Arabia, and hence it is easy to slip into identifying them as 'Arabs' (Gril (2003) vol. 3, p. 393, Böwering (2004) vol. 4, p. 218); consider also Wheeler's 2006 'Arab Prophets of the Qur'an and Bible'). Tottoli calls them 'Arabian Prophets' (2002) p. 45, but also 'Arab stories' Ibid. p. 50, some query their Arabness (Gilliot writes 'Arab Prophets' in inverted commas (2003) vol. 3, p. 525), but these figures tend to be under-problematised in terms of ethnicity.
110. Donner (2010) pp. 203–16 discusses the changing from Believer (*muʾmin*) to Muslim terminology, and the Arabisation of earlier memories (Ibid. pp. 216–20), as does Hoyland (2015) pp. 213–19.
111. Ibn al-Jawzī (1995) vol. 1, p. 6. *Al-Muntaẓam* can reasonably be called a text intended as 'orthodox' also because it is based on al-Ṭabarī's *Tārīkh al-rusul wa-l-mulūk*, a text which, by Ibn al-Jawzī's period, had achieved widespread

acceptance. For Ibn al-Jawzī's borrowings from al-Ṭabarī see de Somogyi (1932) pp. 58–9, 65, 69–76.

112. Ibn al-Jawzī (1995) vol. 1, p. 400.
113. Ibid. vol. 1, p. 402.
114. Ibid. vol. 1, p. 403.
115. Of the opening nine statements in the chapter of *al-Muntaẓam*, seven are ascribed to Muḥammad (Ibid. vol. 1, pp. 400–4).
116. Ibn Qutayba (1994) p. 56.
117. G Vajda dates scepticism to the Ibn al-ᶜAbbās, Wahb ibn Munabbih *Isrāᵓīliyyāt* source milieu to the third/ninth century, noting 'extravagant flights of fancy' which became attached to these stories (*EI*[2] 'Isrāᵓīliyyāt' vol. 4, p. 212). Khouri is more sympathetic, seeking to rehabilitate the image of Wahb as a reliable narrator (*EI*[2] 'Wahb ibn Munabbih' vol. 11, pp. 34–5), and the reality is likely somewhere between: Wahb/Ibn ᶜAbbās anecdotes existed at an early date and were open to later manipulation, as Colby (2008) reveals was the case for narratives of Muhammad's Night Journey. In the third/ninth-century discursive milieu, a prophetic hadith would be deemed more authoritative than potentially suspect *Isrāᵓīliyyāt* tales.
118. Lecomte (1965) pp. 259–64. Ibn Qutayba's familiarity with hadith appears in his section on hadith scholars in *al-Maᶜārif* where he lists brief biographical information typical of contemporary *ᶜilm al-rijāl* texts (1994) pp. 501–27. In *Taᵓwīl mukhtalif al-ḥadīth*, Ibn Qutayba vigorously defends the methods of hadith scholars amongst whom he presumably counted himself aligned (n.d.).
119. Ibn Balbān (1993) vol. 2, p. 77; al-Ājurrī (1989) p. 125. The early fourth/tenth-century al-Ṭabarī's *Tārīkh* (n.d.) vol. 1, pp. 150–1 quotes a mid-way version of the Abū Dharr hadith in which Muḥammad enumerates the prophets since Creation, but without express reference to 'Arab prophets' or other ethnic groups.
120. Muqātil (1979–89) vol. 2, p. 181 in reference to Q9:70.
121. ᶜAlī accepts, with some reservations, the divisions of Arabs into the 'disappeared', 'Arab Arab' and 'Arabised' *ṭabaqāt* (1968–1973) vol. 1, pp. 294–8. In respect of Hūd and ᶜĀd, ᶜAlī notes the genealogies linking first/seventh-century Arabs to the ancient prophet were likely politically motivated and spurious (Ibid. vol. 1, pp. 313–14), but he rejects the 'rulings' of the 'Orientalists' (*aḥkām al-mustashriqīn*) about ᶜĀd's status as myth (Ibid. p. 298), and he does not problematise ᶜĀd's Arabness. See also Nāfiᶜ (1952) pp. 29–32.
122. Muqātil (1979–89) vol. 2, p. 399.
123. Ibid. vol. 3, p. 748.

124. J. Stetkevych (1996) p. 2 analysed Thamūd stories at length through the lens of mythology and the creation of an Arabic cultural 'self'. Studying pre-Islamic history as a literary exercise of mythification is stimulating, but it needs firm roots in historical analysis too. J. Stetkevych grounds his work in two paradigmatic stereotypes critiqued in this book – *al-Jāhiliyya* and Arabness (Ibid. pp. 5–9), and so does not see the Thamūd stories as part of a wider, developing discourse. He instead uses Muslim-era Arabic literature as an essentially monolithic bloc that imported a pre-Islamic myth of Thamūd as the 'Arabic *Götterdämmerung*' (see, especially, Ibid. pp. 69–77), an erudite analogy, though one which transfers Wagner's sophisticated nineteenth-century German secular nationalism to the Late Antique Muhammad and Muqātil ibn Sulaymān. Adding scrutiny of the historical contexts of the Thamūd stories and their use in early Islam (discussed here, pp. 219–20) invites reinterpretation to explain how Thamūd only eventually became part of Arab history.
125. See Azami (1992) for critiques of Goldziher and, particularly Schacht's (1950) scepticism; Motzki (2005) outlines the varied critical, optimistic and intermediate positions.
126. Motzki (1991) and Lucas (2008) demonstrated that Muhammad features in only some 10 per cent of hadith in the legal chapters of al-Ṣanᶜānī and Ibn Abī Shayba; 90 per cent relate the legal opinions of first/seventh-century jurists.
127. See Note 153.
128. See Chapter 3(III), pp. 147–51.
129. Hallaq (1999) p. 90.
130. The likely forgery of hadith to bolster the standing of political factions in early Islam is little studied, though noted with some specific details regarding Quḍāᶜa in Crone (1994a) p. 48.
131. Ibn Wahb (1939–48) p. 1, Ibn al-Kalbī (2005) p. 17, Ibn Saᶜd (1997) vol.1, p. 47, Ibn Khayyāṭ (n.d.) pp. 2–3.
132. Ibn Khayyāṭ (n.d) p. 3.
133. Al-Balādhurī (1997–2004) vol. 1, p. 14.
134. Ibn Durayd (n.d.) pp. 4–5, 32.
135. Ibid. p. 32.
136. Ibn Durayd examines these more ancient, Yemeni 'Arabs' (Ibid. pp. 361–2).
137. Ibn Saᶜd (1997) vol. 1, p. 43; Ibn Wahb (1939–48) p. 5.
138. Al-Zubayrī (1999) pp. 3–4. Ibn Hishām's (d. 218/833) *Sīra* (n.d.) vol. 1, p. 2 posits nine generations between Maᶜadd and Ishmael; Ibn Saᶜd (d. 230/845) reports a range between five and forty-one (1997) vol. 1, pp. 47–8.

139. The hadith appears in Ibn Hishām's *Sīra* (n.d.) vol. 1, p. 8 and the Prophetic biography section in Ibn Sa^cd's *al-Ṭabaqāt* (1997) vol. 1, p. 43.
140. Fāriq notes the importance of Quraysh genealogy in pro-Hashemite discourses such as al-Zubayrī's *Nasab* and Ibn Ḥabīb's *al-Munammaq* intended to bolster Abbasid caliphal authority (1985) pp. 7–8. The articulation of prophetic ancestry in the above hadith renders *all* Arabs as the scion of prophecy, not just the Abbasids, however. Ibn al-Kalbī's more broadly genealogial *al-Jamhara* begins with the Hashemites, betraying the influence of early Abbasid agendas too, but Ibn al-Kalbī neither refers to Abraham nor Ishmael, hence obviating the prophetic legacy, focusing instead on blood-hierarchy of Arabian tribes.
141. Ibn Sa^cd (1997) vol. 1, pp. 42–3.
142. Ibid. vol. 1, p. 43.
143. Ibid. vol. 1, p. 43.
144. Ibid. vol. 1, p. 43–4.
145. Both Firestone (1989) p. 129 and Hawting (1999) p. 38 proposed the Ishmaelite lineage was developed in the first two Islamic centuries, and Dagorn speaks of 'l'inexistence absolue et radicale dans la tradition arabe pré-islamique, des personnages d'Ismaël, d'Agar se mere, et meme d'Abraham' (1981) p. 377. This cannot be proven conclusively because the first-century CE Latin Jewish author Josephus speaks of 'Arabs' who claimed descent from Ishmael (Millar (1993)) and Sozomen's *Ecclesiastical History* (1890) 6:38 describes an Ishmaelite-alleged ancestry of certain 'Saracens' bordering Phoenicia and Palestine. Whilst such anecdotes evidence that certain groups in the Transjordan had a history of claiming ancestry to Ishmael, connecting them to Muhammad's Muslim community is difficult. Josepheus probably intended Nabataeans by his 'Arabs', and Sozomen's 'Saracens' seem to be a matriarchal tribe entirely forgotten in Muslim-era Arabic history. Sozomen's story also concerns the conversion of this tribe to Christianity, hence it is not illogical to read their conversion and the historical reconstruction of their lineage into a biblical structure as connected, much like Muslims three or four centuries later would do. Names related to Ishmael are absent in pre-Islamic poetry, indicating a rather salient lack of symbolic attachment to Ishmael in pre-Islamic central Arabia. The only pre-Islamic onomastic evidence of Ishmaelite names occur in about fifty Safiitic inscriptions from modern Syria (al-Azmeh (2014a) p. 125 n. 150): there is some spatial congruence of these inscriptions with textual evidence from Sozomen, perhaps pointing to a regional Levantine, not pan-Arabian appeal of Ishmael. Since there is little to connect the Levantine references to Muhammad's much later Muslim community in central Arabia, both

Ephʾal (1976) and Bakhos (2006) pp. 159–60 consider the Muslim claims of Ishmaelite legacy to be separate from the earlier records.

146. It is also possible that social changes in the first century of Islam affected a merger between non-Ishmaelite Maᶜadd and smaller pre-Islamic Levantine groups who did imagine Ishmaelite ancestry. Evaluating the non-Arabic references to Levantine Ishmaelite groups (see the previous note) alongside the absence of Arabic-language records referring to Ishmaelite heritage, we could propose that the majority of those people who became 'Arabs' during Islam and spoke Arabic-like languages in pre-Islamic times were originally Ma'addites (and to a lesser extent, Kindites and *Ṭayyāyē*), and lacked Ishmaelite genealogical imagination, but the effect of their adoption of Islam prompted a search for Prophetic origins and they alighted on Ishmael, perhaps as a result of mixing with Ishmaelite groups in the Levant. These Ma'addites and other Muslims adopted Ishmael, sewing his seed, for the first time, on a pan-Arabian level thanks to the wider process of community consolidation inaugurated by Islam.

147. Q19:54–55 are the only verses devoted to Ishmael alone, though they are part of a longer list depicting the continuity of prophethood, and they give no indications that Ishmael was considered to be either Arabian domiciled or an ancestor figure: 'Mention too, in the Qur'an, the story of Ishmael. He was true to his promise, a messenger and a prophet. He commanded his household to pray and give alms, and his Lord was well pleased with him'. A passage in Q2:124–34 offers another view into Qur'anic Ishmael. In the context of the story of the Kaᶜba, Abraham makes the supplication: to God (Q2:128) 'make our descendants into a community [*umma*] devoted to You'. The 'community' is not about genealogy, however, it is based on faith: an *umma muslima*, and the following verses (Q2:129–134) continue the story of a righteous belief community from Abraham to Jacob, ending with 'That community passed away [*khalat*]. What they earned belongs to them, and what you earn belongs to you: you will not be answerable for their deeds'. The Qur'an thus closes the matter with reference to their passing [*khalat*] – a typical device in its treatment of analogies drawn from the past. Accordingly, the Qur'an does not connect Ishmael to Muhammad in terms of blood (and never Arabness, either), but instead invites a symbolic connection through faith.

148. The utter destruction of ᶜĀd and Thamūd is a common Qur'anic refrain: 'He destroyed ancient ᶜĀd, and Thamūd and let nothing remain' (Q53:50–51). As they are symbols of disobedience, it is vital for the Qur'an to express the totality of their destruction as witness to God's power.

149. For discussion of the Yemenis' role in the conquests, see Mad'aj (1988) pp. 64–75 and G. Rex Smith (1990) p. 134.
150. Ibn Khayyāṭ (n.d.) pp. 2–3.
151. Ibid. p. 3.
152. Ibid. p. 3.
153. Ibid. p. 66. This hadith, unlike all other hadith cited in this section, also appears in al-Bukhārī's *Ṣaḥīḥ* (1999) *Manāqib*:4 where it takes an unusual form, describing Muhammad encouraging people to shoot arrows in a marketplace!
154. Ibn Khayyāṭ (n.d.) p. 66. According to my searches, this hadith is not reported in any other text.
155. Ibn Wahb (1939–48) pp. 5–6.
156. Ibn Hishām (n.d.) vol. 1, p. 7.
157. Al-Hamdānī (2004) vol. 1, pp. 129–30.
158. Ibn Ḥazm (1999b) p. 7. The early fourth/tenth century philologist Ibn Durayd (d. 321/933) is, according to my readings, the last Iraqi author to cite the opinion that Qaḥṭān was a descendent of Ishmael: he notes it in his dictionary, *Jamharat al-lugha*'s definition of *ᶜarab* (1987) vol. 1, p. 319. Though even there, the opinion appears as the last option Ibn Durayd lists for Arab genealogy, one of the manuscripts from which the modern version of the dictionary was compiled omits the opinion, and in his genealogical *al-Ishtiqāq*, Ibn Durayd does not mention it at all.
159. In texts dating after the third/ninth century, I found no citations of hadith claiming Ishmael as the father of all Arabs.
160. Ibn Hishām (n.d.) vol. 1, p. 7.
161. See his discussion of Abraham, Ibn al-Kalbī (1988) vol. 2, p. 549.
162. Ibn al-Kalbī details Qaḥṭān's genealogy (1988) vol. 1, pp. 131–3.
163. Ibn Wahb (1939–48) p. 5.
164. For Yemeni narratives of Tubbaᵓ and the pre-Islamic past, see Diᶜbil (1997) pp. 47–51, Wahb ibn Munabbih (1996) pp. 271–311; al-Ḥimyarī (1985) pp. 29, 140–200.
165. Investigating the political intersections between early Muslim Iraq and Thamūd's place in early Muslim memories seems vital to elaborate Thamūd mythology in later Arabic literature; J. Stetkevych refers once to Thaqīf (1996) p. 41, though the interplay of Thaqīf and political alignments seems a more significant piece necessary to reinterpret the later mythology.
166. *Al-Muḥabbar* survives in the recension of al-Sukkarī (d. 275/888 or 290/903), student of Ibn Ḥabīb. The extant text may reflect al-Sukkarī's additions,

evidenced by two mentions in the texts of caliphs who ruled after Ibn Ḥabīb's death (Ibn Ḥabīb (1942) pp. 44, 62).

167. Ibid. pp. 384–5.
168. Ibid. p. 395.
169. Al-Azharī (1994) vol. 2, p. 170. This historical interpretation also has different emphasis to the definition of *ᶜāriba* in the earlier lexicon *al-ᶜAyn*, see Note 3.
170. Al-Balādhurī (1979-) vol. 1.1, pp. 8–9.
171. Ibn al-Kalbī (1988) vol. 1, p. 131.
172. Ibn Ḥabīb (1942) pp. 131–2. He recites three different lists of circumcised prophets, Hūd and Ṣāliḥ feature in two.
173. Bray (2003) pp. 223, 226.
174. Q53:51, 69:8; al-Jāḥiẓ (2003) vol. 1, pp. 187–8. Al-Jāḥiẓ's negative appraisal and al-Jumaḥī's detailed below reveal the difficulty in assuming the 'Muslim tradition' smoothly articulated a monolithic 'Arabic myth' from the past.
175. Al-Jāḥiẓ (2003) vol. 1, p. 188.
176. For the Yemeni-focused narrative, see Ibn Hishām (n.d.) vol. 1, pp. 13–70.
177. Al-Jumaḥī (n.d.) vol. 1, p. 8–9.
178. Ibid. vol. 1, p. 9.
179. Ibid. vol. 1, pp. 9–10.
180. Ibid. vol. 1, pp. 10–11.
181. Ibid. vol. 1, p. 11.
182. Shryock (1997) pp. 30–4.
183. Mad'aj (1988) pp. 86–7, 90.
184. Donner (1981) pp. 75–82, 221–44 discusses the tribal organisation and power structures in which the Thaqīf (alongside Quraysh) played a dominant role over other early Muslim groups. The persecutions of the Thaqafī governor al-Ḥajjāj ibn Yūsuf in Iraq are famous.
185. Note Ibn Wahb's *al-Jāmiᶜ* also relates a hadith with the same *isnād* as the Thaqīf/Ḥimyar hadith in the same section where Muhammad orders his community to not to curse Tubbaᶜ 'because he was a Muslim' (1939–48) p. 1). Ibn Wahb thus resolves the Qur'anic ambiguity and prompts praise of Ḥimyar when his following hadith reveal Ḥimyar as Tubbaᶜ's descendants.
186. This aspect, though not considered in J. Stetkevych (1996), seems an important context in which mythology from pre-Islamic Arabia can be read.
187. Al-Balādhurī (1997–2004) vol. 1, p. 6.
188. Ibid. vol. 1, pp. 5–7.
189. Al-Yaᶜqūbī describes ᶜĀd and Thamūd without mentioning their Arabness

(n.d.) vol. 1, pp. 20–2), and his chapter on the ancestors of Muhammad begins with Abraham and Ishmael (in keeping with the Ma'addite model (Ibid. vol. 1, p. 221)). But when recounting the history of Yemen, al-Yaᶜqūbī notes that the Prophet Hūd's tribe was (possibly, according to al-Yaᶜqūbī's language) the ancestor of the Yemeni Arabs (Ibid. vol. 1, p. 195).

190. Al-Balādhurī discusses the 'Ancient Arabs' (*al-ᶜarab al-ᶜāriba*) when listing the descendants of Noah and includes ᶜĀd and Thamūd, Jurhum and Yaqṭān (whom he later explains is the Yemeni Qaḥṭān) (1997–2004) vol. 1, pp. 5–6. Conversely, he also narrates opinions from late second/eighth-century genealogists (Ibn al-Kalbī and al-Sharqī) that state: 'Ishmael is the father of all Arabs on Earth' (Ibid. vol. 1, pp. 6–7), but al-Balādhurī relieves the confused reader by offering the (now familiar, but unprecedented at his time) observation that Ishmael was the first Arabic speaking son of Abraham – i.e. Ishmael's scion constitute a secondary, later group of Arabic speakers (Ibid. vol. 1, p. 7). Emphasising the Arabness of the ancient Arabs, al-Balādhurī also notes short *akhbār* about ᶜĀd, Thamūd, Jadīs and Jurhum's activities in Arabia before Ishmael and establishes Yemeni lineage from Hūd (Ibid. vol. 1, pp. 7-9).

191. Bray (2003) p. 221 suggests that *al-Maᶜārif* offers a sometimes contradictory menu of details about Arab tribes, and it does leave astute readers with difficult questions regarding Arab origins. But it states clearly that Yaᶜrub ibn Qaḥṭān was the first Arabic speaker (Ibn Qutayba (1994) p. 626) who lived five generations before Ishmael (Ibid. pp. 26–7). *Al-Maᶜārif* is silent on ᶜĀd and Thamūd's Arabness, making them only distant relatives of Qaḥṭān's Arab family and dates them one or two generations before Yaᶜrub and the first Arabic speakers (Ibid. pp. 28–9), making it unclear how Hūd and Ṣāliḥ can be counted as 'Arab Prophets', though Ibn Qutayba expressly identifies them as Arabs elsewhere in *al-Maᶜārif* (Ibid. p. 56).

192. Al-Ṭabarī (n.d.) vol. 1, p. 216; see also vol. 1, p. 204.

193. See herein, pp. 186–7.

194. See al-Qurṭubī (2000) vol. 8, p. 191; al-Zamakhsharī (1995) vol. 2, p. 314; al-Bayḍāwī (1999) vol. 1, p. 426.

195. Ibn Durayd (1987) vol. 1, p. 319.

196. The same backwards progression of Mecca's history occurred simultaneously: early third/ninth-century narratives depicting Abraham/Ishmael as the first builders of Mecca (and progenitors of the Arabs) were replaced by fourth/tenth-century narratives of Mecca's founding at the beginning of time by Adam, alongside narratives of more ancient Arabness (detailed in Webb (2013b)).

5

Arabs as a People and Arabness as an Idea: 750–900 CE

Thus far, we have traced the sociopolitical drivers of Arab ethnogenesis to the second/eighth century, and we found that the exceptional conditions of early Islam fostered a new idea of 'Arab community' as a means for Conquerors to uphold their elite status once the initial burst of conquests had passed. The Conquerors' towns (*al-amṣār*) bear striking parallels to the conditions which catalyse ethnogenesis, but the process of creating shared consciousness of Arab community was nonetheless uneven as a consequence of various obstacles impeding the capacity of Arabness to reconcile the Conquerors into one integrated family. Power struggles, regional rivalries and doctrinal strife, alongside an array of alternative communal identities which the Conquerors could choose to embrace (especially Maᶜadd and Yemen), and the distinction stressed between Arab identity and nomadic Arabian *aᶜrāb* complicated consciousness of unified community and homeland, and we can appreciate why early Arabic literature and poetry express disputed traditions of Arab genealogy and varied terms of communal belonging.

The broad consolidation of Arab genealogies and the definition of *ᶜarab* as a kin-group (*umma/jīl*) in later third/ninth century and subsequent writings surveyed in the last chapter indicate a resolution of earlier Arabness ambiguity, and suggest that key changes occurred in the underlying society and literary circles to facilitate the developed discourses. The contemporaneous consolidation of Arab genealogy alongside the literary recording of pre-Islamic Arabian history and Islam's rise as the cohesive 'Arab story' familiar today marks the third/ninth century as the period when Arabness became furnished with both a consolidated genealogy and ancient history, the familiar trappings of an ethnic identity. That period thus appears a climax of early Islamic Arab ethnogenesis, reflecting an underlying Arabness vigour in a society where a self-aware community of Arabs enjoyed a sense of cohesion and status which fuelled the literary trumpeting of Arab collective identity and achievements. Understanding the social conditions between the second/eighth and third/ninth centuries to explain the emergence of these classic Arabness discourses is the next step to critically interpret the genesis and meanings of the vast Muslim-era literature about Arab lore.

The high point of Arab consciousness, however, soon slid to denouement when the Fourth *Fitna* succession struggle (193–8/809–13) interrupted the old order, and the ever-grinding wheels of social change exerted new pressures on the Arabness idea. Third/ninth-century sociopolitical forces cleared new paths for subsequent writers to rethink Arabness and rewrite Arab history yet again to reflect the new circumstances. This chapter traces the early Abbasid imaginations about Arabs and the changes that in turn inspired new imaginations, which will be studied in our final chapter.

I Arabs in the Early Abbasid Caliphate (132–93/750–809)

Historians had traditionally cited the Abbasid takeover in 132/749–50 as a revolution dividing distinct periods of 'Arabic' and 'Persianate' Caliphates.[1] But now such binary periodisation is critiqued: it is too blunt, too categorical and obscures continuities between Umayyad and Abbasid times.[2] And from our perspective of Arab ethnogenesis, it is important to disengage from the timeworn binary model of Umayyad/Arab versus Abbasid/Persian too. This book maintains that the Umayyads could not have been a self-consciously Arab *Staatsnation*[3] since their elites only began calling themselves Arabs towards the end of the Umayyad period. And theories of ethnicity also reject views that the Abbasid takeover could have signalled a sudden switch to Persian acculturation. Ethnogenic processes are powerful movements which are not simply stopped in their tracks by a change of dynasty, and the momentum of Umayyad-era Arab ethnogenesis should be expected to carry into Abbasid times. With our new critical approach to identity, we no longer need be beholden to racial labels for early Muslim-era political movements, and by reappraising the sources, we shall appreciate that the early Abbasids continued to articulate statecraft around Arabness, and that contemporary

Iraqi society witnessed important developments which enhanced the value and visibility of Arab identity. The Abbasid 'revolution' in fact provided for the healthy continuation of Arab ethnogenesis via the high social and political status retained by groups who called themselves 'Arabs'.

From the outset, the Abbasid takeover involved substantial self-expressed 'Arab' groups: the union of Yamānī and Qaysī affiliations against Muḍar was the decisive stroke that turned the tide against Umayyad fortunes in Iraq,[4] and in the ensuing decades Arab groups retained power as evidenced by continued *ᶜaṣabiyya* (inter-Arab group tensions) across the Caliphate. For instance, during the reign of al-Manṣūr (136–58/754–75), factionalism prompted change from Yamānī to Nizārī control over Azerbaijan in 141/758–9,[5] Qaysī and Yamānī sympathies are accorded a role in caliphal appointments,[6] and rivalry between Rabīᶜa and Yamān flared in Sind in 142/759–60.[7] Arab feuding seemed to have trans-regional cohesion: in the upshot of an apparent collusion of rebellious groups between Yemen and Sind, a Tamīmī governor of Sind, ᶜUyayna ibn Mūsā, was killed by the Yamāniyya, and the caliph's Yamānī officer (*ᶜāmil*) (and later governor of al-Baṣra) ᶜUqba ibn Salam attacked members of Rabīᶜa in al-Baḥrayn in apparent retribution for transgressions of the Rabīᶜa governor in Yemen.[8] *ᶜAṣabiyya* conflict in Sind continued during al-Mahdī's caliphate (158–69/775–85),[9] and Hārūn al-Rashīd's reign (170–93/785–809) experienced wide-ranging *ᶜaṣabiyya* too: Yamānīs and Nizārīs fought in Sind after the appointment of Ṭayfūr ibn ᶜAbd Allāh al-Ḥimyarī, a Yamānī governor,[10] the anti-Abbasid Nizārī Abū al-Haydhām attacked Yamānīs in al-Shām in 176/792–3,[11] and Yamānīs and Nizārīs fought repeatedly over influence in Armenia.[12] The flashes of *ᶜaṣabiyya* in so many parts of the Caliphate indicate that Arab identities remained functional rallying points for organising violence, and the Abbasids were compelled to navigate them just as the Umayyads had done in the generations before.

The continued high status of Arab tribesmen as governors, generals and officials during the reigns of al-Manṣūr and al-Hādī further reflect the political influence Arabs maintained into the early Abbasid Caliphate.[13] In an indication that early Abbasids perhaps even assumed that Arabs must continue in leadership positions under the new regime, al-Fasawī notes there was a debate in the caliphate of al-Manṣūr over whether it was permissible to appoint *mawālī* (non-Arab clients, considered presently) as governors.[14] Al-Fasawī remarks that an Arab was appointed in the circumstance (thus keeping the status quo), though the Caliph reportedly did not reject the possibility of appointing *mawālī* governors, and al-Yaᶜqūbī notes that al-Manṣūr relied on fifteen 'Arab *ᶜummāl*' along with eleven *ᶜummāl* from the *mawālī*.[15] During the reign of al-Rashīd, the appointment of Arab governors continued, but it occurred alongside increasing non-Arab appointments too. For instance, after *ᶜaṣabiyya* in al-Shām, al-Rashīd appointed one of the non-Arab Khurasanian Barmakids, Jaᶜfar ibn Yaḥyā ibn Khālid (which sparked further *ᶜaṣabiyya* unrest in Ḥimṣ);[16] during tribal feuding in Armenia, al-Rashīd appointed an Arab Hashemite, Mūsā ibn ᶜĪsā, to quell the trouble, and then, when that move failed, the Caliph dispatched the Khurasanian al-Ḥarashī with soldiers drawn from the Khurasanians (*ahl al-Khurāsān*), though their presence roused further unrest amongst both Nizārī and Yamānī Arabs.[17] Taking stock, the sources evidence that early Abbasid replacement of Arab commanders with non-Arabs was not pervasive, and therefore we cannot maintain that the Abbasid takeover signalled the political end of the Arab elite: rather the ceding of influence to non-Arabs progressed gradually. Such pace of change over two generations implies that the rise of 'Persians' and other conquered peoples was not the result of specific Abbasid revolutionary platforms, but reflected a deeper, slower evolution in the wider society, and prompts evaluation of Iraq in the late Umayyad and early Abbasid periods from the perspective of ethnogenesis.

Chapter 3 proposed that the initial iterations of Arabness enabled Conquerors to articulate their privileged status around notions of the Qur'an, language and Islam, and for so long as the Conquerors were spatially and culturally distinct in their *amṣār*, they could monopolise Arab identity. But the growing prosperity of the *amṣār* prompted changes. During the Umayyad period, the former, pre-Islamic Iraqi population centres were abandoned as indigenous Iraqis moved into the *amṣār* for economic opportunity, and these immigrants (who acquired the name *mawālī*[18]) began sharing the same social contexts as the descendants of the Conquerors. Considered in relation to theories of ethnicity, such population movements generally rewrite social divisions and thus influenced early Islamic-era Iraq's ethnic boundaries. By the later Umayyad period, many *mawālī* had converted to Islam, spoke Arabic and were born in the same environment as the scion of the Conquerors, so whilst *mawālī* were distinct from the Conquerors in terms of their origins, *mawālī* adoption of Arabic 'cultural stuff' (language and religion) and their rising economic and administrative power thanks to their participation in the success of the *amṣār* reduced barriers between them and the Conqueror elites. By the early second/eighth century, the two generations of reorganising Iraq's urban landscape would have made it difficult to discern *ᶜarab* from many *mawālī*. By the Abbasid takeover, therefore, a familiar paradox of ethnogenesis was in progress: the mixing of populations, which had initially enabled the Conquerors to recognise their collective difference from indigenous Iraqis, gradually transformed into a driver towards assimilation. A transactionist/instrumentalist theoretical perspective reads the regularisation of transactions and the sharing of urban spaces between Arabian Conqueror and Iraqi conquered as a potent moment that blurred former boundaries of difference into opportunities for merger under a hybrid Iraqi-Muslim identity. As a result, the *amṣār* were no longer spaces for purely 'Arab' ethnogenesis, and the rise of non-Arabs in the later second/eighth century can be cogently explained as an inevitable social phenomenon (and not a political policy) emanating from the Caliphate's success that spread riches and power so widely as to overflow the boundaries of the old elite.

Given the specific social context of early Muslim-era Iraqi towns where opportunities enabled manifold groups to establish and reorganise themselves in the political/economic/doctrinal new order, we accordingly do ourselves a disservice by maintaining a binary analytical division of Arab/Persian onto our understanding of Iraqi society. As in all social contexts, individuals negotiated an array of possible identities, and enjoyed the freedom of considerable choice in their decisions about identifying and aligning themselves.[19] Individual Iraqi *amṣār*-dwellers could be expected to assert their Arabness or Persian-ness with varying degrees of intensity depending on their circles of interest, social interaction and personal choice. And furthermore, as discussed in Chapter 4, there were manifold interpretations of the parameters of membership into an 'Arab' community, and so not even all people who identified themselves in historical records as 'Arabs' necessarily can be taken as constituting one cohesive social group. A Ḥimyarī's concept of belonging to Arabness via his ancient imagined communities of Yemeni 'Arab' kings of *al-ᶜāriba* differed from a Ma'addite's Arabness flowing from his sense of language, faith and early Conqueror elite ancestors. We are faced with a pluriform situation in which Conquerors did not cling to an 'innate' sense of Arabness that they imported from pre-Islamic Arabia, nor did they emerge with an agreed pan-Arabian family tree to imagine kin-relationships between each other. As such, we shall stress again that the word *al-ᶜarab* was realistically not a matter of 'who', but rather a question of 'what'. As opposed to a totality that demarcates who people were, Arabness was a mentality, a strategy shaped through several stages of development into an identity, and the same applies for 'Persian' and other *shuᶜūb* (classification of peoples) of Iraqi society. It is accordingly only with some trepidation that we can apply the ethnonyms 'Arab' and 'Persian' onto a given individual in Abbasid-era Iraq, but the proliferation of textual references to *ᶜarab* and *ᶜajam* reveal that these categories became important in the second/eighth century, and are in need of attention that pays due heed to their constructed nature.

At this juncture of pluriform Arabness within a developing Iraqi urban context, we recall Wallman's adage, 'it takes two, ethnicity can only happen at the boundary of us':[20] we shall need to investigate how the meanings of 'Arab' incubated in dialogue over time with the articulations of other Iraqi identities. 'Arab' and *mawālī* both needed each other to define themselves as independent groups, and herein, as part of the often paradoxical path of ethnogenesis, the period when *mawālī* began to imagine an identity for themselves by adopting Arabic language and Islamic faith and were thus poised to deprive the Conquerors of their monopoly over Arabness as a marker of 'elite' can also be expected to have constituted a fertile moment for the Arabness idea to enter a new evolution too. Examining this phenomenon can help explain why Arabness began to define itself around kinship. Because *mawālī* aspirants to social prestige were deftly entering power by mimicking Arabness' linguistic–doctrinal manifestations, Conqueror elites would benefit from keeping assimilating *mawālī* at arms length by inventing a new idea of Arabness that better maintained ethnic boundaries. And because second/eighth-century 'Arabs' possessed only memories of their genealogy and history to readily distinguish themselves from *mawālī*, a recasting of Arabness around closed-ended lineage and heritage seems a logical response to sustain Arab/*mawlā* distinction and preserve Conqueror elite status. In contrast, therefore, to the Umayyad era when intertribal *ʿaṣabiyya* was a source of division, Arab tribalism in the early Abbasid period became a means for elites to articulate shared community. The appearance of Ibn al-Kalbī's pan-Arab genealogical models in the late second/eighth century and the shift to defining Arabness around *nasab* traced in Chapter 4 suggest this is precisely what happened. The coherent Arab family trees emerge as a self-defensive intellectual legacy of the pressures of cosmopolitanism which drove the formerly disparate Arabian groups into a novel recognition of shared interest in becoming kin and celebrating a shared (and no longer competitive) history since their wide collective power structure was being threatened by newly rich and increasingly influential *mawālī*. In short, the early Abbasid era fostered conditions much more amenable to nurturing consciousness of Arab kin-unity than the more competitive environment of Umayyad times.

The rise of shared Arab kinship thus occurred within a framework of a stable, prosperous, cosmopolitan society where generations of consolidating conquests around an elite with a symbolically powerful language, intertwined with a new religion, established a secure structure. The structure, however, was so successful that it could not segregate conquered peoples for long, and the Abbasid founding of Baghdad (142–5/758–62) can also be recognised for its major impact on ethnogenesis by forging new transactional boundaries. The consolidation of the Caliphate's Iraqi imperial capital created an unprecedented system of Iraq-centre versus provinces-periphery which grouped Iraqi Muslims, Arab and non-Arab, into one coherent (and affluent) transactional sphere vis-à-vis the other regions of the Caliphate. The Abbasid–Baghdad system accelerated opportunities for all Iraqi groups to share power, status and prosperity. Theory indicates that such a structure is highly conducive to assimilation and re-articulation of ethnic identities, and studies of early Abbasid Iraq note its cosmopolitanism.[21] Theory also instructs that such a rise of a hegemonic, cosmopolitan identity has an attendant wrinkle of ethnic revival. History again reveals theory's applicability to early Abbasid society, for we read indications of a second/eighth-century phenomenon called *al-shuʿūbiyya*, a cultural partisanship between ethnic groups in Iraq. Modern scholars have written extensively about *al-shuʿūbiyya*, changing their interpretations in step with changes in Western approaches to race, nationalism and identity;[22] but *al-shuʿūbiyya* has not yet been studied as an ethnic revival, and such terms can offer fruitful explanations for the phenomenon's significance and its relevance to Arab identity.

Ethnic revival describes a cultural reaction occurring when subaltern groups assimilate into the identity of a hegemon. The sense of losing old culture leads assimilators towards nostalgic promotion of their heritage, and members of the hegemon may also respond by attempting to maintain their distinctiveness from assimilators. Both sides debate their respective merits, but their efforts are doomed; assimilation is a powerful tide caused by sociopolitical–economic factors that merge groups, and unless major shifts in transactional boundaries or power relations occur, assimilation will prevail, notwithstanding the brief outburst of ethnic revivalists' chauvinism. If *al-shu*ᶜ*ūbiyya* was an ethnic revival, we could then anticipate that it would be short-lived, that subaltern groups would soon be silenced, and that, once time progressed a little, members of both formerly competitive sides would assimilate and eventually sing from the same cultural hymn sheet. Such predictions address salient issues regarding *al-shu*ᶜ*ūbiyya*.

Scholars question why *al-shu*ᶜ*ūbiyya* had limited political legacy and why, considering the many references to it, only one anti-Arab *shu*ᶜ*ūbī* text survives.[23] The phenomenon of ethnic revival offers answers: Arabs and *mawālī* shared the same transactional environment and their interests were aligned in favour of the Iraqi system's survival. As they approached parity in status, rank and material possessions, and as the prosperity of early Abbasid Iraq kept all sides comfortably well funded, competition could not long remain seriously political as to endanger the whole system, and the opposing sides accordingly found their outlet to debate more intangible qualities of culture and memories of communal pasts.[24] The absence of surviving anti-Arab *shu*ᶜ*ūbī* texts stems from ethnic revival's short-lived nature. *Al-shu*ᶜ*ūbiyya* was relevant in second/eighth-century Iraq, but during that century paper technology had not become widespread; as a consequence few books were written, and hence we cannot expect many texts from that period to exist.[25] In the third/ninth century, on the other hand, the proliferation of paper fuelled a dramatic increase in book production, but by then *al-shu*ᶜ*ūbiyya*'s passion had subsided and few anti-Arab partisans remained since there was little left to debate as the process of assimilation had advanced, and so the absence of specifically *shu*ᶜ*ūbī* books can be anticipated. By interpreting *al-shu*ᶜ*ūbiyya* as a necessarily brief outburst, we can apprehend that by the time Arabic literary production began in earnest, *al-shuᶜūbiyya* had already receded into a memory of a past political issue, and constituted merely an intellectual diversion to third/ninth-century writers, thereby explaining why the loudest surviving voices of anti-Arab sentiment are primarily restricted to some second/eighth-century poems of Bashshār ibn Burd and Abū Nuwās that survived into third/ninth-century written poetry collections (though much caution is advised when interpreting even these verses as evidence for *al-shuᶜūbiyya*).[26]

Reading *al-shuᶜūbiyya* as ethnic revival also redresses a traditional oversimplification regarding cultural production in the second/eighth century which directly influences interpretation of early Arabness discourses. It was suggested that Arabs and *mawālī* competed over the power to write pre-Islamic history and that non-Arabs won following *al-shuᶜūbiyya*,[27] but this implies that Arabs 'lost' the struggle. Ethnic revival is not about winners or losers: it is a story of assimilation, and this is reflected in Arabic literature. Many second/eighth-century narrators of the Arab pre-Islamic past such as Ḥammād al-Rāwiya, Khalaf al-Aḥmar, al-Madāʾinī and al-Jāḥiẓ did not claim Arab lineage, but many others did: for example, poetry collectors al-Aṣmaᶜī, al-Mufaḍḍal al-Ḍabbī and Ibn Sallām al-Jumaḥī, the genealogist and historian Ibn al-Kalbī, the belles-lettrist al-Mubarrad and *akhbār* narrators Ibn Ḥabīb and al-Zubayr ibn Bakkār. And while the non-Arab poetry collector Abū ᶜUbayda is cited as the paradigmatic Arab-hater,[28] his surviving work, *al-Naqāʾiḍ* contains such extensive anecdotes about past Arab glories that it is difficult to adduce as anti-Arab invective of a supposedly excited *shuᶜūbī*. It is challenging to find sustained scorn against the Arabs in any surviving Iraqi works, and I am not aware that scholars have demonstrated that 'ethnically Arab' authors wrote different versions of history than their 'ethnically Persian' peers. Reading *al-shuᶜūbiyya* as an ethnic revival enables us to side-step essentialised notions of cultural production on ethnic Arab versus Persian lines and thus grasp that the assimilation had a crucial result of facilitating the outpouring of shared writing on *Arabica* as the process led to widespread praise of the Arab hegemon's past as all Iraqi cultural producers flowed together towards Arabness.

The form of Arabness they would embrace, however, should not be assumed as fixed. We have seen that prior to the third/ninth century, the parameters of Arab identity were ill defined, and ethnic revival and ethnogenesis do not create tidy categories either. The hypothesis that Muslim elites in the early second/eighth century defended their status by reinterpreting past tribal rivalry into a shared sense of Arab kinship is reflected in the development of Arab genealogy (*nasab*), but genealogical senses of Arabness also shared space with the assimilators who remained outside Arab kinship but wanted to participate in the elite language and Arabness' cultural–political system. When an identity is a valuable practical asset in a given social context, manifold voices will assert opinions about it, obstructing the emergence of one clear hegemonic definition, and the 'Arab' as an idea thus spanned several possibilities in early Abbasid Iraq. Some could imagine 'Arab' as symbolising their own kin, a living ethnos and genealogical chain of heroic ancestors; others could imagine 'the Arabs' as a historic group who had brought Islam to Iraq, and they could interpret Arabness as a cultural device to imagine the contours of a broader Iraqi-Muslim identity.

Born in the crucible of conquest, Arabness, perhaps because of its usefulness as an identity, lacked the circumstances for uniform articulation: early Abbasid politics, assimilation and *al-shu*^{c}*ūbiyya* were all steps in the process of Arab ethnogenesis. The result was seminal, for at the dawn of the third/ninth century, shortly following the flash of *al-shu*^{c}*ūbiyya* ethnic revival, Arabness matured into a wide-embracing notion of community shared by members of Arab tribes and non-Arab Iraqis alike. But while Arabness thus gained widespread consent, its flowering leapt out of step with its history. 'Arabs' had only just become an integrated kin-community, yet the demands placed upon Arabness as the signature identity of Muslim Iraq required a deeper and more illustrious past to sustain it. To our good fortune, we possess texts from this period revealing how Iraqi cultural producers set about creating an appropriately ancient and dignified pan-Arab history to imagine the Arabs in as positive a light as possible.

II Forging an Iraqi 'Arab Past'

The Muslim conquest of Iraq was but one event in a continuous ebb and flow of Mesopotamia's settled–nomad relations that traces its history to the establishment of urban states circa 3000 BCE. But the conquest was exceptional in its ability to generate Iraqi interest in Arabian cultures, and extraordinary in its effect of making Iraqis want their history to become Arabian. Prior to Islam, Mesopotamian civilisations expressed limited interest in the deserts beyond Iraq:[29] they policed the borders and engaged in sporadic trade with Arabian populations,[30] but they little investigated Arabia's inhabitants. The Neo-Babylonian Nabonidus (r. 556–539 BCE) appears to be the only ancient Mesopotamian ruler who established a presence in Arabia, but his ten-year sojourn around Tayma was lambasted in Babylonia and was disastrous, as the Neo-Babylonian empire collapsed almost immediately afterwards,[31] and for the next seven centuries, the succession of Achaemenid, Seleucid and Parthian regimes each developed urban centres in Iraq without significant advance into central Arabia.[32] In Late Antiquity, the Sasanians made more substantial Arabian inroads, but their efforts were directed towards influence and competition against Roman and later Byzantine interests. Arabia consequently neither became part of Sasanian 'inside space', a region for Sasanian urban expansion, nor a source of cultural influence.[33] As for Arabian population movements into Iraq in ancient times, Arabian groups continuously infiltrated Iraq's borders and settled in Mesopotamia, but they invariably assimilated, leaving scant trace of literary longings for Arabia.[34] The Muslim-era narratives written by Iraqis from the third/ninth century therefore mark a singular departure from previous Mesopotamian literary traditions that created an unprecedented merger of Iraqi and Arabian heritage, demonstrating the intriguing power the Arabness idea acquired in their imagination. The cumulative effects of their many surviving narratives have conditioned subsequent readers to imagine the cohesiveness of pre-Islamic Arab identity, and to conceptualise Late Antique Arabia and its Iraqi fringes as distinctive 'Arab' places, but the constructed nature of these narratives, as we shall see, calls into question such putative Arabness and invites reappraisal.

The Arabic narratives of pre-Islamic history preserved in al-Yaᶜqūbī, al-Ṭabarī and al-Masᶜūdī's histories,[35] as well as anecdotes in the writings of their contemporaries,[36] reveal a salient role Muslim Iraqi authors accorded Iraq in their pre-Islamic 'Arab story'. Precise details vary, but the common framework dates the Arabs' first settlement in Iraq to the reign of the Neo-Babylonian Nebuchadnezzar.[37] Their story relates that Nebuchadnezzar launched a bloody campaign into Arabia to exterminate the Arabs, and deported survivors to the town of al-Ḥīra on the Euphrates near the site upon which Muslims later founded their city of al-Kūfa in 14/636.[38] The Arab story then skips to the period after Alexander the Great and describes fresh waves of Arabs invading Iraq and establishing kingdoms in al-Ḥīra and al-Anbār.[39] The sources affirm the Arabness of these kingdoms by reference to their Arabian origin and their kin-relation to Arab tribes, and they are portrayed as remaining 'Arab': the texts neither imply that urban settlement affected the invaders' Arabness nor that they ever assimilated or even mixed with the *Nabaṭ* (the usual term for Mesopotamia's ancient agricultural population), the *Aramāniyyūn* (al-Ṭabarī's rendering of Iraqi Aramaeans/Syriac peoples)[40] or the *Furs* (the dynasts of Mesopotamia and Iran).[41] Unlike the fluid notion of ethnic identity embraced by modern anthropologists, our early sources depict unchanging and enduring 'racial' Arabness that renders their depictions of ancient Arabs indistinguishable from their portrayals of Arabs in Muhammad's day. Iraqi Muslim writers seem to have intended to narrate a long, stable Arab presence in Iraq to insinuate the Arabs' time-honoured right to Iraqi kingship, an obviously utilitarian discourse for the post-conquest Middle East.

The Iraqi Muslims' depiction of pre-Islamic Iraq is almost completely at odds with modern reconstructions of Mesopotamian history. There are no Sumerians or Akkadians in the Arabic texts, and Arabic writers only mention Assyrian and Babylonian kings referenced in the biblical tradition such as Sennacherib and Nebuchadnezzar, revealing that the Arabic narratives borrowed particularly from Hebrew sources.[42] Disregarding the Achaemenids, they switch to the Seleucid and Parthian periods (Arabic: *Mulūk al-Ṭawāʾif*), and while the descriptions of Arabian incursions during weak central authority may reflect the nature of nomadic/settled relations at that time,[43] the Muslim-era narratives' stress on the Arabness of the whole succession of Arabian nomads and the express avowals that the nomadic incursions were a 'desire to defeat the non-Arabs (*al-aᶜājim*) in the Iraqi/Arabian borderland, or to share kingship with them',[44] is anachronistic. We have seen that textual and theoretical indicators point to the Islamic-era creation of Arab communal consciousness, and hence Muslim-era Iraqi narratives may contain names of some real tribes and kings, but the recasting of history into one overarching story of *ᶜarab* versus *ᶜajam*, and the inclusion of pre-Islamic Iraqi kingdoms as salient participants in the story of the Arab community, make these accounts not a 'true memory' of ancient Iraq, but instead a projection of the third/ninth-century Iraqi present onto the past. Third/ninth-century Iraqi writers reconceptualised the past into a cyclical 'Arab' pattern with an apparent goal of creating an authentically 'Arab past' for Iraq and foreshadowing/justifying the conquests and Abbasid-era Muslim identity via forged historical precedent. Closer textual analysis affirms this reading.

To create Arab history, the Muslim narratives appropriate real events of the distant past and reformat them in an Arab guise. For instance, they elide memory of the Roman capture of Palmyra in 272 CE and rewrite it as the victory of an Iraqi Arab king Jadhīma ibn Mālik al-Abrash.[45] Muslim writers' depiction of the nomadic/settled relations along the southern and western borders of Iraq as a binary *ᶜarab/ᶜajam* power-sharing structure appropriated memories of various peoples and amalgamated them into putative Arab national independence, a point al-Ṭabarī reiterates.[46] By converting every independent group along Mesopotamia's borders since the Seleucid period into 'Arabs', Muslim authors forged an ancient sense of 'Arab' political independence and tradition of defiance against Mesopotamian hegemons neatly foreshadowing the Muslim conquest. The literary reconstruction of the Battle of Dhū Qār which we saw gained its 'Arab' guise in the Abbasid era complements the narrative too.[47] To enhance the Arabness framework, the stories portray pre-Islamic 'Arab kings' as perpetually oriented towards relations with their 'Arab' kinsmen in the Syrian and Arabian deserts rather than to Iraqi states and populations. The kings remain entirely Arab, eternally Arabic-speaking and aware of their Arab unity,[48] pointing the narratives' attention not into Iraq, but outwards, to Arabia, deftly mirroring the settlement of the conquest-era Muslims on the edges of Iraq in new-founded cities at al-Baṣra and al-Kūfa.

Alongside the appropriation of others' history into an Arab narrative, the Muslim-era texts also contain a generous proportion of poetry to accompany each story about the ancient 'Arab' Iraqi kingdoms during the millennium before Muhammad.[49] This seems a consequence of the widely held view amongst third/ninth-century scholars that poetry was a skill unique to the Arabs.[50] In an era when poetry was called *dīwān al-ᶜarab* (the Archive of the Arabs),[51] poetry emphatically Arabised any narrative, and history furnished with poetry would appear quintessentially 'Arab'.[52] The authenticity of such ancient 'Arabic poetry' was lambasted by both the third/ninth-century poetry critic Ibn Sallām al-Jumaḥī, and the belles-lettrist al-Jāḥiẓ,[53] but historians such as al-Yaᶜqūbī and al-Ṭabarī nonetheless cite more poetry in the stories of pre-Islamic Iraqi Arabs than in any other parts of their histories,[54] revealing the lengths to which the historians went to portray the Iraqi past as 'Arab history', depicting ancient Iraqi populations in the manner which third/ninth-century Muslims imagined 'original Arabness'.

The presence of poetry also betrays the influence of early Islamic storytellers in creating the narratives of pre-Islamic Iraqi Arab history,[55] which explains the volume of dramatic and romantic details in the 'historical' narratives. Lakhmid history (the century immediately preceding Islam), was already more than 250 years in the past when classical writers began to record it, and notwithstanding the 'real' existence of a Lakhmid polity in pre-Islam, the copious poetry, stories of court conspiracies and the prominence of intrigues around women in the Muslim-era narratives about Lakhm indicate romanticisation and reorientation of Lakhmids into a model court history that resonates with the manner in which third/ninth-century historians memorialised their archetype of 'Arab' Umayyad princes. The accounts of more ancient history contain fantastical embellishment too, for example the Iraqi 'Arab' capture of Queen Zabbāʾ's Tadmur (Zenobia's Palmyra) is ascribed to a successful ambush of soldiers hidden in camel saddle-packs – a remarkable parallel to the Trojan Horse,[56] and the legend of the Ṭasm and Jadīs tribes in al-Yamāma whom Muslim writers dated to the Ṭawāʾif period, includes a battle where armies advanced under the cover of bushes akin to Great Birnam Wood.[57] The embellished epics colouring the Arabisation of Iraqi history recreate a time that was too distant, to borrow Bakhtin's reading of epic, to have a tangible connection to any sense of empirical history.[58]

The Arabisation of history also entailed appropriating religious material. In claiming that Nebuchadnezzar first brought Arabs into Iraq, Muslim-era historians borrowed from the biblical story of the Hebrews' Babylonian Captivity following Nebuchadnezzar's destruction of the Temple in 587 BCE. Muslim-era Arabic writers were familiar with the Biblical story and its portrayal of Nebuchadnezzar as a tyrant,[59] whereas Neo-Babylonian records make no record of Nebuchadnezzar's deep foray into Arabia or any mass deportation of Arabs to Babylonia.[60] Muslim accounts of Nebuchadnezzar's Arab war are neither a Mesopotamian nor Arabian memory, but rather a reworking of the Bible to usurp the Hebrews' monopoly on pre-Muhammadic monotheistic heritage. Muslim historians wove Arabs into the ancient struggle of tyrant versus monotheist, and by beginning Arab Iraqi history on this religious note, they offer yet another example of how the Arabisation of history also involved Islamicisation. The slow adoption of the story in Arabic writing may highlight its novelty: Ibn Ḥabīb's mid-third/ninth-century *al-Muḥabbar* appears to be the first extant record,[61] later third/ninth-century historical surveys such as Ibn Qutayba's *al-Maᶜārif*, al-Dīnawarī's *al-Akhbār al-ṭiwāl* and al-Yaᶜqūbī's *Tārīkh* ignore it,[62] the early fourth/tenth-century al-Ṭabarī's *Tārīkh* gives the story's first lengthy articulation, and it was then repeated in all later chronological–prophetic world histories.[63] The 'orthodoxy' of the story thus appears datable to the later third/ninth century, also contemporary with the increasing emphasis of the prophetic angle in Dhū Qār's 'Arab' memorialisation explored in Chapter 2(V).

Muslim-era narratives are thus the first body of Iraqi literature that (1) constructs pre-Islamic Mesopotamian history with an orientation towards Arabia, and (2) portrays Arabians as Iraq's historical heroes. Essentially forgetting millennia of Mesopotamian history in favour of a novel emphasis on Arab heritage, the narratives written by Muslim Arabs and non-Arabs alike reflect the extent to which Arabisation reworked history to feed Muslim–Iraqi identity with a healthy Arab heritage matching Iraq's pre-Islamic Sasanian legacy,[64] and recast the past into a veritable prelude for the Muslim conquests and Iraq's Islamisation.

By assigning a portion of Arab heritage to Iraq, the narrative threads Iraqi heroes from Jadhīma to the Lakhmids into the Arab family. In contrast, therefore, to the pre-Islamic Ma'addite tribes which erected kin-barriers to reflect the transactional boundaries between them and Iraqi power, Muslim-era cultural producers brought Iraq inside their imagined pre-Islamic Arab world which necessitated the construction of the wider Arab family trees traced in Chapter 4(IV). The deconstruction of pre-Islamic groupings such as Maᶜadd, the reorganisation of communities on the Iraqi/Arabian border (such as Lakhm), and the integration of ancient figures into one Arab family betray a concession from Conqueror groups to admit others into their story and create a new sense of community. The result assisted early third/

ninth-century assimilated urban Iraqis to embrace Arab feeling as something essentially indigenous to Iraq, and the stories became the classic framework for Arab history-telling thereafter. They prime subsequent readers to assume the existence of a single Arab community in pre-Islam, but we can appreciate that their Arabness pretensions were directed to explain the idea Arabness as it was circulating in their contemporary context, not as a preservation of a 'true' history, community and identity. Our narrative thus far has related the events Iraqi writers crafted into the frame of their imagined Arab pre-history: we now need to consider characters to probe how the writers invented the identity for their pre-Islamic 'Arabs'.

III *Al-Jāhiliyya* and Imagining Pre-Islamic Arabs

When seeking to recover how early generations of Muslim cultural producers imagined the pre-Islamic Arabs, and to explain the particular forms their portrayals adopted, we confront major questions concerning the interpretation of the sources. The questions lead us into the universe of Muslim imaginations about the pre-Islamic past and their constructions of Islam's pre-history and origin mythology. The manifold different approaches which Muslims adopted across the centuries of classical Islam cannot be epitomised with tidy answers, however, and the study which these questions deserve expands far beyond this book's scope of Arab ethnogenesis. Accordingly, this section concentrates upon challenging the familiar set of stereotypes which hitherto have been commonly assumed to epitomise the way in which Muslims depict pre-Islamic Arabs. By revealing the variations in Arabic literature about pre-Islamic Arabia, and by relating the changing literary portrayals to the changing social contexts of early Islamic Iraq, we develop this book's primary theme of Arabness' essential plasticity to underline the error of holding on to monoliths about 'Arab identity' and 'Arab culture', and through defining the idea of the 'Arab' in early Abbasid Iraq, analysis points towards ways of rethinking the wider Muslim narratives of pre-Islam.[65]

The starting point of analysis is the premise that the pre-Islamic Arab did not really exist, at least not in the guise Muslim-era Iraqi cultural producers imagined pan-Arabian Arabness. As our critical appraisal of pre-Islamic Arab community has demonstrated, there was neither one 'Arab community' nor one monolithic 'Arab culture' to tie all pre-Islamic Arabians together. Instead, it was when urban Iraqi Muslim elites began to imagine themselves as 'Arabs' that the diverse memories from their disparate pasts were homogenised to retrospectively convert their ancient Arabian forebears into one single 'Arab' ancestral story with one uniform 'Arab identity'. The invention of the 'pre-Islamic Arab' in early Muslim-era Iraqi writing consequently deserves attention as one of the most enduring and creative constructions of early Islam. Our findings thereby redress the reservations scholars express about the difficulties of reconciling the proliferation of 'inconsistent' detail in Muslim-era Arabic sources about pre-Islamic Arabia.[66] Since there was no unified 'Arab' community before Islam, there was no single 'Arab heritage' for third/ninth-century Muslims to remember. Muslim writers were compelled to construct their imagined pre-Islamic Arabs from a patchwork of competing memories and diverse agendas, and it should therefore be expected that their literature does not present a wholly cohesive narrative. When we discard the assumption that there was a pan-Arabian Arabness, many problems of the generalisations about 'Arab culture' become redundant: we can study the sources afresh without needing to force the diverse evidence into one composite Arab whole, and we can explore instead how the uneven state of our sources reflects the challenges Iraqi scholars faced when inventing the 'Arab past'.

Gerald Hawting's closing speculation in his *The Idea of Idolatry* that the Muslim-era sources about pre-Islamic Arabia created a 'myth',[67] is thus both accurate and even deeper-reaching than he expressed. Hawting's research revealed the extent to which sources fabricated a panorama of Arab paganism to explain the milieu of the Qur'an's revelation, but we must yet probe much further, since Muslim constructions of pre-Islamic Arabian history were not limited to projecting religious ideas, but actually created the entire notion of Arab identity as a pre-Islamic ethnos, forgetting in the process that Arabness only emerged as a broad communal identity in the Muslim-era. How then can we read the Muslim-era sources as building blocks of a mythic past to construct an edifice of Arab identity?

Source-critical methodologies to date are relatively underdeveloped, since the last century of scholarship predominantly sought to trawl Muslim-era sources for empirical nuggets of what might be 'truth' about the 'real' pre-Islamic Arabia.[68] While correspondences can be found, such approaches rather miss the forest for the trees: the bigger question surely must be the literary achievement itself of creating an origin story for a whole community of imagined 'Arabs'. Such wider-ranging research has been restricted in part because previous studies have tended to presume that the Arabs 'must have' existed in some form of cohesive community before Islam, and hence underestimate the Muslim creative process of imagining pre-Islamic 'Arabs'. And moreover, there is a prevailing argument that Muslims simply imagined pre-Islam as a debased, pre-enlightened age, constructing its history as a simple tale of 'barbarism' familiar through the Arabic word *al-Jāhiliyya* (the pre-Islamic 'Age of Ignorance/Passion').[69] The premise prompts the belief that the sources about pre-Islam can be interpreted straightforwardly as concerted Muslim retrojections to depict pre-Islamic Arabs as 'barbarians' in a disorganised, violent, dimly perceptible swirl of nomadism,[70] epitomised in four *al-Jāhiliyya* topoi of idol worship, tyranny/injustice, ritual killing of baby girls (alongside mistreatment of women generally[71]) and violence of vainglorious tribal antagonisms.[72]

The belief that Muslims imagined *al-Jāhiliyya* in one way, however, is itself a monolithic presumption, and some specialists of Arabic literature offer inspirations for correctives. Susan Stetkevych began with the suggestion that Muslim writers constructed two kinds of pre-Islam: one heroic tableau preserved in poetry, and the other more reprobate anti-Islam discussed in historical writing;[73] Alan Jones invited even deeper reflection into the context of pre-Islamic lore's narration when he observed that pre-Islamic Arabian poetry (and related lore) exists in an 'Abbasid guise', that is, in a shape reworked by Abbasid-era scholars for the purposes of their own discourses.[74] Mirroring Stetkevych and Jones, Rina Drory argued that the stories about *al-Jāhiliyya* are the product of late second/eighth-century non-Arab *mawālī* who created a body of knowledge for themselves to monopolise as 'experts', and thereby created a new sense of pre-Islamic history to suit a caliphal court interested in the faraway desert of the Arabian past.[75] Looking at non-poetic material, however, Hawting adduced theological perspectives to relate Muslim *al-Jāhiliyya* narratives as a means to depict the Qur'an's original audience as 'pagans'.[76] Consequently, these more nuanced studies leave us with an array of possibilities to interpret *al-Jāhiliyya*, but we yet lack a comprehensive survey of literature about pre-Islam with broad synthesis and perspective that can take account of the massive corpus Muslim textual production.[77]

What the current state of research does demonstrate is the richness of the *al-Jāhiliyya* idea as a potent device with varied connotations serving a variety of Muslim-era agendas connected with Islam and Arabness. Probing further, elsewhere I explored the plurality of Jahiliyyas in Muslim writing, revealing the word's development and obtainment of new significations in pre-modern Arabic dictionaries and Qur'anic exegesis over time.[78] Far from the supposed monolith of 'barbaric' pre-Islam, *al-Jāhiliyya* had a plurality of meanings across different genres and discourses, and between different periods and locales. Like the idea of Arab identity itself, therefore, *al-Jāhiliyya* ought to be interpreted as an intellectual construct, which needs to be rigorously historicised and related to the contexts in which its stories were imagined. Reading *al-Jāhiliyya* accordingly transcends the search for empirical information: to elaborate Jones' observation, there were manifold Abbasid guise*s*, each with different aesthetic and discursive purposes. Perhaps foremost then, we ought to conceptualise the texts as having a common purpose of expressing a sense origin and pastness, whereby authors invoked *al-Jāhiliyya* to articulate what they intended as primordial ideas, some serving theological arguments, philological constructions, mythic narratives, or demarcations of community and identity. Here we shall focus on the latter: the place of *al-Jāhiliyya* in early Muslim imaginations of 'original' Arab identity.

To ground our source texts in the realities and worldviews of the places in which they were written, we can observe that the idea of 'barbaric' pre-Islamic *al-Jāhiliyya* past benefits a discourse seeking to validate the venture of Islam, but the attendant creation of the pre-Islamic 'Arab' as a barbarous figure would be embarrassing when viewed from certain second/eighth-century perspectives. For an early Abbasid-era governor who counted himself as an Arab, emphasis on barbarous *al-Jāhiliyya* smears his ancestors' characters and insinuates that his salvation hinged solely on the decision of one of his grandfathers to convert to Islam. For Arabised Iraqi *mawālī* too, the barbarous *al-Jāhiliyya* is equally damning: their cherished Muslim faith would seem to have been carried on the shoulders of brutes, and the society's elite (whom many *mawālī* were avidly emulating) appear as unworthy leaders without pedigree. If we contrast this early Abbasid Iraqi context with the context of Muhammad's Ḥijāzī community, for example, we can appreciate some reasons for fundamental divergences of opinion about *al-Jāhiliyya* in Muslim imaginations. When Muhammad was at war with non-Muslim Arabians, his community possessed evident grounds to lambast their foes and thereby laid the groundwork for what later became the negative ideas of pagan *al-Jāhiliyya* as reprobate, 'barbaric' folly; but by the second/eighth century, on the other hand, when the *Arabians* converted and later became the elite of *Arabs*, the memories of old identities would need new clothes – and preferably good ones.[79] As an origin story, therefore, *al-Jāhiliyya* is like most historical narratives: as a given society changes its composition and identity over time, it develops new senses of the past, building upon and reshaping old memories as much as possible to create new narratives of origins reflective of the new needs of the present.[80]

The hypothesis that early third/ninth-century views on *al-Jāhiliyya* conjured a very different impression of pre-Islamic Arabness than the now familiar barbarism archetypes is confirmed in the sources. Starting from the impressions of Arab society narrated through pre-Islamic poetry, we find that poetry is not an archive of anarchical violence, baby-killing and despotism, and it even lacks references to pagan worship.[81] If some pre-Islamic Arabians did lead a wretched life, early Abbasid poetry narrators suppressed that memory when they constructed 'Arab' origins, and moreover, the legacy of pre-Islam itself was a source of merit as expressed plainly in the verses of the second/eighth-century poet Muḥammad ibn Munādhir (d. 198/813):

> Relate to us some Islamic knowledge (*fiqh*) transmitted from our Prophet
> To nourish our hearts;
> Or relate the stories of our *Jāhiliyya*
> For they are wise and glorious.[82]

Ibn Munādhir's sentiments reflect the sort of Arabness expected from Arab elites in Iraq who sought to conceptualise their religion and heritage as dual sources of honour. The rebranding of pre-Islam extended beyond poetry too, even (somewhat ironically perhaps) to collections of Prophetic hadith, where, in the now canonical collections, a report ascribed to Jābir ibn Samra reads:

> The Prophet – God's blessings upon him – would pray Fajr and then sit in his place of prayer until sunrise and his Companions would converse about

> stories of *al-Jāhiliyya* and they would recite poetry and they would laugh, and he [the Prophet] would smile.[83]

In another hadith, reported in Ibn Ḥabīb's (d. 245/859–60) *al-Muḥabbar*, Muhammad orders his people to 'appoint as your leader he who used to lead you during *al-Jāhiliyya*'.[84] The message underscores *al-Muḥabbar*'s wider discourse by articulating a prophetically sanctioned narrative of continuity between pre-Islamic and Islamic times. Herein, Ibn Ḥabīb presents Arabness as a static identity, akin to the depictions of pre-Islamic Iraqi 'Arabs' noted above: readers are prompted to think that Arabs are always Arabs, and that 'Arab ways' are laudatory and did not fundamentally change with the dawn of Islam.[85] Ibn Ḥabīb's construction of Arabness is rather typically 'ethnic' in the vein of Hobsbawn's theories of European nation-building, inasmuch as it marshals the past to invent a sense of tradition of the 'authentic' Arab way, which has the appearance of being fixed, unchanging and definitive as Arab blood itself. [86] Express indications of such continuity include Ibn Ḥabīb's lists of 'rulings of *al-Jāhiliyya* that correspond with Islamic Law',[87] religious practices of *al-Jāhiliyya* continued in Islam,[88] and an array of positive qualities about *al-Jāhiliyya*: pre-Islamic Arabs who shunned alcohol,[89] were famous for their honesty,[90] praiseworthy traits of pre-Islamic tribes,[91] and six 'merits of the Arabs' in *al-Jāhiliyya*, of which Ibn Ḥabīb notes three survived into Islam while three (hostels for feeding the poor) were closed.[92] And as a consequence, Ibn Ḥabīb's perspective presents *al-Jāhiliyya* as not a time to be repudiated, but rather the basis of Arabness. Contemporary with the articulation of a coherent Arab genealogy traced in our last chapter, Ibn Ḥabīb's anecdotes indicate an agenda to articulate Arabness as a laudatory archetype in which pre-Islam had a formative role.

Ibn Ḥabīb's peers express similar sentiments: al-Jāḥiẓ (d. 255/868) writes in *al-Bayān wa-l-tabyīn*, another compendium of Arabian lore cast in a discourse on language and communication, that

> the Arabs better retain what they hear and better memorise what is narrated; and they have poetry which registers their glories and immortalises their merits. They followed in their Islam the practices from their *Jāhiliyya*. And on the basis of that [the Umayyads] established great honour and glory.[93]

Ibn Qutayba (d. 276/889) repeats the pre-Islamic/Islamic-era Arab continuity theme in his *Faḍl al-ᶜarab* cultural defence of Arabness too, listing 'judgments of *al-Jāhiliyya* affirmed by Islam'[94] within a wider discourse drawn from both pre-Islamic and Umayyad-era anecdotes to demonstrate the extent of the Arabs' longstanding and advanced learning (*ᶜilm*).[95] Given the third/ninth-century definition of *jahl* as the opposite of *ᶜilm*, Ibn Qutayba's emphasis on the Arabs' *ᶜilm* from *al-Jāhiliyya* seems another pointed rehabilitation of the era, rejecting assumptions about its 'ignorance', and, for good measure, he adds also that 'Arabs of *al-Jāhiliyya* were the world's bravest nation'.[96] The genealogist and narrator of Arabian history, Ibn al-Kalbī (d.204/819 or 206/821) appears to have participated in the same discourse of Arab continuities between *al-Jāhiliyya* and Islam, given the title of his (now lost) work, *Kitāb mā kānat al-Jāhiliyya tafᶜaluhu wa-yuwāfiq ḥukm al-Islām* (Book of *Jāhiliyya*–Islam Juridical Correspondence).[97]

'Arab Muslims' Before Muhammad

Early Abbasid-era constructions of laudatory pre-Islamic Arabness also manifested in an important aspect of the earliest textual layers of Arab identity: the invention of pre-Islamic Arab monotheism. Readers will be familiar with the traditional impression that pre-Islamic Arabians were polytheists, and such notions are grounded in much Muslim-era Arabic writing about *al-Jāhiliyya*, but it is less well known that early third/ninth-century writings conversely focus on stories of ancient Arabian monotheism. The stories have manifold literary manifestations, including what is perhaps the most fundamental step of rooting Arab genealogy in the prophetic family of Abraham and Ishmael. According to the stories, Abraham, Hagar and their son Ishmael travelled from the Levant to Mecca where Ishmael and Hagar settled; Abraham periodically visited thereafter, and he and Ishmael constructed Mecca's sanctum where they initiated pure monotheistic worship (*al-ḥanīfiyya*). The stories then marshal genealogy to paint Ishmael as the father of the Arabs (as detailed in Chapter 4(IV)), and they stress the continuation of monotheistic worship across the Arabs' subsequent generations, thereby projecting Arab history as born from prophetic family and following a course of monotheism. The monotheistic aspect of Arab history is unambiguous from the outset of al-Yaᶜqūbī's account of pre-Islamic Ma'addite Arabs in his *Tārīkh*: he opens the story of Abraham and Ishmael with emphasis on Ishmael's foundational role in several parameters of Arabness,[98] and adds:

> The Quraysh and most of the descendants of Maᶜadd ibn ᶜAdnān retained something of the Religion of Abraham, they made pilgrimage to the Sacred House, performed the rites, provided for guests, respected the Holy Months, and eschewed fornication and wickedness, and upheld the laws – and they did so for so long as they were custodians of the Sacred House.[99]

Al-Yaᶜqūbī accepts the Arabs adopted other religious practices based on the beliefs of populations whom they neighboured, and al-Yaᶜqūbī imputes a decline in *ḥanīf* practice four generations after Maᶜadd,[100] but the nexus of monotheism, Hajj and Arabness are nonetheless developed throughout al-Yaᶜqūbī's section on the Arab past, for he grounds his narrative of pre-Islamic Ma'addites (whom he treats synonymous with Arabs) with repeated reference to the Hajj in the progression of Arab nobles from Ishmael to Muhammad.[101] In the same vein, contemporary writers rebranded the Kaᶜba as *bayt al-ᶜarab* (the Sacred House of the Arabs) associated with signature Arab monotheism, not pagan ritual,[102] a theme elaborated in the records of pre-Islamic tribal expressions proclaiming the unity of God (*talbiya*) that engender the impression of widespread attachment to monotheistic ritual.[103]

The Arab/monotheism nexus extended into other realms of scholarly enquiry too, including the study of horsemanship, a trait associated with original 'Arab culture'.[104] Ibn al-Kalbī's *Ansāb al-khayl* (Genealogy of Horses) intimately intertwines Arab horsemanship with Arab prophecy by elaborating the narrative of Arab Ishmaelite origins: he notes that Ishmael was both the first Arabic speaker *and* the first (Arab) horseman, since God produced 100 horses from the sea for him. Ibn al-Kalbī includes further statements that Ishmael was the 'first man to ride horses' and so begins his history of horses by fusing prophecy with Arab origins and the horsemanship of the early Muslim-era Arab elite.[105] Al-Yaᶜqūbī's Ma'addite Arab narrative likewise identifies Ishmael as history's first horseman, again emphasising the community's origins in prophethood, and al-Yaᶜqūbī adds, for good measure, that the horses' first pasture was Mecca, and that part of Mecca's plain known as Ajyād was so named on account of the purebred prophetic stallions that originated there.[106]

In what seems an entrenchment of Arabness, horsemanship and prophecy, Ibn al-Kalbī's *Ansāb al-khayl* offers readers an alternative origin story for Arab stallions, sidelining Ishmael and positing the origins of Arab horses in David and Solomon's stables, specially preserved by God, and procured by the al-Azd when Solomon travelled to marry the Queen of Sheba.[107] The subsequent sections of Ibn al-Kalbī's *Ansāb al-khayl* list famous horses named in poetry and link them to Arab tribes, noting the horses' ancestry in 'prophetic' stallions. It is telling that almost every example of Arab horses dates to two (or at most three) generations before Muhammad, indicating how Muslim narrators of 'Arab history' had a grasp of memories from the century before Islam which they cobbled into a pan-Arab story, and then bridged an enormous gap of millennia to embed the community's roots in monotheism by claiming (or usurping?) legacies of Judaic prophecy.

The association of Arab history with monotheism runs even deeper in oft-overlooked narratives about ancient Yemen. Chapter 4(IV) explored how groups claiming Yemeni ancestry in early Islam attempted to fuse their genealogy onto the Ishmaelite system, or to cast their ancestry deeper into prehistory. The latter model ties Yemeni origins with the prophetic community of Hūd, the Qur'anic prophet whom Muslims dated to the period following Noah, and this genealogical model essentially replicates the Ishmaelite–Ma'addite prophet-parentage scheme but with an even older prophetic heritage for Yemen. Akin to the narratives of Arab history following Ishmael, the Yemeni stories emphasise the survival of monotheism: we possess several third/ninth-century histories which trace Yemeni kings from primeval times to the dawn of Islam, and each portray Yemenis as a community blessed with Islamic guidance via their preservation of Islam's sacred monotheistic message as a nearly unbroken chain from Hūd.[108] The Yemeni narratives so stress the Muslim piety of almost all pre-Islamic Yemeni kings, that readers could wonder why Muhammad's mission was even necessary – this question is left unanswered in favour of an evident overriding interest in depicting ancient South Arabians as both Arabs and monotheists.

A number of modern studies have sought to explain the monotheist/polytheist dichotomy in Arabic accounts of pre-Islam: Hawting's *The Idea of Idolatry* is perhaps the most sustained, and it argues that third/ninth-century Muslims misinterpreted Qur'anic polemic and constructed an anachronistic set of stories to depict pre-Islamic Arab polytheism as a corruption of an early Arabian monotheism.[109] While it seems clear that early Muslim writers tampered with memories of pre-Islamic Arabian religion to create new narratives, two key considerations have been missing from analysis of the material to date: the ancient 'Arab monotheism' stories we related above have received relatively little attention or integration into analysis of Muslim *Jāhiliyya* discourses, and the contexts of the *Jāhiliyya* stories' narration have yet to be placed within a framework of either Arab ethnogenesis or Islamic identity creation. Some remarks here hope to redress the oversights and invite renewed investigation into the vast corpus of Muslim *Jāhiliyya* lore.

Concerning the narratives of pre-Islamic 'Arab' monotheism, it could be imagined that pre-Islamic central Arabia possessed a number of monotheistic communities and was not the idolatrous 'pagan reservation' as traditionally believed.[110] It could therefore be proposed that when Muslim sources describe pre-Islamic Arabian monotheism, they are recording real history,[111] but this does not appear sustainable by the full array of the sources. Muslim-era texts give no impression that their imagined communities of pre-Islamic Arab monotheists constituted Christian or Jewish sects (even though such actually may have been scattered across parts of pre-Islamic Arabia) – on the contrary, they are depicted as descendants of true Abrahamic monotheists (*ḥanīf*) without sectarian labels, and they are represented as one cohesive religious community of Arabs focused around Mecca. Emphasis on the religious cohesion of the *Arab* community is overriding: the Arab monotheistic groups are not attached to any Late Antique Christological arguments, the depictions of the pre-Islamic Arabs are, in many respects, carbon copies of the ways in which Arabic literature describes early Muslim communities. Our texts are thus writing an Arab community into pre-Islamic existence; they are not performing acts of empirical comparative religion. By marshalling Ishmael, Solomon's thoroughbreds and a pan-Arabian allure of Mecca's sanctum, Muslim-era sources are inventing a novel idea of pre-Muhammadic Arabian monotheism to accompany the equally novel Muslim-era invention of an imagined pre-Islamic 'Arab' identity.

Given the profuse inventiveness of the Arab monotheism stories, reading them within the wider context of early third/ninth-century literary production seems crucial to grasp the discourses that prompted their creation. We can now appreciate that the impact of the stories transcends purely religious or exegetical questions – the stories are tied to notions of Arab origins and Arab history, and hence primarily exegetical readings today miss a key substance of this literature. The literature transcends explanation of the Qur'an and/or writing a religious taxonomy of pre-Islamic Arabia; rather, it explains the origins of Arab community. Such a purpose has been overlooked hitherto, doubtless since previous studies have followed the widespread assumption that an Arab community 'must have' existed in pre-Islam, and consequently research has proceeded under the presumption that we should be able to look through the sources and reconstruct something of the pre-Islamic 'Arab religion'. But as there was no single 'Arab community' in pre-Islamic Arabia, there could not have been one 'Arab faith': Iraqi Muslims created this history and pantheon, and the resultant stories we possess are their property and ought to be interpreted as such.

When early Muslim reconstructions of pre-Islamic Arabian religion are thus read on the continuum of Arab ethnogenesis, it becomes apparent that the writers of pre-Islamic Arabian monotheism stories were participating in a wider discourse that was linking Arabisation with Islamisation. For example, Chapter 2(V) traced how the changing representation of the Battle of Dhū Qār transformed it into an 'Arab' victory in tandem with connecting its memory to Muhammad, and the representation of the conquests as an equally Muslim *and* Arab national movement is clear from third/ninth-century accounts of early Islam.[112] Viewed through the theoretical prism of imagining a community, the wedding of Arab history to a monotheistic core has considerable logic. The first conceptions of Arabness in the late Umayyad and early Abbasid periods revolved around a monotheistic community, the *ᶜarabī* Qur'an and the identity of Muslim elite. Hence, embedding contemporary Arab religious identity into the fabric of imagined Arab origins was valuable and enabled the construction of primordial Arabness in a format that neatly mirrored contemporary Arab elites. Moreover, the articulation of Islam in the two centuries following the conquests was such a decisive factor in helping Conquerors imagine their Arab identity, that it follows religion needed to feature in their reconstruction of communal origins, and since their narratives plotted imagined Arab origins long before Muhammad, the similarly imagined pre-Muhammadic Islam would need to travel back in time with them.

The sum of the monotheism stories thus align with the other narratives of *al-Jāhiliyya* traced above. The texts of third/ninth-century cultural producers created a sense of the imagined pre-Islamic Arab in the guise of the self-aware communities of Muslim Arabs, and like so many racial and national stereotypes around the world, writers needed to forget much of the Arabian past in order to convert it into a demonstration of 'authentic' Arab traits.

And so our interpretation proposes a reorientation in reading early Muslim-era Arabic texts about pre-Islamic 'Arab' polytheism. Reading the stories of pre-Islamic Arab idolatrous practice as inventions by Muslim exegetes seems too narrow a focus to grasp their significance, as the wider narrative context and tenor of the anecdotes actually prompts an opposite interpretation. The texts seem defensive and intent to play down ideas of idolatry – as if cognisance of pre-Islamic Arabian idolatry existed, and Muslim authors sought to write their way around such memories in order to create a sense of unified monotheism. For instance, we read authors attempting to prove that anecdotes of polytheism were merely misunderstood by-products of original 'Arab' monotheism. Ibn Ḥabīb reports that pre-Islamic Arabs worshipped idols 'along with God – and there is no God but He';[113] Ibn Qutayba is more explicit, stating that pre-Muhammadic Arabs maintained 'vestiges of pure monotheism *(al-ḥanīfiyya)*',[114] and al-Ya^cqūbī reports that the Arabs' adoption of idols was 'only a means [of worship], they continued to make the Hajj and practice its *talbiya* like their father, Abraham'.[115] If we are to venture empirical conclusions, it would seem that pre-Islamic Arabia had a substantial polytheistic fabric, but the process of Arab ethnogenesis outside of Arabia hastened the forgetting of old doctrines, and a radical recasting of its memory onto a simplified model of (1) initial monotheism, followed by (2) slippage into polytheism, and finally (3) a return to original *ᶜarabī* purity via Muhammad.[116]

The Arab–monotheistic agenda offers another avenue to evaluate Ibn al-Kalbī's oft-cited *Kitāb al-Aṣnām* (Book of Idols). It is a catalogue of Arab idols – ostensibly a monograph on pre-Islamic Arab paganism – but it opens with stress on the monotheistic origins of Arab worship, depicting Arab idolatry as the product of originally sincere and devout Abrahamic monotheism.[117]

Ibn al-Kalbī renders the Arabs inadvertent pagans: they maintained vestiges of monotheism while gradually (and innocently) shifting into misguidedness.[118] *Al-Aṣnām*'s inclusion of references to non-Arabian idols such as those of Noah's era,[119] suggests moreover that idol worship is not uniquely Arab, thus exonerating them from exclusive ridicule.[120] It is also interesting that Ibn al-Kalbī reports the absence of reference to various idols in pre-Islamic poetry – does he intend by this for readers to infer that worship of these idols did not take deep root?[121] *Al-Aṣnām* leaves no doubt that Muhammad's mission against idols was necessary,[122] but Muhammad's purpose appears as righting the Arab ship, not introducing a novel doctrine, and Ibn al-Kalbī narrates no generalised negative conclusions about ancient Arabs either and instead harmonises pre-Muhammadic idol worship, Islam and Ishmaelite origin tales to show Islam as a basic continuity in Arab history.

The third/ninth-century rebranding of pre-Islamic Arabians as a cohesive community of Arab monotheists confronted a difficult task of navigating Qur'anic depictions of Muhammad's actual contemporaries. The Qur'an contains several passages condemning reprobate social practices and chastising idolaters, and since the Qur'an could not be changed, it represented potentially embarrassing testimony of pre-Islamic Arabian paganism. The manner in which third/ninth-century literature navigated these passages sheds further light on a vital part of Arab ethnogenesis too, for it reveals the extent to which Arabian groups whom the Qur'an censured needed to forget polytheistic origins by rehabilitating Arabian belief structures.

Reversals of Qur'anic invective against pagans appears in several guises. The Qur'an relatively rarely levels specific critique against identifiable pagan practices, but in some cases, for example the calendar adjustment (*al-nasīʾ*), the Qur'an is explicit, describing the adjustment as an 'excess of disbelief'.[123] But, intriguingly, when the third/ninth-century historian al-Yaᶜqūbī narrated pre-Islamic Arab history, he counted *al-nasīʾ* as one of the 'virtues' of the Kināna tribe, aside their right to announce the Hajj, and al-Yaᶜqūbī presents the practice as a mark of nobility (*sharaf*) (he also ignores the critical Qur'anic verse).[124] *Sharaf* is a recurring feature in al-Yaᶜqūbī's narratives of pre-Islamic Arabian tribes, and he does not cite it in opposition to Persian nobility (as traditional notions of *al-shuᶜūbiyya* might suppose), rather, in the spirit of the assimilated society proposed here, al-Yaᶜqūbī's notion of *sharaf* is not zero-sum, but shared, and Arabs are accorded a healthy portion. As another example, the Qur'an's several references to *al-waʾd* (female infanticide) which fourth/tenth-century Arabic exegetes roundly lamented as emblematic of barbaric pre-Islamic 'Arab' society,[125] was also rehabilitated to reduce the Qur'anic stigma on Arab origins. Al-Mubarrad's lengthy discourse on infanticide expressly attempts to reinterpret *al-waʾd* as a rare tragic necessity, an abnormal custom, or the practice of just one or a small group of tribes. Al-Mubarrad makes no definitive conclusions, but his text informs readers that *al-waʾd* should not be assumed as an innate pan-Arab trait.[126]

The resultant impression of pseudo-monotheistic Arabs before Muhammad is complimented by third/ninth-century historians' generous depictions of Arabs as 'noble' (*sharīf*),[127] 'generous' (*karīm*),[128] 'forebearing' (*ḥalīm* – the opposite of *jāhil*)[129] and of 'innumerable virtues'.[130] Likewise al-Balādhurī's (d. *c.*279/892) *Ansāb al-ashrāf*, a genealogical history of noblemen, depicts nobility as embodied in Arab families, with *sharaf* beginning in pre-Islamic times. Though al-Balādhurī worked as a courtier of Abbasid caliphs,[131] he interestingly narrates noble biography only to the end of the second/eighth century and thus renders nobility as a property of Arabs from pre-Islamic beginnings to the reigns of the early Abbasids, al-Manṣūr and al-Mahdī,[132] crossing the *Jāhiliyya*/Islam barrier without pause, and ending at the Fourth *Fitna* (193–211/809–20).

The Fourth *Fitna* is also a seminal event in Khalīfa ibn Khayyāṭ's (d. *c.* 250/854–5) annals, *al-Tārīkh* which shuns the history of the *Fitna* and post-*Fitna* events, seemingly in the hope of banishing its memory into oblivion.[133] But whereas al-Balādhurī constructs the effluxion of historical time via genealogy that spans pre-Islam to post-Muhammad without interruption, Ibn Khayyāṭ's annalistic chronology ignores pre-Islam, and instead starts with Year 1 AH.[134] Ibn Khayyāṭ explains his rationale, noting that while all peoples, ancient Arabs included, devised systems of chronological reckoning,[135] Muhammad's *hijra* was a decisive historical juncture since the Prophet's physical movement from the land of *shirk* (polytheism) to the land of *īmān* (faith) represents the moment *ḥaqq* (truth) separated from *bāṭil* (falsehood).[136] Herein Ibn Khayyāṭ sets Muslim communal history in a different light, marking a break with the past. Ibn Khayyāṭ himself differs from all authors mentioned hitherto since he was a hadith scholar by training:[137] perhaps his approach to pre-Islamic history stems from this, or perhaps the absence of a reliable pre-*hijra* (BH?) dating system ran counter to Ibn Khayyāṭ's interests which concerned annalistic synthesis of specifically Islamic history to establish the relative chronology of the generations of hadith scholars.[138]

Early Arabic literature accordingly provides us with a widespread construction of Arabness in the guise of a noble, monotheistic pre-Islamic people – an uncanny mirroring of the status and identity of Muslim Arabs in early Islam. Though Ibn Khayyāṭ's *Tārīkh* reveals an exclusively Islamic-focused account of the community's history, it does not follow that hadith scholars pursued a consistently opposing narrative to denigrate the Arabs: consider, for example, a statement hadith collectors ascribed to Muhammad, reporting that Quraysh 'only recently adopted *Jāhiliyya*' prior to Muhammad's prophecy, a statement offering useful support for the narratives of the Quraysh's longstanding *ḥanīfiyya* (pure religion) before Muhammad.[139] The paradigm of original Arab monotheism, a brief slip into paganism, and then a return to Islam appears to operate across genres, and it was not a fringe fancy of Arab partisans: it was shared by a variety of writers and appears as a logical construct to project Arabian–Arabness as monotheistic, noble and relatively accommodating with Persians – just as Iraqi society was Muslim, powerful and cosmopolitan. Their notion of Arabness was appropriate for both consciously Arab communities who could marshal this imagined history to explain their recently consolidated Arab community's nobility, and for Iraqi converts who could apprehend the Muslim Conquerors as an ancient group with an established heritage, and not fragmented, barbarous, polyglot hordes from an 'outside' Arabia.

For so long as Arab tribes represented cohesive political actors in Iraq, pre-Islamic Arabness would benefit from associations of nobility, learning and prowess, but the marked end of reporting Arab noble lineages after the reign of al-Rashīd and the unusual reporting of the Fourth *Fitna* conflict by its near contemporaries points to important sociopolitical changes which appear to mark the end of this early way to imagine the Arabs and inaugurated a new paradigm.

IV Arabs and Arabia: Changing Relationships in the Third/Ninth Century

Political Disenfranchisement after al-Rashīd

Al-Rashīd's decision to divide the Caliphate between his sons, al-Amīn and al-Maᵓmūn, and the subsequent Fourth *Fitna* war between them initiated various processes that pressured Arab groups and Arabness as an idea. Change took several guises, particularly evident in politics. Al-Amīn's faction was backed by Arab tribal leaders and *al-abnāᵓ* (a Khurasanian collective of mixed genealogies)[140] whereas al-Maᵓmūn relied on Eastern Iranian support. Al-Maᵓmūn seized total victory, but only after violent conflict and a siege of Baghdad that devastated Iraq, marginalised the Iraqi elite Arab tribal groups and inaugurated a 'period of social renegotiation of power roles, [when] individuals began to coalesce around the new caliph and their identities were reconstituted and adapted'.[141] The renegotiations prejudiced the Arab elite, as evidenced in al-Yaᶜqūbī's lists of provincial governors: al-Maᵓmūn appears to have intended a wilful replacement of high officials from the old regime with Eastern Iranian Khurasanians who supported his bid for the Caliphate.[142] He quelled unrest in al-Jazīra with the appointment of the Easterner ᶜAbd Allāh ibn Ṭāhir whom he later granted control over the Caliphate's western provinces of al-Jazīra, al-Shām, Egypt (Miṣr) and al-Maghrib; unrest in Egypt in 211/826–7 resulted in the replacement of an Arab governor with a *mawlā* loyal to the Tahirid house; and al-Maᵓmūn entrusted a Persian from Badghīs to control the unstable Armenia where we noted previous inter-Arab tribal *ᶜaṣabiyya* friction (the new governor was apparently selected for his personal loyalty to the Caliph, as he was known by the *nisba* al-Maᵓmūnī).[143] Al-Maᵓmūn similarly quelled Arab *ᶜaṣabiyya* in Sind, first by appealing to the Arab Muhallabī group, but when that failed, al-Maᵓmūn turned to Khurasanians and dispatched a Barmakid, Mūsā ibn Yaḥyā as governor who expelled the Muhallabī Arabs and reigned over the province, bequeathing it upon his death to his son.[144] Mūsā's appointment marked a wholesale changing of the guard, as never again do we hear of *ᶜaṣabiyya* conflict in Sind.

Al-Muᶜtaṣim (218–27/833–42), al-Maᵓmūn's successor, shifted the military balance of power even further from Arab tribes by building new mercenary armies 'imported' from nomadic communities beyond Abbasid frontiers

– Berber North Africa and the mixed-ethnic Turkestan. Al-Masᶜūdī reports that al-Muᶜtaṣim had mustered 4,000 'slave-soldiers' (*mamālīk/ghilmān*) by the early part of his reign,[145] and between ten and twenty thousand by its end.[146] These soldiers would become known as the 'Turks' (*atrāk*) who rapidly monopolised power in the Caliphate, their leaders famously rose to positions of the highest influence under al-Muᶜtaṣim's successor, al-Wāthiq (227–32/842–7), and by the reign of al-Mutawakkil (232–47/847–61), leaders affiliated to Arab tribes were eclipsed by Turks and Khurasanians.[147] In tandem with the rise of the Turks, reference to *ᶜaṣabiyya* conflicts vanish: al-Yaᶜqūbī, who expressly listed *ᶜaṣabiyya* during the first Abbasid reigns, makes no further reference to such tensions following the Fourth *Fitna* (he only mentions an apparently pseudo-theological *ᶜaṣabiyya* between Mu'tazilites and *al-Jamāᶜa*).[148] The abrupt end of reference to tribal *ᶜaṣabiyya* signals a change in the value of Arab tribal loyalty as a functioning assert in the political area, a consequence of Arab tribal blocs having lost their former influence and stake in the power structure.[149]

The eclipse of Arab tribal military units also accords with the traditional dating of the removal of Arabs from the *dīwān al-ᶜaṭā* (the official stipend payments paid to the descendants of the original Conquerors) which al-Kindī reports was terminated in 218/833.[150] The decree is considered the official end of the entire *dīwān* system, the last perceptible step in the wider process through which ethnic Arabs lost official status and military privilege.[151]

The third/ninth-century rewriting of Iraq's political landscape with Turkic influence also had substantial ramifications on urban settlement patterns. Arabic historians report that al-Muᶜtaṣim's Turkic/Berber armies became unpopular in the capital Baghdad for their rowdy and violent ways, and al-Muᶜtaṣim responded by moving the capital sixty miles north of Baghdad, to Samarra.[152] Samarra was a massive project, requiring construction of a palace city from scratch, and while it was not the first large Abbasid 'second capital' (al-Rashīd made similar construction in al-Raqqa, now in modern Syria), al-Muᶜtaṣim's Samarra was on an unprecedented scale and seems specifically intended to separate his new army and ruling elite from the traditional centres of population.[153] Ensconced with his personal militia and largely Turkic and Khurasanian courtiers in Samarra, the Caliph was spatially separated from the original 'Arab' towns of al-Baṣra and al-Kūfa, as well as

Baghdad, further distancing the loci of political influence in the third/ninth-century Caliphate from the old Arab centres.

The establishment of rule through personal clique epitomised in the caliphs' move to Samarra also traces roots to al-Maʾmūn's *Miḥna* in the aftermath of the Fourth *Fitna*. Long considered a theological debate, *al-Miḥna* has recently been revealed as politically motivated too, whereby the Caliph articulated a personal 'Maʾmūnite platform' to which his courtiers were expected to submit.[154] *Al-Miḥna* was not a concerted purge of Arabs or Arab-Khurasanians,[155] but its ultimate effect inaugurated a paradigm of power articulated via proximity to the Caliph, which directly opposed former structures where Arab lineage defined around membership to a tribal bloc constituted ways to influence.[156]

The multifaceted political changes following the Fourth *Fitna*, therefore, each eroded the value of Arabness in the Caliphate's power structure. Al-Maʾmūn persecuted some of al-Amīn's Arab supporters, promoted his own allies, demoted former Arab power groups, and initiated a new form of Caliphate in which autonomous Arab groups lost power to those people in the caliph's personal circle. Simultaneously, the rise of Turks in the military and the end of the *dīwān al-ʿaṭā* mark the end of economic utility in membership in Arab military units, and the transfer of the capital to Samarra cleaned the house entirely, enabling the caliphs, ministers and Turkic generals to run the Caliphate's affairs with unprecedented autonomy after the mid-third/ninth century. The cumulative effects of the first half of the third/ninth century both banished individual Arabs from the political centre and categorically undermined the practical value of being an Arab. Turkic military–political elites built their own patronage systems and even changed the connotation of *mawālī* from the Umayyad/early-Abbasid designation of a non-Arab to a new meaning of lower order soldier in the Turkic/caliphal patronage ladder,[157] and ethnic Arabs who did remain near the centre of power would need to merge with the new cliques and subsume their Arabness into other identities to avoid stigmas of the old *ʿaṣabiyya* feuding and allegiances to the defeated al-Amīn.

The suggestion of the gradual but absolute decline of Arab fortunes in the two generations following the Fourth *Fitna* helps explain a comment of the contemporary observer al-Jāḥiẓ in his *al-Bayān wa-l-tabyīn* who described the Caliphate in his day (the 220–30s/830–40s) as 'non-Arab and Khurasanian' *(ᶜajamiyya khurāsāniyya)*.[158] By this terminology, al-Jāḥiẓ contrasted his contemporary Caliphate with the 'Arab' Caliphate of the previous generations (that is, both the Umayyads and early Abbasids), signalling recognition that the aftermath of the Fourth *Fitna* and the move to Samarra marked a cultural shift, whereby mid-third/ninth-century observers could periodise their conception of the Caliphate as definitively leaving 'Arab hands'. To this point, al-Jāḥiẓ draws examples of good Arabic skills throughout *al-Bayān* almost entirely from the 'Arab' Umayyads and, to a significantly lesser extent, the Abbasids up to al-Maᵓmūn, mirroring the chronological end-point of the portrayals of Arab nobility in al-Balādhurī's *Ansāb al-ashrāf.* Cultural producers point to a periodising of 'proper Arabness' as something past before their time, which tallies with the fall of Arab elites and the sociopolitical processes we have traced herein. As Weber would remind us, changes in the underlying society and political power structures can alter paths of ethnogenesis,[159] and the changes in third/ninth-century Iraq's case prompt the expectation of a decline in the usefulness of Arabness as either a group or elite identity.

Outside the court, old attachments to Arabness slipped away in wider society too. Judith Ahola's study of al-Khaṭīb al-Baghdādī's biographical dictionary, *Tārīkh Baghdād* and Maxim Romanov's computational reading of al-Dhahabī's *Tārīkh al-Islām* both reveal a sharp decline in individuals claiming affiliation (*nisba*) to Arabian tribes during the third/ninth century.[160] Whereas the majority of second/eighth-century scholars and important urban figures listed in the biographical dictionaries are recorded as members of Arabian tribes, the proportion drops sharply in the generations after the Fourth *Fitna*, and by the mid-fourth/tenth century, most Iraqis had eschewed all tribal labels to identify themselves.[161] Combining and interpreting Ahola's and Romanov's independent studies, we can note that the decline in the use of tribal *nisba* corresponds with the sudden end of *ᶜaṣabiyya* tension noted from the historical sources. The disengagement from tribal faction as a form of political mobilisation and the manifest drop in individuals using Arabian tribal identifiers in the generations after the Fourth *Fitna* paints a distinct retreat from expressions of identity in 'Arab' terms, both at the level of political blocs and in individual cases. Ahola's and Romanov's computational surveys offer a numerical basis to rethink Arabness in later Abbasid Iraq: together with the textual evidence and theoretical considerations of identity considered in this book, the signs indicate a wholesale decline in Arab self awareness during the third/ninth century. Urban Iraqis seem to have been changing how they articulated their senses of self, choosing to no longer identify with Arab linages.[162] Their choices harmonise with the fate of Arab elites in the political sphere as noted above, and the decline can be further sustained with reference to economic factors, which Weber also would remind us play a key role in ethnogenesis.[163] The devastation of Iraq during the Fourth *Fitna* inaugurated a rapid downward spiral in the Iraqi economy and destruction of agricultural yields, evidenced particularly sharply in the deteriorating tax revenues during the first half of the third/ninth century.[164] Although more work is needed to determine the full social effects of the economic depression, the dual pressures of political evacuation to Samarra and the collapse of economic relations in the traditional Iraqi urban centres would have abruptly affected the transactional boundaries that had flourished and nourished the stable relationships of Arab/non-Arab over the previous 150 years. In contrast to the first 150 years of post-conquest settlement in Iraq when transactional boundaries and the value of Arabic symbolic capital aligned to generate value in expressing Arab identity as a social commodity, each of the particular factors which had been conducive to Arab ethnogenesis in Iraq fell away or changed forms during the third/ninth century, thereby pointing individuals, political groups and economic elites into new directions. Even graver changes were ahead, unleashing dramatic consequences for the Arabness idea in Iraq.

Insurrection in Arabia

From the mid-third/ninth century, the Arabian Peninsula underwent an unprecedented separation from caliphal authority. Previously, early Abbasid caliphs, al-Manṣūr, al-Mahdī and al-Rashīd, expended tremendous energies to develop Arabia and connect their Iraqi capital with the pilgrimage sites of Mecca and Medina. Their collective works during the second half of second/eighth century are now known as the *Darb Zubayda*:[165] a well-provisioned and carefully managed network of roads, water storage systems, food supply networks, way-stations and traveller amenities that facilitated smooth transit across the 750 miles between al-Kūfa and Mecca. Archaeological surveys confirm the scale of their operations,[166] and by the reign of al-Rashīd, classical sources describe pilgrim travel on the *Darb Zubayda* in remarkably luxurious terms.[167] The effect of caliphal infrastructure projects on Arabia's nomadic population should not be overlooked either: official attention to Hajj roads provided employment to Bedouin, and steady pilgrim traffic provided them bountiful charity and food.[168] Following the war between al-Amīn and al-Maʾmūn, however, Iraq's economy declined, and the fifty years of caliphal attention to the road abruptly ceased. Hārūn al-Rashīd was the last caliph to ever perform the pilgrimage in person, and between the reign of al-Amīn (193–8/809–13) and al-Wāthiq's accession in 227/842, no works are reported along the *Darb Zubayda*, and only limited construction is attested in Mecca. Pilgrimage continued, but official energies following al-Maʾmūn's victory in the Fourth *Fitna* were directed to rebuilding Baghdad, and then from al-Muʿtaṣim's reign, state revenues were even further sapped by the massive greenfield project at Samarra. The nature of *Darb Zubayda*'s infrastructure works demanded continuous attention to maintain its wells and supplies, and lack of attention across the first half of the third/ninth century necessarily degraded infrastructural integrity.[169]

Al-Wāthiq planned a major overhaul of the Hajj routes: his brother Jaʿfar led the Hajj of 227/842 to mark the Caliph's accession (the highest ranking prince to make a Hajj in over a generation) and al-Wāthiq's mother also made the pilgrimage in the same year (though she died en route).[170] Al-Wāthiq declared his intention to perform the Hajj himself in 231/846, the first time a caliph would consider leaving his court for Arabia since 186/802, but circumstances intervened. Al-Wāthiq's Hajj was impossible due to a water shortage stemming from the neglect over the preceding twenty years which left the *Darb Zubayda* in a precarious state. For example, during the pilgrimage of 229/843, a draught of water cost forty dirhams (perhaps a 600 per cent increase since al-Rashīd's reign),[171] and whilst al-Wāthiq ordered emergency repairs,[172] he died in 232/847, and for the next fifty years the road was again neglected as caliphal attention, caliphal power and the Iraqi economy further weakened. In sum, the century between the death of al-Rashīd and the reign of al-Muqtadir (295–320/908–32) was marked by official inattention and steady decline of the Arabian networks.[173]

For the Arabian Bedouin, the sudden end to the lavish expenditure and charity which they had come to expect from the caliphs, courtiers and ordinary pilgrims must have caused economic hardship and famine (especially given that the 'fat' decades of building on the *Darb Zubayda* likely swelled Bedouin populations), and these hardships resulted in a security collapse. In 230/845, Bedouin from the Banū Sulaym raided pilgrim caravans, threatened Medina and killed its governor when he opposed them. Al-Wāthiq dispatched his Turkic army under the command of Bughā into Arabia with initial success, but the Bedouin proved difficult to contain and unrest spread. Banū Sulaym regrouped and began a kind of guerrilla war, and the tribes of Hilāl, Fazāra, Ghaṭafān and Murra also took arms, raiding the Hajj roads and markets in Arabia. In 231/846 Bughā engaged them again, and eventually restored control, but the caliphs failed to capitalise on Bughā's peace, and the continued lack of building works for the next fifty years caused more shortages, making pilgrimage very difficult. A vicious cycle ensued, whereby insecurity curbed pilgrim numbers and the dwindling pilgrim traffic in turn made the Bedouin increasingly desperate and rapacious, rendering the Hajj an evermore difficult undertaking for Iraqi pilgrims.[174]

Water shortages are reported for the Hajj of 258/871, Banū Asad revolts in 265/878 claimed the life of Mecca's governor, and in 268/882 groups of Bedouin attacked returning pilgrims between Tūz and Samīrā, robbing them, stealing 5,000 camels and taking prisoners. In 285/898 Ṭayyiʾ Bedouin attacked returning pilgrims at al-Ajfar, killing their Turkic guards and plundering two million dinars and capturing women pilgrims.[175] In 286/899, the Banū Shaybān from the desert near al-Kūfa, evidently emboldened by the successes of Ṭayyiʾ and the lack of security in the Iraqi countryside, took to marauding Iraq itself, attacking villages, killing locals who defended their land and stealing livestock. The Ṭayyiʾ defeated detachments from Baghdad, and they spread through the Iraqi/Arabian border zone with impunity. Finally, a large force was dispatched from al-Raqqa to corral them, but the Bedouin retreated back into the desert and central authority took no punitive measures.[176] Ṭayyiʾ attacks continued in 287/900, and while their force of 3,000 Bedouin was eventually defeated,[177] by this time pilgrim caravans now required heavy guards and insecurity nonetheless continued. Ṭayyiʾ raids are recorded in 293/906 and 294/907 too.

Unprecedented disaster soon followed in the form of the Qarāmiṭa whose bold and utterly ruthless attack on pilgrims in 286/899 and subsequent consolidation of power across Arabia during the early 300s/920s devastated pilgrim traffic. The Qarāmiṭa sacked Mecca and al-Kūfa, effectively severing Iraqi contact with Arabia, and from the later third/ninth and through the fourth/tenth centuries, Arabia disappears from the literary historical record.[178] A sharp decline of pilgrims' graffiti in the site of al-Ṣuwaydira on the *Darb Zubayda* pilgrimage road provides evidence confirming the extent of Arabia's isolation after the early third/ninth century.[179]

Arabness After the Third/Ninth Century: Conclusions

Anarchy in Arabia was traumatic and deprived urban Iraqis of their connection to Hajj and the birthplace of Islam. The fact that Arab tribal groups were responsible was yet another blow to the status of Arab tribal identities in urban Iraq, infusing the Arabness idea with an embarrassing stigma of barbarous outsider. The negative impact of Qarāmiṭa and Bedouin incursions precisely coincided with the loss of Arabness' political status inside Iraq following the Fourth *Fitna* devastation and subsequent terminal economic decline too. The old Arab centres waned as wealth and power shifted to the Caliphate's former periphery. And so the symbolic and economic value of Arabness was definitively undercut and Iraqis began recasting their identities away from Arabian tribal affiliations. For intriguing specific examples, Romanov's empirical enumeration of the declining frequency of reference to tribal lineages in the biographies of urban Iraqis can be related chronologically to particular insurrections in Arabia considered here. The use of the affiliation Sulamī (from the Banū Sulaym) begins its sharp decline in urban Iraq from the mid-third/ninth century: tellingly close on the heels of the Arabian Banū Sulaym's raids against Hajj pilgrims and Abbasid authorities. Likewise, the number of Iraqi individuals claiming descent from Ṭayyiʾ began regressing one generation later, in the later third/ninth century – the period when the Arabian Ṭayyiʾ began their predations on pilgrims.[180] Imputing a collective revulsion to news of outrage on the Hajj roads thus finds some substantiation in the numbers of urban Sulamīs and Ṭāʾīs dropping ostensible connection to their eponymous Bedouin 'kinsmen'.

In contrast, therefore, to the early Abbasid period when self-professed Arabs in Iraq drove articulations of Arab identity as Islam's elite, by the late third/ninth century Arabness was changing from a relevant symbol of power to a relic of the past, abetted by Arabia's growing isolation and transformation into a seemingly anarchical, unfamiliar outside world. At the moment when Arabic literature was about to flourish and the encyclopedic process of writing Arab history began, sociopolitical changes had dramatically reduced the footprint of Arab groups in Iraq's urban milieu. Cultural producers wrote in Arabic, but they were no longer calling themselves Arabs, and they no longer could travel safely to Arabia either. The fourth/tenth-century writers about the Arabs were thus no longer writing about their own senses of kin, the early third/ninth-century narratives of Arabness no longer spoke to the new circumstances. The decline of Arab political factions and the pervasive decoupling of Arabic-speaking scholars in urban Iraq from 'Arab' tribal identities points to an environment of detachment in which Arab genealogy could be discussed dispassionately, and thereby ossified into those neat models which became established in genealogical writings from the late third/ninth and early fourth/tenth centuries (see Chapter 4(IV)). The wider changes to the Arabness idea flowing from the new urban Iraqi perspectives are the subject of our final chapter.

Notes

1. The foundational periodisation is evident in Goldziher (1889–90); Wellhausen (1927).
2. Critique of the racialising Arab vs Persian lens to categorise the opposing sides in the Abbasid takeover begins with the observation that the seminal modern studies, Goldziher and Wellhausen, were written at the height of Europe's aggressive nationalist ideologies. The Medieval Arabic sources do not draw such stark racial dichotomies, and count 'Arab' support of the Abbasids (particularly Yemenis) as key for Abbasid success (e.g. al-Dīnawarī (2001) pp. 513–8). After the decline of racialist thinking in Europe, studies have also critiqued the Arab/Persian binary of the Abbasid takeover (see Lassner (1980) and Sharon (1990) pp. 112–15, 263–301). Agha (2003) pp. 239–73 views the early Abbasids, following the allegiance poem of Naṣr ibn Sayyār, as a purposely 'invisible' movement whose members were neither strictly Arab nor *mawālī*, though in the background of his analysis is the assumption that the Umayyads constituted an 'Arab empire' (Ibid. p. 324). Other recent analysis

also underlines the inaccuracy of interpreting the events as a racial venture, Cobb (2010) pp. 266–8; Borrut (2011) pp. 330–8). The complex identities of members involved in the Abbasid movement will prevent earlier simplifications, though once the movement gained momentum and became visible, established power bases, such as Arab groups in Iraq did engage, and many of them were supportive.

3. The identification of Umayyads as an 'Arab kingdom' returns to Wellhausen (1927), and the elaboration of *Staatsnation* is by von Grunebaum (1963); as this book critiques von Grunebaum's notion of pre-Islamic *Kulturnation*, our analysis of Umayyad-era Arab ethnogenesis precludes generalising Umayyad statecraft as wholly 'Arab'; see Montgomery (2006) for further critique of von Grunebaum's *Staatsnation* thesis.
4. Writers traditionally identified the *abnā*ʾ (Arab-Khurasanians of mixed background) as the collective identity of much early Abbasid support, but Crone's 1998 and Turner's 2004 reappraisals demonstrate that the faction is not cited with regularity or coherence before, at the very earliest, the reign of al-Rashīd.
5. Al-Yaᶜqūbī (n.d.) vol. 2, p. 371. Al-Yaᶜqūbī is a rich and early source: his narrative counts *ᶜaṣabiyya* tensions as one of the basic ingredients of caliphal eras, and pays particular attention to them; al-Ṭabarī's *Tārīkh* usually furnishes corroboration.
6. Al-Ṭabarī (n.d.) vol. 7, p. 532.
7. Al-Yaᶜqūbī (n.d.) vol. 2, p. 372, al-Ṭabarī notes the conflict without express mention of *ᶜaṣabiyya* (n.d.) vol. 7, p. 512.
8. Al-Yaᶜqūbī (n.d.) vol. 2, pp. 372–3, 385. Al-Ṭabarī is silent here.
9. Al-Yaᶜqūbī (n.d.) vol. 2, p. 398. Al-Ṭabarī notes these changes in governorship in Sind in 161/777–8, but does not elaborate details.
10. Al-Yaᶜqūbī (n.d.) vol. 2, p. 409.
11. Ibid. vol. 2, p. 410, al-Ṭabarī calls it a *fitna* between Yamānīs and Nizārīs (n.d.) vol. 8, pp. 251–2.
12. Al-Yaᶜqūbī (n.d.) vol. 2, pp. 426–7. Al-Ṭabarī (n.d.) vol. 8, p. 270 adds that in 183/799–800 a Khazar invasion in Armenia started when *ᶜaṣabiyya* feuding spilled over and members of one tribal faction sought revenge against the Abbasid governor Yazīd ibn Mazyad al-Shaybānī by inviting Khazar incursions.
13. Al-Yaᶜqūbī (n.d.) vol. 2, pp. 371–2.
14. Al-Fasawī (1989–90) vol. 1, p. 123.
15. al-Yaᶜqūbī (n.d.) vol. 2, p. 384.
16. Ibid. vol. 2, p. 410.

17. Ibid. vol. 2, p. 427.
18. The process of conversion to Islam has much regional variation. In the case of Iraq, conversion begins in the first/seventh century, but neither Morony (1984) pp. 119, 431, nor Kennedy (1986) pp. 199–200 postulate early mass conversion. Bulliet dates wide-scale conversion to Iraq's urbanisation during the early Abbasid period (1979) p. 87. Anecdotally, *Mawālī* play an important role in al-Mukhtār's 66/685 revolt in al-Kūfa, though Crone views *mawālī* in that early period as neither all converts nor wholly assimilated (1980) p. 49, n. 358. Iraqi *Mawālī* conversion remains debated, but substantial conversion during the course of the second/eighth century seems reasonable given the population concentrations in the Muslim cities of al-Baṣra, al-Kūfa, al-Wāsiṭ and Baghdad. Ahola (2004) pp. 75–100 provides statistical support for rapid urban conversion against slower rates in the countryside.
19. The ability for individuals to choose between a plurality of identities, and even to adopt several, depending on changing circumstances in their everyday life is noted as a matter of theory, and constitutes an important critique of nationalist paradigms which assert a one-to-one relationship between an individual and his 'national' identity. In a pre-national period, where notions of ethnos lacked the bureaucratic control of nation states, the scope for plurality is evident, as outlined in Pohl (1998).
20. Wallman (1979) p. 3. See the summary of the theories of ethnogenesis in the Introduction of this book.
21. Pellat (1953) pp. 21–42; Lassner (1980) pp. 116–18.
22. During Europe's nationalist heyday, scholars cast *al-shuʿūbiyya* as an analogous nationalist struggle between Arab and Persian (Goldziher (1889–90) vol. 1, p. 137–97; Gibb (1962) pp. 62–73); as political nationalism subsided in post-World War II Europe, so the political ramifications of *al-shuʿūbiyya* were rejected (Norris (1990) pp. 31, 34–8; Mottahedeh (1976) p. 162). Postmodern scholars speak of cultural *shuʿūbiyya* (Enderwitz, *EI*² 'Shuʿūbiyya' vol. 9, p. 514). See Crone (2006) and Webb (forthcoming (B)) for further discussion of the faces of *al-shuʿūbiyya* in Western thought. See pp. 13–14 for anthropological groundwork on ethnic revivals.
23. Recorded in Ibn ʿAbd Rabbihi's *al-ʿIqd* (n.d.) vol. 3, pp. 407–11, 413–15.
24. Brief political tensions did flare in *Zindīq* persecution during al-Mahdī's reign (158–69/775–85) (Gutas (1998) pp. 65–9). Goldziher links *Zandaqa* and *al-shuʿūbiyya* (1889–90) vol. 1, p. 148, as does Gibb (1962) p. 69, but Taheri-Iraqi (1982) pp. 161-73 doubts the connection.

25. Schoeler (2006) and (2009) details the rise of book writing, and Bloom (2001) pp. 47–56, 100–16 traces the vital link between the introduction of paper manufacture in the late second/eighth and third/ninth centuries and the subsequent proliferation of Arabic literature.
26. It is traditional to identify Bashshār ibn Burd and Abū Nuwās as *shuᶜūbīs* (Badawi (1990) p. 157; Schoeler (1990) p. 276), and praise of Persians alongside disparagement of Arabness is present across both their *dīwāns*, see, for example, Bashshār ibn Burd (1976) vol. 1, p. 389, vol. 3, pp. 241–5; Abū Nuwās (2012) vol. 2, p. 1–35, vol. 5, p. 175. Interpreting these poets and their ostensibly pro-*ᶜajam* and/or anti-Arab poems is a difficult question, however. Bashshār's poetry also has a healthy praise of Arabs and Arab lineages, and as for Abū Nuwās, we have a number of indications that he consciously acted the role of 'ritual clown'. Should we thus ascribe anti-Arab, pro-wine rants to clowning, erudite fun, a real dislike of Arab-Islamic identity, or a volatile mixture of the three? See Hamori (1974) pp. 31–77 and Harb (1990) p. 228 for fruitful discussions of Abū Nuwās' poetry and functions.
27. Drory (1996) pp. 40–2 elaborates on *mawālī* construction of Arab identity with emphasis on the power non-Arabs won to create Arab history in the second/eighth century. Her framework embraces the relatively binary paradigm of early Abbasid society's Arab/non-Arab distinction which seems to need modification in the light of Abbasid-era Iraq's assimilating cultural boundaries.
28. See depictions of Abū ᶜUbayda in Gibb *EI*² 'Abū ᶜUbayda' vol. 1, p. 158; Lecker (1995a) p. 97 rightly shies away from labelling Abū ᶜUbayda a single-minded Arab-hater.
29. Mesopotamian trade with 'Dilmun' – Arabia's Gulf littoral – is dated to the fourth millennium BCE (Potts (2010) p. 71), central Arabian trade is inferred from at least the early third millennium BCE (Mallowan (1971) p. 285), but no Mesopotamian records refer to central and western Arabia (i.e. Najd, al-Ḥijāz, Tihāma) before the eighth century BCE (Potts (2010) pp. 71, 74).
30. Macdonald (2009f) pp. 338–9 identifies the eighth-century BCE Sūr Jarᶜā tablet as the earliest Mesopotamian cuneiform record about central Arabia. But it is noteworthy that Sūr Jarᶜā is removed from Mesopotamia's Babylonian heartland, and only from the later Assyrian period do Mesopotamian records reveal interest in controlling trade into Arabia (Ephᵓal (1982); Potts (2010)).
31. Lewy cites the cuneiform 'Verse Account' blaming Nabonidus 'for having built, in the far-off oasis town of Tēmā, a palace as his residence like the palace of Babylon' ((1971) p. 737). Lewy comments on a Babylonian aversion

to shifting the capital–residence anywhere outside of Babylon, an important observation regarding notions of ritual space in Mesopotamian culture retained by the Muslims (through the location of Baghdad), but also modified, through their novel interests in the desert. See also Potts (2010).

32. See Bosworth (1983) pp. 593–6.
33. The Achaemenids, Seleucids and Parthians engaged in trade and interest in the Eastern Arabian Gulf, particularly with Dilmun (Bahrain) and Gerrha (al-Hasa region of modern Saudi Arabia). The Sasanians intensified these interests: their first monarch, Ardashir I, captured Bahrain and Oman from the Parthians and installed his son, Shapur, as governor; Shapur II campaigned against Arabian incursions in Iraq and the Gulf littoral; his victories and punishment of Arabian leaders are memorialised in Muslim-era Arabic literature, where Shapur II is named *Dhū al-Aktāf* ('Master of the Shoulders'). The Sasanians also developed the Lakhmid client network to extend influence in Eastern and central Arabia, but without infrastructural or urban development. In the late sixth century CE, the Sasanians also extended influence to Southern Arabia, eventually capturing and settling garrisons in parts of modern Yemen. Arabic sources report that Sasanian rule ended *c.*628 with the conversion of the Persian governor Badhān to Islam, though details of the collapse of Persian control are unclear. For this history, see Bosworth (1983) pp. 579–609, Hoyland (2001) and Bowersock (2013).
34. Ephᵓal studied the seventh-century BCE arrival into Mesopotamia of peoples identified in Assyrian texts as *Arba-ā*. He observed the newcomers maintained the nomadic moniker *Arba-ā* for almost a century, but references to them disappear by the beginning of the sixth century BCE and the term later returns to designate nomads outside of Babylonia. In terms of ethnic articulation, the immigrants' settling in Iraq, their adoption of new lifestyles and the political reorganisation of Iraq after the fall of the Assyrians in 612 BCE cleft the *Arba-ā* from desert ties and integrated them as Iraqis. The complete forgetting of their nomadic roots took three generations (1982) pp. 113–15). In early Islam, the rise of express Arab identity conversely arose two or three generations after the arrival of groups from Arabia.
35. Al-Yaᶜqūbī (n.d.) vol. 1, pp. 208–16; al-Ṭabarī (n.d.) vol. 1, pp. 558–65, 609–32, vol. 2, pp. 95–8, 213–18; al-Masᶜūdī (1966–79) §§1037–75.
36. See Ibn Ḥabīb (1942) pp. 6–7 for Nebuchadnezzar; for the Iraqi 'Arab' king Jadhīma and the Syrian 'Arab' Queen Zabbāᵓ, see: al-Mubarrad (2008) vol. 3, pp. 1443–4); Ibn Qutayba (1994) pp. 108, 618; Abū al-Faraj al-Iṣfahānī (1992) vol. 15, pp. 305–10.

37. Nebuchadnezzar reigned 605–562 BCE. Arabic sources place him in ancient pasts, but with less precision, Ibn Ḥabīb (1942) p. 2 dates his reign 2,240 years after the founding of Jerusalem.
38. Ibn Ḥabīb (1942) pp. 6–7, al-Ṭabarī (n.d.) vol. 1, pp. 558–61. Bosworth notes a rival tradition from the earlier Ibn al-Kalbī that dates the founding of al-Ḥīra to the reign of the Sasanian Ardashir (r. *c.*224–40 CE), which Bosworth considers 'improbable' (1983) p. 597. Yāqūt's *Mu*ᶜ*jam al-buldān* (1993) vol. 2, p. 329 gives a variety of narratives.
39. Al-Ṭabarī (n.d.) vol. 1, pp. 609–11.
40. Al-Ṭabarī (n.d.) vol. 1, p. 611 equates *Aramāniyyūn* with the Nabaṭ, and muses over folk-etymological arguments positing their descent from ᶜĀd of Iram given the lexical similarity between Iram and *Aramānī*.
41. See al-Ṭabarī's discussion (n.d.) vol. 1, p. 609 of the first wave of 'Arabs' deported to al-Ḥīra whom he describes as subsequently departing (leaving the town in ruins for centuries), and joining the 'Arab tribes' in the town of al-Anbār where an Arab community was maintained. Al-Ṭabarī gives no indication that any joined the Nabaṭ.
42. See al-Masᵓūdī's Babylonian king list which contains mostly unknown names, the recognisable of which are only those mentioned in the Bible (1966–79) §§524–6. Al-Ṭabarī does not even offer a king list as he deems Babylonian history part of Persian kingship (n.d.) vol. 1, pp. 453–6); he counts Sennacherib as 'King of Babylon' and, again in keeping with the hypothesis of a biblical source milieu, al-Ṭabarī places Sennacherib's war against Judah (recorded in Kings II.19.6–36) within his narrative of Hebrew history (al-Ṭabarī (n.d.) vol. 1, pp. 532–8).
43. Al-Ṭabarī (n.d.) vol. 1, pp. 610–11. Modern historians note 'romantic legend' in these accounts (Bosworth (1983) p. 596), but seek to use them empirically, identifying names of tribes and kings which they reconstruct into alternative narratives (Hoyland (2009), Bosworth (1983)).
44. Al-Ṭabarī (n.d.) vol. 1, p. 611
45. The 'Arab' capture of Palmyra is widely cited: al-Yaᶜqūbī (n.d.) vol. 1, pp. 208-9; al-Ṭabarī (n.d.) vol. 1, pp. 618–28. Macdonald (2009b) rejects the Palmyrenes' Arabness on the basis of pre-Islamic evidence.
46. '[The Arab kings] were not subjugated by the *a*ᶜ*ājim*, nor did they subjugate the *a*ᶜ*ājim*' (al-Ṭabarī (n.d.) vol. 1, pp. 611–12, 627).
47. See Chapter 2(V).
48. See for example, al-Masᶜūdī's references to the collective 'Arab people' in

his reconstructions of dialogue among the early kings of al-Ḥīra (1966–79) §1051.

49. Al-Yaᶜqūbī (n.d.) vol. 1, pp. 209–14, Ḥamza al-Iṣfahānī even records lines of poetry ascribed to Arab immigrants during the 'Ṭawāᵓif period' between Alexander and the Sasanians (Ḥamza al-Iṣfahānī (n.d.) p. 75).
50. See Chapter 2, pp. 64–5.
51. Al-Jumaḥī (n.d.) vol. 1, p. 24–5; Ibn Qutayba (1925) vol. 2, p. 185, (1998) p. 150.
52. Heinrichs (1997) notes poetry's role in creating authentic *ᶜilm*; see also van Gelder's consideration of prosimetrum in classical literature (2011). See Webb (2013a) pp. 122, 133–8 for the role of poetry in early narratives of 'Arab history' and constructing heroic 'Arab' archetypes.
53. Al-Jumaḥī (n.d.) vol. 1, pp. 8–12, 108–9. Less impassioned, but to the same point, al-Jāḥiẓ observes that the oldest Arabic poetry pre-dates Muhammad by a maximum of 200 years (1998) vol. 1, p. 53.
54. See Webb (2013a) pp. 120–4.
55. The enhanced status of poetry in second/eighth-century Arabic historiography has connection with the storytelling *Quṣṣāṣ* (Webb (2013a) pp. 131–3).
56. Al-Yaᶜqūbī (n.d.) vol. 1, p. 209; al-Ṭabarī (n.d.) vol. 1, pp. 624–5.
57. Al-Ṭabarī (n.d.) vol. 1, p. 630; al-Masᶜūdī (1966–79) §1157. Al-Ṭabarī also relates memories of Ṭasm and Jadīs with the Iraqi 'Arab' king Jadhīma al-Abrash (n.d.) vol. 1, p. 613.
58. Bakhtin (1981) pp. 3–40.
59. Ibn Ḥabīb (1942) p. 394 identifies Nebuchadnezzar and Nimrod as 'non-believer' (*kāfir*) world kings, in apposition to Dhū al-Qarnayn (Alexander the Great) and Solomon, the 'believer' (*muᵓmin*) kings. This quartet was oft repeated: see Ibn Qutayba (1994) 32; Ibn Kathīr (d. 774/1373) notes that the story was known by the 'exegetes and other scholars of genealogy and reports from the past' (n.d.) vol. 1, p. 139.
60. Nebuchadnezzar recorded campaigns against *Arabi* in the Transjordan and Palestine (Ephᵓal (1982) pp. 171–2), but these cannot be the kernel of the Muslim-era narratives: Nebuchadnezzar's campaign did not penetrate Arabia, and it was not even very decisive in stemming nomadic pressures (Ibid. p. 179), hence it unlikely sparked Arabian epic, and moreover, we have noted that no other historical events between ancient Mesopotamians and Arabians were remembered in Muslim historical narratives.
61. Ibn Ḥabīb (1942) pp. 6–7.

62. Each relates Nebuchadnezzar's deportation of the Hebrews without mentioning campaigns in Arabia (Ibn Qutayba (1994) pp. 46–8; al-Dīnawarī (2001) pp. 63–4; al-Yaᶜqūbī (n.d.) vol. 1, pp. 65–6).
63. Al-Ṭabarī (n.d.) vol. 1, pp. 557–60. For later chronicles: Ibn al-Jawzī (1995) vol. 1, p. 281; Ibn al-Athīr (1979) vol. 1, pp. 271–3; Ibn Kathīr (n.d.) vol. 2, pp. 180, 196–7.
64. Most Iraqi writers also included Persian heritage alongside their 'Arab' stories of pre-Islam. The extent to which they rewrote the past wholesale to forge an Arab heritage is an interesting background to reappraise the 'Persian-ness' of the Sasanian Muslim-era Arabic narratives. Strategies for manipulation and re-remembrance of the Persian material are discussed in Savant (2013).
65. The Muslim-era construction of *al-Jāhiliyya*, the narratives and interplay of memory and myth in creating an 'Arab past' are the subject of a British Academy Postdoctoral Fellowship (pf150079) which I am commencing as this book goes to press.
66. Consider, in particular Lecker's questioning of why the sources stress the idea of Bedouinism as defining original Arabness (2010) pp. 153–4, and Hawting's detailed critique of narratives about pre-Islamic Arabian polytheism (1999) pp. 118–22.
67. Hawting (1999) p. 151.
68. The search for kernels of truth takes numerous turns and prompts varied interpretations of pre-Islamic history: Hoyland (2009) and al-Azmeh (2014a) offer the most comprehensive comparisons of Arabic sources with epigraphic finds. On the other hand, Hawting (1999) critiques many modern reconstructions, and, to develop Hawting's thesis, more concerted analysis of the narratives in Muslim-era accounts is needed to better place their details within the discourses by which writers employed memories of the past.
69. Goldziher (1889–90) vol. 1, p. 202 began the discourse on *al-Jāhiliyya* as reprobate not-Islam, followed by Izutsu (1966) p. 228. See also Hawting (1999) pp. 1–3; Hoyland (2001) p. 9. Difficulties inherent in translating *al-Jāhiliyya* are discussed in Shepard (2001) and Webb (2014).
70. After Goldziher's essay on *al-Jāhiliyya* (1889–90) vol. 1, p. 202, the barbarism epithet was much followed: Izutsu (1966) p. 228; Peters (1994) pp. 21, 36, 39–40; Khalidi (1994) pp. 1–3, Robinson (2003) p. 14, McCants (2011) p. 2.
71. Wadud (1999) and Barlas (2002) relate various examples of misogynistic 'Arab *Jāhiliyya*' society which both argue overtook the articulation of early Islam.

72. See Webb (2014) pp. 69–70 for a summary of current interpretations of *al-Jāhiliyya* society.
73. S. Stetkevych (1979) p. 51.
74. Jones (1996), a view endorsed in Montgomery (1997).
75. Drory (1996).
76. Hawting (1999) pp. 33–6.
77. Drory (1996) makes the call for such concerted narratological analysis; her tragic early death sadly prevented further publications, and my present research (see Note 65) seeks to reopen the enquiry.
78. Webb (2014) pp. 76–84.
79. This view is an amalgamation of Donner (1998) and Drory (1996) who address the drivers for scholarly interest in the pre-Islamic past in the first/seventh and the second/eighth centuries, respectively. A diachronic approach can shift from identifying *the* one driver for the Muslim memorialisation of *al-Jāhiliyya* and pursues explanations as to how and why interest in *al-Jāhiliyya* changed over time, and how such changes influenced the idea of 'pre-Islam' and the narration of its history.
80. The pervasive reshaping of the past to suit needs of the present is the basis of narratological historiography's critique of empirical historiography's search for 'kernels of truth' (see White (1980) and (1987), Ricoeur (1988) and Lowenthal (1985)).
81. Hawting (1999) p. 30. Hawting cites Carl Brocklemann's 'Allah und Die Götzen, der Ursprung des islamischen Monotheismus' *Archiv für Religionswissenschaft* 21 (1922) pp. 99–121: Brocklemann notes that references to the apparently monotheistic *Allāh* in pre-Islamic poetry far outnumber citations of pagan idols; and I found no reference to the pre-Islamic Hajj in the well-known Arabic poetry collections (Webb (2013b) p. 13, n. 3).
82. Al-Nuwayrī (2004) vol. 3, p. 268. Ibn ᶜAbd Rabbihi (n.d.) vol. 2, p. 314 narrates the same poem with 'wonders [*aᶜājīb*] of *al-Jāhiliyya*', not 'stories [*aḥādīth*]'. Yāqūt ascribes the poem to Muḥammad ibn ᶜAbd al-Malik al-Zayyāt, with 'stories [*aḥādīth*]' (1991) vol. 1, p. 61.
83. Al-Nasāᵓī (1999) *al-Sahw*:90. See a similar hadith in al-Tirmidhī (1999) *al-Adab*:70.
84. Ibn Ḥabīb (1942) p. 500.
85. For further consideration of this discourse, see Webb (2014) pp. 87–91.
86. Hobsbawm's now classic study (1990) was restricted to the nation state, particularly the European variety, but his concept of 'inventing tradition' fits

within the current thrust of the Vienna school and its students who pursue the construction of pre-modern identities. This section's discussion of how an imagined community of Arabs invented a past and 'pre-Islamic Arab traditions' to articulate their own particularism seem to be exemplars of Hobsbawm's thesis.

87. Ibn Ḥabīb (1942) p. 236 reports the will of ᶜĀmir ibn Jusham who decreed his son's share would be twice each daughter's, anticipating the Islamic rule. For other examples from *al-Muḥabbar*, see Webb (2014) pp. 87–90.
88. Ibn Ḥabīb (1942) pp. 309–11.
89. Ibid. pp. 237–40.
90. Ibid. pp. 312–20.
91. Ibid. p. 146.
92. Ibid. pp. 241–3.
93. Al-Jāḥiẓ (2003) vol. 3, p. 366. Al-Jāḥiẓ's text compares the 'Arab/Arabian' Umayyads to what he calls the 'Persian Khurasanian' Caliphate of his day. See Chapter 6(I) for further consideration of al-Jāḥiẓ's construction of this dichotomy.
94. Ibn Qutayba (1998) p. 89.
95. Ibid. *passim*, in particular pp. 89, 141, 146.
96. Ibid. p. 84.
97. Ibn al-Nadīm (1988) p. 109.
98. Al-Yaᶜqūbī (n.d.) vol. 1, p. 221–2.
99. Ibid. vol. 1, p. 254.
100. Ibid. vol. 1, p. 254.
101. Ibid. vol. 1, p. 239. See also Ibid. vol.1, p. 248
102. See Chapter 2, pp. 82–3.
103. Al-Yaᶜqūbī (n.d.) vol. 1, p. 239; Ibn Ḥabīb (1942) pp. 311–15 and Ibn al-Kalbī (1924) p. 7 list tribal *talbiya*s with express statements that the repetition of these proclaimed the unity of God, stressing their link to monotheistic Abrahamic/Ishmaelite origins.
104. Ibn Qutayba (1998) pp. 120–7. The proliferation of monographs entitled *al-Khayl* ('The Book of Horses') by late second/eighth and third/ninth-century philologists and poetry collectors further embedded the idea of horsemanship as a defining element of *Arabica*, as does the lexical invention of the term *khayl ᶜirāb* to describe purebred Arabian stallions (see, e.g. Ibn Durayd (1987) vol. 1, p. 319). I propose the term's Muslim-era invention, as I am unaware of its citation in any horse descriptions from pre-Islamic poetry: to the extent of my

searches, the word only appears in prose comments written by Muslims to describe the poetry. The absence of ʿ-r-b cognates to describe purebred horses in pre-Islamic poetry seems significant given the incredibly profuse horse vocabulary the corpus contains.

105. Ibn al-Kalbī (2009) p. 12.
106. Al-Yaʿqūbī (n.d.) vol. 1, p. 221. The association of the place Ajyād with horses is conjectural: *ajyād* could be a plural of *jīd*, the common word to describe the long necks of desirable thoroughbreds, and folk-etymological predilections seem operative to 'prove' the truth of Ishmael's stallions via the toponym. Writing almost two centuries after al-Yaʿqūbī, and after the Ishmael cum-father of all Arabs stories had subsided, al-Bakrī is more circumspect regarding the association of Mecca's Ajyād with horses (1947) vol. 1, p. 115.
107. Ibn al-Kalbī (2009) pp. 13–17.
108. See Diʿbil (d. 246/860) *Waṣāyā al-Mulūk* (1997) (possibly written by Diʿbil's son); Wahb ibn Munabbih (1996) and ʿUbayd ibn Sharya (1996). Ibn Hishām's *Sīra* also includes a prologue of Yemeni prophetic history as the condition precedent of Muhammad's prophethood (n.d.) vol. 1, pp. 11–42.
109. See Hawting's re-evaluation of traditional interpretations of the Qur'an with his new reading of its references to idolatry (1999) pp. 48–66, and one of his hypotheses that 'early scholars did not really understand the koranic polemic' (Ibid. p. 150).
110. The term 'pagan reservation' is a centrepiece of al-Azmeh's study of pre-Islamic Arabia (2014a) pp. 249–63. Shahid (1985–) offers the counterargument of substantial Christian groups across pre-Islamic Arabia.
111. Given Hawting's argument that the Qur'an's polemic is primarily directed at other monotheists (Hawting (1999) pp. 67–87), a reader could suppose part of the Qur'anic discourse emanated from a pre-Islamic Arabian inter-Christian or Jewish debate.
112. Hoyland rightly notes the retrospective Arabisation of memories of the rise of Islam (2015) pp. 56–60, for specific examples of the working of such Arabisation in memories of the conquest of Syria, see Webb (2015) pp. 20–3.
113. Ibn Ḥabīb (1942) p. 315.
114. Ibn Qutayba (1998) pp. 87–9.
115. Al-Yaʿqūbī (n.d.) vol. 1, p. 255.
116. The significance of the polytheistic anecdotes suggests alternative conclusions to Hawting's thesis (1999) that Muslims constructed polytheism to reinterpret Qur'anic polemic, since the early sources betray more substantial emphasis on

monotheism than Hawting accorded them (he did not, for example, consider the place of the Yemeni Hūd narratives or the Muslim-era construction of Ishmaelite genealogy which seem vital parts of the wider discourse). Hawting's main argument nonetheless remains crucial: Muslim-era writers give a mostly non-empirical picture of pre-Islamic Arabia, and it is difficult to reconstruct a 'real' sense of pre-Islamic polytheism from Muslim-era texts.

117. Ibn al-Kalbī (1924) p. 6, see also his reinterpretation of the idols Isāf and Nā'ila (Ibid. p. 29).
118. Ibn al-Kalbī notes that Arabs changed Abraham and Ishmael's religion (1924) pp. 6–8, but backtracks when later declaring that: 'the descendants of Ma'add preserved part of the religion of Ishmael. Rabī'a and Muḍar also followed this' (Ibid. p. 13). The political importance of those three groups in Islam is a noteworthy factor guiding their memorialisation.
119. Ibid. pp. 13, 53.
120. Consider Ibn al-Kalbī's narrative about the origins of idolatry after Adam: Adam's sons establish a monument to pay respect, but afterwards a son of Cain misinterprets the monument and sets his people on the path of idolatry (Ibid. pp. 53–4). The narratives' mirroring of the origins ascribed for Arab idolatry is apparent.
121. For example, Ibn al-Kalbī notes that while Hamdān and Ḥimyar were associated with the idols Ya'ūq and Nasr, neither names were recorded in pre-Islamic poetry (Ibid. pp. 10–11). Ibn al-Kalbī follows this with a reference to Ḥimyar's conversion to Judaism. Regarding the idol Ri'ām, Ibn al-Kalbī reports: 'The Arabs did not remember [Ri'ām] in poetry except shortly before Islam' (Ibid. p. 12), an observation reminiscent of the hadith regarding Quraysh's only 'recent' adoption of *Jāhiliyya* before Muhammad (see Note 139).
122. Ibn al-Kalbī details the Muslims' destruction of idols, often by fire (1924) pp. 17, 31. This is perhaps a deliberate contrast to his accounts of idol destruction during the Flood (Ibid. pp. 53–4): fire's more total destructive power signals that after Muhammad, there will be no more false worship.
123. Q9:36.
124. Al-Ya'qūbī (n.d.) vol. 1, p. 237.
125. Q16:58–9; 81:8–9; see also 6:137, 140, 151; 17:31; 60:12. See Lee Bowen (2002) vol. 2, p. 511.
126. Al-Mubarrad (2008) vol 2, pp. 604–8.
127. Al-Ya'qūbī (n.d.) vol 1, pp. 223, 237, 241.
128. Ibid. vol 1, p. 226.

129. Ibid. vol. 1, p. 226.
130. Ibid. vol. 1, pp. 232, 228.
131. Al-Balādhurī's connection with the court is recounted in Yāqūt (1991) 2:50–4 and al-Kutubī (1973) 1:155–7. He was also entrusted to teach the son of the Caliph al-Muᶜtazz, ᶜAbd Allāh (Ibn al-ᶜAdīm (1988) 3:1220).
132. These are the last two caliphs for whom al-Balādhurī narrates a biography (1997–2004) vol. 3, pp. 289–321. There is brief mention of al-Rashīd and his contemporaries (Ibid. vol. 3, p. 316).
133. Ibn Khayyāṭ devotes only 15 per cent of *al-Tārīkh* to the century 132–232/749–846 (1993) pp. 330–95; events after al-Rashīd (d. 193/809) are particularly abbreviated: the siege of Baghdād is very curt, and Ibn Khayyāṭ never mentions al-Amīn by name, preferring the pointed *al-makhlūᶜ* (the deposed) (Ibid. pp. 384–5).
134. Barring a brief discussion of the year of Muhammad's birth (Ibid. pp. 26–8).
135. Ibid. p. 24.
136. Ibid. p. 25. The reference to journey (*hijra*) and the theological statement are narrated in separate *akhbār*, though their juxtaposition adjacent to each other suggests Ibn Khayyāṭ intends his readers to make the connection.
137. Ibn Khayyāṭ's biographies are found in compendiums of hadith narrators: we may think of him as a 'historian', but his contemporaries counted him amongst the *aṣḥāb al-ḥadīth* (Ibn al-Nadīm (1988) p. 288); see also al-Rāzī (1952) vol. 3, p. 378; Ibn Ḥajar (1907–9) vol. 3, p. 160). Another early annalistic text entitled *Tārīkh* by Abū Zurᶜa (1996), similarly begins 'history' with the Prophet's *hijra*; and again, Abū Zurᶜa was a hadith specialist, and his 'history' text primarily concerns the life histories of early jurists.
138. Dating hadith scholars is the goal of Ibn Khayyāṭ's other surviving text, *al-Ṭabaqāt*.
139. Al-Nasāʾī (1999) *al-Sahw*:99; al-Tirmidhī (1999) *Manāqib*:65.
140. Arguing against Crone (1998) p. 3, Turner (2004) indicates the sources more strongly suggest *al-abnāʾ* gathered into a collective during the *fitna* between al-Amīn and al-Maʾmūn.
141. Turner (2004) p. 22.
142. Al-Yaᶜqūbī (n.d.) vol. 2, p. 445.
143. Ibid. vol. 2, pp. 456, 460, 464.
144. Ibid. vol. 2, p. 458.
145. Al-Masᶜūdī (1966–79) §2801. See Gordon (2001) for analysis of the 'Turks' third/ninth-century rise.

146. Ibn al-Jawzī (1995) vol. 6, p. 358. Modern scholars estimate the Turks numbered between 100,000 (Kennet) and 20,000 (Töllner): see Gordon (2001) p. 73 who prefers the lower estimate. Northedge (2007) p. 192 also argues for lower estimates, but his excavations revealing large expansions in the Karkh and Dūr 'cantonments' indicate dramatic increases in the size of Turkic soldiers procured for al-Muᶜtaṣim.
147. El-Hibri (2010) p. 296. Gordon (2001) pp. 111–18 details the networks of influence of these prominent Turks.
148. Al-Yaᶜqūbī (n.d.) vol. 2, p. 462.
149. See Gordon (2001) pp. 75–88 for the ramifications of the rise of Turks in the public sphere at the expense of old elites between the reigns of al-Muᶜtaṣim to al-Mutawakkil.
150. Al-Kindī (1912) pp. 193–4.
151. Ayalon (1994) pp. 21–2. More nuanced, but ultimately similar conclusions are expressed in Gordon (2001) pp. 39–40 and Mikhail (2008) pp. 383–4.
152. Al-Ṭabarī (n.d.) vol. 9, pp. 17–18; al-Masᶜūdī (1996–79) §§2801–2, al-Kutubī (1973) vol. 4, p. 49. The widely-reported story may exaggerate the causal connection between Turkish rowdiness and the move to Samarra, but the effect of Samarra's establishment, whatever its initial prompt, exerted seminal changes on Iraq's urban and political landscape.
153. El-Hibri (2010) p. 296.
154. Nawas (1994) p. 624; Gutas (1998) pp. 75–83.
155. Nawas (1996) p. 707 critiques the earlier interpretations of al-Miḥna as a markedly anti-Arab-Khurasanian purge as hypothesised by Lapidus (1975) and Madelung (1990).
156. Gordon (2001) p. 105.
157. Ibid. p. 106.
158. Al-Jāḥiẓ (2003) vol. 3, p. 366.
159. Weber (1996) pp. 35–6.
160. Ahola (2004) pp. 107–10. Romanov (2013) pp. 133–5 identifies the process as 'de-tribalisation', counting it as 'one of the most striking processes that the onomastic data allows us to discover' (2016) p. 129.
161. Romanov (2013) pp. 133–5 notes that up to 85 per cent of individuals recorded in al-Dhahabī's *Tārīkh al-Islām* from the later part of Islam's first century were identified by tribal *nisba*, but by 350 AH, only circa 20 per cent were, and this count includes a considerable proportion of Quraysh and *Anṣār nisbas* which Romanov suggests were more a marker of social status (via linkage to the two

communities most closely associated the memory of Muhammad) than tribal organisation. See also the individual tribal nisba charts in Romanov (2013) Appendix 2.

162. The computational evidence appears particularly applicable in this analysis since both Ahola and Romanov, working from a different source text and independently, found a curve of decreasing reference to tribal *nibsa*, not an instantaneous break. Statistically, the curve implies an organic process by which increasing numbers of individuals chose to change their self-designations over two or three generations.
163. Weber (1996) pp. 35–6.
164. The classic account of Iraqi economic decline is Waines (1977) pp. 285–8. For enlightening exploration of the political-economic nexus of crisis and decline, see Kennedy (2004) pp. 13–16; Mårtensson (2011).
165. Zubayda was the wife of al-Rashīd: many of the Arabian infrastructural works were named after their benefactors, and various women in the Abbasid Court were particularly active and left their names in the memories recorded in the detailed late third/ninth-century *Kitāb al-Manāsik* (al-Ḥarbī (attrib.) 1999). The naming of the entire network of roads under the one name *Darb Zubayda* occurred in the later Abbasid period.
166. See al-Rashid's survey (1980) and his revisions (1993). Various Arabic sources provide the literary evidence of the scale and enormous cost of the buildings: Ibn Khurdādbih, al-Ḥarbī (his work *Kitāb al-Manāsik* perhaps should be entitled *Kitāb al-Ṭarīq* and be ascribed to al-Ḥarbī's student, al-Qāḍī al-Wakīᶜ (d. 306/918–19, see al-Ḥarbī (attrib) (1999) p. 21–3), Qudāma ibn Jaᶜfar, al-Ṭabarī, and Ibn al-Athīr relate the pertinent information collated in al-Rashid (1980) pp. 12–45.
167. Ibn ᶜAbd Rabbihi (n.d.) vol. 5, p. 124. Al-Rashid and Webb (2016) pp. 68–73 suggest some later hyperbole exaggerating memories of al-Rashīd's Hajjes, but the *Darb Zubayda* was undoubtedly a major and successful undertaking.
168. See al-Rashid and Webb (2016) pp. 109–10.
169. Al-Rashid and Webb (2016) pp. 111–16.
170. Al-Ṭabarī (n.d.) vol. 9, p. 123.
171. Ibid. vol. 9, p. 124.
172. See al-Ḥarbī (attrib.) (1999) pp. 286–7.
173. There are cursory mentions of caliphal appointments of governors over Mecca to oversee roadworks, but apart from scattered reports for the reigns of al-Muᶜtaḍid (279–89/892–902) and al-Muktafī (289–95/902–8), nothing

else is mentioned (al-Rashid (1980) 24–5). The most detailed account of the Hajj route from Iraq, al-Ḥarbī/al-Wakīʿ's *Kitāb al-Manāsik/al-Ṭarīq* illustrates the extent of decline by the almost ubiquitous reference to 'effaced', 'ruined' and 'no longer existing' places along the route (al-Ḥārbī attrib. (1999) pp. 44–107), and only scant reference to work following the reign of al-Maʾmūn (e.g. Ibid. pp. 40, 45, 73, 90).

174. Al-Rashid and Webb (2016) pp. 119–40, Landau-Tasseron (2010) pp. 406–12, and al-Rāshid (1993) pp. 83–100.
175. Al-Ṭabarī (n.d.) vol. 10, p. 67. Al-Ṭabarī's language casts some doubts suggestive that the figure of two million dinars may have been inflated by the time it reached the historical record.
176. Al-Ṭabarī (n.d.) vol. 10, pp. 71–2.
177. Ibid. vol. 10, p. 74.
178. Landau-Tasseron (2010) p. 413.
179. Al-Rāshid (2009) catalogues graffiti at the site of al-Ṣuwaydira dated on the basis of epigraphy. Of the 257 inscriptions, two are dated to the first/seventh century, 109 to the first/seventh–second/eighth century, ninety-four to the second/eighth century, forty-four to the second/eighth or third/ninth century, and only seven date to the third/ninth century (one is undatable). The concentration in the second/eighth century corresponds with the literary evidence of the Darb Zubayda's heyday and the dramatic drop in the third/ninth century underlines the sudden disruptive power of the tribal raiding and lack of administrative attention to the pilgrim road.
180. Romanov (2013) pp. 318, 336.

6

Philologists, 'Bedouinisation' and the 'Archetypal Arab' after the Mid-Third/Ninth Century

In the face of assimilation and the seismic changes in the political structure which deprived Arab groups of their status in third/ninth-century Iraq, it is remarkable that scholarly interest in ancient *Arabica* paradoxically blossomed after the mid-third/ninth century. Despite urban Iraqi society's abandonment of Arab tribal affiliations (*nisba*) and the severance of urban Iraq from desert Arabia in the wake of the escalating Qarāmiṭa crisis and the collapse of Hajj traffic, Iraqi writers produced an unprecedented outpouring of literature about Arabness and Arab history, resulting in what today constitute the 'primary sources' about pre-Islamic Arabia. When reading these sources, it is therefore material to reflect upon the effects of the curious context of their creation. In earlier periods, memorialising the Arab past had political ramifications: in the first/seventh century, tribal genealogy and memories of pre-Islamic battles of Arabian groups (*ayyām al-ᶜarab*) directly impacted the reputations and relative merits of the different groups of Conquerors, and during the second/eighth century, Arab groups marshalled history to establish their heritage vis-à-vis conquered populations.[1] Political interests and status thus exerted significant pressures on imagining the Arabs, but very few writings survive from those early periods. In contrast, the voluminous fourth/tenth-century and later compendiums emanate from a peculiar moment when, for the first time, Iraqi scholars were detached from practical ramifications of writing about Arabness and when Arabness discourses no longer impacted politically significant communities.

With the new context in mind, we need also consider that the authors of our major sources for the *ayyām al-ᶜarab* Arabian pre-Islamic battle histories and genealogy are, intriguingly, philologists and belles-lettrists, and not specialised historians, nor partisans of particular 'Arab' or other groups. Books expressly intended as chronicles (*tārīkh*) have very little to say about *ayyām al-ᶜarab*, and make scant attempt to integrate Arabian pasts into world history.[2] Instead, our view into *ayyām al-ᶜarab* relies upon poetry anthologies compiled by scholars known for their knowledge of philology,[3] the *adab* encyclopedic compendium by the Andalusian Ibn ᶜAbd Rabbihi (d. 328/940), and Abū al-Faraj al-Iṣfahānī's (d. 356/967) *al-Aghānī*, a collection of and commentary on popular songs derived from pre-Islamic and Umayyad-era poetry. The *ayyām al-ᶜarab* tales we possess, therefore, are transplants from a period when they impacted actual political arrangements into a new era where they spoke to a range of discourses which were all different from the earlier, politicised contexts.

The recording of Arab genealogy (*nasab*) also shifted from the preserve of authors identifiable as 'historians' to a more belles-lettristic milieu. The earliest extant genealogies were written by Ibn al-Kalbī during the momentous changes following al-Maᵓmūn's capture of Baghdad, and three other survivals of the third/ninth century were written by authors identifiable as 'historians' with evident political interests;[4] but the later and major surviving genealogical texts are by philologists (al-Mubarrad's (d. 285/898) *Nasab ᶜAdnān wa Qaḥṭān* and Ibn Durayd's (d. 321/933) *al-Ishtiqāq*), the Andalusian jurist Ibn Ḥazm's (d. 456/1064) *Jamharat ansāb al-ᶜarab* and the Eastern encyclopedist Yāqūt's (d. 626/1228) *al-Muqtaḍab*.

Beyond enumerating surviving texts, we can further quantify the shift in scholarly interest in pre-Islamic Arab history from a larger data sample in the extensive list of books catalogued in 377/987 in the Baghdadi bookseller Ibn al-Nadīm's *al-Fihrist*. *Al-Fihrist* devotes a chapter to 'genealogists and narrators of events from the past' (*akhbāriyyūn, nassābūn* and *aṣḥāb al-aḥdāth*) who lived from the beginning of the Arabic scholarly tradition to Ibn al-Nadīm's day. Up to the mid-second/eighth century (when tribal infighting was at its peak) 29 per cent of the *akhbāriyyūn* are noted for expertise in *ayyām al-ᶜarab* and 65 per cent for *nasab*.[5] From the mid-second/eighth century to the mid-third/ninth, when Arab and other elements of society argued the merits of *al-shuᶜūbiyya*, 23 per cent of the *akhbāriyyūn* wrote about *ayyām al-ᶜarab* and 45 per cent composed books of *nasab*.[6] But after the mid-third/ninth century, only 12 per cent of scholars are accorded books on *ayyām al-ᶜarab* and 35 per cent on *nasab*, and the *nasab* works from this period primarily concern the genealogy of the Abbasids, implying a shift in *nasab* study's purpose to extoll the Caliphate specifically, not to rehearse Arab glories more generally.[7] Ibn al-Nadīm's lists and our extant sources dovetail to reveal specialists of history and genealogy after the mid-third/ninth century distinctly turned away from writing about the Arab past and lineage.

It may seem ironic that 'historians' grew less interested in Arab history than philologists, poetry experts and *adab* belles-lettrists, but the precise coincidence with the decline of Arabness' practical political importance can explain the shift. After the third/ninth century in Iraq, remembering the discrete differences between the relative glories of individual Arab tribes had little relevance in a world where no important individuals claimed membership to such groups. The detailed preservation and re-narration of the old, seemingly obsolescent tribalist material therefore prompts a number of practical questions. Why did *Arabica* continue to be so interesting for Iraqi grammarians and *littérateurs*? Why did they assume mastery over these subjects, and what did they need the 'Arabness' idea to do? Analysis of these questions will reveal wholesale changes in the definitions of Arabness and a new paradigm that canonised a wholly new way of imagining the Arabs.

I Philologists and Arabness: Changing Conceptions of Arabic between the Late Second/Eighth and Fourth/Tenth Centuries

Grammarians' and lexicographers' interest in pre-Islamic Arabness extended beyond antiquarian curiosity. They sought to codify and explain every detail of the Arabic language as they imagined it existed in the pre-Islamic period in part to determine the correct interpretation of the Qur'an.[8] Since the Arabics spoken in the philologists' Iraqi urban milieu no longer retained Qur'anic syntax, morphology or lexicon, grammarians were compelled to look to the past. They needed a historical reconstruction of Arabic as it really was spoken.

The philologists' speculations are consequently fertile ground for historical investigation. Grammarians supported their linguistic arguments via historical narratives built upon anecdotes from the past that contained phrases which proved their rules of 'correct' Arabic. Such an empiricist–historical discourse resonates with other kinds of historical writing that seek to recreate the past as it really happened. Recently, narratological theories of Hayden White, Paul Ricoeur and like-minded historiographers have critiqued historians' remonstrations to recover absolute truth from the past,[9] and we ought therefore to be wary of the Abbasid-era philologists' claims to reconstruct pre-Islamic Arabic as it really was spoken. Like any historical reconstruction, the philologists' enterprise of recreating a 300-year-old language did not invent the Arab past entirely, but they chose to remember it in ways apposite to their discourses. In so doing, as we shall see, they directed the paradigm of 'original' Arabness onto unprecedented trajectories.

Arabia, Arabic and Arabness: a Mid-Third/Ninth-Century Perspective

The polymath, philologist, humanist and belles-lettrist al-Jāḥiẓ[10] offers one of the most detailed extant mid-third/ninth-century discourses about Arabic and Arabness in his *al-Bayān wa-l-tabyīn*, an expansive text on language and communication. The manner in which *al-Bayān* employs Arabness offers an insightful window to enter the universe of the practical uses of *Arabica* amongst Iraqi philologists.

Al-Bayān establishes a linguistic–geographical framework for Arabia (*Jazīrat al-ᶜarab*,[11] or just *al-Jazīra*[12]) which al-Jāḥiẓ projects as outside his Iraqi world by demarcating Arabia's border at the edge of his hometown, al-Baṣra.[13] He turns the spatial border into a linguistic boundary, exemplified in an anecdote about Zayd ibn Kathwa, a poet originally from Arabia who settled in al-Baṣra. Al-Jāḥiẓ describes Zayd's house as situated at 'the last place of Pure Speech [*mawḍiᶜ al-faṣāḥa*], and at the first place of Non-Arabic Speech [*mawḍiᶜ al-ᶜujma*]',[14] articulating the division of Arabian/non-Arabian land as a divide between what al-Jāḥiẓ portrays as 'correct', 'pure' Arabic and the 'adulterated' Arabic of his Iraqi compatriots. The Zayd anecdote is situated immediately following al-Jāḥiẓ's explication of the basis of good communication,[15] and when lamenting that Zayd's ability to speak eloquent Arabic was affected when he left Bedouin life in Peninsula, we perceive an emphasis on Arabian space underpinning al-Jāḥiẓ's construction of proper Arabic language.

Al-Jāḥiẓ develops his spatial portrayal of eloquence throughout *al-Bayān*. He contrasts the city ('the abode which corrupts language [*tufsid al-lugha*] and diminishes eloquence [*tanquṣ al-bayān*]')[16] with Arabian deserts (the 'land of the pure Bedouin [*bilād al-a*ᶜ*rāb al-khullaṣ*] and the source of the correct/pure Arabic [*ma*ᶜ*din al-faṣāḥa al-tāmma*]').[17] And he articulates the purity of the Arabic language as a function of Arabian geography:

> [The Arabic] language only runs correctly, stands upright, flows mellifluously, and reaches perfection by virtue of the aspects which come together in that Peninsula [*jazīra*] and between its neighbours [*jīra*], and because other peoples [*umam*, that is, non-'natural' Arabic speakers] do not tread there.[18]

Arabia's particular geographical difference from Iraq seems to have been important for al-Jāḥiẓ's discourse in *al-Bayān*, for he later reiterates a more explicit statement of Arabness' pan-Arabian unity by virtue that

> [the Arabs] have one home, the Peninsula . . . and their resemblance is erected upon the soil and the character of the air and water. Hence they are unified in nature, language, ambition, good qualities, pasture and waters, artifice and desire.[19]

Why does al-Jāḥiẓ erect such a boundary between Iraq and the unique characteristics of Arabia? In practical terms, the division enables him to argue that his urban environment intrinsically lacks eloquence in contrast to desert Arabia where he nudges forward an argument that Bedouin perpetuate ideal Arabic.

Al-Jāḥiẓ's praise for Arabia and derision of his own milieu may seem to bolster his noted Arab partisanship in the context of the 'Arab versus non-Arab' cultural debate (*al-shu*ᶜ*ūbiyya*).[20] *Al-Bayān* does express antagonism to anti-Arab partisans,[21] and his thesis that town-dwellers (*baladiyyūn* or *qarawiyyūn*) and non-Arabian Muslim converts (*muwalladūn*) are largely incapable of replicating the most correct Arabic[22] sustains a cultural defence of Arabness,[23] but al-Jāḥiẓ's argument in *al-Bayān* pushes further. The construction of Arabia as pure Arabic (linguistic) space is not strictly an apparatus for praising ethnic Arabs, for the division of desert/city and pure speech/corrupt speech intersects with one of *al-Bayān*'s more fundamental themes concerning the essence of *bayān* and *balāgha* (eloquence and good rhetoric).[24] Al-Jāḥiẓ's discourse transcends ethnic divisions: via his Mu'tazilite theology, he posits that *bayān* is the cornerstone of all aspects of life including the means to understand God and the meaning of the Qur'an.[25] He explains that intellectual culture is only perpetuated by the communication of knowledge (*ᶜilm*), which occurs via eloquence (*bayān*) and necessarily begins with the Qur'an since its excellent *bayān* is the means by which God teaches His ultimate knowledge. Ideal *bayān* and *ᶜilm* thus belong to God, not any one group of people, and the first pages of *al-Bayān* discuss the primacy of God's *bayān* and its centrality to His revelation for mankind.[26] Because the Qur'an is in Arabic, and pure Arabic (*faṣīḥ*) at that, the Arabic language becomes the object of al-Jāḥiẓ's effusive praise:

> There is no speech more enjoyable or elegant, nor sweeter to hear, nor so in accordance with sound reason, nor more freeing for the tongue nor finer upon which one can discover eloquence than long hours listening to the clever, eloquent desert Arabians [*al-aᶜrāb al-ᶜuqalāᵓ al-fuṣaḥāᵓ*], or articulate scholars [*al-ᶜulamāᵓ al-bulaghāᵓ*].[27]

The theoretical basis for Arabic's primacy as emanating from God means that al-Jāḥiẓ's construction transcends Arab ethnicity. He never intimates that Arabs all speak his perfect Arabic ideal, instead he repeatedly stresses that good Arabic vests in Arabian Bedouin (*aᶜrāb*) and Arabs of the past (until the end of the Umayyad era).[28] His third/ninth-century contemporary 'modern Arabs', especially city-dwellers, would thus find only limited ammunition for defence against *al-shuᶜūbiyya* critique as al-Jāḥiẓ only guardedly lauds the Arabic spoken since the Abbasid takeover.[29] Al-Jāḥiẓ's ideal Arabic is in the 'Land of the *aᶜrāb* [Bedouin]', not 'Land of the Arabs [*ᶜarab*]',[30] and hence his philological theory does not actually champion the *Arab* ethnos, but results in praise for *Arabian* space as the closest terrestrial equivalent to the ultimate standard of Qur'anic Arabic.

While al-Jāḥiẓ's discourse about Arabia seems constructed to validate his reverence for the language of the Qur'an, there also seems an even deeper motive behind his reasoning. By equating the best terrestrial Arabic with that spoken in Arabia, and especially the past Arabic of Muhammad's day, al-Jāḥiẓ marshals both space and time to categorically distance ideal Arabic from his own urban, third/ninth-century Iraq. As a result, al-Jāḥiẓ presents his contemporary society in a linguistic crisis of inexpressiveness, and he develops this notion, chastising his contemporaries for the impurity of their language. By arguing that any mixing with impure speech will spread bad-language contagion,[31] al-Jāḥiẓ renders it practically impossible for an urbanite to avoid tainting his language, yet by opening *al-Bayān wa-l-tabyīn* with an elaborate prayer for eloquence,[32] al-Jāḥiẓ instils a holy fear of bad language. The connection of excellent speech with excellent knowledge will therefore lead al-Jāḥiẓ's readers to want to perfect their own idiom to perfect their knowledge, and here al-Jāḥiẓ's argument becomes cunning. Since he repeatedly stresses that Arabian space and isolated Bedouin embody the terrestrial apex of speech,[33] al-Jāḥiẓ neatly inspires his urban readers to want to perfect their *bayān*, but axiomatically denies them the opportunity because he has established that their domicile already 'corrupted' their language *ipso facto*.

Al-Bayān's readers are accordingly thrust into an uncomfortable bind, and here al-Jāḥiẓ offers a solution. We recall above that he noted the best Arabic could be heard from 'long hours listening to the clever, eloquent Arabian Bedouin [*al-aᶜrāb al-ᶜuqalāʾ al-fuṣaḥāʾ*], or articulate scholars [*al-ᶜulamāʾ al-bulaghāʾ*]'.[34] The addition of 'scholars' is key, for it means that al-Jāḥiẓ's narrative ultimately results in self-praise. He presents himself and his community of scholars as the only city-dwellers who, through their efforts to study Qur'anic Arabic, can approach the putative linguistic ideal. In locking Arabic away in Arabia, al-Jāḥiẓ left himself the key and projected his scholarly companions as the urbanites' surrogate Bedouin.[35]

Al-Jāḥiẓ thus needs to construct a belief that Bedouin and isolated desert linguistic purity are the standard to which all should strive, and which scholars nearly obtain.[36] The geographical differentiation al-Jāḥiẓ draws between desert and city make tangible the difference between urban and desert language, and it will leave the urbanite craving for Bedouin teachers. But since the desert in al-Jāḥiẓ's day was virtually inaccessible given the dramatic decline in Arabian security shortly before he wrote *al-Bayān*,[37] the Bedouin 'experts' were out of reach, nomadic raiders were too dangerous to rationally contemplate visiting for grammatical pursuits, and so city-dwellers were left with little option but to employ al-Jāḥiẓ for the necessary instruction. *Al-Bayān*'s discourse affirms the value of al-Jāḥiẓ's (and his colleagues') expertise as they monopolise the terrestrial share of eloquence.

Al-Jāḥiẓ's Arabian linguistic reservation seems more imagined than real, and perhaps Arabia's quintessential distance and isolation facilitated its construction as the idealised locus of pure Arabic. Herein we find al-Jāḥiẓ, the mid-third/ninth-century Iraqi urbanite, taking it upon himself to construct an image of historical Arabia which ultimately promotes himself (and not ethnic Arabs) as the intermediary for urban Iraqis to approach proper *bayān* and *ᶜilm*. The political eclipse of Iraqi Arab groups and Arabia's isolation seem to facilitate the discourse too – as ethnic Arabs were retreating from claiming their tribal lineages, al-Jāḥiẓ was left with increasing power to define Arabness with less risk of dissent. The grammarians' inroads into power relations have attracted some consideration,[38] but the ways in which al-Jāḥiẓ and his contemporaries developed new archetypes for Arabness remain under-examined and need to be brought into dialogue with notions of the wider notions of Arabness in their contemporary society. This now becomes our task.

Arabians and Arabic between the Second/Eighth and Fourth/Tenth Centuries

Al-Jāḥiẓ's discourse may seem entirely typical of the Arabic grammatical tradition, and Western scholarship since the nineteenth century tends to treat Arabian Bedouin dialects as the most 'authentic' Arabic too,[39] but something seems amiss. We have seen that stereotyping Arabs as primordial Bedouin lacks empirical basis: the Qur'an's *ᶜarabī* was not a Bedouin vernacular, and the first evidential stirrings of Arab communal consciousness emerged from the towns of early Islam, not inner Arabian deserts. Closer analysis of the development of Arabic philology will reveal that al-Jāḥiẓ's apparent orthodoxy was in fact part of a radical third/ninth-century departure from earlier philological thought by which grammarians invented the 'eloquent Bedouin' paradigm.

In proposing that philologists helped remodel Arab ethnic identity, I borrow from recent studies that stress the importance of situating classical Arabic philology within the broader Arabic 'discourse community',[40] but we must be careful when reconstructing the members and aims of that 'discourse community' lest we impose one essentialised purpose of language standardisation across all grammatical writing, and thereby homogenise the first four centuries of Islam into one contiguous exercise of Arab identity formation.[41] We have seen that cultural/political contexts changed significantly during early Islam, and the dynamic of the inter-ethnic strife in the first centuries of Islam was not operative when the most complete grammars were written after the mid-third/ninth century. Moreover, the lexicons surveyed in Chapter 4(I) revealed that language had been a touchstone of Arabness, but from the fourth/tenth century genealogy became paramount, and assumptions that fourth/tenth- and fifth/eleventh-century Arabic speakers thought of themselves as members of one Arab ethnos thus seem quite inaccurate.[42] Definitions of Arabness shifted away from identifying Arabic speakers as 'the Arabs' in favour of delineating the identity via those born with pure Arab blood. Rodinson proposed that later Arab ethnic unity was not conceptualised around the shared Arabic language until the sixteenth century,[43] and so we ought to disengage from axiomatically identifying all Arabic speakers as members of one ethnos. When we differentiate the sources chronologically without anachronistic interpolations, we can uncover paradigmatic shifts in the construction of Arabness and the Arabic language between the second/eighth and fourth/tenth centuries.

Some scholars of Arabic philology have already queried the Bedouin qua pure Arabic speaker paradigm: Bohas, Guillaume and Kouloughli refer to the role of the Bedouin as an 'afterthought' in philological works pre-dating the late third/ninth century,[44] and Versteegh suggests that the early Bedouin may have preserved some aspects of an ancient Arabic koine, but he questions the extent to which Bedouin vernaculars corresponded to the rules of the early urbanite grammarians, and whether early grammarians even valued Bedouin vernacular at all when codifying grammatical rules.[45] Fresh review of the relationships between Arabic language, Arab identity and Bedouin from the earliest extant grammatical texts, through al-Jāḥiẓ, and into the fourth/tenth century shall link them with the sociopolitical processes traced in the last chapter and discern how and why the 'eloquent Bedouin' archetype eventually dominated conceptions of Arab identity.

From Sībawayh (d. 180/796) to al-Akhfash (d. 215/830)

The earliest extant Arabic grammar, Sībawayh's *al-Kitāb*, intriguingly makes only sparse mention of inner Arabian Bedouin. In its first three volumes (that is, more than two-thirds of the work), I found only four references to nomadic Arabians (*a*^{c}*rāb*) as sources of grammar,[46] and Sībawayh expresses misgivings about one of them, describing the example of Bedouin speech cited by his contemporary Basran grammarian colleague, Yūnus ibn Ḥabīb (d. 182/798) as 'queer [*ba*ᶜ*īd*], the Arabs do not speak like that, nor do many [*nās kathīr*] use it'.[47] In another instance, Sībawayh specifies a particular Bedouin informant as 'one of the most correct-speaking people' (*min afṣaḥ al-nās*),[48] implying that Sībawayh (unlike al-Jāḥiẓ sixty years later) did not operate under a blanket assumption that all Bedouin intrinsically embodied correct-Arabic and identified some as more right-speaking than others. It is also suggested that the Bedouin to whom Sībawayh refers were not from inner Arabia, but instead lived near al-Baṣra (and perhaps specifically those who frequented the market Mirbad).[49]

Modern interpretations of Sībawayh's system of grammar thus encounter difficulties reconciling the lack of his citation of *a*ᶜ*rāb* Bedouin with the traditional assumptions that grammarians always esteemed Bedouin Arabic.[50] One could interpret every reference to ᶜ*arabī* in *al-Kitāb* as meaning Bedouin, but then why does Sībawayh specifically mention *a*ᶜ*rāb* in some cases, and why does Sībawayh also expressly state that *a*ᶜ*rāb* connote a separate group from ᶜ*arab*?[51] Melding Arab and Bedouin identity into one conceptual category blurs distinctions that were very important for early Muslim cultural producers, and furthermore, modern scholars also concede that Sībawayh 'relied far more on indirect evidence' than personal interaction with the Bedouin, and that 'not everything was accepted merely because it came from a Bedouin Arab'.[52] Hence the problem with interpreting the status of Bedouin in *al-Kitāb* may be one we have imposed upon ourselves. Sībawayh may not have felt the need to refer to Bedouin as the arbiters of Arabic at all, and further analysis of *al-Kitāb* without the prejudice of later grammatical paradigms can better grasp Sībawayh's own conception of the language he sought to codify.

If the language detailed in *al-Kitāb* is not Bedouin Arabic, then what is it? The text lacks an introduction expressing Sībawayh's precise aims: he clearly intended to codify Arabic grammar, but in stark contrast to later grammatical texts where philologists ubiquitously ground their arguments in the linguistic ideal of *kalām al-*ᶜ*arab* (the speech of the Arabs), Sībawayh only sparingly invokes the term *kalām al-*ᶜ*arab*. In my review of the first two volumes of *al-Kitāb* (some 840 pages and approximately 40 per cent of the work), I found only eighteen references to *kalām al-*ᶜ*arab*.[53] The infrequency calls for scrutiny – in what context does Sībawayh invoke the term and how does it relate to his codification of Arabic grammar? Of the eighteen citations, Sībawayh uses *kalām al-ᶜarab* ten times as quantitative measure: 'this is frequent/more frequent (*kathīr*) in *kalām al-ᶜarab*',[54] or 'this is infrequent/less frequent (*qalīl/aqall*)'.[55] Only in four cases does he cite *kalām al-ᶜarab* as the basis for a strict grammatical rule,[56] in another case a construction is 'known (*maᶜrūf*) in *kalām al-ᶜarab*' (implying acceptability, not absolute correctness),[57] and in another, he describes a construction as 'permissible (*jawāz*) in *kalām al-ᶜarab*, but it is weak'[58] – Sībawayh, the non-Arab, asserts his right to judge grammatical correctness outside of merely copying what is heard from Arabs. Elsewhere he explains:

> You have the choice to make [the word] *Zayd* [in the exceptive grammatical construction] *badal* or an adjective (*ṣifa*) [and in a specific case] it can only be an adjective; this has a correspondence (*naẓīr*) with the *kalām al-ᶜarab* . . .[59]

The notion of 'correspondence' suggests that the *kalām al-ᶜarab* exists parallel to and resembles what Sībawayh predominantly refers to as 'your speech'.[60] Another citation of *kalām al-ᶜarab* makes this more explicit: 'the Arabs do not speak like this, the grammarians only derived the rule from analogy . . . it is ugly amongst the Arabs . . . and the Arabs say [*x*] – this is the *kalām al-ᶜarab*'.[61] Sībawayh does not strongly reproach grammarians for breaches of *kalām al-ᶜarab*, however, and his sparse reference to *kalām al-ᶜarab* and his particular use of it suggests that it is a reference of permissibility, not a rigid model. If a given construction is frequent in *kalām al-ᶜarab*, then it is clearly worthy of repetition, but in turn, 'infrequent'/*qalīl* constructions are surely not recommended for imitation. Quite why the 'Speech of the Arabs' is not firmly the centre stage in *al-Kitāb* can be ascertained via closer consideration of his use of the words *ᶜarab* and *ᶜarabī*.

Sībawayh makes frequent reference to grammatical constructions being 'good Arabic' (*ᶜarabī jayyid*)[62] or just 'Arabic' (*ᶜarabī*),[63] whereby *ᶜarabī* is a byword for 'correct', or 'permissible'. The notion of permissibility engenders impressions of Arabic as something more fluid than a single language of the Arab people. Sometimes Sībawayh deems an Arabic expression 'pure' (*maḥḍ*)[64] or 'mellifluous' (*muṭṭarad*)[65] which are eminently good, but the relative infrequency of these adjectives in the voluminous *al-Kitāb* indicates that 'Arabs' are marshalled as guides to the language, but not the only source of Sībawayh's rules. Versteegh makes a similar observation in noting that the language of 'Arabs' cited in *al-Kitāb* predominantly relates to poetry, and that the actual spoken vernacular was less important,[66] that is, the Arabs' language was not the ultimate source for the rules of all spoken language, but rather, only evidence for specific points of grammar encountered in poetry.

Further consideration reveals that Sībawayh primarily cites 'Arabs' as exceptions to overarching grammatical rules. Sībawayh usually accepts these as vernacular oddities ascribed to *baᶜḍ al-ᶜarab* ('one Arab'):[67] he does not deny that these Arabs speak correct Arabic, but as they are cited in a singular fashion, he renders them unique specimens within a wider linguistic system. His common reference to 'a trustworthy Arabic speaker',[68] also implies that not all Arabic speakers inherently embody correct Arabic. A reference to one 'whose Arabic pleases',[69] indicates that power remains with Sībawayh's readership to appraise the language. Sībawayh neither depicts 'Arabs' as unquestionable authorities for 'correct Arabic', nor envisions the language he codifies as the sole property of ethnic Arabs.

If 'Arabs' are not *al-Kitāb*'s primary source, then what is Sībawayh's criterion of correctness? It appears that he actually considers his own readers the primary creators of language. Most sections of *al-Kitāb* contain, at their outset, the expression 'you say *x*', and/or 'you say *x* because you intend/mean *y*',[70] that is, Sībawayh seeks to explore the logic behind how his readers speak, and he engages in an intellectual exercise to codify the proper workings of that language, or, as it has been proposed, its ethical rules.[71] The second-person singular could be impersonal, translatable as 'one says', but the personal 'you' seems to better capture Sībawayh's intention. Firstly, book composition at that time was transitioning from oral lecture to written text:[72] books were still dialogical, written in a direct, personal style of address between a teacher and his audience, which, in Sībawayh's case, was a conversation between teacher and his Arabic-speaking students. Secondly, the statements following Sībawayh's 'you' formula are usually simple, non-controversial constructions which seem reflective of the standard idiom of his audience. And thirdly, Sībawayh adduces no other consistent standard for 'correct' language. The ways 'Arabs' speak are interspersed throughout, especially where they do not correspond to regular speech patterns, but *al-Kitāb* is not a cultural defence of Arabs. It offers no expressions of innate Arab (and certainly not Bedouin) eloquence, nor does it intimate Arab superiority via their linguistic excellence. This leads to the conclusion that Sībawayh accepts that his readership constitute members of an Arabic speech community and the ways he observes that they convert their ideas into speech are the roots of his grammatical rules which he analyses with reference to 'trustworthy Arabs' and their poetry in particular.

By according his reader, 'you', such a prominent role, Sībawayh accords with the definition of *ᶜarabī* in *al-ᶜAyn* composed in the same period. We recall from Chapter 4(I) that *al-ᶜAyn* conceptualised Arabs as a speech community and signalled out the 'Arab Arabs' (*al-ᶜarab al-ᶜāriba*) as the 'pure of them' (*al-ṣarīḥ minhum*).[73] It could be argued therefore that, at the close of the second/eighth century, some discourses portrayed Arabs as a broad speech community of varied dialects (akin also to the Qur'an's references to the indefinite *ᶜarabī*). As grammarians codified the rules, certain Arabs, especially those who transmitted poetry from the past, emerged as embodying the purest form of the language presumably on account of their proximity to the period of the Qur'an's revelation,[74] but while interest in old poetry reveals a special appeal of old Arabic, the absence of a homogeneous notion of *kalām al-ᶜarab* as the property of ancient Arabs and the 'gold standard' of correct Arabic (*al-fuṣḥā*) found in later grammatical texts, reveals that in Sībawayh's grammatical system, the differences between past Arabic and the Arabic of his day did not render his contemporaries' Arabic inauthentic. In emphasising his own speech community's autonomy to create 'correct speech', there is no role for the Bedouin to emerge as a cohesive group of 'superior Arabic speakers', and, as Versteegh hinted, the notion of their linguistic purity is merely a topos that post-dates Sībawayh's *al-Kitāb*.[75] The codification of language as an exercise in national identity creation, as was the case in early modern Europe, is not applicable to Sībawayh since he did not cast language rules as the basis of an ethnic Arab 'imagined community'.[76]

Written a generation after Sībawayh, the second earliest extant grammatical text, al-Akhfash's (d. 215/830) *Maᶜānī al-Qurʾān*, differs from *al-Kitāb* as it is a commentary on the correct ways to read the Qur'an and an exposition on its more complicated grammatical structures. But while it is not a comprehensive grammar of the Arabic language, its approach to the Arabic language and the status it accords Arabs have salient similarities with *al-Kitāb*. When read together, both texts contrast the conceptualisations of Arabic in later classical philology.

Akin to *al-Kitāb*, the Bedouin *aʿrāb* are conspicuous in *Maʿānī al-Qurʾān* for their absence. Across the 593 pages of the modern edition, I only identified three express citations of *aʿrāb*,[77] and in two, the *aʿrābī* cited is described as 'eloquent/correct' (*faṣīḥ*),[78] again suggesting that early third/ninth-century readership did not axiomatically equate all *aʿrāb* with paragons of eloquence, and needed assurance of the particular *aʿrābī*'s suitability as a source. Two of the three instances also describe the manner in which a Bedouin recited poetry,[79] supportive of Versteegh's proposal that the early grammarians were not so interested in the Bedouin vernacular as they were in a poetic koine.[80] Most interestingly, al-Akhfash cites each Bedouin anecdote with *isnād*. Elsewhere, al-Akhfash eschews *isnād*, and hence reveals that he did not encounter the Bedouin himself. Arabia was accessible during al-Akhfash's lifetime – he lived during the height of the centrally planned development of the *Darb Zubayda* between Iraq and Mecca – so his infrequent reference to Bedouin, and the fact that each Bedouin anecdote is related second-hand, suggests that the early generations of grammarians did not make concerted efforts to explore inner Arabia's vernacular.

Compared with *al-Kitāb*, al-Akhfash's *Maʿānī al-Qurʾān* makes more frequent reference to the *kalām al-ʿarab*, but when compared with later grammatical texts, al-Akhfash is nonetheless more akin to Sībawayh. He refers to *kalām al-ʿarab* relatively sparingly,[81] and he invokes it in the same manner as Sībawayh – usually accompanied by old poetry connected to complex points of grammar.[82] His *kalām al-ʿarab* primarily concerns a poetic koine, as opposed to Bedouin or the exclusively 'pure'/'correct' vernacular of the Arab 'nation'. Since al-Akhfash's text is specifically focused on studying the ritual *ʿarabī* of the Qur'an (unlike Sībawayh's general grammar), the increased reference to *kalām al-ʿarab* insinuate early ritual-poetic connotations.

Al-Akhfash also cites 'Arabs' more frequently than Sībawayh,[83] but this does not engender a more certain notion of a national Arab eloquence because al-Akhfash's many mentions of 'Arab' concern grammatical differences, not linguistic unity. Al-Akhfash usually cites Arabs in formulations such as 'one of the Arabs vowels [a given word] in *x* manner [differing from 'usual' usage]',[84] or 'some Arabs say/one Arab says [*x*]'[85] – again where they differ from 'usual' readings; or 'one of the Arabs/some of the Arabs elide [a given letter/vowel – whereas most readers do not]'.[86] These expressions will be familiar to readers of Sībawayh where 'one of the Arabs' is the grammatical outlier. Hence, while al-Akhfash cites Arabs quantitatively more than Sībawayh, in qualitative terms, both authors treat them similarly. Except in a very limited number of circumstances, the language al-Akhfash conceptualises as spoken by 'the Arabs' is divisive and indicative of variety. As such, al-Akhfash is not codifying, but observing fluidity.

The reader of al-Akhfash's *Maᶜānī al-Qurᵓān* will apprehend, therefore, that the text does not impose rules about Arabic, but instead reveals the variety of Arabics. This should not be surprising, since al-Akhfash's aim is to justify the multiple manners in which words in the Qur'an are read, and so allusion to a varied, unsystematic way Arabs speak (as evidenced in old poetry) enables him to accept Qur'an readings that disagree with common speech practice. Again like Sībawayh, al-Akhfash does not imply all old poetic grammar should be axiomatically embraced, as he calls some readings 'ugly'/ *qabīḥ*,[87] and even notes that 'some Arabs speak this way, but it is ugly and infrequent'.[88] In sum, al-Akhfash distinguishes his group of grammarians/ Qur'an readers and outlying 'Arabs' who provide different readings, but this cannot be interpreted as a rigid separation of 'correct' Arab and 'incorrect' non-Arab, but rather an encyclopedia aimed to explain the full panoply of Qur'anic readings.

In other cases, al-Akhfash describes how 'Arabs' and 'Qur'an Readers' (*al-qurrāᵓ*) share common notions of correctness,[89] and he frequently mentions the second-person 'you' pronoun, again akin to Sībawayh. Al-Akhfash compares 'your language' (that is, his readers') with that of the Arabs, and notes some similarities,[90] as well as differences.[91] In refraining from upbraiding his readers where their readings do not conform to *kalām al-ᶜarab* (or some versions of Arab speech), al-Akhfash, like Sībawayh, allows his readers autonomy over their communication, evidencing a paradigm that permits them to create language depending on what *they* want to say.[92]

In the generation preceding al-Jāḥiẓ, therefore, two major grammatical texts both depict Arabic as a set of contemporary speech rules with awareness that some Arabs follow different rules which are either *ḥasan*/good models correctness, or *qabīḥ*/ugly phrases to be avoided. The grammarians reserve a right to judge what is laudable and what is ugly; Qur'anic Arabic and most old Arabic poetry is good, but there is no indication that there is one definitive version of Arabic – even for reading/reciting the Qur'an. The grammarians neither undertake a historical reconstruction of an ancient Arabic language nor create an Arab imagined community around a systematised grammar. The absence of express reverence for Bedouin dialects also reveals that neither grammarian required his readers to correct their own speech to bring it into conformity with Bedouin *kalām*. Ethnic 'Arabs', at the dawn of the third/ninth century therefore do not monopolise Arabic, and given the rate of assimilation and spread of Arabic as the language of everyday transactions by the outset of the second/eighth century, the grammarians' discourse is logical. Long gone were the conditions of the first/seventh century when the conquering elites' Arabic-like dialects differentiated them from the conquered populations and constituted a means for elites to express their distinctiveness. By the second/eighth century the language had become the vernacular of Conqueror and conquered alike, and so it can be expected to have lost ethnic connections to define Arab identity which, as demonstrated in Chapter 4, was at that time also shifting away from language as the touchstone of Arabness in favour of closed-ended genealogical models that expressly operated to exclude Arabic speakers from the ambit of *al-ᶜarab*.

Arabians and Arabic at the Beginning of the Fourth/Tenth Century

Al-Jāḥiẓ's privileging of Arabia's linguistic superiority over urban Iraq accordingly marks a departure from earlier texts. Analysis of philological writing after the mid-third/ninth century in turn evidences the entrenchment of al-Jāḥiẓ's discourse, indicating that classical philology did enter a new phase, as evidenced in Ibn al-Sarrāj's (d. 316/928–9) *al-Uṣūl fi-l-naḥw*, a lengthy grammatical treatise written two generations after al-Jāḥiẓ's *al-Bayān*.

Ibn al-Sarrāj reconfigures the second/eighth-century grammarians' model of language based on the formula 'you say *x* because you want to express *y*' with a statement at the outset of his text: '*al-naḥw* [grammar] specifically refers to a speaker's copying of the *kalām al-ᶜarab*, this is a science which earlier scholars derived from close reading of the *kalām al-ᶜarab*'.[93]

He continues, 'my aim in this book is to mention the grammatical causes (*ᶜilla*) which, if you pursue them, will lead you to [the Arabs'] speech'.[94] Hence, while Ibn al-Sarrāj retains Sībawayh's proverbial 'you' to illustrate how his readers speak, in crucial distinction to earlier texts, the notion of the speaker's will is absent. Ibn al-Sarrāj's introduction makes it clear that people do not speak Arabic in correspondence to their wishes, but rather they speak in imitation of the *kalām al-ᶜarab*. Ibn al-Sarrāj also reorients the 'ugly' or 'irregular' (*shādhdh*) language away from Sībawayh's identification of them as attested Arabic ways of speaking which do not correspond to Sībawayh's usual grammatical rules. For Ibn al-Sarrāj, such ethical/aesthetic terms connote speech which does not correspond to the way in which 'they [the Arabs] use a word'.[95] He places the onus on his readers to memorise how the Arabs spoke,[96] and so subordinates grammar to the essentially monolithic way in which he records *historical* Arabic.

In distinction to earlier notions of Arabic's fluidity and Sībawayh's comments on the relative aesthetic merits of different grammatical constructions, Ibn al-Sarrāj leaves no room to imagine that 'Arabs' speak incorrectly. The structure of Ibn al-Sarrāj's *al-Uṣūl* reveals a consistent pattern to embed this discourse. He begins a grammatical topic by detailing the way in which his readers speak, using the 'you' similar to Sībawayh, but he denies his readers the right to forge rules themselves, and instead codifies a set of logically derived principles checked against the *kalām al-ᶜarab*. Difficulties and exceptions to the rules are also supplied by the *kalām al-ᶜarab*, and hence the contemporary speaker of Arabic is demoted from speech producer to rule follower. Language cannot be formulated to accord with logic or ethics of the grammarians, Ibn al-Sarrāj merely allows grammarians the right to *qiyās* (analogy) and posits *kalām al-ᶜarab* as the arbiter.[97]

Absent too are the hints of Arabic heterogeneity: Ibn al-Sarrāj readily accepts that different tribes had different dialects, but he renders all as constituent parts of *kalām al-ᶜarab*. He consolidates the language into a comprehensive and rationally constructed edifice and a relic of the past: this enables the Arabic language to be observed as a foreign object, not a living, evolving organism. Shifting from messy, multi-faceted present speech discourse to an ossified statuesque monument from the past gives Ibn al-Sarrāj's Arabic grammar an elegant simplicity and definiteness, which in turn enables a new conception of a historical ethnic Arab as the representative of *the* perfect language. Ibn Al-Sarrāj transforms Arabs from partners in a present living language to architects of a monolithic past Arabic.

The model of *al-Uṣūl fi-l-naḥw* has prompted scholars to identity it as one of the first codifications of Arabic grammar in terms of 'correct principles' (*uṣūl*) backed by a rational framework (*ᶜilal*).[98] It has also been noted that Ibn al-Sarrāj conceptualises grammar as the language of the Bedouin Arabs, he strives to teach his readers to speak like them, and through study of the old dialects, he reveals this language to his readers.[99] These changes extend beyond the boundaries of philology, since they impinge on the depiction of Arabness itself. In presenting *kalām al-ᶜarab* as a certain, tangible relic, Ibn al-Sarrāj needs history more than any previous grammarian hitherto in order to present a perfect model of the past in which the Arabs can be presented as homogeneous.

Ibn al-Sarrāj thus required a very different Arab past than first/seventh-century narrators of *ayyām al-ᶜarab* for whom divisive conflict was a major theme. Ibn al-Sarrāj's gravitation towards Bedouin is also noteworthy, for it switches discourse about the Arab past from the progress of kingdoms and wars to a cyclical, unchanging Bedouin ideal of language preservation across time. Ibn al-Sarrāj intensifies al-Jāḥiẓ's paradigm written fifty years earlier, and champions what, in comparison to earlier grammatical texts, is a novel discourse about the absolute correctness of historical Arabic speech that homogenises and elevates the status of *kalām al-ᶜarab*, strips language autonomy from contemporary readers, and compels them to listen to and mimic an idealised language speaking to them from a distant desert in a distant past.

The new perceptions about Bedouin Arabia are also evidenced in a statement of Ibn al-Sarrāj's near contemporary Abū Naṣr al-Fārābī (d. 339/950) who, in positing that the most correct Arabic is that which is least corrupted by other linguistic influence, ventured a framework degrading Syrian and Iraqi vernaculars on account of their intermixing with non-Arabs. Similarly, he degraded the tribal dialects of ᶜAbd al-Qays for their residence near the Persians in Bahrain, and Yemenis too on account of their contact with Ethiopia. Interestingly, even the town-dwellers of the Ḥijāz (*ḥāḍirat al-Ḥijāz*) fell short of al-Fārābī's standard, though he did not specify the cause of their impurity, remarking only that their Arabic was mixed with 'members of foreign nations' (*ghayrihim min al-umam*).[100] His vague comment against the Ḥijāzīs is instructive: Ḥijāzī 'urban' Arabic was esteemed in Sībawayh's system,[101] yet al-Fārābī appears set on devaluing it, even without specific cause. To understand Ḥijāzī Arabic's downfall in al-Fārābī's opinion, we need look no further than his assertion that the best Arabic was Najdī, that spoken by central Arabian Bedouin. When contextualising al-Fārābī's preference, we will observe that he lived at the height of the Qarāmiṭa threat when Najd was completely out of bounds for urban Muslims and when the Hajj itself was either outright cancelled or attempted only at extreme risk. Al-Fārābī's seemingly rational argument is an elaborate reasoning to prove that the ideal Arabic is Bedouin, and by locating this Arabic in an inaccessible void, his ideal is in fact wholly idealised. The shifting goalposts of Arabic linguistic 'perfection' from Sībawayh's system to al-Fārābī's desertscape are palpable, and the germ of prevalent modern stereotypes about idealised Bedouin vernacular seem emergent from fourth/tenth-century urbanite philologists' imaginations. Texts from the later fourth/tenth century develop the discourse to its logical conclusion.

Arabians and Arabic at the Close of the Fourth/Tenth Century

The reverence for idealised Arabian Arabic projected into an ancient past manifests with unprecedented clarity a generation after Ibn al-Sarrāj and al-Farābī in Ibn Fāris' (d. 395/1004) *al-Ṣāḥibī fī fiqh al-lugha*. Ibn Fāris raises Arabic to the status of God-given language (*tawqīf*),[102] he argues that the best speakers of Arabic are the prophets,[103] and, by extension, insinuates that the Arabs of Muhammad's day existed on an exalted status somewhere between humans and prophethood. Ibn Fāris adopts the logic of al-Jāḥiẓ's *al-Bayān* in basing his praise of Arabic on the expressiveness of Qur'anic Arabic, but he chooses starker words: 'inasmuch as God bestowed on the Arabic language its special clarity, it was made known that all other languages lack its clarity and fall short of it'.[104]

Modern scholars have commented on the fourth/tenth-century debates around Arabic's *tawqīf* nature as part of the theological proofs of the Qur'an's divine/pseudo-divine nature,[105] and references to the inferiority of Persian in Ibn Fāris' text[106] seem to correspond to a pro-Arab/Islam (that is, anti-*shuᶜūbī*) discourse, but a pro-Arab/Islam agenda is unlikely to be Ibn Fāris' goal in *al-Ṣāḥibī*. The Qur'an's divinity and the ethnic tension between Arab and Persian are issues that would have interested scholars since the second/eighth century if not earlier, hence we need to consider why Ibn Fāris, a later fourth/tenth-century author, would engage with these issues in a fashion not evidenced so starkly before. Reading *al-Ṣāḥibī* in the context of the development of Arabic philology uncovers new explanations.

Just as Ibn Fāris develops al-Jāḥiẓ's argument about Arabic's quality into a simplified, direct praise of the language and disparagement of other languages, Ibn Fāris also intensifies the fixedness of the grammatical framework of Ibn al-Sarrāj. We noted Ibn al-Sarrāj's promulgation of a rational grammatical system, borrowing the jurisprudential term 'legal principles' (*uṣūl*) as the title of his treatise in order to portray Arabic as more coherent and historically certain than second/eighth-century grammarians did.[107] Ibn Fāris borrows further from jurisprudence, explaining that the Arabic language was the '*sunan* [customs, hence law][108] of the Arabs in their speech', and their Arabic grammar has fundamental principles, the *uṣūl*, and 'branches' (*furū*ᶜ – another jurisprudential term) such as its rare vocabulary.[109] The technical terminology enables Ibn Fāris to entitle his work the *Jurisprudence (*fiqh*) of Language* and to elevate Arabic to the rank of *ᶜilm* – a formal science – which he dubs the 'science of the Arabs'.[110] The 'scientific' approach to language prompts Ibn Fāris to imagine ancient Arabs in a new fashion, inasmuch as third/ninth-century texts such as al-Jāḥiẓ's *al-Bayān* and Ibn Qutayba *Faḍl al-ᶜarab* refrain from depicting pre-Islamic Arabs as technical language specialists. Ibn Qutayba enumerates the 'Arab sciences' (*ᶜulūm*), including horsemanship, astrology, reading signs in nature, poetry and oratory, and while the expressiveness and breadth of Arabic vocabulary is cited as evidence of the Arabs' excellence,[111] the language itself is not counted as one of their 'sciences'. Similarly, al-Jāḥiẓ argued that the expressiveness of the Arabic language enabled Arabs to develop authoritative and worthwhile knowledge (*ᶜilm*),[112] but al-Jāḥiẓ stopped short of declaring the Arabic language to be a science in its own right, and, as noted at the outset of this chapter, his praise focused on the Bedouin *aᶜrāb*, not all Arabs.

The third/ninth-century authors' refraining from classifying Arabic as a science (*ᶜilm*) seems attributable to the fact that grammarians had not yet fully codified the language in one definite form of *al-ᶜarabiyya*, nor specifically fixed it onto their historical notion of the Arab ethnos. Since early grammarians conceptualised Arabic as a living idiom shared between Abbasid Iraqis and pre-Islamic Arabians, they did not treat it as a relic of an Arab past.[113] Ibn al-Sarrāj's detailed codification of Arabic, however, facilitated new conceptualisation of Arabic as a cohesive and specifically Arab language which Ibn Fāris could thus develop into a more coherent Arab science than his third/ninth-century forebears could have imagined.

Ibn Fāris also parries the risks of fragmentation of his perfect monolithic model of *kalām al-ᶜarab* posed by the varied Arabian dialects by whitewashing them. He admits that different dialects existed, and that Arabian groups had chastised each other on account of dialectical differences,[114] but he denies that regional shibboleths affected the unity of Arab lineage,[115] and he deposits dialectical differences into a schema of three categories which transforms exceptions into regularities and renders robust unity for *kalām al-ᶜarab*.[116] To a degree unlike his predecessors, Ibn Fāris can articulate a comprehensive theoretical framework in which the Arabic language emerges as a perfect object of study, created in the past via revelation to prophets and perpetuated by generic, homogeneously eloquent Arabs.[117] By arguing that the original speakers of Arabic treated this language as their *ᶜilm*, he legitimises his own scholarly study of Arabic, and expressly denies Muslim-era philologists (such as himself and his peers) the status of intellectual trailblazers or inventors of language rules: Ibn Fāris notes they merely revived the Arabs' primordial Arabic science.[118]

By treating the Arabic language as more than a mere terrestrial vernacular, and declaring that no new rules of grammar can be invented by philologists,[119] Ibn Fāris in fact does himself a tremendous service of which al-Jāḥiẓ would have been proud. Ibn Fāris notes that the Arabic language is too vast for any human to know completely,[120] but at the same time, its status as the world's most expressive language and the idiom of the Qur'an make it eminently, and even urgently, learnable. In considering then, how one can learn such a difficult yet crucial language, Ibn Fāris enumerates three options: (1) being raised by Arab parents, (2) 'inspiration' (*talqīn*), that is, the manner in which God inspired the prophet Ishmael to learn Arabic, or (3) listening to 'trustworthy, honest narrators'.[121] Of the three options, neither *talqīn* nor innate Arabness have much practical value: *talqīn* appears only to have been available to prophets, and acquiring Arabic from birth is unlikely to have applied to many readers of *al-Ṣāḥibī* since, by its late fourth/tenth-century date, very few urban Muslims had purely Arab parents, Arabness was a relic of the impenetrable deserts of long cut-off Arabia, and few Iraqis even identified themselves as 'Arabs'.[122] As for the third, remaining option to learn Arabic – narration, Ibn Fāris laments that much of the Arabic language has been lost, and that only scattered reports from the past remain to learn the depths of the language.[123] In the final analysis, therefore, Ibn Fāris leaves us no option but to read the rest of his book to learn Arabic properly. He forces us to concede that only scholars like himself can teach us Arabic, and since Arabic is so tidily codified, the rules taught to us by the philologists appear faithful reproductions of the 'real' *kalām al-ᶜarab*, and since different dialects no longer affect the unity of Arabness, anything we learn from the past builds our knowledge of Arabic. Scholars therefore have the ultimate power to reveal Arabic to us. Arabic teachers ever since have been revealing this knowledge and been remunerated by grateful students for the opportunity.

Ibn Fāris' model was embraced by contemporary philologists too: Ibn Jinnī's (d. 392/1002) *al-Khaṣāʾiṣ*, a more voluminous study of Arabic, opens with a long discourse describing how 'real Arabs' possess 'correct Arabic' by nature, not by learning, a necessary construction to ensure that any reports from Arabs can be axiomatically assumed as correct Arabic. Arabs, by their nature (according to Ibn Jinnī) cannot make grave grammatical mistakes.[124] Like Ibn Fāris, Ibn Jinnī notes that Bedouin are the speakers of true Arabic, and he disparages 'urbanites' (*baladiyyūn*) for their inability to possess the same innate ability for correct Arabic.[125] Whilst this resembles both al-Jāḥiẓ and al-Fārābī, Ibn Jinnī pursues the analysis of Bedouin Arabic further, arguing that only Bedouin of the past exemplified correct Arabic, since his contemporary Bedouin had lost their purity and no longer counted as valid informants.[126] Ibn Jinnī thus permanently locks Arabic away – confined into the vast and impenetrable desert, and even further buried in a bygone historical time – and so he emphatically echoes Ibn Fāris: one can only learn Arabic from trustworthy teachers (evidently, himself included).[127]

Arabic and Arabians: Conclusions

Reading the two centuries of grammatical writing between Sībawayh and Ibn Jinnī diachronically unfurls a progressive reconceptualisation of Arabic and the role of Bedouin within Arabic's linguistic construct. Ideas of the homogeneity of *kalām al-ᶜarab*, the definiteness of *al-ᶜarabiyya*, the association of Bedouin with innate eloquence and the situating of the best Arabic in a distant desert past emerged gradually and were accentuated precisely following Arabia's security collapse when the region became virtually inaccessible. Whereas Sībawayh and al-Akhfash afforded ethnic Arabs an undoubted high status in the system of Arabic grammar, they left the language replete with oddities of speech that enabled their contemporaries to consider themselves, within reason, genuine Arabic speakers. The early grammarians would have had the opportunity to explore Bedouin Arabic thanks to the security of the early Abbasid *Darb Zubayda*, but they did not do so. Ironically, it was only after desert Arabia was detached from the urban Iraqi community that it acquired the status of the unique situs of the Arabic language and Iraqis lost their right to 'native' Arabic fluency. It is pointed that contemporary dictionary definitions of *ᶜarab* traced in Chapter 4(I) underline the shift by expressly removing linguistic mastery of Arabic from the criteria of Arab identity. The lexicographers were keeping up with the development of Arabic philology when compiling their dictionaries.

The temporal congruence of Arabian security collapse and the decline of powerful Arab ethnic groups in Iraq (traced in Chapter 5(IV), and the change in the philological depictions of Arabic are surely not coincidental. The promotion of Arabic as a perfect, self-contained and unchanging language has manifest advantages for philologists who could assert themselves as the sole experts capable of teaching that language, and the circumstances of the mid-third/ninth century conveniently fed this agenda. Arabia's isolation meant that most Iraqis could not easily challenge the philologists' hegemony by venturing into Arabia to experience its language for themselves, and the gradual decline in Arab ethnic groups inside Iraq meant that the philologists would not face opposition to their claims of 'owning' the best Arabic either. Not all philologists after 250 AH clubbed together to monopolise Arabic as a kind of scholarly mafia, nor ought we conclude that urban philologists concocted their models of pure Arabic outright and independent of any input from Bedouin informants or, at least, some preserved memories of earlier Bedouin interactions, but a trend is perceptible, afforded by opportunities to mould Arabic into a field over which philologists controlled expert knowledge. The desert Bedouin provided their ideal proof: Arabia offered a conceptual test tube that shielded *kalām al-ᶜarab* from the idiosyncrasies and uneven evolution inherent in spoken vernaculars and transformed it into a technically perfect archetype and definite object of study, while Bedouin lifestyle that seems so unchanging and primordial from an urban perspective provided an appropriate image of unchanging Arabian life to support the discourse that the Arabic language itself had remained unchanged since time immemorial.

The period of *c.*250–400 AH thus evidences the rise of new spokesmen for the Arabness idea – philologists. They depicted Arabic as a primary basis for an Arab identity in a manner strikingly similar to the language codification enterprises in early modern Europe, but with a crucial distinction. The Iraqis who argued that the *kalām al-ᶜarab* was the 'property' of ethnic Arabs did not claim to be Arabs themselves. Their construction of an Arab identity is therefore the polar opposite of the European nationalist model: the Iraqi philologists elaborated an identity of an 'other' people situated in an environment that was isolated and radically different from their own. I am unaware of any grammarian asserting that his own genealogical Arabness entitled him to better grammatical knowledge; grammarians from at least the time of al-Jāḥiẓ positioned themselves in a position of awe, looking and yearning towards an unattainable linguistic object, and the tension between Arabia's bygone past and the Arabic language's present religious potency embeds a sense or urgency and necessity upon which grammarians capitalised. While they debased themselves before the mightily eloquent paragon of *kalām al-ᶜarab*, the philologists left themselves in a good position to generate a perpetual demand for their knowledge.

By the fourth/tenth century, therefore, philologists had become the most vocal advocates of the Arabness idea and became masters of ancient *Arabica*. This coincides with the shifts in the narration of the pre-Islamic Arabian battles (*ayyām al-ᶜarab*) and genealogy (*nasab*) identified at the outset of this chapter, whereby philologists came to dominate the production of the Arab past. The 'philological turn' in Iraqi study of pre-Islamic Arabia had powerful ramifications for the notion of Arabness itself. Unlike earlier generations of narrators, philologists reconstructed pre-Islamic Arabia as the linguistic preserve of the Arabic language maintained by archetypal, unchanging Bedouin: their discourse demanded a new, coherent archetype of Arabness to support their more monolithic reconstructions of the *kalām al-ᶜarab*. They had no use for a model of Arabian history as a patchwork of different groups split along antagonistic lines as the warring pre-Islamic Arabian tribes appear in earlier narrators of *al-ayyām*. Accordingly, one could expect (and does find) that no chronological history (*tārīkh*) of *al-Jāhiliyya* would be written in the fourth/tenth or fifth/eleventh centuries: despite the enormous cultural interest in the pre-Islamic past, scholars were more concerned to create a cyclical and undifferentiated pre-Islamic Arabness that contained essentially interchangeable details about the past which could be cited as evidence of the one model of 'original Arabness' to match their ideal of the original *kalām al-ᶜarab*.

Analogous shifts are discernable in the narration of the *al-ayyām* pre-Islamic battles. For reasons of space, I only introduce this topic here, but comparison of a third/ninth-century narrative with fourth/tenth-century versions reveals interesting parallels with the *kalām al-ᶜarab* paradigm. For example the famous Dāḥis wa-l-Ghabrāᵓ War between Banū ᶜAbs and Banū ᶜĀmir was narrated in al-Balādhurī's third/ninth-century *Ansāb al-ashrāf* within his genealogy of the super-tribe Qays. Al-Balādhurī tracks the history of Qays through accounts of its prominent members arranged chronologically from its earliest generations into Islamic times, and Dāḥis wa-l-Ghabrāᵓ is narrated in its place on the continuum of hereditary succession.[128] Specific dates are lacking, but its 'time' is fixed by its position in the sequence of generations; time is chronological within a progressive 'biological history'.[129] When the war was narrated in the fourth/tenth-century *al-ᶜIqd* and *Kitāb al-Aghānī*, however, it was cleft from its chronological moorings. *Al-ᶜIqd* lists it in a chapter about all the *ayyām* where a jumble of wars are related out of chronological order,[130] and in *al-Aghānī* it is narrated as part of the biography of one of the war's poetic/hero protagonists, al-Rabīᶜ ibn Ziyād, but it is sandwiched between the biography of the Umayyad-era Medinan singer ᶜAzza al-Maylāᵓ and a short chapter on the poetry and love interest of Yazīd ibn Muᶜāwiya.[131] Removed from its genealogical/chronological context, Dāḥis wa-l-Ghabrāᵓ becomes difficult to qualitatively differentiate from other pre-Islamic Arabian battles: they are all equally exemplarist, consisting of heroism, bravery and fine poetry sung by standardised protagonists. It is tempting to consider the fourth/tenth century's achronological presentation of Dāḥis and al-Ghabrāᵓ as a sort of parataxis whereby the reader is left to make sense of the apparently haphazard arrangement of the battles, and can conclude that pre-Islamic *al-Jāhiliyya* was an era of constant ebb and flow of war and heroes, thereby engendering an impression of a cyclical, noble and virile time where wars only led to more wars, without beginning and without end: timeless *Jāhiliyya* to go with a timeless Arabic language that likewise experienced no development in that great monolith of Bedouin Arabia.

Arabness thus metamorphosed between the second/eighth and fourth/tenth centuries from the expression of an urban/Muslim elite identity in the new towns of the Islamic conquests to a desert/Bedouin 'pre-historical' identity championed by non-ethnic Arab philologists and literary scholars in Iraq who 'othered' Arabic to proclaim their mastery over a deliberately isolated language. This transplanted conceptions of ethnic Arabness from the Iraqi community into the desert, and entailed a dramatic about-face in the relationship between Bedouin and Arab identities and early Muslim imaginations about the Arabs.

II The Transformation of Arabness into Bedouin-ness

The philological agendas promoting Bedouin-ness as the most authentic form of Arabness and the emergence of a discipline of *al-ᶜarabiyya* for Iraqi philologists offered an interested group of scholars long-term practical benefits to fuel a sustained process of rewriting history and reshaping Arab identity to suit the new discourse. But to succeed, the philologists required a novel merger of Arab identity with archaic Bedouinism, and since communities of Arabs (*al-ᶜarab*) had previously been rigorously distinguished from nomads (*al-aᶜrāb*), Arabness and Arab history would need to be reimagined in a completely new fashion. To our good fortune, we possess texts written during the period of this philological turn that enable exploration of the process inaugurating a striking new way of imagining the Arabs.

Arabs and Bedouin Distinguished in Early Islam

The difference between *ᶜarab* (Arab) and *aᶜrāb* (Bedouin) may seem trifling today given the ready association of Arabness and Bedouinism, and from a strictly grammatical perspective, the nearly identical morphology of *ᶜarab* and *aᶜrāb* suggest that *aᶜrāb* is the correct plural form of *ᶜarab*.[132] But in terms of analysing historical identities, morphological possibility is less pertinent than actual perceptions: identity is, at its root, a function of self-perception and changing circumstances, and in the case of *a*ᶜ*rāb*/ᶜ*arab*, the perceptions of early Muslims were adamantly stacked against grammatical theory, rejecting suppositions that Bedouin could be called 'Arabs'.[133]

Chapter 3 explored the Qur'anic disparagement of *a*ᶜ*rāb* Bedouin and the barrier the Qur'an erected between Muhammad's community and *a*ᶜ*rāb* outliers, and following Donner's interpretation of early Islamic-era terminology, the distinction between Believer/*mu*ʾ*min* and Bedouin/*muslim*[134] does appear to enforce some confessional divide between the groups. The division was maintained in the earliest levels of Arabic literature where al-Khalīl ibn Aḥmad's dictionary, *al-*ᶜ*Ayn*, and Sībawayh's grammar, *al-Kitāb*, both depict *a*ᶜ*rāb* as a collective noun not equivalent to the ᶜ*arab* collective.[135] Muqātil's second/eighth-century exegesis gives no indication that the *a*ᶜ*rāb* of the Qur'an shared a common Arabness with the Muslim Medinans either,[136] and early jurists also differentiated Bedouin *a*ᶜ*rāb* from other Muslims in terms of legal rights and obligations. For example, Bedouin (*a*ᶜ*rāb*) were not permitted the same level of *fay*ʾ payments which Emigrants (*muhājirūn*) communities could receive, Bedouin testimony was deemed inadmissible against testimony of a townsman (*ṣāḥib qarya*), and according to one hadith, Bedouin were not required to hold Friday prayers, thus ritually segregating them from the settled Muslim community.[137] From the perspective of second/eighth-century textual indicators, *a*ᶜ*rāb* are consistently relegated to low status and separated from 'Arab'.

The outsider, second-class status accorded to *a*ᶜ*rāb* reflects the social contexts of Islam's first generations. The Qur'an's equation of *a*ᶜ*rāb* with nomad at the dawn of Islam was perpetuated as a practical matter when Muslims settled in their *amṣār* towns, and thus positioned *a*ᶜ*rāb* outside the boundaries of the developing Arab ethnos, both physically (via their desert domicile), and conceptually (as lesser-class groups). Whilst a number of 'Arabs' in the *amṣār* were descended from formerly Bedouin communities, 'former' is the operative word: *a*ᶜ*rāb*'s connotations of nomadism and tenuous Islamic faith were opposed to the basic ingredients of the Arab identity which Muslim urbanites cultivated for themselves. It is also noteworthy that the two key terms of social identification of early Muslims, *muhājirūn* and then ᶜ*arab*, were both axiomatically distinguished from *a*ᶜ*rāb* who were deemed to have no *hijra* and lesser confessional purity. The idea of *a*^c^*rāb* Bedouin as an opposite to *muhājir*/^c^*arab* could have assisted the creation of an urban/Muslim identity for ^c^*arab*, and early Islam thus perpetuated the long Middle Eastern tradition of Assyrians, Hebrews and Sabaic Yemenis of treating *a*^c^*rāb* as quintessential outsiders. Earlier studies have highlighted the many anecdotes in other genres of early Arabic literature that negatively stereotype Bedouin, and the sum bears witness to the rigid barrier excluding *a*^c^*rāb* from the parameters of ^c^*arab*.[138]

Turning Arabs into Bedouin

The lower-class status of *a*^c^*rāb*, the depiction of them as 'outsiders' in early Arabic literature, and the fact that the core of Arab identity as connoting urban, Muslim elite during the first centuries of Islam had nothing in common with the idea of Bedouin life, left little room or reason for Arabic writings to praise Bedouin groups. Against this background, the mid-third/ninth-century philological arguments about Bedouin Arabic purity thus sat uneasily with over a century of urbanite disparagement of Bedouinism, and if the philologists were to succeed in promoting their imagined eloquent-Bedouin ideal amongst urban audiences, they would need to give the Bedouin unprecedentedly positive spin. Most fundamentally, the old barrier between ^c^*arab* and *a*^c^*rāb* would need to be overcome such that Bedouin could appear as legitimately Arab–Arabic speakers. Given the rigorous distinction between Arabs and Bedouin in previous generations, the philologists needed to redefine Arabness with entirely new orientations. From dictionaries to historical writings, we can trace the new fashion of imagining Arab identity through a Bedouinisation of memory which we can link to the context of the Iraqi society in which the new ideas circulated.

Starting with lexicons and the definition of *a*^c^*rāb*, material developments appear in al-Azharī's *Tahdhīb al-lugha*, written almost 200 years after Sībawayh's *al-Kitāb* and contemporary with Ibn Fāris and Ibn Jinnī's arguments that the pre-Islamic Bedouin embodied *the* model of correct Arabic. Al-Azharī maintains the traditional differentiation of ^c^*arab* (village-dwellers or other settled groups) from *a*^c^*rāb* (desert-dwellers),[139] but closer analysis reveals that the barrier is superficial since al-Azharī implies permeability between 'Arab' and 'Bedouin' worlds by adding that an *a*^c^*rābī* Bedouin can join the *ᶜarab* Arabs if he settles in a permanent habitation, and vice versa.[140] He reiterates the relative superiority of the 'Arabs' in a statement that an *ᶜarab* would become upset if one were to call him an *aᶜrābī*, whereas the *aᶜrābī* would be delighted to be counted as an *ᶜarab*(!),[141] which seems a fair reflection of early Muslim society, but the dichotomy has little practical effect given al-Azharī's wider definition of *ᶜarab*. He defines Arabs as those of Arabic lineage (*nasab*) thus merging both *ᶜarab* and *aᶜrāb* into one collective, and in al-Azharī's final analysis, he renders all Arabic-speaking Arabians as Arabs (*ᶜarab*) irrespective of lifestyle.[142]

The conceptual merger of Arab–Bedouin is affirmed in al-Azharī's introduction to *Tahdhīb al-lugha* where he relates a remarkable story of his long imprisonment with Hawāzin tribal nomads following his capture by the Qarāmiṭa when attempting the Hajj. Echoing the spirit of Ibn Fāris and Ibn Jinnī's philological theories of Arabic purity, al-Azharī explains how he rather enjoyed his enslavement, as such close-quarter living enabled him to experience the 'superior' Bedouin Arabic speech first-hand, and he remarks that their Bedouin-ness was the root of their enhanced Arabic abilities. They

> originated from the desert steppe (*al-bādiya*), they followed the rainfall in search of pasture after the springtime, then returned to the permanent waterholes. They pastured sheep and lived off their milk. They spoke with their Bedouin character and their [linguistic] genius as is their wont – in their speech there is almost no mistake or serious error. I stayed with them as a prisoner for a long time . . . and benefited from addressing them and from [hearing] their conversations with each other.[143]

While al-Azharī counts his Hawāzin captors as quintessential Bedouin, he never calls them *aᶜrāb*, and instead always calls them *ᶜarab*.[144] His dictionary's separation of *ᶜarab*/*aᶜrāb* thus seems to reflect a technical replication of earlier dictionaries written when such distinction was maintained across Arabic writing,[145] but in al-Azharī's vernacular usage, he did not maintain the old division, and assimilated Bedouin with *ᶜarab*.

Al-Azharī's contemporary Ibn Fāris exhibits a similar Bedouinisation of the definition of Arabness in his dictionary, *Maqāyīs al-lugha*. Ibn Fāris' exuberant feelings about desert Arabic expressed in his grammar, *al-Ṣāḥibī* considered above crossed over into a novel innovation in the definition of the 'non-Arabic speaker' *a^cjamī* whom Ibn Fāris defines as 'one who does not speak [Arabic] correctly, even if the *a^cjamī* resides in the desert (*bādiya*)'.[146] The clear presumption here is that the desert is the locus of good speech, and Ibn Fāris also augments the definition of *^carab* to include references to the Arabic language's superior expressiveness.[147]

In the following generation, al-Wazīr al-Maghribī's (d. 418/1027) *Adab al-khawāṣṣ*, makes an express departure from earlier philology by asserting that '*a^crāb* is the plural of *^carab*'.[148] This is the first text of which I am aware that morphologically conflates *^carab* and *a^crāb*, and significantly, the text post-dates the 'Bedouin turn' in classical Arabic philology. The point appears to have been debated at this juncture, for his contemporary al-Jawharī's dictionary *al-Ṣiḥāḥ* expressly instructs that *a^crāb* is not the plural of *^carab*.[149] This perhaps explains al-Wazīr al-Maghribī's equivocation, for his *Adab al-khawāṣṣ* ultimately leaves debate open as to the origin of the word *^carab* (he focuses on the notions of clear speech and Qur'anic *^carabī*).[150] But in the succeeding century, the association of *^carab* and *a^crāb* becomes clearer: al-Khaṭīb al-Tabrīzī (d. 502/1108–9) states in a philological discussion of Arab-related words: '*a^cārīb* is the plural of *a^crāb* and *a^crāb* is the plural of *^carab*'. Negotiating the earlier literature which maintained the opposite view, al-Tabrīzī whitewashes it by noting 'people differentiated between the two . . . but they would do this for clarificatory purposes', and he repeats the point that both share the same *nasab* genealogical relation.[151] Likewise, Nashwān al-Ḥimyarī's (d. 573/1178) *Shams al-^culūm* includes *a^crāb* ('people of the steppe/desert' (*ahl al-bādiya*)) within its definition of *^carab*, which is significant since the dictionary is arranged by word pattern and not by root: hence his inclusion of *a^crāb* within his definition of *^carab* implies he considered them parts of one unit.[152] The difference between the words is merely habitat: both *^carab* and *a^crāb* share the same ethnic identity. And two centuries later, the process reached a logical extreme in Ibn Manẓūr's definition of *^carab* in *Lisān al-^carab* which notes an Arab is a person of Arabic lineage 'even if he is not a Bedouin'[153] – a complete reversal of the first dictionaries, now implying, prima facie, that 'Arab' is equal to 'Bedouin'.

Over the course of several centuries, beginning from the fourth/tenth, lexicographers and philologists had succeeded in changing the definition of *^carab* to include *a^crāb* as one of its basic components. From a second/

eighth-century perspective, this is otiose because the elite of the early Muslim community considered themselves *ᶜarab*, distinctly different from low-class *aᶜrāb*, and Bedouin values had no intersection with the marks of status cultivated by the elite in the *amṣār*. But we noted that from the later third/ninth century, Arab groups lost political power, most urban Muslims had ceased identifying with Arab tribes, and hence the stakeholder with the most to lose from a merger of *ᶜarab* with *aᶜrāb* was largely removed from the equation. It is tempting to place the lexicons in this context – philologists could avail themselves of the decline of urban Arab communal power and adopt Arabness for themselves, merge it with Bedouin-ness and wrap it into a new model of primordialism and eloquence. Other literature furnishes further indications of such shifts between the third/ninth and fourth/tenth centuries.

Deconstructing the Bedouin/Arab Distinction from the Mid-third/Ninth Century

Paradigm shifts as substantial as merging Arabness into Bedouin-ness occur gradually: an Iraqi readership accustomed to conceptualising *aᶜrāb* and *ᶜarab* as separate identities cannot suddenly forget tradition and instantly meld them, and instead the re-imagining of Arab identity in a novel Bedouin guise and the deconstruction of the former conceptual barrier between *ᶜarab* and *aᶜrāb* can only have been achieved as a process over a protracted period of time. Diachronic analysis of four important texts about Arab history and culture give insightful indicators as to how urban Iraqi writers developed the new discourse: they are (1) al-Jāḥiẓ's (d. 255/868) *al-Bayān wa-l-tabyīn*, (2) Ibn Qutayba's (d. 276/889) *Faḍl al-ᶜarab wa-l-tanbīh ᶜalā ᶜulūmihā*, an express cultural defence of the Arabs and detailed description of what Ibn Qutayba presents as the quintessence of Arabness,[154] (3) al-Yaᶜqūbī's (d. *c.*275/888 or 292/905) *Tārīkh*'s description of pre-Islamic Arab history and culture, and (4) al-Masᶜūdī's (d. 346/957) *Murūj al-dhahab* which ostensibly follows al-Yaᶜqūbī's model, but with crucial amendments that point to a culmination of a changed depiction of Arabness.

Alongside al-Jāḥiẓ's linguistic theories that laud *kalām al-ᶜarab* and Qur'anic *lisān ᶜarabī*,[155] al-Jāḥiẓ disengages from the Qur'an's *aᶜrāb*/*ᶜarabī* distinction by pervasively maintaining that the best speakers of Arabic are the *aᶜrāb*. We saw above that he describes *aᶜrāb* as *khullaṣ* (pure),[156] implying that they best embody the speech of the *ᶜarab*, and in *al-Bayān*'s most spirited defence of 'Arabs' against their detractors – the *Kitāb al-ᶜaṣā* – al-Jāḥiẓ specifically cites the *aᶜrāb* as the living proof of the Arabs' linguistic superiority.[157] We also noted that al-Jāḥiẓ's discourse is ultimately self-serving since the invitation he extends to readers to visit inner desert *aᶜrāb* and experience their eloquence was hollow, given the insecurity and remoteness of the Peninsula from the mid-third/ninth century, and readers were forced to rely on al-Jāḥiẓ and his peers to learn the bountiful *bayān* of Arabic. In order for the clever discourse to function, it critically relies on depicting Arabic eloquence via Bedouin, and hence it needs to link *aᶜrāb* firmly with *ᶜarab*, and al-Jāḥiẓ seems aware of this. Towards the end of *al-Bayān* he summarises the idea of culture and his contemporary world, and praises Arabness, but specifically the Arabness of the past which al-Jāḥiẓ counts as the 'great honour and glory' of the Umayyads. Al-Jāḥiẓ remarks that his late second/eighth-century scholarly predecessors had lost much of that valuable knowledge since they discontinued the 'Arab' methods of the Umayyads whom al-Jāḥiẓ describes with the remarkable phrase: *dawla ᶜarabiyya aᶜrābiyya* (an Arab–Bedouin state).[158] Herein Arabness and Bedouin-ness are made complimentary in a manner which the Umayyad caliphs themselves could not have accepted: al-Jāḥiẓ calls them *ᶜarab* (which they doubtless would have liked to hear), but also *aᶜrāb* (a surprising association that would have offended their sensibilities). History is written by the present, however: al-Jāḥiẓ sought to construct a nostalgic longing for pure Arabic language and culture, and hence needed to lock it away in a Bedouin past. In order to do so, he needed the bygone Umayyads to appear as a Bedouin state with essential Arab qualities, and he describes them in that image, deconstructing the Umayyad era's own conceptual/theological/legal barrier between *ᶜarab* and *aᶜrāb* in the process.[159] Al-Jāḥiẓ's portrayal of Arab history in a Bedouin guise did not completely reverse older discourses: al-Jāḥiẓ does not deem *ᶜarab* and *aᶜrāb* as synonymous and does not use the terms interchangeably, but by positing *aᶜrāb* as the purest Arabs and citing *ᶜarab* and *aᶜrāb* in tandem, he deconstructs the difference and prompts readers to reconceptualise Arabness via the desert.

The increasing envelopment of Arabs into a Bedouin ideal can be traced in Ibn Qutayba's *Faḍl al-ᶜarab* which echoes al-Jāḥiẓ's Arab–Bedouin nexus by adducing anecdotes about the Bedouin to praise Arabs, and so both (1) rehabilitates *aʿrāb* from the Qur'anic disparagement into a worthy people, and (2) merges *aʿrāb* and *ʿarab* into one united heritage. This is most evident in *al-Tanbīh*, the second section of Ibn Qutayba's text which champions the Arabs' cultural achievement by enumerating the 'sciences' in which Arabs excelled over all other peoples.[160] Those sciences are horse husbandry, observation of the stars and clouds, physiognomy (*al-firāsa*), somatomancy (*al-qiyāfa*), augury (*al-ʿiyāfa*), geomancy (*al-khaṭṭ*), divination (*al-kihāna*), medicine,[161] poetry and oratory. All are skills of nomads and pertain to oral culture and the observation of natural phenomena. Knowledge of stars and clouds is expressly noted as a skill the Arabs needed for seasonal migrations in search of pasture;[162] *al-khaṭṭ* is a specific desert science involving drawing divination lines in the sand;[163] what survives now as an only very fragmentary section on Arab medicine relates an anecdote on the efficacy of cures derived from camel urine and desert plants; and Ibn Qutayba expressly notes that poetry and oratory are skills of oral literature, not sedentary, literate civilisations.[164] Ibn Qutayba's list thus shifts Arab cultural superiority away from urban centres and *amṣār* in the Fertile Crescent, and redraws 'Arab' cultural achievement in the desert. In so doing, Ibn Qutayba separates Arabs from the established cultures of the Middle East, particularly the memory of Iran – a clearly practical device, for it spares Arabs from like-for-like comparison with older civilisations, and presents Arab cultural achievement as a unique set of knowledge, bypassing the fact that Arabs lacked the cultural trappings of more ancient urban peoples. To make his argument stick, Ibn Qutayba emphasises original Arabness as a Bedouin identity, and his discourse thus aligns with the contemporary philological emphasis on the Arabic language's Bedouin purity.

A wide-scope urban Iraqi discourse to reconceptualise Arabness begins to appear. Merging Arabness into Bedouin-ness was advantageous for philologists specifically, as it bequeathed them mastery over a fixed construct of *the* Arabic language, and it benefitted urban Muslims generally, as it enabled them to conceptualise their religious identity as definitely separate from older civilisations and praiseworthy in and of itself: a new creed brought into the Fertile Crescent as a gust of fresh air borne by a simple Bedouin people who cleared away the old order and showed Iraqis a bright new future. The conceptual benefits of imaging the Arabs as Bedouin, of course conflicted with empirical history. Pre-Islamic Arabians were not all Bedouin, nor did they call themselves Arabs, and Arab identity only emerged in the urban centres of the Fertile Crescent during the generations following the conquests. The late third/ninth-century discourse accordingly needed to write a new sense of Arab identity to remove Arabness from the very cities where Arabness had developed, and transplant it into an imaginary historical 'Arab desert'.

Since Arabs had long lost political influence and demographic distinctiveness in the cities of Ibn Qutayba's world, and since Islam's rise was one quarter-millennium removed from Ibn Qutayba's era, the opportunity to replace old facts with a more useful narrative existed, though not every reader of *Faḍl al-ᶜarab* was persuaded. The Eastern Iranian al-Bīrūnī expressed disagreement, noting that any nomadic people possess the kinds of knowledge which Ibn Qutayba considered exclusively 'Arab',[165] but his reservations appear to have been mostly overlooked: Ibn Qutayba's Arab–Bedouin model offered an elegant means to extol Arabness and the Islamic culture wrought by Arabian Conquerors as a novel and worthy origin for the new world order of Islam, and we shall see that subsequent writers effectively and inexorably change Arabness to suit the new agenda.

From the perspective of terminology, Ibn Qutayba's depiction of Arab sciences and culture around the desert leaves a reader wondering how *ᶜarab* and *aᶜrāb* can be distinguished. The logical result is for the two terms to merge, but the persistence of the word *aᶜrāb* in Ibn Qutayba's text suggests that he is situated at the beginning of the process. His citations of *aᶜrāb* are invariably positive,[166] he cites individual Bedouin (*aᶜrābī*) informants for examples of eloquent Arabic,[167] and in one case, Ibn Qutayba cites a settled Arab from Medina alongside a Bedouin *aᶜrābī* as joint examples of eloquence.[168] Herein we perceive an important aspect of *al-Faḍl*'s terminology: despite the persistence of *aᶜrāb* as a reference to Bedouin, Ibn Qutayba accords them an equal place within the wider Arab collective. Ibn Qutayba also deftly shifts on occasion into calling Bedouin *ᶜarab*, and adjusts his terminology accordingly, for example, '*Arabs* from the desert steppe' (*al-bādūn min al-ᶜarab*)[169] or an '*Arab* king of the desert steppe' (*malik al-ᶜarab bi-l-bādiya*),[170] and Ibn Qutayba calls all of Arabia 'the land of the Arabs' (*arḍ al-ᶜarab*).[171] Moreover, the nomadic skills of travelling about the desert are ascribed to *ᶜarab* and not *aᶜrāb*,[172] and in his analysis of individual sciences in *al-Tanbīh*, Ibn Qutayba makes no reference to *aʿrāb* at all, referring to each nomadic science exclusively in terms of 'Arab' knowledge. The terminological sublimation of Arabness into Bedouin-ness is developing, but not yet complete.

Contemporary with Ibn Qutayba, al-Yaʿqūbī's narrative of pre-Islamic Arabian history in his world history, *al-Tārīkh*, presents an account of Arab origins complementary with Ibn Qutayba's *al-Faḍl*, emphasising, as noted in Chapter 5(III), the admirable qualities of nobility and the prophetic origins of pre-Islamic 'Arabs'. Al-Yaʿqūbī promulgates a two-fold narrative of pre-Islamic Arabian history, separating 'Arab kingdoms' from central Ma'addite Arabians, which ostensibly divides settled from nomad, but the 'kingdoms' include the nomadic Kinda from the deserts of south-central Arabia and the semi-nomadic Lakhm in the Syrian Desert,[173] and his account of the central Arabians includes a long section on the settled population of Mecca.[174] Al-Yaʿqūbī's narrative of 'Arab' history thus admits an equal role for Bedouin and settled groups, while promoting nomadic polities as centrepieces of the Arab story wherein his lengthy enumerations of religious practice, poetry, customs and seasonal nomadic fairs are listed as the basis of pan-Arabian shared Arab culture.[175] It is perhaps for this reason that al-Yaʿqūbī never refers to pre-Islamic nomadic Arabians as *aʿrāb*: his laudatory impressions of pre-Islamic 'Arab' nomad nobility descended from Abraham's prophetic family would be undermined if they were classified with the derogatory connotations of the outsider *aʿrāb* nomenclature.

Tellingly, as far as my reading has uncovered, al-Yaʿqūbī only invokes the term *aʿrāb* when recounting Abbasid-era history, where *aʿrāb* are counted amongst an array of disorganised and violent ad hoc groups marshalled in those conflicts (noted in Chapter 5(IV)) which plagued Arabia in al-Yaʿqūbī's third/ninth century.[176] The references to Fourth *Fitna*-era vagabonds as *aʿrāb* illustrates a preservation of the ancient Middle Eastern tradition of labelling undesirable outsider rabble as *aʿrāb*, while al-Yaʿqūbī's avoidance of the word to describe pre-Islamic Arabian nomads underlines a discourse to promote a novel sense of a pan-Arabian 'inside' sense of unified 'Arab' ethnic community with the quintessential ethnic traits of consolidated genealogy and shared history, traditions and cultural practices. By eschewing the terminological divide of *ʿarab* and *aʿrāb*, al-Yaʿqūbī also helps entrench the single name to refer to these groups, and hence it becomes very easy for readers to conceptualise all of pre-Islamic Arabia's population into one communal mould. Al-Yaᶜqūbī's *al-Tārīkh* thus places the cohesive entity of 'Arabs' into a distinct compartment of world history, presenting them as a single ethnos across pre-Islamic Arabia, comprehensively praised for noble history with emphasis on Arab culture's desert component alongside the narratives of the more urban, dynastic Arab history of pre-Islamic empire-building.

Two generations following al-Yaᶜqūbī, al-Masᶜūdī's *Murūj al-dhahab* written, according to the text itself, in 332/943–4,[177] relates world history on al-Yaᶜqūbī's model,[178] but with key differences in the presentation of Arab history. Mirroring al-Yaᶜqūbī, al-Masᶜūdī divides Arab history into 'kingdoms' and 'Arabians', but unlike al-Yaᶜqūbī's opening of central Arabian history with the story of Abraham and Ishmael's founding of Mecca, al-Masᶜūdī's section on the Arabians begins with a long excursus on nomadism. Whereas al-Yaᶜqūbī's narrative insinuated Arab origins in prophecy, al-Masᶜūdī depicts Arabs as the quintessential people of the desert steppe (*al-bawādī*) whom he considers akin to other nomads such as Kurds,[179] Turks, Eastern Iranian Sijistānīs,[180] Berbers,[181] and Ethiopic Africans.[182] And whilst al-Masᶜūdī effects a thorough Bedouinisation of the idea of Arabness, he makes no reference to *aᶜrāb* – only the collective *ᶜarab*. By the expression 'Bedouin Arabs' (*al-ᶜarab al-badw*), al-Masᶜūdī implies that Arabs are not necessarily all Bedouin, but his discourse does conceptualise the Arabs as originally all Bedouin. In contrast, therefore, to earlier, prophetic-tinged accounts of noble Arab origins al-Masᶜūdī peels the layers of history back to the Flood to note that certain peoples chose the desert over settlements for their homeland.[183] The Arabs were amongst those people, and al-Masᶜūdī ascribes a statement to these ancient Arabs that 'we were skilled in travelling the earth and we live where we want, that is more salubrious than other lifestyles'. Accordingly, readers are to perceive that Arabs chose to live as desert nomads,[184] a point al-Masᶜūdī makes expressly: 'the ancient Arabs' (*al-qudamāʾ min al-ᶜarab*) chose desert life because they saw in urban settlement shame and shortcomings', and 'the knowledgeable amongst them (*dhawū al-maᶜrifa*) declared that the desert was more healthy and more conducive to a strong, salubrious life'.[185] Nomadism emerges as the Arab (and not *aᶜrāb*) way since their beginnings.

Following these anecdotes, al-Masᶜūdī asserts that 'all of the Arabs (*jamīᶜ al-ᶜarab*) gather around waterholes'[186] (the quintessence of nomadic existence), and importantly, he identifies the first/pure Arabs (*al-ᶜarab al-ᶜāriba*) as 'all Bedouin who spread through the land',[187] reporting that 'experts of history (*ahl al-siyar wa-l-akhbār*) note that all of the [first Arab] tribes . . . were people of tents, nomads living in temporary settlements across the land'.[188] Al-Masᶜūdī concludes that Arabs did not construct cities and settlements until later in their history – and not once does he refer to any Bedouin as *aᶜrāb*. Al-Masᶜūdī shifts the discourse of nomadism towards primitivism, with his emphasis on Arab Bedouin-ness leading him to posit that Muhammad's Islamic mission was a special catalyst that brought Arabs out of the desert for the first time. In this vein, he relates an anecdote attributed to the second caliph, ᶜUmar ibn al-Khaṭṭāb, in which the Caliph reportedly asked 'a wise man' upon the Muslim armies' conquest of the Middle East:

> We are an Arab people [*unās ᶜarab*]; God granted us conquest over the lands, and we want to settle them and live in walled towns [*amṣār*]; so tell us about cities [*mudun*], their climates and settlements, and how their earth and climate affects their inhabitants.[189]

Arabness even at the dawn of Islam is cast as an unchanged relic of ancient, primordial Bedouin-ness.

Al-Masᶜūdī continues, relating a story about the pre-Islamic Sasanian Persian emperor Kisrā and 'one of the Arab orators' in which the Persian asks the Arab why Arabs live in the desert steppe (*al-bādiya*) and chose to be Bedouin (*al-badw*). In accordance with each anecdote in this chapter of *al-Murūj*, the 'Arab' describes the salutary desert environment and the nobility and courage which it fosters.[190] Al-Masᶜūdī's emphasis on the physically salubrious primitivism departs from Ibn Qutayba's narrative praising Bedouin intellectual heritage too; the ramifications of this will be considered in the next section. As regards the conception of Arab identity as a specifically Bedouin identity, *Murūj al-dhahab* is a pivotal marker in the history of the word *aᶜrāb* for it makes no reference to *aᶜrāb*: the term *ᶜarab* suffices to convey essential Bedouin-ness. Tracing backwards seventy-five years through al-Yaᶜqūbī, Ibn Qutayba and al-Jāḥiẓ we can perceive what, in retrospect, is an inexorable decline in the citation of *aᶜrāb* accompanied by an emphatic shift of Arabness into the desert. It is likely not coincidental that the beginning of clear discourses about the single, uniform *kalām al-ᶜarab* in philological writings coincides with the emergence of *al-ᶜarab* in historical narratives as the cohesive, uniform inhabitants of desert Arabia who, like the language itself, were most intimately associated with the desert, evidencing a fourth/tenth-century watershed for the Bedouinisation of the Arab that broke down the spatial barrier formerly separating *ᶜarab* and *aᶜrāb*, and rendered the term *aᶜrāb* obsolete.

The supplanting of *aᶜrāb* by *ᶜarab* as the signifier of Bedouin occurs in other genres too. In exegesis, for example, Qur'an 81:4's description of the terror of Judgment Day warns that 'heavily pregnant camels (*sawālif*) will be abandoned'. Exegetes interpret this reference to mean that people will be so frightened that they will forget even their most prized possessions. The first extant exegete, Muqātil ibn Sulaymān, explains that the reference to pregnant camels proves the verse was addressed to desert Arabians, since 'nothing is more beloved to the *aᶜrāb* than a pregnant camel'.[191] The later *tafsīrs* make the same point, but with the terminological shift we have noted: al-Qurṭubī (d. 671/1273) relates the pregnant camel is the thing 'most dear to the *ᶜarab*',[192] and similarly, al-Biqāᵓī's (d. 885/1480) *Naẓm al-Durar* explains, 'they are the most beloved of the possessions of the *ᶜarab*'.[193] Inasmuch as early texts indicate that *ᶜarab* was a designator of urban Muslims in the second/eighth century and had no connotation with Bedouin, Muqātil's choice of *aᶜrāb* to describe camel herders is consistent with his contemporaries' discourses, whereas the replacement of *aᶜrāb* with *ᶜarab* in later exegesis reflects the critical lexical change when *ᶜarab* replaced *aᶜrāb* as signifier of Bedouin.[194] The 'Bedouinisation' of the Arab was complete.

Examples of the convergence of *ᶜarab* and *aᶜrāb* extend also to political titulature in material culture. A brass basin from Mosul dated 1275–1300 CE (*c.*670–700 AH) (Berlin, Museum für Islamische Kunst I.6581) refers to its courtly owner as ruler of *al-aᶜrāb wa-l-ᶜajam*, whereas a brass plate from Shiraz dated 1345–60 CE (745–60 AH) refers to rule over *al-ᶜarab wa-l-ᶜajam*.[195] The shared message of the 'world domination' enjoyed by their Il-Khanid patrons is clear – the interchangability of *ᶜarab* and *aᶜrāb* is instructive.

Indications thus point strongly to a reimagination of the Arab as a desert outsider from the perspective of urban Muslim communities across the Middle East. When 'Arab' became a widely used byword for nomads, it could no longer connote a sense of self for a Muslim urbanite, and this aligns with Ahola's and Romanov's findings noted Chapter 5(IV) that Iraqis rapidly discarded Arab tribal affiliations after the mid-third/ninth century. The reworking of dictionary definitions of *ᶜarabī* away from a speech community to a tribal family are further steps indicating that the Arabic-speaking communities in the Fertile Crescent were actively defining Arabness away from themselves, and it seems wrong to think that populations in Egypt, Syria, Iraq and Iran after the fourth/tenth century were 'Arabs': their intellectuals had expelled the trappings of Arab identity to a faraway and inaccessible desert. The findings are also aligned with Rodinson's offhand, but important observation that Arabic-speaking peoples in the Middle East did not return to express their identity as 'Arabs' until the Ottoman period.[196] The fate of Arab identity following the fourth/tenth century needs much reappraisal, but in testing Rodinson's point, it is noteworthy that Ibn Īyās' (d. *c.*930/1523) *Badāʾiᶜ al-Zuhūr*, the last Egyptian historical chronicle written before the Ottoman defeat of the Mamluks, is consistent in its use of the word *ᶜarab* to connote Bedouin groups in Arabia and raiding bands from the Delta and Egyptian Desert.[197] The Arabic-speaking Cairene Ibn Īyās never uses *ᶜarabī* as an adjective to describe himself or his own community: the word signifies 'outsider'. A pressing question for future study must carefully investigate which, if any groups in the Middle East from the fourth/tenth to tenth/sixteenth century ever called themselves 'Arabs'.[198]

III Bedouin Arabness and the Emergence of a *Jāhiliyya* Archetype

The merger of Arab identity with Bedouin, the fading of the term *aᶜrāb* and the projection of pure *kalām al-ᶜarab* into an ancient desert language established new foundations to conceptualise Arab history. Unlike earlier Iraqi discourses that constructed a noble past for the Arabs, befitting the status of Arab groups in the early Abbasid Caliphate,[199] fourth/tenth-century Iraqi cultural producers did not have to contend with powerful Arab groups, and their process of imagining the Arabs as Bedouin 'others', and not 'self', opened unprecedented opportunity for them to turn Arabness into an external object, and thus conceptualise pre-Islamic Arab history as the binary opposite of the fourth/tenth-century *littérateurs*' world. Herein, we can discern conditions conducive to generating the archetypes of the now familiar reprobate *al-Jāhiliyya*, and by comparing al-Masᶜūdī's fourth/tenth-century *Murūj al-dhahab* with earlier narratives of Arab history, we can focus on three salient departures Masᶜūdī makes from his predecessors' narratives which alter the thrust of imagining Arabness and pre-Islamic *al-Jāhiliyya*, and which lay the groundwork for subsequent generations of Arabic writers to embed negative connotations of *al-Jāhiliyya* across multiple genres.

Firstly, al-Masᶜūdī tempers the narratives of pre-Muhammadic Arab monotheism. He accepts that Northern Arabs descend from Abraham through Ishmael and that Southern Arabs have a connection to the prophetic mission of Hūd from Noah, but in both cases, and unlike writers of the century before, al-Masᶜūdī declares that Arabia's monotheism was fleeting. In the case of Hūd's people ᶜĀd, al-Masᶜūdī remarks that 'confusions [*shubah*] entered their minds . . . since they stopped reasoning and considering religion, and they turned to inactivity and followed pleasure and tradition . . . and they worshipped statues'.[200] Al-Masᶜūdī records Hūd's escape with 'those believers who followed him',[201] but narrates nothing more about them and ends the passage with a poem describing their total destruction, leaving little scope to imagine that Yemeni kings continued Hūd's mission, as earlier Yemeni histories asserted.[202] In conformity with this notion of Hūd's unheeded message, al-Masᶜūdī makes no mention of Hūd in his chapter on pre-Islamic Yemeni kings,[203] and accepts that only one king, Abū Karib al-Ḥimyarī, was a believer 'seven hundred years before Muhammad's mission'.[204] While al-Masᶜūdī cites two poems also recorded in Diᶜbil's history of Muslim pre-Islamic Yemeni kings, al-Masᶜūdī does not situate Abū Karib within a line of Muslim Yemeni kings as Diᶜbil's narrative does, and gives no explanation for Abū Karib's apparent Islam, nor indication that monotheistic belief continued after him. Al-Masᶜūdī thus retains some names made famous by earlier Yemeni narratives, but the glue which held together those monotheism-inscribed narratives of pre-Islamic Yemen – the passing of Hūd's prophetic message from one king to the next – is erased in al-Masᶜūdī's *Murūj*.

As for the Northern Arabians, al-Masᶜūdī only accepts that a small number espoused monotheistic belief before Muhammad, naming Khuss ibn Sāᶜida al-Iyādī and two members of the ᶜAbd al-Qays tribe (Baḥīrā al-Rāhib and Riʾāb al-Shannī) amongst five other Arab tribal 'believers of the period between Jesus and Muhammad'.[205] Otherwise, al-Masʿūdī does not connect Arab descent from Ishmael and the presence of the Kaʿba in Mecca with the maintenance of Arabian monotheism before Muhammad. In a related vein, al-Masʿūdī also twists the emphasis of earlier narratives about ʿAbd al-Muṭṭalib, Muhammad's uncle.[206] Earlier historians portrayed ʿAbd al-Muṭṭalib as a pious pre-Islamic Meccan, part of a wider group who maintained Abrahamic monotheism before Muhammad,[207] but al-Masʿūdī turns the tables and portrays him instead as a maverick against what al-Masʿūdī presents as otherwise prevailing idolatrous polytheism of Mecca before Muhammad, rendering ʿAbd al-Muṭṭalib not a continuation of monotheistic tradition as earlier emphasised, but instead one of the few who 'abandoned [idolatrous] tradition and espoused monotheism'.[208] Understanding al-Masʿūdī's reworking of ʿAbd al-Muṭṭalib into a lone paragon of monotheism is understandable in the context of Abbasid rule: Abbasid caliphs claimed descent from the Hāshim clan of which ʿAbd al-Muṭṭalib was a major ancestor figure, hence a nod to his piety upheld the propriety of the Caliphate, the growing power of Twelver Shi'a Islam and even the dignity of the Turkic generals whose legitimacy during al-Masʿūdī's time relied on their ostensible 'protection' of the caliph. None of those agendas required a wider extolling of Arabness – conversely, from a rhetorical perspective, it would have behoved later Abbasid elites to portray ʿAbd al-Muṭṭalib as a rare shining light in an otherwise pagan past in order to emphasise the special importance of those Abbasid-era groups connected to ʿAbd al-Muṭṭalib's memory. Similar to al-Masʿūdī's retention of the 'believer' Yemeni king Abū Karīb, the presentation of pre-Muhammadic Northern Arab faith in *Murūj al-dhahab* incorporates names so celebrated across earlier texts that al-Masʿūdī could not obliterate their memory, but otherwise he expunges earlier intimations of widespread pre-Muhammadic Arab monotheism.

Secondly, al-Masʿūdī writes pre-Islamic Arab history with newly marked emphasis on what are today familiar negative stereotypes of *al-Jāhiliyya*. He renders *Jāhiliyya* an innate trait of the pre-Islamic Arabs: he begins a chapter on pre-Islamic Arabian religion with the telling statement: 'The Arabs, in their *Jāhiliyya* were divided into sects' (each non-Islamic).[209] When considering Arab notions of the soul, al-Masʿūdī similarly begins his chapter 'The Arabs had several schools of thought in the *Jāhiliyya*',[210] and he dismisses them along with a host of other supernatural beliefs: 'The Arabs had, before the rise of Islam, opinions and schools of thought regarding the soul, ghouls, wraiths and jinn.'[211] With a sceptical air (accompanied by the incredulous phrase 'one alleged' (*zaᶜama*)), al-Masᶜūdī proceeds to explain the pre-Islamic Arabs' belief in supernatural beings,[212] and narrates their skills in somatomancy (*qīyāfa*), augury (*ᶜiyāfa*) and other divination (*zajr* and *kihāna*).[213] Herein lie two crucial departures from earlier writing: (1) al-Masᶜūdī separates *al-Jāhiliyya* from Islam, denying the continuity expressed by Ibn Ḥabīb, Ibn Qutayba and others, and (2) he reverses Ibn Qutayba's analysis of pre-Islamic Arab sciences by naming the exact same fields which Ibn Qutayba enumerated a century before as 'sciences' (*ulūm*) to praise Arabs, and making them instead part of a disparaging and sceptical account of pre-Islamic belief in the supernatural, demoting the 'sciences' to superstitions. Again, al-Masᶜūdī turns material about pre-Islamic Arabs narrated by his third/ninth-century predecessors on its head and constructs a discourse of Arab *Jāhiliyya* as irrational pagandom before Islam.

And lastly, al-Masᶜūdī tempers the former depictions of pre-Islamic Arab nobility. He mentions the conquests of the ancient Yemeni Arabians which earlier generations of Yamānī authors emphasised with fabulous tales,[214] but al-Yaᶜqūbī's lexicon of *sharaf* and *majd* is absent. Al-Masᶜūdī's emphasis on pre-Islamic Arabian *Jāhiliyya* would seem to explain his less than generous attitude towards pre-Islamic Arabs, and al-Masᶜūdī's emphasis on the Arabs' innate Bedouin-ness restricts scope for praising ancient Arab kingdoms. He makes brief notes in one paragraph to the Yemeni kings who 'constructed buildings', 'took to large-scale settlement' and even 'constructed Samarqand' – all claims earlier made by Yamānī partisans such as Diᶜbil al-Khuzāᶜī (whom al-Masᶜūdī expressly cites as a source).[215] But these succinct 'admissions' occur at the opening of al-Masᶜūdī's chapter on the Arabs' primordial Bedouin nature, and so they appear as exceptions to what al-Masᶜūdī argues over the next thirty paragraphs to be the real primitive/nomadic essence of Arabness. His emphasis on Bedouin-ness leads towards contradiction – as he cites an anecdote that argues all Arabs before Umaym al-Khayr lived in tents and that Umaym was the first to construct roofed buildings.[216] According to al-Masᶜūdī's genealogical scheme, Umaym lived after Hūd, but Qur'an

89:7–8 notes that Hūd's people lived in fabulous buildings, so al-Masᶜūdī has problems with chronology. This can be expected if we recognise that al-Masᶜūdī converted older material into new discourses where old memories did not entirely fit new visions. His turn to primitivism converted Arabs into primordial, pre-historical peoples whose role in history is no longer to prop the nobility of Muslim elites, but can, with the new emphasis, represent the antithetical precursor of Islam: Arab memory is Bedouinised.

Arabness as Archetype

Al-Masᶜūdī's reorientations of the pre-Islamic Arab past are significant, not only for their departure from earlier models, but also for their longevity. As opposed to al-Yaᶜqūbī's model of pre-Islamic nobility and monotheism, subsequent Arabic writers across a wide array of genres would copy al-Masᶜūdī's model of Bedouin paganism. As examples, al-Bakrī's (d. 487/1094) world geography's section on Arabia and the Arabs copies almost verbatim from al-Masᶜūdī's *Murūj*, sometimes acknowledging the earlier source, and sometimes not.[217] Al-Bakrī's depiction of the Arabs accordingly focuses on their pagan superstitions and their wild Bedouin life before Islam, making no reference to the impressions of earlier writers about widespread monotheism or the nobility of pre-Islamic Arab ancestors. Al-Masᶜūdī's model of the Arab past also spread to the field of heresiography where al-Shahristānī's *al-Milal wa-l-Niḥal* cites abbreviated, but largely identical, examples of pre-Islamic Arabness, describing their pre-Islamic superstitions, polytheism and atheism in the same terms familiar to readers of al-Masᶜūdī's *al-Murūj*.[218] Al-Shahristānī lists the same Arab 'superstitions' (formerly, Ibn Qutayba's 'sciences'),[219] and also like al-Masᶜūdī, he classifies the vast majority of Arabs as atheists and polytheists, reducing reference to pre-Muhammadic Arabian monotheists to exactly the same list as found in *Murūj al-dhahab* with emphasis on ᶜAbd al-Muṭṭalib.[220]

In historical writing, al-Maqdisī's (d. 507/1112) *al-Badʾ wa-l-tārīkh* depicts the pre-Islamic Arabs within the same conceptual categories of al-Masᶜūdī's *Murūj*. His Arab history section opens with a nod to Bedouinism and names ᶜAkk ibn ᶜAdnān as the 'first Arab who took to nomadic life'.[221] The Arab past is called the blind *Jāhiliyya* (*al-Jāhiliyya al-ᶜamyāʾ*),[222] and this reference colours his portrayal of Arabian society. It allows al-Maqdisī to depict pre-Islamic glory (*majd*) as vainglorious boasting about supernatural magic – a pointed reversal of al-Yaᶜqūbī's stress on Arab nobility and Ibn Qutayba's 'Arab sciences'.[223] In another reversal, al-Maqdisī reinterprets Meccan history: whereas al-Yaᶜqūbī depicts each change of control over Mecca's sanctum in pre-Islamic time as a handover of the noble office (with reference to *sharaf* – inherited glory), al-Maqdisī refers to it with the neutral phrase '*x* then took over the affair' (*qāma bi-l-amr*).[224] This is a consequence of al-Maqdisī's narrative that the prophetic legacy established in Mecca via Abraham and Ishmael was lost after a few generations, when the right religion (*dīn*) was replaced with whimsy (*wahm*) and the Meccans made unlawful acts lawful and became wicked people (*istaḥallū haram . . . fa-ẓalamū*).[225] Accordingly, al-Maqdisī does not count the Arabs' descent from Ishmael as monotheistic heritage,[226] and he makes no mention of Hūd's prophetic mission being perpetuated by pre-Muhammadic Yemeni kings either.[227] Like al-Masᶜūdī, al-Maqdisī leaves his readers with the impression that pre-Islamic Arabs primarily excelled in sorcery and magic.[228]

A fifth/eleventh-century reader thus would have encountered a consistent impression of pre-Islamic Arabness across history, geography and heresiography, and it is perhaps at this period that we can begin to speak of the creation of a vulgate for *Jāhiliyya* history and Arabness. The modern stereotype of pre-Islamic Arabs as Arabian Bedouin pagans must derive from somewhere, and I suggest that its genesis can be traced to this later period when such a variety of authors, embracing a range of agendas, all depicted the Arabs with essential uniformity.

IV Conclusions: a Bedouinisation of Memory

The fourth–fifth/tenth–eleventh-century creation of the Arab *Jāhiliyya* archetype logically progressed from the third–fourth/ninth–tenth-century philological discourses. By casting Arabs into the sand and othering their language as a vernacular of a past, distant place, the philologists separated Arabness from Islam. Their *ᶜarab* were conceptually much closer to the Qur'an's *aᶜrāb* – a desert people outside of Islam and distinct from the Muslims who wrote about them. Such a depiction of Arabs, abetted by the disappearance of ethnic Arab power centres at the same time, meant that the Arabs could be imagined as a *pre*-Islamic people who were saved by the mission of Islam and who brought Islam to the Fertile Crescent from Arabia. Such a discourse had to purge the notion that early Islam and pre-Islamic Arabia shared continuities and converted positive memories of pre-Islamic Arabness into a reprobate state to underscore Islam's mission of salvation. The retreat from genealogical identifications of Ishmael as the 'father of all Arabs' traced in Chapter 4(IV) also coincides chronologically with the fourth/tenth-century literary emphasis on the wickedness of *al-Jāhiliyya*, and the two processes seem related. Arab power brokers no longer dominated society, and hence there was no longer a pressing need for concocted family trees that connected contemporary Arabs to a long chain of prophetic heritage. With Arab interest groups removed from the centre of sociopolitical attention, Ishmael could be rebranded as a 'false start' in the story of monotheism, and Muhammad's mission could then be portrayed as wholesale rectification of society. The narrative emphasising Muhammad as a world saviour emerged at the expense of the earlier belief in prophet-infused Arab blood, but with few so powerful Arab groups left in fourth/tenth-century Iraqi society, Ishmaelite genealogy and the second/eighth-century stories of the pre-Islamic Arabian monotheism 'surviving' amongst his descendants had become an anachronism, and they could be easily forgotten in favour of new stories of *al-Jāhiliyya* and Muhammad as a world prophet.

The resultant depiction of Arabness is beset with a difficult contradiction: on the one hand, the perfection of the Bedouin vernacular led philologists to praise the pre-Islamic Arabs (and so do a good service to their value of their own 'expertise'), but the development of the pre-Islamic *Jāhiliyya* paradigm involved a comprehensive degrading of Arab culture before Islam to highlight Islam's supreme salvation. As the notion of pre-Islamic Arabic was synthesised, each of the conflicting notions of past-Arabness had to be placed in the literary reconstruction of the Arab story, and the manners in which Muslim writers from the fourth/tenth century constructed pre-Islam and mythologised Arab origins presents itself as a vast topic for future study.[229]

The difference between the third/ninth-century histories of the Arabs and those written in the subsequent centuries can also be epitomised as the change from an Arab 'national' history to a Muslim 'world' history. The narratives in al-Yaᶜqūbī and Diᶜbil depict Arabs as the champions of monotheism since the earliest times where Arab nobles perpetuate tribal glory, whereas al-Masʿūdī converts them to a precursor in the global story of Islam where the focus becomes the succession of failed prophecy in the world before Muhammad. Other historians from the fourth/tenth century such as al-Ṭabarī and Ibn al-Jawzī make this explicit, narrating world history without substantial material on pre-Islamic Arabs, instead focusing on predominantly non-Arab prophets, diluting the Arabs' share in pre-Muhammadic monotheism and portraying Islam as a more expressly global phenomenon.

The crux of the fourth/tenth-century discourses that so Bedouinise Arab memory is the comprehensive othering of Arabness. Whereas the *aʿrāb* Bedouin were, since the earliest Arabic writings, depicted on the outside of the Muslim community, in contrast to the Arabs on the inside, the merging of Bedouin with Arab did not bring the Bedouin inside, but rather cast the Arabs outside too. The Arab ethnos thus inherited Bedouin otherness, no doubt augmented by Arabian insecurity and the disappearance of Arab communities in Iraq. I have stressed that this enabled urbanite Iraqi *littérateurs* to promote themselves as 'experts', but the model had additional advantages, which can explain why it became so widely adopted. By drawing such a rigid line between pre-Islamic and Islamic, and by portraying Islam's roots in primordial desert Arabness, Muslim writers detached their civilisation from those of the Middle East. As opposed to a continuity of millennia of urban development in the Fertile Crescent, Islam could be projected as a phenomenon from the outside, brought by the swords of desert Arabs. Since the later Abbasid writers stressed no ethnic connection with those Arabs, the denigration of Arab primitivism had no effect on Iraqis' own self-image: they were merely Islam's inheritors.

Although Arabness developed within the urban Middle East, the Muslim discourse which eventually placed Arabness on the outside is perhaps why Islam is considered such a historical and cultural break in the region's history, why Islamic arts are accorded their own room in museums and galleries, and why 'Islam' so commonly over-determines analysis of the Middle East historically and today. Muslims wanted to believe that they had inherited a new world order, and their portrayal of the Arabs helped them achieve that goal. Modern students, however, must be very careful: neither tales from Arabia nor modern Bedouin anthropology take us back to Islam's real origins: rather, Bedouin-ness brings us to the urban imagination of fourth/tenth-century Iraqi writers who reconstructed their past so comprehensively.

Notes

1. See, for the first/seventh century, Donner (1998) pp. 197–8; for the second/eighth century, see Gibb (1962) p. 69, Norris (1990) pp. 34–8, Drory (1996). See also Chapter 5(I–III).
2. For example, Khalīfa ibn Khayyāṭ's (d. 250/854–5) *Tārīkh* contains no pre-Islamic material, al-Dīnawarī's *al-Akhbār al-ṭiwāl* narrates nothing relevant to *ayyām al-ᶜarab*, and al-Ṭabarī's *Tārīkh* only details *ayyām* which intersect with pre-Islamic Persian royal history. Al-Masᶜūdī's *Murūj* has only one paragraph on *al-ayyām* (1966–79) §1120, Ḥamza al-Iṣfahānī's *Tārīkh* concentrates its pre-Islamic Arabian chapter on Meccan events (Ḥamza al-Iṣfahānī (n.d.) pp. 113–16), and al-Maqdisī's *al-Badᵓ wa-l-tārīkh*'s chapter on Arabs focuses exclusively on pre-Islamic Mecca too (n.d.) vol. 4, pp. 105–30). Al-Iṣfahānī indicates that the lack of precise chronology for non-Meccan Arabian pre-Islamic history dissuaded him from narrating it, but creating chronology was evidently possible, as evidenced by the much later Ibn al-Athīr's (d. 630/1232–3) narrative of *al-ayyām* in his *al-Kāmil*, so the lack of fourth/tenth century attempts is intriguing.
3. Abū ᶜUbayda's (d. 210/825) *Naqāᵓiḍ Jarīr wa-l-Farazdaq*, Abū Tammām's (d. 231/845) *Naqāᵓiḍ Jarīr wa-l-Akhṭal* (attrib.) and to a lesser extent, al-Sukkarī's (d. 275/888 or 290/903) *Sharḥ ashᶜār al-Hudhaliyyīn* and Abū Muḥammad al-Qāsim al-Anbārī's (d. 304/916–7) *Sharḥ Dīwān al-Mufaḍḍaliyyāt.*
4. Al-Zubayrī's *Nasab Quraysh* and Ibn Bakkār's *Jamharat nasab Quraysh* both vaunt the Quraysh tribe as part of a wider phenomenon of lauding the Abbasid caliphs via positive depictions of the history of pre-Islamic Quraysh. Chapter 5(III) noted al-Balādhurī's *Ansāb al-ashrāf* and its construction of Arab elites around the idea of nobility.
5. Of the fourteen *akhbārī* scholars Ibn al-Nadīm associated with this period, four are associated with *al-ayyām* and nine with *nasab* (Ibn al-Nadīm (1988) pp. 101–4).
6. Of sixty-two named scholars, fourteen are ascribed works on *al-ayyām* and twenty-eight on *nasab* (Ibid. pp. 104–20).
7. Ibid. pp. 120–8.
8. Levin (2004) pp. 1, 13 argued that the motivation of second/eighth-century

grammarians such as Sībawayh was not as religious as often assumed, and while this is possible (see also Carter (2004) pp. 56–73), by the early third/ninth century, the emergence of al-Farrā᾽ and al-Akhfash's *Ma᾽ānī al-Qur᾽ān* does suggest early connection between philology and the study of Islam's scripture.

9. Ricoeur (1988) vol. 3, p. 142. White (1980) pp. 8, 27.
10. Al-Jāḥiẓ's 'humanism' is described in the collected essays in Heinemann et al. (2009); see also Anghelescu (1995) pp. 63, 66; Pellat (1953), (1966).
11. Al-Jāḥiẓ (2003) vol. 1, p. 308.
12. Ibid. vol. 1, p. 163. In its context, this citation cannot be confused with *al-Jazīra*, a term commonly used by Arabic authors to refer to the land between the Tigris and Euphrates.
13. Ibid. vol. 1, p. 163.
14. Ibid. vol. 1, p. 163.
15. Al-Jāḥiẓ argues that merely intelligible communication is not deserving of the label for proper rhetoric (*balāgha*). The argument begins in *al-Bayān* (2003) vol. 1, p. 88, and is made emphatically at vol. 1, p. 162, immediately preceding the Zayd anecdote.
16. Ibid. vol. 1, p. 163.
17. Ibid. vol. 3, p. 29.
18. Ibid. vol. 1, p. 163.
19. Ibid. vol. 3, p. 291.
20. Norris (1990) pp. 36, 39, 43–5 and Pellat (1990) p. 88. Norris (1990) p. 34, n. 10 also refers to 'ambiguous examples' of *al-shu᾿ūbiyya*, including an epistle of al-Jāḥiẓ. The ambivalence accords with our identification of *al-shu᾿ūbiyya* as a second/eighth-century ethnic revival, underlining the shortcomings in labelling the third/ninth-century al-Jāḥiẓ via essentialised *shu᾿ūbī* terms.
21. Al-Jāḥiẓ (2003) vol. 1, p. 383. See also the famous *Kitāb al-᾿aṣā* (Ibid. vol. 3, pp. 14–93).
22. Ibid. vol. 1, pp. 145–6, 163–4.
23. See Pellat (1953) pp. 224–34, (1966), (1969) p. 3; Webb (2012a) pp. 48–50. Enderwitz (2009) pp. 235–7 argues that *al-Ḥayawān* defends Arabness by blending Arab/non-Arab culture together into *adab*.
24. Montgomery (2009a) and (2009b) describe the centrality of this theme.
25. See Behzadi (2009a) and (2009b).
26. Al-Jāḥiẓ (2003) vol. 1, pp. 8–9. He expands the argument at vol. 1, pp. 75–88. The argument's connection with al-Jāḥiẓ's contemporary book culture is considered in Webb (2012a) pp. 41–7.

27. Al-Jāḥiẓ (2003) vol. 1, p. 145.
28. Ibid. vol. 1, pp. 11, 91, 383; vol. 3, p. 366.
29. Ibid. vol. 3, pp. 366–7.
30. Ibid. vol. 3, p. 29.
31. Ibid. vol. 1, p. 162.
32. Ibid. vol. 1, p. 3: 'Mighty God! We seek refuge in You from the trials of speech as we seek Your protection from the trials of action. We seek Your protection from having affectation when we are not proficient, and from conceit when we are. We seek Your protection from having caustic tongues, or babbling ones, and from stammering and spluttering speech!'
33. A point made repeatedly (Ibid. vol. 1, pp. 162–4).
34. Ibid. vol. 1, p. 145.
35. Ibid. vol. 1, p. 145. *Al-Bayān*'s narrative shortly afterwards denies scholars the ability to exactly replicate Bedouin Arabic (Ibid. vol. 1, pp. 162–4).
36. Al-Jāḥiẓ instructs supporters of Arabic *bayān* to lead the hypothetical *shu*ᶜ*ūbī* doubters 'by the hand' into desert Arabia (*bilād al-a*ᶜ*rāb*) to test the eloquence of language there, offering the Bedouin as 'living proof' of his theories about language (2003) vol. 3, p. 29.
37. Pellat considers *al-Bayān* was written 'anterieur à 237' ((1984) p. 133), uncannily correspondent to the collapse of Arabian security from 230/845.
38. See Carter (1983) p. 66; Suleiman (2003) pp. 32, 202.
39. Tidrick (1990) pp. 153–4 recounts the opinions of Palgrave (1865), Doughty (1936) and Burton, nineteenth-century English explorers in Arabia who expressed the superiority of Desert Arabic. She reasons that Burton's familiarity with classical Arabic philological texts may be the route by which the stereotypes of Bedouin linguistic purity entered English scholarship. See also Doughty (1936) vol. 1, pp. 35, 84, 100, 143 for typical expressions of Bedouin/Arab primitivism and 'purity'. As examples of modern endorsement of Bedouin vernacular purity, see Levin (2004) pp. 3–10; Suleiman (2003) pp. 36–48.
40. Suleiman (2011) pp. 10–11.
41. Suleiman (2003) pp. 44–66 tends to read classical grammars as a single, ongoing exercise in Arab identity formation, leaving aside the prospect that different grammarians at different times articulated varied notions of Arab identity; this is the task of this chapter.
42. Suleiman (2011) p. 20 argues that fourth/tenth-century writers particularly used language as a means to define Arab identity; however, this appears to be at

odds with the lexical definitions of *^{c}arab* which shifted away from language as the basis to define Arabness, see Chapters 4(I) and 5(IV).

43. Rodinson (1981) pp. 5–6, 22. He relates a fascinating anecdote about the 'Arab Mosque' in seventeenth-century Istanbul to substantiate his hypothesis.
44. Bohas et al. (1990) p. 42.
45. Versteegh (1997) pp. 50-1.
46. Sībawayh (1966–77) vol. 2, p. 411; vol. 3, pp. 81, 300, 314.
47. Ibid. vol. 2, p. 411.
48. Ibid. vol. 3, p. 300, Sībawayh's use of the verb *za^{c}ama* (to allege) here also implies a degree of mistrust regarding the point raised in the Bedouin testimony.
49. Levin (2004) pp. 2–3. The absence of reference to *a^{c}rāb* does not mean Sībawayh did not use *any* Bedouin informants, but I suggest Levin too quickly assumed the Bedouin-ness of Sībawayh's grammar and adopted later impressions about Bedouin linguistic purity without problematising the paradigm.
50. Carter (2004) p. 40.
51. Sībawayh (1966–77) vol. 3, p. 379. The distinction is considered further in Section II of this chapter.
52. Carter (2004) pp. 40–1. Compare citation of *a^{c}rāb* in *al-Kitāb* with, for example, their ubiquitous presence in al-Jāḥiẓ's *al-Bayān*, written one generation later.
53. Sībawayh (1966–77) vol. 1, p. 122, 303, 339, 428; vol. 2, pp. 57, 102, 121, 181, 185, 228, 241, 250, 334, 349, 364, 390, 401, 421.
54. Ibid. vol. 1, p. 339; vol. 2, pp. 102, 136, 181, 185, 241, 349.
55. Ibid. vol. 1, p. 303; vol. 2, p. 250.
56. Ibid. vol. 1, p. 122; vol. 2, pp. 228, 364, 421.
57. Ibid. vol. 1, p. 428.
58. Ibid. vol. 2, p. 57.
59. Ibid. vol. 2, p. 334. See also vol. 2, p. 401, where Sībawayh refers to 'similarities' between a grammatical construction and what is heard in *kalām al-^{c}arab*.
60. Most sections begin with a description of the rule followed by the expressions: 'this is like your statement (*naḥw qawlik*) . . .' or 'this is your statement (*dhālika qawluk*)' (Ibid. vol. 2, pp. 5, 19, 22, 23, 25, 28).
61. Ibid. vol. 2, p. 364.
62. This is a common expression in *al-Kitāb*, see for examples vol. 1, pp. 54, 80; vol. 2, pp. 127, 158.

63. Ibid. vol. 2, p. 63.
64. Ibid. vol. 2, p. 120.
65. Ibid. vol. 1, p. 197.
66. Versteegh (1997) notes that grammarians extracted what they wanted from Bedouin via poetry reports and paid little regard to their vernacular. Carter's work on Sībawayh's *al-Kitāb* tends to disagree (2004) pp. 40–2; and the issue appears unresolved. As is evident from my findings, I support Versteegh's hypothesis, as does Brustad (forthcoming).
67. Sībawayh (1966–77) vol. 1, pp. 47, 51, 70, 86, 169, 183.
68. The expression is usually 'we heard from one of the Arabs who is trustworthy' (*ba*ᶜ*ḍ al-*ᶜ*arab al-mawthūq bi-hi/bi-him*' (Ibid. vol. 1, pp. 309, 319, 329, 330, 395, 423; vol. 2, pp. 92, 329, 336, 337, 345); or, interestingly, 'the Arabs whose Arabic is trustworthy' (*al-*ᶜ*arab al-mawthūq bi-*ᶜ*arabiyyatihā*) Ibid. vol. 2 pp. 20, 319.
69. Ibid. vol. 1, p. 182.
70. The verb *arāda* 'to want' in the second person singular is almost ubiquitous. See also Ibid. vol. 2, p. 28 for the interaction between what 'you say' and how 'one Arab' says a similar construction – both are accepted as correct.
71. Levin's analysis (2004) seems right in judging Sībawayh's goal as extending beyond interpreting the Qur'an or recreating old Arabic. For ethics and *al-Kitāb*, see Carter (2004) pp. 61–5.
72. Schoeler (2006) pp. 40–1 describes the development towards books. He interprets Sībawayh's employment of the second-person pronoun as 'address[ing] the reader directly' (2006) p. 49.
73. See Chapter 4(I).
74. Al-Jumaḥī (n.d.) vol. 1, pp. 23–5 gives a contemporary gloss to the interest in pre-Islamic Arabic, stating the philologists' required evidence specifically from shortly before the time of Muhammad to re-construct the linguistic universe of the Qur'an. It is noteworthy that al-Jumaḥī considered the idiom of ancient Arabians, especially Yemenis, to be different from the Arabic (ᶜ*arabiyya*) of Muhammad's community (Ibid. vol. 1, pp. 9–10).
75. Versteegh (1997) pp. 50–1.
76. Anderson (1991) pp. 13, 71–84 and Hobsbawm (1990) pp. 102–3 demonstrate the role of language codification in promoting European national identities. Suleiman's argument that Arabic was codified for similar nationalistic purposes, though in different circumstances ((2003) pp. 34–68) does not tally well with Sībawayh's seeming disinterest in ethnic Arabness. It is perhaps

unsurprising, therefore, that Suleiman makes no reference to *al-Kitāb*. In only one instance he refers to Sībawayh as one of the two 'foremost grammarians in the Arabic linguistic tradition' ((2003) p. 149), but he does not explain why *al-Kitāb* is otherwise absent in his analysis.

77. Al-Akhfash (2010) vol. 1, pp. 32, 126, 162.
78. Ibid. vol. 1, pp. 32, 162.
79. Ibid. vol. 1, pp. 32, 126.
80. The third reference in *Maᶜānī al-Qurʾān* does relate a Bedouin vernacular expression (Ibid. vol. 1, p. 162), but the small sample size makes extrapolation difficult. Surely, it is more significant that all *aᶜrāb* speech, verse or prose, is markedly absent in al-Akhfash's *Maᶜānī*.
81. There are only six references in *Maᶜānī*'s first 100 pages: Ibid. vol. 1, pp. 21, 25, 55, 61, 67, 81.
82. Ibid. vol. 1, pp. 21, 25, 55, 81.
83. Unlike Sībawayh's *al-Kitāb*, al-Akhfash expressly mentions the 'Arabs' in almost all sections of his work.
84. Al-Akhfash (2010) vol. 1, p. 36.
85. Ibid. vol. 1, pp. 37, 39, 60, 80, 83, 99.
86. Ibid. vol. 1, pp. 28, 78. Al-Akhfash also notes 'there are those Arabs who pronounce a double case ending, and those who do not', and 'some Arabs add a *hamza*, other Arabs do not' (Ibid. vol. 1, pp. 80, 106).
87. Ibid. vol. 1, pp. 30, 83, 96.
88. Ibid. vol. 2, p. 508.
89. Ibid. vol. 1, p. 110.
90. Ibid. vol. 1, pp. 26, 32, 105.
91. Ibid. vol. 1, pp. 49, 89, 91–2.
92. For an express example, consider his expression 'don't you see that you speak in this way' – indicating the touchstone of correctness is not a conscious copying of old Arabic, but the natural manner in which his contemporaries speak (Ibid. vol. 1, p. 57). See also vol. 1, pp. 52–3.
93. Ibn al-Sarrāj (1993) vol. 1, p. 35.
94. Ibid. vol. 1, p. 36.
95. Ibid. vol. 1, p. 57.
96. Ibid. vol. 1, p. 57.
97. For the importance of memorisation (*ḥifẓ*) over analogy (*qiyās*) see Ibid. vol. 1, pp. 57, 76.
98. Bohas et al. (1990) pp. 5–6.

99. Levin (2004) pp. 10–11.
100. Cited in al-Suyūṭī (1976) pp. 56–7; discussed in Suleiman (2003) pp. 51–5, (2011) p. 7.
101. It is difficult to argue that Sībawayh preferred one particular version of Arabic, but in considering Sībawayh's preferences, Carter argues the case for Ḥijazī (2004) p. 41. If this is correct, it is noteworthy that Sībawayh selected the more urban al-Ḥijāz over pastoral/Bedouin Najd.
102. I.e. it was created perfect by God and does not develop via human agency (Ibn Fāris (1993) pp. 36–41).
103. Ibid. pp. 37–40; see also p. 49: 'Only a prophet can fully know Arabic'.
104. Ibid. p. 44. Ibn Fāris manifestly echoes al-Jāḥiẓ's claim that Arabic is the most expressive language, but al-Jāḥiẓ did not flatly disparage all non-Arabic communication. For an appraisal of al-Jāḥiẓ's opinion on non-Arabic communication see Pellat (1966) pp. 95–8, Anghelescu (1995) pp. 55–9; and for examination of his sometimes ambivalent opinions, Webb (2012a) pp. 35–7, 46–7.
105. Weiss (1984) p. 99.
106. Ibn Fāris (1993) pp. 46–7.
107. The term *uṣūl*, though most common in jurisprudence, had wide usage: e.g. Ibn al-Muqaffa^{c} (d. *c.*140/757) uses it in a text defining *adab* (1960) p. 69–71, implying that any field of knowledge is composed of both *uṣūl* (roots – principles) and *furū^{c}* (branches – specialisations). Ibn al-Sarrāj's incorporation of *uṣūl* into grammar need not be read as a strict emulation of jurisprudence, therefore, but as part of a transformation of *al-^{c}arabiyya* towards a self-contained field/^{c}*ilm*.
108. *Sunan* could also be read *sanan*, implying a 'way/path'. I prefer *sunan* given Ibn Fāris' seeming intention to use words with legal resonances (*uṣūl*, *furū^{c}*, *fiqh*) in this section of his text.
109. Ibn Fāris (1993) p. 33.
110. Ibid. p. 33.
111. See, for example, the Arabic vocabulary regarding horse husbandry and Ibn Qutayba's argument that this meant the Arabs must have possessed superior knowledge of this field over other peoples (1998) p. 120. Ibn Qutayba does not proceed from this particular point to a general praise of Arabic linguistic pre-eminence, unlike Ibn Fāris' construction of Arabness.
112. Webb (2012a) pp. 48–9.
113. The sharing of 'Arabic' between scholars and Bedouin served al-Jāḥiẓ's purposes

by enabling him to praise both pre-Islamic Arabs and his own literary output, as I argue in Webb (2012a) pp. 42–50.

114. Ibn Fāris (1993) pp. 50–5, 56–60.
115. Ibid. p. 59.
116. Ibid. pp. 50–1.
117. Ibid. p. 37.
118. Ibid. p. 41.
119. Ibid. p. 67.
120. Ibid. pp. 34–5.
121. Ibid. p. 64.
122. Ahola (2004) pp. 110–11. Romanov (2013) pp. 133–5. See discussion in Chapter 5(IV).
123. Ibn Fāris (1993) pp. 67–71.
124. Ibn Jinnī (2006) p. 110.
125. Ibid. p. 169.
126. Ibid. pp. 311–13.
127. Ibid. p. 77.
128. Al-Balādhurī (1997–2004) vol. 12, pp. 90–109.
129. For fuller discussion of the notion of genealogical time and the chronological order it bestows by presenting a biological progression of a family/dynasty see Spiegel (1997) pp. 99–110.
130. For example, Dāḥis wa-l-Ghabrā° is narrated after the battle of Shi°b Jabala, which was a later episode (Ibn °Abd Rabbihi (n.d.) vol. 5, pp. 146–53).
131. Abū al-Faraj al-Iṣfahānī (1992) vol. 21, pp. 191–210. The biography of °Azza is vol. 21, pp. 164–82, and Yazīd vol. 21, pp. 211–5.
132. Pietruschka (2001) p. 214. Notwithstanding the logic of treating *a°rāb* as the plural of *°arab* (on the basis that *af°āl* is a usual plural for *fa°al*), this seems an example of grammatical hyper-correctness ignoring both history and lexical usage of *°arab/a°rāb*. Lexically, *°arab* is itself a plural: I am unaware of any citation of *°arab* to connote 'one Arab' – a singular Arab is invariably *°arabī*, and the connection is rendered further remote in light of the possibility that *°arab* and *a°rāb* entered the Arabic language from different origins: see Chapter 3(II) for my hypothesis.
133. Or even 'cousins' of the Arabs, as suggested in Retsö (2003) pp. 82–93.
134. Donner (2010) pp. 57–8, 71–2.
135. Al-Khalīl (1980) vol. 2, p. 128; Sībawayh (1966–77) vol. 3, p. 379.

136. Consider Muqātil's commentary on the multiple citations of *a^c^rāb* in Qur'an Chapter 9 (1979–89) vol. 2, pp. 189–203.
137. The *fay*ʾ and *ṣadaqa* payments are considered in Steppat (1986) pp. 406–11. For Bedouin testimony, see Abū Dāwūd (1999) *al-Qaḍā*ʾ:17 and discussion in Ibn Qudāma (n.d.) vol. 12, p. 31; Ibn Qudāma also discusses the Friday prayer issue (Ibid. vol. 2, p. 171).
138. Athamina (1987) discusses *aʿrāb* as second-class peoples in early Islam. See also Leder (2005) pp. 400–2 and Binay (2006) pp. 55–9. Donner (1981) elaborates that original conquerors were urbanites who mobilised Bedouin for the purpose of conquest, and then treated those remaining in the desert as second-class *aʿrāb*.
139. Al-Azharī (2004) vol. 2, 166–7.
140. Ibid. vol. 2, p. 167.
141. Ibid. vol. 2, p. 166.
142. Ibid. vol. 2, p. 171.
143. Ibid. vol. 1, p. 21.
144. Ibid. vol. 1, p. 21.
145. The replication of old definitions irrespective of contemporary language development has been noted in the context of Arabic lexicography, whereby dictionaries have been called 'deliberate instruments of conservatism' (Carter (1990) p. 116).
146. Ibn Fāris (1946–52) vol. 4, p. 240.
147. Ibid. vol. 4, p. 300.
148. Al-Wazīr al-Maghribī (1980) vol. 1, p. 115.
149. Al-Jawharī (1956) vol. 1, p. 178.
150. Al-Wazīr al-Maghribī (1980) vol. 1, pp. 87–115.
151. Al-Tabrīzī (2000) vol. 2, p. 906.
152. Al-Ḥimyarī (1999) vol. 7, pp. 4456–7.
153. Ibn Manẓūr (1990) vol. 1, p. 586.
154. Ibn Qutayba (1998) pp. 35, 51–5.
155. *Al-Bayān wa-l-tabyīn* opens with this praise (al-Jāḥiẓ (2003) vol. 1, pp. 8–12). Note in this passage al-Jāḥiẓ deftly shifts the Qur'anic indefinite 'an Arabic tongue' into definite Arabness via his discussion of the language of 'the Arabs' and 'the Quraysh tribe'. See the analysis in Section I of this chapter.
156. Ibid. vol. 2, p. 7; vol. 3, p. 29.
157. Ibid. vol. 3, p. 29.

158. Ibid. vol. 3, p. 366.
159. Note in Ibid. vol. 1, p. 91; al-Jāḥiẓ similarly groups 'orators of Banū Hāshim [the Umayyads]' with 'eloquent tribesmen [*qabāʾil* – i.e. *aʿrāb*]'.
160. Ibn Qutayba (1998) p. 119.
161. The modern edition of Ibn Qutayba's *Faḍl al-ʿarab wa-l-tanbīh ʿalā ʿulūmihā* does not contain a section on medicine, but it does relate a fragmentary passage left unidentified at p. 135. My searches uncovered the same anecdote as part of discourse on Bedouin medicine in al-Dīnawarī's *al-Mujālasa wa-jawāhir al-ʿilm* (1998) vol. 5, p. 368. Review of a digital copy of the manuscript reveals an apparent tear between f. 37 and f. 38: the medical anecdote constitutes the first lines of f. 38r, suggesting that an unknown number of folios with other medical anecdotes are missing.
162. Ibid. pp. 131–3.
163. Ibid. p. 143.
164. Ibid. p. 161.
165. Al-Bīrūnī (1923) pp. 238–9.
166. The one derogatory reference in *Faḍl al-ʿarab* to *aʿrāb* as riffraff (*aʿlāj*) is not in Ibn Qutayba's own words: it is direct quotation from Muḥammad ibn ʿAlī, the early second/eighth-century spiritual leader of the nascent Abbasid movement (Ibn Qutayba (1998) p. 99).
167. Ibid. pp. 61, 78.
168. Ibid. p. 78.
169. Ibid. p. 66.
170. Ibid. p. 86.
171. Ibid. p. 105. Contrast with al-Jāḥiẓ's *bilād al-aʿrāb* (2003) vol. 3, p. 29.
172. Ibn Qutayba (1998) pp. 125, 131.
173. Al-Yaʿqūbī (n.d.) vol. 1, pp. 208–20.
174. Ibid. vol. 1, pp. 221–53.
175. Ibid. vol. 1, pp. 254–71.
176. Ibid. vol. 2, pp. 448, 498. Gordon (2001) p. 87, n. 147 considers other third/ninth century-associations of 'Arab troops' with 'vagabonds', 'street thugs' and 'outlaws'.
177. Al-Masʿūdī (1966–79) §1136.
178. Both al-Yaʿqūbī's *Tārīkh* and al-Masʿūdī's *Murūj* begin with a history of all peoples since Creation, including the pre-Islamic Arabs, following which they narrate the history of Islam organised by caliphal reign.
179. Al-Masʿūdī (1966–79) §1118.

180. Ibid. §1117.
181. Ibid. §1104.
182. Ibid. §1105.
183. Ibid. §1102.
184. Ibid. §1108.
185. Ibid. §1109.
186. Ibid. §1112.
187. Ibid. §1150.
188. Ibid. §1166.
189. Ibid. §973.
190. Ibid. §1111.
191. Muqātil (1979–89) vol. 4, p. 601.
192. Al-Qurṭubī (2000) vol. 19, p. 149.
193. Al-Biqāᶜī (1995) vol. 8, p. 337.
194. References to *aᶜrāb* occur in post-fourth/tenth-century literature, but as a technical term related to the Qur'anic citations of *aᶜrāb* – e.g. al-Bīrūnī's *al-Āthār* (1923) pp. 238–9 considers the negative stereotypes of the Qur'anic *aᶜrāb* and Ibn Ḥazm's *al-Fiṣal* (1999a) vol. 3, pp. 28–9 uses the term *aᶜrāb* as the technical marker of Arabian nomads at the time of Muhammad, again when citing the Qur'an. When these authors consider ancient Arabians generally, they use *al-ᶜarab*.
195. See R. Ward (2014) pp. 133–5, 142–4 for images of the objects.
196. Rodinson (1981) p. 22.
197. In events he records from his own lifetime, Ibn Īyās refers to *al-ᶜarab* or *al-ᶜurbān* almost exclusively for raiders and people who disrupt the countryside (e.g. Ibn Īyās (2008) vol. 4, pp. 20, 79, 90, 193, 217, 229, 264, 353, 359).
198. The rise of Arab identity as a form of self-expression in writings from Muslim Spain in the fourth/tenth and fifth/eleventh centuries is a case in point to develop our understanding of Arabness' variability in medieval Islam. In contrast to Iraqi writers, Andalusians do refer to themselves as 'Arabs' and were especially interested in the pre-Islamic Arab past after the third/ninth century. The 'Umayyad' identity of Andalusia's caliphs, their interaction with different socio-political groups of Berbers and independent Catholic kings, and their separation from the traditional font of Arabness constitute a very different context for their process of imagining the Arabs, which can be expected to have yielded different results. Quantitatively, the literary production is reflected in Romanov's observation that Andalusian individuals from the fourth/tenth

and fifth/eleventh century continued to be identified by Arab tribal *nisbas* in contrast to Iraqi domiciles (2016) p. 130.

199. See Chapter 5(II–III).
200. Al-Masᶜūdī (1966–79) §1171.
201. Ibid. §1175.
202. Ibid. §1175. See also Chapter 5(III).
203. Ibid. §§1000–35.
204. Ibid. §134.
205. Ibid. §§130–51, 1122.
206. Ibid. §§1126–40.
207. Ibn Ḥabīb (1985) pp. 86–9, Ibn Hishām (n.d.) vol. 1, pp. 137–55.
208. Al-Masᶜūdī (1966–79) §1126.
209. Ibid. §1122.
210. Ibid. §1190.
211. Ibid. §1189.
212. Ibid. §§1196–1216.
213. Ibid. §§1217–49.
214. See Ibid. §§927, 1000–16.
215. Ibid. §1086.
216. Ibid. §1166.
217. Al-Bakrī's frequent borrowings from al-Masᶜūdī are discussed in the introduction to *al-Masālik wa-l-mamālik* (1992) vol. 1, pp. 18–19.
218. Al-Shahristānī (n.d.) vol. 3, pp. 248–61.
219. Ibid. vol. 3, pp. 272–5.
220. Ibid. vol. 3, pp. 276–88.
221. Al-Maqdisī (n.d.) vol. 4, p. 107.
222. Ibid. vol. 4, p. 122.
223. Ibid. vol. 4, p. 122.
224. Ibid. vol. 4, pp. 111, 113, 129.
225. Ibid. vol. 4, p. 124.
226. Ibid. vol. 4, p. 113.
227. Ibid. vol. 3, pp. 174–6, vol. 4, pp. 116–18.
228. Ibid. vol. 4, pp. 114, 116, 122.
229. Such narratives and mythmaking to construct *al-Jāhiliyya*, will be the subject of a British Academy Postdoctoral Fellowship (pf150079) which I am commencing as this book goes to press.

Imagining and Reimagining the Arabs: Conclusions

By unfastening Arab identity from conventional cultural stereotypes, Bedouinism and ancient pre-Islamic Arabian bloodlines, this book sought to reveal the complexities and changing nature of historic Arab identity. The book was intended as an invitation to begin rethinking Arabness afresh, and by highlighting the shortcomings inherent in the static, monolithic manner in which historical Arab communities have often been discussed, our analysis sought to reappraise historic Arabness as an ethnicity, tracking its evolution and contextualising its development with close attention to the sociopolitical and 'cultural stuff' factors that sustain ethnogenesis.

Taking stock, ethnogenesis and Max Weber's ideas seem to do a world of good for our understanding of Arab origins, pre-Islamic Arabia and the rise of Islam. Theorising the origin of Arab communities as a Muslim-era phenomenon helped unblock difficulties in interpreting memories of pre-Islamic Arabia, for we are relieved of the search for pre-Islamic Arabs and can focus on studying the region's communities as the wholly diverse panoply of peoples as they actually were. Our model of Arab ethnogenesis also prompts reassessment of the traditional interpretation of Islam's rise as a 'national movement' of Arabs and the customary focus on the 'Arab conquests' as the history of a militarised migration. Instead, the rise of the novel community of 'Arabs' in the wake of the conquests signals deeper currents were at work, and can reorient study towards the Conquerors' achievements of crafting novel forms of statecraft, urban networks and societies as a consequence of the unprecedented circumstances their conquests created. We ought no longer assume with confidence that 'Saracen barbarians' occupied the ailing body of Late Antiquity and 'civilised' themselves in its trappings: instead the Conquerors knew of themselves as Emigrants (*muhājirūn*) with a distinct message and code, and as they developed their doctrines into the religion of Islam and distinguished themselves from conquered populations, they took on a new Arab guise for themselves and creatively tried to reorganise their world in its image. Creating the 'Muslim World' was equally a process of imagining the Arabs, and the study of early Islam will benefit from a more sensitive approach to community and increased attention to the diversity of the early Muslims who were embroiled in a process amongst themselves of negotiating what it meant to be an 'Arab'.

The theories of ethnogenesis at last offer grounded perspective to interpret the longstanding conundrum of pre-Islamic references to 'Arabs' too. Reconsidering the sources which mention 'Arabs' from Assyrian scribes in the ninth century BCE to South Arabian inscriptions in the fifth century CE, we can propose with some confidence that 'Arab'-cognates connoted 'nomad' and ideas of outsider-ness, and were labels for 'other', neither signifiers for 'self' nor the 'Arab people'. Populations inside Arabia gave no indication of awareness of attachment to a pan-regional community, and the transactional boundaries and cultural zones across the Peninsula underline the theoretical problems inherent in trying to find Arabs in pre-Islamic Arabia on a 'must-have-been' basis. If it were not for the vociferous Muslim-era Arabic literary tradition's claims that Arabia was full of Arabs, I doubt modern readers would ever have expected to find any communal homogeneity in pre-Islamic Arabia. The considerable divergence in opinions about pre-Islamic Arab origins expressed over the last century is therefore a corollary of the fact that a cohesive community of 'pre-Islamic Arabs' did not actually exist, or at least it did not exist in the form that we were conditioned to expect. Scouring pre-Islam to find the first stirrings of the Arab ethnos somewhere in the darkness of the 'Empty Ḥijāz', tending camels, singing poetry and jealously guarding their tribal honour will be futile since such Bedouin stereotypes are not a relic of pre-Islamic Arabia, rather they are a construct of Muslim imaginations championed in fourth/tenth-century writings. In the pre-Islamic era itself, 'Arab' was a label without a people, it was the property of outsiders who used the word without close consideration of the actual status of Arabian communities.

The spectre of an Arabless pre-Islamic Arabia does not require us to conjure Arabs from nothing in the Islamic period, however. The curious disjoint between the stark lack of evidence of communities expressing a sense of Arab identity before Islam, and the ample reference to self-designated Arabs once the Caliphate was well established is bridged by the circumstances fostered by the Muslim Conquerors' settlement patterns. The conquests moved populations, the *amṣār* settlement concentrated groups of co-confessionalists, the success of the conquests gave the Conquerors a preponderance of power and status, and the challenges of maintaining their gains prompted circumstances conducive to generating new consciousness of community. The absence of a unifying pre-Islamic background common to the varied Conqueror groups coupled with their potent shared symbolic capital emanating from nascent Islam pointed to new building blocks around which the new community could form. The novel arrangement of peoples into webs of never before shared interests point emphatically to the reason why they would embrace a new identity of Arabness that had hitherto never been expressed, and the derivation of their name from the Qur'an and its unique meaning of *ᶜarabī* to connote, for the first time in recorded history, something other than 'nomadic outsiders' underlines the role of religion in giving meaning to the new community's identity. And so the novel idea that people could imagine themselves as 'Arabs' slid into history – not in one swoop of caliphal decree, but gradually and unevenly as groups found, for matters of convenience, necessity or simply pride in the their elite Conqueror status, value in becoming 'Arab' and sharing that identity with others of similar sociopolitical ranks and confessional alignments.

The formation stage of Arab identity remains cloudy and observable through narrow windows of surviving evidential shards, but such is the expected state of an ethnos' origins. In the Umayyad era, Arabness needed to replace old identities as Conqueror groups obliterated divisive pre-Islamic senses of community to reorganise themselves into an Arab family. Moreover, the enduring appeal of Ma'addite communal consciousness, the rise of new regional power bases in Syria and Iraq, and new senses of solidary between 'Yemenis' and other smaller-scale groups brought together in post-conquest settlement offered early Muslims manifold alternative identities, and as the precise parameters of Arabness were not yet fully articulated, we cannot expect later Umayyad-era Muslims to instantly turn into 'Arabs' and describe Arabness to us in coherent and consistent terms. But we can grasp that Arabness, with its significations of 'purity' and connection with the specific 'monotheistic purity' of *al-ḥanīfiyya*, constituted a tangible means to identify the Conqueror elite in terms of their proprietary scripture and the elevated status which their vernaculars attained by virtue of their similarity to the Qur'anic koine. Arabness thus encompassed powerful symbols and 'cultural stuff', and aided by the background of the particular transactional boundaries between social groups in the post-conquest Middle East, Arab identity had the theoretical potential to appeal to groups of 'Emigrants' who were no longer emigrating, and thus needed new paradigms to conceptualise their community to uphold their status above conquered populations. The discernable rise in the citation of *al-ᶜarab* in poetry of the late first/seventh century, marshalled in the way that the ethnonym 'Maᶜadd' had previously pervaded central Arabian pre-Islamic poetry, is key evidence that the theoretical potential for ethnogenesis following the Muslim conquests became real in the late first/seventh century. A new sense of Arabness as a broad-based community of elites from Central Asia to North Africa took shape within two or three generations of the first conquests.

The rise of Arab self-awareness in poetry coincides closely with the confident articulation of the Islamic state under ᶜAbd al-Malik ibn Marwān (r. 65–86/685–705), and prompts further inferences. First, the congruence of new-found Arabness and reinvigorated Caliphate supports our proposal that *ᶜarabī* initially connoted a sense of 'monotheistic purity'. We know that ᶜAbd al-Malik was intent on broadcasting Islam as the Caliphate's creed, and identifying his elites via a term redolent of religious purity would appeal. Arabness offered ᶜAbd al-Malik a means to create a sense of a legitimate community out of the fragmentation and mistrust of the Second *Fitna* war, which had brought him to power. Second, the link of Arabness with the newly vigorous Marwanid Caliphate can explain the success of Arabness as a name and community: it was associated with winners – the scion of the Conquerors and their state – and hence it was a valuable asset backed by the authority of a stable regime. As the Marwanid Caliphate remained stable for two generations, Arabness had the requisite time to gain traction, prompting increasing numbers of groups, Ma'addites, Yemenis and others, to want to join of their own accord. The quite clearly articulated Arab community of the early Abbasid Caliphate can then be counted as one of the major legacies of Marwanid-era society building. Third, the chronology of Arabness' formation seems to accord with Donner's theory of Islam's transition from a 'Believers movement' to the 'Muslim state' during the reign of ᶜAbd al-Malik. As Donner hypothesised, Arab unity did not drive the conquests: the label of 'Arab conquest' is a hazardous misnomer that essentially invents an anachronistic ethnicity to explain the conquests in a way its participants themselves would not have understood. Likewise, the first generations of post-conquest settlers did not define their community in 'Arab' terms either, and the notion that the early Umayyads constituted an 'Arab state' is as hollow as 'Arab conquests', but when the religious creed was articulated as the system of Islam, Arab identity soon followed, indicating that a sense of kinship was indeed the result, not the cause, of Islam's establishment. And fourth, from a theoretical perspective, the formation of Arab identity appears an ideal test case to explore the role of faith in shaping ethnic communities. Islam emerges as a precondition and catalyst of Arab ethnogenesis, whereby a community of co-religionists in the particular circumstances of the post-conquest Middle East rearticulated their religious community into an ethnic guise, giving it a name, genealogy, history and cultural trappings which were all tied to the symbolic capital of their faith, but became articulated in exclusive kinship forms.

The role of shared faith in Arab ethnogenesis and the resultant notion of Arabness' communal boundaries also offer intriguing grounds to contrast the Arab case with the nearly contemporary processes of European community formation. Conquests and resettlements occurred elsewhere in Late Antiquity, but they created distinct ethnic communities of Franks, Lombards, Anglo-Saxons and Avars, and some groups such as the Vandals acquired very tenuous identities. The conquests of the early Muslims, on the other hand, created a system in which the elite became cognisant of one salient and novel identity of Arabness across a vast area, their community neither dissolved into regionalised fragments, nor looked to previous imperial regimes for legitimacy: they engrained instead a new faith and a novel interest in 'being Arabian' across cultural centres in the Middle East. In both the European and Arab cases, the emergence of new ethnic groups coincided with the embracing of monotheism, but the 'pure' *ᶜarabī* monotheism seems to have possessed an unprecedented magnitude, presumably thanks to the fact that its foundational scripture called itself *ʿarabī*, that maintained social cohesion and a sense of new purpose across the vast conquered regions and eventually spawned an 'Arabic' *ʿarabī* people.

To further grasp the 'formation' stage of Arab community, we shall need renewed attention into the competing forms of identity in early Islam and the ways which Umayyad society was organised,[1] while also exploring how urban networks, the economy, the development of the Caliphate and Islamic doctrines interacted with Arab ethnogenesis to give post-conquest society its unique form. And the formation of Arabness is yet only a part of the Arab story. This book's purpose was to critique generalisation about Arab identity, and hence we also needed to evaluate the fate of the Arab idea once it had become established as a group's own identity. Therein, we uncovered the disagreement, debate and evolution that accompanied the mental processes of imagining the Arabs, bringing us to the 'maintenance and renewal' stage as different groups grappled with the meaning of being 'Arab' and writers began to pick up the pieces of old debates and elevated the idea of the 'Arab' to the foundational block of Arabic literature.

Our analysis of texts and society from the second/eighth to the fourth/tenth centuries probed both the nexus between Arabness as the identity of actual groups, and Arabness as an intellectual construct. Considerable segments of society in the second/eighth and third/ninth centuries self-designated as 'Arabs', but their socio-economic and political status was in flux and the practical value of Arabness as an asset and the symbolic significations of Arabness as an idea in society shifted in turn. When Arabness had practical value, disparate groups sought to join the Arabs, and so foisted their traditions and ideas onto the concept of Arab identity and an Arab race (*shaʿb*) linked through varied notions of bloodlines and history. But when Arab groups began to fall from political grace, membership of Arab communities dwindled as people abandoned former claims to tribal lineages, and their retreat from Arab self-designation left a door open for new cultural producers to take over the 'Arab idea' and fill the identity with new significations.

Amongst the many ramifications of the complex fate of the Arabness idea in early Islam as it was buffeted by assimilation, conversion and ethnic revival, two salient discourses merit particular attention: *al-Jāhiliyya* and the Bedouin. Chapters 5 and 6 revealed that these two concepts evolved during early Islam as Muslims developed new senses of their own identities. Communities need to construct a shared sense of the past in order to gel their members into one cohesive group, and because a given group's members hail from diverse backgrounds, that sense of past unity is quite often imaginary. In the Arab case, the narratives of pre-Islam played a vital role in creating a sense of 'Arab pre-history' to forget the fact that consciousness of Arab identity only coalesced in the Islamic era, and to understand the place of Islam in the sweep of world history. As Muslim communities developed and as the status of Arab groups changed, impressions of the Arab pre-history evolved in turn, and to open our sources to the full wealth of their discourses, a new approach to 'Jahiliyya studies' is needed that marshals narratological and mythopoeic methods to probe the different and changing Jahiliyyas in Muslim imaginations across time.

Chapter 6 also aimed to explain why Arabs have been so customarily associated with Bedouin, especially given the vociferous claims of the first self-designated *ᶜarab* (Arabs) to distinguish themselves from *aᶜrāb* (Bedouin). We found that the familiar Bedouin archetype can be traced to Muslim philologists from the mid-third/ninth century, who rearticulated models of 'correct-Arabic' and projected it into a distant and dangerous desert, championing the absent nomad as the paragon of linguistic purity. As members of urban societies were contemporaneously retreating from Arab self-designation, the Bedouin archetype in the imaginations of Muslim philologists became the primary stakeholder in the definition of Arabness and, over the course of a century, the Bedouin was crafted by the weight of much consistent writing, into the idealised 'Arab'. The efforts of the philologists were practically useful for their own purposes of championing themselves as the second-best (but best available) sources of Arabic knowledge, and their discourse of Bedouinising Arab memories had manifold other advantages too. Foremost, it enabled fourth/tenth-century Muslims to imagine Islam's origins in a guise of Bedouin primitivism, bestowing a sublime sense of purity onto Islam's formative milieu. The Arab-turned-Bedouin idea became a device that narrated Islam's origins onto a *tabula rasa*, presenting a perfect language possessed by perfect fools in a pristine desert. The Bedouin played an Islamic

Parsifal, and the story of his enlightenment via Muhammad offered global redemption.

Edward Said famously noted the problematic legacy which Orientalism bequeathed the study of the Middle East when Western writers 'othered' Middle Eastern peoples as a means to explore their own civilisation and assert their feelings of superiority. Fourth/tenth-century Muslim discourses appear to mirror this process exactly: Iraqi scholars wielded the power to create the 'Arab' in the image they desired and so generated the stereotypes of Bedouin primitivism that persist to this day. Before Colonial-era European Orientalism, therefore, there was a Muslim Arabism that modern researchers must confront as one of the most pervasive and important intellectual constructs of the Abbasid era that generated long-lasting narratives to explain Islam's origins and the essence of its urban, 'civilised' culture.

We are now left with more questions to better elaborate the full panoply of the Arabness idea. Outside of Iraq, how did Arab communities form in Egypt, Syria and Iran, and why did fourth/tenth-century Andalusians embrace Arabness as one of their cherished identities while Iraqis were conversely dropping Arab tribal affiliations? What messages were the Fatimids broadcasting when naming their succession of caliphs in North Africa Ismāᶜīl, Maᶜadd and Nizār, mirroring Ma'addite Arab genealogy? Did any peoples in the Middle East call themselves Arabs across the half-millennium between the fifth/eleventh and tenth/seventeenth centuries, and if so, why and what meanings did Arab identity convey? And how did nineteenth-century Arab nationalist discourses reassemble the pieces of the medieval Arabness heritage to reimagine the Arabs yet again?

It is my hope that this book has offered a new and credible narrative to conceptualise the rise and early development of Arab communities. I construct this story to make the past understandable for the present, and I am handicapped by the spatial and temporal gap between my study in which I write and the material which I study. Nevertheless, I am but only a little more removed from pre-Islamic Arabia than al-Jāḥiẓ and al-Masᶜūdī were when they expounded on the 'authentic habits' of the 'original Arabs'. Readers shall continue investigating the complexities of Arabness, and in so doing they shall better understand the rise and significance of one of the world's most discussed and oft-misinterpreted peoples.

Note

1. Such work could revisit the old debate between Shaban (1971) and Crone (1994a), rethinking the Yamāniyya and other groups, not in stark terms of 'political parties', but as other forms of group mobilisation and regional identities. A study of Ma'addite identity in early Islam is the subject of Webb (forthcoming (A)).

Bibliography

Abbott, Nabia (1941), 'Pre-Islamic Arab Queens', *The American Journal of Semitic Languages and Literatures* 58, pp. 1–22.

—— (1949), 'A Ninth-Century Fragment of the 'Thousand Nights': New Light on the Early History of the Arabian Nights', *Journal of Near Eastern Studies* 8, pp. 129–64.

—— (1967), *Studies in Arabic Literary Papyri, II: Qurʾānic Commentary and Tradition*. Chicago: University of Chicago Press.

Abdel Haleem, M. A. S. (trans.) (2004), *The Qurʾān: A New Translation*. Oxford: Oxford UP.

Abū Dahbal al-Jumaḥī (1972), *Dīwān*. ᶜAbd al-ᶜAẓīm ᶜAbd al-Muḥsin (ed.). Najaf: Maṭbaᶜat al-Qaḍā.

Abū Dāwūd, Sulaymān (1999), *Sunan Abī Dāwūd*. Riyadh: Dār al-Salām.

Abū Nuwās, al-Ḥasan ibn Hāniʾ [1972–2003] (2012), *Dīwān Abī Nuwās*. Ewald Wagner (ed.). Beirut, Orient Institut.

Abū Tammām al-Ṭāʾī (1987), *al-Waḥshiyyāt*. ᶜAbd al-ᶜAzīz al-Maymanī al-Rājkūtī (ed.). Cairo: al-Maᶜārif.

Abū Tammām al-Ṭāʾī (attrib.) (1922), *Naqāʾiḍ Jarīr wa-l-Akhṭal*. Anṭūn Ṣāliḥānī (ed.). Beirut: Dār al-Kutub al-ᶜIlmiyya.

Abū ᶜUbayda, Maᶜmar ibn al-Muthannā (1905–12), *Naqāʾiḍ Jarīr wa-l-Farazdaq*. A. A. Bevan (ed.). Leiden: Brill.

Abū Zurᶜa al-Dimashqī (1996), *Tārīkh Abī Zurᶜa*. Khalīl al-Manṣūr (ed.). Beirut: Dār al-Kutub al-ᶜIlmiyya.

Agha, Said Saleh (2003), *The Revolution Which Toppled the Umayyads: Neither Arab Nor Abbasid*. Leiden: Brill.

—— (2011), 'Of Verse, Poetry, Great Poetry and History', in Ramzi Baalbaki,

Saleh Said Agha and Tarif Khalidi (eds), *Poetry and History: the Value of Poetry in Reconstructing Arab History*. Beirut: American University of Beirut, pp. 1–35.

Agius, Dionysius (1980), 'The Shu'ubiyya Movement and its literary manifestation', *Islamic Quarterly* 24, pp. 76–88.

Ahola, Judith (2004), 'The community of scholars: an analysis of the biographical data from the Ta'rīkh Baghdād'. Unpublished PhD Thesis, University of St Andrews.

al-Ājurrī, Abū Bakr Muḥammad (1989), *al-Arbaᶜūn ḥadīthan*. ᶜAlī Ḥusayn ᶜAlī ᶜAbd al-Ḥamīd (ed.). Beirut: al-Maktab al-Islāmī.

al-Akhfash, Abū al-Ḥasan Saᶜīd (2010), *Maᶜānī al-Qurᵓān*. Hudā Maḥmūd Qarrāᶜa (ed.). Cairo: al-Khānjī.

Alexander, Paul J. (1985), *The Byzantine Apocalyptic Tradition*. Berkeley: University of California Press.

ᶜAlī, Jawād (1968–73), *al-Mufaṣṣal fi-tārīkh al-ᶜarab qabla al-Islām*. Beirut: Dār al-ᶜIlm li-l-Malāyīn.

Ammianus Marcellinus (1989), *History: Books 20–26*. John C. Rolfe (trans.). Cambridge, MA: Loeb.

al-Anbārī, Abū Muḥammad al-Qāsim (2003), *Sharḥ Dīwān al-Mufaḍḍaliyyāt*. Muḥammad Nabīl Ṭarīfī (ed.). Beirut: Dār Ṣādir.

Anderson, Benedict (1991), *Imagined Communities*. London: Verso.

Anghelescu, Nadia (1995), *Langage et Culture dans la civilisation Arabe*. Viorel Visan (trans.). Paris: L'Harmattan.

al-Anṣārī, A. R. (1982), *Qaryat al-Fau*. Al-Riyadh: University of al-Riyadh.

ᶜĀqil, Nabīh (1969), *Tārīkh al-ᶜarab al-qadīm wa-ᶜaṣr al-Rasūl*. Damascus: Silsilat Tārīkh al-ᶜArab wa-l-Islām.

Arafat, Walid (1966), 'The Historical Significance of Later Anṣārī Poetry – I', *Bulletin of the School of Oriental and African Studies* 29, pp. 1–11.

—— (1970), 'The Historical Background to the Elegies on ᶜUthmān b. ᶜAffān attributed to Ḥassān b. Thābit', *Bulletin of the School of Oriental and African Studies* 33, pp. 276–82.

Arḥīla, ᶜAbbās (2004), *al-Kitāb wa-ṣināᶜat al-taᵓlīf ᶜinda-l-Jāḥiẓ*. Marrakech: al-Warrāqa al-Waṭaniyya.

al-Aᶜshā, Qays ibn Maymūm (1974), *Dīwān*. Muḥammad Muḥammad Ḥusayn (ed.). Beirut: Dār al-Nahḍa al-ᶜArabiyya.

al-Aṣmaᶜī, ᶜAbd al-Malik ibn Qurayb (2005), *al-Aṣmaᶜiyyāt*. Muḥammad Nabīl Ṭarīfī (ed.). Beirut: Dār Ṣādir.

Assyrian Dictionary (1964–2010), Martha T. Roth (ed.). Chicago: Oriental Institute of the University of Chicago.

Atallah, W., 'al-Kalbī', *EI*[2], 4:494–6.

Athamina, Khalil (1987), 'A'rāb and Muhājirūn in the Environment of Amṣār', *Studia Islamica* 66, pp. 5–25.

—— (1992) 'Al-Qasas: Its Emergence, Religious Origin and Its Socio-political Impact on Early Muslim Society', *Studia Islamica* 76, pp. 53–74.

Attwood, Bain (1989), *The Making of the Aborigines*. Sydney: Allen & Unwin.

Ayalon, David (1994), 'The Military Reforms of Caliph al-Muᶜtasim: Their Background and Consequence', in Ayalon (ed.), *Islam and the Abode of War*. Farnham: Ashgate Variorum, pp. 1–39.

Azami, M. M. (1992), *Studies in Ḥadīth methodology and literature*. Indianapolis: American Trust Publications.

al-Azharī, Muḥammad ibn Aḥmad (2004), *Tahdhīb al-lugha*. Muḥammad ᶜAbd al-Raḥmān Mukhaymir (ed.). Beirut: Dār al-Kutub al-ᶜIlmiyya.

al-Azmeh, Aziz (2014a), *The Emergence of Islam in Late Antiquity*. Cambridge: Cambridge UP.

—— (2014b) *Arabs and Islam in late antiquity: a critique of approaches to Arabic sources*. Berlin: Gerlach.

Bachelard, Gaston [1958] (1994), *The Poetics of Space*. Maria Jolas (trans.). Boston: Beacon.

Badawi, M. M. (1990), 'ᶜAbbāsid poetry and its antecedents', in Julia Ashtiany, T. M. Johnstone, J. D. Latham, R. B. Serjeant and G. Rex Smith (eds), *ᶜAbbāsid Belles-Lettres*. Cambridge: Cambridge UP, pp. 146–66.

al-Baghdādī, al-Khaṭīb (1997), *Tārīkh Baghdād*. Muṣṭafā ᶜAbd al-Qādir ᶜAṭā (ed.). Beirut: Dār al-Kutub al-ᶜIlmiyya.

al-Bājī, Sulaymān ibn Khalaf (1999), *al-Muntaqā sharḥ Muwaṭṭaᵓ Mālik*. Muḥammad ᶜAbd al-Qādir ᶜAṭā (ed.). Beirut: Dār al-Kutub al-ᶜIlmiyya.

Bakhos, Carol (2006), *Ishmael on the Border: Rabbinic Portrayals of the First Arab*. Albany, NY: State University of New York Press.

Bakhtin, M. M. (1981), *The Dialogic Imagination*. Michael Holquist (ed.), Caryl Emerson and Michael Holquist (trans.). Austin: University of Texas.

al-Bakrī, Abū ᶜUbayd (1947), *Muᶜjam mā istaᶜjam*. Muṣṭafā al-Saqā (ed.). Cairo: Lajnat al-Taᵓlīf wa-l-Tarjama wa-l-nashr.

—— (1992), *al-Masālik wa-l-mamālik*. Adrian Van Leeuwen and André Ferré (eds). Tunis: al-Dār al-ᶜArabīya li-l-Kitāb.

al-Balādhurī, Aḥmad ibn Yaḥyā (1979–), *Ansāb al-ashrāf*. Iḥsān ᶜAbbās, Ramzī

Ba^c^albaki, ^c^Abd al-^c^Azīz al-Dūrī, Wilferd Madelung, Yūsuf al-Mar^c^ashlī, ^c^Iṣām ^c^Uqla (eds). Beirut: Orient-Institut.

—— (1997–2004), *Ansāb al-ashrāf.* Maḥmūd al-Firdaws al-^c^Aẓam (ed.). Damascus: Dār al-Yaqaẓa al-^c^Arabiyya.

Banton, Michael (2007), 'Max Weber on "ethnic communities": a critique', *Nations and Nationalism* 13, pp. 19–35.

Barlas, Asma (2002), *Believing Women in Islam.* Austin: University of Texas.

Barth, Fredrik (1969), *Ethnic groups and boundaries: The social organization of culture difference.* Oslo: Universitetsforlaget.

—— (1994), 'Enduring and emerging issues in the analysis of ethnicity', in H. Vermeulen and C. Govers (eds), *The Anthropology of Ethnicity: Beyond Ethnic Groups and Boundaries.* Amsterdam: Het Spinhuis, pp. 11–32.

Bashear, Suliman (1984), *Muqaddima fī tārīkh al-ākhar.* Jerusalem: (no publisher).

—— (1997), *The Arabs and Others in Early Islam.* Princeton: Darwin.

Bāshmīl, Muḥammad (1973), *al-^c^Arab fī al-Shām qabla al-Islām.* Beirut: Dār al-Fikr.

Bashshār ibn Burd (1976), *Dīwān Bashshār ibn Burd.* Muḥammad al-Ṭāhir ibn ^c^Āshūr (ed.). Tunis: al-Sharika al-Tūnisiyya li-l-Tawzī^c^.

al-Bayḍāwī, Abū Sa^c^īd (1999), *Tafsīr al-Bayḍāwī.* Beirut: Dār al-Kutub al-^c^Ilmiyya.

Bayṭār, Muḥammad Shafīq (1999), 'al-Muqaddima' in Zuhayr ibn Janāb al-Kalbī, *Dīwān*, Muḥammad Shafīq Bayṭār (ed.). Beirut: Dār Ṣādir, pp. 9–50.

Becker, C. H. (1913), 'The Expansion of the Saracens', in H. M. Gwatkin and J. P. Whitney (eds), *The Cambridge Medieval History Volume 2: The Rise of the Saracens and the Foundation of the Western Empire.* Cambridge: Cambridge UP, pp. 329–65.

Beeston, A. F. L. (1977), 'On the Correspondence of Hebrew *s* to ESA *s2*', *Journal of Semitic Studies* 22, pp. 50–7.

—— (1984), 'Himyarite Monotheism', in ^c^Abd al-Qādir Maḥmūd, Richard Abdalla and Sami al-Sakkar (eds), *Studies in the History of Arabia II: Pre-Islamic Arabia.* Riyadh: King Saud University, pp. 149–54.

Beeston, A. F. L., M. A. Ghul, W. W. Müller, J. Ryckmans (1982), *Sabaic Dictionary.* Louvain-la-Neuve: Éditions Peeters.

Behzadi, Lale (2009a), 'Al-Jāḥiẓ and his Successors on Communication and the Levels of Language', in Arnim Heinemann, John L. Meloy, Tarif Khalidi and Manfred Kropp (eds), *Al-Jāḥiẓ: A Muslim Humanist for our Time.* Beirut: Orient-Institut and Ergon Verlag, pp. 125–32.

—— (2009b), *Sprache und Verstehen: al-Ǧāḥiẓ über die Vollkommenheit des Ausdrucks.* Wiesbaden: Harrassowitz.

Bell, H. I. (ed.) (1910), *Greek Papyri in the British Museum, Vol IV: The Aphrodito Papyri*, London: British Museum.

—— (1945), 'The Arabic Bilingual Entagion', *Proceedings Of The American Philosophical Society* 89 (1945), pp. 538–9.

Bellamy, James A. (1985), 'A New Reading of the Namārah Inscription', *Journal of the American Oriental Society* 105, pp. 31–51.

—— (1990) 'Arabic verses from the first/second century: The inscription of ᶜEn ᶜAvdat', *Journal of Semitic Studies* 25, pp. 73–9.

Berkey, Jonathan P. (2003), *The formation of Islam: religion and society in the Near East, 600–1800*. Cambridge: Cambridge UP.

Berkhofer Jr, Robert (1978), *The White Man's Indian*. New York: Alfred Knopf.

Biella, Joan Copeland (2004), *Dictionary of Old South Arabic: Sabaean Dialect*. Winona Lake, IN: Eisenbrauns.

Binay, Sara (2006), *Die Figur des Beduinen in der arabischen Literatur 9.–12. Jahrhundert*. Wiesbaden: Reichert.

Binggeli, A. (2007), 'Foires et pèlerinages sur la route du ḥajj', *Aram* 18–19, pp. 559–82.

al-Biqāᶜī, Burhān al-Dīn Abū al-Ḥasan (1995), *Naẓm al-durar fī tanāsub al-āyāt wa-l-suwar*. ᶜAbd al-Razzāq Ghālib al-Mahdī (ed.). Beirut: Dār al-Kutub al-ᶜIlmiyya.

al-Bīrūnī, Muḥammad ibn Aḥmad (1923), *al-Āthār al-bāqiya ᶜan al-qurūn al-khāliya*. C. E. Sachau (ed.). Leipzig: Otto Harrassowitz.

Blankinship, Khalid Yahya (1994), *The End of the Jihād State: the reign of Hishām Ibn 'Abd Al-Malik and the collapse of the Umayyads*. Albany, NY: State University of New York Press.

Blau, J. (1982), 'The Transcription Of Arabic Words And Names In The Inscription Of Mu'āwiya From Hammat Gader', *Israel Exploration Journal* 32, p. 102.

Bloom, Jonathan (2001), *Paper before Print: the History and Impact of Paper in the Islamic World*. New Haven: Yale UP.

Bohas, Georges, Jean-Patrick Guillaume, Djamel Kouloughli (1990), *The Arabic Linguistic Tradition*. Washington, DC: Georgetown UP.

Borrut, Antoine (2005), 'Entre tradition et histoire: genèse et diffusion de l'image de 'Umar II', *Mélanges de l'Université Saint-Joseph* 58, pp. 329–78.

—— (2011), *Entre mémoire et pouvoir: l'espace syrien sous les derniers Omeyyades et les premiers Abbassides (v. 72–193/692–809)*. Leiden: Brill.

Bosworth, C. E. (1983), 'Iran and the Arabs before Islam', in Ehsan Yarshater (ed.), *The Cambridge History of Iran Volume 3(1): The Seleucid, Parthian and Sasanian Periods*. Cambridge: Cambridge UP, pp. 593–612.

—— (1989), 'A note on Ta^carrub in early Islam', *Journal of Semitic Studies* 34, pp. 355–62.

Böwering, Gerhard (2004), 'Prayer', in Jane D. McAuliffe (ed.), *Encyclopaedia of the Qur^ɔān*. Leiden: Brill, vol. 4, pp. 215–31.

—— (2008), 'Recent research on the construction of the Qur^ɔān', in Gabriel Said Reynolds (ed.), *The Qur^ɔān in its Historical Context*. London: Routledge, pp. 70–87.

Bowersock, G. W. (2013), *The Throne of Adulis*. Oxford: Oxford UP.

Boyarin, Daniel (1999), *Dying for God: Martyrdom and the Making of Judaism and Christianity*. Stanford: Stanford UP.

—— (2004), 'The Christian Invention of Judaism', *Representations* 85, pp. 21–57.

Bray, Julia (2003), 'Lists and Memory: Ibn Qutayba and Muḥammad ibn Ḥabīb', in F. Daftary and J. W. Meri (eds), *Culture and Memory in Medieval Islam*. London: I. B. Tauris in association with the Institute of Ismaili Studies, pp. 210–31.

Brett, Michael and Elizabeth Fentress (1997), *The Berbers*. London: Wiley-Blackwell.

Brock, S. (2005), 'The Use Of Hijra Dating In Syriac Manuscripts: A Preliminary Investigation', in J. J. Van Ginkel, H. Murre-Van den Berg and T. M. van Lint (eds), *Redefining Christian Identity: Cultural Interaction In The Middle East Since The Rise Of Islam*. Louvain: Peeters, pp. 275–90.

Brustad, Kristen (forthcoming), 'The Story of al-^cArabiyya'.

Bucholtz, Mary and Kira Hall (2004), 'Language and Identity', in Alessandro Duranti (ed.), *A Companion to Linguistic Anthropology*. Oxford: Blackwell, pp. 369–94.

al-Buḥturī, al-Walīd ibn ^cUbayd (1910), *al-Ḥamāsa*. Shaykhu al-Yasū^cī (ed.). Beirut: Mélanges de la Faculté Orientale.

al-Bukhārī, Muḥammad ibn Ismā^cīl (1941–64), *al-Tārīkh al-kabīr*. Hyderabad: Dā^ɔirat al-Ma^cārif al-Uthmānīyya.

—— (1999), *Ṣaḥīḥ al-Bukhārī*. Riyadh: Dār al-Salām.

Bulliet, Richard (1979), *Conversion to Islam in the Medieval Period: an essay in quantitative history*. Cambridge, MA: Harvard UP.

Calder, N. (1990), 'The ummī in early Islamic juristic literature', *Der Islam* 67, pp. 111–23.

Carmichael, Joel (1967), *The Shaping of the Arabs: a study in ethnic identity*. New York: Macmillan.

Carter, M. G. (1983), 'Language Control as People Control in Medieval Islam: the Aims of the Grammarians in their Cultural Context', *Al-Abhath* 31, pp. 65–84.

—— (1990), 'Arabic Lexicography', in M. J. L. Young, D. Latham and R. B.

Serjeant (eds), *Religion Learning and Science in the Abbasid Period.* Cambridge: Cambridge UP, pp. 106–17.

—— (2004), *Sībawayhi.* London: I. B. Tauris.

Caskel, Werner (1954), 'The Bedouinisation of Arabia', *American Anthropologist* 56, pp. 36–46.

Cheikho, Louis (1890), *Shuᶜarā al-Naṣrāniyya.* Beirut: Maṭbaᶜa al-Ābā al-Mursalīn al-Yasūᶜiyyīn.

Chronicle of Zuqnīn: Parts III and IV A.D. 488–775 (1999). Amir Harrak (trans.). Toronto: Pontifical Institute of Mediaeval Studies.

Cobb, Paul M. (2010), 'The Empire in Syria, 705–763', in Chase Robinson (ed.), *The New Cambridge History of Islam Volume 1.* Cambridge: Cambridge UP, pp. 226–68.

Colby, Frederick S. (2008), *Narrating Muḥammad's Night Journey.* Albany, NY: State University of New York Press.

Conrad, Lawrence (1987), 'Abraha and Muhammad: some observations apropos of chronology and literary topoi in the early Arabic historical tradition', *Bulletin of the School of Oriental and African Studies* 50, pp. 225–40.

—— (2000), 'The Arabs', in Averill Cameron, Byran Ward-Perkins and Michael Whitby (eds), *The Cambridge Ancient History Volume XIV: Late Antiquity: Empire and Successors.* Cambridge: Cambridge UP, pp. 678–700.

Cook, Michael (1981), *Early Muslim Dogma: A Source Critical Study.* Cambridge: Cambridge UP.

—— (1986), 'The Emergence of Islamic Civilisation', in S. Eisenstadt (ed.), *The Origins and Diversity of Axial Age Civilisation.* Albany, NY: State University of New York Press, pp. 476–83.

Corm, Georges and Marie Foissy (2012), 'Forgotten Memory and Heritages', in Marie Foissy (ed.), Timothy Stroud, Simon Pleasance, David Hunter and Christ Atkinson (trans.), *Museum Album.* Paris: Institut du Monde Arabe, pp. 25–32.

Courbage, Youssef and Philippe Fargues [1992] (1997), *Christians and Jews under Islam.* Judy Mabro (trans.). London: I. B. Tauris.

Cragg, Kenneth (1992), *The Arab Christian: A History in the Middle East.* London: Mowbray.

Crone, Patricia (1980), *Slaves on Horses: the Evolution of the Islamic Polity.* Cambridge: Cambridge UP.

—— (1987), *Meccan Trade.* Oxford: Oxford UP.

—— (1994a), 'Were the Qays and Yemen of the Umayyad Period Political Parties?', *Der Islam* 71, pp. 1–57.

—— (1994b), 'The First-Century concept of Higra', *Arabica* 41, pp. 352–87.

—— (1998), 'The ᶜAbbāsid Abnāᵓ and Sasanid Cavalrymen', *Journal of the Royal Asiatic Society* 8, pp. 1–19.

—— (2006), 'Imperial Trauma: the case of the Arabs', *Common Knowledge* 12, pp. 107–16.

—— (2008), 'Barefoot and Naked: What did the Bedouin of the Arab Conquests look like?', *Muqarnas* 25, pp. 1–10.

Crone, Patricia and Michael Cook (1977), *Hagarism: the Making of the Islamic World*. Cambridge: Cambridge UP.

Crone, Patricia and Martin Hinds (1986), *God's Caliph: Religious authority in the first centuries of Islam*. Cambridge: Cambridge UP.

Cuyler Young Jr, T. (1988), 'The Consolidation of the empire and its limits of growth under Darius and Xerxes', in John Boardman, N. G. L. Hammond, D. M. Lewis and M. Ostwald (eds), *The Cambridge Ancient History IV*. Cambridge: Cambridge UP, pp. 53–111.

Dagorn, René (1981), *La Geste d'Ismaël d'après l'onomastique et la tradition arabes*. Geneva: Droz.

Daryaee, Touraj (2009), *Sasanian Persia: the Rise and Fall of an Empire*. London: I. B. Tauris.

Dennett, D. C. (1950), *Conversion and the poll tax in early Islam*. Cambridge, MA: Harvard UP.

Déroche, François (2003), 'Manuscripts of the Qurᵓān', in Jane D. McAuliffe (ed.), *Encyclopaedia of the Qurᵓān*. Leiden: Brill, vol. 3, pp. 254–75.

Dhū al-Rumma (1972–4), *Dīwān*. ᶜAbd al-Quddūs Abū Ṣāliḥ (ed.). Damascus: Majmaᶜ al-Lugha al-ᶜArabiyya.

Diᶜbil ibn ᶜAlī al-Khuzāᶜī (1983), *Shᶜir*. ᶜAbd al-Karīm al-Ashtar (ed.). Damascus: Majmaᶜ al-Lugha al-ᶜArabiyya.

—— (1997), *Waṣāyā al-mulūk*. Nizār Abāẓa (ed.). Damascus: Dār al-Bashāᵓir.

al-Dīnawarī, Abū Bakr Aḥmad (1998), *al-Mujālasa wa-jawāhir al-ᶜilm*. Abū ᶜUbayda Mashhūr ibn Ḥasan Āl Salmān (ed.). Beirut: Dār Ibn Ḥazm.

al-Dīnawarī, Abū Ḥanīfa Aḥmad (2001), *al-Akhbār al-ṭiwāl*. ᶜIṣām Muḥammad al-Ḥājj ᶜAlī (ed.). Beirut: Dār al-Kutub al-ᶜIlmiyya.

Diodorus Siculus (1935), *Library of History*. C. H. Oldfather (trans.). Cambridge, MA: Loeb Classical Library.

Diqqa, Muḥammad ᶜAlī (1999), *Dīwān Banī Asad*. Beirut: Dār Ṣādir.

Djaït, Hichem (1986), *al-Kūfa: Naissance de la ville islamique*. Paris: Maisonneuve & Larouse.

Donner, Fred McGraw (1980), 'The Bakr B. Wā'il Tribes and Politics in Northeastern Arabia on the Eve of Islam', *Studia Islamica* 51, pp. 5–38.

—— (1981), *The Early Islamic Conquests*. Princeton: Princeton UP.

—— (1986), 'The Formation of the Islamic State', *Journal of the American Oriental Society* 106, pp. 283–96.

—— (1998), *Narratives of Islamic origins: the beginning of Islamic historical writing*. Princeton: Darwin.

—— (2008), 'The Qur'an in Recent Scholarship – Challenges and Desiderata', in Gabriel S. Reynolds (ed.), *The Qur'an in its Historical Context*. Abingdon: Routledge, pp. 29–50.

—— (2010), *Muhammad and the Believers: At the Origins of Islam*. Cambridge, MA: Harvard UP.

—— (2015), 'Review: Robert Hoyland, *In God's Path: The Arab Conquests and the Creation of an Islamic Empire*', *al-ᶜUṣūr al-Wusṭā* 23, pp. 134–40.

Doughty, Charles [1888] (1936), *Travels in Arabia Deserta*. London: Jonathan Cape.

Dousse, Michel (2012), 'A Few Fundamental Aspects of Arab Identity', in Marie Foissy (ed.), Timothy Stroud, Simon Pleasance, David Hunter and Christ Atkinson (trans.), *Museum Album*. Paris: Institut du Monde Arabe, pp. 42–5.

Drory, Rina (1996), 'The Abbasid Construction of the Jāhiliyya: Cultural Authority in the Making', *Studia Islamica* 83, pp. 33–49.

Duranti, A. and C. Goodwin (eds) (1992), *Rethinking Context: Language as an Interactive Phenomenon*. Cambridge, Cambridge UP.

Duri, A. A. (1962), 'The Iraq School of History to the Ninth Century – a sketch', in Bernard Lewis and P. M. Holt (eds), *Historians of the Middle East*. London: Oxford UP.

—— (1987), *The Historical Formation of the Arab Nation*. Lawrence Conrad (trans.). London: Croom Helm.

al-Dūrī, ᶜAbd al-ᶜAzīz and Aḥmad Ṭarabīn (eds) (1989), *Al-Waḥda al-ᶜarabiyya: tajāribuhā wa tawaqquᶜātuhā*. Beirut: Markaz Dirāsat al-Waḥda al-ᶜArabiyya.

Enderwitz, Susanne (2009), 'Culture, History and Religion: À propos the Introduction of the Kitāb al-Ḥayawān', in Arnim Heinemann, John L. Meloy, Tarif Khalidi and Manfred Kropp (eds), *Al-Jāḥiẓ: A Muslim Humanist for our Time*. Beirut: Orient-Institut and Ergon Verlag, pp. 229–38.

—— 'al-Shuᶜūbiyya', *EI²*, 9:513–16.

Enloe, Cynthia (1980), 'Religion and Ethnicity: Some General Considerations', in Peter Sugar (ed.), *Ethnic Diversity and Conflict in Eastern Europe*. Santa Barbara: ABC-Clio, pp. 347–71.

Ephal, Israel (1976), 'Ishmael and 'Arab(s)': A Transformation of Ethnological Terms', *Journal of Near Eastern Studies* 35, pp. 225–35.

—— (1982), *The ancient Arabs: nomads on the borders of the Fertile Crescent, 9th–5th century B.C.* Jerusalem: Magnus.

—— (1988), 'Syria-Palestine under Achaemenid rule', in John Boardman, N. G. L. Hammond, D. M. Lewis and M. Ostwald (eds), *The Cambridge Ancient History IV*. Cambridge: Cambridge UP, pp. 139–64.

Epstein, A. L. (1978), *Ethos and Identity: Three Studies in Ethnicity*. London: Tavistock.

Eriksen, Thomas Hylland (1997), 'Mauritian Society between the Ethnic and the non-Ethnic', in Hans Vermeulen and Cora Govers (eds), *The Politics of Ethnic Consciousness*. London: Macmillan, pp. 250–76.

al-Farazdaq (1983), *Sharḥ Dīwān al-Farazdaq*. Īliyā al-Ḥāwī (ed.). Beirut: Dār al-Kitāb al-Lubnānī.

Fāriq, Khurshīd Aḥmad (1985), *Muqaddima*, in Muḥammad Ibn Ḥabīb, *al-Munammaq*, Khurshīd Aḥmad Fāriq (ed.). Beirut: ᶜĀlam al-Kutub, pp. 3–17.

al-Farrāʾ, Yaḥyā ibn Ziyād (n.d.), *Maᶜānī al-Qurʾān*. Aḥmad Yūsuf Najātī and Muḥammad ᶜAli al-Najjār (eds). Cairo: Dār al-Surūr.

Farrin, Raymond (2011), *Abundance from the Desert*. Syracuse: Syracuse UP.

al-Fasawī, Yaᶜqūb (1989–90), *al-Maᶜrifa wa-l-tārīkh*, Akram Ḍiyāʾ al-ᶜUmarī (ed.). Medina: al-Dār.

Fenwick, Corisande (2013), 'From Africa to Ifrīqiya: Settlement and Society in Early Medieval North Africa 650–800', *al-Masāq* 25, pp. 9–33.

Firestone, Reuven (1989), 'Abraham's Son as the Intended Sacrifice (*Al-Dhabīḥ*, Qurʾān 37:99–113): Issues in Qurʾānic Exegesis', *Journal of Semitic Studies* 34, pp. 95–131.

Fisher, Greg (2011a), *Between Empires: Arabs, Romans, and Sasanians in Late Antiquity*. Oxford: Oxford UP.

—— (2011b), 'Kingdoms or Dynasties: Arabs, History and Identity before Islam', *Journal of Late Antiquity* 4, pp. 245–67.

—— (2013), *Rome and the Arabs Before the Rise of Islam: A Brief Introduction*. CreateSpace Independent Publishing Platform.

Fowden, Elizabeth Key (1999), *The Barbarian Plain: St. Sergius between Rome and Iran*. Berkeley, UCLA.

Geary, P. (1983), 'Ethnic identity as a situational construct in the Early Middle Ages', *Mitteilungen der Anthropologischen Gesellschaft in Wien* 113, pp. 15–26.

Gelder, Geert Jan van (2011), 'Poetry in Historiography: the case of *al-Fakhrī* by

Ibn Ṭiqtaqā', in Ramzi Baalbaki, Saleh Said Agha and Tarif Khalidi (eds), *Poetry and History: the Value of Poetry in Reconstructing Arab History*. Beirut: American University of Beirut, pp. 61–94.

Gellner, Ernst (1983), *Nations and Nationalism*. Ithaca, NY: Cornell.

Genequand, Denis (2012), *Les Établissements des Élites Omeyyades en Palmyrène et au Proche-Orient*. Beirut: Institut Français du Proche-Orient.

Genequand, Denis and Christian Robin (eds) (2015), *Les Jafnides: des rois arabes au service de Byzance (VIe siècle de l'ère chrétienne)*. Paris: De Boccard.

Ghabban, Ali Ibrahim, Béatrice André-Salvini, Françoise Demange, Carne Juvin and Marianne Cotty (eds) (2010), *Roads of Arabia: Archaeology and History of the Kingdom of Saudi Arabia*. Paris: Louvre.

al-Ghul, Omar (2004), 'An Early Arabic Inscription From Petra Carrying Diacritic Marks', *Syria* 81, pp. 105–18.

Gibb, H. A. R. (1940), *The Arabs*. Oxford: Clarendon.

—— (1962), 'The social significance of the Shu'ubiya', in S. Shaw and W. Polk (eds), *Studies on the Civilisation of Islam*. London, pp. 62–73.

—— 'Abū ʿUbayda', *EI*², 1:158–9.

Gibbon, Edward [1776–89] (1994), *Decline and Fall of the Roman Empire*. London: Everyman.

Gilliot, Claude (2003), 'Narratives', in Jane D. McAuliffe (ed.), *Encyclopaedia of the Qurʾān*. Leiden: Brill, vol. 3, pp. 516–28.

—— (2006), 'Creation of a Fixed Text', in Jane D. McAuliffe (ed.), *The Cambridge Companion to the Qur'an*. Cambridge: Cambridge UP, pp. 41–57.

Goldziher, Ignáz [1889–90] (1967–71), *Muslim Studies (Muhammedanische Studien)*, S. M. Stern (ed.), C. R. Barber and S. M. Stern (trans.). London: George Allen & Unwin.

Gordon, Matthew S. (2001), *The Breaking of a Thousand Swords*. Albany, NY: State University of New York Press.

Grayson, A. K. (1996), *Assyrian Rulers of the Early First Millennium* BC *II (858–745 BC)*. Toronto: University of Toronto.

Griffith, Sidney (2008), *The church in the shadow of the mosque: Christians and Muslims in the world of Islam*. Princeton: Princeton UP.

Gril, Denis (2003), 'Miracles' in Jane D. McAuliffe (ed.), *Encyclopaedia of the Qurʾān*. Leiden: Brill, vol. 3, pp. 392–9.

Gruen, Erich S. (ed.) (2011a), *Cultural Identity: In the Ancient Mediterranean*. Los Angeles: Getty Research Institute.

—— (2011b), *Rethinking the Other in Antiquity*. Princeton: Princeton UP.

Gruendler, Beatrice (1993), *The Development of the Arabic Scripts: from the Nabatean Era to the first Islamic century according to dated texts*. Atlanta: Scholars Press.

Grunebaum, G. E. von (1963), 'The Nature of Arab Unity before Islam', *Arabica* 10, pp. 4–23.

Günther, Sebastian (2002), 'Muḥammad, the Illiterate Prophet. An Islamic Creed in the Qur'ān and Qur'ānic Exegesis', *Journal of Qur'anic Studies* 4, pp. 1–26.

—— (2006), 'Praise to the Book! Al-Jāḥiẓ and Ibn Qutayba on the Excellence of the Written Word in Medieval Islam', *Franz Rosenthal Memorial Volume, Jerusalem Studies in Arabic and Islam* 32, pp. 125–43.

—— (2006), 'Ummī', in Jane D. McAuliffe (ed.), *Encyclopaedia of the Qur'ān*. Leiden: Brill, vol. 5, pp. 399–403.

Gutas, Dimitri (1998), *Greek Thought, Arabic Culture*. Abingdon: Routledge.

Haar Romeny, Bas ter (ed.) (2010), *Religious Origin of Nations? The Christian Communities of the Middle East*. Leiden: Brill.

—— (2012), 'Ethnicity, ethnogenesis and the identity of Syriac Orthodox Christians', in Walter Pohl, Clemens Gantner and Richard Payne (eds), *Visions of Community in the Post-Roman World: The West, Byzantium, and the Islamic World*. Aldershot: Ashgate, pp. 183–204.

Haar Romeny, Naures Atto, Jan J. van Ginkel, Mat Immerzeel and Bas Snelders (2010), 'Formation of a Communal Identity among West Syrian Christians', in Bas ter Haar Romeny (ed.), *Religious Origin of Nations? The Christian Communities of the Middle East*. Leiden: Brill, pp. 1–52.

Haldon, John and Hugh Kennedy (2012), 'Regional Identities and Military Power: Byzantium and Islam ca. 600–750', in Walter Pohl, Clemens Gantner and Richard Payne (eds), *Visions of Community in the Post-Roman World*. Farnham: Ashgate, pp. 317–53.

Halevi, Leor (2007), *Muhammad's Grave*. New York: Columbia.

Hallaq, Wael (1999), 'The Authenticity of Prophetic Ḥadîth: A Pseudo-Problem', *Studia Islamica* 89, pp. 75–90.

al-Hamdānī, al-Ḥasan (2004), *al-Iklīl Vol.1*. Muḥammad ibn ʿAlī al-Akwaʿ (ed.). Sana'a: Wizārat al-Thaqāfa wa-l-Siyāḥa.

Hamori, Andras (1974), *On the Art of Medieval Arabic Literature*. Princeton, Princeton UP.

Harb, F. (1990), 'Wine poetry', in Julia Ashtiany, T. M. Johnstone, J. D. Latham, R. B. Serjeant and G. Rex Smith (eds), *ʿAbbāsid Belles-Lettres*. Cambridge: Cambridge UP, pp. 219–34.

al-Ḥarbī, Abū Isḥāq Ibrāhīm (attrib.) (1999), *al-Manāsik wa-amākin ṭuruq al-ḥajj wa-ma*ᶜ*ālim al-Jazīrah*. ᶜAbd Allāh Nāsir al-Wuhaybī (ed.). Riyadh: Dār al-Yamāma li-l-Baḥth wa-l-Nashr.

Ḥassān ibn Thābit (1974), *Dīwān*. Walīd ᶜArafāt (ed.). Beirut: Dār Ṣādir.

Hawting, Gerald (1999), *The Idea of Idolatry and the Emergence of Islam*. Cambridge: Cambridge UP.

—— (2003), 'Kaᶜba', in Jane D. McAuliffe (ed.), *Encyclopaedia of the Qur*ᵓ*ān*. Leiden: Brill, vol. 3, pp. 75–9.

Healey, J. F. (1989), 'Were the Nabataeans Arabs?', *Aram* 1, pp. 38–44.

Heath, Peter (2011), 'Some Facets of Poetry in Pre-modern Historical and Pseudo-historical Texts', in Ramzi Baalbaki, Saleh Said Agha and Tarif Khalidi (eds), *Poetry and History: the Value of Poetry in Reconstructing Arab History*. Beirut: American University of Beirut, pp. 39–60.

Heck, Gene W. (2003), '"Arabia without Spices": An Alternative Hypothesis'. *Journal of the American Oriental Society* 123, pp. 547–76.

Heinemann, Arnim, John L. Meloy, Tarif Khalidi and Manfred Kropp (2009), 'Introduction', in Arnim Heinemann, John L. Meloy, Tarif Khalidi and Manfred Kropp (eds), *Al-Jāḥiẓ: a Muslim humanist for our time*. Beirut: Orient-Institut and Ergon Verlag, pp. v–vii.

Heinrichs, Wolfhart (1997), 'Prosimetrical Genres in Classical Arabic Literature', in Joseph Harris, Karl Reichl (eds), *Prosimetrum: Cross-Cultural Perspectives on Narrative in Prose and Verse*. Cambridge, MA: Harvard UP, pp. 249–75.

Herodotus (1992), *The Histories*. Henry Cary (trans.), Chris Scarre (ed). London: Folio.

Herrmann, Georgina and K. Kurbansakhatov et al. (1995), 'The International Merv Project: Preliminary Report on the Third Season (1994)', *Iran* 33, pp. 31–60.

El-Hibri, Tayeb (2010), 'The Empire in Iraq, 763–861', in Chase Robinson (ed.), *The New Cambridge History of Islam Volume 1*. Cambridge: Cambridge UP, pp. 269–304.

al-Ḥimyarī, Nashwān (1985), *Mulūk Ḥimyar wa-aqyāl al-Yaman*. ᶜAlī ibn Ismāᶜīl al-Muᵓayyad and Ismāᶜīl ibn Aḥmad al-Jarāfī (eds). Beirut: Dār al-Tanwīr.

—— (1999), *Shams al-*ᶜ*ulūm*. Ḥusayn ibn ᶜAbd Allāh al-ᶜUmarī (ed.). Damascus: Dār al-Fikr.

Hitti, Philip K. (1946), *History of the Arabs*. London: Macmillan.

Hobsbawm, Eric (1990), *Nations and Nationalism since 1780*. Cambridge: Cambridge UP.

Hofstee, Willem (2010), 'Family Matters: Community, Ethnicity and Multiculturalism', in Bas ter Haar Romeny (ed.), *Religious Origin of Nations? The Christian Communities of the Middle East*. Leiden: Brill, pp. 53–64.

Holm, Tom (2002), 'American Indian Warfare', in Philip Delorint and Neal Salisbury (eds), *A Companion to American Indian History*. Malden, MA: Blackwell, pp. 154–72.

Hourani, Albert (1991), *A History of the Arab Peoples*. London: Faber and Faber.

Howell, William (1680–5), *An Institution of General History; or the History of the World*. London: Henry Herringman.

Hoyland, Robert (1997), *Seeing Islam as others saw it*. Princeton: Darwin.

—— (2001), *Arabia and the Arabs*. London: Routledge.

—— (2006), 'New Documentary Texts and the Early Islamic State', *Bulletin of the School of Oriental and African Studies* 69, pp. 395–416.

—— (2008), 'Epigraphy And The Linguistic Background Of The Qur'ān', in G. S. Reynolds (ed.), *The Qur'ān In Its Historical Context*. London: Routledge, pp. 51–70.

—— (2009), 'Arab kings, Arab tribes and the beginnings of Arab historical memory in Late Roman Epigraphy', in H. Cotton, R. Hoyland, J. Price and D. Wasserstein (eds), *From Hellenism to Islam: Cultural and Linguistic Change in the Roman Near East*. Cambridge: Cambridge UP, pp. 374–400.

—— (2010), 'Mount Nebo, Jabal Ramm, and the status of Christian Palestinian Aramaic and Old Arabic in Late Roman Palestine and Arabia', in Michael Macdonald (ed.), *The development of Arabic as a written language* (Supplement to the Proceedings of the Seminar for Arabian Studies 40). Oxford: Archaeopress, pp. 29–46.

—— (2012), 'Fred M. Donner: Muhammad and the Believers: At the Origins of Islam', *International Journal of Middle East Studies* 44, pp. 573–6.

—— (2015), *In God's Path*. Oxford: Oxford UP.

Humphreys, Stephen (2006), *Muᶜawiya*. Oxford: Oneworld.

Ḥusayn, Ṭāhā (1926), *Fī al-shiᶜr al-jāhilī*. Cairo: Dār al-Kutub al-Miṣriyya.

Hutchison, John and Anthony Smith (1996), *Ethnicity*. Oxford: Oxford UP.

Ibn ᶜAbd Rabbihi, Abū ᶜUmar Aḥmad (n.d.), *al-ᶜIqd al-farīd*. Ibrahīm al-Abyārī (ed.). Beirut: Dār al-Kitāb al-ᶜArabī.

Ibn Abī Shayba, ᶜAbd Allāh (2010), *al-Muṣannaf*. Muḥammad ᶜAwwāma (ed.). Jeddah: Dār al-Qibla.

Ibn al-ᶜAdīm, Kamāl al-Dīn (1988), *Bughyat al-Ṭalab fī Tārīkh Ḥalab*, Suhayl Zakkār (ed.). Beirut: Dār al-Fikr.

Ibn al-Anbārī, Muḥammad ibn al-Qāsim (2005), *Sharḥ al-qaṣā'id al-sab^c al-ṭiwāl al-jāhiliyyāt*. ^cAbd al-Salām Muḥammad Hārūn (ed.). Cairo: al-Ma^cārif.

Ibn al-Athīr, ^cIzz al-Dīn (1979), *al-Kāmil fī al-tārīkh*. C. J. Tornberg (ed.). Beirut: Dār Ṣādir.

Ibn Bakkār, al-Zubayr (1962), *Jamharat nasab Quraysh wa-akhbārihā*. Maḥmūd Muḥammad Shākir (ed.). Cairo: al-Madanī.

Ibn Balbān, ^cAlā' al-Dīn al-Fārisī (1993), *Ṣaḥīḥ Ibn Ḥibbān*. Shu^cayb al-Arna'ūṭ (ed.). Beirut: Mu'assasat al-Risāla.

Ibn Durayd, Abū Bakr Muḥammad (1987), *Jamharat al-lugha*. Ramzī Ba^calbakī (ed.). Beirut: Dār al-^cIlm li-l-Milāyīn.

—— (n.d.), *al-Ishtiqāq*. ^cAbd al-Salām Muḥammad Hārūn (ed.). Cairo: al-Khānjī.

Ibn Fāris, Abū al-Ḥasan Aḥmad (1946–52), *Maqāyīs al-lugha*. ^cAbd al-Salām Muḥammad Hārūn (ed). Cairo: al-Bābī al-Ḥalabī.

—— (1993), *al-Ṣāḥibī fī fiqh al-lugha*. ^cUmar Fārūq al-Ṭabbā^c (ed.). Beirut: Maktabat al-Ma^cārif.

Ibn Ḥabīb, Muḥammad (1942), *al-Muḥabbar*. Ilse Lichtenstadter (ed.). Hyderabad: Dā'irat al-Ma^cārif al-^cUthmāniyya.

—— (1985), *al-Munammaq*. Khurshīd Aḥmad Fāriq (ed). Beirut: ^cĀlam al-Kutub.

Ibn Ḥajar al-^cAsqalānī (1907–9), *Tahdhīb al-Tahdhīb*. Hyderabad: Dā'irat al-Ma^cārif al-^cUthmāniyya.

—— (2011), *Fatḥ al-Bārī bi-sharḥ Ṣaḥīḥ al-Bukhārī*. Naẓar Muḥammad al-Faryābī (ed.). Al-Riyadh: Dār Ṭayba.

Ibn Ḥanbal, Aḥmad (1983), *Faḍā'il al-Ṣaḥāba*. Waṣī Allāh ibn Muḥammad ^cAbbās (ed.). Mecca: Markaz al-Baḥth al-^cIlmī.

—— (1988), *Masā'il al-Imām Aḥmad ibn Ḥanbal*. Zuhayr al-Shāwīsh (ed.). Beirut: al-Maktab al-Islāmī.

—— (1993), *Musnad Aḥmad ibn Ḥanbal*. Muḥammad ^cAbd al-Salām ^cAbd al-Shāfī (ed.). Beirut: Dār al-Kutub al-^cIlmiyya.

Ibn Ḥazm, Abū Muḥammad ^cAli (1999a), *al-Fiṣal fī al-milal wa-l-niḥal*. Aḥmad Shams al-Dīn (ed.). Beirut: Dār al-Kutub al-^cIlmiyya.

—— (1999b), *Jamharat ansāb al-^carab*. ^cAbd al-Salām Muḥammad Hārūn (ed.). Cairo: al-Ma^cārif.

Ibn Hishām, ^cAbd al-Malik (n.d.), *al-Sīra al-nabawiyya*. Muṣṭafā al-Saqqā, Ibrāhīm al-Abyārī and ^cAbd al-Ḥafīẓ Shalabī (eds). Beirut: Dār al-Ma^crifa.

Ibn Īyās, Muḥammad ibn Aḥmad (2008), *Badā'i^c al-Zuhūr fī Waqā'i^c al-Duhūr*. Muḥammad Muṣṭafā (ed.). Cairo: Dār al-Kutub wa-l-Wathā'iq al-Qawmiyya.

Ibn al-Jawzī, Abū al-Faraj (1995), *al-Muntaẓam*. Suhayl Zakkār (ed.). Beirut: Dār al-Fikr.

Ibn Jinnī, Abū al-Fatḥ ᶜUthmān (2006), *al-Khaṣāʾiṣ*. Muḥammad ᶜAlī al-Najjār (ed.). Beirut: ᶜĀlam al-Kutub.

Ibn al-Kalbī, Hishām ibn Muḥammad (1924), *al-Aṣnām*, Aḥmad Zakī Bāshā (ed.). Cairo: Dār al-Kutub.

—— (1988), *Nasab Maᶜadd wa-l-Yaman*. Nājī Ḥasan (ed.). Beirut: ᶜĀlam al-Kutub.

—— (2005), *Jamharat al-nasab*. Nājī Ḥasan (ed.). Beirut: ᶜĀlam al-Kutub.

—— (2009), *Ansāb al-khayl*. Aḥmad Zakī Bāshā (ed.). Cairo: Dār al-Kutub.

Ibn Kathīr, Abū al-Fidā' (n.d.), *al-Bidāya wa-l-nihāya*. Ahmad Abū Mulhim, ᶜAlī Mujīb al-ᶜAtwī, Fuʾād al-Sayyid, Mahdī Nāṣir al-Dīn and ᶜAlī ᶜAbd al-Sātir (eds). Beirut: Dār al-Kutub al-ᶜIlmiyya.

—— (1994), *Tafsīr Ibn Kathīr*. Beirut: Dār al-Kutub al-ᶜIlmiyya.

Ibn Khallikān, Shams al-Dīn (1968), *Wafayāt al-aᶜyān*. Iḥsān ᶜAbbās (ed.). Beirut: Dār Ṣādir.

Ibn Khayyāṭ, Khalīfa (n.d.), *al-Ṭabaqāt*. Akram Ḍiyāʾ al-ᶜUmarī (ed.). Baghdad: Jāmiᶜat Baghdād.

—— (1993), *Tārīkh Khalīfa ibn Khayyāṭ*. Suhayl Zakkār (ed.). Beirut: Dār al-Fikr.

Ibn Manẓūr, Muḥammad ibn Makram (1990), *Lisān al-ᶜarab*. Beirut: Dār Ṣādir.

Ibn al-Muqaffaᶜ, ᶜAbd Allāh (1960), *al-Adab al-ṣaghīr wa-l-adab al-kabīr*. Beirut: Dār Ṣādir.

Ibn Muzāḥim, Naṣr (1981), *Waqᶜat Ṣiffīn*. ᶜAbd al-Salām Muḥammad Hārūn (ed.). Cairo: al-Khānjī.

Ibn al-Nadīm, Muḥammad ibn Isḥāq (1988), *al-Fihrist*. Riḍā Tajaddud (ed.). Beirut: al-Masīra.

Ibn Qudāma, Muwaffaq al-Dīn (n.d.), *al-Mughnī*. Beirut: Dār al-Kitāb al-ᶜArabī.

Ibn Qutayba, ᶜAbd Allāh (n.d.), *Taʾwīl mukhtalif al-ḥadīth*. Cairo: Maktabat al-Mutanabbī.

—— (1925), *ᶜUyūn al-akhbār*. Cairo: Dār al-Kutub.

—— (1994), *al-Maᶜārif*. Tharwat ᶜUkāsha (ed.). Qum: al-Sharīf Riḍā.

—— (1998), *Faḍl al-ᶜarab wa-l-tanbīh ᶜala ᶜulūmiha*. Walīd Maḥmūd Khāliṣ (ed.). Abu Dhabi: al-Majmaᶜ al-Thaqāfī.

—— (2006), *al-Shiᶜr wa-l-shuᶜarāʾ*. Aḥmad Muḥammad Shākir (ed.). Cairo: Dār al-Ḥadīth.

Ibn Saᶜd, Muḥammad (1997), *al-Ṭabaqāt al-kubrā*. Muḥammad ᶜAbd al-Qādir ᶜAṭā (ed.). Beirut: Dār al-Kutub al-ᶜIlmiyya.

Ibn al-Sarrāj, Abū Bakr Muḥammad (1993), *al-Uṣūl fī al-naḥw*. ᶜAbd al-Ḥusayn al-Fatlī (ed.). Beirut: Muᵓassasat al-Risāla.

Ibn Wahb, ᶜAbd Allāh (1939–48), *Jāmiᶜ Ibn Wahb*. J. David-Weill (ed.). Cairo: Imprimerie de l'Institut français d'archéologie orientale.

Ibrahim, Vivian (2011), 'Ethnicity', in Stephen M. Caliendo and Charlton D. McIlwain (eds), *The Routledge Companion to Race and Ethnicity*. London: Routledge, pp. 12–20.

Imruᵓ al-Qays (1990), *Dīwān*. Muḥammad Abū al-Faḍl Ibrāhīm (ed.). Cairo: Dār al-Maᶜārif.

Irwin, Robert (2006), *A Lust for Knowing: the Orientalists and their Enemies*. London: Penguin/Allen Lane.

al-Iṣfahānī, Abū al-Faraj (1992), *al-Aghānī*. ᶜAbd Allāh ᶜAlī Muhanna and Samīr Jābir (eds). Beirut: Dār al-Kutub al-ᶜIlmiyya.

al-Iṣfahānī, Ḥamza ibn al-Ḥasan (n.d.), *Tārīkh sinī mulūk al-arḍ wa-l-anbiyāᵓ*. Beirut: Maktabat al-Ḥayāt.

Izutsu, Toshihiko [1966] (2002), *Ethico-Religious Concepts in the Qurᵓān*. Montreal: McGill Queens.

al-Jāḥiẓ, ᶜAmr ibn Baḥr, (1963–79) *al-Rasāᵓil*. ᶜAbd al-Salām Muḥammad Hārūn (ed.). Cairo: Al-Khānjī.

—— (1998), *Kitāb al-Ḥayawān*. Muḥammad Bāsil ᶜUyūn al-Sūd (ed.). Beirut: Dār al-Kutub al-ᶜIlmiyya.

—— (2003), *al-Bayān wa-l-tabyīn*. ᶜAbd al-Salām Muḥammad Hārūn (ed.). Cairo: al-Khānjī 2003.

al-Jallad, Ahmad (2014), 'On the genetic background of the Rbbl bn Hfᶜm grave inscription at Qaryat al-Fāw'. *Bulletin of the School of Oriental and African Studies* 77, pp. 1-21.

—— (2015), *An outline of the grammar of the Safaitic Inscriptions*. Leiden: Brill.

—— (forthcoming) 'Graeco-Arabica I: The Southern Levant', in F. Briquel-Chatonnet, M. Debié and L. Nehmé (eds), *Le contexte de naissance de l'écriture arabe. Écrit et écritures araméennes et arabes au 1er millénaire après J.-C.* Louvain: Orientalia Lovaniensa Analecta.

Jamme, Albert (1962), *Sabaean inscriptions from Maḥram Bilqīs (Mārib)*. Baltimore: Johns Hopkins UP.

Jarīr (1969), *Dīwān*. Nuᶜmān Muḥammad Amīn Ṭāhā (ed.). Cairo: Dār al-Maᶜārif.

al-Jawālīqī, Abū Manṣūr Mawhūb ibn Aḥmad (1969), *al-Muᶜarrab min al-kalām al-aᶜjamī ᶜalā ḥurūf al-muᶜjam*. Aḥmad Muḥammad Shākir (ed.). Cairo: Dār al-Kutub.

al-Jawharī, Ismāʿīl ibn Ḥammād (1956), *al-Ṣiḥāḥ*. Aḥmad ʿAbd al-Ghafūr ʿAṭṭār (ed.). Cairo: Dār al-Kitāb al-ʿArabī.

Jenkins, Richard (2008), *Rethinking Ethnicity*. London: Sage.

Johns, Jeremy (2003), 'Archaeology and the History of Early Islam: The First Seventy Years', *Journal of the Economic and Social History of the Orient* 46, pp. 411–36.

Jones, Alan (1992), *Early Arabic Poetry Volume One*. Reading: Ithaca.

—— (1996),'The Oral and the Written: some thoughts about the Quranic Text', in K. Dévényi and T. Iványi (eds), *Proceedings of the Colloquium on Logos, Ethnos, Mythos in the Middle East and North Africa Part One: Linguistics and Literature*. Budapest: Eötvös Loránd University & Csoma de Körös Society Section of Islamic Studies, pp. 57–66.

al-Jumaḥī, Ibn Sallām (n.d.), *Ṭabaqāt fuḥūl al-shuʿarāʾ*. Maḥmūd Muḥammad Shākir (ed.). Cairo: al-Khānjī.

Juynboll, G. H. A. (1982), 'On the Origins of Arabic Prose: Reflections on Authenticity', in G. H. A. Juynboll (ed.), *Studies on the First Century of Islamic Society*. Carbondale, IL: Southern Illinois UP, pp. 161–75.

Kennedy, Hugh (1981), 'Central government and provincial élites in the early ʿAbbāsid caliphate', *Bulletin of the School of Oriental and African Studies* 44, pp. 26–38.

—— (1986), *The Prophet and the Age of the Caliphates: the Islamic Near East from the sixth to the eleventh century*. London: Longman.

—— (1997), 'From Oral Tradition to Written Record in Arabic Genealogy', *Arabica* 44, pp. 531–44.

—— (2004), 'The Decline and Fall of the First Muslim Empire', *Der Islam* 81, pp. 3–30.

—— (2007), *The Great Arab Conquests*. London: Weidenfeld and Nicolson.

Kerr, Robert (2014), 'Der Islam, die Araber und die Hiğra', in H. Ohlig und M. Gross (eds), *Die Entstehung einer Weltreligion III*. Berlin–Tübingen: Schiler Verlag, pp. 46–51.

Khalidi, Tarif (1994), *Arabic Historical Thought in the Classical Period*. Cambridge: Cambridge UP.

—— (2001), 'Arabs', in Jane D. McAuliffe (ed.), *Encyclopaedia of the Qurʾān*. Leiden: Brill, vol. 1, pp. 144–5.

al-Khalīl ibn Aḥmad (1980), *al-ʿAyn*. Mahdī al-Makhzūmī and Ibrāhīm al-Sāmarrāʾī (eds). Baghdad: Wizārat al-Thaqāfah wa-l-Iʿlām.

al-Khaṭīb, ʿAbd al-Laṭīf (2002), *Muʿjam al-qirāʾāt*. Damascus: Dār Saʿdal-Dīn.

Khoury, R. G., 'Wahb ibn Munabbih', *EI²*, 11:34–6.

al-Kindī, Muḥammad ibn Yūsuf (1912), *The Governors and Judges of Egypt*. Rhuvon Guest (ed.). London: Luzac.

Kister, M. J. (1989), 'Do Not Assimilate Yourselves', *Jerusalem Studies in Arabic and Islam* 12, pp. 321–71.

—— (1991), 'Land property and jihād: A discussion of some early traditions', *Journal of the Economic and Social History of the Orient* 34 pp. 270–311.

—— 'Kuḍāᶜa', *EI²*, 5:315–18.

Kister, M. J. and M. Plessner (1976), 'Notes on Caskel's Ǧamharat an-nasab', *Oriens* 25/26, pp. 48–68.

Kramsch, Claire (1998), *Language and Culture*. Oxford: Oxford UP.

Kubiak, Wladislaw (1987), *Al-Fustat: Its Foundation and Early Urban Development*. Cairo: American University of Cairo.

al-Kutubī, Muḥammad ibn Shākir (1973), *Fawāt al-wafayāt*. Iḥsān ᶜAbbās (ed.). Beirut: Dār Ṣādir.

Labīd (1962), *Dīwān*. Iḥsān ᶜAbbās (ed.). Kuwait: Wizārat al-Irshād wa-l-Anbāᵓ.

Lancaster, William (1981), *The Rwala Bedouin Today*. Cambridge: Cambridge UP.

Landau-Tasseron, Ella (1996), 'Ḏū Qār', *Encyclopaedia Iranica*, vol. 7, pp. 574–5.

—— (2010), 'Arabia', in Chase Robinson (ed.), *The New Cambridge History of Islam Volume 1*. Cambridge: Cambridge UP, pp. 395–447.

Lapidus, Ira M. (1975), 'The Separation of State and Religion in the Development of Early Islamic Society', *International Journal of Middle East Studies* 6, pp. 363–85.

Lassner, Jacob (1980), *The Shaping of Abbāsid Rule*. Princeton: Princeton UP.

—— (1986), *Islamic Revolution and Historical Memory*. New Haven: American Oriental Society.

Lecker, Michael (1995a), 'Biographical Notes on Abū 'Ubayda Maᶜmar b. al-Muthannā', *Studia Islamica* 81, pp. 71–100.

—— (1995b), *Muslims, Jews and Pagans: Studies on Early Islamic Medina*. Leiden: Brill.

—— (2010), 'Pre-Islamic Arabia', in Chase Robinson (ed.), *The New Cambridge History of Islam Volume 1*. Cambridge: Cambridge UP, pp. 153–70.

Lecomte, Gérard (1965), *Ibn Qutayba*. Damascus: Institut Français.

Leder, Stefan (2002), 'The Literary Use of the *Khabar*', in Stefan Leder (ed.), *Studies in Arabic and Islam: Proceedings of the 19th Congress, Union Européenne des Arabisants et Islamisants, Halle 1998*. Leuven: Peeters, pp. 277–315.

—— (2005), 'Nomadic and Sedentary Peoples – A Misleading Dichotomy? The Bedouin and Bedouinism in the Arab Past', in Stefan Leder and Bernhard Streck (eds), *Shifts and Drifts in Nomad-Sedentary Relations*. Wiesbaden: Reichert, pp. 401–20.

Lefebvre, Henri [1974] (1991), *The Production of Space*. Donald Nicholson-Smith (trans.). Oxford: Blackwell.

Levin, A. (2004), 'The Status of the Science of Grammar among Islamic Sciences', *Jerusalem Studies in Arabic and Islam* 29, pp. 1–16.

Levtzion, Nehemiah (ed.) (1979), *Conversion to Islam*. New York: Holmes and Meier.

—— (1990), 'Conversion to Islam in Syria and Palestine, and the Survival of Christian Communities', in M. Gerversand and R. J. Bikhazi (eds), *Conversion and Continuity: Indigenous Christian Communities in Medieval Islamic Lands*. Toronto: Pontifical Institute of Medieval Studies, pp. 289–312.

Levy-Rubin, Milka (2000), 'New Evidence Relating to the Process of Islamization in Palestine', *Journal of the Economic and Social History of the Orient* 43, pp. 257–76.

—— (2011), *Non-Muslims in the Early Islamic Empire*. Cambridge: Cambridge UP.

Lewy, Hildegard (1971), 'Assyria c.2600–1816 BC', in I. E. S. Edwards, C. J. Gadd and N. G. L. Hammond (eds), *The Cambridge Ancient History I.2*. Cambridge: Cambridge UP, pp. 729–70.

Lindstedt, Ilkka (2015), '*Muhājirūn* as a name for the first/seventh century Muslims', *Journal of Near Eastern Studies* 74, pp. 67–73.

Lint, Theo Maarten van (2010), 'The Formation of Armenian Identity in the First Millennium', in Bas ter Haar Romeny (ed.), *Religious Origin of Nations? The Christian Communities of the Middle East*. Leiden: Brill, pp. 251–79.

Lowenthal, David (1985), *The Past is a Foreign Country*. Cambridge: Cambridge UP.

Lucas, Scott (2008), 'Where are the Legal Hadith? A Study of the *Muṣannaf* of Ibn Abī Shayba', *Islamic Law and Society* 15, pp. 283–314.

Luxenberg, Christoph (2007), *The Syro-Aramaic reading of the Koran*. Berlin: Hans Schiller.

Macdonald, Michael [2001] (2009a), 'Arabians, Arabias and the Greeks: contact and perceptions', in Michael Macdonald (ed.), *Literacy and Identity in Pre-Islamic Arabia*. Farnham: Ashgate, V pp. 1–33.

—— [2003] (2009b), ''Les Arabes en Syrie' or 'La penetration des Arabes en Syrie': a question of perceptions?', in Michael Macdonald (ed.), *Literacy and Identity in Pre-Islamic Arabia*. Farnham: Ashgate, VI pp. 303–18.

—— [1991] (2009c), 'Was the Nabataean Kingdom a Bedouin State?', in Michael Macdonald (ed.), *Literacy and Identity in Pre-Islamic Arabia*. Farnham: Ashgate, VII pp. 102–19.

—— [1995] (2009d), 'On Saracens, the Rawwāfah inscription and the Roman army', in Michael Macdonald (ed.), *Literacy and Identity in Pre-Islamic Arabia*. Farnham: Ashgate, VIII pp. 1–26.

—— [2000] (2009e), 'Reflections on the linguistic map of pre-Islamic Arabia', in Michael Macdonald (ed.), *Literacy and Identity in Pre-Islamic Arabia*. Farnham: Ashgate, III pp. 28–79.

—— [1997] (2009f), 'Trade Routes and trade goods at the northern end of the 'incense road' in the first millennium B.C.', in Michael Macdonald (ed.), *Literacy and Identity in Pre-Islamic Arabia*. Farnham: Ashgate, IX pp. 333–49.

—— [1998] (2009g) 'Some Reflections on Epigraphy and Ethnicity', in Michael Macdonald (ed.), *Literacy and Identity in Pre-Islamic Arabia*. Farnham: Ashgate, IV pp. 177–90.

—— [2005] (2009h), Literacy in an oral environment', in Michael Macdonald (ed.), *Literacy and Identity in Pre-Islamic Arabia*, Farnham: Ashgate, I pp. 49–118.

—— (2008), 'Old Arabic (Epigraphic)', in Kees Versteegh (ed.), *Encyclopedia of Arabic Language and Linguistics*. Leiden: Brill, vol. 3, pp. 464–77.

al-Madāᵓinī, Aḥmad ibn Muḥammad (2011), *Majmaᶜ al-amthāl*. Muḥammad Abū al-Faḍl Ibrāhīm (ed.). Beirut: al-Maktaba al-ᶜAṣriyya.

Madʿaj, Abd al-Muhsin Madʿaj M. (1988), *The Yemen in early Islam (9–233/630–847): a political history*. London: Ithaca Press, for the Centre for Middle Eastern and Islamic Studies, University of Durham.

Madelung, Wilferd (1990), 'The Vigilante Movement of Sahl b. Salama al-Khurasani and the Origins of Hanbalism Reconsidered', *Journal of Turkish Studies* (*Fahir Iz Festschrift, I*) 14, pp. 331–7.

Mahler, 'ᶜArūba', *EI*¹, 1:463.

Malik ibn Anas (1979), *al-Muwaṭṭaᵓ*. Muḥammad ibn al-Ḥasan al-Shaybānī (transmitter), ᶜAbd al-Wahhāb ᶜAbd al-Laṭīf (ed.). Beirut (?): al-Maktabat al-ᶜIlmiyya.

—— (1994), *al-Muwaṭṭaᵓ*. Yaḥyā ibn Yaḥyā (transmitter), Saᶜīd Muḥammad al-Laḥḥām (ed.). Beirut: Dār Iḥyāᵓ al-ᶜulūm.

Mallowan, Max (1971), 'The Early Dynastic Period in Mesopotamia', in I. E. S. Edwards, C. J. Gadd and N. G. L. Hammond (eds), *The Cambridge Ancient History I.2*. Cambridge: Cambridge UP, pp. 238–314.

Mandeville, John (1953), *Mandeville's Travels*. London: Hakluyt Society.

al-Maqdisī, al-Muṭahhar ibn Ṭāhir (n.d.), *al-Badᵓ wa-l-tārīkh*. Cairo: Maktabat al-Thaqāfa al-Dīniyya.

Margoliouth, D. S. (1925), 'The Origins of Arabic Poetry', *Journal of the Royal Asiatic Society* 3, pp. 417–49.

Marsham, Andrew (2009), *Rituals of Islamic Monarchy: accession and succession in the first Muslim empire*. Edinburgh: Edinburgh UP.

Mårtensson, Ulrika (2011), '"It's the economy stupid": Al-Ṭabarī's Analysis of the Free Rider Problem in the ᶜAbbāsid Caliphate', *Journal of the Economic and Social History of the Orient* 54, pp. 203–38.

Martinez, Jean-Luc and Néguine Mathieux (2015), 'La Thrace dans l'imaginaire antique et modern', in Jean-Luc Martinez, Alexandre Baralis, Néguine Mathieux, Totko Stoyanov and Milena Tonkova, *L'Épopée des rois thraces*. Paris: Louvre, pp. 28–51.

al-Marzūqī, Aḥmad ibn Muḥammad (1968), *Sharḥ Dīwān al-Ḥamāsa*, Aḥmad Amīn and ᶜAbd al-Salām Hārūn (eds). Cairo: Maṭbaᶜat Lajnat al-Taᵓlīf wa-l-Tarjama wa-l-Nashr.

al-Masᶜūdī, ᶜAlī ibn al-Ḥusayn (1966–79), *Murūj al-dhahab*. Charles Pellat (ed.). Beirut: al-Jāmiᶜa al-Lubnāniyya.

McCants, William (2011), *Founding Gods, Inventing Nations: Conquest and Culture Myths from Antiquity to Islam*. Princeton: Princeton UP.

McCrone, D. (1998), *The Sociology of Nationalism*. London: Routledge.

Merrills, A. H. (ed.) (2004), *Vandals, Romans and Berbers: New Perspectives on Late Antique North Africa*. London: Ashgate.

Mikhail, Maged (2008), 'Notes on the "Ahl al-Dīwān": The Arab–Egyptian Army of the Seventh through the Ninth Centuries C.E.', *Journal of the American Oriental Society* 128, pp. 273–84.

Millar, Fergus (1993), 'Hagar, Ishmael, Josepheus and the Origins of Islam', *Journal of Jewish Studies* 44.1, pp. 23–45.

—— (2013), *Religion, Language and Community in the Roman Near East*. Oxford: Oxford UP.

Monroe, James (1972), 'Oral Composition in pre-Islamic Poetry', *Journal of Arabic Literature* 3, pp. 1–53.

Montgomery, James (1997), *The Vagaries of the Qaṣīdah: the Tradition and Practice of Early Arabic Poetry*. Cambridge: E. J. W. Gibb Memorial Trust.

—— (2006), 'The Empty Hijaz', in James Montgomery (ed.), *Arabic Theology, Arabic Philosophy. From the Many to the One: Essays in Celebration of Richard M. Frank*. Leuven: Peeters, pp. 37–97.

—— (2009a), 'Speech and Nature: Jāḥiẓ, Bayān 2.175–207, Part 3', *Middle Eastern Literatures* 12, pp. 107–25.

—— (2009b), 'Speech and Nature: Jāḥiẓ, Bayān 2.175–207, Part 4', *Middle Eastern Literatures* 12, pp. 213–32.

—— (2013), *al-Jāḥiẓ: in Praise of Books*. Edinburgh: Edinburgh UP.

Morony, M. (1984), *Iraq after the Muslim Conquest*. Princeton: Princeton UP.

Mottahedeh, Roy (1976), 'The Shu'ubiyya Controversy and the Social History of Early Islamic Iran', *International Journal of Middle East Studies* 7, pp. 161–82.

Motzki, Harold (1991), 'The Musannaf of `Abd al-Razzaq Al-San`ani as a Source of Authentic Ahadith of the First Century A.H.', *Journal of Near Eastern Studies* 50, pp. 1–21.

—— (2005), 'Dating Muslim Traditions: A Survey', *Arabica* 52, pp. 204–53.

al-Mubarrad, Muḥammad ibn Yazīd (1936), *Nasab ᶜAdnān wa Qaḥṭān*. ᶜAbd al-ᶜAzīz al-Maymanī al-Rājkūtī (ed.). [Cairo]: Lajnat al-Taᵓlīf wa-l-Tarjama wa-l-Nashr.

—— (2008), *al-Kāmil*. Muḥammad Aḥmad al-Dālī (ed.). Beirut: Muᵓassasat al-Risāla.

Müller, D. H. (1896), 'Arabia', *Paulys Real-Encyclopädie der Classischen Altertumswissenschaften*. Stuttgart: J. B. Meltzer Sohn, pp. 344–59.

Munt, Harry (2015), 'No Two Religions: Non-Muslims in the early Islamic Ḥijāz', *Bulletin of the School of Oriental and African Studies* 78, pp. 249–69.

Muqātil ibn Sulaymān (1979–89), *Tafsīr al-Qurᵓān al-ᶜaẓīm*. ᶜAbd Allāh Maḥmūd al-Shaḥāta (ed.). Cairo: Al-Hayᵓa al-Miṣriyya al-ᶜĀmma li-l-Kutub.

Muslim ibn al-Ḥajjāj (1999), *Ṣaḥīḥ Muslim*. Riyadh: Dār al-Salām.

Muṣṭafā, Maḥmūd and Sayf al-Dīn ᶜAbd al-Faṭṭāḥ (eds) (2006), *al-Lugha wa-l-huwiyya wa ḥiwār al-ḥaḍārāt*. Cairo: Kulliyyat al-Iqtiṣād.

al-Nābigha al-Dhubyānī (1990), *Dīwān*. Muḥammad Abū al-Faḍl Ibrāhīm (ed.). Cairo: Dār al-Maᶜārif.

Nāfiᶜ, Muḥammad Mabrūk (1952), *Tārīkh al-ᶜarab: ᶜaṣr mā qabl al-Islām*. Cairo: al-Saᶜāda.

al-Nasāᵓī, Aḥmad ibn Shuᶜayb (1999), *Sunan al-Nasāᵓī*. Riyadh: Dār al-Salām.

Naṣṣār, Nāṣif (1992), *Mafhūm al-umma bayna l-dīn wa-l-tārīkh*. Beirut: Dār al-Amwāj.

Nawas, John A. (1994), 'A Reexamination of Three Current Explanations for al-Mamun's Introduction of the Mihna', *International Journal of Middle East Studies* 26, pp. 615–29.

—— (1996), 'The *Miḥna* of 218 A.H./833 A.D. Revisited: An Empirical Study', *Journal of the American Oriental Society* 116, pp. 698–708.

Negev, A., A. J. Naveh and S. Shaked (1986), 'Obodas the God'. *Israel Exploration Journal* 36, pp. 56–60.

Nehmé Laïla (forthcoming), 'The Rampart and the South-eastern Gate (Area 35). Survey and Excavation Seasons 2011 and 2014'.

—— (2015), 'Can one speak of Arabic script in northwest Arabia in the 5th century AD?', in F. Briquel-Chatonnet, M. Debié and L. Nehmé (eds), *Le contexte de naissance de l'écriture arabe. Écrit et écritures araméennes et arabes au 1er millénaire après J.-C.* Louvain: Orientalia Lovaniensa Analecta.

Nehmé Laïla, Daifallah Al-Talhi and François Villeneuve (2010), 'Hegra of Arabia Felix', in Ali Ibrahim al-Ghabban, Béatrice André-Salvini, Françoise Demange, Carne Juvin and Marianne Cotty (eds), *Roads of Arabia: Archaeology and History of the Kingdom of Saudi Arabia*. Paris: Louvre, pp. 286–307.

Newby, Gordon Darnell (1988), *A History of the Jews of Arabia*. Columbia, SC: University of South Carolina Press.

Nöldeke, Theodor (1899), 'Arabia, Arabians', in T. K. Cheyne (ed.), *Encyclopaedia Biblica Volume I*. London: Black, pp. 272–5.

—— (2009), *Ghassān*, Bandalī Jawzī and Qusṭanṭīn Razīq (trans.). London: Al-Warrāq.

Nora, Pierre (ed.) (1996–8), *Realms of Memory*. New York: Columbia.

Norris, H. T. (1990), '*Shuᶜūbiyyah* in Arabic Literature', in Julia Ashtiany, T. M. Johnstone, J. D. Latham, R. B. Serjeant and G. Rex Smith (eds), *ᶜAbbāsid Belles-Lettres*. Cambridge: Cambridge UP, pp. 31–47.

Northedge, Alastair (2007), *The Historical Topography of Samarra*. London: British School of Archaeology in Iraq.

Noth, Albrecht (1994), *The Early Arabic Historical Tradition*. Princeton: Darwin.

al-Nuwayrī, Shihāb al-Dīn (2004), *Nihāyat al-arab fī funūn al-adab*. Ḥasan Nūr al-Dīn (ed.). Beirut: Dār al-Kutub al-ᶜIlmiyya.

Oppenheimer, Stephen (2007), *The Origins of the British*. London: Robinson.

Palgrave, William Gifford (1865), *Narrative of a Year's Journey through Central and Eastern Arabia – 1862–63*. London: Macmillan.

Payne, Richard (2012), 'Avoiding Ethnicity: Uses of the Ancient Past in Late Sasanian Northern Mesopotamia', in Walter Pohl, Clemens Gantner and Richard Payne (eds), *Visions of Community in the Post-Roman World*. Farnham: Ashgate, pp. 183–204.

Payne Smith, J. (1903), *Syriac English Dictionary*. Oxford: Clarendon.

Pedersen, Johannes (1953), 'The Criticism of the Islamic Preacher', *Die Welt des Islams* 2.4, pp. 215–231.

Pellat, Charles (1953), *Le milieu Baṣrien et la formation de Ǧāḥiẓ*. Paris: Librairie d'Amérique et d'Orient.

—— (1966), 'Djâhiz et la littérature comparée', *Cahiers Algériens de Littérature Comparée* 1, pp. 95–108.

—— (1969), *The Life and Works of al-Jāḥiẓ*. D. M. Hawke (trans.). Berkeley: University of California Press.

—— (1984), 'Nouvel essai d'inventaire de l'ouvre ǧāḥiẓienne', *Arabica* 31, pp. 117–64.

—— (1991),'al-Jāḥiẓ', in Julia Ashtiany, T. M. Johnstone, J. D. Latham, R. B. Serjeant and G. Rex Smith (eds), *ʿAbbāsid Belles-Lettres*. Cambridge: Cambridge UP, pp. 78–95.

—— 'Ḳāṣṣ', *EI*², 4:733–73.

Peters, F. E. (1994), *The Hajj*. Princeton: Princeton UP.

Pietrushka, Ute (2001), 'Bedouin', in Jane D. McAuliffe (ed.), *Encyclopaedia of the Qur'ān*. Leiden: Brill, vol. 1, pp. 214–17.

Pohl, Walter (1998), 'Conceptions of Ethnicity in Early Medieval Studies', in Lester K. Little and Barbara H. Rosenwein (eds), *Debating the Middle Ages: Issues and Readings*. London: Blackwell, pp. 13–24.

Pohl, Walter, Clemens Gantner and Richard Payne (eds) (2012), *Visions of Community in the Post-Roman World*. Farnham: Ashgate.

Pohl, Walter and Helmut Reimitz (eds) (1998), *Strategies of Distinction: the Construction of Ethnic Communities (300–800)*. Leiden: Brill.

Polk, William (1991), *The Arab World Today*. Cambridge, MA: Harvard UP.

Potts, Robert (1990), *The Arabian Gulf in Antiquity Volume II*. Oxford: Oxford UP.

—— (2010), 'The Story of Origins', in Ali Ibrahim al-Ghabban, Béatrice André-Salvini, Françoise Demange, Carne Juvin and Marianne Cotty (eds), *Roads of Arabia: Archaeology and History of the Kingdom of Saudi Arabia*. Paris: Louvre, pp. 70–89.

Pourshariati, Parvaneh (2008), *Decline and Fall of the Sasanian Empire*. London: I. B. Tauris.

Price, Richard (2010), 'The Development of Chalcedonian Identity in Byzantium (451–553), in Bas ter Haar Romeny (ed.), *Religious Origin of Nations? The Christian Communities of the Middle East*. Leiden: Brill, pp. 307–25.

Procopius (1914), *History of the Wars Books 1-2*. H. B. Dewing (trans.). Cambridge, MA: Loeb Classical Library.

al-Qadi, Wadad (2010), 'The Names of Estates in State Registers Before and After the Arabization of the 'Dīwāns', in Antoine Borrut and Paul Cobb (eds),

Umayyad Legacies: Medieval Memories from Syria to Spain. Leiden: Brill, pp. 255–280.

Qaṭṭāṭ, Ḥayāt (2006), *al-ᶜArab fi-l-Jāhiliyya al-akhīra wa-l-Islām al-mubakkir*. Tunis: Dār al-Amal.

al-Qurṭubī, Muḥammad ibn Aḥmad (2000), *al-Jāmiᶜ li-aḥkām al-Qurʾān*. Sālim Muṣṭafā al-Badrī (ed.). Beirut: Dār al-Kutub al-ᶜIlmiyya.

Ragib Y. (2007), 'Une Ère Inconnue D'Égypte Musulmane: L'ère De La Juridiction Des Croyants', *Annales Islamologiques* 41, pp. 187–207.

al-Rāᶜī al-Numayrī (1980), *Dīwān*. Reinhard Weipert (ed.). Beirut: Franz Steiner.

Ranger, Terence (1983), 'The Invention of Tradition in Colonial Africa' in Eric Hobsbawn and Terence Ranger (eds), *The Invention of Tradition*. Cambridge: Cambridge UP, pp. 211–62.

—— (1993), 'The Invention of Tradition Revisited: the Case of Colonial Africa' in Terence Ranger and Olufemi Vaughan (eds), *Legitimacy and the State in Twentieth Century Africa*. Houndmills, Basingstoke: Macmillan, pp. 5–50.

al-Rāshid, Saᶜd (1980), *Darb Zubaydah: the pilgrim road from Kufa to Mecca*. Riyadh: Riyadh University Libraries.

—— (1993), *Darb Zubayda: ṭarīq al-ḥajj min al-Kūfa ilā Makka al-mukarrama: dirāsa tārīkhiyya wa-ḥaḍāriyya wa-athariyyah*. Riyadh: Dār al-Waṭan.

—— (2009) *al-Ṣuwaydira*. Riyadh: al-Layyān.

al-Rāshid, Saᶜd and Peter Webb (2016), *Medieval Roads to Mecca: The Darb Zubayda*. London: Gilgamesh.

Raum, Johannes W. (1995), 'Reflections on Max Weber's thoughts concerning ethnic groups', *Zeitschrift für Ethnologie* 120, pp. 73–87.

al-Rāzī, ᶜAbd al-Raḥmān ibn Abī Ḥātim (1952), *al-Jarḥ wa-l-taᶜdīl*. Hyderabad: Dāʾirat al-Maᶜārif al-ᶜUthmāniyya.

Reinink, Gerrit (2010), 'Tradition and the Formation of the "Nestorian" Identity in Sixth- to Seventh-Century Iraq', in Bas ter Haar Romeny (ed.), *Religious Origin of Nations? The Christian Communities of the Middle East*. Leiden: Brill, pp. 217–50.

Renan, Ernst (1857), *Études d'histoire religieuse*. Paris: M. Lévy.

Rentz, G., 'Djazīrat al-ᶜArab', *EI²*, 1:533–56.

Retsö, Jan (1993), 'The Road to Yarmuk: The Arabs and the Fall of Roman Power in the Middle East' in Lennart Rydén and Jan Olof Rosenqvis (eds), *Aspects of Late Antiquity and Early Byzantium*. Stockholm: Swedish Research Institute, pp. 31–41.

—— (1999), 'Nabataean origins – once again', *Proceedings of the Seminar for Arabian Studies* 29, pp. 115–18.

—— (2000), 'Where and What was Arabia Felix?', *Proceedings for the Seminar for Arabian Studies* 30, pp. 189–92.

—— (2003), *The Arabs in antiquity: their history from the Assyrians to the Umayyads*. London: RoutledgeCurzon.

—— (2012), 'The Nabataeans: Problems Defining Ethnicity in the Ancient World', in Walter Pohl, Clemens Gantner and Richard Payne (eds), *Visions of Community in the Post-Roman World*. Farnham: Ashgate, pp. 73–9.

Ricoeur, Paul [1985] (1988), *Time and Narrative*. Kathleen Blamey and David Pellauer (trans.). Chicago: University of Chicago Press.

Rippen, Andrew (1991), 'Raḥmān and the Ḥanīfs', in W. B. Hallaq and D. P. Little (eds), *Islamic studies presented to Charles J. Adams*, Leiden: Brill, pp. 154–68.

—— 'Tafsīr', *EI*², 10:84–7.

Robin, Christian Julien (1991), 'La pénétration des Arabes nomade au Yemen', *L'Arabie antique de Karib'il a Mahomet: nouvelles données sur l'histoire des Arabes grâce aux inscriptions*. Paris: Revue du monde musulman et de la Méditerranée 61, pp. 71–88.

—— (2006), 'Les Arabes vus de Ḥimyar', *Topoi* 14, pp. 121–37.

—— (2010), 'Antiquity', in Ali Ibrahim al-Ghabban, Béatrice André-Salvini, Françoise Demange, Carne Juvin and Marianne Cotty (eds), *Roads of Arabia: Archaeology and History of the Kingdom of Saudi Arabia*. Paris: Louvre, pp. 81–99.

—— (2012), 'The Birth of an Arab Identity', in Marie Foissy (ed.), Timothy Stroud, Simon Pleasance, David Hunter and Christ Atkinson (trans.), *Museum Album*. Paris: Institut du Monde Arabe, pp. 47–50.

Robinson, Chase (2000), *Empire and Elites after the Muslim Conquest*. Cambridge: Cambridge UP.

—— (2003), *Islamic Historiography*. Cambridge: Cambridge UP.

—— (2005), *ᶜAbd al-Malik*. Oxford: Oneworld.

Rodinson, Maxime (1966), *Islam et capitalisme*. Paris: Éditions du Seuil.

—— [1979] (1981), *The Arabs*, Arthur Goldhammer (trans.). Chicago: University of Chicago Press.

Romanov, Maxim (2013), 'Computational Reading of Arabic Biographical Collections with Special Reference to Preaching in the Sunnī World (661–1300 CE)'. Unpublished PhD Thesis, University of Michigan.

—— (2016) 'Toward Abstract Models for Islamic History', in Elias I. Muhanna (ed.), *The Digital Humanities and Islamic & Middle East Studies*. Berlin: De Gruyter, pp. 118–45.

Roosens, Eugene (1989), *Creating Ethnicity: the Process of Ethnogenesis*. Newbury Park: Sage.

—— (1994), 'The Primordial Nature of Origins in Migrant Ethnicity', in Hans Vermeulen and Cora Govers (eds), *The Anthropology of Ethnicity: Beyond 'Ethnic Groups and Boundaries'*. Amsterdam: Het Spinhuis, pp. 81–104.

Rosenthal, Franz (1968), *A History of Muslim Historiography*. Leiden: Brill.

—— (1970), *Knowledge Triumphant: the concept of knowledge in medieval Islam*. Leiden: Brill.

—— 'Nasab', *EI*², 7:967–8.

Rubin, Uri (1990), 'Ḥanīfiyya and Kaᶜba', *Jerusalem Studies in Arabic and Islam* 13, pp. 85–112.

Saḥḥāb, Victor (1992), 'Īlāf Quraysh'. Unpublished PhD Thesis, Lebanese University.

Said, Edward (1991), *Orientalism*. London: Penguin.

Sālim, ᶜAbd al-ᶜAzīz (1970), *Tārīkh al-ᶜarab fī al-ᶜaṣr al-jāhilī*. Beirut: al-Nahḍa al-ᶜArabiyya.

Sansone, Livio (1997), 'The New Politics of Black Culture in Bahia', in Hans Vermeulen and Cora Govers (eds), *The Politics of Ethnic Consciousness*. London: Macmillan, pp. 277–309.

Schacht, Joseph (1950), *The Origins of Muhammadan Jurisprudence*. Oxford: Clarendon.

Schmidt, Erich F. (1953), *Persepolis I: Structures, Reliefs, Inscriptions*. Chicago: Oriental Institute of the University of Chicago.

Schoeler, Gregor (1990), 'Bashshār b. Burd, Abū ᵓl-ᶜAtāhiyah and Abū Nuwās', in Julia Ashtiany, T. M. Johnstone, J. D. Latham, R. B. Serjeant and G. Rex Smith (eds), *ᶜAbbāsid Belles-Lettres*. Cambridge: Cambridge UP, pp. 275–99.

—— (2006), *The Oral and the Written in Early Islam*. Uwe Vagelpohl (trans.), James Montgomery (ed.). London and New York: Routledge.

—— (2009), *The Genesis of Literature in Islam: from the Aural to the Read*. Shawkat Toorawa (trans.). Edinburgh: Edinburgh UP.

Serjeant, R. B. (1962), 'Haram and Hawtah: the Sacred Enclaves in Arabia', in A. Badawi (ed.), *Mélanges Taha Husain*. Cairo: Dār al-Maᶜārif, pp. 41–58.

—— (1990), 'Meccan Trade and the Rise of Islam: Misconceptions and Flawed Polemics', *Journal of the American Oriental Society* 111, pp. 472–86.

Sezgin, Fuat (1967–84), *Geschichte des arabischen Schrifttums*. Leiden: Brill.

Shaban, M. A. (1971), *Islamic History: AD 600–750 (AH 132): A New Interpretation*. Cambridge: Cambridge UP.

al-Shāfiᶜī, Muḥammad ibn Idrīs (1996), *Kitāb al-Umm*. Aḥmad Badr al-Dīn Ḥassūn (ed.). Beirut: Dār Qutayba.

Shahid, Irfan (1970), 'Pre-Islamic Arabia', in P. M. Holt, Anne S. K. Lambton and Bernard Lewis (eds), *The Cambridge History of Islam*. Cambridge: Cambridge UP, vol. 1, pp. 3–29.

—— (1984), *Byzantium and the Arabs in the Fourth Century*. Washington, DC: Dumbarton Oaks.

—— (1989), *Byzantium and the Arabs in the Fifth Century*. Washington, DC: Dumbarton Oaks.

—— (1995–2009), *Byzantium and the Arabs in the Sixth Century*. Washington, DC: Dumbarton Oaks.

al-Shahristānī, Abū al-Fatḥ (n.d.), *al-Milal wa-l-niḥal*. Aḥmad Fahmī Muḥammad (ed.). Beirut: Dār al-Kutub al-ᶜIlmiyya.

Sharon, Moshe (1990), *Revolt: The Social and Military Aspects of the 'Abbasid Revolution*. Jerusalem: Hebrew University.

Shepard, William E. (2001), 'The Age of Ignorance', in Jane D. McAuliffe (ed.), *Encyclopaedia of the Qurᵓān*. Leiden: Brill, vol. 1, pp. 37–40.

Shryock, Andrew (1997), *Nationalism and the Genealogical Imagination*. Berkeley: University of California Press.

Sībawayh, ᶜAmr ibn ᶜUthmān (1966–77), *al-Kitāb*. ᶜAbd al-Salām Muḥammad Hārūn (ed.). Cairo: Al-Hayᵓa al-Miṣriyya al-ᶜĀmma li-l-Kitāb.

Sijpesteijn, Petra (2013), *Shaping a Muslim State*. Oxford, Oxford UP.

Smith, Anthony (1986), *The Ethnic Origins of Nations*. Oxford: Blackwell.

—— (2003), *Chosen Peoples: Sacred Sources of National Identity*. Oxford: Oxford UP.

Smith, G. Rex (1990), 'Yemenite history – problems and misconceptions', *Proceedings of the Seminar for Arabian Studies* 20, pp. 131–41.

Smith, Sidney (1954), 'Events in Arabia in the sixth century', *Bulletin of the School of Oriental and African Studies* 16, pp. 425–68.

Snir, Reuven (1993), 'The Inscription of 'En 'Abdat: An Early Evolutionary Stage of Ancient Arabic Poetry', *Abr Nahrain* 31, pp. 110–25.

Sokoloff, Michael (2009), *A Syriac Lexicon: A Translation of the Latin, Correction, Expansion and Update of C Brockelmann's Lexicon Syriacum*. Winona Lake, IN: Eisenbrauns.

Somogyi, Joseph de (1932), 'The 'Kitāb al-muntaẓam' of Ibn al-Jauzī'. *Journal of the Royal Asiatic Soceity* 1, pp. 49–76.

Sozomen, Hermias (1890), *The Ecclesiastical History of Sozomen: Comprising a History of the Church from A.D. 323 To A.D. 425*., C. D. Hartranft (trans.), in H. Wace and P. Schaff, *A Select Library of Nicene and Post Nicene Fathers*. Oxford: Parker, vol. 2, pp. 327–698.

Spiegel, Gabrielle (1997), *The Past as Text*. Baltimore: Johns Hopkins UP.

Steinberg, Stephen (1989), *The Ethnic Myth: Race, Ethnicity and Class in America*. Boston: Beacon Press.

Steppat, Fritz (1986), '"Those who believe and have not emigrated". The Bedouin as the Marginal Group of Islamic Society', in Adel Sidarus (ed.), *Islão e Arabismo na Península Ibérica: Actas do XI Congresso da União Europeia de Arabistas e Islamólogos*. Évora: Universidade de Évora, pp. 403–12.

Stetkevych, Jaroslav (1993), *The Zephyrs of Nejd*. Chicago: University of Chicago Press.

—— (1996), *Muḥammad and the golden bough: reconstructing Arab myth*. Bloomington, IN: Indiana UP.

Stetkevych, Susanne (1979), 'The ᶜAbbasid Poet Interprets History: Three Qaṣīdahs by Abū Tammām', *Journal of Arabic Literature* 10, pp. 49–64.

—— (1993), *The mute immortals speak: pre-Islamic poetry and the poetics of ritual*. Ithaca, NY: Cornell UP.

Stillman, Norman (1979), *The Jews of Arab Lands*. Philadelphia: the Jewish Publication Society of America.

Strabo (1930), *Geography*. Horance Leonard Jones (trans.). Cambridge, MA: Loeb Classical Library,

Stroumsa, Rachel (2008), 'People and Identities in Nessana', Unpublished PhD Thesis, Duke University.

al-Sukkarī, Abū Saᶜīd al-Ḥasan (n.d.), *Sharḥ ashᶜār al-Hudhaliyyīn*. ᶜAbd al-Sattār Aḥmad Farrāj and Maḥmūd Muḥammad Shākir (eds). Cairo: Maktabat Dār al-ᶜUrūba.

Suleiman, Yasir (2003), *The Arabic Language and National Identity*. Edinburgh: Edinburgh UP.

—— (2011), 'Ideology, Grammar-Making and the Standardization of Arabic' in Bilal Orfali (ed.), *In the shadow of Arabic the centrality of language to Arabic culture*. Leiden: Brill, pp. 3–30.

al-Suyūṭī, Jalāl al-Dīn (1976), *al-Iqtirāḥ fī ᶜilm uṣūl al-naḥw*. Aḥmad Muḥammad Qāsim (ed.). Cairo: Maṭbaᶜat al-Saᶜāda.

Szombathely, Zoltán (2002), 'Genealogy in Medieval Muslim Societies, *Studia Islamica* 95, pp. 5–35.

al-Ṭabarānī, Abū Qāsim Sulaymān (198-), *al-Muᶜjam al-kabir*. Ḥamdi ᶜAbd al-Majīd al-Salafī (ed.). Beirut: Maktabat al-tawᶜīya al-Islāmīyya.

al-Ṭabarī, Muḥammad ibn Jarīr (1999), *Tafsīr jāmi*ᶜ *al-bayān*. Ṣidqī Jamīl al-ᶜAṭṭār (ed.). Beirut: Dār al-Fikr.

—— (n.d.) *Tārīkh al-rusul wa-l-mulūk*. Muḥammad Abū al-Faḍl Ibrāhīm (ed.). Beirut: Rawāᵓiᶜ al-Turāth al-ᶜArabi.

al-Tabrīzī, al-Khaṭīb (2000), *Sharḥ Dīwān al-Ḥamāsa*. Gharīd al-Shaykh (ed.). Beirut: Dār al-Kutub al-ᶜIlmiyya.

Taheri-Iraqi, Ahmad (1982), 'Zandaqa in the Early Abbasid Period with special reference to the poetry'. Unpublished PhD Thesis, University of Edinburgh.

Tannous, Jack (2013), 'You Are What You Read', in Philip Wood (ed.), *History and Identity in the Late Antique Middle East*. Oxford: Oxford UP, pp. 83–102.

Testen, David (1996), 'On the Arabic of the 'En 'Avdat Inscription', *Journal of Near Eastern Studies*, 55, pp. 281–92.

Thaᶜlab, Abū ᶜAbbās (2004), *Sharḥ dīwān Zuhayr ibn Abī Sulmā*. Ḥanā Naṣr al-Ḥittī (ed.). Beirut: Dār al-Kitāb al-ᶜarabī.

al-Thaᶜālibī, Abū Manṣūr (n.d.), *Fiqh al-lugha wa-sirr al-*ᶜ*arabiyya*. Muṣṭafā Saqqā, Ibrāhīm al-Abyārī and ᶜAbd al-Ḥafīz Shalabī (eds). Beirut: Dār al-Fikr.

Tidrick, Kathryn (2010), *Heart Beguiling Araby*. London: Tauris Park.

al-Tirmidhī, Muḥammad (1999), *Jāmi*ᶜ *al-Tirmidhī*. Riyadh: Dār al-Salām.

Tolan, John (2002), *Saracens: Islam in the Medieval European Imagination*. New York: Columbia UP.

Toral-Niehoff, Isabel (2014), *al-Ḥīra*. Leiden: Brill.

Tottoli, Roberto (2002), *Biblical Prophets in the Qur*ᵓ*ān and Muslim Literature*. Richmond, Surrey: Curzon.

Trimingham, John Spencer (1979), *Christianity among the Arabs in pre-Islamic times*. London: Longman.

Turner, John (2004), 'The abnāᵓ al-dawla: The Definition and Legitimation of Identity in Response to the Fourth Fitna', *Journal of the American Oriental Society* 124, pp. 1–22.

ᶜUbayd ibn Sharya (1996), *Akhbār al-Yaman*. Cairo: al-Hayᵓa al-ᶜĀmma li-Quṣūr al-Thaqāfa.

Vail, Leroy (1989), 'Introduction: Ethnicity in Southern African History', in Leroy Vail (ed.), *The Creation of Tribalism in Southern Africa*. Berkeley: University of California Press.

Vajda, G., 'Isrāᵓīliyyāt', *EI*², 4:211–12.

Vayda, Andrew (1994), 'Actions, variations, and change: the emerging anti-essentialist view in anthropology', in Robert Borofsky (ed.), *Assessing Cultural Anthropology*. New York: McGraw Hill, pp. 320–30.

Vermeulen, Hans and Cora Govers (1997), 'From Political Mobilisation to the Politics of Consciousness', in Hans Vermeulen and Cora Govers (eds), *The Politics of Ethnic Consciousness*. London: Macmillan, pp. 1–30.

Versteegh, C. H. M. (1997), *The Arabic Language*. Edinburgh: Edinburgh UP.

Waardenburg, Jacques (1981), 'Towards a Periodization of Earliest Islam According to its Relations with Other Religions', in Rudolf Peters (ed.), *Proceedings of the Ninth congress of the Union Européenne des Arabisants et Islamisants*. Leiden: Brill, pp. 304–26.

Wadud, Amina (1999), *Qur'an and Women*. Oxford: Oxford UP.

Wahb ibn Munabbih (1996), *Kitāb al-Tījān fi mulūk Ḥimyar*. Cairo: al-Hayᵓa al-ᶜĀmma li-Quṣūr al-Thaqāfa.

Waines, David (1977), 'The Third Century Internal Crisis of the Abbasids', *Journal of the Economic and Social History of the Orient* 20, pp. 282–306.

al-Walīd ibn Yazīd (1998), *Dīwān*. Wāḍiḥ al-Ṣamad (ed.). Beirut: Dar Ṣādir.

Wallman, Sandra (1979), 'Introduction: the scope for ethnicity', in S. Wallman (ed.), *Ethnicity at Work*. London: Macmillan, pp. 1–14.

Wansbrough, John (1977), *Quranic Studies*. Oxford: Oxford UP.

al-Wāqidī, Muḥammad ibn ᶜUmar (1966), *Kitāb al-Maghāzī*. Marsden Jones (ed.). London: Oxford UP.

Ward, Rachel (ed.) (2014), *Court and Craft: A Masterpiece from Northern Iraq*. London: Courtauld Gallery and Paul Holdberton Publishing.

Ward, Walter David (2008), 'From Provincia Arabia to Palaestina Tertia'. Unpublished PhD Thesis, University of California, Los Angeles.

Washburn, Wilcomb and Bruce Trigger (1996), 'Native peoples in Euro-American historiography', in Wilcomb E. Washburn and Bruce G. Trigger (eds), *The Cambridge History of the Native Peoples of the Americas Volume 1: North America*. Cambridge: Cambridge UP, vol. 1, pp. 61–124.

Wasserstein, D. J. (2010), 'Conversion and the ahl al-dhimma', in Robert Irwin (ed.), *The New Cambridge History of Islam Volume 4*. Cambridge: Cambridge UP, pp. 184–208.

Wasserstrom, Steven (1995), *Between Muslim and Jew*. Princeton: Princeton UP.

al-Wazīr al-Maghribī, al-Ḥusayn ibn ᶜAlī (1980), *Adab al-Khawāṣṣ*. Ḥamad al-Jāsir (ed.). Al-Riyadh: Dār al-Yamāma.

Webb, Peter, (2012a), '"Foreign books" in Arabic literature: discourses on books, knowledge and ethnicity in the writings of al-Jāḥiẓ', *Journal of Arabic and Islamic Studies* 12, pp. 16–55.

—— (2012b), 'Muḥammad's ascension to the Heavenly Spheres: "Utopian Travel": Fact and Fiction in making Utopias', *Middle Eastern Literatures* 15, pp. 240–56.

—— (2013a), 'Poetry and the Early Islamic Historical Tradition: Poetry and narratives of the Battle of Ṣiffīn', in Hugh Kennedy (ed.), *Poetry and Warfare in Middle Eastern Literatures*. London: I. B. Tauris, pp. 119–48.

—— (2013b), 'The Hajj before Muhammad: Journeys to Mecca in Muslim Narratives of Pre-Islamic History', in Venetia Porter and Liana Saif (eds), *The Hajj: Collected Essays*. London: British Museum Press, pp. 6–14.

—— (2014), '*al-Jāhiliyya*: Uncertain Times of Uncertain Meanings'. *Der Islam* 91, pp. 69–94.

—— (2015), 'Pre-Islamic *al-Shām* in Classical Arabic Literature: Spatial Narratives and History-telling. *Studia Islamica* 110, pp. 135–64.

—— (forthcoming (A)) 'Ethnicity and power in the Umayyad era: the case of Maᶜadd', in Andrew Marsham (ed.), *The Umayyad World*. London: Routledge.

—— (forthcoming (B)) 'Swansong of the *Dhimmis*: *al-Shuᶜūbiyya* and ethnic revival'.

—— (forthcoming (C)) 'Identity and Social Formation in the Early Caliphate', in Herbert Berg (ed.), *Routledge Handbook on Early Islam*. London: Routledge.

Weber, Max [1922] (1996), 'The Origins of Ethnic Groups', in John Hutchinson and Anthony D. Smith (eds), *Ethnicity*. Oxford: Oxford UP, pp. 35–9.

Weiss, Bernard (1984), 'Language and tradition in medieval Islam: the question of al-Ṭarīq Ilā Maᶜrifat al-Lugha', *Der Islam* 61, pp. 91–9.

—— (1992), *The Search for God's Law: Islamic Jurisprudence in the Writings of Sayf al-Din al-Amidi*. Salt Lake City: Utah UP.

Wellhausen, Julius (1927), *The Arab Kingdom and its Fall*. Margaret Graham Weir (trans.). Calcutta: University of Calcutta.

Wensinck, A. J. (1932), *The Muslim Creed: its genesis and historical development*. Cambridge: Cambridge UP.

Wenskus, Reinhard (1961), *Stammesbildung und Verfassung: Das Werden der frühmittelalterlichen gentes*. Cologne: Böhlau Verlag.

Wessels, Antoine (1995), *Arab and Christian? Christians in the Middle East*. Kampen: Pharos.

Wheeler, Brannon (2006), 'Arab Prophets of the Qur'an and Bible', *Journal of Qur'anic Studies* 8, pp. 24–57.

Whitcomb, Donald (1994), 'Amsar in Syria? Syrian Cities after the Conquest', *Aram* 6, pp. 13–33.

—— (1995) 'The Misr of Ayla: New Evidence for the Early Islamic City', in G. Bisheh (ed.), *Studies in the History and Archaeology of Jordan V*. Amman: Department of Antiquities, pp. 277–88.

White, Hayden (1980), 'The value of narrativity in the representation of reality', *Critical Inquiry*, 7, pp. 5–27.

—— (1987), *The Content of the Form*. Baltimore: Johns Hopkins UP.

al-Ya^c^qūbī, Aḥmad ibn Abī Ya^c^qūb (n.d.), *Tārīkh al-Ya^c^qūbī*. Beirut: Dār Ṣādir.

Yāqūt al-Ḥamawī (1991), *Mu^c^jam al-udabā^ɔ^*. Beirut: Dār al-Kutub al-^c^Ilmiyya.

—— (1993), *Mu^c^jam al-buldān*. Beirut: Dār Ṣādir.

Yarduman, Aram and Theodore Shcurr (2011), 'Who Are the Anatolian Turks?', *Anthropology & Archaeology of Eurasia* 50, pp. 6–42.

al-Zabīdī, Murtaḍā (1994), *Tāj al-^c^Arūs min Jawāhir al-Qāmūs*. ^c^Alī Shīrī (ed.). Beirut: Dār al-Fikr.

al-Zamakhsharī, Ibn ^c^Umar (1992), *Asās al-balāgha*. Beirut: Dār Ṣādir, 1992.

—— (1995), *Tafsīr al-Kashshāf*. Muḥammad ^c^Abd al-Salām Shāhīn (ed.). Beirut: Dār al-Kutub al-^c^Ilmiyya.

al-Zubayrī, Muṣ^c^ab (1999), *Nasab Quraysh*. E. Levi-Provençal (ed.). Cairo: al-Ma^c^ārif.

Zuhayr ibn Abī Sulmā (1988), *Dīwān*. ^c^Alī Ḥasan Fāghūr (ed.). Beirut: Dār al-Kutub al-^c^Ilmiyya.

Zuhayr ibn Janāb al-Kalbī (1999), *Dīwān*. Muḥammad Shafīq al-Bayṭār (ed.). Beirut: Dār Ṣādir.

Zwettler, M. (1978), *The Oral Tradition of Classical Arabic Poetry: Its Character and Implications*. Columbus, OH: Ohio UP.

—— (2000), 'Ma'add in Late–Ancient Arabian Epigraphy and Other Pre-Islamic Sources', *Wiener Zeitschrift für die Kunde des Morgenlandes*. Vienna: Selbstvlg. d. Institutes f. Orientalistik, pp. 223–309.

Index

EU representative:
Easy Access System Europe
Mustamäe tee 50, 10621 Tallinn, Estonia
Gpsr.requests@easproject.com

www.ingramcontent.com/pod-product-compliance
Lightning Source LLC
Chambersburg PA
CBHW050624280326
41932CB00015B/2509